Worlds of History

A Comparative Reader

Volume One: To 1550

Worlds of History

A Comparative Reader

Volume One: To 1550

Third Edition

Kevin Reilly
Raritan Valley College

Bedford/St. Martin's
Boston • New York

To those who taught me to think historically: Eugene Meehan, Donald Weinstein, and Peter Stearns; and to the memory of Warren Susman and Traian Stoianovich

For Bedford/St. Martin's

Publisher for History: Mary V. Dougherty
Executive Editor for History: Katherine Meisenheimer
Director of Development for History: Jane Knetzger
Senior Developmental Editor: Louise Townsend
Editorial Assistant: Holly Dye
Senior Production Supervisor: Joe Ford
Production Associate: Maureen O'Neill
Senior Marketing Manager: Jenna Bookin Barry
Project Management: Books By Design, Inc.
Cover Design: Billy Boardman
Cover Art: *Constructing the Norman Fleet*. Detail of the Bayeux Tapestry. 11th c. embroidery. Musée de la Tapisserie, Bayeux, France © Erich Lessing / Art Resource, N.Y.; *Carpenter Squatting on a Scaffolding and Working on a Wooden Object with His Adze*. Painted relief fragment. Egyptian, 19th dynasty. Staatliche Museen zu Berlin, Berlin, Germany © Werner Forman / Art Resource, N.Y.
Composition: Pine Tree Composition, Inc.
Printing and Binding: RR Donnelley & Sons Company

President: Joan E. Feinberg
Editorial Director: Denise B. Wydra
Director of Marketing: Karen Melton Soeltz
Director of Editing, Design, and Production: Marcia Cohen
Manager, Publishing Services: Emily Berleth

Library of Congress Control Number: 2006927524

2 1 0 9 8 7
f   e   d   c   b

For information, write: Bedford/St. Martin's, 75 Arlington Street, Boston, MA 02116   (617-399-4000)

ISBN-10: 0-312-44687-X
ISBN-13: 978-0-312-44687-1

Acknowledgments

Preface

Teaching introductory world history to college students for more than thirty-five years has helped me appreciate three enduring truths that provide the framework for this book. The first is that any introductory history course must begin by engaging with the students, as they sit before us in their remarkable diversity. The second is that world history requires a wide lens; it embraces all, the entire past, the whole world. The third is that students need to learn to think historically, critically, and independently, and realize that the subject matter of history can teach them how. With these truths in mind, I have constructed chapters in *Worlds of History* that pique student interest, teach broad trends and comparative experiences, and develop what today we call "critical thinking skills" and the Romans used to call "habits of mind."

The primary and secondary source selections in this reader address specific topics that I believe can imbue a general understanding of world history while helping students develop critical thinking skills. The reader's format helps students (and instructors) make sense of the overwhelming richness and complexity of world history. First, the reader has a **topical organization** that is also chronological, with each chapter focusing on an engaging topic within a particular time period. I am convinced that students are generally more interested in topics than eras, and that an appreciation of period and process can be taught by concentrating on topics. Into these topical chapters I've woven a **comparative approach,** examining two or more cultures at a time. In some chapters students can trace parallel developments in separate regions, such as the role of women in ancient China, India, and the Greco-Roman world in Volume One, or the rise of capitalism and industrialization in Latin America, India, Europe, and Japan in Volume Two. In other cases students examine the enduring effects of contact and exchange between cultures, as in Volume One's chapter on Mongol and Viking raiding and settlements from the tenth to the fourteenth centuries or Volume Two's chapter on the scientific revolution in Europe, the Americas, and Asia.

A wealth of **pedagogical tools** helps students unlock the readings and hone their critical thinking skills. Each chapter begins with **"Historical Context,"** an introduction to the chapter's topic that sets the stage for directed comparisons among the readings. A separate **"Thinking Historically"** section follows, exploring a particular critical thinking skill — reading primary and secondary sources or distinguishing causes of change — that ties to the chapter's selections. These skills build students' capacity to analyze, synthesize, and interpret one step at a time. A set of **"Reflections"** that both summarizes and extends the chapter's lessons concludes each chapter.

Each volume's fourteen chapters should correspond to general survey texts and to most instructors' syllabi. Understanding that some variation might exist, I have included a correlation chart in the **Instructor's Resource Manual** that matches each reading in this text with related chapters in more than a dozen of the most widely used survey texts. The manual, available at **bedfordstmartins.com/reilly** as well as in a one-volume print version, provides the rationale for the selection and organization of the readings, suggestions for teaching with the documents, and information about additional resources, including films and Internet sites.

NEW TO THIS EDITION

While I am continually testing selections in my own classroom, I appreciate input from readers and adopters, and I want to thank them for their many suggestions. Having incorporated some of this feedback, I think those who have used the reader previously will find the third edition even more geographically and topically comprehensive, interesting, and accessible to students. Twenty-five to 30 percent new documents on regions and topics from Latin America to Polynesia and from genocide to women in politics in the twentieth century have allowed me to introduce fresh material into each volume. In addition, I have included one new chapter in each volume, coincidentally, both Chapter 12: "The Black Death" in Volume One offers an in-depth look at this momentous event in Afro-Eurasian history; in Volume Two, "Religion and Politics: Israel, Palestine, and the West" provides a compelling and troubling look at contemporary conflict in the Middle East and its historic antecedents. Finally, I have also included five new "Thinking Historically" exercises across the volumes: "Distinguishing Historical Understanding from Moral Judgments," "Considering Cause and Effect," "Understanding and Explaining the Unforgivable," "Evaluating Grand Theories," and "Making Use of the Unexpected."

Another exciting substantive change to this edition is the inclusion of more visuals as documents and increased emphasis on their importance as historical evidence. Four chapters in each volume incorporate visual evidence, including Egyptian wall paintings, Fayum portraits of women, images of the Black Death, and illustrations of humans and the environment in Volume One; and contrasting views of Amerindians, Japanese images of Westernization, World War I propaganda posters, and "Global Snapshots" of the world's energy use, population, and wealth distribution in Volume Two.

Two more changes to this edition of *Worlds of History* I hope have made the reader even more accessible. Improved and new maps in almost every chapter — for example, "The Expansion of Islam to 750" in Volume One, Chapter 7, and "U.S. Involvement in Central America" in Volume

Two, Chapter 11— will help students locate the regions and cultures under consideration. A running pronunciation guide at the base of the page that sounds out difficult-to-pronounce terms and names for readers should help students discuss the sources with greater confidence.

I am not a believer in change for its own sake; when I have a successful way of teaching a subject, I am not disposed to jettison it for something new. Consequently, many of my most satisfying changes are incremental: a better translation of a document or the addition of a newly discovered source. In some cases I have been able to further edit a useful source, retaining its muscle, but providing room for a precious new find. I begin each round of revision with the conviction that the book is already as good as it can get. And I end each round with the surprising discovery that it is much better than it was.

ACKNOWLEDGMENTS

A book like this cannot be written without the help and advice, even if sometimes unheeded, of a vast army of colleagues and friends. I consider myself enormously fortunate to have met and known such a large group of gifted and generous scholars and teachers during my years with the World History Association. Some were especially helpful in the preparation of this new edition. They include Jean Berger, *University of Wisconsin–Fox Valley*; Fred Bilenkis, *John Jay College, CUNY*; John Bohstedt, *University of Tennessee, Knoxville*; Jason Freitag, *Ithaca College*; Jesse Hingson, *Georgia College*; Theodore Kallman, *San Joaquin Delta College*; Andrew J. Kirkendall, *Texas A&M University*; Leonora Neville, *The Catholic University of America*; Lauren Ristvet, *Georgia State University*; Fulian Patrick Shan, *Grand Valley State University*; Anthony J. Steinhoff, *University of Tennessee-Chattanooga*; and Stephen Tallackson, *Purdue University Calumet*.

Over the years I have benefited from the suggestions of innumerable friends and fellow world historians. Among them: Michael Adas, *Rutgers University*; Jerry Bentley, *University of Hawaii*; David Berry, *Essex County Community College*; Edmund (Terry) Burke III, *UC Santa Cruz*; Catherine Clay, *Shippensburg University*; Philip Curtin, *Johns Hopkins University*; S. Ross Doughty, *Ursinus College*; Ross Dunn, *San Diego State University*; Marc Gilbert, *North Georgia College*; Steve Gosch, *University of Wisconsin at Eau Claire*; Gregory Guzman, *Bradley University*; Brock Haussamen, *Raritan Valley College*; Allen Howard, *Rutgers University*; Sarah Hughes, *Shippensburg University*; Stephen Kaufman, *Raritan Valley College*; Karen Jolly, *University of Hawaii*; Maghan Keita, *Villanova University*; Pat Manning, *University of Pittsburgh*; John McNeill, *Georgetown University*; William

H. McNeill, *University of Chicago*; Gyan Prakash, *Princeton University*; Robert Rosen, *UCLA*; Heidi Roupp, *Aspen High School*; John Russell-Wood, *Johns Hopkins University*; Lynda Shaffer, *Tufts University*; Robert Strayer, *UC Santa Cruz*; Robert Tignor, *Princeton University*; and John Voll, *Georgetown University*.

I also want to thank the people at Bedford/St. Martin's. Joan Feinberg and Denise Wydra remained involved and helpful throughout, as did Mary Dougherty, Katherine Meisenheimer, and Jane Knetzger. Amy Leathe provided invaluable help in reviewing the previous edition, and Holly Dye developed the instructor's manual and companion Web site for the book. I want to thank my production managers, Nancy Benjamin, for her project management, and Emily Berleth, for overseeing the entire production process (some thirty-five years after she first made me an author). I would also like to thank Mary Sanger for copyediting, Billy Boardman and Donna Dennison for the cover design, and Jenna Bookin Barry for advertising and promotion. Finally, it was a pleasure to work with senior developmental editor Louise Townsend. Rarely is an editor so knowledgeable in a field as vast as world history, so vigorous and insightful in her comments and suggestions, and so ready and able to do more.

While writing this book, memories of my own introduction to history and critical thinking came flooding back to me. I was blessed at Rutgers in the 1960s with teachers I still aspire to emulate. Eugene Meehan taught me how to think and showed me that I could. Traian Stoianovich introduced me to the world and an endless range of historical inquiry. Warren Susman lit up a room with more life than I ever knew existed. Donald Weinstein guided me as a young teaching assistant to listen to students and talk with them rather than at them. And Peter Stearns showed me how important and exciting it could be to understand history by making comparisons. I dedicate this book to them.

Finally, I want to thank my own institution, Raritan Valley College, for nurturing my career, allowing me to teach whatever I wanted, and entrusting me with some of the best students one could encounter anywhere. I could not ask for anything more. Except, of course, a loving wife like Pearl.

                                                          Kevin Reilly

Introduction

You have here fourteen lessons in world history, each of which deals with a particular historical period and topic from human origins to the 1500s. (A companion volume addresses the last five hundred years.) Some of the topics are narrow and specific, covering events such as the First Crusade and the Black Death in detail, while others are broad and general, such as urbanization or the spread of universal religions.

As you learn about historical periods and topics, you will also be learning to explore history by analyzing primary and secondary sources systematically. The "Thinking Historically" exercises in each chapter encourage habits of mind that I associate with my own study of history. They are not necessarily intended to turn you into historians but, rather, to give you skills that will help you in all of your college courses and throughout your life. For example, the first chapter leads you to become more perceptive about time, the passage of time, measuring time, the time between events, all of which are useful throughout life. Similarly, a number of chapters help you in various ways to distinguish between fact and opinion and otherwise to build critical thinking, clearly abilities as necessary at work, on a jury, in the voting booth, and in discussions with friends as they are in the study of history.

World history is nothing less than everything ever done or imagined, so we cannot possibly cover it all. In his famous novel *Ulysses*, James Joyce imagines the thoughts and actions of a few friends on a single day in Dublin, June 16, 1904. The book runs almost a thousand pages. Obviously, there were many more than a few people in Dublin on that particular day, countless other cities in the world, and infinitely more days than that one particular day in world history. So we are forced to choose among different places and times in our study of the global past.

In this volume our choices do include some particular moments in time, like the one in 195 B.C.E., when Roman women demonstrated against the Oppian Law that forbade them from buying certain luxury goods, but our attention will be directed toward much longer periods as well. And while we will visit particular places in time like Republican Rome in the second century B.C.E., typically we will study more than one place at a time by using a comparative approach.

Comparisons can be enormously useful in studying world history. When we compare urbanization in Egypt and Mesopotamia, the religious origins of Christians and Buddhists, and the raiding and trading of Vikings and Mongols, we learn about the general and the specific at the same time. My hope is that by comparing some of the various *worlds* of history, a deeper and more nuanced understanding of our global past will emerge. With that understanding, we are better equipped to make sense of the world today and to confront whatever the future holds.

Contents

The agricultural revolution ten thousand years ago and the urban revolution five thousand years ago were probably the two most important events in human history. Did they "revolutionize" the power of women or begin the age of male domination? Thinking in "stages" can be more useful than thinking in years.

The urban revolution created writing and interpretation, war and law, individual anonymity, money and taxes, paupers and kings. Did Mesopotamia and Egypt undergo the same development and changes? We have primary (written and visual) as well as secondary sources to find the answers.

3. Identity in Caste and Territorial Societies

Greece and India, 1000–300 B.C.E.   66

Ancient Greece and India developed with different ideas of society. Does who we are depend on where we are or who we know? While finding out, we explore the relationship between facts and opinions, sources and interpretations.

4. Classical Civilizations and Empires

China and Rome, 300 B.C.E.–300 C.E. 108

Two thousand years ago the Chinese Han dynasty and the Roman Empire spanned Eurasia. In comparing these ancient empires, we seek to understand more about ancient empires, empires in general, and the course of change in ancient societies. A good comparison can lead us to consider new questions and topics, and generate new comparisons as well.

5. Women in Classical Societies

India, China, and the Mediterranean,
500 B.C.E.–500 C.E. 154

The experiences of women varied greatly over time both within and among the classical cultures of India, China, and the Greco-Roman world. The written and visual documents in this chapter allow us to explore the differences and similarities. At the same time we also examine both moments and processes in the history of women in classical antiquity to understand two different ways of thinking about the past.

6. From Tribal to Universal Religion
Hindu-Buddhist and Judeo-Christian Traditions, 1000 B.C.E.–100 C.E.   187

Two religious traditions transformed themselves into universal religions at about the same time in two different parts of Asia as each became part of a more connected world. Their holy books reveal the changes as well as the desire to hold on to the tried and true.

7. Encounters and Conversions: Monks, Merchants, and Monarchs
Expansion of Salvation Religions, 400 B.C.E.–1400 C.E.

Christianity, Buddhism, and later, Islam, spread far across Eurasia often along the same routes in the first thousand years of the Common Era. To understand their success, we explore the evolution of religions in a larger context.

8. Medieval Civilizations

European, Islamic, and Chinese Societies,
600–1400 C.E.   *268*

Three great civilizations spanned Eurasia between 500 and 1500. Of the three, China and Islam were the strongest, Europe the weakest. But their differences can be best understood by looking separately at the social structure, economy, politics, and culture of each.

HISTORICAL CONTEXT   *268*

THINKING HISTORICALLY
Distinguishing Social, Economic, Political,
and Cultural Aspects   *268*

9. Love and Marriage

Medieval Europe, India, and Japan, 400–1200 C.E.   *301*

Love and marriage make the world go 'round today, but not a thousand years ago. Love meant different things to different people in Europe, India, and Japan, and we use cultural comparisons to find out how and why.

HISTORICAL CONTEXT   *301*

THINKING HISTORICALLY
Analyzing Cultural Differences   *302*

Reflections   *335*

10. The First Crusade

Muslims, Christians, and Jews during the First Crusade, 1095–1099 C.E.

The First Crusade initiated a centuries-long struggle and dialogue between Christians and Muslims that would have a lasting impact on both. Wars are windows on cultures, but they also make moving narratives. Using the selections here, put together your own version of the story.

HISTORICAL CONTEXT   *337*

THINKING HISTORICALLY
Analyzing and Writing Narrative   *339*

11. Raiders of Steppe and Sea: Vikings and Mongols
Eurasia and the Atlantic, 750–1350 C.E. 375

From the late ninth through the tenth century, waves of Viking ships attacked across Europe; a few centuries later beginning in 1200, the Mongols swept across Eurasia, conquering all in their path and creating the largest empire the world had ever seen. What was the impact of these raiding peoples on settled societies and vice versa? In considering this question and the violent and destructive nature of these "barbarian" raids, we will consider the relationship of morality to history.

HISTORICAL CONTEXT 375

THINKING HISTORICALLY
Distinguishing Historical Understanding from
Moral Judgments 377

12. The Black Death
Afro-Eurasia, 1346–1350 C.E. 422

The pandemic plague ravaged the population of Afro-Eurasia, killing about one-third of the population of Europe and Egypt. In this chapter, looking at both written and visual evidence, we examine the impact of the plague in various locales while also contemplating its causes and the relation between cause and effect.

HISTORICAL CONTEXT 422

THINKING HISTORICALLY
Considering Cause and Effect 422

13. On Cities

European, Chinese, Islamic, and Mexican Cities, 1000–1550 C.E.   455

What did increasing urbanization from the medieval period on mean for those who lived in cities and those who did not? Wandering through some of the great cities of medieval Europe, China, and the Islamic world, we attempt to answer this question while also considering the validity and merits of one historian's famous comparative thesis about urbanization.

HISTORICAL CONTEXT   455

THINKING HISTORICALLY
Evaluating a Comparative Thesis   455

14. Ecology, Technology, and Science
Europe, Asia, Oceania, and Africa, 500–1550 C.E.   *493*

Since the Middle Ages, the most significant changes have occurred in the fields of ecology, technology, and science. In this chapter we read and assess three grand theories about the origins of our technological transformation and of our environmental problems, drawing on written and visual primary source evidence to develop our conclusions.

HISTORICAL CONTEXT   *493*

THINKING HISTORICALLY
Evaluating Grand Theories   *494*

List of Maps

Worlds of History

A Comparative Reader

Volume One: To 1550

1

Prehistory and the Origins of Patriarchy

Gathering, Agricultural, and Urban Societies, 20,000–3000 B.C.E.

HISTORICAL CONTEXT

Men control more of the world's income, wealth, and resources; enjoy more opportunities, freedoms, and positions of power; and exercise greater control over the bodies, wishes, and lives of others than do women. In most of the world, men dominate, parents prefer sons to daughters, and most people—even women—associate maleness with strength, energy, reason, science, and the important public sphere. A system of male rule—"patriarchy"—seems as old as humanity itself. But is it? This chapter will ask if patriarchy is natural or historical. If patriarchy did not always exist, did it have a historical beginning, middle, and, therefore, potentially a historical end? If patriarchy had human causes, can humans also create a more equal world?

The selections in this chapter span the three types of societies known to human history: hunting and gathering (the earliest human lifestyle), agricultural and pastoral (beginning about ten thousand years ago), and urban (beginning about five thousand years ago). Thus, we can speak of the agricultural revolution (8000 B.C.E.) and the urban revolution (3000 B.C.E.) as two of the most important changes in human history. These events drastically transformed the way people earned a living and led to increased populations, greater productivity, and radically changed lifestyles.

How did the lives of men and women change with these revolutions? How did the relationships between men and women change? As people settled in agricultural villages, and later in cities, economic and social differences between groups became more marked. Did differences

1

between the sexes increase as well? Did men and women have relatively equal power before the development of agriculture and the rise of cities? Did patriarchy originate as part of the transition from agricultural to urban society, or did men always have more power?

THINKING HISTORICALLY
Thinking about History in Stages

To answer these questions, one must think of early human history in broad periods or stages. History does not develop in neat compartments, however, one clearly distinguished from the other. Historians must organize and analyze disparate events and developments that occur over time in order to make sense of them. This chapter follows a widely accepted division of early history into the hunting-gathering, agricultural/pastoral, and urban stages. You might reflect on how this system of structuring the past makes history more intelligible; you might also consider the shortcomings of such a system. What challenges to the idea of historical stages do the readings in the chapter pose? On balance, does organizing history into stages make it easier or more difficult to understand complex changes, such as evolving gender roles?

NATALIE ANGIER

Furs for Evening, But Cloth Was the Stone Age Standby

The female "Venus" statues discussed in the following article date back over 20,000 years and are the earliest sculptures of humans. Archaeologists have long considered them symbols of fertility, given their exaggerated depiction of the female anatomy. As *New York Times* science writer Natalie Angier reports, some archaeologists have recently begun to reinterpret these "Venuses," emphasizing the detailed clothing and reconsidering what these costumes might reveal

Natalie Angier, "Furs for Evening, But Cloth Was the Stone Age Standby," *New York Times*, December 15, 1999, p. F1.

about the role of women in hunting and gathering societies. What conclusions do archaeologists draw from these new interpretations? What conclusions might you draw from these statues about the roles of women and their relative status in prehistoric society?

Thinking Historically

Grouping prehistory into the hunting-gathering, agricultural/pastoral, and urban stages emphasizes how early people sustained themselves. Archaeologists and historians also divide prehistory into eras defined by the tools that humans developed. They also call the age of hunters and gatherers the Old Stone Age, or Paleolithic era, because of the rough stone tools and arrow points that humans fashioned in this period. The age of agriculture is called the New Stone Age, or Neolithic era, because of the use of more sophisticated stone tools. The urban age is often called the Bronze Age because city people began to smelt tin and copper to make bronze tools. Angier's article asks us to reconsider the importance of these designations by highlighting what Dr. Elizabeth Wayland Barber has termed "the string revolution." What is the string revolution, and what was its significance? According to Angier, how might the string revolution prompt us to reconsider stages of prehistory?

Ah, the poor Stone Age woman of our kitschy imagination. When she isn't getting bonked over the head with a club and dragged across the cave floor by her matted hair, she's hunched over a fire, poking at a roasting mammoth thigh while her husband retreats to his cave studio to immortalize the mammoth hunt in fresco. Or she's Raquel Welch, saber-toothed sex kitten, or Wilma Flintstone, the original Soccer Mom. But whatever her form, her garb is the same: some sort of animal pelt, cut nasty, brutish, and short.

Now, according to three anthropologists, it is time to toss such hidebound clichés of Paleolithic woman on the midden heap of prehistory. In a new analysis of the renowned "Venus" figurines, the hand-size statuettes of female bodies carved from 27,000 to 20,000 years ago, the researchers have found evidence that the women of the so-called upper Paleolithic era were far more accomplished, economically powerful, and sartorially gifted than previously believed.

As the researchers see it, subtle but intricate details on a number of the figurines offer the most compelling evidence yet that Paleolithic women had already mastered a revolutionary skill long thought to have arisen much later in human history: the ability to weave plant fibers into cloth, rope, nets, and baskets.

And with a flair for textile production came a novel approach to adorning and flaunting the human form. Far from being restricted to a wardrobe of what Dr. Olga Soffer, one of the researchers, calls "smelly animal hides," Paleolithic people knew how to create fine fabrics that very likely resembled linen. They designed string skirts, slung low on the hips or belted up on the waist, which artfully revealed at least as much as they concealed. They wove elaborate caps and snoods for the head, and bandeaux for the chest—a series of straps that amounted to a cupless brassiere. [See Figure 1.1.]

"Some of the textiles they had must have been incredibly fine, comparable to something from Donna Karan or Calvin Klein," said Dr. Soffer, an archaeologist with the University of Illinois in Urbana-Champaign.

Archaeologists and anthropologists have long been fascinated by the Venus figurines and have theorized endlessly about their origin and purpose. But nearly all of that speculation has centered on the exaggerated body parts of some of the figurines: the huge breasts, the bulging thighs and bellies, the well-defined vulvas. Hence, researchers have suggested that the figurines were fertility fetishes, or prehistoric erotica, or gynecology primers.

"Because they have emotionally charged thingies like breasts and buttocks, the Venus figurines have been the subject of more spilled ink than anything I know of," Dr. Soffer said. "There are as many opinions on them as there are people in the field."

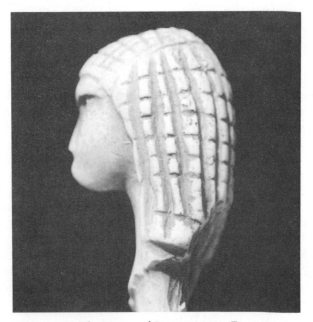

Figure 1.1   The Venus of Brassempouy, France.
Source: Steve Holland, University of Illinois.

In their new report, which will be published in the spring in the journal *Current Anthropology*, Dr. Soffer and her colleagues, Dr. James M. Adovasio and Dr. David C. Hyland of the Mercyhurst Archaeological Institute at Mercyhurst College in Erie, Pa., point out that voluptuous body parts notwithstanding, a number of the figurines are shown wearing items of clothing. And when they zeroed in on the details of those carved garments, the researchers saw proof of considerable textile craftsmanship, an intimate knowledge of how fabric is woven.

"Scholars have been looking at these things for years, but unfortunately, their minds have been elsewhere," Dr. Adovasio said. "Most of them didn't recognize the clothing as clothing. If they noticed anything at all, they misinterpreted what they saw, writing off the bandeaux, for example, as tattoos or body art." [See Figure 1.2.]

Scrutinizing the famed Venus of Willendorf, for example, which was discovered in lower Austria in 1908, the researchers paid particular attention to the statuette's head. The Venus has no face to speak of, but detailed coils surround its scalp. Most scholars have interpreted the coils as a kind of paleo-coiffure, but Dr. Adovasio, an authority on

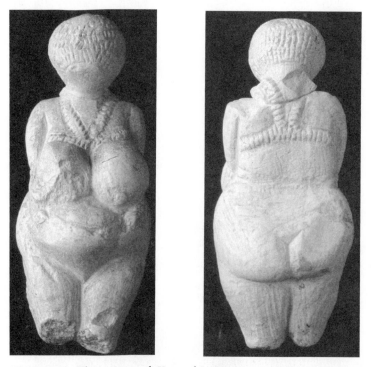

Figure 1.2 The Venus of Kostenki (Russia), wearing a woven bandeau.

Source: Bill Wiegand, University of Illinois.

textiles and basketry, recognized the plaiting as what he called a "radially sewn piece of headgear with vertical stem stitches."

Willendorf's haberdashery "might have looked like one of those woven hats you see on Jamaicans on the streets of New York," he said, adding, "These were cool things."[See Figure 1.3.]

On the Venus of Lespugue, an approximately 25,000-year-old figurine from southwestern France, the anthropologists noticed a "remarkable" degree of detail lavished on the rendering of a string skirt, with the tightness and angle of each individual twist of the fibers carefully delineated. The skirt is attached to a low-slung hip belt and tapers in the back to a tail, the edges of its hem deliberately frayed.

"That skirt is to die for," said Dr. Soffer, who, before she turned to archaeology, was in the fashion business. "Though maybe it's an acquired taste."

Figure 1.3   The Venus of Willendorf
Source: Visual Arts Library (London)/Alamy.

To get an idea of what such an outfit might have looked like, she said, imagine a hula dancer wrapping a 1930s-style beaded curtain around her waist. "We're not talking protection from the elements here," Dr. Soffer said. "This would have been ritual wear, if it was worn at all, a way of communicating with higher powers."

Other anthropologists point out that string skirts, which appear in Bronze-Age artifacts and are mentioned by Homer, may have been worn at the equivalent of a debutantes' ball, to advertise a girl's coming of age. In some parts of Eastern Europe, the skirts still survive as lacy elements of folk costumes.

The researchers presented their results earlier this month at a meeting on the importance of perishables in prehistory that was held at the University of Florida in Gainesville. "One of the most common reactions we heard was, 'How could we have missed that stuff all these years?'" Dr. Adovasio said.

Dr. Margaret W. Conkey, a professor of anthropology at the University of California at Berkeley, and co-editor, with Joan Gero, of *Engendering Archaeology* (Blackwell Publishers, 1991) said, "They're helping us to look at old materials in new ways, to which I say bravo!"

Not all scholars had been blinded by the Venusian morphology. Dr. Elizabeth Wayland Barber, a professor of archaeology and linguistics at Occidental College in Los Angeles, included in her 1991 volume *Prehistoric Textiles* a chapter arguing that some Venus figurines were wearing string skirts. The recent work from Dr. Soffer and her colleagues extends and amplifies on Dr. Barber's original observations.

The new work also underscores the often neglected importance of what Dr. Barber has termed the "string revolution." Archaeologists have long emphasized the invention of stone and metal tools in furthering the evolution of human culture. Even the names given to various periods in human history and prehistory are based on heavyweight tools: the word *Paleolithic*—the period extending from about 750,000 years ago to 15,000 years ago—essentially means "Old Stone Age." And duly thudding and clanking after the Paleolithic period were the Mesolithic and Neolithic, or Middle and New Stone Age, the Bronze Age, the Iron Age, the Industrial Age.

But at least as central to the course of human affairs as the invention of stone tools was the realization that plant products could be exploited for purposes other than eating. The fact that some of the Venus figurines are shown wearing string skirts, said Dr. Barber, "means that the people who made them must also have known how to make twisted string."

With the invention of string and the power to weave, people could construct elaborate yet lightweight containers in which to carry, store, and cook food. They could fashion baby slings to secure an infant snugly against its mother's body, thereby freeing up the woman to work and wander. They could braid nets, the better to catch prey animals without the risk of hand-to-tooth combat. They could lash together wooden logs or planks to build a boat.

"The string revolution was a profound event in human history," Dr. Adovasio said. "When people started to fool around with plants and plant byproducts, that opened vast new avenues of human progress."

In the new report, the researchers argue that women are likely to have been the primary weavers and textile experts of prehistory, and may have even initiated the string revolution in the first place—although men undoubtedly did their share of weaving when it came to making hunting and fishing nets, for example. They base that conclusion on modern crosscultural studies, which have found that women constitute the great bulk of the world's weavers, basketry makers, and all-round mistresses of plant goods.

But while vast changes in manufacturing took the luster off the textile business long ago, with the result that such "women's work" is now accorded low status and sweatshop wages, the researchers argue that weaving and other forms of fiber craft once commanded great prestige. By their estimate, the detailing of the stitches shown on some of the Venus figurines was intended to flaunt the value and beauty of the original spinsters' skills. Why else would anybody have bothered etching the stitchery in a permanent medium, if not to boast, whoa! Check out these wefts!

"It's made immortal in stone," Dr. Soffer said. "You don't carve something like this unless it's very important."

The detailing of the Venusian garb also raises the intriguing possibility that the famed little sculptures, which rank right up there with the Lascaux cave paintings in the pantheon of Western art, were hewn by women—moonlighting seamstresses, to be precise. "It's always assumed that the carvers were men, a bunch of guys sitting around making their zaftig Barbie dolls," Dr. Soffer said. "But maybe that wasn't the case, or not always the case. With some of these figurines, the person carving them clearly knew weaving. So either that person was a weaver herself, or he was living with her. He's got an adviser."

Durable though the Venus figurines are, Dr. Adovasio and his co-workers are far more interested in what their carved detailing says about the role of perishables in prehistory. "The vast bulk of what humans made was made in media that hasn't survived," Dr. Adovasio said. Experts estimate the ratio of perishable objects to durable objects generated in the average culture is about 20 to 1.

"We're reconstructing the past based on 5 percent of what was used," Dr. Soffer said.

Because many of the items that have endured over the millennia are things like arrowheads and spear points, archaeologists studying the Paleolithic era have generally focused on the ways and means of that noble savage, a.k.a. Man the Hunter, to the exclusion of other members of the tribe.

"To this day, in Paleolithic studies we hear about Man the Hunter doing such boldly wonderful things as thrusting spears into woolly mammoths, or battling it out with other men," Dr. Adovasio said. "We've emphasized the activities of a small segment of the population—healthy young men—at the total absence of females, old people of either sex, and children. We've glorified one aspect of Paleolithic life ways at the expense of all the other things that made that life way successful."

Textiles are particularly fleeting. The oldest examples of fabric yet discovered are some carbonate-encrusted swatches from France that are about 18,000 years old, while pieces of cordage and string dating back 19,000 years have been unearthed in the Near East, many thousands of years after the string and textile revolution began.

In an effort to study ancient textiles in the absence of textiles, Dr. Soffer, Dr. Adovasio, and Dr. Hyland have sought indirect signs of textile manufacture. They have pored over thousands of ancient fragments of fired and unfired clay, and have found impressions of early textiles on a number of them, the oldest dating to 29,000 B.C.E. But the researchers believe that textile manufacture far predates this time period, for the sophistication of the stitchery rules out its being, as Dr. Soffer put it, "what you take home from Crafts 101." Dr. Adovasio estimates that weaving and cord-making probably goes back to the year 40,000 B.C.E. "at a minimum," and possibly much further.

Long before people had settled down into towns with domesticated plants and animals, then, while they were still foragers and wanderers, they had, in a sense, tamed nature. The likeliest sort of plants from which they extracted fibers were nettles. "Nettle in folk tales and mythology is said to have magic properties," Dr. Soffer said. "In one story by the Brothers Grimm, a girl whose two brothers have been turned into swans has to weave them nettle shirts by midnight to make them human again." The nettles stung her fingers, but she kept on weaving.

But what didn't make it into Grimms' was that when the girl was done with the shirts, she took out a chisel, and carved herself a Venus figurine.

MARJORIE SHOSTAK

From Nisa: The Life and Words
of a !Kung Woman

Marjorie Shostak, a writer and photographer, interviewed Nisa, a woman of the hunting-gathering !Kung people of the Kalahari Desert of Southern Africa. (The exclamation point at the beginning of !Kung indicates one of the clicking sounds used in their language.) From these interviews, which took place between 1969 and 1971, Shostak compiled Nisa's story in Nisa's own words.

As you read Nisa's account of her early adulthood, consider how it is similar to, and how it is different from, that of a young woman growing up today in modern society. If Nisa is typical of women in her world, do !Kung women have more or less authority, prestige, or power than women in your own society?

Finally, what does Nisa's story tell us about women in hunting-gathering societies?

Thinking Historically

Keep in mind that Nisa exists in the late twentieth century. When we think of stages of history, we are abstracting the human past in a way that vastly oversimplifies what happened but allows us to draw important conclusions. We know hunting and gathering did not end ten thousand years ago when agriculture first began. Hunters and gatherers still live in the world today—in places like the Arctic, the Amazon, and the Kalahari. That is why we use Nisa's account, which we are lucky to have. We have no vivid first-person accounts from those ancient hunters and gatherers—writing was not invented until the first cities developed five thousand years ago. So we generalize from Nisa's experience because we know that in some ways her life is like that of our hunting-gathering ancestors. But there are ways in which it is not. At the very least, the hunters and gatherers in the world today have been pushed by farmers and city people into the most remote parts of the globe—like the Kalahari Desert.

Using a contemporary of ours, like Nisa, as a kind of representative of our most distant ancestors is clearly a strange thing to do. Does

Marjorie Shostak, *Nisa: The Life and Words of a !Kung Woman* (Cambridge: Harvard University Press, 1981), 51, 56–59, 61–62, 89–90, 132–38.

it work? What precautions should we take when using a contemporary account as evidence of life in the Paleolithic Era?

One time, my father went hunting with some other men and they took dogs with them. First they saw a baby wildebeest and killed it. Then, they went after the mother wildebeest and killed that too. They also killed a warthog.

As they were coming back, I saw them and shouted out, "Ho, ho, Daddy's bringing home meat! Daddy's coming home with meat!" My mother said, "You're talking nonsense. Your father hasn't even come home yet." Then she turned to where I was looking and said, "Eh-hey, daughter! Your father certainly has killed something. He *is* coming with meat."

I remember another time when my father's younger brother traveled from far away to come and live with us. The day before he arrived he killed an eland. He left it in the bush and continued on to our village. When he arrived, only mother and I were there. He greeted us and asked where his brother was. Mother said, "Eh, he went to look at some tracks he had seen near a porcupine hole. He'll be back when the sun sets." We sat together the rest of the day. When the sun was low in the sky, my father came back. My uncle said, "Yesterday, as I was coming here, there was an eland—perhaps it was just a small one—but I spent a long time tracking it and finally killed it in the thicket beyond the dry water pan. Why don't we get the meat and bring it back to the village?" We packed some things, left others hanging in the trees, and went to where the eland had died. It was a huge animal with plenty of fat. We lived there while they skinned the animal and the meat into strips to dry. A few days later we started home, the men carrying the meat on sticks and the women carrying it in their karosses.

At first my mother carried me on her shoulder. After a long way, she set me down and I started to cry. She was angry, "You're a big girl. You know how to walk." It was true that I was fairly big by then, but I still wanted to be carried. My older brother said, "Stop yelling at her, she's already crying," and he picked me up and carried me. After a long time walking, he also put me down. Eventually, we arrived back at the village.

We lived, eating meat; lived and lived. Then, it was finished. . . .

When adults talked to me, I listened. When I was still a young girl with no breasts, they told me that when a young woman grows up, her parents give her a husband and she continues to grow up next to him.

When they first talked to me about it, I said, "What kind of thing am I that I should take a husband? When I grow up, I won't marry. I'll just lie by myself. If I married, what would I be doing it for?"

My father said, "You don't know what you're saying. I, I am your father and am old; your mother is old, too. When you marry, you will gather food and give it to your husband to eat. He also will do things for you. If you refuse, who will give you food? Who will give you things to wear?"

I said, "There's no question about it, I won't take a husband. Why should I? As I am now, I'm still a child and won't marry." I said to my mother, "You say you have a man for me to marry? Why don't you take him and set him beside Daddy? You marry him and let them be co-husbands. What have I done that you're telling me I should marry?"

My mother said, "Nonsense. When I tell you I'm going to give you a husband, why do you say you want me to marry him? Why are you talking to me like this?"

I said, "Because I'm only a child. When I grow up and you tell me to take a husband, I'll agree. But I haven't passed through my childhood yet and I won't marry!" . . .

When I still had no breasts, when my genitals still weren't developed, when my chest was without anything on it, that was when a man named Bo came from a distant area and people started talking about marriage. Was I not almost a young woman?

One day, my parents and his parents began building our marriage hut. The day we were married, they carried me to it and set me down inside. I cried and cried and cried. Later, I ran back to my parents' hut, lay down beside my little brother, and slept, a deep sleep like death.

The next night, Nukha, an older woman, took me into the hut and stayed with me. She lay down between Bo and myself, because young girls who are still children are afraid of their husbands. So, it is our custom for an older woman to come into the young girl's hut to teach her not to be afraid. The woman is supposed to help the girl learn to like her husband. Once the couple is living nicely together and getting along, the older woman leaves them beside each other.

That's what Nukha was supposed to do. Even the people who saw her come into the hut with me thought she would lay me down and that once I fell asleep, she would leave and go home to her husband.

But Nukha had within her clever deceit. My heart refused Bo because I was a child, but Nukha, she liked him. That was why, when she laid me down in the hut with my husband, she was also laying me down with her lover. She put me in front and Bo was behind. We stayed like that for a very long time. As soon as I was asleep, they started to make love. But as Bo made love to Nukha, they knocked into me. I kept waking up as they bumped me, again and again.

I thought, "I'm just a child. I don't understand about such things. What are people doing when they move around like that? How come Nukha took me into my marriage hut and laid me down beside my husband, but when I started to cry, she changed places with me and lay down next to him? Is he hers? How come he belongs to her yet Mommy and Daddy said I should marry him?"

I lay there, thinking my thoughts. Before dawn broke, Nukha got up and went back to her husband. I lay there, sleeping, and when it started getting light, I went back to my mother's hut.

The next night, when darkness sat, Nukha came for me again. I cried, "He's your man! Yesterday you took me and brought me inside the hut, but after we all lay there, he was with you! Why are you now bringing me to someone who is yours?" She said, "That's not true, he's not mine. He's *your* husband. Now, go to your hut and sit there. Later, we'll lie down."

She brought me to the hut, but once inside, I cried and cried and cried. I was still crying when Nukha lay down with us. After we had been lying there for a very long time, Bo started to make love to her again. I thought, "What is this? What am I? Am I supposed to watch this? Don't they see me? Do they think I'm only a baby?" Later, I got up and told them I had to urinate. I passed by them and went to lie down in mother's hut and stayed there until morning broke.

That day, I went gathering with my mother and father. As we were collecting mongongo nuts and klaru roots, my mother said, "Nisa, as you are, you're already a young woman. Yet, when you go into your marriage hut to lie down, you get up, come back, and lie down with me. Do you think I have married you? No, I'm the one who gave birth to you. Now, take this man as your husband, this strong man who will get food, for you and for me to eat. Is your father the only one who can find food? A husband kills things and gives them to you; a husband works on things that become your things; a husband gets meat that is food for you to eat. Now, you have a husband, Bo; he has married you."

I said, "Mommy, let me stay with you. When night sits, let me sleep next to you. What have you done to me that I'm only a child, yet the first husband you give me belongs to Nukha?" My mother said, "Why are you saying that? Nukha's husband is not your husband. Her husband sits elsewhere, in another hut."

I said, "Well . . . the other night when she took me and put me into the hut, she laid me down in front of her; Bo slept behind. But later, they woke me up, moving around the way they did. It was the same last night. Again, I slept in front and Bo behind and again, they kept bumping into me. I'm not sure exactly what they were doing, but that's why tonight, when night sits, I want to stay with you and sleep next to you. Don't take me over there again."

My mother said, "Yo! My daughter! They were moving about?" I said. "Mm. They woke me while I was sleeping. That's why I got up and came back to you." She said, "Yo! How horny that Bo is! He's screwing Nukha! You are going to leave that man, that's the only thing I will agree to now."

My father said, "I don't like what you've told us. You're only a child, Nisa, and adults are the ones responsible for arranging your marriage. But when an adult gives a husband and that husband makes love to someone else, then that adult hasn't done well. I understand what you have told us and I say that Bo has deceived me. Therefore, when Nukha comes for you tonight, I will refuse to let you go. I will say, 'My daughter won't go into her marriage hut because you, Nukha, you have already taken him for a husband.' "

We continued to talk on our way back. When we arrived at the village, I sat down with my parents. Bo walked over to our marriage hut, then Nukha went over to him. I sat and watched as they talked. I thought, "Those two, they were screwing! That's why they kept bumping into me!"

I sat with Mother and Father while we ate. When evening came, Nukha walked over to us. "Nisa, come, let me take you to your hut." I said, "I won't go." She said, "Get up. Let me take you over there. It's your hut. How come you're already married but today you won't make your hut your home?"

That's when my mother, drinking anger, went over to Nukha and said, "As I'm standing here, I want you to tell me something. Nisa is a child who fears her husband. Yet, when you took her to her hut, you and her husband had sex together. Don't you know her husband should be trying to help bring her up? But that isn't something either of you are thinking about!"

Nukha didn't say anything, but the fire in my mother's words burned. My mother began to yell, cursing her, "Horny, that's what you are! You're no longer going to take Nisa to her husband. And, if you ever have sex with him again, I'll crack your face open. You horny woman! You'd screw your own father!"

That's when my father said, "No, don't do all the talking. You're a woman yet, how come you didn't ask me? I am a man and I will do the talking now. You, you just listen to what I say. Nisa is my child. I also gave birth to her. Now, you are a woman and will be quiet because I am a man."

Then he said, "Nukha, I'm going to tell you something. I am Gau and today I'm going to pull my talk from inside myself and give it to you. We came together here for this marriage, but now something very bad has happened, something I do not agree to at all. Nisa is no longer going to go from here, where I am sitting, to that hut over there, that hut which you have already made your own. She is no longer going to look for anything for herself near that hut."

He continued, "Because, when I agree to give a man to my daughter, then he is only for my daughter. Nisa is a child and her husband isn't there for two to share. So go, take that man, he's already yours. Today my daughter will sit with me; she will sit here and sleep here. Tomorrow I will take her and we will move away. What you have already done to this marriage is the way it will remain."

Nukha didn't say anything. She left and went to the hut without me. Bo said, "Where's Nisa? Why are you empty, returning here alone?" Nukha said, "Nisa's father refused to let her go. She told him that you had made love to me and that's what he just now told me. I don't know what to do about this, but I won't go back to their hut again." Bo said, "I have no use for that kind of talk. Get the girl and come back with her." She said, "I'm not going to Gau's hut. We're finished with that talk now. And when I say I'm finished, I'm saying I won't go back there again."

She left and walked over to her own hut. When her husband saw her, he said, "So, you and Bo are lovers! Nisa said that when you took her to Bo, the two of you . . . how exactly *did* Bo reward you for your help?" But Nukha said, "No, I don't like Bo and he's not my lover. Nisa is just a child and it is just a child's talk she is talking."

Bo walked over to us. He tried to talk but my father said, "You, be quiet. I'm the one who's going to talk about this." So Bo didn't say anything more, and my father talked until it was finished.

The next morning, very early, my father, mother, and aunt packed our things and we all left. We slept in the mongongo groves that night and traveled on until we reached another water hole where we continued to live.

We lived and lived and nothing more happened for a while. After a long time had passed, Bo strung together some trade beads made of wood, put them into a sack with food, and traveled the long distance to the water hole where we were living.

It was late afternoon; the sun had almost left the sky. I had been out gathering with my mother, and we were coming back from the bush. We arrived in the village and my mother saw them, "Eh-hey, Bo's over there. What's he doing here? I long ago refused him. I didn't ask him to come back. I wonder what he thinks he's going to take away from here?"

We put down our gatherings and sat. We greeted Bo and his relatives — his mother, his aunt, Nukha, and Nukha's mother. Bo's mother said, "We have come because we want to take Nisa back with us." Bo said, "I'm again asking for your child. I want to take her back with me."

My father said, "No, I only just took her from you. That was the end. I won't take her and then give her again. Maybe you didn't hear me the first time? I already told you that I refused. Bo is Nukha's husband and my daughter won't be with him again. An adult woman does not make love to the man who marries Nisa."

Then he said, "Today, Nisa will just continue to live with us. Some day, another man will come and marry her. If she stays healthy and her eyes stand strong, if God doesn't kill her and she doesn't die, if God stands beside her and helps, then we will find another man to give to her."

That night, when darkness set, we all slept. I slept beside mother. When morning broke, Bo took Nukha, her mother, and the others and they left. I stayed behind. They were gone, finally gone.

We continued to stay at that water hole, eating things, doing things, and just living. No one talked further about giving me another husband, and we just lived and lived and lived.

3

ELISE BOULDING

Women and the Agricultural Revolution

Because women were the foragers or gatherers in hunting-gathering societies (while men were normally the hunters), women probably developed agriculture. The earliest form of agriculture was horticulture, a simple process of planting seeds with a digging stick and tending the plants in a garden. Sociologist Elise Boulding imagines how the planting of wild einkorn, a wheatlike grain of the ancient Middle East, must have transformed the lives of men and women about ten thousand years ago. How might this early agriculture or horticulture have contributed to women's power or prestige?

Thinking Historically

Boulding draws a distinction between the early horticultural stage of agriculture and the later agriculture that depended on animal-drawn plows. How did this later stage of agriculture change the roles of men and women?

Is agriculture one stage for the history of women, or are there two stages? How does our idea of stages of history depend on what we are studying?

Elise Boulding, *The Underside of History: A View of Women Through Time* (Boulder, CO: Westview Press, 1976; Rev. ed., Sage, 1992), 114–17, 118–19.

There is some disagreement about whether the domestication of animals or plants came first. In fact, both were probably happening at the same time. There is evidence from campfire remains as long ago as 20,000 B.C.E. that women had discovered the food value of einkorn, a kind of wild wheat that grows all through the fertile crescent.[1] An enterprising Oklahoma agronomist, Professor Jack Harlan of the University of Oklahoma, noticed several years ago, on an expedition to eastern Turkey, how thick these stands of wild einkorn grew. He tried harvesting some, and once he had resorted to a nine-thousand-year-old flint sickle blade set in a new wooden handle (he tried to use his bare hands first, with disastrous results), he was able to come away with an excellent harvest. After weighing what he had reaped, he estimated that a single good stand of einkorn would feed a family for a whole year. He also found that the grains had 50 percent more protein than the wheat we use now in North America for bread flour. Einkorn grains are found everywhere on the ancient home-base sites of the fertile crescent, either as roasted hulls in cooking hearths, or as imprints in the mud-and-straw walls of the earliest preagriculture huts.

It would be inevitable that grains from sheaves of einkorn carried in from a distant field would drop in well-trodden soil just outside the home base, or perhaps in a nearby pile of refuse. When the band returned the following year to this campsite—perhaps a favorite one, since not all campsites were revisited—there would be a fine stand of einkorn waiting for them right at their doorstep. We might say that the plants taught the women how to cultivate them. Planting, however, was quite a step beyond just leaving some stalks at the site where they were picked, to seed themselves for the next year. There was less reason for deliberate planting as long as bands were primarily nomadic and there was plenty of game to follow. But in time there was a premium on campsites that would have abundant grain and fruit and nuts nearby, and then there was a point in scattering extra grain on the ground near the campsite for the next year. Because of the construction of the seed, einkorn easily plants itself, so it was a good plant for initiating humans into agriculture.

Gradually, bands lengthened their stays at their more productive home bases, harvesting what had been "planted" more or less intentionally, and letting the few sheep they had raised from infancy graze on nearby hills. One year there would be such a fine stand of wheat at their favorite home base, and so many sheep ambling about, that a band would decide just to stay for a while, not to move on that year.

If any one band of nomads could have anticipated what lay in store for humankind as a result of that fateful decision (made separately by

---

[1]The Tigris-Euphrates river valley, so called because it forms a crescent of highly fertile land between the Persian Gulf and the uplands near the Mediterranean Sea. [Ed.]

thousands of little bands over the next ten thousand years), would they after all have moved on? While it may have been a relief not to be on the move, they in fact exchanged a life of relative ease, with enough to eat and few possessions, for a life of hard work, enough to eat, and economic surplus. As [archaeologist V. Gordon] Childe says, "a mild acquisitiveness could now take its place among human desires."

Successful nomads have a much easier life than do farmers. Among the !Kung bushmen today, the men hunt about four days a week and the women only need to work two-and-a-half days at gathering to feed their families amply for a week. (At that, meat is a luxury item, and most of the nourishment comes from nuts and roots.) The rest of their time is leisure, to be enjoyed in visiting, creating, and carrying out rituals, and just "being."

The First Settlements

For better or worse, the women and the men settled down. They settled in the caves of Belt and Hotu to a prosperous life of farming and herding on the Caspian. They settled in Eynan, Jericho, Jarmo, Beidha, Catal Huyuk, Hacilar, Arpachiyah, and Kherokitia in Cyprus, and in uncounted villages that no archaeologist's shovel has touched. These places were home-base sites first, some going back thousands of years. By 10,000 B.C.E. Eynan had fifty houses, small stone domes, seven meters in diameter, around a central area with storage pits. This was probably preagricultural, still a hunting and gathering band, but a settled one. The village covered two thousand square meters. Each hut had a hearth, and child and infant burials were found under some of the floors. Three successive layers of fifty stone houses have been found at the same site, so it must have been a remarkably stable site for a settlement.

What was life like, once bands settled down? This was almost from the start a woman's world. She would mark out the fields for planting, because she knew where the grain grew best, and would probably work in the fields together with the other women of the band. There would not be separate fields at first, but as the former nomads shifted from each sleeping in individual huts to building houses for family groups of mother, father, and children, a separate family feeling must have developed and women may have divided the fields by family groups.

Their fire-hardened pointed digging sticks, formerly used in gathering, now became a multipurpose implement for planting and cultivating the soil. At harvest time everyone, including the children, would help bring in the grain. The women also continued to gather fruit and nuts, again with the help of the children. The children watched the sheep and goats, but the women did the milking and cheese making. Ethnologists who have studied both foraging and agricultural societies comment on the change in the way of life for children that comes with agriculture. Whereas in foraging societies they have no responsibilities beyond feeding themselves and learning the hunting and foraging skills they will need, and therefore they have much leisure, it is very common in agricultural societies to put children to work at the age of three, chasing birds from the food plots. Older children watch the animals, and keep them out of the planted areas.

The agriculture practiced by these first women farmers and their children, producing enough food for subsistence only, must be distinguished from that agriculture which developed out of subsistence farming and which produced surpluses and fed nonfarming populations in towns. The first type is commonly called horticulture and is carried out with hand tools only. The second is agriculture proper, and involves intensive cultivation with the use of plow and (where necessary) irrigation. In areas like the hilly flanks of the fertile crescent in the Middle East, horticulture moved fairly rapidly into agriculture as it spread to the fertile plains. As we shall see, trading centers grew into towns and cities needing food from the countryside. Women and children could not unaided produce the necessary surpluses, and by the time the digging stick had turned into an animal-drawn plow, they were no longer the primary workers of the fields.

The simpler form of farming continued in areas where the soil was less fertile, and particularly in the tropical forest areas of Africa. Here soils were quickly exhausted, and each year the village women would enlist the men in helping to clear new fields which were then burned over in the slash-and-burn pattern which helped reconstitute the soils for planting again. The slash-and-burn pattern of horticulture has continued into this century, since it is a highly adaptive technique for meager tropical soils. Where the simple horticultural methods continued to be used, women continued as the primary farmers, always with their children as helpers. In a few of these societies women continued also in the positions of power; these are usually the tribes labeled by ethnologists as matrilocal. Not many tribes have survived into the twentieth century with a matrilocal pattern, however, though traces of matrilineal descent reckoning are not infrequent.

The first women farmers in the Zagros foothills were very busy. Not only did they tend the fields and do the other chores mentioned above, they also probably built the round stone or mud-brick houses in the first villages. The frequency with which women construct shelters in foraging societies has already been cited.

Women also began to spend more time on making tools and containers. No longer needing to hold the family possessions down to what they could carry, women could luxuriate in being able to choose larger and heavier grinding stones that crushed grain more efficiently. They could make containers to hold food stores that would never have to go on the road. They ground fine stone bowls, made rough baskets, and in the process of lining their baskets with mud accidentally discovered that a mudlined basket placed in the hearth would come out hardened—the first pottery. [Archaeologist] Sonja Cole suggests that pottery was invented in Khartoum in Africa about 8000 B.C.E., spreading northwest to the Mediterranean, but the same process probably happened over and over again as people became more sedentary.

The evidence from food remains in these early villages, 10,000 to 6000 B.C.E., indicates that men were still hunting, to supplement the agriculture and modest domestic herds. This means that they were not around very much. When they were, they probably shared in some of the home-base tasks.

Evidence from some of the earliest village layouts suggests that adults lived in individual huts, women keeping the children with them. Marriage agreements apparently did not at first entail shared living quarters. As the agricultural productivity of the women increased, and the shift was made to dwellings for family units, husband-wife interaction probably became more frequent and family living patterns more complex.

With the accumulation of property, decisions about how it was to be allocated had to be made. The nature of these agreements is hardly to be found in the archaeological record, so we must extrapolate from what we know of the "purest" matrilineal tribes of the recent past.

The senior woman of a family and her daughters and sons formed the property-holding unit for the family. The senior woman's *brother* would be the administrator of the properties. His power, whether over property or in political decision making, would be derivative from his status as brother (usually but not always the oldest) to the senior woman in a family. This role of the brother, so important in present-day matrilineal societies, may not have been very important in the period we are now considering, between 12,000 and 8000 B.C.E.

4

GERDA LERNER

The Urban Revolution:
Origins of Patriarchy

Often called "the rise of civilization," the urban revolution ushered in
many changes five thousand years ago. The city societies or city-states
that developed in Mesopotamia, Egypt, and the Indus River Valley
after 3000 B.C.E. gave rise to the first kings, temples, priests, and social
classes, as well as to writing, laws, metallurgy, warfare, markets, and
private property. With the city-state came patriarchy, the assertion of
male power, and the subordination of women—the signs of which
were clear in Sumer and Mesopotamia, both ruled by assemblies of
men or kings. Mesopotamian law codes favored men: Women could
be divorced, punished, or sold into slavery for adultery, while men
could not. Laws also required that women wear veils, restricted
women's freedom of movement, and treated women as the property of
fathers or husbands.

People in ancient Egypt worshiped their kings as gods. Cities worshiped Sky Father Gods. One Egyptian creation myth describes the
great god Ra emerging from the waters of Nun and creating the
Egyptian universe from his own body. A Mesopotamian creation
story, the *Enuma Elish,* recounts a primordial battle between the male
god Marduk and the mother goddess Tiamat: Marduk splits Tiamat's
heart with his arrow and then cracks her dead body in half like a
shellfish, her hollowed-out form becoming heaven and earth.

In this selection, *The Creation of Patriarchy,* the author, modern
historian Gerda Lerner, gives considerable attention to the way in
which religious ideas changed as city-based states replaced the world
of small Neolithic villages. At the beginning of the selection, Lerner
notes the impact of urban social classes and patriarchy. Because cities
legislated the rule of the rich and powerful classes above the poor and
slaves, there were periods in which some women—the wives and
daughters of wealthy and powerful men—benefited at the expense of
other women. Eventually, though, city law curtailed the freedom of all
women, rich and poor. Despite these restrictions, some women continued to play a role in popular religion. What was that role? How important do you think it was?

Gerda Lerner, *The Creation of Patriarchy* (Oxford: Oxford University Press, 1986), 141–45.

What do you think of the author's comparison of Ishtar and the Virgin Mary? Does this comparison suggest that Christianity was more patriarchal? Do we live in a patriarchy today? What would suggest the presence of patriarchy in modern society? What would suggest its absence?

Thinking Historically

Any stage theory of history depends on a series of broad generalizations. We might distinguish two here. First, Lerner suggests that cities, archaic states, kings, gods, militarism, and patriarchy are all related, that they appeared at about the same time as part of the same process of change. Notice how Lerner links some of these elements, one to the other. Which of these couplings is persuasive?

Second, notice the absence of specific dates in this selection. The kinds of evidence Lerner uses here cannot be dated very precisely. She uses phrases like "the first half of the third millennium B.C.," which would mean between 3000 and 2500 B.C.E. When would you date the origins of patriarchy? Notice the time lag between the imposition of patriarchal laws and the slower process of replacing goddesses with gods. How does Lerner account for this time lag?

Do you think religion would be slower to change than law or social custom? Could the worship of Ishtar have been representative of an earlier, more agricultural, religious tradition?

. . . In Mesopotamian societies the institutionalization of patriarchy created sharply defined boundaries between women of different classes, although the development of the new gender definitions and of the customs associated with them proceeded unevenly. The state, during the process of the establishment of written law codes, increased the property rights of upper-class women, while it circumscribed their sexual rights and finally totally eroded them. The lifelong dependency of women on fathers and husbands became so firmly established in law and custom as to be considered "natural" and god-given. In the case of lower-class women, their labor power served either their families or those who owned their families' services. Their sexual and reproductive capacities were commodified, traded, leased, or sold in the interest of male family members. Women of all classes had traditionally been excluded from military power and were, by the turn of the first millennium B.C., excluded from formal education, insofar as it had become institutionalized.

Yet, even then, powerful women in powerful roles lived on in cultic service, in religious representation, and in symbols. There was a considerable time lag between the subordination of women in patriarchal society and the declassing of the goddesses. As we trace below changes in the position of male and female god figures in the pantheon of the gods in a period of over a thousand years, we should keep in mind that the power of the goddesses and their priestesses in daily life and in popular religion continued in force, even as the supreme goddesses were dethroned. It is remarkable that in societies which had subordinated women economically, educationally, and legally, the spiritual and metaphysical power of goddesses remained active and strong.

We have some indication of what practical religion was like from archaeological artifacts and from temple hymns and prayers. In Mesopotamian societies the feeding of and service to the gods was considered essential to the survival of the community. This service was performed by male and female temple servants. For important decisions of state, in warfare, and for important personal decisions one would consult an oracle or a diviner, who might be either a man or a woman. In personal distress, sickness, or misfortune the afflicted person would seek the help of his or her household-god and, if this was of no avail, would appeal to any one of a number of gods or goddesses who had particular qualities needed to cure the affliction. If the appeal were to a goddess, the sick person also required the intercession and good services of a priestess of the particular goddess. There were, of course, also male gods who could benefit one in case of illness, and these would usually be served by a male priest.

For example, in Babylonia a sick man or woman would approach the Ishtar temple in a spirit of humility on the assumption that the sickness was a result of his or her transgression. The petitioner would bring appropriate offerings: food, a young animal for sacrifice, oil, and wine. For the goddess Ishtar such offerings quite frequently included images of a vulva, the symbol of her fertility, fashioned out of precious lapis lazuli stone. The afflicted person would prostrate himself before the priestess and recite some appropriate hymns and prayers. A typical prayer contained the following lines:

> Gracious Ishtar, who rules over the universe,
> Heroic Ishtar, who creates humankind,
> who walks before the cattle, who loves the shepherd . . .
> You give justice to the distressed, the suffering you give
>   them justice.
> Without you the river will not open,
> the river which brings us life will not be closed,
> without you the canal will not open,
> the canal from which the scattered drink,
> will not be closed . . . Ishtar, merciful lady . . .
> hear me and grant me mercy.

Mesopotamian men or women, in distress or sickness, humbled themselves before a goddess-figure and her priestly servant. In words reflecting the attitude of slave toward master, they praised and worshiped the goddess's power. Thus, another hymn to Ishtar addresses her as "mistress of the battle field, who pulls down the mountains"; "Majestic one, lioness among the gods, who conquers the angry gods, strongest among rulers, who leads kings by the lead; you who open the wombs of women . . . mighty Ishtar, how great is your strength!" Heaping praise upon praise, the petitioner continued:

> Where you cast your glance, the dead awaken, the sick arise;
> The bewildered, beholding your face, find the right way.
> I appeal to you, miserable and distraught,
> tortured by pain, your servant,
> be merciful and hear my prayer! . . .
> I await you, my mistress; my soul turns toward you.
> I beseech you: Relieve my plight.
> Absolve me of my guilt, my wickedness, my sin,
> forget my misdeeds, accept my plea!

We should note that the petitioners regarded the goddess as all-powerful. In the symbol of the goddess's vulva, fashioned of precious stone and offered up in her praise, they celebrated the sacredness of female sexuality and its mysterious life-giving force, which included the power to heal. And in the very prayers appealing to the goddess's mercy, they praised her as mistress of the battlefield, more powerful than kings, more powerful than other gods. Their prayers to the gods similarly extolled the god's virtues and listed his powers in superlatives. My point here is that men and women offering such prayers when in distress must have thought of women, just as they thought of men, as capable of metaphysical power and as potential mediators between the gods and human beings. That is a mental image quite different from that of Christians, for example, who in a later time would pray to the Virgin Mary to intercede with God in their behalf. The power of the Virgin lies in her ability to appeal to God's mercy; it derives from her motherhood and the miracle of her immaculate conception. She has no power for herself, and the very sources of her power to intercede separate her irrevocably from other women. The goddess Ishtar and other goddesses like her had power in their own right. It was the kind of power men had, derived from military exploits and the ability to impose her will on the gods or to influence them. And yet Ishtar was female, endowed with a sexuality like that of ordinary women. One cannot help but wonder at the contradiction between the power of the goddesses and the increasing societal constraints upon the lives of most women in Ancient Mesopotamia.

Unlike the changes in the social and economic status of women, which have received only tangential and scattered attention in Ancient Mesopotamian studies, the transition from polytheism to monotheism and its attendant shift in emphasis from powerful goddesses to a single male god have been the subject of a vast literature. The topic has been approached from the vantage point of theology, archaeology, anthropology, and literature. Historical and artistic artifacts have been interpreted with the tools of their respective disciplines; linguistic and philosophical studies have added to the richness of interpretation. With Freud and Jung and Erich Fromm, psychiatry and psychology have been added as analytic tools, focusing our attention on myth, symbols, and archetypes. And recently a number of feminist scholars from various disciplines have discussed the period and the subject from yet another vantage point, one which is critical of patriarchal assumptions.

Such a richness and diversity of sources and interpretations makes it impossible to discuss and critique them all within the confines of this volume. I will therefore focus, as I have done throughout, on a few analytic questions and discuss in detail a few models which, I believe, illustrate larger patterns.

Methodologically, the most problematic question is the relation between changes in society and changes in religious beliefs and myths. The archaeologist, art historian, and historian can record, document, and observe such changes, but their causes and their meaning cannot be given with any kind of certainty. Different systems of interpretation offer varying answers, none of which is totally satisfying. In the present case it seems to me most important to record and survey the historical evidence and to offer a coherent explanation, which I admit is somewhat speculative. So are all the other explanations including, above all, the patriarchal tradition.

I am assuming that Mesopotamian religion responded to and reflected social conditions in the various societies. Mental constructs cannot be created from a void; they always reflect events and concepts of historic human beings in society. Thus, the existence of an assembly of the gods in "The Epic of Gilgamesh" has been interpreted as indicating the existence of village assemblies in pre-state Mesopotamian society. Similarly, the explanation in the Sumerian Atrahasis myth that the gods created men in order that men might serve them and relieve them of hard work can be regarded as a reflection of social conditions in the Sumerian city-states of the first half of the third millennium B.C.E., in which large numbers of people worked on irrigation projects and in agricultural labor centered on the temples. The relation between myth and reality is not usually that direct, but we can assume that no people could invent the concept of an assembly of the gods if they had not at some time experienced and known a like institution on earth. While we cannot say with certainty that certain political and economic changes "caused" changes in religious beliefs and myths, we cannot help but notice a pattern in the changes of religious beliefs in a number of societies, following upon or concurrent with certain societal changes.

My thesis is that, just as the development of plow agriculture, coinciding with increasing militarism, brought major changes in kinship and in gender relations, so did the development of strong kingships and of archaic states bring changes in religious beliefs and symbols. The observable pattern is: first, the demotion of the Mother-Goddess figure and the ascendance and later dominance of her male consort/son; then his merging with a storm-god into a male Creator-God, who heads the pantheon of gods and goddesses. Wherever such changes occur, the power of creation and of fertility is transferred from the Goddess to the God.

REFLECTIONS

A historical stage is a specific example of a larger process that historians call *periodization*. Dividing history into periods is one way historians make the past comprehensible. Without periodization, history would be a vast, unwieldy continuum, lacking points of reference, form, intelligibility, and meaning.

One of the earliest forms of historical periodization—years of reign—was a natural system of record keeping in the ancient cities dominated by kings. Each kingdom had its own list of kings, and each marked the current date by numbering the years of the king's reign. Some ancient societies periodized their history according to the years of rule of local officials or priesthoods. In the ancient Roman Republic, time was figured according to the terms of the elected consuls. The ancient Greeks used four-year periods called Olympiads, beginning with the first Olympic games in 776 B.C.E.

The ancient Greeks did not use "B.C." or "B.C.E.," of course. The periodization of world history into B.C. ("before Christ") and A.D. (*anno Domini*, "the Year of Our Lord" or "after Christ") did not come until the sixth century A.D., when a Christian monk named Dionysius Exiguus hit upon a way to center Christ as the major turning point in history. We use a variant of this system in this text, when designating events "B.C.E." for "before the common era" or "C.E." for "of the common era." This translation of "B.C." and "A.D." avoids the Christian bias of the older system but preserves its simplicity. A common dating system can be used worldwide to delineate time and coordinate different dynastic calendars.

All systems of periodization implicitly claim to designate important transitions in the past. The periodization of Dionysius inscribed the Christian belief that Christ's life, death, and resurrection fundamentally changed world history: Because Christ died to atone for the sins of humankind, only those who lived after Christ's sacrifice could be saved when they died. Few other systems of periodization made such a sweeping claim, though, of course, most people today—even many non-Christians—use it because of its convenience. Muslims count the years from a year one A.H. (*anno Hegire*, designating the year of the prophet Muhammad's escape from Mecca to Medina) in 622 A.D. of the Christian calendar, and Jews date the years from a Biblical year one.

Millennia, centuries, and decades are useful periods for societies that count in tens and (after the spread of Indian numerals) use the zero. While such multiples are only mathematical, some historians use them for rough periodization, to distinguish between the 1950s and the 1960s or between the eighteenth and nineteenth centuries, for example, as if there were a genuine and important transition between one period and the other. Sometimes historians "stretch" the boundaries of centuries or decades in order to account for earlier or later changes. For example, some historians speak of "the long nineteenth century," embracing the period from the French Revolution in 1789 to the First World War in 1914, on the grounds that peoples' lives were transformed in 1789 rather than in 1800 and in 1914 rather than in 1900. Similarly, the "sixties," as a term for American society and culture during the Vietnam War era, often means the period from about 1963 to about 1975, since civil rights and antiwar activity became significant a few years after the beginning of the decade and the war continued until 1975.

Characterizing and defining a decade or century in chronological terms is only one method of periodization, however. Processes can also be periodized. In this chapter we have periodized world history by process. All of world history can be divided into three periods—hunting-gathering, agricultural/pastoral, and urban. These are overlapping and continuing periods, and we can date only the beginning of the agricultural/pastoral and the urban periods, at about ten thousand and five thousand years ago, respectively. None of these periods has ended, as there are still hunters and gatherers as Nisa's story shows, and many farmers and pastoralists in the world. Still, the periodization is useful, because both the agricultural/pastoral revolution and the urban revolution brought about widespread and permanent changes.

We have also tried to locate patriarchy in a historical period, suggesting that it was a product of the urban revolution. We have not attempted to periodize changes in patriarchy over the course of the last five thousand years, but we could investigate this as well. Many people would say that patriarchy has been declining in recent decades. Is this a valid view, or is it a view specific to North America? If patriarchy is a product of cities and if the world is becoming more urban, can patriarchy be declining globally? What forces do you see bringing a decline or end to patriarchy?

To periodize something like the history of patriarchy would require a good deal of knowledge about the history of male and female relations over the course of the last five thousand years. That is a tall order for anyone. But you can get a sense of how the historian goes about periodizing and a feeling for its value if you periodize something you know a lot about. You might start, for instance, with your own life. Think of the most important change or changes in your life. How have these changes divided your life into certain periods? Outline your autobiography by marking these periods as parts or chapters of the story of your life so far. As you review these periods of your life, recognize how periodization must be grounded in reality. Defining these periods may help you understand yourself better.

To gain a sense of how periodization is imposed on reality, imagine how a parent or good friend would periodize your life. How would you periodize your life ten or twenty years from now? How would you have done it five years ago?

2

The Urban Revolution and "Civilization"

Mesopotamia and Egypt, 3500–1000 B.C.E.

HISTORICAL CONTEXT

The urban revolution that began approximately five thousand years ago produced a vast complex of new inventions, institutions, and ideas in cities that dominated surrounding farms and pastures. The first selection in this chapter surveys the wide range of innovations in these earliest civilizations.

The term *civilization* has to be used cautiously. Especially when the idea of civilization is used as a part of a stage theory of human history, we tend to assume that technological advancement means moral advancement. For instance, one hundred years ago scholars described ancient history as the progression from "savagery" to "barbarism" to "civilization."

It would be a shame to throw out the word *civilization* because it has been written more often with an axe than with a pen. The fact remains that the ancient cities created new ways of life for better or worse that were radically different from the world of agricultural villages. If we discard the word *civilization* as too overburdened with prejudice, we will have to find another one to describe that complex of changes. The term *civilization* comes from the Latin root word for city, *civitas*, from which we also get *civic, civilian,* and *citizen*. But, as the first reading argues, cities also created social classes, institutionalized inequalities, and calls to arms; most civilizations created soldiers as well as civilians.

Note: Pronunciations of difficult-to-pronounce terms will be given throughout the book. The emphasis goes on the syllables appearing in all capitals. [Ed.]

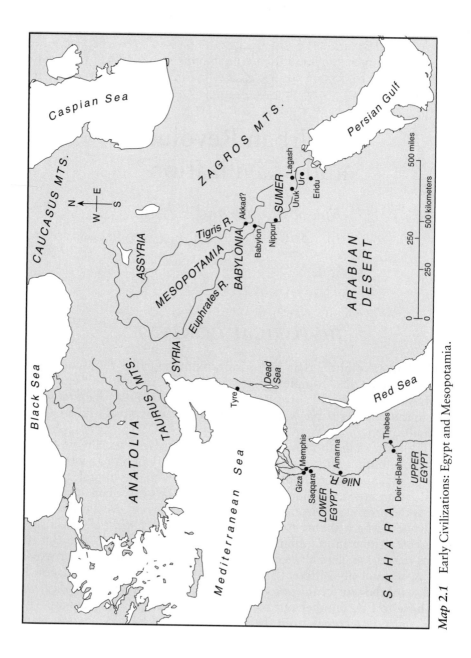

Map 2.1 Early Civilizations: Egypt and Mesopotamia.

The earliest cities, the small city-states on the Tigris and Euphrates* in ancient Sumer, included King Gilgamesh's Uruk, which is recounted in the second reading. Later cities, like Hammurabi's† Babylon, united Sumerian city-states and upriver pastoral kingdoms into giant empires (see Map 2.1). The third reading presents excerpts from Hammurabi's law code.

The ancient Egyptian empire depended less on cities than on the power of the king or pharaoh, but life along the Nile was magnified in the pharaoh's residence city and in his future home in the City of the Dead.

As you examine these selections, consider the overall transformation of the urban revolution in both Mesopotamia and Egypt. Note also the differences between Mesopotamian and Egyptian civilizations.

THINKING HISTORICALLY
Distinguishing Primary and Secondary Sources

For some historians, the "age of cities" is the beginning of history because cities invented writing. The period before city building and the creation of writing systems thus is often called "prehistory."

Our knowledge of ancient cities is enormously enhanced by ancient writings, art, and artifacts which we call primary sources. These would include literature, law codes, and inscriptions, but also sculpture, murals, building remains, tools, and weapons, indeed virtually anything from the time and place being studied. Secondary sources differ: They are written after the fact. History books or historical interpretations are secondary sources. They are secondary in that they rely on primary sources for information. Historians read, study, and interpret primary sources to compose secondary sources. In this chapter you will read one secondary source and examine three primary sources to help you learn ways to discern sources and extrapolate information from them.

*TY gruhs and yu FRAY teez
†ha muh RAH bee

KEVIN REILLY

Cities and Civilization

This selection from a college textbook is an obvious secondary source. You know it is a secondary source because it was written long after the events described by a modern historian—me.

From my perspective, this selection does two things. First, it explores the wide range of changes brought about by the urban revolution, from particulars like writing and money and metallurgy to abstractions like social class, visual acuity, and anonymity. After you read the selection, you might make a list of all of the inventions and new phenomena of cities. You will likely be surprised by the great number of ideas, institutions, and activities that originated in the first cities. You might also find it interesting to place pluses and minuses next to the items on your list to help you determine whether "civilization" (city life) was, on balance, beneficial or harmful.

Second, the selection compares the "civilizations" of Mesopotamia and Egypt. According to the selection, what are the chief differences between Mesopotamian and Egyptian civilization? What accounts for these differences?

Thinking Historically

To get a feel for the differences between a primary source and a secondary source, try to determine what primary sources might lead to some of these interpretations. Choose a sentence or two that appear specific enough to be based on a primary source. What kind of source could lead to such an interpretation? Conversely, find interpretations in this selection that *could not* possibly derive from a primary source and ask yourself, why not? Finally, consider what kind of non-written sources and evidence inform this account.

Kevin Reilly, *The West and the World: A History of Civilization*, 2nd ed. (New York: Harper & Row, 1989), 48–54, 56, 58, 60.

The Urban Revolution: Civilization and Class

The full-scale urban revolution occurred not in the rain-watered lands that first turned some villages into cities, but in the potentially more productive river valleys of Mesopotamia around 3500 B.C.E. Situated along the Tigris and Euphrates rivers, large villages like Eridu, Erech, Lagash, Kish, and later Ur and Babylon built irrigation systems that increased farm production enormously. Settlements like these were able to support five thousand, even ten thousand people, and still allow something like 10 percent of the inhabitants to work full-time at non-farming occupations.

A change of this scale was a revolution, certainly the most important revolution in human living since the invention of agriculture five thousand years earlier. The urban revolution was prepared by a whole series of technological inventions in agricultural society. Between 6000 and 3000 B.C.E. people not only learned how to harness the power of oxen and the wind with the plow, the wheeled cart, and the sailboat; they also discovered the physical properties of metals, learned how to smelt copper and bronze, and began to work out a calendar based on the movements of the sun. River valleys like those of the Tigris and Euphrates were muddy swamps that had to be drained and irrigated to take advantage of the rich soil deposits. The dry land had literally to be built by teams of organized workers.

Therefore, cities required an organizational revolution that was every bit as important as the technological one. This was accomplished under the direction of the new class of rulers and managers—probably from the grasslands—who often treated the emerging cities as a conquered province. The work of irrigation itself allowed the rulers ample opportunity to coerce the inhabitants of these new cities. Rain knows no social distinctions. Irrigated water must be controlled and channeled.

It is no wonder then that the first cities gave us our first kings and our first class societies. In Mesopotamia, along the Nile of Egypt, in China, and later in Middle America the king is usually described as the founder of cities. These kings were able to endow their control with religious sanction. In Egypt and America the king was god. In Mesopotamia a new class of priests carried out the needs of the king's religion of control.

In some cities the new priesthood would appoint the king. In others, the priests were merely his lieutenants. When they were most loyal, their religion served to deify the king. The teachings of the new class of Mesopotamian priests, for instance, were that their god had created the people solely to work for the king and make his life easier. But even when the priesthood attempted to wrest some of the king's power from him, the priests taught the people to accept the divided society, which benefited king and priesthood as providers of a natural god-given order. The priesthood, after all, was responsible for measuring time, bounding space, and predicting seasonal events. The mastery of people was easy for those who controlled time and space.

The priesthood was only one of the new classes that insured the respectability of the warrior-chieftain turned king. Other palace intellectuals—scribes (or writers), doctors, magicians, and diviners—also struggled to maintain the king's prestige and manage his kingdom. This new class was rewarded, as were the priests, with leisure, status, and magnificent buildings, all of which further exalted the majesty of the king and his city.

Beneath the king, the priesthood, and the new class of intellectuals-managers was another new class charged with maintaining the king's law and order. Soldiers and police were also inventions of the first cities. Like the surrounding city wall, the king's military guard served a double function: it provided defense from outside attack and an obstacle to internal rebellion.

That these were the most important classes of city society can be seen from the physical remains of the first cities. The archeologist's spade has uncovered the monumental buildings of these classes in virtually all of the first cities. The palace, the temple, and the citadel (or fort) are, indeed, the monuments that distinguish cities from villages. Further, the size of these buildings and the permanency of their construction (compared with the small, cheaply built homes of the farmers) attest to the fundamental class divisions of city society.

Civilization: Security and Variety

The most obvious achievements of the first civilizations are the monuments—the pyramids, temples, palaces, statues, and treasures—that were created for the new ruling class of kings, nobles, priests, and their officials. But civilized life is much more than the capacity to create monuments.

Civilized life is secure life. At the most basic level this means security from the sudden destruction that village communities might suffer. Civilized life gives the feeling of permanence. It offers regularity, stability, order, even routine. Plans can be made. Expectations can be realized. People can be expected to act predictably, according to the rules.

The first cities were able to attain stability with walls that shielded the inhabitants from nomads and armies, with the first codes of law that defined human relationships, with police and officials who enforced the laws, and with institutions that functioned beyond the lives of their particular members. City life offered considerably more permanence and security than village life.

Civilization involves more than security, however. A city that provided only order would be more like a prison than a civilization. The first cities provided something that the best-ordered villages lacked. They provided far greater variety: More races and ethnic groups were speaking more languages, engaged in more occupations, and living a greater variety of lifestyles. The abundance of choice, the opportunities for new sensations, new experiences, knowledge—these have always been the appeals of city life. The opportunities for growth and enrichment were far greater than the possibilities of plow and pasture life.

Security plus variety equals creativity. At least the possibility of a more creative, expressive life was available in the protected, semipermanent city enclosures that drew, like magnets, foreign traders and diplomats, new ideas about gods and nature, strange foods and customs, and the magicians, ministers, and mercenaries of the king's court. Civilization is the enriched life that this dynamic urban setting permitted and the human creativity and opportunity that it encouraged. At the very least, cities made even the most common slave think and feel a greater range of things than the tightly knit, clannish agricultural village allowed. That was (and still is) the root of innovation and creativity—of civilization itself.

The variety of people and the complexity of city life required new and more general means of communication. The villager knew everyone personally. Cities brought together people who often did not even speak the same language. Not only law codes but written language itself became a way to bridge the many gaps of human variety. Cities invented writing so that strangers could communicate, and so that those communications could become permanent—remembered publicly, officially recorded. [Writer and philosopher Ralph Waldo] Emerson was right when he said that the city lives by memory, but it was the official memory that enabled the city to carry on its business or religion beyond the lifetime of the village elders. Written symbols that everyone could recognize became the basis of laws, invention, education, taxes, accounting, contracts, and obligations. In short, writing and records made it possible for each generation to begin on the shoulders of its ancestors. Village life and knowledge often seemed to start from scratch. Thus, cities cultivated not only memory and the past, but hope and the future as well. City civilizations invented not only history and record keeping but also prophecy and social planning.

Writing was one city invention that made more general communication possible. Money was another. Money made it possible to deal with anyone just as an agreed-upon public language did. Unnecessary in the village climate of mutual obligations, money was essential in the city society of strangers. Such general media of communication as writing and money vastly increased the number of things that could be said and thought, bought and sold. As a consequence, city life was more impersonal than village life, but also more dynamic and more exciting.

The "Eye" and "I"

[Communication theorist] Marshall McLuhan has written that "civilization gave the barbarian an eye for an ear." We might add that civilization also gave an "I" for an "us." City life made the "eye" and the "I" more important than they had been in the village. The invention of writing made knowledge more visual. The eye had to be trained to recognize the minute differences in letters and words. Eyes took in a greater abundance of detail: laws, prices, the strange cloak of the foreigner, the odd type of shoes made by the new craftsworker from who-knows-where, the colors of the fruit and vegetable market, and elaborate painting in the temple, as well as the written word. In the village one learned by listening. In the city seeing was believing. In the new city courts of law an "eyewitness account" was believed to be more reliable than "hearsay evidence." In some villages even today, the heard and the spoken are thought more reliable than the written and the seen. In the city, even spoken language took on the uniformity and absence of emotion that is unavoidable in the written word. Perhaps emotions themselves became less violent. "Civilized" is always used to mean emotional restraint, control of the more violent passions, and a greater understanding, even tolerance, of the different and foreign.

Perhaps empathy (the capacity to put yourself in someone else's shoes) increased in cities — so full of so many different others that had to be understood. When a Turkish villager was recently asked, "What would you do if you were president of your country?" he stammered: "My God! How can you ask such a thing? How can I ... I cannot ... president of Turkey ... master of the whole world?" He was completely unable to imagine himself as president. It was as removed from his experience as if he were master of the world. Similarly, a Lebanese villager who was asked what he would do if he were editor of a newspaper accused the interviewer of ridiculing him, and frantically waved the interviewer on to another question. Such a life was beyond his comprehension. It was too foreign to imagine. The very variety of city life must have increased the capacity of the lowest commoner to imagine, empathize, sympathize, and criticize.

The oral culture of the village reinforced the accepted by saying and singing it almost monotonously. The elders, the storytellers, and the minstrels must have had prodigious memories. But their stories changed only gradually and slightly. The spoken word was sacred. To say it differently was to change the truth. The written culture of cities taught "point of *view*." An urban individual did not have to remember everything. That was done permanently on paper. Knowledge became a recognition of different interpretations and the capacity to look up things. The awareness of variety meant the possibility of criticism, analysis, and an ever-newer synthesis. It is no wonder that the technical and scientific knowledge of cities increased at a geometric rate compared with the knowledge of villages. The multiplication of knowledge was implicit in the city's demand to recognize difference and variety. Civilization has come to mean that ever-expanding body of knowledge and skill. Its finest achievements have been that knowledge, its writing, and its visual art. The city and civilization (like the child) are to be seen and not heard.

It may seem strange to say that the impersonal life of cities contributed greatly to the development of personality—the "I" as well as the "eye." Village life was in a sense much more personal. Everything was taken personally. Villagers deal with each other not as "the blacksmith," "the baker," "that guy who owes me a goat," or "that no-good bum." They do not even "deal" with each other. They know each other by name and family. They love, hate, support, and murder each other because of who they are, because of personal feelings, because of personal and family responsibility. They have full, varied relationships with each member of the village. They do not merely buy salt from this person, talk about the weather with this other person, and discuss personal matters with only this other person. They share too much with each other to divide up their relationships in that way.

City life is a life of separated, partial relationships. In a city you do not know about the butcher's life, wife, kids, and problems. You do not care. You are in a hurry. You have too many other things to do. You might discuss the weather—but while he's cutting. You came to buy meat. Many urban relationships are like that. There are many business, trading, or "dealing" relationships because there are simply too many people to know them all as relatives.

The impersonality of city life is a shame in a way. (It makes it easier to get mugged by someone who does not even hate you.) But the luxurious variety of impersonal relationships (at least some of the time) provides the freedom for the individual personality to emerge. Maybe that is why people have often dreamed of leaving family and friends (usually for a city) in the hope of "finding themselves." Certainly, the camaraderie and community of village life had a darker side of surveillance and conformity. When everything was known about everyone, it was difficult for the individual to find his or her individuality. Family ties and village custom were often obstacles to asserting self-identity. The city offered its inhabitants a huge variety of possible relationships and personal identities. The urban inhabitant was freer than his village cousin to choose friends, lovers, associates, occupation, housing, and lifestyle. The city was full of choices that the village could not afford or condone. The village probably provided more security in being like everyone else and doing what was expected. But the city provided the variety of possibilities that could allow the individual to follow the "inner self" and cultivate inner gardens.

The class divisions of city society made it difficult for commoners to achieve an effective or creative individuality. But the wealthy and powerful—especially the king—were able to develop models of individuality and personality that were revolutionary. No one before had ever achieved such a sense of the self, and the model of the king's power and freedom became a goal for the rest of the society. The luxury, leisure, and opportunity of the king was a revolutionary force. In contrast to a village elder, the king could do whatever he wanted. Recognizing that, more and more city inhabitants asked, "Why can't we?" City revolutions have continually extended class privilege and opportunities ever since.

Once a society has achieved a level of abundance, once it can offer the technological means, the educational opportunities, the creative outlets necessary for everyone to lead meaningful, happy, healthy lives, then classes may be a hindrance. Class divisions were, however, a definite stimulus to productivity and creativity in the early city civilizations. The democratic villagers preferred stability to improvement. As a result, their horizons were severely limited. They died early, lived precipitously, and suffered without much hope. The rulers of the first cities discovered the possibilities of leisure, creation, and the good life. They invented heaven and utopia—first for themselves. Only very gradually has the invention of civilization, of human potential, sifted down to those beneath the ruling class. In many cases, luxury, leisure, freedom, and opportunity are still the monopolies of the elite. But once the powerful have exploited the poor enough to establish their own paradise on earth and their own immortality after death, the poor also have broader horizons and plans.

Mesopotamian and Egyptian Civilizations: A Tale of Two Rivers

Experts disagree as to whether Mesopotamian or Egyptian civilization is older. Mesopotamian influence in Egypt was considerable enough to suggest slightly earlier origins, but both had evolved distinct civilizations by 3000 B.C.E. Indeed, the difference between the two civilizations attests to the existence of multiple routes to civilized life. In both cases, river valleys provided the necessary water and silt for an agricultural surplus large enough to support classes of specialists who did not have to farm. But the differing nature of the rivers had much to do with the different types of civilization that evolved.

The Egyptians were blessed with the easier and more reliable of the two rivers. The Nile overflowed its banks predictably every year on the parched ground in the summer after August 15, well after the harvest had been gathered, depositing its rich sediment, and withdrawing by early October, leaving little salt or marsh, in time for the sowing of winter crops. Later sowings for summer crops required only simple canals that tapped the river upstream and the natural drainage of the Nile Valley. Further, transportation on the Nile was simplified by the fact that the prevailing winds blew from the north, while the river flowed from the south, making navigation a matter of using sails upstream and dispensing with them coming downstream.

The Euphrates offered none of these advantages as it cut its way through Mesopotamia. The Euphrates flowed high above the flood plain (unlike the neighboring Tigris) so that its waters could be used, but it flooded suddenly and without warning in the late spring, after the summer crops had been sown and before the winter crops could be harvested. Thus, the flooding of the Euphrates offered no natural irrigation. Its waters were needed at other times, and its flooding was destructive. Canals were necessary to drain off water for irrigation when the river was low, and these canals had to be adequately blocked, and the banks reinforced, when the river flooded. Further, since the Euphrates was not as easily navigable as the Nile, the main canals had to serve as major transportation arteries as well.

In Mesopotamia the flood was the enemy. The Mesopotamian deities who ruled the waters, Nin-Girsu and Tiamat, were feared. The forces of nature were often evil. Life was a struggle. In Egypt, on the other hand, life was viewed as a cooperation with nature. Even the Egyptian god of the flood, Hapi, was a helpful deity, who provided the people's daily bread. Egyptian priests and philosophers were much more at ease with their world than were their Mesopotamian counterparts. And, partly because of their different experiences with their rivers, the Mesopotamians developed a civilization based on cities, while the Egyptians did not. From the first Sumerian city-states on the lower Euphrates to the later northern Mesopotamian capital of Babylon, civilization was the product and expression of city life. Egyptian civilization, in contrast, was the creation of the pharaoh's court rather than of cities. Beyond the court, which was moved from one location to another, Egypt remained a country of peasant villages.

A prime reason for Egypt's lack of urbanization was the ease of farming on the banks of the Nile. Canal irrigation was a relatively simple process that did not demand much organization. Small market towns were sufficient for the needs of the countryside. They housed artisans, shopkeepers, the priests of the local temple, and the agents of the pharaoh, but they never swelled with a large middle class and never developed large-scale industry or commerce.

In Sumer, and later in Mesopotamia, the enormous task of fighting the Euphrates required a complex social organization with immediate local needs. Only communal labor could build and maintain the network of subsidiary canals for irrigation and drainage. Constant supervision was necessary to keep the canals free of silt, to remove salt deposits, to maintain the riverbanks at flood-time, and to prevent any farmer from monopolizing the water in periods of drought. Life on the Euphrates required cooperative work and responsibility that never ceased. It encouraged absolute, administrative control over an area larger than the village, and it fostered participation and loyalty to an irrigated area smaller than the imperial state. The city-state was the political answer to the economic problems of Sumer and Mesopotamia.

The religious practices in the Euphrates Valley reflected and supported city organization. Residents of each local area worshiped the local god while recognizing the existence of other local gods in a larger Sumerian, and eventually Mesopotamian, pantheon of gods. The priests of the local temple supervised canal work, the collection of taxes, and the storage of written records, as well as the proper maintenance of religious rituals. Thus, religious loyalty reinforced civic loyalty. Peasant and middle-class Sumerians thought of themselves as citizens of their particular city, worshipers of their particular city god, subjects of their particular god's earthly representative, but not as Sumerian nationals. By contrast, the Egyptian peasant was always an Egyptian, a subject of the pharaoh, but never a citizen.

The local, civic orientation of Mesopotamian cities can be seen in the physical structure of the capital city of Sumer, the city of Ur. Like other cities on the Euphrates, Ur was surrounded by a wall. It was dominated by the temple of Nannar, the moon-god who owned the city, and the palace complex beneath the temple. The residential areas were situated outside of the sacred Temenos, or temple compound, but within the walls, between the river and the main canal. The well-excavated remains of Ur of the seventeenth century B.C.E. show a residential street plan that looks like many Middle Eastern cities of today. A highly congested area of winding alleys and broad streets sheltered one- and two-story houses of merchants, shopkeepers, tradespeople, and occasional priests and scribes that suggest a large, relatively prosperous middle class. Most houses were built around a central courtyard that offered shade throughout the day, with mud-brick, often even plastered, outside walls that protected a number of interior rooms from the sun and the eyes of the tax inspector. The remains of seventeenth-century Ur show both the variety and the density of modern city life. There are specialized districts throughout the city. Certain trades have their special quarters: a bakers' square, probably special areas for the dyers, tanners, potters, and metalworkers. But life is mixed together as well. Subsidiary gods have temples outside the Temenos. Small and large houses are jumbled next to each other. There seems to be a slum area near the Temenos, but there are small houses for workers, tenant farmers, and the poor throughout the city. And no shop or urban professional is more than a short walking distance away. The entire size of the walled city was an oval that extended three-quarters of a mile long and a half a mile wide.

A well-excavated Egyptian city from roughly the same period (the fourteenth century B.C.E.) offers some striking contrasts. Akhetaton, or Tell el Amarna, Pharaoh Akhenaton's capital on the Nile, was not enclosed by walls or canals. It merely straggled down the eastern bank of the Nile for five miles and faded into the desert. Without the need for extensive irrigation or protection, Tell el Amarna shows little of the crowded, vital density of Ur. Its layout lacks any sense of urgency. The North Palace of the pharaoh is a mile and a half north of the temple complex and offices, which are three and a half miles from the official pleasure garden. The palaces of the court nobility and the large residences of the court's officials front one of the two main roads that parallel the river, or they are situated at random. There is plenty of physical space (and social space) between these and the bunched villages of workers' houses. The remains suggest very little in the way of a middle class or a merchant or professional class beyond the pharaoh's specialists and retainers. Life for the wealthy was, judging from the housing, more luxurious than at Ur, but for the majority of the population, city life was less rich. In many ways, the pharaoh's court at Tell el Amarna was not a city at all.

6

From The Epic of Gilgamesh

The Epic of Gilgamesh is the earliest story written in any language. It also serves as a primary source for the study of ancient Mesopotamia—the land between the two great rivers, the Tigris and Euphrates.

Gilgamesh was an ancient king of Sumer, who lived about 2700 B.C.E. Since *The Epic* comes from a thousand years later, we can assume Sumerians kept telling this tale about King Gilgamesh for some time before it was written down. In Sumer, writing was initially used

The Epic of Gilgamesh, trans. N. K. Sanders (London: Penguin Books, 1972), 61–69, 108–13.

by temple priests to keep track of property and taxes. Soon, however, writing was used to preserve stories and to celebrate kings.

The more you know about the Sumerian people, the more information you will be able to mine from your source. In the previous secondary selection, you read some historical background that will help you make sense of this story. Look in *The Epic* for evidence of the urban revolution discussed in the previous selection. What is the meaning of the story of the taming of Enkidu by the harlot? Does Enkidu also tame Gilgamesh? What two worlds do Enkidu and Gilgamesh represent?

Do the authors or listeners of *The Epic* think city life is better than life in the country? According to *The Epic*, what are the advantages of the city? What problems does it have?

What does the story of the flood tell you about life in ancient Mesopotamia? Would you expect the ancient Egyptians to tell a similar story?

Thinking Historically

Reading a primary source differs markedly from reading a secondary source. Primary sources were not written with you or me in mind. It is safe to say that the author of *The Epic of Gilgamesh* never even imagined our existence. For this reason, primary sources are a bit difficult to access. Reading a primary source usually requires some intensive work. You have to keep asking yourself, why was this story told? How would a story like this help or teach people at that time? That is, you must put yourself in the shoes of the original teller and listener.

Primary sources offer us a piece of the past. No historian is in your way explaining things. With your unique perspective, you have an advantage over the intended audience: You can ask questions about the source that the author and original audience never imagined or, possibly, would not have dared ask.

Ask a question for which this primary source can provide an answer, then find the answer.

Prologue: Gilgamesh King in Uruk

I will proclaim to the world the deeds of Gilgamesh. This was the man to whom all things were known; this was the king who knew the countries of the world. He was wise, he saw mysteries and knew secret things, he brought us a tale of the days before the flood. He went on a long journey, was weary, worn-out with labor; returning he rested, he engraved on a stone the whole story.

When the gods created Gilgamesh they gave him a perfect body. Shamash the glorious sun endowed him with beauty, Adad the god of the storm endowed him with courage, the great gods made his beauty perfect, surpassing all others, terrifying like a great wild bull. Two thirds they made him god and one third man.

In Uruk he built walls, a great rampart, and the temple of blessed Eanna for the god of the firmament Anu, and for Ishtar the goddess of love. Look at it still today: the outer wall where the cornice runs, it shines with the brilliance of copper; and the inner wall, it has no equal. Touch the threshold; it is ancient. Approach Eanna the dwelling of Ishtar, our lady of love and war, the like of which no latter-day king, no man alive can equal. Climb upon the wall of Uruk; walk along it, I say; regard the foundation terrace and examine the masonry; is it not burnt brick and good? The seven sages laid the foundations.

The Coming of Enkidu

Gilgamesh went abroad in the world, but he met with none who could withstand his arms till he came to Uruk. But the men of Uruk muttered in their houses, "Gilgamesh sounds the tocsin for his amusement, his arrogance has no bounds by day or night. No son is left with his father, for Gilgamesh takes from all, even the children; yet the king should be a shepherd to his people. His lust leaves no virgin to her lover, neither the warrior's daughter nor the wife of the noble; yet this is the shepherd of the city, wise, comely, and resolute."

The gods heard their lament, the gods of heaven cried to the Lord of Uruk, to Anu the god of Uruk: "A goddess made him, strong as a savage bull, none can withstand his arms. No son is left with his father, for Gilgamesh takes them all; and is this the king, the shepherd of his people? His lust leaves no virgin to her lover, neither the warrior's daughter nor the wife of the noble." When Anu had heard their lamentation the gods cried to Aruru, the goddess of creation, "You made him, O Aruru, now create his equal; let it be as like him as his own reflection, his second self, stormy head for stormy heart. Let them contend together and leave Uruk in quiet."

So the goddess conceived an image in her mind, and it was of the stuff of Anu of the firmament. She dipped her hands in water and pinched off clay, she let it fall in the wilderness, and noble Enkidu* was created. There was virtue in him of the god of war, of Ninurta himself. His body was rough; he had long hair like a woman's; it waved like the hair of Nisaba, the goddess of corn. His body was covered with matted hair like Samuqan's, the god of cattle. He was innocent of mankind; he knew nothing of cultivated land.

*EHN kee doo

Enkidu ate grass in the hills with the gazelle and lurked with wild beasts at the water-holes; he had joy of the water with the herds of wild game. But there was a trapper who met him one day face to face at the drinking-hole, for the wild game had entered his territory. On three days he met him face to face, and the trapper was frozen with fear. He went back to his house with the game that he had caught, and he was dumb, benumbed with terror. His face was altered like that of one who has made a long journey. With awe in his heart he spoke to his father: "Father, there is a man, unlike any other, who comes down from the hills. He is the strongest in the world, he is like an immortal from heaven. He ranges over the hills with wild beasts and eats grass; he ranges through your land and comes down to the wells. I am afraid and dare not go near him. He fills in the pits which I dig and tears up my traps set for the game; he helps the beasts to escape and now they slip through my fingers."

His father opened his mouth and said to the trapper, "My son, in Uruk lives Gilgamesh; no one has ever prevailed against him, he is strong as a star from heaven. Go to Uruk, find Gilgamesh, extol the strength of this wild man. Ask him to give you a harlot, a wanton from the temple of love; return with her, and let her woman's power overpower this man. When next he comes down to drink at the wells she will be there, stripped naked; and when he sees her beckoning he will embrace her, and then the wild beasts will reject him."

So the trapper set out on his journey to Uruk and addressed himself to Gilgamesh saying, "A man unlike any other is roaming now in the pastures; he is as strong as a star from heaven and I am afraid to approach him. He helps the wild game to escape; he fills in my pits and pulls up my traps." Gilgamesh said, "Trapper, go back, take with you a harlot, a child of pleasure. At the drinking-hole she will strip, and when he sees her beckoning he will embrace her and the game of the wilderness will surely reject him."

Now the trapper returned, taking the harlot with him. After a three days' journey they came to the drinking-hole, and there they sat down; the harlot and the trapper sat facing one another and waited for the game to come. For the first day and for the second day the two sat waiting, but on the third day the herds came; they came down to drink and Enkidu was with them. The small wild creatures of the plains were glad of the water, and Enkidu with them, who ate grass with the gazelle and was born in the hills; and she saw him; the savage man, come from far-off in the hills. The trapper spoke to her: "There he is. Now, woman, make your breasts bare, have no shame, do not delay but welcome his love. Let him see you naked, let him possess your body. When he comes near uncover yourself and lie with him; teach him, the savage man, your woman's art, for when he murmurs love to you the wild beasts that shared his life in the hills will reject him."

She was not ashamed to take him, she made herself naked and welcomed his eagerness; as he lay on her murmuring love she taught him the woman's art. For six days and seven nights they lay together, for Enkidu had forgotten his home in the hills; but when he was satisfied he went back to the wild beasts. Then, when the gazelle saw him, they bolted away; when the wild creatures saw him they fled. Enkidu would have followed, but his body was bound as though with a cord, his knees gave way when he started to run, his swiftness was gone. And now the wild creatures had all fled away; Enkidu was grown weak, for wisdom was in him, and the thoughts of a man were in his heart. So he returned and sat down at the woman's feet, and listened intently to what she said. "You are wise, Enkidu, and now you have become like a god. Why do you want to run wild with the beasts in the hills? Come with me. I will take you to strong-walled Uruk, to the blessed temple of Ishtar and of Anu, of love and of heaven: there Gilgamesh lives, who is very strong, and like a wild bull he lords it over men."

When she had spoken Enkidu was pleased; he longed for a comrade, for one who would understand his heart. "Come, woman, and take me to that holy temple, to the house of Anu and of Ishtar, and to the place where Gilgamesh lords it over people. I will challenge him boldly, I will cry out aloud in Uruk, 'I am the strongest here, I have come to change the old order, I am he who was born in the hills, I am he who is strongest of all.'"

She said, "Let us go, and let him see your face. I know very well where Gilgamesh is in great Uruk. O Enkidu, there all the people are dressed in their gorgeous robes, every day is holiday, the young men and the girls are wonderful to see. How sweet they smell! All the great ones are roused from their beds. O Enkidu, you who love life, I will show you Gilgamesh, a man of many moods; you shall look at him well in his radiant manhood. His body is perfect in strength and maturity; he never rests by night or day. He is stronger than you, so leave your boasting. Shamash the glorious sun has given favors to Gilgamesh, and Anu of the heavens, and Enlil, and Ea the wise has given him deep understanding. I tell you, even before you have left the wilderness, Gilgamesh will know in his dreams that you are coming."

Now Gilgamesh got up to tell his dream to his mother, Ninsun, one of the wise gods. "Mother, last night I had a dream. I was full of joy, the young heroes were round me and I walked through the night under the stars of the firmament, and one, a meteor of the stuff of Anu, fell down from heaven. I tried to lift it but it proved too heavy. All the people of Uruk came round to see it, the common people jostled and the nobles thronged to kiss its feet; and to me its attraction was like the love of woman. They helped me, I braced my forehead and I raised it with thongs and brought it to you, and you yourself pronounced it my brother."

Then Ninsun, who is well-beloved and wise, said to Gilgamesh, "This star of heaven which descended like a meteor from the sky; which you tried to lift, but found too heavy, when you tried to move it it would not budge, and so you brought it to my feet; I made it for you, a goad and spur, and you were drawn as though to a woman. This is the strong comrade, the one who brings help to his friend in his need. He is the strongest of wild creatures, the stuff of Anu; born in the grasslands and the wild hills reared him; when you see him you will be glad; you will love him as a woman and he will never forsake you. This is the meaning of the dream."

Gilgamesh said, "Mother, I dreamed a second dream. In the streets of strong-walled Uruk there lay an axe; the shape of it was strange and the people thronged round. I saw it and was glad. I bent down, deeply drawn towards it; I loved it like a woman and wore it at my side." Ninsun answered, "That axe, which you saw, which drew you so powerfully like love of a woman, that is the comrade whom I give you, and he will come in his strength like one of the host of heaven. He is the brave companion who rescues his friend in necessity." Gilgamesh said to his mother, "A friend, a counsellor has come to me from Enlil, and now I shall befriend and counsel him." So Gilgamesh told his dreams; and the harlot retold them to Enkidu.

And now she said to Enkidu, "When I look at you you have become like a god. Why do you yearn to run wild again with the beasts in the hills? Get up from the ground, the bed of a shepherd." He listened to her words with care. It was good advice that she gave. She divided her clothing in two and with the one half she clothed him and with the other herself; and holding his hand she led him like a child to the sheepfolds, into the shepherds' tents. There all the shepherds crowded round to see him, they put down bread in front of him, but Enkidu could only suck the milk of wild animals. He fumbled and gaped, at a loss what to do or how he should eat the bread and drink the strong wine. Then the woman said, "Enkidu, eat bread, it is the staff of life; drink the wine, it is the custom of the land." So he ate till he was full and drank strong wine, seven goblets. He became merry, his heart exulted and his face shone. He rubbed down the matted hair of his body and anointed himself with oil. Enkidu had become a man; but when he had put on man's clothing he appeared like a bridegroom. He took arms to hunt the lion so that the shepherds could rest at night. He caught wolves and lions and the herdsmen lay down in peace; for Enkidu was their watchman, that strong man who had no rival.

He was merry living with the shepherds, till one day lifting his eyes he saw a man approaching. He said to the harlot, "Woman, fetch that man here. Why has he come? I wish to know his name." She went and called the man saying, "Sir, where are you going on this weary journey?" The man answered, saying to Enkidu, "Gilgamesh has gone into the marriage-house and shut out the people. He does strange things in

Uruk, the city of great streets. At the roll of the drum work begins for the men, and work for the women. Gilgamesh the king is about to celebrate marriage with the Queen of Love, and he still demands to be first with the bride, the king to be first and the husband to follow, for that was ordained by the gods from his birth, from the time the umbilical cord was cut. But now the drums roll for the choice of the bride and the city groans." At these words Enkidu turned white in the face. "I will go to the place where Gilgamesh lords it over the people, I will challenge him boldly, and I will cry aloud in Uruk, 'I have come to change the old order, for I am the strongest here.'"

Now Enkidu strode in front and the woman followed behind. He entered Uruk, that great market, and all the folk thronged round him where he stood in the street in strong-walled Uruk. The people jostled; speaking of him they said, "He is the spit of Gilgamesh." "He is shorter." "He is bigger of bone." "This is the one who was reared on the milk of wild beasts. His is the greatest strength." The men rejoiced: "Now Gilgamesh has met his match. This great one, this hero whose beauty is like a god, he is a match even for Gilgamesh."

In Uruk the bridal bed was made, fit for the goddess of love. The bride waited for the bridegroom, but in the night Gilgamesh got up and came to the house. Then Enkidu stepped out, he stood in the street and blocked the way. Mighty Gilgamesh came on and Enkidu met him at the gate. He put out his foot and prevented Gilgamesh from entering the house, so they grappled, holding each other like bulls. They broke the doorposts and the walls shook, they snorted like bulls locked together. They shattered the doorposts and the walls shook. Gilgamesh bent his knee with his foot planted on the ground and with a turn Enkidu was thrown. Then immediately his fury died. When Enkidu was thrown he said to Gilgamesh, "There is not another like you in the world. Ninsun, who is as strong as a wild ox in the byre, she was the mother who bore you, and now you are raised above all men, and Enlil has given you the kingship, for your strength surpasses the strength of men." So Enkidu and Gilgamesh embraced and their friendship was sealed.

The Story of the Flood

"You know the city Shurrupak, it stands on the banks of Euphrates? That city grew old and the gods that were in it were old. There was Anu, lord of the firmament, their father, and warrior Enlil their counsellor, Ninurta the helper, and Ennugi watcher over canals; and with them also was Ea. In those days the world teemed, the people multiplied, the world bellowed like a wild bull, and the great god was aroused by the clamour. Enlil heard the clamour and he said to the gods in council, 'The uproar of mankind is intolerable and sleep is no longer possible by reason of the babel.' So the gods agreed to exterminate mankind. Enlil did this, but Ea because of his oath warned me in a dream. He whispered their words to my house of reeds, 'Reed-house, reed-house! Wall, O wall, hearken reed-house, wall reflect; O man of Shurrupak, son of Ubara-Tutu; tear down your house and build a boat, abandon possessions and look for life, despise worldly goods and save your soul alive. Tear down your house, I say, and build a boat. These are the measurements of the barque as you shall build her: let her beam equal her length, let her deck be roofed like the vault that covers the abyss; then take up into the boat the seed of all living creatures.'

"When I had understood I said to my lord, 'Behold, what you have commanded I will honour and perform, but how shall I answer the people, the city, the elders?' Then Ea opened his mouth and said to me, his servant, 'Tell them this: I have learnt that Enlil is wrathful against me, I dare no longer walk in his land nor live in his city; I will go down to the Gulf to dwell with Ea my lord. But on you he will rain down abundance, rare fish and shy wild-fowl, a rich harvest-tide. In the evening the rider of the storm will bring you wheat in torrents.'

"In the first light of dawn all my household gathered round me, the children brought pitch and the men whatever was necessary. On the fifth day I laid the keel and the ribs, then I made fast the planking. The ground-space was one acre, each side of the deck measured one hundred and twenty cubits, making a square. I built six decks below, seven in all, I divided them into nine sections with bulkheads between. I drove in wedges where needed, I saw to the punt-poles, and laid in supplies. The carriers brought oil in baskets, I poured pitch into the furnace and asphalt and oil; more oil was consumed in caulking, and more again the master of the boat took into his stores. I slaughtered bullocks for the people and every day I killed sheep. I gave the shipwrights wine to drink as though it were river water, raw wine and red wine and oil and white wine. There was feasting then as there is at the time of the New Year's festival; I myself anointed my head. On the seventh day the boat was complete.

"Then was the launching full of difficulty; there was shifting of ballast above and below till two thirds was submerged. I loaded into her all that I had of gold and of living things, my family, my kin, the beast of the field both wild and tame, and all the craftsmen. I sent them on board, for the time that Shamash had ordained was already fulfilled when he said 'In the evening, when the rider of the storm sends down the destroying rain, enter the boat and batten her down.' The time was fulfilled, the evening came, the rider of the storm sent down the rain. I looked out at the weather and it was terrible, so I too boarded the boat and battened her down. All was now complete, the battening and the caulking; so I handed the tiller to Puzur-Amurri the steersman, with the navigation and the care of the whole boat.

"With the first light of dawn a black cloud came from the horizon; it thundered within where Adad, lord of the storm, was riding. In front over hill and plain Shullat and Hanish, heralds of the storm, led on. Then the gods of the abyss rose up; Nergal pulled out the dams of the nether waters, Ninurta the war-lord threw down the dykes, and the seven judges of hell, the Annunaki, raised their torches, lighting the land with their livid flame. A stupor of despair went up to heaven when the god of the storm turned daylight to darkness, when he smashed the land like a cup. One whole day the tempest raged, gathering fury as it went, it poured over the people like the tides of battle; a man could not see his brother nor the people be seen from heaven. Even the gods were terrified at the flood, they fled to the highest heaven, the firmament of Anu; they crouched against the walls, cowering like curs. Then Ishtar the sweet-voiced Queen of Heaven cried out like a woman in travail: 'Alas the days of old are turned to dust because I commanded evil; why did I command this evil in the council of all the gods? I commanded wars to destroy the people, but are they not my people, for I brought them forth? Now like the spawn of fish they float in the ocean.' The great gods of heaven and of hell wept, they covered their mouths.

"For six days and six nights the winds blew, torrent and tempest and flood overwhelmed the world, tempest and flood raged together like warring hosts. When the seventh day dawned the storm from the south subsided, the sea grew calm, the flood was stilled; I looked at the face of the world and there was silence, all mankind was turned to clay. The surface of the sea stretched as flat as a roof-top; I opened a hatch and the light fell on my face. Then I bowed low, I sat down and I wept, the tears streamed down my face, for on every side was the waste of water. I looked for land in vain, but fourteen leagues distant there appeared a mountain, and there the boat grounded; on the mountain of Nisir the boat held fast, she held fast and did not budge. One day she held, and a second day on the mountain of Nisir she held fast and did not budge. A third day, and a fourth day she held fast on the mountain and did not budge; a fifth day and a sixth day she held fast on the mountain. When the seventh day dawned I loosed a dove and let her go. She flew away, but finding no resting-place she returned. Then I loosed a swallow, and she flew away but finding no resting-place she returned. I loosed a raven, she saw that the waters had retreated, she ate, she flew around, she cawed, and she did not come back. Then I threw everything open to the four winds, I made a sacrifice and poured out a libation on the mountain top. Seven and again seven cauldrons I set up on their stands, I heaped up wood and cane and cedar and myrtle. When the gods smelled the sweet savour, they gathered like flies over the sacrifice. Then, at last, Ishtar also came, she lifted her necklace with the jewels of heaven that once Anu had made to please her. 'O you gods here present, by the lapis lazuli round my neck I shall remember these days as I remember the jewels of my throat; these last days I shall not forget. Let all the gods gather round the sacrifice, except Enlil. He shall not approach this offering, for without reflection he brought the flood; he consigned my people to destruction.'

"When Enlil had come, when he saw the boat, he was wrath and swelled with anger at the gods, the host of heaven, 'Has any of these mortals escaped? Not one was to have survived the destruction.' Then the god of the wells and canals Ninurta opened his mouth and said to the warrior Enlil, 'Who is there of the gods that devise without Ea? It is Ea alone who knows all things.' Then Ea opened his mouth and spoke to warrior Enlil, 'Wisest of gods, hero Enlil, how could you so senselessly bring down the flood?

> Lay upon the sinner his sin,
> Lay upon the transgressor his transgression,
> Punish him a little when he breaks loose,
> Do not drive him too hard or he perishes;
> Would that a lion had ravaged mankind
> Rather than the flood,
> Would that a wolf had ravaged mankind
> Rather than the flood,
> Would that famine had wasted the world
> Rather than the flood,
> Would that pestilence had wasted mankind
> Rather than the flood.

It was not I that revealed the secret of the gods; the wise man learned it in a dream. Now take your counsel what shall be done with him.'

"Then Enlil went up into the boat, he took me by the hand and my wife and made us enter the boat and kneel down on either side, he standing between us. He touched our foreheads to bless us saying, 'In time past Utnapishtim was a mortal man; henceforth he and his wife shall live in the distance at the mouth of the rivers.' Thus it was that the gods took me and placed me here to live in the distance, at the mouth of the rivers."

From Hammurabi's Code

King Hammurabi of Babylon conquered the entire area of Meso-potamia (including Sumer) between 1793 and 1750 B.C.E. His law code provides us with a rare insight into the daily life of ancient urban society.

Law codes give us an idea of a people's sense of justice and notions of proper punishment. This selection includes only parts of Hammurabi's Code, so we cannot conclude that if something is not mentioned here it was not a matter of legal concern. We can, however, deduce much about Babylonian society from the laws mentioned in this essay.

What do these laws tell us about class divisions or social distinctions in Babylonian society? What can we learn from these laws about the roles of women and men? Which laws or punishments seem unusual today? What does that difference suggest to you about ancient Babylon compared to modern society?

Thinking Historically

As a primary source, law codes are extremely useful. They zero in on a society's main concerns, revealing minutiae of daily life in great detail. But, for a number of reasons, law codes cannot be viewed as a precise reflection of society.

We cannot assume, for instance, that all of Hammurabi's laws were strictly followed or enforced, nor can we assume that for our own society. If there was a law against something, we can safely assume that some people obeyed it and some people did not. (That is, if no one engaged in the behavior, there would be no need for the law.) Therefore, law codes suggest a broad range of behaviors in a society.

While laws tell us something about the concerns of the society that produces them, we cannot presume that all members of society share the same concerns. Recall that, especially in ancient society, laws were written by the literate, powerful few. What evidence do you see of the upper-class "patrician" composition of Babylonian law in this code?

Finally, if an ancient law seems similar to our own, we cannot assume that the law reflects motives, intents, or goals similar to our own laws. Laws must be considered within the context of the society in which they were created. Notice, for instance, the laws in Hammurabi's Code that may seem, by our standards, intended to protect women. On closer examination, what appears to be their goal?

"Hammurabi's Code," from C. H. Johns, *Babylonian and Assyrian Laws, Contracts and Letters* (Library of Ancient Inscriptions) (New York: Charles Scribner's Sons, 1904), 33–35.

Theft

6. If a man has stolen goods from a temple, or house, he shall be put to death; and he that has received the stolen property from him shall be put to death.

8. If a patrician has stolen ox, sheep, ass, pig, or goat, whether from a temple, or a house, he shall pay thirtyfold. If he be a plebeian, he shall return tenfold. If the thief cannot pay, he shall be put to death.

14. If a man has stolen a child, he shall be put to death.

15. If a man has induced either a male or female slave from the house of a patrician, or plebeian, to leave the city, he shall be put to death.

21. If a man has broken into a house he shall be killed before the breach and buried there.

22. If a man has committed highway robbery and has been caught, that man shall be put to death.

23. If the highwayman has not been caught, the man that has been robbed shall state on oath what he has lost and the city or district governor in whose territory or district the robbery took place shall restore to him what he has lost.

Family

128. If a man has taken a wife and has not executed a marriage-contract, that woman is not a wife.

129. If a man's wife be caught lying with another, they shall be strangled and cast into the water. If the wife's husband would save his wife, the king can save his servant.

130. If a man has ravished another's betrothed wife, who is a virgin, while still living in her father's house, and has been caught in the act, that man shall be put to death; the woman shall go free.

131. If a man's wife has been accused by her husband, and has not been caught lying with another, she shall swear her innocence, and return to her house.

138. If a man has divorced his wife, who has not borne him children, he shall pay over to her as much money as was given for her bride-price and the marriage-portion which she brought from her father's house, and so shall divorce her.

139. If there was no bride-price, he shall give her one mina of silver, as a price of divorce.

140. If he be a plebeian, he shall give her one-third of a mina of silver.

148. If a man has married a wife and a disease has seized her, if he is determined to marry a second wife, he shall marry her. He shall not divorce the wife whom the disease has seized. In the home they made together she shall dwell, and he shall maintain her as long as she lives.

149. If that woman was not pleased to stay in her husband's house, he shall pay over to her the marriage-portion which she brought from her father's house, and she shall go away.

153. If a man's wife, for the sake of another, has caused her husband to be killed, that woman shall be impaled.

154. If a man has committed incest with his daughter, that man shall be banished from the city.

155. If a man has betrothed a maiden to his son and his son has known her, and afterward the man has lain in her bosom, and been caught, that man shall be strangled and she shall be cast into the water.

156. If a man has betrothed a maiden to his son, and his son has not known her, and that man has lain in her bosom, he shall pay her half a mina of silver, and shall pay over to her whatever she brought from her father's house, and the husband of her choice shall marry her.

186. If a man has taken a young child to be his son, and after he has taken him, the child discovers his own parents, he shall return to his father's house.

188, 189. If a craftsman has taken a child to bring up and has taught him his handicraft, he shall not be reclaimed. If he has not taught him his handicraft that foster child shall return to his father's house.

Assault

195. If a son has struck his father, his hands shall be cut off.

196. If a man has knocked out the eye of a patrician, his eye shall be knocked out.

197. If he has broken the limb of a patrician, his limb shall be broken.

198. If he has knocked out the eye of a plebeian or has broken the limb of a plebeian's servant, he shall pay one mina of silver.

199. If he has knocked out the eye of a patrician's servant, or broken the limb of a patrician's servant, he shall pay half his value.

200. If a patrician has knocked out the tooth of a man that is his equal, his tooth shall be knocked out.

201. If he has knocked out the tooth of a plebeian, he shall pay one-third of a mina of silver.

Liability

229. If a builder has built a house for a man, and has not made his work sound, and the house he built has fallen, and caused the death of its owner, that builder shall be put to death.

230. If it is the owner's son that is killed, the builder's son shall be put to death.

231. If it is the slave of the owner that is killed, the builder shall give slave for slave to the owner of the house.

232. If he has caused the loss of goods, he shall render back whatever he has destroyed. Moreover, because he did not make sound the house he built, and it fell, at his own cost he shall rebuild the house that fell.

237. If a man has hired a boat and a boatman, and loaded it with corn, wool, oil, or dates, or whatever it be, and the boatman has been careless, and sunk the boat, or lost what is in it, the boatman shall restore the boat which he sank, and whatever he lost that was in it.

238. If a boatman has sunk a man's boat, and has floated it again, he shall pay half its value in silver.

251. If a man's ox be a gorer, and has revealed its evil propensity as a gorer, and he has not blunted its horn, or shut up the ox, and then that ox has gored a free man, and caused his death, the owner shall pay half a mina of silver.

252. If it be a slave that has been killed, he shall pay one-third of a mina of silver.

8

Advice to the Young Egyptian: "Be a Scribe"

Writing was a hallmark of the urban revolution five thousand years ago. Egyptian society, like Mesopotamian, prospered through written laws, records, and knowledge. Urban societies required many occupations that had not existed in the agricultural village, but foremost among these was the writer, or scribe. Sometimes a priest, often an official, the scribe, by virtue of his ability to read and write, provided the glue that held complex societies together.

Excavations of ancient Egypt have unearthed many papyri like these from the 20th Dynasty (twelfth century B.C.E.) that urge young Egyptians to become scribes. Because these papyri often contain spelling mistakes and other errors, archaeologists have concluded they are probably writing exercises for future scribes. How would the assignment to copy

Miriam Lichtheim, *Ancient Egyptian Literature: A Book of Readings, Volume II: The New Kingdom* (Berkeley: University of California Press, 1976), 169–72.

these paragraphs help train writers in ancient Egypt? What do these papyri tell you about the life of the scribe in ancient Egypt?

Thinking Historically

These paragraphs tell us about other occupations besides that of the scribe. What, according to the papyri, were some of the other occupations common in ancient Egypt? How accurate do you think the descriptions of these occupations are? This document is sometimes called "the satire on the trades." Why would it be called that? How might you use this document to argue that Egyptian society was reasonably fair and egalitarian for the ancient world? How might you use this document to argue that Egyptian society was a deeply divided class society? Which do you think it was?

All Occupations Are Bad Except That of the Scribe

See for yourself with your own eye. The occupations lie before you.

The washerman's day is going up, going down. All his limbs are weak, (from) whitening his neighbors' clothes every day, from washing their linen.

The marker of pots is smeared with soil, like one whose relations have died. His hands, his feet are full of clay; he is like one who lives in the bog.

The cobbler mingles with vats. His odor is penetrating. His hands are red with madder,[1] like one who is smeared with blood. He looks behind him for the kite, like one whose flesh is exposed.

The watchman prepares garlands and polishes vase-stands. He spends a night of toil just as one on whom the sun shines.

The merchants travel downstream and upstream. They are as busy as can be, carrying goods from one town to another. They supply him who has wants. But the tax collectors carry off the gold, that most precious of metals.

The ships' crews from every house (of commerce), they receive their loads. They depart from Egypt for Syria, and each man's god is with him. (But) not one of them says: "We shall see Egypt again!"

The carpenter who is in the shipyard carries the timber and stacks it. If he gives today the output of yesterday, woe to his limbs! The shipwright stands behind him to tell him evil things.

His outworker who is in the fields, his is the toughest of all the jobs. He spends the day loaded with his tools, tied to his tool-box. When he returns home at night, he is loaded with the tool-box and the timbers, his drinking mug, and his whetstones.

The scribe, he alone, records the output of all of them. Take note of it!

---

[1]A plant used to make red dye. [Ed.]

The Misfortunes of the Peasant

Let me also expound to you the situation of the peasant, that other tough occupation. [Comes] the inundation and soaks him————, he attends to his equipment. By day he cuts his farming tools; by night he twists rope. Even his midday hour he spends on farm labor. He equips himself to go to the field as if he were a warrior. The dried field lies before him; he goes out to get his team. When he has been after the herdsman for many days, he gets his team and comes back with it. He makes for it a place in the field. Comes dawn, he goes to make a start and does not find it in its place. He spends three days searching for it; he finds it in the bog. He finds no hides on them; the jackals have chewed them. He comes out, his garment in his hand, to beg for himself a team.

When he reaches his field he finds [it] "broken up." He spends time cultivating, and the snake is after him. It finishes off the seed as it is cast to the ground. He does not see a green blade. He does three plowings with borrowed grain. His wife has gone down to the merchants and found nothing for "barter." Now the scribe lands on the shore. He surveys the harvest. Attendants are behind him with staffs, Nubians with clubs. One says (to him): "Give grain." "There is none." He is beaten savagely. He is bound, thrown in the well, submerged head down. His wife is bound in his presence. His children are in fetters. His neighbors abandon them and flee. When it's over, there's no grain.

If you have any sense, be a scribe. If you have learned about the peasant, you will not be able to be one. Take note of it!

Be a Scribe

The scribe of the army and commander of the cattle of the house of Amun, Nebmare-nakht, speaks to the scribe Wenemdiamun, as follows. Be a scribe! Your body will be sleek; your hand will be soft. You will not flicker like a flame, like one whose body is feeble. For there is not the bone of a man in you. You are tall and thin. If you lifted a load to carry it, you would stagger, your legs would tremble. You are lacking in strength; you are weak in all your limbs; you are poor in body.

Set your sight on being a scribe; a fine profession that suits you. You call for one; a thousand answer you. You stride freely on the road. You will not be like a hired ox. You are in front of others.

I spend the day instructing you. You do not listen! Your heart is like an [empty] room. My teachings are not in it. Take their ["meaning"] to yourself!

The marsh thicket is before you each day, as a nestling is after its mother. You follow the path of pleasure; you make friends with revellers. You have made your home in the brewery, as one who thirsts for beer. You sit in the parlor with an idler. You hold the writings in contempt. You visit the whore. Do not do these things! What are they for? They are of no use. Take note of it!

The Scribe Does Not Suffer Like the Soldier

Furthermore. Look, I instruct you to make you sound; to make you hold the palette freely. To make you become one whom the king trusts; to make you gain entrance to treasury and granary. To make you receive the ship-load at the gate of the granary. To make you issue the offerings on feast days. You are dressed in fine clothes; you own horses. Your boat is on the river; you are supplied with attendants. You stride about inspecting. A mansion is built in your town. You have a powerful office, given you by the king. Male and female slaves are about you. Those who are in the fields grasp your hand, on plots that you have made. Look, I make you into a staff of life! Put the writings in your heart, and you will be protected from all kinds of toil. You will become a worthy official.

Do you not recall the (fate of) the unskilled man? His name is not known. He is ever burdened [like an ass carrying] in front of the scribe who knows what he is about.

Come, [let me tell] you the woes of the soldier, and how many are his superiors: the general, the troop-commander, the officer who leads, the standard-bearer, the lieutenant, the scribe, the commander of fifty, and the garrison-captain. They go in and out in the halls of the palace, saying: "Get laborers!" He is awakened at any hour. One is after him as (after) a donkey. He toils until the Aten sets in his darkness of night. He is hungry, his belly hurts; he is dead while yet alive. When he receives the grain-ration, having been released from duty, it is not good for grinding.

He is called up for Syria. He may not rest. There are no clothes, no sandals. The weapons of war are assembled at the fortress of Sile. His march is uphill through mountains. He drinks water every third day; it is smelly and tastes of salt. His body is ravaged by illness. The enemy comes, surrounds him with missiles, and life recedes from him. He is told: "Quick, forward, valiant soldier! Win for yourself a good name!" He does not know what he is about. His body is weak, his legs fail him. When victory is won, the captives are handed over to his majesty, to be taken to Egypt. The foreign woman faints on the march; she hangs herself [on] the soldier's neck. His knapsack drops, another grabs it while he is burdened with the woman. His wife and children are in their village; he dies and does not reach it. If he comes out alive, he is worn out from marching. Be he at large, be he detained, the soldier suffers. If he leaps and joins the deserters, all his people are imprisoned. He dies on the edge of the desert, and there is none to perpetuate his name. He suffers in death as in life. A big sack is brought for him; he does not know his resting place.

Be a scribe, and be spared from soldiering! You call and one says: "Here I am." You are safe from torments. Every man seeks to raise himself up. Take note of it!

Images of Ancient Egypt

Thanks to the preservative dry climate and the ancient Egyptian interest in illustrating books of papyrus and painting the interiors of pyramids, temples, and tombs, we have excellent visual primary sources on the daily life of ancient Egypt. The first two images are from a papyrus called Hunefer's *Book of the Dead*. Hunefer was a royal official of the 13th century B.C.E. Like other wealthy or powerful Egyptians, Hunefer had a version of the *Book of the Dead*, with all its prayers and incantations, prepared especially for him.

In Figure 2.1, Hunefer's mummy is prepared to enter the afterlife. His wife and daughter dab their heads with dirt. Three priests administer the rituals. The priest on the far left, dressed in a lion skin, burns incense and readies the food offerings. Two others prepare the important ceremony of opening the mummy's mouth so that it can breathe and eat. Anubis, the jackal-headed god of death, holds the mummy. Behind him we can read an enlarged version of Hunefer's tombstone, which will be placed in front of his tomb, a miniature image of which we see on the far right.

In Figure 2.2 we see Hunefer led by Anubis, about to be judged. In the center of the frame Hunefer's heart is weighed against a feather. If his heart is lighter than the feather he will be admitted to the presence of Osiris and enter the afterlife. If not, his heart will be devoured by the demon Ammut, whose crocodile head is turned to the ibis-headed god Thoth, standing to the right of the scales and writing the verdict. In that case, his existence will end forever. Fortunately, Hunefer's artist assures him of a happy ending. Thoth conducts Hunefer to Osiris seated on a throne, behind his four sons standing on a lotus leaf and in front of his wife, the goddess Isis, and her sister. What do these

Book of the Dead of Hunefer Thebes, Egypt, 19th Dynasty, around 1275 B.C.E.

images tell you about Egyptian society? How do they compare to your own ideas of death?

Egyptians also celebrated life. Figures 2.3 and 2.4 are representative of countless paintings from Egyptian tombs that were made to ensure the deceased a happy immortality. In this case, we see images from a vineyard and a bakery. What do these images tell you about Egyptian society?

Thinking Historically

Reading primary sources, whether they be words or images, is always tricky. Unlike secondary sources, they were not written, painted, or left for us. The assumptions and intentions of the writer or artist may be very different from our own, and so we may misunderstand the meaning or purpose of a work.

Entering an Egyptian tomb today, one cannot help being overwhelmed by the beauty of the paintings. Their vitality can be breathtaking. To the modern viewer, especially in museums where paintings and papyrus are torn from their original setting, they appear to us as beautiful works of art. And so they are. But for the ancient Egyptians, these images were more than representations, more than art. They were the things depicted. The food that was displayed was food for the deceased in the afterlife; the people painted on the walls were there to provide and serve. The pictures were intended to be more vital than we can imagine. Are visual images more or less reliable as primary sources than written words? What visuals add to our understanding? How might they mislead us?

Images are different from written words in another way. You are able to make sense of these images from Hunefer's *Book of the Dead* because primary and secondary texts enable us to provide a summary of the story behind them. But the Egyptian artist and viewer knew that story, and hundreds of subplots, by heart. Imagine "reading" the images the way an ancient Egyptian viewer would have. Would the difference between your modern interpretation and the Egyptian viewer's interpretation be similar to the difference between seeing a movie and reading the book? And if "the book" was the wisdom of the ages as everyone knew it, and images could be real, what sort of movie would that be?

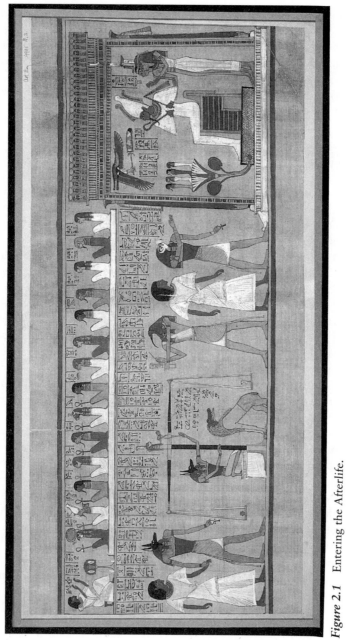

Figure 2.1 Entering the Afterlife.

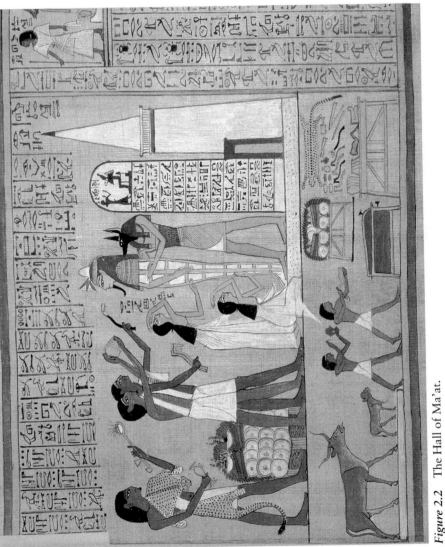

Figure 2.2   The Hall of Ma'at.
Source: © The Trustees of The British Museum.

Figure 2.3   Making Wine.
   Source: The Image Works.

Figure 2.4   Making Bread.
   Source: The Image Works.

REFLECTIONS

To focus our subject in a brief chapter we have examined Mesopotamia and Egypt almost exclusively. This enabled us to observe the beginnings of the urban revolution in Mesopotamia and one of the most spectacular and best preserved of ancient civilizations in Egypt. The city-states of Mesopotamia and the territorial state of Egypt were the two extremes of ancient civilization. City-states packed most people tightly within their walls. Eighty percent of Mesopotamians lived within city walls by 2800 B.C.E. By contrast, less than 10 percent of Egyptians lived in cities—if we can call their unwalled settlements, palace compounds, and pyramid construction sites "cities" at all. The lesser role of cities in Egypt has led some historians to drop the term "urban revolution" for "the rise of civilization." Other historians, objecting to the moralistic implications of the term "civilization," prefer "the rise of complex societies." "Complex" is not a very precise term, but it would refer to the appearance of social classes, the mixing of different populations, a multilayered governmental structure with rulers, officials, and ordinary people, and numerous specialists who are not full-time farmers or herders. More specifically, we might include kings, priests, writing, wheels, monumental building, markets, and money.

If we broaden our view, however, to include the "complex societies" of South Asia, China, and the Americas, cities—even city-states—pop up like mushrooms after a spring rain. Along the Indus River in Pakistan dozens of small and midsize cities formed independent clones of Harappa and Mohenjodaro. These numerous cities seem to have enjoyed the independence of city-states since there is no evidence of kings, soldiers, or warfare along the Indus. Instead of being bound to a territorial sovereign, these cities and dozens of others in what is today Iran, Afghanistan, India, and surrounding areas communicated and traded with each other in a web of economic interactions.

Territorial states, more like Egypt than Mesopotamia, integrated the Yellow River valley of northern China and the settlements of the high Andes in South America, but they also constructed large cities as administrative and spiritual centers. In Mexico, early civilizations were centered in cities: the Zapotec at Monte Alban, the Toltec at Teotihuacan, the Aztec at Tenochtitlan, and the Mayan at numerous ceremonial and residential centers. Cities defined the complex societies of the Americas more than wheels (used only for toys) and writing, which remained highly pictorial in Mexico, and, in the Andes, a matter of reading colored strings where the place of knots signified meaning like an ancient system of digital computing.

Thus, a larger lens raises more questions than we have allowed in our brief examination of Mesopotamia and Egypt. How important were such "urban inventions" as kings, soldiers, warfare, wheels, and writing if they did not exist everywhere cities were created? Further, how important were cities in the creation of the complex lives we have lived for the last five thousand years?

We might also ask the larger question: Has the urban revolution improved our lives? The belief that it has lies behind the use of the word *civilization*. Though the root of the word is the same as city, civil, and civilian, the word *civilization* came into the modern vocabulary of historians and social scientists in the nineteenth century. At this time anthropologists were working to distinguish stages of history and to illustrate the differences between what were then called "primitive" peoples and people of the modern world whom anthropologists considered "civilized." Thus, they contended there had been three stages of history that could be summarized, in chronological order, as savagery, barbarism, and civilization. By the early twentieth century, in the work of the great prehistorian V. Gordon Childe, these terms stood for hunting-gathering, agricultural, and urban societies.

The belief that the world of the anthropologists and the "moderns" of the nineteenth and twentieth centuries was more civilized than the pre-urban world that they studied was more than a bit presumptuous. But this presumption continues today, in the popular mythology of "country bumpkins" who lack the manners and savoir faire of their city cousins. Interestingly, it was also the assumption of the earliest founders of cities. *The Epic of Gilgamesh* tells of the need of the city to tame the wild Enkidu so that he can take his place in:

> . . . ramparted Uruk,
> Where fellows are resplendent in holiday clothing,
> Where every day is set for celebration.

There are many reasons to be skeptical of the so-called achievements of city life: increased inequality, suppression of women, slavery, organized warfare, conscription, heavy taxation, forced labor, to name some of the most obvious. But our museums are full of the art and artifacts that testify to what the ancients meant by "civilization." The pyramids of Egypt and of Mexico and the ziggurats of Mesopotamia are among the wonders of the world. Does it matter that the great pyramids of Egypt were built from the forced labor of thousands to provide a resting place for a single person and that people were entombed alive in order to serve him? We can view the pyramids today as a remarkable achievement of engineering and organization while still condemning the manner of their execution. We can admire the art in the tombs, thrill to the revealing detail of ancient Egyptian life, marvel at the persistence of vivid colors mixed almost five thousand years ago, and treasure the art for what it reveals of the world of its creators, while we still detest its purpose.

We can do this because these monuments have become something different for us than what they were for the ancients. They have become testaments to human achievement, regardless of the cost. These ancient city-based societies were the first in which humans produced abundant works of art and architecture, which still astound us in their range, scope, and design.

The significance of the urban revolution was that it produced things that lasted beyond their utility or meaning—thanks to new techniques in stone cutting and hauling; baking brick, tile, and glass; and smelting tin, copper, and bronze—as a legacy for future generations. Even three thousand years ago, Egyptian engineers studied the ancient pyramids to understand a very distant past, 1,500 years before, and to learn, adapt, revive, or revise ancient techniques. In short, the achievement of the urban revolution is that it made knowledge cumulative, so that each generation could stand on the shoulders of its predecessors.

3

Identity in Caste and Territorial Societies

Greece and India, 1000–300 B.C.E.

HISTORICAL CONTEXT

Both India and Greece developed ancient city-based civilizations within a thousand years of the urban revolution. In India that civilization was concentrated on the Indus River valley in what is today Pakistan. (See Map 3.1.) In Greece the Minoan civilization on the island of Crete was followed by the Mycenaean civilization on the mainland. (See Map 3.2.) But both ancient Indian and ancient Greek civilizations were transformed by new peoples from the grasslands of Eurasia, who settled in both areas between 1500 and 1000 B.C.E. Called by later generations the Aryans in India and the Dorians in Greece, these pastoral peoples arrived with horses, different customs, and new technologies. The Aryans came with chariots (as had the early Mycenaeans), while the Dorians, somewhat later, brought iron tools and weapons.

Despite the similar origins of the newcomers and the similar urban experience of the lands in which they settled, Aryan India and Dorian Greece developed in significantly different ways. As William H. McNeill writes in the first selection, by the year 500 B.C.E. Indian and Greek civilizations had found entirely different ways of organizing and administering their societies. And these differences had profound effects on the subsequent history of Indian and European society.

THINKING HISTORICALLY

Interpreting Primary Sources in Light of a Secondary Source

In Chapter 2, we distinguished between primary and secondary sources. Similarly, we begin here with a secondary source, or an interpretation. We then turn, as we did in the last chapter, to a series of primary sources. But while the last chapter focused on recognizing and distinguishing primary from secondary sources, here we concentrate on the relationship of the primary sources to the secondary interpretation — how one affects our reading of the other.

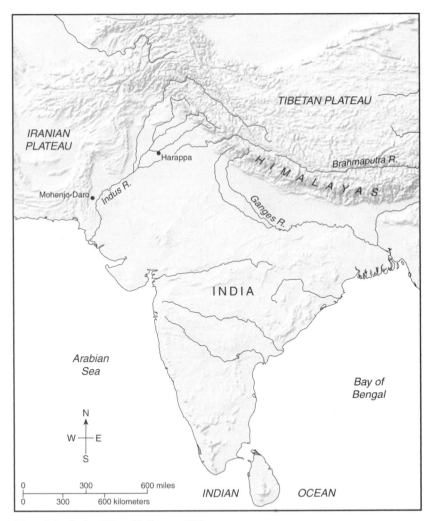

Map 3.1 Indus River Valley, c. 500 B.C.E.

In this chapter, the primary sources were chosen to illustrate points made in the introductory interpretation. This provides an opportunity to understand the interpretation in some detail and with some degree of subtlety. The primary sources do not give you enough material to argue that McNeill is right or wrong, but you will be able to flesh out some of the meaning of his interpretation. You might also reflect more generally on the relationship of sources and interpretations. You will be asked how particular sources support or even contradict the interpretation. You will consider the relevance of sources for other interpretations, and you will imagine what sort of sources you might seek for evidence.

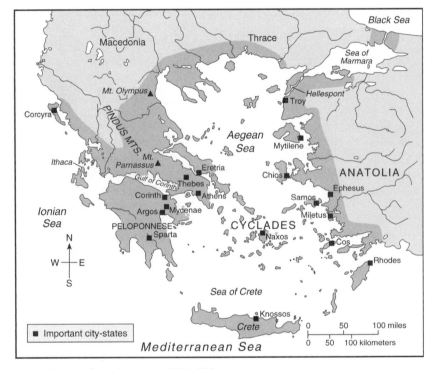

Map 3.2   Archaic Greece, c. 750–500 B.C.E.

10

WILLIAM H. McNEILL

Greek and Indian Civilization

William H. McNeill is one of the leading world historians in the United States. In this selection from his college textbook *A World History*, he compares the different ways in which Indian and Greek civilizations of the classical age (by around 500 B.C.E.) organized themselves. He distinguishes between Indian *caste* and Greek *territorial sovereignty*. These concepts are complex but useful to distinguish between two of the basic ways societies organize and identify themselves. As you read, try to define what each term means. McNeill argues that caste and territorial sovereignty had enormously different effects on the subsequent development of Indian and European society. What were some of these different effects?

Thinking Historically

As you read this secondary source or historical interpretation, consider what sort of primary sources might have led McNeill to this view or support his interpretation. Notice especially that in the first half of the selection, McNeill mentions specific ancient Indian writings: These are obvious primary sources for his interpretation. Not having read McNeill's primary sources, can you imagine what in them would lead to this interpretation?

Less of McNeill's interpretation of Greece is included in this selection and, consequently, there is no mention of primary sources. In this chapter, you will read a number of Greek primary sources, but at this point can you speculate about what types of sources would demonstrate the Greek idea of territorial sovereignty?

Keep in mind that caste and territorial sovereignty are modern terms not known or used by the ancients; therefore, you will not find them in the primary sources that follow. What words might the ancient Indians or Greeks have used to denote these concepts?

William H. McNeill, *A World History*, 2nd ed. (New York: Oxford University Press, 1971), 78–83, 88, 90, 95, 99–100.

Caste

A modern caste is a group of persons who will eat with one another and intermarry, while excluding others from these two intimacies. In addition, members of any particular caste must bear some distinguishing mark, so that everyone will know who belongs and who does not belong to it. Definite rules for how to behave in the presence of members of other castes also become necessary in situations where such contacts are frequent. When an entire society comes to be organized on these principles, any group of strangers or intruders automatically becomes another caste, for the exclusive habits of the rest of the population inevitably thrust the newcomers in upon themselves when it comes to eating and marrying. A large caste may easily break into smaller groupings as a result of some dispute, or through mere geographical separation over a period of time. New castes can form around new occupations. Wanderers and displaced individuals who find a new niche in society are automatically compelled to eat together and marry one another by the caste-bound habits of their neighbors.

How or when Indian society came to be organized along these lines remains unclear. Perhaps the Indus civilization itself was built upon something like the caste principle. Or perhaps the antipathy between Aryan invaders and the dark-skinned people whom they attacked lay at the root of the caste system of later India. But whatever the origins of caste, three features of Indian thought and feeling were mobilized to sustain the caste principle in later times. One of these was the idea of ceremonial purity. Fear of contaminating oneself by contact with a member of a lower, "unclean" caste gave Brahmans and others near the top of the pyramid strong reasons for limiting their association with low-caste persons.

From the other end of the scale, too, the poor and humble had strong reasons for clinging to caste. All but the most miserable and marginal could look down upon somebody, a not unimportant psychological feature of the system. In addition, the humbler castes were often groups that had only recently emerged from primitive forest life. They naturally sought to maintain their peculiar customs and habits, even in the context of urban or mixed village life, where men of different backgrounds and different castes lived side by side. Other civilized societies usually persuaded or compelled newcomers to surrender their peculiar ways, and assimilated them in the course of a few generations to the civilized population as a whole. In India, on the contrary, such groups were able to retain their separate identities indefinitely by preserving their own peculiar customs within the caste framework, generation after generation.

The third factor sustaining the caste principle was theoretical: the doctrine of reincarnation and of "varna." The latter declared that all men were naturally divided into four castes: the Brahmans who prayed, the Kshatriyas* who fought, the Vaisyas† who worked, and the Sudras who performed unclean tasks. Official doctrine classified the first three castes as Aryan, the last as non-Aryan, and put much stress on caste rank, from Brahmans at the top to Sudras at the bottom. Reality never corresponded even remotely to this theory. There were hundreds if not thousands of castes in India, rather than the four recognized in Brahmanical teaching. But apparent injustices and anomalies disappeared when the doctrine of reincarnation was combined with the doctrine of varna. The idea of reincarnation, indeed, gave logical explanation and justification to the system by explaining caste as a divinely established institution, hereditary from father to son, and designed to reward and punish souls for their actions in former lives. This undoubtedly helped to stabilize the confused reality. A man of unblemished life, born into the lowest caste, could hope for rebirth higher up the ladder. Conversely, a man of high caste who failed to conform to proper standards could expect rebirth in a lower caste. A man even risked reincarnation as a worm or beetle, if his misbehavior deserved such a punishment.

Clearly, the caste system as observed today did not exist in ancient India. Yet modern castes are the outgrowth of patterns of social organization that are as old as the oldest records. Early Buddhist stories, for instance, reveal many episodes turning upon caste distinctions, and passages in the *Rig Veda*‡ and other ancient writings imply caste-like practices and attitudes. By 500 B.C.E. we can at least be sure that the seeds from which the modern caste organization of society grew had already sprouted luxuriantly on Indian soil.

Caste lessened the significance of political, territorial administration. Everyone identified himself first and foremost with his caste. But a caste ordinarily lacked both definite internal administration and distinct territorial boundaries. Instead, members of a particular caste mingled with men of other castes, observing the necessary precautions to prevent contamination of one by the other. No king or ruler could command the undivided loyalty of people who felt themselves to belong to a caste rather than to a state. Indeed, to all ordinary caste members, rulers, officials, soldiers, and tax collectors were likely to seem mere troublesome outsiders, to be neglected whenever possible

*KSHAH tree uh
†VYS yuh
‡rihg VAY dah

and obeyed only as far as necessary. The fragile character of most Indian states resulted in large part from this fact. A striking absence of
information about war and government is characteristic of all early
Indian history; and this, too, presumably reflects Indian peoples'
characteristic emotional disengagement from the state and from
politics. . . .

The Vedas and Brahmanas

Our knowledge of Aryan religion derives from the Vedas. The Vedas,
used as handbooks of religious ritual, consist of songs that were recited
aloud during sacrifices, together with other passages instructing the
priests what to do during the ceremony. In course of time, the language
of the Vedas became more or less unintelligible, even to priests. A great
effort was thereupon made to preserve details of accent and pronunciation, by insisting on exact memorization of texts from master to pupil
across the generations. Every jot and tittle of the inherited verses was
felt to matter, since a misplaced line or mispronounced word could nul-
lify a whole sacrifice and might even provoke divine displeasure.

Preoccupation with correctness of detail speedily shifted emphasis
from the gods of the Aryan pantheon to the act of worship and invocation itself. Aryan priests may also have learned about magical powers
claimed by priests of the Indus civilization. At any rate, some Brahmans
began to argue that by performing rituals correctly they could actually
compel the gods to grant what was asked of them. Indeed, proper sacrifice and invocation created the world of gods and men anew, and sta-
bilized afresh the critical relation between natural and supernatural reality. In such a view, the importance and personalities of the separate
gods shrank to triviality, while the power and skill of the priesthood
was greatly magnified. These extravagant priestly claims were freely put
forward in texts called Brahmanas. These were cast in the form of commentaries on the Vedas, purportedly explaining what the older texts really meant, but often changing meanings in the process.

The Upanishads and Mysticism

Priestly claims to exercise authority over gods and men were never
widely accepted in ancient India. Chiefs and warriors might be a bit
wary of priestly magic, but they were not eager to cede to the priests
the primacy claimed by the Brahmanas. Humbler ranks of society also
objected to priestly presumption. This is proved by the fact that a rival
type of piety took hold in India and soon came to constitute the most
distinctive element in the whole religious tradition of the land. Another

body of oral literature, the Upanishads,* constitutes our evidence of this religious development. The Upanishads are not systematic treatises nor do they agree in all details. Yet they do express a general consensus on important points.

First of all, the Upanishads conceive the end of religious life in a radically new way. Instead of seeking riches, health, and long life, a wise and holy man strives merely to escape the endless round of rebirth. Success allows his soul to dissolve into the All from whence it had come, triumphantly transcending the suffering, pain, and imperfection of existence.

In the second place, holiness and release from the cycle of rebirths were attained not by obedience to priests nor by observance of ceremonies. The truly holy man had no need of intermediaries and, for that matter, no need of gods. Instead, by a process of self-discipline, meditation, asceticism, and withdrawal from the ordinary concerns of daily life, the successful religious athlete might attain a mystic vision of Truth — a vision which left the seer purged and happy. The nature and content of the mystic vision could never be expressed in words. It revealed Truth by achieving an identity between the individual soul and the Soul of the universe. Such an experience, surpassing human understanding and ordinary language, constituted a foretaste of the ultimate bliss of self-annihilation in the All, which was the final goal of wise and holy life. . . .

While India worked its way toward the definition of a new and distinctive civilization on one flank of the ancient Middle East, on its other flank another new civilization was also emerging: the Greek. The principal stages of early Greek history closely resemble what we know or can surmise about Indian development. But the end product differed fundamentally. The Greeks put political organization into territorial states above all other bases of human association, and attempted to explain the world and man not in terms of mystic illumination but through laws of nature. Thus despite a similar start, when fierce "tamers of horses" — like those of whom Homer[1] later sang — overran priest-led agricultural societies, the Indian and Greek styles of civilization diverged strikingly by 500 B.C.E. . . .

The self-governing city-states created by Greeks on the coast of Asia Minor had . . . great . . . importance in world history. For by inventing the city-state or *polis* (hence our word "politics"), the Greeks of Ionia established the prototype from which the whole Western world derived its penchant for political organization into territorially defined

---

*oo PAH nee shahdz
[1]Greek poet c. 800 B.C.E.; author of *The Iliad* and *The Odyssey*. [Ed.]

sovereign units, i.e., into states. The supremacy of territoriality over all other forms of human association is neither natural nor inevitable, as the Indian caste principle may remind us. . . .

Dominance of the Polis in Greek Culture

So powerful and compelling was the psychological pull of the polis that almost every aspect of Greek cultural activity was speedily caught up in and — as it were — digested by the new master institution of Greek civilization. Religion, art, literature, philosophy, took shape or acquired a new accent through their relationship with the all-engulfing object of the citizens' affection. . . .

Despite the general success of the polis ordering of things, a few individuals fretted over the logical inconsistencies of Greek religion and traditional world view. As trade developed, opportunities to learn about the wisdom of the East multiplied. Inquiring Greeks soon discovered that among the priestly experts of the Middle East there was no agreement about such fundamental questions as how the world was created or why the planets periodically checked their forward movement through the heavens and went backward for a while before resuming their former motion. It was in Ionia that men first confronted this sort of question systematically enough to bother recording their views. These, the first philosophers, sought to explain the phenomena of the world by imaginative exercise of their power of reason. Finding conflicting and unsupported stories about the gods to be unsatisfactory, they took the drastic step of omitting the gods entirely, and boldly substituted natural law instead as the ruling force of the universe. To be sure, the Ionian philosophers did not agree among themselves when they sought to describe how the laws of nature worked, and their naive efforts to explain an ever wider range of phenomena did not meet with much success.

Nevertheless, their attempts at using speculative reason to explain the nature of things marked a major turning point in human intellectual development. The Ionian concept of a universe ruled not by the whim of some divine personality but by an impersonal and unchangeable law has never since been forgotten. Throughout the subsequent history of European and Middle Eastern thought, this distinctively Greek view of the nature of things stood in persistent and fruitful tension with the older, Middle Eastern theistic explanation of the universe. Particular thinkers, reluctant to abandon either position entirely, have sought to reconcile the omnipotence of the divine will with the unchangeability of natural law by means of the most various arguments. Since, however, the two views are as logically incompatible with one another as were the myths from which the Ionian philosophers started, no formulation or reconciliation ever attained lasting and universal consent. Men always had to start over again to reshape for themselves a more satisfactory metaphysic and theology. Here, therefore, lay a growing point for all subsequent European thought which has not yet been exhausted.

Indeed, the recent successes of natural science seem to have vindicated the Ionian concept of natural law in ways and with a complexity that would have utterly amazed Thales* (d. c. 546 B.C.E.) or any of his successors, who merely voiced what turned out to be amazingly lucky guesses. How did they do it? It seems plausible to suggest that the Ionians hit upon the notion of natural law by simply projecting the tight little world of the polis upon the universe. For it was a fact that the polis was regulated by law, not by the personal will or whim of a ruler. If such invisible abstractions could govern human behavior and confine it to certain roughly predictable paths of action, why could not similar laws control the natural world? To such a question, it appears, the Ionians gave an affirmative answer, and in doing so gave a distinctive cast to all subsequent Greek and European thought.

Limitations of the Polis

It would be a mistake to leave the impression that all facets of Greek life fitted smoothly and easily into the polis frame. The busy public world left scant room for the inwardness of personal experience. Striving for purification, for salvation, for holiness, which found such ample expression in the Indian cultural setting, was almost excluded. Yet the Greeks were not immune from such impulses. Through the ancient mystery religions, as well as through such an association as the "Order" founded by Pythagoras,† the famous mathematician and mystic (d. c. 507 B.C.E.), they sought to meet these needs. But when such efforts took organized form, a fundamental incompatibility between the claims of the polis to the unqualified loyalty of every citizen and the pursuit of personal holiness quickly became apparent. This was illustrated by the stormy history of the Pythagorean Order. Either the organized seekers after holiness captured the polis, as happened for a while in the city of Croton in southern Italy, or the magistrates of the polis persecuted the Order, as happened in Pythagoras' old age. There seemed no workable ground of compromise in this, the earliest recorded instance of conflict between church and state in Western history.

The fundamental difference between Greek and Indian institutions as shaped by about 500 B.C.E. was made apparent by this episode. The loose federation of cultures allowed by the caste principle in India experienced

*THAY leez
†py THAG uhr ahs

no difficulty at all in accommodating organized seekers after holiness such as the communities of Buddhist monks. By contrast, the exclusive claim upon the citizens' time, effort, and affection which had been staked out by the Greek polis allowed no sort of corporate rival.

Enormous energies were tapped by the polis. A wider segment of the total population was engaged in cultural and political action than had been possible in any earlier civilized society, and the brilliant flowering of classical Greek civilization was the consequence. Yet the very intensity of the political tie excluded ranges of activity and sensitivity that were not compatible with a territorial organization of human groupings, and sowed seeds of civil strife between the Greek cities which soon proved disastrous. But every achievement involves a surrender of alternatives: It is merely that the Greek achievement, by its very magnitude, casts an unusually clear light upon what it also excluded.

11

From the Rig Veda:
Sacrifice as Creation

As McNeill discusses in the previous selection, the Vedas are the writings of the ancient Brahman priests in India. They cover a wide variety of religious subjects and concerns: ritual, sacrifice, hymns, healing, incantations, allegories, philosophy, and the problems of everyday life. In general, the earliest Vedas (like the Rig Veda) focus more on the specifics of ritual and sacrifice, reflecting the needs and instructions of the priests during the Aryan conquest. The last of the Vedas (like the Upanishads) are more philosophical and speculative.

This selection is from the Rig Veda. What happened when Purusha was sacrificed? What is the meaning of this first sacrifice? How does this story support the role of priests?

Thinking Historically

Consider how this primary source supports the division of Indian society into castes, as McNeill discusses in the previous selection. How does this story suggest that the people who wrote the Rig Veda thought the division of society into four castes was pretty basic? Can

---

"Rig Veda," 10.90, in *Sources of Indian Tradition*, 2nd ed., ed. and rev. Ainslie T. Embree (New York: Columbia University Press, 1988), 18–19.

you deduce from this source which of the four castes was most likely the originator of the story? Does this support anything else that McNeill said in his interpretation?

Thousand-headed Purusha, thousand-eyed, thousand-footed — he, having pervaded the earth on all sides, still extends ten fingers beyond it.

Purusha alone is all this — whatever has been and whatever is going to be. Further, he is the lord of immortality and also of what grows on account of food.

Such is his greatness; greater, indeed, than this is Purusha. All creatures constitute but one-quarter of him, his three-quarters are the immortal in the heaven.

With his three-quarters did Purusha rise up; one-quarter of him again remains here. With it did he variously spread out on all sides over what eats and what eats not.

From him was Virāj born, from Virāj the evolved Purusha. He, being born, projected himself behind the earth as also before it.

When the gods performed the sacrifice with Purusha as the oblation, then the spring was its clarified butter, the summer the sacrificial fuel, and the autumn the oblation.

The sacrificial victim, namely, Purusha, born at the very beginning, they sprinkled with sacred water upon the sacrificial grass. With him as oblation, the gods performed the sacrifice, and also the Sādhyas [a class of semidivine beings] and the rishis [ancient seers].

From that wholly offered sacrificial oblation were born the verses [*ṛc*] and the sacred chants; from it were born the meters [*chandas*]; the sacrificial formula was born from it.

From it horses were born and also those animals who have double rows [i.e., upper and lower] of teeth; cows were born from it, from it were born goats and sheep.

When they divided Purusha, in how many different portions did they arrange him? What became of his mouth, what of his two arms? What were his two thighs and his two feet called?

His mouth became the brāhman; his two arms were made into the rajanya; his two thighs the vaishyas; from his two feet the shūdra was born.

The moon was born from the mind, from the eye the sun was born; from the mouth Indra and Agni, from the breath [*prāna*] the wind [*vāyu*] was born.

From the navel was the atmosphere created, from the head the heaven issued forth; from the two feet was born the earth and the quarters (the cardinal directions) from the ear. Thus did they fashion the worlds.

Seven were the enclosing sticks in this sacrifice, thrice seven were the fire-sticks made when the gods, performing the sacrifice, bound down Purusha, the sacrificial victim.

With this sacrificial oblation did the gods offer the sacrifice. These were the first norms [*dharma*] of sacrifice. These greatnesses reached to the sky wherein live the ancient Sādhyas and gods.

$$\boxed{12}$$

From the Upanishads: Karma and Reincarnation

The idea of karma (cause and effect, appropriate consequences) appears in the earliest Upanishads. Karma meant: "As you sow, so shall you reap." Good karma would be enhanced; bad karma would lead to more bad karma. The universe was a system of complete justice in which all people got what they deserved. The idea that the soul might be reborn in another body may have been an even older idea, but in the Upanishads it combined easily with the idea of karma. That a good soul was reborn in a higher life, or a bad soul in a lower, was perhaps a more material, less subtle, version of the justice of karma. The idea of reincarnation, or the transmigration of souls, united justice with caste.

What effect would these ideas have on people? In what ways would these ideas aid people in gaining a sense of power over their lives? How might these ideas be tools of control? What does "morality" mean in this tradition?

Thinking Historically

How does the idea of karma presented in this primary source support McNeill's interpretation of the importance of the caste system in India? Would the idea of reincarnation make caste organization stronger or weaker?

According as one acts, according as one conducts himself, so does he become. The doer of good becomes good. The doer of evil becomes evil. One becomes virtuous by virtuous action, bad by bad action.

Brihad Aranyaka, IV:4:5–6, in *The Thirteen Principal Upanishads*, ed. and trans. R. E. Hume (Bombay: Oxford University Press, 1954), 140–41. *Chandogya*, V:10:7, in Hume, quoted in *The Hindu Tradition: Readings in Oriental Thought*, ed. Ainslee T. Embree (New York: Vintage, 1966, copyright renewed 1994), 62–63.

But people say: "A person is made not of acts, but of desires only." In reply to this I say: As is his desire, such is his resolve; as is his resolve, such the action he performs; what action (*karma*) he performs, that he procures for himself.

On this point there is this verse: —

Where one's mind is attached — the inner self
Goes thereto with action, being attached to it alone.

> *Obtaining the end of his action,*
> *Whatever he does in this world,*
> *He comes again from that world*
> *To this world of action.*

— So the man who desires.

Now the man who does not desire. — He who is without desire, who is freed from desire, whose desire is satisfied, whose desire is the Soul — his breaths do not depart. Being very Brahman, he goes to Brahman.

Accordingly, those who are of pleasant conduct here — the prospect is, indeed, that they will enter a pleasant womb, either the womb of a Brahman, or the womb of a Kshatriya, or the womb of a Vaishya. But those who are of stinking conduct here — the prospect is, indeed, that they will enter a stinking womb, either the womb of a dog, or the womb of a swine, or the womb of an outcaste (*candāla*).

13

From the Upanishads: Brahman and Atman

In this selection *Brahman* does not refer to priests or to a specific god. In the late Vedas, or Upanishads, Brahman is all divinity, and all is Brahman. Even the individual soul or *atman* can be one with the universal Brahman, "as the Father of Svetaketu demonstrates to his son through the examples of a banyan tree and salt water." How would ideas like these challenge the caste system?

Chandogya Upanishad, in *The Upanishads,* trans. Juan Mascaro (Harmondsworth: Penguin Press, 1965), 113–14.

Thinking Historically

McNeill suggests that the Upanishads expressed a religious vision that challenged the power of priests, sacrifice, and caste. How does this selection from the Upanishads support that interpretation?

Great is the Gayatri, the most sacred verse of the Vedas; but how much greater is the Infinity of Brahman! A quarter of his being is this whole vast universe: the other three quarters are his heaven of Immortality. (3.12.5)

There is a Light that shines beyond all things on earth, beyond us all, beyond the heavens, beyond the highest, the very highest heavens. This is the Light that shines in our heart. (3.13.7)

All this universe is in the truth Brahman. He is the beginning and end and life of all. As such, in silence, give unto him adoration.

Man in truth is made of faith. As his faith is in this life, so he becomes in the beyond: with faith and vision let him work.

There is a Spirit that is mind and life, light and truth and vast spaces. He contains all works and desires and all perfumes and all tastes. He enfolds the whole universe, and in silence is loving to all.

This is the Spirit that is in my heart, smaller than a grain of rice, or a grain of barley, or a grain of mustard-seed, or a grain of canary-seed, or the kernel of a grain of canary-seed. This is the Spirit that is in my heart, greater than the earth, greater than the sky, greater than heaven itself, greater than all these worlds.

He contains all works and desires and all perfumes and all tastes. He enfolds the whole universe and in silence is loving to all. This is the Spirit that is in my heart, this is Brahman. (3.14)

"Bring me a fruit from this banyan tree."
"Here it is, father."
"Break it."
"It is broken, Sir."
"What do you see in it?"
"Very small seeds, Sir."
"Break one of them, my son."
"It is broken, Sir."
"What do you see in it?"
"Nothing at all, Sir."
Then his father spoke to him: "My son, from the very essence in the seed which you cannot see comes in truth this vast banyan tree.

Believe me, my son, an invisible and subtle essence is the Spirit of the whole universe. That is Reality. That is Atman. THOU ART THAT."

"Explain more to me, father," said Svetaketu.

"So be it, my son.

Place this salt in water and come to me tomorrow morning."

Svetaketu did as he was commanded, and in the morning his father said to him: "Bring me the salt you put into the water last night."

Svetaketu looked into the water, but could not find it, for it had dissolved.

His father then said: "Taste the water from this side. How is it?"

"It is salt."

"Taste it from the middle. How is it?"

"It is salt."

"Taste it from that side. How is it?"

"It is salt."

"Look for the salt again and come again to me."

The son did so, saying: "I cannot see the salt. I only see water."

His father then said: "In the same way, O my son, you cannot see the Spirit. But in truth he is here.

An invisible and subtle essence is the Spirit of the whole universe. That is Reality. That is Truth. THOU ART THAT." (6.12–14)

$$\boxed{14}$$

From the Bhagavad Gita: Caste and Self

The *Bhagavad Gita** is the best-known work in Hindu religious literature. It is part of a larger epic called the *Mahabharata*,† a story of two feuding families that may have had its origins in the Aryan invasion of 1500 B.C.E. The *Bhagavad Gita* is a philosophical interlude that interrupts the story just before the great battle between the two families. It poses some fundamental questions about the nature of life, death, and proper religious behavior. It begins as the leader of one of the battling armies, Arjuna, asks why he should fight his friends and relatives on the other side. The answer comes from none other than the god Krishna, who has taken the form of Arjuna's charioteer.

*BUH guh vahd GEE tuh
†mah hah BAH rah tah

Bhagavad Gita, trans. Barbara Stoler Miller (New York: Bantam Books, 1986), 31–34, 52, 86–87.

What is Krishna's answer? What will happen to the people Arjuna kills? What will happen to Arjuna? What would happen to Arjuna if he refused to fight the battle? What does this selection tell you about Hindu ideas of life, death, and the self?

Thinking Historically

In some ways this work reconciles the conflict in the Upanishads between caste and *atman.* Performing the *dharma,* or duty, of caste is seen as a liberating act. Would the acceptance of this story support or challenge the caste system? Does this primary source support McNeill's interpretation of Indian society?

Lord Krishna

You grieve for those beyond grief,
and you speak words of insight;
but learned men do not grieve
for the dead or the living.

Never have I not existed,
nor you, nor these kings;
and never in the future
shall we cease to exist.

Just as the embodied self
enters childhood, youth, and old age,
so does it enter another body;
this does not confound a steadfast man.

Contacts with matter make us feel
heat and cold, pleasure and pain.
Arjuna, you must learn to endure
fleeting things — they come and go!

When these cannot torment a man,
when suffering and joy are equal
for him and he has courage,
he is fit for immortality.

Nothing of nonbeing comes to be,
nor does being cease to exist;
the boundary between these two
is seen by men who see reality.

Indestructible is the presence
that pervades all this;

no one can destroy
this unchanging reality.

Our bodies are known to end,
but the embodied self is enduring,
indestructible, and immeasurable;
therefore, Arjuna, fight the battle!

He who thinks this self a killer
and he who thinks it killed,
both fail to understand;
it does not kill, nor is it killed.

It is not born,
it does not die;
having been,
it will never not be;
unborn, enduring,
constant, and primordial,
it is not killed
when the body is killed.

Arjuna, when a man knows the self
to be indestructible, enduring, unborn,
unchanging, how does he kill
or cause anyone to kill?

As a man discards
worn-out clothes
to put on new
and different ones,
so the embodied self
discards
its worn-out bodies
to take on other new ones.

Weapons do not cut it,
fire does not burn it,
waters do not wet it,
wind does not wither it.

It cannot be cut or burned;
it cannot be wet or withered;
it is enduring, all-pervasive,
fixed, immovable, and timeless.

It is called unmanifest,
inconceivable, and immutable;

since you know that to be so,
you should not grieve!

If you think of its birth
and death as ever-recurring,
then too, Great Warrior,
you have no cause to grieve!

Death is certain for anyone born,
and birth is certain for the dead;
since the cycle is inevitable,
you have no cause to grieve!

Creatures are unmanifest in origin,
manifest in the midst of life,
and unmanifest again in the end.
Since this is so, why do you lament!

Rarely someone
sees it,
rarely another
speaks it,
rarely anyone
hears it —
even hearing it,
no one really knows it.

The self embodied in the body
of every being is indestructible;
you have no cause to grieve
for all these creatures, Arjuna!

Look to your own duty;
do not tremble before it;
nothing is better for a warrior
than a battle of sacred duty.

The doors of heaven open
for warriors who rejoice
to have a battle like this
thrust on them by chance.

If you fail to wage this war
of sacred duty,
you will abandon your own duty
and fame only to gain evil.

People will tell
of your undying shame,

and for a man of honor
shame is worse than death.

> In this next passage from the *Bhagavad Gita*, Krishna reveals a deeper
> meaning to his message to Arjuna. Not only must Arjuna act like a war-
> rior because that is his caste, but he must also act without regard to the
> consequences of his action. What does Krishna seem to mean by this?
> How does one do "nothing at all even when he engages in action"?

Abandoning attachment to fruits
of action, always content, independent,
he does nothing at all
even when he engages in action.

He incurs no guilt if he has no hope,
restrains his thought and himself,
abandons possessions,
and performs actions with his body only.

Content with whatever comes by chance,
beyond dualities, free from envy,
impartial to failure and success,
he is not bound even when he acts.

When a man is unattached and free,
his reason deep in knowledge,
acting only in sacrifice,
his action is wholly dissolved.

When devoted men sacrifice
to other deities with faith,
they sacrifice to me, Arjuna,
however aberrant the rites.

I am the enjoyer
and the lord of all sacrifices;
they do not know me in reality,
and so they fail.

Votaries of the gods go to the gods,
ancestor-worshippers go to the ancestors,
those who propitiate ghosts go to them,
and my worshippers go to me.

The leaf or flower or fruit or water
that he offers with devotion,
I take from the man of self-restraint
in response to his devotion.

Whatever you do — what you take,
what you offer, what you give,
what penances you perform —
do as an offering to me, Arjuna!

You will be freed from the bonds of action,
from the fruit of fortune and misfortune;
armed with the discipline of renunciation,
your self liberated, you will join me.

I am impartial to all creatures,
and no one is hateful or dear to me;
but men devoted to me are in me,
and I am within them.

If he is devoted solely to me,
even a violent criminal
must be deemed a man of virtue,
for his resolve is right.

His spirit quickens to sacred duty,
and he finds eternal peace;
Arjuna, know that no one
devoted to me is lost.

If they rely on me, Arjuna,
women, commoners, men of low rank,
even men born in the womb of evil,
reach the highest way.

How easy it is then for holy priests
and devoted royal sages —
in this transient world of sorrow,
devote yourself to me!

Keep me in your mind and devotion,
sacrifice to me, bow to me,
discipline yourself toward me,
and you will reach me!

15

ARISTOTLE

The Athenian Constitution:
Territorial Sovereignty

The process of establishing political authority based on the territorial state was not achieved at one particular moment in history. Much of Greek history (indeed much of world history since the Greeks) witnessed the struggle of territorial authority over family, blood, and kinship ties.

The process of replacing kinship and tribal alliances with a territorial "politics of place" can, however, be seen in the constitutional reforms attributed to the Athenian noble Cleisthenes* in 508 B.C.E. Cleisthenes was not a democrat; his reform of Athenian politics was probably intended to win popular support for himself in his struggle with other noble families. But the inadvertent results of his reforms were to establish the necessary basis for democracy: a territorial state in which commoners as citizens had a stake in government. A description of those reforms is contained in a document called "The Athenian Constitution," discovered in Egypt only a hundred years ago and thought to have been written by the philosopher Aristotle (384–322 B.C.E.) around 330 B.C.E.

Modern scholars doubt that Cleisthenes created the *demes*† (local neighborhoods) that were the basis of his reforms. Some existed earlier. But by making the *demes* the root of political organization, he undoubtedly undercut the power of dominant families. As *demes* were given real authority, power shifted from relatives to residents. Also, as Cleisthenes expanded the number of citizens, the *deme* structure became more "*deme*-ocratic."

Notice how the constitutional reform combined a sense of local, residential identity with citizenship in a larger city-state by tying city, country, and coastal *demes* together in each new "tribe." Why were these new tribes less "tribal" than the old ones? What would be the modern equivalent of these new tribes? Was democracy possible without a shift from kinship to territorial or civic identity? Was it inevitable?

*KLYS thuh neez
†deems

Aristotle, "The Athenian Constitution," in *Aristotle, Politics, and the Athenian Constitution,* trans. John Warrington (London: David Campbell Publishers, 1959).

Thinking Historically

Territorial sovereignty is something we take for granted. It means the law of the land. Regardless of the beliefs of our parents or ancestors, we obey the law of the territory. In the United States, we are bound to observe the law of the nation and the law of the state and municipal ordinances. We do not take our own family law with us when we move from one town or state or country to another. When we go to Japan, we are bound by Japanese law, even if we are not Japanese. In the modern world, sovereignty, ultimate authority, is tied to territory. Because this is so obvious to us in modern society, it is difficult to imagine that this was not always the case.

Historians have to acknowledge that things they and their societies take for granted may not have always existed; rather, they have developed throughout history. McNeill's interpretation of the essential difference between India and Greece makes such a leap. Many people have pointed out the unique Athenian invention of democracy. But McNeill recognized that the Athenians invented democracy because they had already invented something more fundamental — territorial sovereignty, politics, government, citizenship. How does "The Athenian Constitution" support McNeill's interpretation?

The overthrow of the Peisistratid tyranny left the city split into two actions under Isagoras and Cleisthenes respectively. The former, a son of Tisander, had supported the tyrants; the latter was an Alcmaeonid. Cleisthenes, defeated in the political clubs, won over the people by offering citizen rights to the masses. Thereupon Isagoras, who had fallen behind in the race for power, once more invoked the help of his friend Cleomenes and persuaded him to exorcise the pollution; that is, to expel the Alcmaeonidae, who were believed still to be accursed. Cleisthenes accordingly withdrew from Attica with a small band of adherents, while Cleomenes proceeded to drive out seven hundred Athenian families. The Spartan next attempted to dissolve the Council and to set up Isagoras with three hundred of his supporters as the sovereign authority. The Council, however, resisted; the populace flew to arms; and Cleomenes with Isagoras and all their forces took refuge in the Acropolis, to which the people laid siege and blockaded them for two days. On the third day it was agreed that Cleomenes and his followers should withdraw. Cleisthenes and his fellow exiles were recalled.

The people were now in control, and Cleisthenes, their leader, was recognized as head of the popular party. This was not surprising; for the Alcmaeonidae were largely responsible for the overthrow of the tyrants, with whom they had been in conflict during most of their rule.

... The people, therefore, had every grounds for confidence in Cleisthenes. Accordingly, three years after the destruction of the tyranny, in the archonship of Isagoras, he used his influence as leader of the popular party to carry out a number of reforms. (A) He divided the population into ten tribes instead of the old four. His purpose here was to intermix the members of the tribes so that more persons might have civic rights; and hence the advice "not to notice the tribes," which was tendered to those who would examine the lists of the clans. (B) He increased the membership of the Council from 400 to 500, each tribe now contributing fifty instead of one hundred as before. His reason for not organizing the people into *twelve* tribes was to avoid the necessity of using the existing division into trittyes, which would have meant failing to regroup the population on a satisfactory basis. (C) He divided the country into thirty portions — ten urban and suburban, ten coastal, and ten inland — each containing a certain number of demes. These portions he called trittyes, and assigned three of them by lot to each tribe in such a way that each should have one portion in each of the three localities just mentioned. Furthermore, those who lived in any given deme were to be reckoned fellow demesmen. This arrangement was intended to protect new citizens from being shown up as such by the habitual use of family names. Men were to be officially described by the names of their demes; and it is thus that Athenians still speak of one another. Demes had now supplanted the old naucraries,[1] and Cleisthenes therefore appointed Demarchs whose duties were identical with those of the former Naucrari. He named some of the demes from their localities, and others from their supposed founders; for certain areas no longer corresponded to named localities. On the other hand, he allowed everyone to retain his family and clan and religious rites according to ancestral custom. He also gave the ten tribes names which the Delphic oracle had chosen out of one hundred selected national heroes.

---

[1]Forty-eight subdivisions of the old four tribes, each responsible for one galley of the Athenian navy. [Ed.]

16

THUCYDIDES

The Funeral Oration of Pericles

The most famous statement of Greek loyalty to the city-state is the following account of the funeral speech of the Athenian statesman Pericles in the classic *History of the Peloponnesian War* by the ancient historian Thucydides.* The speech eulogized the Athenian soldiers who had died in the war against Sparta in 431 B.C.E.

Notice the high value placed on loyalty to Athens and service to the state. Here is the origin of patriotism. Pericles also insists that Athens is a democratic city-state. He praises Athenian freedom as well as public service. Could there be a conflict between personal freedom and public service? If so, how would Pericles resolve such a conflict? You might also notice that Pericles is praising Athenian citizen-soldiers who died defending not their home but the empire. Could there be a conflict between Athenian democracy and the ambitious empire?

Thinking Historically

Are the sentiments that Pericles expresses a consequence of territorial sovereignty? Could such sentiments be expressed in defense of caste? Notice how Pericles speaks of ancestors, family, and parents. Do his words suggest any potential conflict between family ties and loyalty to the state? How is Pericles able to convince his audience of the priority of the state over kinship ties? How does this primary source provide evidence for McNeill's interpretation?

I will speak first of our ancestors, for it is right and seemly that now, when we are lamenting the dead, a tribute should be paid to their memory. There has never been a time when they did not inhabit this land, which by their valour they have handed down from generation to generation, and we have received from them a free state. But if they were worthy of praise, still more were our fathers, who added to their inheritance, and after many a struggle transmitted to us their sons this great

*thoo SIH duh deez

The History of Thucydides, Book II, trans. Benjamin Jowett (New York: Tandy-Thomas, 1909).

empire. And we ourselves assembled here today, who are still most of us in the vigour of life, have carried the work of improvement further, and have richly endowed our city with all things, so that she is sufficient for herself both in peace and war. Of the military exploits by which our various possessions were acquired, or of the energy with which we or our fathers drove back the tide of war, Hellenic or Barbarian [non-Greek], I will not speak: for the tale would be long and is familiar to you. But before I praise the dead, I should like to point out by what principles of action we rose to power, and under what institutions and through what manner of life our empire became great. For I conceive that such thoughts are not unsuited to the occasion, and that this numerous assembly of citizens and strangers may profitably listen to them.

Our form of government does not enter into rivalry with the institutions of others. We do not copy our neighbours, but are an example to them. It is true that we are called a democracy, for the administration is in the hands of the many and not of the few. But while the law secures equal justice to all alike in their private disputes, the claim of excellence is also recognised; and when a citizen is in any way distinguished, he is preferred to the public service, not as a matter of privilege, but as the reward of merit. Neither is poverty a bar, but a man may benefit his country whatever be the obscurity of his condition. There is no exclusiveness in our public life, and in our private intercourse we are not suspicious of one another, nor angry with our neighbour if he does what he likes; we do not put on sour looks at him which, though harmless, are not pleasant. While we are thus unconstrained in our private intercourse, a spirit of reverence pervades our public acts; we are prevented from doing wrong by respect for the authorities and for the laws, having an especial regard to those which are ordained for the protection of the injured as well as to those unwritten laws which bring upon the transgressor of them the reprobation of the general sentiment.

And we have not forgotten to provide for our weary spirits many relaxations from toil; we have regular games and sacrifices throughout the year; our homes are beautiful and elegant; and the delight which we daily feel in all these things helps to banish melancholy. Because of the greatness of our city the fruits of the whole earth flow in upon us; so that we enjoy the goods of other countries as freely as of our own.

Then, again, our military training is in many respects superior to that of our adversaries. Our city is thrown open to the world, and we never expel a foreigner or prevent him from seeing or learning anything of which the secret if revealed to an enemy might profit him. We rely not upon management or trickery, but upon our own hearts and hands. And in the matter of education, whereas they from early youth are always undergoing laborious exercises which are to make them brave, we live at ease, and yet are equally ready to face the perils which they face. And here is the proof. . . .

If then we prefer to meet danger with a light heart but without laborious training, and with a courage which is gained by habit and not enforced by law, are we not greatly the gainers? Since we do not anticipate the pain, although, when the hour comes, we can be as brave as those who never allow themselves to rest; and thus too our city is equally admirable in peace and in war. For we are lovers of the beautiful, yet simple in our tastes, and we cultivate the mind without loss of manliness. Wealth we employ, not for talk and ostentation, but when there is a real use for it. To avow poverty with us is no disgrace; the true disgrace is in doing nothing to avoid it. An Athenian citizen does not neglect the state because he takes care of his own household; and even those of us who are engaged in business have a very fair idea of politics. We alone regard a man who takes no interest in public affairs, not as a harmless, but as a useless character; and if few of us are originators, we are all sound judges of policy. The great impediment to action is, in our opinion, not discussion, but the want of that knowledge which is gained by discussion preparatory to action. For we have a peculiar power of thinking before we act and of acting too, whereas other men are courageous from ignorance but hesitate upon reflection. And they are surely to be esteemed the bravest spirits who, having the clearest sense both of the pains and pleasures of life, do not on that account shrink from danger. In doing good, again, we are unlike others; we make our friends by conferring, not by receiving favours. Now he who confers a favour is the firmer friend, because he would fain by kindness keep alive the memory of an obligation; but the recipient is colder in his feelings, because he knows that in requiting another's generosity he will not be winning gratitude but only paying a debt. We alone do good to our neighbours, not upon a calculation of interest, but in the confidence of freedom and in a frank and fearless spirit.

To sum up: I say that Athens is the school of Hellas, and that the individual Athenian in his own person seems to have the power of adapting himself to the most varied forms of action with the utmost versatility and grace. This is no passing and idle word, but truth and fact; and the assertion is verified by the position to which these qualities have raised the state. For in the hour of trial Athens alone among her contemporaries is superior to the report of her. No enemy who comes against her is indignant at the reverses which he sustains at the hands of such a city; no subject complains that his masters are unworthy of him. And we shall assuredly not be without witnesses; there are mighty monuments of our power which will make us the wonder of this and of succeeding ages; we shall not need the praises of Homer or of any other panegyrist whose poetry may please for the moment, although his representation of the facts will not bear the light of day. For we have compelled every land and every sea to open a path for our valour, and have everywhere planted eternal memorials of our friendship and of our enmity. Such is the city of whose sake these men nobly fought and died; they could not bear the thought that she might be taken from them; and every one of us who survive should gladly toil on her behalf.

I have dwelt upon the greatness of Athens because I want to show you that we are contending for a higher prize than those who enjoy none of these privileges, and to establish by manifest proof the merit of these men whom I am now commemorating. Their loftiest praise has been already spoken. For in magnifying the city I have magnified them, and men like them whose virtues made her glorious. And of how few Hellenes can it be said as of them, that their deeds when weighed in the balance have been found equal to their fame! . . . They resigned to hope their unknown chance of happiness; but in the fact of death they resolved to rely upon themselves alone. And when the moment came they were minded to resist and suffer, rather than to fly and save their lives; they ran away from the word of dishonour, but on the battlefield their feet stood fast, and in an instant, at the height of their fortune, they passed away from the scene, not of their fear, but of their glory.

Such was the end of these men; they were worthy of Athens, and the living need not desire to have a more heroic spirit, although they may pray for a less fatal issue. The value of such a spirit is not to be expressed in words. Any one can discourse to you forever about the advantages of a brave defence, which you know already. But instead of listening to him I would have you day by day fix your eyes upon the greatness of Athens, until you become filled with the love of her; and when you are impressed by the spectacle of her glory, reflect that this empire has been acquired by men who knew their duty and had the courage to do it, who in the hour of conflict had the fear of dishonour always present to them, and who, if ever they failed in an enterprise, would not allow their virtues to be lost to their country, but freely gave their lives to her as the fairest offering which they could present at her feast. The sacrifice which they collectively made was individually repaid to them; for they received again each one of himself a praise which grows not old, and the noblest of all sepulchres — I speak not of that in which their remains are laid, but of that in which their glory survives, and is proclaimed always and on every fitting occasion both in word and deed. For the whole earth is the sepulchre of famous men; not only are they commemorated by columns and inscriptions in their own country, but in foreign lands there dwells also an unwritten memorial of them, graven not on stone but in the hearts of men. Make them your examples, and, esteeming courage to be freedom and freedom to be happiness, do not weigh too nicely the perils of war. The unfortunate who has no hope of a change for the better has less reason to throw away his life than the prosperous who, if he survives, is always liable to a change for the worse, and to whom any accidental fall makes the most serious difference. To a man of spirit, cowardice and disaster coming together are far more bitter than death striking him unperceived at a time when he is full of courage and animated by the general hope.

Wherefore I do not now commiserate the parents of the dead who stand here; I would rather comfort them. You know that your life has been passed amid manifold vicissitudes; and that they may be deemed fortunate who have gained most honour, whether an honourable death like theirs, or an honourable sorrow like yours, and whose days have been so ordered that the term of their happiness is likewise the term of their life. I know how hard it is to make you feel this, when the good fortune of others will too often remind you of the gladness which once lightened your hearts. And sorrow is felt at the want of those blessings, not which a man never knew, but which were a part of his life before they were taken from him. Some of you are of an age at which they may hope to have other children, and they ought to bear their sorrow better; not only will the children who may hereafter be born make them forget their own lost ones, but the city will be doubly a gainer. She will not be left desolate, and she will be safer. For a man's counsel cannot have equal weight or worth, when he alone has no children to risk in the general danger. To those of you who have passed their prime, I say: Congratulate yourselves that you have been happy during the greater part of your days; remember that your life of sorrow will not last long, and be comforted by the glory of those who are gone. For the love of honour alone is ever young, and not riches, as some say, but honour is the delight of men when they are old and useless.

To you who are the sons and brothers of the departed, I see that the struggle to emulate them will be an arduous one. For all men praise the dead, and, however pre-eminent your virtue may be, hardly will you be thought, I do not say to equal, but even to approach them. The living have their rivals and detractors, but when a man is out of the way, the honour and good-will which he receives is unalloyed. And, if I am to speak of womanly virtues to those of you who will henceforth be widows, let me sum them up in one short admonition: To a woman not to show more weakness than is natural to her sex is a great glory, and not to be talked about for good or for evil among men.

I have paid the required tribute, in obedience to the law, making use of such fitting words as I had. The tribute of deeds has been paid in part; for the dead have been honourably interred, and it remains only that their children should be maintained at the public charge until they are grown up; this is the solid prize with which, as with a garland, Athens crowns her sons living and dead, after a struggle like theirs. For where the rewards of virtue are greatest, there the noblest citizens are enlisted in the service of the state. And now, when you have duly lamented, everyone his own dead, you may depart.

PLATO

From The Republic

This selection is from one of the world's most famous books of philosophy. Two events dominated the early life of Plato (428–348 B.C.E.), turning him away from the public life he was expected to lead. Plato was born in the shadow of the Peloponnesian War, which ended with the defeat of Athens in his twenty-third year. Disillusioned with the postwar governments, especially the democracy that condemned his teacher Socrates in 399 B.C.E., Plato forsook the political arena for a life of contemplation.

Plato's philosophical books, called dialogues because of the way they develop ideas from discussion and debate, follow Plato's teacher Socrates around the city-state of Athens. Often they begin, like *The Republic*, with a view of Socrates and other Athenian citizens enjoying the public spaces and festivals of the city. Notice in this introduction how territorial sovereignty creates public places and public activities.

Thinking Historically

Plato was neither a democrat nor politically active. Nevertheless, his life and his philosophy exemplify a commitment to the world of what McNeill calls "territorial sovereignty."

A primary source can support a particular viewpoint by espousing it, as Plato espouses the benefits of living in a territorial state or thinking about government. But a source can also provide clues about the

Plato, *The Republic of Plato*, trans. F. M. Cornford (London: Oxford University Press, 1941), 2–3, 177–79, 227–35.

society from which it comes. What clues in Plato's text show that his life and the lives of the people around him are shaped by the city-state?

Chapter 1

SOCRATES. I walked down to the Piraeus yesterday with Glaucon, the son of Ariston, to make my prayers to the goddess. As this was the first celebration of her festival, I wished also to see how the ceremony would be conducted. The Thracians, I thought, made as fine a show in the procession as our own people, though they did well enough. The prayers and the spectacle were over, and we were leaving to go back to the city, when from some way off Polemarchus, the son of Cephalus, caught sight of us starting homewards and sent his slave running to ask us to wait for him. The boy caught my garment from behind and gave me the message.

I turned around and asked where his master was.

There, he answered; coming up behind. Please wait.

Very well, said Glaucon; we will.

A minute later Polemarchus joined us, with Glaucon's brother, Adeimantus, and Niceratus, the son of Nicias, and some others who must have been at the procession.

Socrates, said Polemarchus, I do believe you are starting back to town and leaving us.

You have guessed right, I answered.

Well, he said, you see what a large party we are?

I do.

Unless you are more than a match for us, then, you must stay here.

Isn't there another alternative? said I; we might convince you that you must let us go.

How will you convince us, if we refuse to listen?

We cannot, said Glaucon.

Well, we shall refuse; make up your minds to that.

Here Adeimantus interposed: Don't you even know that in the evening there is going to be a torch-race on horseback in honour of the goddess?

On horseback! I exclaimed; that is something new. How will they do it? Are the riders going to race with torches and hand them on to one another?

Just so, said Polemarchus. Besides, there will be a festival lasting all night, which will be worth seeing. We will go out after dinner and look on. We shall find plenty of young men there and we can have a talk. So please stay, and don't disappoint us.

It looks as if we had better stay, said Glaucon.

Well, said I, if you think so, we will.

Accordingly, we went home with Polemarchus.

At the home of Polemarchus, the participants meet a number of other old friends. After the usual greetings and gossip, the discussion begins in response to Socrates' question, what is justice?

Each of the participants poses an idea of justice that Socrates challenges. Then Socrates outlines an ideal state that would be based on absolute justice. In the following selection he is asked how this ideal could ever come about.

Aside from the specifics of Socrates' argument, notice the way in which public issues, for Socrates, are passionate personal concerns.

Chapter 18

But really, Socrates, Glaucon continued, if you are allowed to go on like this, I am afraid you will forget all about the question you thrust aside some time ago; whether a society so constituted can ever come into existence, and if so, how. No doubt, if it did exist, all manner of good things would come about. I can even add some that you have passed over. Men who acknowledged one another as fathers, sons, or brothers and always used those names among themselves would never desert one another; so they would fight with unequalled bravery. And if their womenfolk went out with them to war, either in the ranks or drawn up in the rear to intimidate the enemy and act as a reserve in case of need, I am sure all this would make them invincible. At home, too, I can see many advantages you have not mentioned. But, since I admit that our commonwealth would have all these merits and any number more, if once it came into existence, you need not describe it in further detail. All we have now to do is to convince ourselves that it can be brought into being and how.

This is a very sudden onslaught, said I; you have no mercy on my shilly-shallying. Perhaps you do not realize that, after I have barely escaped the first two waves, the third, which you are now bringing down upon me, is the most formidable of all. When you have seen what it is like and heard my reply, you will be ready to excuse the very natural fears which made me shrink from putting forward such a paradox for discussion.

The more you talk like that, he said, the less we shall be willing to let you off from telling us how this constitution can come into existence; so you had better waste no more time.

Well, said I, let me begin by reminding you that what brought us to this point was our inquiry into the nature of justice and injustice.

True; but what of that?

Merely this: suppose we do find out what justice is, are we going to demand that a man who is just shall have a character which exactly corresponds in every respect to the ideal of justice? Or shall we be satisfied if he comes as near to the ideal as possible and has in him a larger measure of that quality than the rest of the world?

That will satisfy me.

If so, when we set out to discover the essential nature of justice and injustice and what a perfectly just and a perfectly unjust man would be like, supposing them to exist, our purpose was to use them as ideal patterns: we were to observe the degree of happiness or unhappiness that each exhibited, and to draw the necessary inference that our own destiny would be like that of the one we most resembled. We did not set out to show that these ideals could exist in fact.

That is true.

Then suppose a painter had drawn an ideally beautiful figure complete to the last touch, would you think any the worse of him, if he could not show that a person as beautiful as that could exist?

No, I should not.

Well, we have been constructing in discourse the pattern of an ideal state. Is our theory any the worse, if we cannot prove it possible that a state so organized should be actually founded?

Surely not.

That, then, is the truth of the matter. But if, for your satisfaction, I am to do my best to show under what conditions our ideal would have the best chance of being realized, I must ask you once more to admit that the same principle applies here. Can theory ever be fully realized in practice? Is it not in the nature of things that action should come less close to truth than thought? People may not think so; but do you agree or not?

I do.

Then you must not insist upon my showing that this construction we have traced in thought could be reproduced in fact down to the last detail. You must admit that we shall have found a way to meet your demand for realization, if we can discover how a state might be constituted in the closest accordance with our description. Will not that content you? It would be enough for me.

And for me too.

Then our next attempt, it seems, must be to point out what defect in the working of existing states prevents them from being so organized, and what is the least change that would effect a transformation into this type of government — a single change if possible, or perhaps two; at any rate let us make the changes as few and insignificant as may be.

By all means.

Well, there is one change which, as I believe we can show, would bring about this revolution — not a small change, certainly, nor an easy one, but possible.

What is it?

I have now to confront what we called the third and greatest wave. But I must state my paradox, even though the wave should break in laughter over my head and drown me in ignominy. Now mark what I am going to say.

Go on.

Unless either philosophers become kings in their countries or those who are now called kings and rulers come to be sufficiently inspired with a genuine desire for wisdom; unless, that is to say, political power and philosophy meet together, while the many natures who now go their several ways in the one or the other direction are forcibly debarred from doing so, there can be no rest from troubles, my dear Glaucon, for states, nor yet, as I believe, for all mankind; nor can this commonwealth which we have imagined ever till then see the light of day and grow to its full stature. This it was that I have so long hung back from saying; I knew what a paradox it would be, because it is hard to see that there is no other way of happiness either for the state or for the individual.

Socrates, exclaimed Glaucon, after delivering yourself of such a pronouncement as that, you must expect a whole multitude of by no means contemptible assailants to fling off their coats, snatch up the handiest weapon, and make a rush at you, breathing fire and slaughter. If you cannot find arguments to beat them off and make your escape, you will learn what it means to be the target of scorn and derision.

Well, it was you who got me into this trouble.

Yes, and a good thing too. However, I will not leave you in the lurch. You shall have my friendly encouragement for what it is worth; and perhaps you may find me more complaisant than some would be in answering your questions. With such backing you must try to convince the unbelievers.

I will, now that I have such a powerful ally.

In arguing that philosophers should be kings, Plato (or Socrates) was parting ways with the democratic tradition of Athens. Like other conservative Athenians, he seems to have believed that democracy degenerated into mob rule. The root of this antidemocratic philosophy was the belief that the mass of people was horribly ignorant and only the rare philosopher had true understanding. Plato expressed this idea in one of the most famous passages in the history of philosophy: the parable of the cave.

Next, said I, here is a parable to illustrate the degrees in which our nature may be enlightened or unenlightened. Imagine the condition of men living in a sort of cavernous chamber underground, with an entrance open to the light and a long passage all down the cave. Here they have been from childhood, chained by the leg and also by the neck, so that they cannot move and can see only what is in front of them, because the chains will not let them turn their heads. At some distance higher up is the light of a fire burning behind them; and between the prisoners and the fire is a track with a parapet built along it, like the screen at a puppet-show, which hides the performers while they show their puppets over the top.

I see, said he.

Now behind this parapet imagine persons carrying along various artificial objects, including figures of men and animals in wood or stone or other materials, which project above the parapet. Naturally, some of these persons will be talking, others silent.

It is a strange picture, he said, and a strange sort of prisoners.

Like ourselves, I replied; for in the first place prisoners so confined would have seen nothing of themselves or of one another, except the shadows thrown by the firelight on the wall of the Cave facing them, would they?

Not if all their lives they had been prevented from moving their heads.

And they would have seen as little of the objects carried past.

Of course.

Now, if they could talk to one another, would they not suppose that their words referred only to those passing shadows which they saw?

Necessarily.

And suppose their prison had an echo from the wall facing them? When one of the people crossing behind them spoke, they could only suppose that the sound came from the shadow passing before their eyes.

No doubt.

In every way, then, such prisoners would recognize as reality nothing but the shadows of those artificial objects.

Inevitably.

Now consider what would happen if their release from the chains and the healing of their unwisdom should come about in this way. Suppose one of them was set free and forced suddenly to stand up, turn his head, and walk with eyes lifted to the light; all these movements would be painful, and he would be too dazzled to make out the objects whose shadows he had been used to see. What do you think he would say, if someone told him that what he had formerly seen was meaningless illusion, but now, being somewhat nearer to reality and turned towards more real objects, he was getting a truer view? Suppose further that he were shown the various objects being carried by and were made to say, in reply to questions, what each of them was. Would he not be perplexed and believe the objects now shown him to be not so real as what he formerly saw?

Yes, not nearly so real.

And if he were forced to look at the firelight itself, would not his eyes ache, so that he would try to escape and turn back to the things which he could see distinctly, convinced that they really were clearer than these other objects now being shown to him?

Yes.

And suppose someone were to drag him away forcibly up the steep and rugged ascent and not let him go until he had hauled him out into the sunlight, would he not suffer pain and vexation at such treatment, and, when he had come out into the light, find his eyes so full of its radiance that he could not see a single one of the things that he was now told were real?

Certainly he would not see them all at once.

He would need, then, to grow accustomed before he could see things in that upper world. At first it would be easiest to make out shadows, and then the images of men and things reflected in water, and later on the things themselves. After that, it would be easier to watch the heavenly bodies and the sky itself by night, looking at the light of the moon and stars rather than the Sun and the Sun's light in the daytime.

Yes, surely.

Last of all, he would be able to look at the Sun and contemplate its nature, not as it appears when reflected in water or any alien medium, but as it is in itself in its own domain.

No doubt.

And now he would begin to draw the conclusion that it is the Sun that produces the seasons and the course of the year and controls everything in the visible world, and moreover is in a way the cause of all that he and his companions used to see.

Clearly he would come at last to that conclusion.

Then if he called to mind his fellow prisoners and what passed for wisdom in his former dwelling-place, he would surely think himself happy in the change and be sorry for them. They may have had a practice of honouring and commending one another, with prizes for the man who had the keenest eye for the passing shadows and the best memory for the order in which they followed or accompanied one another, so that he could make a good guess as to which was going to come next. Would our released prisoner be likely to covet those prizes or to envy the men exalted to honour and power in the Cave? Would he not feel like Homer's Achilles, that he would far sooner "be on earth as a hired servant in the house of a landless man" or endure anything rather than go back to his old beliefs and live in the old way?

Yes, he would prefer any fate to such a life.

Now imagine what would happen if he went down again to take his former seat in the Cave. Coming suddenly out of the sunlight, his eyes would be filled with darkness. He might be required once more to deliver his opinion on those shadows, in competition with the prisoners who had never been released, while his eyesight was still dim and unsteady; and it might take some time to become used to the darkness. They would laugh at him and say that he had gone up only to come back with his sight ruined; it was worth no one's while even to attempt the ascent. If they could lay hands on the man who was trying to set them free and lead them up, they would kill him.

Yes, they would.

Every feature in this parable, my dear Glaucon, is meant to fit our earlier analysis. The prison dwelling corresponds to the region revealed to us through the sense of sight, and the firelight within it to the power of the Sun. The ascent to see the things in the upper world you may take as standing for the upward journey of the soul into the region of the intelligible; then you will be in possession of what I surmise, since that is what you wish to be told. Heaven knows whether it is true; but this, at any rate, is how it appears to me. In the world of knowledge, the last thing to be perceived and only with great difficulty is the essential Form of Goodness. Once it is perceived, the conclusion must follow that, for all things, this is the cause of whatever is right and good; in the visible world it gives birth to light and to the lord of light, while it is itself sovereign in the intelligible world and the parent of intelligence and truth. Without having had a vision of this Form no one can act with wisdom, either in his own life or in matters of state.

So far as I can understand, I share your belief.

Then you may also agree that it is no wonder if those who have reached their height are reluctant to manage the affairs of men. Their souls long to spend all their time in that upper world — naturally enough, if here once more our parable holds true. Nor, again, is it at all strange that one who comes from the contemplation of divine things to the miseries of human life should appear awkward and ridiculous when, with eyes still dazed and not yet accustomed to the darkness, he is compelled, in a law court or elsewhere, to dispute about the shadows of justice or the images that cast those shadows, and to wrangle over the notions of what is right in the minds of men who have never beheld Justice itself.

It is not at all strange.

No; a sensible man will remember that the eyes may be confused in two ways — by a change from light to darkness or from darkness to light; and he will recognize that the same thing happens to the soul. When he sees it troubled and unable to discern anything clearly, instead of laughing thoughtlessly, he will ask whether, coming from a brighter existence, its unaccustomed vision is obscured by the darkness, in which case he will think its condition enviable and its life a happy one; or whether, emerging from the depths of ignorance, it is dazzled by excess of light. If so, he will rather feel sorry for it; or, if he were inclined to laugh, that would be less ridiculous than to laugh at the soul which has come down from the light.

That is a fair statement.

If this is true, then, we must conclude that education is not what it is said to be by some, who profess to put knowledge into a soul which does not possess it, as if they could put sight into blind eyes. On the contrary, our own account signifies that the soul of every man does possess the power of learning the truth and the organ to see it with; and that, just as one might have to turn the whole body round in order that the eye should see light instead of darkness, so the entire soul must be turned away from this changing world, until its eye can bear to contemplate reality and that supreme splendour which we have called the Good. Hence there may well be an art whose aim would be to effect this very thing, the conversion of the soul, in the readiest way; not to put the power of sight into the soul's eye, which already has it, but to ensure that, instead of looking in the wrong direction, it is turned the way it ought to be.

Yes, it may well be so.

It looks, then, as though wisdom were different from those ordinary virtues, as they are called, which are not far removed from bodily qualities, in that they can be produced by habituation and exercise in a soul which has not possessed them from the first. Wisdom, it seems, is certainly the virtue of some diviner faculty, which never loses its power, though its use for good or harm depends on the direction towards which it is turned. You must have noticed in dishonest men with a reputation for sagacity the shrewd glance of a narrow intelligence piercing the objects to which it is directed. There is nothing wrong with their power of vision, but it has been forced into the service of evil, so that the keener its sight, the more harm it works.

Quite true.

And yet if the growth of a nature like this had been pruned from earliest childhood, cleared of those clinging overgrowths which come of gluttony and all luxurious pleasure and, like leaden weights charged with affinity to this mortal world, hang upon the soul, bending its vision downwards; if, freed from these, the soul were turned round towards true reality, then this same power in these very men would see the truth as keenly as the objects it is turned to now.

Yes, very likely.

Is it not also likely, or indeed certain after what has been said, that a state can never be properly governed either by the uneducated who know nothing of truth or by men who are allowed to spend all their days in the pursuit of culture? The ignorant have no single mark before their eyes at which they must aim in all the conduct of their own lives and of affairs of state; and the others will not engage in action if they can help it, dreaming that, while still alive, they have been translated to the Islands of the Blest.

Quite true.

It is for us, then, as founders of a commonwealth, to bring compulsion to bear on the noblest natures. They must be made to climb the ascent to the vision of Goodness, which we called the highest object of knowledge; and, when they have looked upon it long enough, they must not be allowed, as they now are, to remain on the heights, refusing to come down again to the prisoners or to take any part in their labours and rewards, however much or little these may be worth.

Shall we not be doing them an injustice, if we force on them a worse life than they might have?

You have forgotten again, my friend, that the law is not concerned to make any one class specially happy, but to ensure the welfare of the commonwealth as a whole. By persuasion or constraint it will unite the citizens in harmony, making them share whatever benefits each class can contribute to the common good; and its purpose in forming men of that spirit was not that each should be left to go his own way, but that they should be instrumental in binding the community into one.

True, I had forgotten.

You will see, then, Glaucon, that there will be no real injustice in compelling our philosophers to watch over and care for the other citizens. We can fairly tell them that their compeers in other states may quite reasonably refuse to collaborate: there they have sprung up, like a self-sown plant, in despite of their country's institutions; no one has fostered their growth, and they cannot be expected to show gratitude for a care they have never received. "But," we shall say, "it is not so with you. We have brought you into existence for your country's sake as well as for your own, to be like leaders and king-bees in a hive; you have been better and more thoroughly educated than those others and hence you are more capable of playing your part both as men of thought and as men of action. You must go down, then, each in his turn, to live with the rest and let your eyes grow accustomed to the darkness. You will then see a thousand times better than those who live there always; you will recognize every image for what it is and know what it represents, because you have seen justice, beauty, and goodness in their reality; and so you and we shall find life in our commonwealth no mere dream, as it is in most existing states, where men live fighting

one another about shadows and quarrelling for power, as if that were a
great prize; whereas in truth government can be at its best and free
from dissension only where the destined rulers are least desirous of
holding office."

Quite true.

Then will our pupils refuse to listen and to take their turns at sharing in the work of the community, though they may live together for
most of their time in a purer air?

No; it is a fair demand, and they are fair-minded men. No doubt,
unlike any ruler of the present day, they will think of holding power as
an unavoidable necessity.

Yes, my friend; for the truth is that you can have a well-governed
society only if you can discover for your future rulers a better way of
life than being in office; then only will power be in the hands of men
who are rich, not in gold, but in the wealth that brings happiness, a
good and wise life. All goes wrong when, starved for lack of anything
good in their own lives, men turn to public affairs hoping to snatch
from thence the happiness they hunger for. They set about fighting for
power, and this internecine conflict ruins them and their country. The
life of true philosophy is the only one that looks down upon offices of
state; and access to power must be confined to men who are not in love
with it; otherwise rivals will start fighting. So whom else can you compel to undertake the guardianship of the commonwealth, if not those
who, besides understanding best the principles of government, enjoy a
nobler life than the politician's and look for rewards of a different
kind?

There is indeed no other choice.

REFLECTIONS

Caste and territorial sovereignty were alternate but equally effective
systems of social organization in the ancient world. Both worked. Both
allocated jobs and rewards, arranged marriages and created families,
assured the peace and fought wars. Neither was necessarily more just,
tyrannical, expensive, or arbitrary. Yet each system created its own
complex world of ideas and behavior.

Caste and territorial sovereignty were not the only bases for identity in the ancient world. In many societies, a person's identity was
based on family ties of a different sort than caste. In China, the family
lineage, constituting many generations of relatives, was particularly important. Almost every society in human history organized itself around
families to a certain extent, and most societies also had a sense of

multiple family units called clans or tribes. The Indian caste system was only one variant of these multifamily systems, and some non-Indian societies had divisions resembling castes.

Family, clan, and tribe are still important determinants of identity in the modern world. In some societies, the authority of a tribal leader, clan elder, or family patriarch rivals that of the state. Nevertheless, the modern world is made up of states. We live according to the law of the land, not that of kinship. In the United States, one obeys the laws of the United States, regardless of who one knows. If the police pull you over for driving through a red light, you do not say that your father gave you permission or your uncle ordered you to drive through red lights. In the territory of the United States, you obey the laws of the United States and the particular state in which you find yourself. When a citizen of the United States goes to Canada, he or she must obey the laws of Canada. This is the world of states, of territorial sovereignty.

One of the major transitions in human history in the last five thousand years has been the rise of territorial sovereignty and the supplanting of the authority of the law of the state over the rule of family, clan, tribe, and caste. This is what developed in ancient Greece twenty-five hundred years ago. It did not occur completely and finally with Cleisthenes or even with the rise of Greek democracy in the fifth century B.C.E. Tribal alliances reasserted themselves periodically in Greece and elsewhere, in the Middle Ages and in modern society. The establishment of territorial sovereignty and ultimately of civil society, where political parties replaced tribes, was gradual and interrupted and is still continuing. Aristotle tells us that after Cleisthenes, Greeks took new surnames based on their new civic "tribes." That would have ended the rule of the old family-based tribes, but we know the old tribal names did not disappear. A thorough transition would mean that political parties would express entirely civic goals without a trace of tribal identity, but that too is a process that still continues. In modern Ireland, for instance, one of the political parties, Finn Gael, means literally the tribe of the Gael. In the wake of the U.S. invasion of Iraq in 2003, many Americans have learned how difficult it is to impose a system of territorial sovereignty on a society where tribal identities are strong.

India today is also a modern state in which the law of the land applies to all regardless of caste, family, or tribe. In fact, recent Indian governments have outlawed discrimination based on caste, and created affirmative action programs on behalf of Dahlits, the outcastes or untouchables. Nevertheless, Indian newspapers still run matrimonial ads that specify caste, though international Web sites often do not.

Modern society encourages us to be many things. Family and caste can still play a role. Religion, ethnicity, national origin, even race are given an importance in modern society that was often absent or irrelevant in ancient societies. But with the civic society produced by territorial sovereignty comes not only citizenship but also a range of chosen identities based on career, education, job, hobbies, friends, and a wide range of living possibilities. These choices can sometimes overwhelm. Sometimes the indelibility of family, caste, or birth can seem a comfort. But over the long term of history, the range and choice of identities seem likely to increase, and more and more of them will likely be voluntary rather than stamped on the birth certificate.

Classical Civilizations and Empires

China and Rome,
300 B.C.E.–300 C.E.

HISTORICAL CONTEXT

Both China and Rome expanded from small states to large empires around 200 B.C.E. (See Maps 4.1 and 4.2.) Each empire ruled at least fifty million people in an area of over one and a half million square miles. Both regimes managed to fund and field enormous armies, tax and control competitors for power in their own aristocracies, and convert millions to their cultural ideas. After the second century C.E., however, both empires became increasingly vulnerable to the nomadic peoples on their frontiers whom they called "barbarians."

This simultaneous development of the two great empires of the classical age did not occur without contact or mutual interaction. During this period the great Silk Road developed across central Asia, Roman senators complained of the price of Chinese silks, and Roman coins were found throughout China. Nevertheless, these two great empires developed largely independently of each other. The Greek roots of Roman civilization were well developed in the Roman Republic of the last centuries B.C.E., and Han China continued the traditions of earlier Chinese dynasties stretching back a thousand years. For these reasons, a comparison of the two great empires broadens our understanding of the possibilities, and limits, of life in the classical age two thousand years ago.

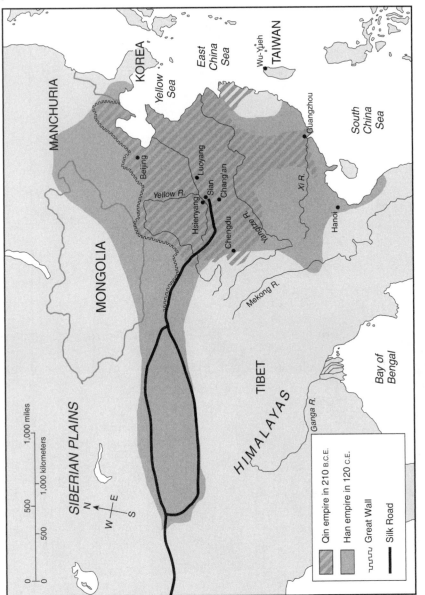

Map 4.1 Imperial China, 210 B.C.E. and 120 C.E.

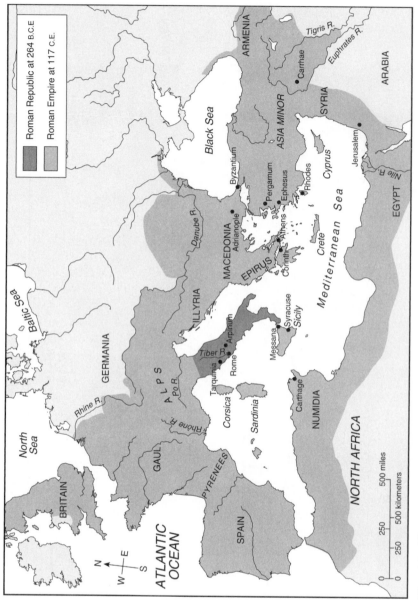

Map 4.2 The Roman Empire, 264 B.C.E. and 117 C.E.

THINKING HISTORICALLY
Making Comparisons

"Compare and contrast" is one of the most common types of exam instructions and is not limited to history courses. Students know that the instruction asks them to find similarities and differences. Even when one is asked simply to "compare" two things, the process usually involves looking for similarities and differences because likenesses have no meaning except in reference to those things which are not alike. To understand something, perhaps even to *see* it, we must first perceive how it is different from other things.

In our daily lives, when we encounter something new, we sift through our memory for similarities and differences. We learn through a process of almost instinctively going back and forth between those things that are similar and those that are different. When we try to be more systematic, however, we might focus on similarities and differences separately. We might notice and list similarities first because generally differences make more sense in terms of similarities, rather than vice versa. For example, if we want to buy a car we begin with those that have a similar appeal, price range, or features, and then examine the differences. We wouldn't start with cars that were radically different and then look for similarities.

Historians also generally begin with cases that are similar, as we have here with our comparison of the Chinese Han and Roman empires. Given all of the similarities mentioned in the first paragraph of this chapter, it becomes interesting to ask about the differences. There would not be much point in beginning with two different entities, say the Chinese Han Empire and medieval Albania, and asking how, despite their differences, they were similar. The chances are that any similarities we discovered would be too general (they both had agriculture), coincidental, or meaningless (they both later became communist).

Ultimately, we compare to understand more than we might learn from examining each case in isolation. In comparing the ancient Chinese and Roman empires, we might seek to understand more about ancient empires, the course of change in ancient societies, or empires in general. Almost invariably, by comparison we also learn something about each of the things compared: in this case China and Rome. Often a good comparison also leads us to new questions, new topics, and new comparisons as well.

S. A. M. ADSHEAD

China and Rome Compared

In this selection a modern historian of China compares the Chinese Han dynasty with the Roman Empire. You will have to read carefully because his analysis is quite dense. He uses a complex vocabulary and covers a wide range of factors — from food to social classes to writing and roads. How, according to the author, were these two empires similar? How were they different? Which of these factors (showing similarities or differences) would you judge to be the most important, and why? In addition, can you think of any similarities or differences between Rome and China that are not mentioned in this reading? If so, how important are they?

Thinking Historically

The easiest way to make a comparison is to list the similarities in one column and the differences in another. You might do this for Rome and China, according to Adshead. Thus in the similarities column, you might begin with such items as empire, 1.5 million square miles, conquered aristocracies, and so on. After you have listed as many items as you can in each column, it might be useful to ask yourself what relation exists between the similarities and differences.

Notice that Adshead begins with similarities and then turns to differences. As we said in the introduction, this is a standard procedure, because differences are only meaningful in terms of some assumed or recognized similarities. Generally, we assume that the similarities are more important than the differences. The differences are mere variations on the larger similarity. Here, however, Adshead says that the differences between Rome and China are greater than the similarities. What might he mean? Are Adshead's differences more important? Are the similarities more superficial? Return to your list of similarities and differences and decide.

This section examines first the similarities between Han China and the classical, pre-Constantinian Roman empire and second, the differences. The conclusion will be that the differences outweighed the similarities.

S. A. M. Adshead, *China in World History*, 3rd ed. (London: Macmillan and New York: St. Martin's, 2000), 4–7, 9–16, 17–19.

Similarities

These may be divided into origin, organization and outcome.

Origin

Both the Han and Roman empires began in the third century BC with the military expansion of conservative, relatively unideological aristocratic states on the western peripheries of their respective civilized zones. The Roman republic was not a full member of the Hellenistic world; the duchy of Ch'in[1] was an outsider in the Chou confederacy. Both expansions were based on a combination of political stability, abundant rural manpower nourished by advanced agriculture, and disciplined infantry, which was pitted against political instability, artificial urban growth and over-specialized military technology. Both were directed first against mercantile rivals: Carthage, the emporium of tin and silver in the West and Ch'i, the emporium of salt and iron in the East; and then against colonial frontiers: the Hellenistic east and Gaul, Ch'u and Wu-yueh. In both cases conquest was followed by civil war. It ended in the elimination of the aristocracies which had organized the expansion and the establishment of bureaucracies which disguised their novelty by archaizing their ideology and exaggerating their continuity. Thus the neotraditionalist refoundation of the republic by Augustus was paralleled by Han-Wu-ti' *feng* and *shan* sacrifices in imitation of the sage rulers of antiquity. In both cases the *novi homines*[2] of the bureaucracy came to be supplied by men from the defeated but more educated east, freedmen, from Greece and scholars from Honan, through the patronage of aggressive and colourful empress-dowagers: Agrippina in the West, empress-dowager Teng in the East.

Organization

In terms of organization the Han and Roman empires had much in common, both problems and solutions. The Roman empire under Hadrian covered 1,763,000 square miles; the Han empire towards the end of the second century AD covered 1,532,000 square miles. Both faced similar problems of distance and time in administering an area half the size of the United States with a technology in which nothing went faster than a horse. Both sought a solution in the cultural solidarity of elites: the spontaneous coordination produced by the shared values, institutions,

---

[1]Duchy of Ch'in (256–206 B.C.E.). Unified China in 221 B.C.E. by conquering the larger Chou confederacy (1050–256 B.C.E.). [Ed.]

[2]Latin for "new men." Usually refers to a newly created class of powerful or wealthy men. In this case, Adshead means new recruits to the bureaucracies. [Ed.]

vocabulary and reactions of, on the one hand, the classical *paedeia**
and, on the other, the Confucian *wen-yen*.[3] Both empires relied on this
solidarity as their foundation, both built roads to foster it and facilitate
military flexibility, and both constructed great walls to give that flexibility time to operate and to avoid the costly continuous mass mobilization
which might destroy culturalism by militarism. In both empires, the
dominant element of the army was the infantry; the dominant colour of
the culture, literary, with poetry giving way to prose. In both the army
was opposed by cavalry enemies, the Iranian cataphract[4] and the Hsu-
ing-nu light horseman, and in both the culture of the elite was challenged by barbarians, *sectaries*,[5] soldiers, and peasants in varying degrees of alienation from it. In both the challenge was for a long time
contained by political skill, social flexibility, economic prosperity and
cultural syncretism, underpinned by military effectiveness. When the
system needed reconstruction, the Severi of 193–235, provincial lawyers
turned soldiers, populists and patrons of exotic religions, were closely
paralleled by Ts'ao Ts'ao and the Wei dynasty of 184–265, outsiders
from a eunuch background, meritocrats, founders of military colonies,
and friends of unorthodox, new-style philosophy.

Outcome

Despite reconstruction, by the Severi and the tetrarchy and by the Wei
and the Chin, the long-term outcome was the same: the rise of barbarism and religion; the collapse of the too-costly superstructure in one
half of the empire; its survival, reformed, in the other. Both the Roman
and the Han empires collapsed in their north-western halves through a
mixture of institutional hypertrophy, military pronunciamentos, ecclesiastical non-cooperation, and barbarian invasions. Both survived in
slightly new forms in their south-eastern halves with a new capital and
the establishment of a foreign, previously "sectarian," ecumenical religion which gradually conquered the north-west as well. In the northwest, the leaders of the invading barbarian armies, often ex-imperial
foederati,[6] set up kingdoms but, except in the vicinity of the *limes*,[7]
there was no serious linguistic change. In both China and the West, society ruralized and centred itself upon self-contained aristocratic es-

---

*py DEE oh
[3]*Paedeia* and *wen-yen* are names for the educational systems of Rome and China, respectively. *Paedeia* or *paideia* refers to humanistic Greek culture; *wen-yen* refers to humanistic
Confucian education. [Ed.]
[4]Heavily armed horsemen. [Ed.]
[5]Members of religious sects, especially Christians and Buddhists. [Ed.]
[6]Allies of Rome by treaty (*foedus*). [Ed.]
[7]Roman frontier or wall at Roman boundary. [Ed.]

tates, lay and monastic which, with their immunities, vassals, retainers, "guests," and servants, were more sociological than economic units. In both, a new superstructure, a medieval civilization with deeper roots and firmer foundations than its antique predecessor, was eventually constructed, but in neither was it built on the old plan or centred on the segment of the old system which had survived in the south-east. Neither Constantinople nor Nanking were to be a basis for the medieval world.

Differences

These may be grouped as contrasts of foundation, architectonics, and decay which paralleled the similarities of origin, organization, and outcome, qualified their genuineness, and limited their significance.

Foundation

. . . In the Roman west, the principal crop was wheat or its relatives barley and oats. In Han China, on the other hand, although wheat and rice were known, the principal crop was millet. Millet is a less palatable grain than wheat, but it had a higher productivity in pre-modern conditions in both quantity sown and area sown. Before the nineteenth century, the ratio of wheat harvested to wheat sown was seldom more than 6:1, while the rate for millet was 10:1. Similarly, while the average pre-modern yield of wheat was 6 quintals a hectare, that of millet was 12 quintals a hectare.

The original difference in productivity was compounded by the difference of natural milieu. In the Roman west, grain was grown on light downland soils which, to maintain their nitrogen content and hence fertility, required fallowing in alternate years. In China, on the other hand, grain was grown on the porous loess[8] of the north-west hills which, because of its permeability by the chemicals of the air and subsoil, was self-renewing and did not require either fallowing or manuring. The amount of arable land under grain at any one time in China was thus double that in Rome.

By the Han period, a higher percentage of [China's] arable acreage was irrigated than in the Roman west, and a larger proportion of the irrigation was by large-scale macrohydraulic means than elsewhere. . . . If this advantage be added to those of millet yields and the absence of fallowing, then average Chinese grain yields would have been eight times those of the Roman west. The two societies had different nutritional bases.

---

[8]Wind-blown dusty but fertile soil of northern China. [Ed.]

A corollary of this greater intensity of Chinese grain farming was a difference in the role of animal husbandry between China and the Roman west. The difference was not as pronounced as it was later to become, but already the two societies were oriented in different directions. Because of the self-renewal of the loess, Chinese arable farming did not require animals for manure; because it did not need to lie fallow there were no unsown fields free for temporary stocking; and because farms could be smaller thanks to the higher grain yields, there was less marginal land for permanent pasture and less need for ploughing animals. Thus, though China and Europe shared the same domestic animals—cows, horses, sheep, goats, pigs—and, as we shall see, China in antiquity used the horse more efficiently than did the West, in China animals were ancillary while in Europe they were essential. True, in antiquity, animals, in particular horses, were much fewer in Europe than they subsequently became (why could Pheidippides[9] not find a mount between Athens and Sparta?), while the opposite was true in China, but already the Chinese farmer was oriented to pure arablism in contrast to the European farmer who was oriented to a mixture of arablism and pastoralism.

This difference, in turn, contributed to others: different attitudes to space (the pastoralist can never have too much of it); to mobility (the pastoralist has both ends and means for it); to energy (the pastoralist will be lavish with it so long as it is non-human); to nomadic pastoralism (the mixed farmer can compromise, the pure arablist cannot); to food (the pastoralist will structure his meal round a main course of meat where the arablist will blend a collection of vegetable dishes); and even to human relations generally (the pastoralist is a herder whereas the arablist is a grower). In *Pilgrim's Regress*, C. S. Lewis[10] called the Jews the "shepherd people": it would be an appropriate name for all westerners. Chinese regalia never included the sword. Even more significant is that Chinese official insignia never included the shepherd's crook, the pastoral staff.

Chinese agriculture was further differentiated from Roman by China's superiority in metallurgy in antiquity, particularly iron. Needham[11] has shown that while the West could not liquify and cast iron until the fourteenth century AD, so that all ancient and medieval iron in the West was low-carbon wrought iron, China produced cast-iron hoes, ploughshares, picks, axes, and swords from the fourth century BC. This metallurgical superiority affected both agriculture and war. The Chinese arable farmer, in addition to his other advantages,

[9]Greek hero who, according to legend, ran the twenty-six miles from Marathon to Athens to announce the Greek victory over the Persians. Aspiring "marathon" runners should also know he collapsed and died after announcing the news. [Ed.]

[10]Twentieth-century English Christian writer. [Ed.]

[11]Joseph Needham was a famous scholar of Chinese science. [Ed.]

had more and better iron implements than his Roman counterpart. If China clung to infantry where Constantinople switched to cavalry, it was partly because the Chinese footsoldier was better armed and was better able to cope with his equestrian opponent than the Roman legionary. For example, it is doubtful if Roman artisans could have produced the precision-made bronze trigger mechanism required for the Chinese cross-bow. Consequently the Han never suffered a Carrhae or an Adrianople.[12] The capacity to cast iron, in turn, raised the level of steel production both in quantity and quality. Wrought iron is low in carbon, cast iron is high in carbon, and steel lies in between. For premodern siderurgy it was easier to decarbonize than recarbonize. So, by the Han period, the Chinese, starting with cast iron, could produce considerable quantities of good steel by what was, in essence, the Bessemer process of oxygenation, i.e., liquifying the iron while simultaneously blowing away part of the carbon; while the West, starting with wrought iron, could only produce limited amounts of poor steel by heating the iron in charcoal. The Damascus and Toledo blades,[13] which were later to so impress the Crusaders, were the products of transplanted Chinese technology and when Pliny the Younger spoke admiringly of Seric iron, he was probably thinking of Chinese steel.

Intellectual technology.   All four primary civilizations shared the primary human tool of articulate speech. Western Eurasia, East Asia, and Amerindia all possessed the basic tool for higher organization: a system of writing. In China and the West, but not in Amerindia, writing was sufficiently old and diffused to constitute the necessary vehicle for education: a literary tradition. As between China and the West, however, there was significant differences in all three intellectual techniques; speech, writing, and literary tradition.

Languages, one might assume are born equal. Each can express the full range of human consciousness and each is completely translatable into every other: as Leonardo Bruni[14] put it: "Nothing is said in Greek that cannot be said in Latin." All languages are equal vehicles of speech and writing, prose and poetry, even though one may think, with Robert Frost, that poetry is what gets lost in translation. The Chomskyan hypothesis of a single transformational grammar or syntactic structure governing all languages supports the assumption of linguistic equivalence. Yet, it may be argued, at a more superficial level, languages are not equal and the inequality may have implications for the thought

---

[12]In the Battle of Carrhae in 53 B.C.E. the Romans suffered a serious defeat at the hands of the Parthians whose calvary and archery tactics overwhelmed the Roman soldiers. The Battle of Adrianople in 378 C.E. against the Huns was the beginning of the end for the Roman Empire. [Ed.]

[13]Muslim steel made in Syrian and Spanish cities. [Ed.]

[14]Leonardo Bruni (c. 1370–1444) was a leading humanist and historian from Tuscany.

expressed in them. In particular one may consider whether or not the different sound/meaning ratio in Chinese as compared to the Indo-European languages influenced thought patterns in China and the West. Chinese, it has been said, "is exceptionally rich in homophones," or, to put it another way, it operates with a "poverty of sounds." Thus modern Mandarin uses only 1280 sounds to express what must be presumed to be the same gamut of meaning as the phoneme-rich Indo-European languages. Although archaic and ancient Chinese, the languages of Confucius and the middle ages, may have had a wider phonological range than Mandarin, economy in phonemes seems to be an original and basic characteristic of Chinese speech. The effect has been a wider indeterminacy of meaning *vis-à-vis* sound, a greater dependence on context and audience to establish signification, and a bias in favour of nuance, indirection, allusion and paradigm, as compared to the cruder, more direct, less allusive, more syntagmatic[15] languages of the West. The medium does not prescribe the content of the message. It may be that nothing is said in Chinese that cannot be said in English, and vice versa: but it does determine the level of articulation, the degree of thematization, the place on the implicit/explicit scale. In this sense, the Chinese language with its peculiar sound/meaning ratio was an invitation both to the collective introversion which Jung[16] found characteristic of the eastern mind and to the protocol thinking which Granet[17] ascribed to the Chinese. . . .

Signification, already depotentiated by the sound/meaning ratio, was further beclouded by the accommodating but unresponsive script. The alphabet was an arithmetic tailored exactly to sound and significance; the *tzu*[18] were an algebra which could mean everything or nothing. Once again the medium smothered the message.

By the beginning of the Christian era, both China and the West possessed a body of literature and a tradition of study which was, on one hand, a vehicle of education and, on the other, both a means and end of government. Both the Han and the Roman empires, as we saw above, were founded upon a *paedeia*. The character of the *paedeias*, however, were different. The Chinese tradition was paradigmatic, introverted to concepts, ethical; the Western tradition was syntagmatic, extraverted to things, metaphysical. In both cultures there was a certain transition from mythology to philosophy, but it had been made to different degrees and in opposite directions. In Greece the concrete myth-

---

[15]Ordered into a collection of statements or propositions (usually logically ordered). [Ed.]

[16]Carl Jung was a Swiss student of Sigmund Freud who generalized about cultural traits. [Ed.]

[17]Marcel Granet was an early twentieth-century French scholar of Chinese civilization. [Ed.]

[18]Chinese characters. [Ed.]

ology of Homer and Hesiod was overlaid by the equally concrete pre-Socratic cosmologies, and both gods and cosmologies were eventually subsumed in the mathematical *Dieu cosmique* of orthodox Platonism or the transcendent *Dieu inconnu*[19] of gnosticism. Concrete paradigm was replaced by concrete syntagmata and then by abstract syntagmata. There was a complete transition from mythology to philosophy. In China, *per contra*, the concrete mythology of the Shang and the early Chou was dissolved by, on the one hand, historicization (conversion of gods to heroes and dynastic founders, an inverse Euhemerism[20]) and, on the other, ritualization (absorption of myth in liturgy), leaving only abstractions like *t'ien, tao,* and *te*[21] behind. Paradigm was reinforced by theoretical abstraction and practical concreteness and philosophy's problem was not the structure of the cosmos but the method of elucidating the paradigms. There was only a partial transition from mythology to philosophy.

The Chinese *paideia*, more than the Western, was centred on form rather than content. It was a communications system rather than a body of doctrine. The *Shih-ching*[22] provided the model for poetry, the *Shu-ching*[23] for prose, and poetry was preferred to prose as being more highly formalized. In both China and the West, the past was a prototype for the present, but where Alexander the Great used the model of Achilles to assert his personality and break continuity, the Han emperors used the model of the sage-emperors to conceal theirs and buttress it. History was understood not, as in Thucydides, as tragedy or pathology, but, as in the *Ch'un-ch'iu*, as annals where morality taught by example. In the *Li-chi*, ethics were reduced to protocol and the *I-ching* provided not an actual cosmology but a repository of concepts for all possible cosmologies.

Similarly, Confucius (author of *Lun-yu*) and Lao-tzu* (author of *Tao-te ching*) had no doctrine to teach, no wisdom to impart. They

---

[19]*Dieu cosmique* and *dieu inconnu*: literally "cosmic god" of science and "unknown god" of gnosticism. The argument is that Greek philosophy led to the idea of a governing god of the universe and that later religious mystics, for whom the visible world was less "real," believed the world was run by an unknown or invisible god. [Ed.]

[20]Euhemerus (ca. 300 B.C.E.) was a Greek philosopher who argued that the gods were once heroic people who had been turned into mythical beings and that mythological stories were elaborations of actual events. This process of rationalizing mythology is called euhemerism. It is sometimes used more broadly for an extremely rational, debunking, or nonreligious attitude. Here, however, Adshead uses it literally, suggesting that Chinese philosophers did just the opposite: turning gods into real people and treating myths as if they were real and abstractions as if they were concrete. [Ed.]

[21]*T'ien* means heaven, god, or nature. *Tao* means the "way" as in the way of nature. *Te* means power or virtue. Adshead's point is that Chinese retained abstractions while the Greeks looked for specific and concrete origins for abstract concepts. [Ed.]

[22]The first and classic collection of Chinese poetry. [Ed.]

[23]The classic collection of documents, or history. [Ed.]

*low TZOO

were concerned not to advance views, but to define the conditions for any views: linguistic reform in the one case, the recognition of the inadequacy of language in the other. They defined the conditions for debate, not as a modern philosopher to clear the ground for argument, but because for them to settle the medium was to settle the message: the categories of thought are thought, thought and reality are isomorphic, and all thought needs are the proper paradigms, the little red book of reality. This tradition was in marked contrast with that of the West where, whether in Indian cosmology, Zoroastrian ethical prophecy, Greek empiricism and logic, or Old Testament theocentrism, there was a recognition of the duality of paradigm and syntagma and the primacy of the latter. In this major intellectual contrast with China, all the minor contrasts within the West—the one and the many, metaphysics and ethics, rationalism and religion, science and intentionality analysis—were swallowed up.

Architectonics

In addition to the contrast of physical and intellectual foundations between China and the West, there was also a contrast in architectonics. The social and political structures erected on the foundations differed in ground plan, spatial relations, and decor.

Ground plans. The Roman empire was laid out like an amp[h]itheatre around the arena of the Mediterranean. Rome itself was the imperial box, the older coastal provinces were the stalls, the new inland *limes* provinces were the heavily buttressed upper circle. The internal differentiation was between, on the one hand, upper and lower, *limes* and city, and on the other, sun and shade, the old urbanization of the east, the new urbanization of the west. The Han empire, *per contra*, was laid out like a wheel. The region of the two imperial capitals, Ch'ang-an and Lo-yang, formed the hub; the converging valleys of the Wei, the Fen, the Ching, the Lo, the Han, and the Huang-ho formed the spokes. The internal differentiation was between centre and circumference, capital and provinces. Both empires in antiquity were centrally planned, but Rome in a series of concentric circles, China in a series of radiating lines. The Roman empire was the work of a city state which sought to stabilize its dominion by universalizing cities, city life, institutions, and values. It tended therefore to homogenization, a general rise in the level of urbanization, a Conrad Hilton civilization[24] of everywhere-similar fora, basilicas, theatres, baths, circuses, and insulae. The Chinese em-

---

[24]Adshead means a civilization that spreads the same hotels (Hiltons), buildings, foods, and chain-culture everywhere. [Ed.]

pire, on the other hand, was the work of a bureaucratic territorial state which sought to stabilize its dominion by monopolizing for the court capital resources, amenities, protection, and prestige. It tended therefore to heterogenization, to a fall in the general level of urbanization following the unification of the empire and a growing disparity between the lifestyles of court and country. Both empires lived by and for cultural glamour and conspicuous consumption but in the one case they were diffused, in the other concentrated.

Spatial relations.   A comparison of the extent and character of the communications systems of the two areas suggests that Han China was less integrated than the Roman empire. According to Needham, the Roman empire under Hadrian covered 1,763,000 square miles and had 48,500 miles of road, an average of 27.5 miles of road per 1000 square miles of territory. Han China, on the other hand, covered 1,532,000 square miles and had 22,000 miles of road, an average of only 14.35 miles of road per 1000 square miles of territory. Moreover, while for Han China, roads were the essence of the communications system, for Rome they were only an adjunct to the Mediterranean whose sea lanes will have at least doubled the total length of routes. Needham suggests that the greater use of rivers and canals for transportation in China as compared to Europe counterbalanced the advantage of the Mediterranean. This may be true for the later periods of Chinese history, the T'ang and the Sung, for example, when the Grand Canal had been completed, but it is doubtful for the Han. Neither the Yellow River nor its tributaries, in whose valleys Chinese civilization was then centred, are good for navigation and most Han hydraulic activity was for irrigation, not communication. Like the Achaemenid empire, Han China was a road state on a plateau, and this in itself ensured inferiority in spatial integration to a Mediterranean empire, since in pre-modern conditions land transport was twenty to forty times more expensive than water transport. . . .

Decor.   Even allowing for accidents of survival, it is difficult not to conclude from the archaeological remains that Han China was a less splendid society than Imperial Rome. The Great Wall no doubt is a stupendous monument, though most of its imposing appearance dates from Ming rather than Han times, but it stands by itself, and though Chinese cities had impressive walls, they did not contain the monumental public buildings of the Classical West—the amphitheatres, aqueducts, arches, basilicas, baths, circuses, theatres, and temples. Rome was a federation of city states, Han China was a swollen court; but in addition, the difference between their towns was rooted in different options for building materials and different conceptions of what a house was for. The fundamental options of Rome and, following her, Europe generally, were for stone, diffusion of heat by hypocausts or multiple fireplaces, and durability. A house was a capital investment, perhaps the prototype of all fixed capital investment, an assertion of culture in the face of nature. The fundamental Chinese options, on the other hand, were for wood, concentration of heat at the *k'ang* or heated divan, and repairability. A house was a charge on income, an extension of consumer non-durables, an adaptation of culture to nature. In the West, buildings were in principle winter palaces, exclusions of weather, permanent embodiments of hearth and family. In China, buildings were in principle summer houses, modifications of weather, makeshift additions to the real home which was the loess cave or the family tomb. The one option produced monumentality and splendour, the other convenience and harmony. . . .

Decay

Finally, besides these contrasts of foundations and architectonics, there was a contrast between the two empires in the pattern of their decay. Although there were superficial similarities between the fall of the Roman empire and the fall of the Han empire, there were more profound differences which in the end made the two episodes more unlike than like: differences in health, pathology, and prognosis.

The body politic of the Han was healthier than that of the Roman empire. With its superior physical technology in arable farming and metallurgy and its lower degree of urbanization, intercommunication and luxury building, the Han world did not suffer from irremediable contradictions between superstructure and base, state and society. Frictions there were, no doubt, but they were adjustable without cataclysm. In the Roman body politic, on the other hand, with its more primitive physical technology yet more grandiose and more parasitic sociology, there were such contradictions, especially after the Illyrian emperors, in response to the military mutinies and barbarian invasions of the mid-third century, doubled the army and multiplied fortifications without sufficient provision for increased agricultural productivity behind the front. . . .

Both the Han and the Roman empires were the work of elites — educated, civilian, and urban. Both coexisted with and were threatened by non-elites: barbarians beyond the frontier, sectaries outside the *paedeia*, soldiers separated from the civilian community, and peasants below the level of urbanization. . . . All four non-elites — barbarians, sectaries, soldiers, and peasants — played some part in the fall of the Roman empire: it was a social revolution.

In China on the other hand, under the Han and its successor states down to 400 A.D., the San-kuo and the Chin, pathology came from within the elite. It came from the aristocracy of great families, the equivalent, *mutatis mutandis*[25] of the senatorial aristocracy of the Western empire or the *pronoia*-holding[26] magnates of medieval Byzantium. These people, the Ma, the Tou, the Liang, the Wang, the Ssu-ma, who as a Chin catch-phrase put it "share the world," were not primarily a landed aristocracy though they owned estates and, especially, the newly invented watermill. Rather their substance consisted in men: *k'o*, literally guests, that is clients, retainers, tenants, servants, and slaves. For their *k'o*, as evidence of their power and prestige, patrons sought exemption from tax lists and muster rolls and thus weakened the fiscal and military foundations of the central government. The Han empire rested on a base of tax-paying and conscription-bearing free farmers. A vicious circle began: the more privileges for *k'o*, the greater the fiscal and draft pressures on the remaining free farmers, the greater the temptation to escape such freedom by commendation and an increase in the number of *k'o*. The Han empire died slowly by financial and military asphyxiation.

[25]After the same changes. [Ed.]
[26]*Pronoia* were land grants made to nobility by the Byzantine or Eastern Roman emperor. [Ed.]

19

CONFUCIUS

From The Analects

Confucius (551–479 B.C.E.) was a son of a low-level noble family in China who, despite some political success in his early years, spent most of his later life teaching and looking for a governmental appointment. His *Analects*, a collection of sayings or teachings compiled by his students, touch on all of his major concerns: filial piety (or respect of sons for fathers), virtuous conduct, governance by good example, tradition, rites, music, and dance. Confucius, the person and model, and Confucianism, the school or writings known as *wen-yen*, had an enormous impact on Chinese thought and culture.

The Analects of Confucius, http://classics.mit.edu//Confucius/analects.html.

What kind of society would ideas like these encourage? In the previous reading, Adshead writes that both the Chinese and the Romans solved the problem of ruling vast empires by increasing the "cultural solidarity of elites: the spontaneous coordination produced by the shared values, institutions, vocabulary, and reactions of, on the one hand, the classical *paedeia* and, on the other, the Confucian *wen-yen*." How would these Confucian *wen-yen* (writings) do what Adshead suggests?

Thinking Historically

A common response that people have when they read writings like this from a famous philosopher or religious figure is to nod in agreement, reflect on the wisdom, and speculate about the similarities among great philosophies. On a second or third reading, we might find more matters of difference and disagreement. We might be more struck by the differences between Confucius and other classical writers: whether Jesus, Plato, or Plutarch or Cicero. What similarities do you see between Confucius and Plato or some other philosophers you have read? After you read Plutarch (selection 20), we will ask how the writings of Confucius and Plutarch are similar and different, and how those differences reflect differences between Chinese and Roman cultures.

Section 1

Part 1

The Master said, "Is it not pleasant to learn with a constant perseverance and application?

"Is it not delightful to have friends coming from distant quarters?

"Is he not a man of complete virtue, who feels no discomposure though men may take no note of him?"

The philosopher Yu said, "They are few who, being filial and fraternal, are fond of offending against their superiors. There have been none, who, not liking to offend against their superiors, have been fond of stirring up confusion.

"The superior man bends his attention to what is at the root. That being established, all practical courses naturally grow up. Filial piety and fraternal submission, are they not the root of all benevolent actions?"

The Master said, "Fine words and an insinuating appearance are seldom associated with true virtue."

The philosopher Tsang said, "I daily examine myself on three points: whether, in transacting business for others, I may have been not faithful; whether, in intercourse with friends, I may have been not sincere; whether I may have not mastered and practiced the instructions of my teacher."

The Master said, "To rule a country of a thousand chariots, there must be reverent attention to business, and sincerity; economy in expenditure, and love for men; and the employment of the people at the proper seasons."

The Master said, "A youth, when at home, should be filial, and, abroad, respectful to his elders. He should be earnest and truthful. He should overflow in love to all, and cultivate the friendship of the good. When he has time and opportunity, after the performance of these things, he should employ them in polite studies."

Tsze-hsia said, "If a man withdraws his mind from the love of beauty, and applies it as sincerely to the love of the virtuous; if, in serving his parents, he can exert his utmost strength; if, in serving his prince, he can devote his life; if, in his intercourse with his friends, his words are sincere: although men say that he has not learned, I will certainly say that he has."

The Master said, "If the scholar be not grave, he will not call forth any veneration, and his learning will not be solid.

"Hold faithfulness and sincerity as first principles.

"Have no friends not equal to yourself.

"When you have faults, do not fear to abandon them."

The philosopher Tsang said, "Let there be a careful attention to perform the funeral rites to parents, and let them be followed when long gone with the ceremonies of sacrifice; then the virtue of the people will resume its proper excellence." . . .

Part 4

The Master said, "It is virtuous manners which constitute the excellence of a neighborhood. If a man in selecting a residence does not fix on one where such prevail, how can he be wise?"

The Master said, "Those who are without virtue cannot abide long either in a condition of poverty and hardship, or in a condition of enjoyment. The virtuous rest in virtue; the wise desire virtue."

The Master said, "It is only the truly virtuous man, who can love, or who can hate, others."

The Master said, "If the will be set on virtue, there will be no practice of wickedness."

The Master said, "Riches and honors are what men desire. If they cannot be obtained in the proper way, they should not be held. Poverty and meanness are what men dislike. If they cannot be avoided in the proper way, they should not be avoided." . . .

Part 9

The subjects of which the Master seldom spoke were profitableness, and also the appointments of Heaven, and perfect virtue.

A man of the village of Ta-hsiang said, "Great indeed is the philosopher K'ung! His learning is extensive, and yet he does not render his name famous by any particular thing."

The Master heard the observation, and said to his disciples, "What shall I practice? Shall I practice charioteering, or shall I practice archery? I will practice charioteering."

The Master said, "The linen cap is that prescribed by the rules of ceremony, but now a silk one is worn. It is economical, and I follow the common practice.

"The rules of ceremony prescribe the bowing below the hall, but now the practice is to bow only after ascending it. That is arrogant. I continue to bow below the hall, though I oppose the common practice."

There were four things from which the Master was entirely free. He had no foregone conclusions, no arbitrary predeterminations, no obstinacy, and no egoism. . . .

Section 3

Part 13

Tsze-lu asked about government. The Master said, "Go before the people with your example, and be laborious in their affairs."

He requested further instruction, and was answered, "Be not weary in these things."

Chung-kung, being chief minister to the head of the Chi family, asked about government. The Master said, "Employ first the services of your various officers, pardon small faults, and raise to office men of virtue and talents."

Chung-kung said, "How shall I know the men of virtue and talent, so that I may raise them to office?" He was answered, "Raise to office those whom you know. As to those whom you do not know, will others neglect them?"

Tsze-lu said, "The ruler of Wei has been waiting for you, in order with you to administer the government. What will you consider the first thing to be done?"

The Master replied, "What is necessary is to rectify names."

"So! indeed!" said Tsze-lu. "You are wide of the mark! Why must there be such rectification?"

The Master said, "How uncultivated you are, Yu! A superior man, in regard to what he does not know, shows a cautious reserve.

"If names be not correct, language is not in accordance with the truth of things. If language be not in accordance with the truth of things, affairs cannot be carried on to success.

"When affairs cannot be carried on to success, proprieties and music do not flourish. When proprieties and music do not flourish, punishments will not be properly awarded. When punishments are not properly awarded, the people do not know how to move hand or foot.

"Therefore a superior man considers it necessary that the names he uses may be spoken appropriately, and also that what he speaks may be carried out appropriately. What the superior man requires is just that in his words there may be nothing incorrect." . . .

Part 15

The Duke Ling of Wei asked Confucius about tactics. Confucius replied, "I have heard all about sacrificial vessels, but I have not learned military matters." On this, he took his departure the next day.

When he was in Chan, their provisions were exhausted, and his followers became so ill that they were unable to rise.

Tsze-lu, with evident dissatisfaction, said, "Has the superior man likewise to endure in this way?" The Master said, "The superior man may indeed have to endure want, but the mean man, when he is in want, gives way to unbridled license."

$$20$$

PLUTARCH

On Education

Plutarch (46 C.E.–120 C.E.) was born in Greece but taught philosophy in Rome and wrote widely on morality, literature, and history. He is known best for his biographies of Greeks and Romans, which he presented as parallel lives from which he drew moral lessons.

No Greek or Roman shaped Mediterranean culture in the way that Confucius influenced Chinese and East Asian culture. Nevertheless, Plutarch's interest in morality and education offers points of comparison

Adapted from Oliver J. Thatcher, ed., *The Library of Original Sources*, vol. III: *The Roman World* (Milwaukee: University Research Extension Co., 1907), 370–91.

with Confucius. In what ways was Plutarch's moral and educational philosophy similar to that of Confucius? In what ways was it different? What do those differences say about the differences between Roman and Chinese culture?

Thinking Historically

One way to draw out a comparison of two major thinkers like Plutarch and Confucius is to list the key concerns and to note the words used by each. You have already read, and we have already listed, some of Confucius's main concerns. You might compose a similar list for Plutarch noting also any key words you see repeated. How do these two lists compare?

Although Plutarch does not represent Roman or Greco-Roman thought as thoroughly as Confucius stands for China, his work was part of what Adshead calls the classical *paedeia* (taught morality) that increased the cultural solidarity of elites. How might these ideas have helped Greek and Roman upper classes identify with their counterparts in the broader empire?

Adshead also suggests that the "sound/meaning ratio" in Chinese (a high percentage of homophones, or sounds that could convey a number of different meanings) made Chinese less explicit than Greek, Latin, or other Indo-European languages. The wider range of phonemes (distinct sounds units) in Indo-European languages, according to Adshead, tends to make Greek and Latin speakers more precise or blunt, less evasive or poetic. Does your reading of Plutarch and Confucius support this judgment? Compare Confucius and Plutarch to Plato or Thucydides (in Chapter 3). Whose writing is more syntagmatic (organized in a logical order of statements)?

1. THE COURSE that ought to be taken for the training of freeborn children, and the means whereby their manners may be rendered virtuous, will, with the reader's permission, be our present subject.

2. We should begin with their very procreation. I would therefore, in the first place, advise those who desire to become the parents of famous and eminent children, that they keep not company with all women that they light on; I mean such as harlots, or concubines. For such children as are blemished in their birth, either by the father's or the mother's side, are liable to be pursued, as long as they live, with the indelible infamy of their base extraction, . . .

[Discussion of birth and childhood follows.]

8. In brief therefore I say (and what I say may justly challenge the repute of an oracle rather than of advice), that the one chief thing in that mat-

ter—which comprises the beginning, middle, and end of all—is good education and regular instruction; and that these two afford great help and assistance toward the attainment of virtue and felicity. For all other good things are but human and of small value, such as will hardly recompense the industry required to the getting of them. It is, indeed, a desirable thing to be well-descended; but the glory belongs to our ancestors. Riches are valuable; but they are the goods of Fortune, who frequently takes them from those that have them, and carries them to those that never so much as hoped for them. Yes, the greater they are, the fairer mark they are for those to aim at who design to make our bags their prize; I mean evil servants and accusers. But the weightiest consideration of all is, that riches may be enjoyed by the worst as well as the best of men. Glory is a thing deserving respect, but unstable; beauty is a prize that men fight to obtain, but, when obtained, it is of little continuance; health is a precious enjoyment, but easily impaired; strength is a thing desirable, but apt to be the prey of disease and old age. And, in general, let any man who values himself upon strength of body know that he makes a great mistake; for what indeed is any proportion of human strength, if compared to that of other animals, such as elephants and bulls and lions? But learning alone, of all things in our possession, is immortal and divine. And two things there are that are most peculiar to human nature, reason and speech; of which two, reason is the master of speech, and speech is the servant of reason, impregnable against all assaults of fortune, not to be taken away by false accusation, nor impaired by sickness, nor enfeebled by old age. For reason alone grows youthful by age; and time, which decays all other things before it carries them away with it, leaves learning alone behind. Whence the answer seems to me very remarkable, which Stilpo, a philosopher of Megara, gave to Demetrius, who, when he leveled that city to the ground and made the citizens slaves, asked Stilpo whether he had lost anything. Nothing, he said, for war cannot plunder virtue. To this saying that of Socrates also is very agreeable; who, when Gorgias (as I take it) asked him what his opinion was of the king of Persia, and whether he judged him happy, returned answer, that he could not tell what to think of him, because he knew not how he was furnished with virtue and learning—as judging human felicity to consist in those endowments, and not in those which are subject to fortune. . . .

11. In the next place, the exercise of the body must not be neglected; but children must be sent to schools of gymnastics, where they may have sufficient employment that way also. This will conduce partly to a more handsome carriage, and partly to the improvement of their strength. For the foundation of a vigorous old age is a good constitution of the body in childhood. Wherefore, as it is expedient to provide those things in fair weather which may be useful to the mariners in a storm, so is it to keep good order and govern ourselves by rules of temperance in youth, as the best provision we can lay in for age. Yet must they husband their strength, so as not to become dried up (as it were) and destitute of strength to follow their studies. For, according to Plato, sleep and weariness are enemies to the arts.

But why do I stand so long on these things? I hasten to speak of that which is of the greatest importance, even beyond all that has been spoken of; namely, I would have boys trained for the contests of wars by practice in the throwing of darts, shooting of arrows, and hunting of wild beasts. For we must remember in war the goods of the conquered are proposed as rewards to the conquerors. But war does not agree with a delicate habit of body, used only to the shade; for even one lean soldier that has been used to military exercises shall overthrow whole troops of mere wrestlers who know nothing of war. But, somebody may say, while you profess to give precepts for the education of all free-born children, why do you carry the matter so as to seem only to accommodate those precepts to the rich, and neglect to suit them also to the children of poor men and plebeians? To which objection it is no difficult thing to reply. For it is my desire that all children whatsoever may partake of the benefit of education alike; but if yet any persons, by reason of the narrowness of their estates, cannot make use of my precepts, let them not blame me that give them for Fortune, which disabled them from making the advantage by them they otherwise might. Though even poor men must use their utmost endeavor to give their children the best education; or, if they cannot, they must bestow upon them the best that their abilities will reach. Thus much I thought fit here to insert in the body of my discourse, that I might the better be enabled to annex what I have yet to add concerning the right training of children. . . .

17. And in sum, it is necessary to restrain young men from the conversation of debauched persons, lest they take infection from their evil examples. This was taught by Pythagoras in certain enigmatical sentences, which I shall here relate and expound, as being greatly useful to further virtuous inclinations. Such are these: *Taste not of fish that have black tails*; that is, converse not with men that are smutted with vicious qualities. *Stride not over the beam of the scales*; wherein he teaches us the regard we ought to have for justice, so as not to go beyond its measures. *Sit not on a phoenix*, wherein he forbids sloth, and requires us to take care to provide ourselves with the necessaries of life. *Do not strike hands with every man*; he means we ought not to be over hasty to make acquaintants or friendships with others. *Wear not a tight string*; that is, we are to labor after a free and independent way of living, and to submit to no fetters. *Stir not up the fire with a sword*; signifying that we ought not to provoke a man more when he is angry already (since this is a most unseemly act), but we should rather comply with him while his passion is in its heat. *Eat not your heart*; which forbids to afflict our souls, and waste them with vexatious cares. *Abstain from beans*; that is, keep out of public offices, for anciently the choice of the officers of state was made by beans. *Put not food in a chamber-pot*; wherein he declares that elegant discourse ought not to be put into an impure mind; for discourse is the food of the mind, which is rendered unclean by the foulness of the man who receives it. *When men are arrived at the goal, they should not turn back*; that is, those who are near

the end of their days, and see the period of their lives approaching, ought to entertain it contentedly, and not to be grieved at it. . . .

18. These counsels which I have now given are of great worth and importance; what I have now to add touches certain allowances that are to be made to human nature. Again, therefore, I would not have fathers of an over-rigid and harsh temper, but so mild as to forgive some slips of youth, remembering that they themselves were once young. . . .

I will add a few words more, and put an end to these advices. The chief thing that fathers are to look to is that they themselves become effectual examples to their children, by doing all those things which belong to them and avoiding all vicious practices, which in their lives, as in a glass, their children may see enough to give them an aversion to all ill words and actions. For those that chide children for such faults as they themselves fall into unconsciously accuse themselves, under their children's names. And if they are altogether vicious in their own lives, they lose the right of reproaching their very servants, and much more do they forfeit it towards their sons. Yes, what is more than that, they make themselves even counselors and instructors to them in wickedness. For where old men are impudent, there of necessity must the young men be so too. Wherefore we are to apply our minds to all such practices as may conduce to the good breeding of our children. And here we may take example from Eurydice of Hierapolis, who, although she was an Illyrian, and so thrice a barbarian, yet applied herself to learning when she was well advanced in years, that she might teach her children. Her love towards her children appears evidently in this Epigram of hers, which she dedicated to the Muses:

> *Eurydice to the Muses here doth raise*
> *This monument, her honest love to praise;*
> *Who her grown sons that she might scholars breed,*
> *Then well in years, herself first learned to read.*

And thus have I finished the precepts which I designed to give concerning this subject. But that they should all be followed by any one reader is rather, I fear, to be wished than hoped. And to follow the greater part of them, though it may not be impossible to human nature, yet will need a concurrence of more than ordinary diligence joined with good fortune.

21

G. E. R. LLOYD

Chinese and Greco-Roman Innovation

In this selection, a modern historian of ideas compares the Chinese and Greco-Roman paths to invention. He focuses on three areas — warfare, agriculture, and civil engineering. His point is not to determine which society was more advanced; they excelled in different areas. He focuses, instead, on how ideas were applied to new technologies in both societies. The different methods of turning ideas into inventions tell us far more about how differently the two societies functioned. What were the different routes to innovation in China and the Greco-Roman world? What does that tell us about the difference between Chinese and Roman societies?

Thinking Historically

Lloyd focuses on a much narrower field than did Adshead. The subject of how a society innovates is minuscule compared to the range of issues compared by Adshead. Yet Lloyd's attempt to answer this simple question in two societies leads to a larger understanding about those two societies. What is that larger understanding?

Notice also that Lloyd's method of comparing is different from Adshead's. He does not list similarities and then list differences. Instead he chooses an action (or three) that all societies must perform: inventing new techniques (in warfare, agriculture, and civil engineering). Then he asks how these two societies did it. Do you find either of these methods preferable? Does Lloyd's method lead you to add another difference between Rome and China to Adshead's list?

I shall consider each of three main subject areas, first warfare, then agriculture, then civil engineering, though it will be immediately apparent that there is some overlap between that third area and the other two. These three, between them, certainly do not cover everything that might be discussed under the heading of the practical applications of theory: but they will give us some idea of the scope of the problems.

G. E. R. Lloyd, *The Ambitions of Curiosity* (Cambridge: Cambridge University Press, 2002), 72–73, 74–76, 77, 79, 80–82, 84–86, 88, 91–92, 94–97.

WARFARE is a subject that no state, no ruler, can afford to ignore. But ideas about the aims and methods of waging war, and about the winning of battles, have varied enormously, as also has the attention paid to improving the efficiency of armies whether by employing better tactics or better weaponry. Both the Greeks and the Chinese were conscious of certain differences between their own ideas, techniques, and practices, and those of the foreign peoples with whom they were familiar. Contacts with other peoples were one source of influence on Greek and Chinese battle tactics themselves. We are told by Vitruvius that certain types of siege engines that came into general use in the Greco-Roman world originated among Tyrian and Carthaginian engineers. The Chinese derived their horses (used first in chariots, then in cavalry engagements) from the people of the steppes.

At the same time efficiency was not the sole criterion, at least, in Greece. For the Greeks, the use of the bow was thought inferior—morally—to fighting hand to hand with spear, sword, and shield. From Homer onwards, the individual's performance in battle was a crucial factor in the moral evaluation of the man. The *Iliad* is organised around the consecutive *aristeia*, deeds of valour, of the Greek heroes who take centre stage in turn in the absence of Achilles. But even when victory in battle depended, as it later did, on the disciplined manoeuvring of the heavy-armed troops—the hoplites—in the massed formation of the phalanx, playing one's part there was the prime test of courage, *andreia*, literally manhood.

Evidence of the increasing complexity of warfare begins already in Herodotus and more especially Thucydides. Thucydides refers to the development of the trireme, the ship on which victory at sea for long depended. In his accounts of the various sieges that took place during the Peloponnesian war, he refers at one point to a primitive kind of flame-thrower. Not much later, in the fourth century BCE, we have our first extant specialist Greek military treatise, the *poliorketika*—siege-warfare—of Aeneas Tacticus, part (it seems) of a series of works he wrote on military matters, the rest of which have not survived. . . .

A comparison between these Chinese and Greco-Roman works yields immediately several points of similarity and two important contrasts. Both Aeneas and *Sunzi* stress the importance of experience, of military intelligence (knowledge of the enemy's strength, whereabouts and intentions) and especially of morale. Both describe the use of spies; both devote attention to the problems of passwords and signalling; both describe various tricks or ploys to gain a psychological or tactical advantage over the enemy.

But for *Sunzi*[1] the supreme skill of the commander consists in securing victory with a minimum of cost, indeed if possible without

---

[1]Sunzi or Sun Tzu, author of *The Art of War*, c. 500 B.C.E.

having to fight a battle. The idea is that you so manoeuvre your troops that the enemy comes to realise the hopelessness of his own position and surrenders without an engagement. For *Sunzi* the value of victory is seriously diminished if the enemy's land is destroyed or his population decimated: the prime prize is to take over and occupy the territory of the vanquished more or less unharmed. . . .

A second major difference lies in the preoccupation, throughout the pages of Aeneas, with the possibility that the city being defended may be betrayed by disaffected elements in the population who disagreed with the policies of those in command. He gives advice on the dangers of having a lot of poor people, or debtors, in the defending army, and on how to counter the plots of would-be revolutionaries. Considerable sections of the work are devoted to guarding against the possibility of the city-gates being opened *from within*. The problems posed by *political* disagreements, among the *citizen* body, on the conduct of the war, just do not figure in our Chinese texts, for all that disagreements between *generals* often do.

The second type of text that has come down to us on the Greco-Roman side deals with military weaponry. Archimedes' reputation as a practical genius depended partly on the stories of the engines he devised to repel the forces of Marcellus besieging Syracuse: but our evidence there is second-hand and anecdotal. However, Philo, Vitruvius, and Hero all deal with the construction and improvement of the various types of catapults—scorpions and ballistae—designed to hurl bolts or stones, in both torsion and non-torsion varieties. Starting with the arrow-shooting *gastraphetes*, or cross-bow, these underwent considerable developments from the early fourth century BCE, as did other types of weapons and siege-engines (battering-rams, for example, and "tortoises" designed to protect attacking forces and so on). . . .

On the Chinese side, the emphasis is not so much on experimental research to prove a mathematical formula setting out the relevant proportionalities. On the other hand, there is a deep concern with what will work and with efficient performance. The main Chinese weapon was the cross-bow, introduced maybe as early as 400 BCE, an extremely powerful weapon, once equipped with an efficient trigger mechanism and once the problems of arming it were overcome. . . .

We could certainly not claim that Greco-Roman engineers were less ingenious, less curious, less inventive, in their attempts to improve weapons of war, than their Chinese counterparts. Indeed the Greeks went further than the Chinese in their admittedly only partially successful efforts to reduce the problems to mathematical terms. Yet where the Chinese had a net advantage was in the organisations that existed for exploiting and implementing new ideas once they were proposed. Although the success of Chinese advisers in gaining the ear of rulers obviously varied, what rulers and advisers alike shared was an intense concern for every aspect of the art of war and a sense of the need to explore any possibility of an advantage and a determination to do so.

These comments will prove relevant also to the next domain we have to consider, namely AGRICULTURE. Every society, large or small, must be concerned with ensuring an adequate food-supply and most call on considerable collective knowledge of the relevant local ecological conditions to achieve that end. In hunting, fishing, herding, sowing, and planting, once certain methods and techniques prove to be effective, there may be little incentive—indeed possibly great risk—in trying to change them. Experimenting with new crops has always been a dangerous business, has it not? In the domain of agriculture, in other words, the forces of conservatism have generally been particularly strong. Departure from tried and tested methods has, accordingly, to be motivated either by necessity—say the need to feed an increasing population—or by some perceived desirable end, the acquisition of wealth or prestige. . . .

We may begin with two fundamental differences in the perception of the importance of agriculture in our two ancient civilisations. First, for the ancient Chinese, agriculture came under the auspices of important divinities and culture heroes, Shennong, the tutelary deity or spirit of agriculture, Hou Ji, the Lord of Millet, and Yu the Great. Of course the Greeks had Demeter, the Romans Ceres. But they did not combine the role of corn goddesses with presiding over technological skills, which were the province, rather, of Athena and in a different way of Prometheus. Yu the Great was responsible for taming the flood, for land clearance, for inaugurating agriculture itself. Flood stories in Greece or the ancient Near East, by contrast, did not culminate in the celebration of the activities of a hero-figure whose efforts *countered* the flood and so enabled agriculture to begin.

The second important difference relates to the role of the Prince or Emperor himself, who in China was personally in charge of agriculture and presided over agricultural activities season by season. Thus he inaugurated the ploughing of the fields every year, just as the Queen started the picking of the mulberry leaves for the silkworms. In *Huainanzi*[2] the ruler does not just sacrifice to the appropriate deities at the appropriate moments of the year: he oversees each and every important agricultural activity. If he fails in his duty, the consequences this text predicts are dire, the failure of crops, drought, unseasonable rains, floods, fire, disease, and not just "natural" calamities but others, such as the invasions of barbarians and the proliferation of bandits. To be sure, the Romans had a ruler—Cincinnatus—who came from

---

[2]A second century B.C.E. Chinese philosophical classic that deals with agriculture, among other things.

ploughing the fields to rule. But even though Columella, in reporting that story, nostalgically approves of the connection between ruling and agriculture, that just points to their normal dissociation in Roman eyes.

Agriculture, one may say, had a far higher ideological profile in China than in the Greco-Roman world, and this is reflected in the amount of literature devoted to the subject. Agricultural topics are discussed in texts from the third to the first centuries BCE in the *Zhouli*, *Guanzi*, and *Lüshi chunqiu*, for example sections defining the responsibilities of the many different types of officials concerned, planning the most efficient use of the available land of different types, specifying what should be done in each season and stressing the importance of the care of agricultural implements. Specialist treatises begin not much later, as well as monographs dealing with particular crops and the vast *bencao* literature dealing with medicinal plants, pharmacopoeia in other words.

Ancient China suffered, we know, from time to time, from terrible famines, brought about by floods or drought or crop failures of one kind or another. Nevertheless the increase of yields by crop rotation, by large-scale irrigation works, by hybridising strains of corn and rice, by manuring, was impressive. New devices for harrowing, ridging, seed-drilling, rolling, were introduced, and the design of the plough underwent considerable modification. These advances came, in the main, from the peasant-farmers themselves, rather than from the members of the literate elite who wrote the treatises. The latter were not, on the whole, themselves innovators: yet they *recorded* the innovations that were made, and, given the prestige and imperial support their writings often enjoyed, this helped to ensure the diffusion of those innovations.

In the Greco-Roman world, too, we have extensive extant writings, ranging from didactic poems such as Hesiod's *Works and Days*, through general works discussing household and estate management, such as Xenophon's *Economica*, to specialist treatises dealing with plants and plant uses (as by Theophrastus) or with agriculture as a whole. Those last go back to the fifth century BCE, though our chief extant examples are from Latin writers of the second century BCE to the first century CE, the works of Cato, Varro and Columella. Some of the mechanical devices useful in agriculture, meanwhile, are described in other treatises as well, in Vitruvius, for example, or in Pliny's encyclopedic *Natural History*. These devices include most notably the mills and presses used in the manufacture of oil and wine, the water-wheel, water-lifting devices, and even such complex machines as the Gallic corn-harvester: the machine is very effective, but the terrain must be level; the design is close to that first adopted when the combine harvester came to be reinvented in modern times—not that the Gallic antecedent was known to the reinventors.

Some of these Greek and Roman machines exhibit a considerable sophistication, and those that employ the screw in its various forms (screw-presses or the Archimedean screw) depend on an understanding of the geometrical principles involved, as well as the all-important empirical know-how necessary to manufacture screws. Although the Greeks and Romans missed out on some simple devices, such as the wheel-barrow, in other areas they exhibit both curiosity and inventiveness.

Yet one key difference marks the Greco-Roman literature out from the Chinese. This is that the specialist agricultural treatises are mainly addressed to private estate-owners—to give individual rich landlords the information they needed for the profitable running of their estates. They could be the audience of Chinese works too, but in China the prime target was often grander—to provide the Emperor with the wherewithal to ensure the prosperity of all under his control. True, Vitruvius does address his "architectural" treatise to Augustus, and his hopes of thereby securing favour and employment are strictly comparable to those of many Chinese writers who presented memorials to the throne with similar ambitions. Yet Vitruvius writes first and foremost as an architect-engineer, not as an agronomist. He entertains no general expectation that the mechanical devices for use in agriculture that he describes will forthwith be taken up and exploited right across the Roman empire. Indeed in the case of the water-wheel, we can confirm from the archaeological record that its diffusion through the Greco-Roman world was both slow and limited in extent.

At this point the factor that many would invoke to explain the technological weaknesses in the Greco-Roman world is the widespread dependence on slave labour, often represented as the chief factor inhibiting the search for and exploitation of labour-saving devices. Their relevance to the problem must certainly be granted, but should not be exaggerated, for three main reasons.

First, slaves, while expendable, still involved their owners in the expense of their upkeep and were far from necessarily always cheaper than machines. That depended crucially on the outlay needed for the machines.

Moreover, secondly, as between the Greco-Roman world and China, although chattel slaves were not common in China, the use of other types of unfree labour, such as conscripts, certainly was. I shall come back to this when considering civil engineering in the next section.

Thirdly, in the domain of agriculture itself, the existence of slaves will hardly be enough to explain the slow diffusion of mechanical devices, for the simple reason that they were everywhere present throughout the Greco-Roman world. If we ask why the water-wheel was not immediately exploited, once the principle had been discovered, or why the Gallic combine harvester was never used in antiquity outside Gaul, then the existence of slaves *by itself* hardly provides the whole answer, since it offers no discriminating factor. Among the other considerations we have to add is the one we noted before, the lack of state structures taking overall responsibility for agricultural production. In the Greco-Roman world this meant that decisions concerning the running of estates, about the use of slaves or of machines, rested with individual landlords and their perception of where their private profits—or prestige—lay.

The third main subject area I identified is what I called CIVIL ENGINEERING, where there are obvious overlaps with military engineering (as in the siege-engines mentioned before) and with agriculture—insofar as irrigation projects, for example, in China especially, could involve considerable problems of planning and construction.

On the Greek side, the chief large-scale projects undertaken in the early classical period related to the building of cities and particularly to their embellishment, with public buildings, theatres, gymnasia, and especially temples. Much remains unclear about how precisely the "architects" in charge worked, the extent to which they made use of models or plans, how they made the often very subtle adjustments on site to produce the effects they did, as for example in connection with entasis (the curvature of columns and entablatures). But here is certainly an example where major works were undertaken on a corporate basis, not (as was usually the case in the running of estates) for private profit, but rather for public prestige.

Moreover considerable mechanical devices came to be deployed in connection with monumental building. Vitruvius describes how the problems of transporting large blocks of marble were overcome, reporting the devices used by Chersiphron and his son Metagenes in this connection in the construction of the classical temple of Artemis at Ephesus. One such consisted essentially in a pair of rollers between which the marble block was suspended, enabling it to be dragged along. That suggests that already in the sixth century BCE considerable ingenuity was being brought to bear to surmount the difficulties, as there was also in connection with lifting devices, where Vitruvius provides evidence of the development of elaborate cranes, especially those using compound pulleys.

Here is another instance where we can be sure that the theoretical principles involved attracted attention and study. We can infer that from the stories about Archimedes. When he was challenged by King Hiero about his claim to be able to move the whole earth, he is said to have arranged a demonstration in which, with a system of compound pulleys, he dragged a fully laden merchant ship across land singlehanded. The story is preposterous, but we can still see it as useful evidence for an *interest* in exploring the extrapolations of mechanical devices. Similarly the potential applications of the lever and related devices are the subject of elaborate discussions in Hero and Pappus.

The second main area where more than just a private individual's interests were at stake, was in the matter of the delivery of water-supplies to cities. This culminated in the vast networks of aqueducts that served Rome, feats of great engineering skill and again the topic of much ancient discussion. It is clear that those responsible never solved satisfactorily the problem of measuring the quantities of water delivered from sluice gates or openings of different apertures set at different angles to the flow of water: rather they used very rough-and-ready rules of thumb, not precise methods of calculation. While the major aqueducts were Roman achievements, the supply of water to the *polis* of Samos had already been the subject of another, different feat of engineering in the sixth century BCE, when Eupalinus constructed a tunnel through the mountain behind the city to achieve this end. As an inspection of the site reveals, he was confident enough of his technique to start tunnelling from both ends simultaneously. The theory of how to do this by using geometrical methods is set out in Hero's *Dioptra*. But it is now abundantly clear that Eupalinus did not proceed by triangulation, but used dead reckoning with sights set up in a straight line over the top of the mountain.

On the Chinese side, the construction of elaborate temples took second place to that of massive tombs. Many of them, we are told, were equipped with complex devices to deter anyone who might try to enter. These included stones that dropped into place automatically to block an entrance if a door was forced, and cross-bows that fired, again automatically, if anyone attempted to pass. The construction of the tombs themselves (sited always after extensive geomantic investigations) is one of the two most vivid illustrations of the Chinese ability to plan and carry out massive projects of civil engineering. In the case of the first Emperor's tomb, outside modern Xian, guarded by the famous terracotta warriors, we are told by Sima Qian (*Shiji Histories*) that 700,000 conscripts worked on it. All who had been involved in its construction and provision with treasure were subsequently executed—so they had no chance to divulge its secrets.

The second main illustration of those same Chinese capabilities is provided by vast irrigation projects, again involving the marshalling of immense labour forces and demonstrating extraordinary skills in overcoming practical difficulties. The most famous of these is the project started by Li Bing, around 270 BCE, and continued by his son Zhengguo. They divided the river Min north of Chengdu and thereby solved at a stroke both the problem of the recurrent flooding to which the river was liable, and that of providing water to irrigate vast stretches of what is now the province of Sichuan. One uncontrollable river was thereby turned into two controllable ones. To achieve this dual aim, Li Bing had to overcome the problems of the seasonal variations in the quantities of water in the river, and those of silting, over and above the main one of dividing the main channel of the river into two. Although theory, in the sense of applied physical theory, was not much involved, here, even so, practical ingenuity of the highest order was displayed.

Grand generalisations about the development of technology in China or in the Greco-Roman world inevitably fall foul of the actual diversities we find between periods and across fields. To have any pretensions to comprehensiveness, my rapid survey of just these three main areas would need to be supplemented by a review of such other domains as transport, navigation, time-keeping devices, astronomical and geological instruments (such as Zhang Heng's famous second-century CE water-driven armillary and his seismoscope): metallurgy, the applications of pneumatics, catoptrics, and acoustics, not to mention such other fields as pharmaceutics which involve non-mechanical applications of theory. But while recognising that I have had to be selective, I shall now ask how far we can answer the principal questions I posed at the outset. What part did theorists play in the advances in technology that were made, in these three fields at least? How far did they manifest an interest in applying their theoretical ideas to practical problems? To what extent did the actual advances we can identify happen without any theoretical input at all? Should all these questions be answered differently for China and for the Greco-Roman world, and if so, what was responsible for the differences?

We may use the last question as a point of entry for suggesting answers to the others. There is, I argued, a far greater similarity between China and the Greco-Roman world than the contrasting stereotypes of practical Chinese and impractical, head-in-the-clouds Greeks would allow for. Many members of the Chinese literate elite were as reluctant to get their hands dirty as were many educated Greeks or Romans.

Against the stereotype of the theoretically oriented, impractical, Greeks, a considerable body of counter-evidence can be adduced. Some of the mechanical devices recorded in the literature are, to be sure, no more than toys, exhibiting a certain ingenuity but of no practical consequence. Such are the ball rotated by steam described by Hero of Alexandria in *Pneumatics* (drastically misnamed his "steam engine"), and many of his pneumatic and hydraulic devices, designed to amuse diners at a symposium, or to impress religious worshippers, as in his idea for temple doors that open automatically when a fire is lit on an altar. That was no practical proposition, but plenty of his other gadgets can be made to work. One such device is a water-pump incorporating one-way valves that was used as a fire-extinguisher. Even though Pappus amazingly included the gadgets of the "wonder-workers" among what he calls the "most necessary" parts of the mechanical arts, not all Greek mechanics was like that. Improvements in weapons of war, in lifting devices using compound pulleys, in the development of applications of the screw in oil and wine presses and in water-lifting devices, all owe something to the researches of Greek and Roman theorists.

It is certainly the case that many of the actual technological advances we can trace in both civilisations cannot now be assigned to named inventors—nor maybe could they ever have been. Many, probably most, were the work of anonymous individuals or groups directly engaged in the business of food-producing and processing, of fighting battles or whatever. Yet both civilisations produced a considerable technical literature devoted to the description and analysis of practical problems. If the driving force was often necessity, many gifted individuals saw the opportunity (and took it) to make a reputation for themselves and were duly celebrated for their achievements, as hydraulic engineers, builders, inventors, whether in the military or the civil domain. While some texts content themselves with recording the devices used, some individuals and groups (the Mohists, Li Bing, Zhang Heng, Archimedes, the Alexandrian engineers, Hero) evidently engaged in more or less sustained investigations into the problems on their own account.

Yet certain differences may be detected, first in the nature of the theoretical discussions to be found in that literature, and then, more fundamentally, in the matter of the structures that existed for the implementation of new ideas.

On the first score, two features appear particularly striking, first the Greek predilection for geometrical idealisations, and second the Chinese focus on exploring the propensities of things, *shi*. I have remarked before that in such fields as statics, Greek geometrical analysis led both to a successful isolation of the key factors in play, and to the bonus that the results could be presented in the form of axiomatic-deductive demonstrations. . . .

On the Chinese side, geometrisation was not the route that theoretical analysis of these questions took, though that cannot be put down to an alleged Chinese lack of interest in geometry as such. . . . But over a range of technological problems, the Chinese interest is less in attempting to *master* the materials they worked with, than in getting those materials to work *for* them. Li Bing's success would be better described not as overcoming the river Min, but as getting it to cooperate with his aims. Similarly, in warfare, the goal of the Chinese strategist was not to annihilate the enemy, but to have him do what you want — surrender. The means to this end was the exploitation of the potentialities of the situation, from the lie of the land to the disposition and morale of your own and the enemy forces. Both the early military classics, *Sunzi* and *Sun Bin*, have chapters devoted to *shi*, understanding and using the propensities of things, and as François Jullien has shown, the concept plays a similar role, as the focus of interest and theoretical elaboration, across a variety of fields where the goal is effect.

Different emphases, such as these, may, then, be found in the *motifs* given prominence, when Chinese, or when Greek or Latin, authors discuss the keys to the solution of practical problems. But there are far more marked differences, between the two civilisations, in the matter of the exploitation of whatever new ideas the theorists and others proposed.

The exceptional nature of the Ptolemies' support for their military engineers just highlights the contrast with the *norm* in the Greco-Roman world. Where, in that world, civic or state interests *were* at stake—in temple building or in the construction of aqueducts—there we find great projects seen through to successful completion. But that was the *norm* in China, increasingly so after the unification of the empire under Qin Shi Huang Di, with the systematic engagement of the Emperor himself (and so of all his many officials under him) in agriculture, in warfare, in the welfare of all under heaven. It was not that the Emperor sought to ensure the prosperity of his people *solely* in a spirit of disinterested magnanimity. Rather, that prosperity had often been, and continued to be, taken as a sign of his virtue and of his mandate from heaven. So where the Roman agronomists (for example) targeted private landowners whose desire for greater efficiency was driven largely by the profit motive, many of the Chinese—not unmoved by profit themselves of course, despite Mencius—were further influenced by the ideal of the welfare of the empire as a whole. But that was not just in a spirit of idealism, but also one of self-interest, for the apparently altruistic ideal of the welfare of the empire coincided with the egoistic one of a secure job in the imperial service.

22

The Salt and Iron Debates

The Chinese state, as selection 21 points out, was much more centralized than the Roman Empire. One of the great centralizers was the Han dynasty Emperor Wu (r. 140–87 B.C.E.). He sent large armies to drive the nomadic Xiongnu* out of Chinese territory and into central Asia, increased domestic and foreign trade, and introduced a system of government bureaus, staffed by graduates of his newly created Confucian Academy. To pay for the greater costs of defense and government administration and services, Emperor Wu initiated government monopolies on salt and iron. The central control of iron production (performed by conscripts and convicts) and the manufacture of iron weapons and tools (everything from cooking pots and scissors to

*zhee yong NOO

"The Debate on Salt and Iron," trans. Pat Ebrey, in *Chinese Civilization: A Sourcebook*, ed. Pat Ebrey (New York: The Free Press, 1993), 60–63.

farm tools and salt drills) were particularly profitable for the government. In addition, Emperor Wu established licenses for the production and sale of alcoholic beverages and set up bureaus to purchase grain when the price was low and sell it when the price was high, called the system of "equable marketing."

In 86 B.C.E. Emperor Wu's successor called a conference to investigate the economic problems of the people. In 81, debate was held between government ministers and the "learned men" who were mainly Confucian scholars. This is part of the record of that debate. What was the disagreement between the government ministers and the "learned men" regarding the salt and iron monopolies? What signs do you see that the Chinese economy and society had become centralized?

Thinking Historically

Our tendency in reading a debate is to notice where the two sides disagree. It is also useful, however, to notice where they agree. What assumptions do the government ministers and Confucians share in this debate? What does that agreement tell you about Han China?

Other comparisons might usefully be drawn from this selection. Since you have read some of Confucius, you might compare the ideas of the Master with the ideas of these Confucian scholars. How similar or different are these two sets of ideas? How might you explain that similarity or difference?

You might also usefully relate this reading to the previous one. Lloyd discusses innovation. What Chinese innovations are discussed in this selection? How do you imagine the Romans might have struggled with the same sort of problems?

In 81 B.C. an imperial edict directed the chancellor and chief minister to confer with a group of wise and learned men about the people's hardships.

The learned men responded: We have heard that the way to rule lies in preventing frivolity while encouraging morality, in suppressing the pursuit of profit while opening the way for benevolence and duty. When profit is not emphasized, civilization flourishes and the customs of the people improve.

Recently, a system of salt and iron monopolies, a liquor excise tax, and an equable marketing system have been established throughout the country. These represent financial competition with the people which undermines their native honesty and promotes selfishness. As a result, few among the people take up the fundamental pursuits [agriculture] while many flock to the secondary [trade and industry]. When artificiality thrives, simplicity declines; when the secondary flourishes, the basic decays. Stress on the secondary makes the people decadent; emphasis on the basic keeps them unsophisticated. When the people are unsophisticated, wealth abounds; when they are extravagant, cold and hunger ensue.

We desire that the salt, iron, and liquor monopolies and the system of equable marketing be abolished. In that way the basic pursuits will be encouraged, and the people will be deterred from entering secondary occupations. Agriculture will then greatly prosper. This would be expedient.

The minister: The Xiongnu rebel against our authority and frequently raid the frontier settlements. To guard against this requires the effort of the nation's soldiers. If we take no action, these attacks and raids will never cease. The late emperor had sympathy for the long-suffering of the frontier settlers who live in fear of capture by the barbarians. As defensive measures, he therefore built forts and beacon relay stations and set up garrisons. When the revenue for the defense of the frontier fell short, he established the salt and iron monopolies, the liquor excise tax, and the system of equable marketing. Wealth increased and was used to furnish the frontier expenses.

Now our critics wish to abolish these measures. They would have the treasury depleted and the border deprived of funds for its defense. They would expose our soldiers who defend the frontier passes and walls to hunger and cold, since there is no other way to supply them. Abolition is not expedient.

The learned men: Confucius observed, "The ruler of a kingdom or head of a family does not worry about his people's being poor, only about their being unevenly distributed. He does not worry about their being few, only about their being dissatisfied." Thus, the emperor should not talk of much and little, nor the feudal lords of advantage and harm, nor the ministers of gain and loss. Instead they all should set examples of benevolence and duty and virtuously care for people, for then those nearby will flock to them and those far away will joyfully submit to their authority. Indeed, the master conqueror need not fight, the expert warrior needs no soldiers, and the great commander need not array his troops.

If you foster high standards in the temple and courtroom, you need only make a bold show and bring home your troops, for the king who practices benevolent government has no enemies anywhere. What need can he then have for expense funds?

The minister: The Xiongnu are savage and cunning. They brazenly push through the frontier passes and harass the interior, killing provincial officials and military officers at the border. Although they have long deserved punishment for their lawless rebellion, Your Majesty has taken pity on the financial exigencies of the people and has not wished to expose his officers to the wilderness. Still, we cherish the goal of raising a great army and driving the Xiongnu back north.

I again assert that to do away with the salt and iron monopolies and equable marketing system would bring havoc to our frontier military policies and would be heartless toward those on the frontier. Therefore this proposal is inexpedient.

The learned men: The ancients honored the use of virtue and discredited the use of arms. Confucius said, "If the people of far-off lands do not submit, then the ruler must attract them by enhancing his refinement and virtue. When they have been attracted, he gives them peace."

At present, morality is discarded and reliance is placed on military force. Troops are raised for campaigns and garrisons are stationed for defense. It is the long-drawn-out campaigns and the ceaseless transportation of provisions that burden our people at home and cause our frontier soldiers to suffer from hunger and cold.

The establishment of the salt and iron monopolies and the appointment of financial officers to supply the army were meant to be temporary measures. Therefore, it is expedient that they now be abolished.

The minister: The ancient founders of our country laid the groundwork for both basic and secondary occupations. They facilitated the circulation of goods and provided markets and courts to harmonize the various demands. People of all classes gathered and goods of all sorts were assembled, so that farmers, merchants, and workers could all obtain what they needed. When the exchange of goods was complete, everyone went home. The *Book of Changes* says, "Facilitate exchange so that the people will not be over-worked." This is because farmers are deprived of tools, and without merchants, desired commodities are unavailable. When farmers lack tools, grain is not planted, just as when valued goods are unavailable, wealth is exhausted.

The salt and iron monopolies and the equable marketing system are intended to circulate accumulated wealth and to regulate consumption according to the urgency of need. It is inexpedient to abolish them.

The learned men: If virtue is used to lead the people, they will return to honesty, but if they are enticed with gain, they will become vulgar. Vulgar habits lead them to shun duty. Vulgar habits lead them to shun duty and chase profit; soon they throng the roads and markets. Laozi said, "A poor country will appear to have a surplus." It is not that it possesses abundance, but that when wishes multiply the people become restive. Hence, a true king promotes the basic and discourages the secondary. He restrains the people's desires through the principles of ritual and duty and arranges to have grain exchanged for other goods. In his markets merchants do not circulate worthless goods nor artisans make worthless implements.

The purpose of merchants is circulation and the purpose of artisans is making tools. These matters should not become a major concern of the government.

The minister: Guanzi[1] said: "If a country possesses fertile land and yet its people are underfed, the reason is that there are not enough tools. If it possesses rich natural resources in its mountains and seas and yet the people are poor, the reason is that there are not enough artisans and merchants." The scarlet lacquer and pennant feathers from the kingdoms of Long and Shu; the leather goods, bone, and ivory from Jing and Yang; the cedar, catalpa, bamboo, and reeds from Jiangnan; the fish, salt, felt, and furs from Yan and Qi; the silk yarn, linen, and hemp cloth from Yan and You—all are needed to maintain our lives or be used in our funerals. We depend upon merchants for their distribution and on artisans for their production. For such reasons the ancient sages built boats and bridges to cross rivers; they domesticated cattle and horses to travel over mountains and plains. By penetrating to remote areas, they were able to exchange all kinds of goods for the benefit of the people.

Thus, the former emperor set up iron officials to meet the farmers' needs and started the equable marketing system to assure the people adequate goods. The bulk of the people look to the salt and iron monopolies and the equable marketing system as their source of supply. To abolish them would not be expedient.

The learned men: If a country possesses a wealth of fertile land and yet its people are underfed, the reason is that merchants and workers have prospered while agriculture has been neglected. Likewise, if a country possesses rich natural resources in its mountains and seas and yet its people are poor, the reason is that the people's necessities have not been attended to while luxuries have multiplied. A spring cannot fill a leaking cup; the mountains and seas cannot satisfy unlimited desires. This is why [the ancient emperor] Pan Geng practiced communal living, [the ancient emperor] Shun concealed the gold, and [the Han dynasty founder] Gaozu prohibited merchants and shopkeepers from becoming officials. Their purpose was to discourage habits of greed and to strengthen the spirit of sincerity. Now, even with all of the discriminations against commerce, people still do evil. How much worse it would be if the ruler himself were to pursue profit!

The *Zuo Chronicle* says: "When the feudal lords take delight in profit, the officers become petty; when the officers are petty, the gentle-

---

[1]Guan Zhong, a famous minister of the seventh century B.C. noted for his economic policies.

men become greedy; when the gentlemen are greedy, the common people steal." Thus to open the way for profit is to provide a ladder for the people to become criminals!

The minister: Formerly the feudal lords in the commanderies and kingdoms sent in the products of their respective regions as tribute. Transportation was troublesome and disorganized and the goods often of such bad quality as not to be worth the transport cost. Therefore, transport officers were appointed in every commandery and kingdom to assist in speeding the delivery of tribute and taxes from distant regions. This was called the equable marketing system. A receiving bureau was established at the capital for all the commodities. Because goods were bought when prices were low and sold when prices were high, the government suffered no loss and the merchants could not speculate for profit. This was called the balancing standard.

The balancing standard safeguards the people from unemployment; the equable marketing system distributes their work fairly. Both of these measures are intended to even out goods and be a convenience for the people. They do not provide a ladder for the people to become criminals by opening the way to profit!

The learned men: The ancients in placing levies and taxes on the people would look for what they could provide. Thus farmers contributed their harvest and the weaving women the products of their skill. At present the government ignores what people have and exacts what they lack. The common people then must sell their products cheaply to satisfy the demands of the government. Recently, some commanderies and kingdoms ordered the people to weave cloth. The officials caused the producers various difficulties and then traded with them. They requisitioned not only the silk from Qi and Tao and the broadcloth from Shu and Han, but also the ordinary cloth people make. These were then nefariously sold at "equable" prices. Thus the farmers suffered twice over and the weavers were doubly taxed. Where is the equability in this marketing?

The government officers busy themselves with gaining control of the market and cornering commodities. With the commodities cornered, prices soar and merchants make private deals and speculate. The officers connive with the cunning merchants who are hoarding commodities against future need. Quick traders and unscrupulous officials buy when goods are cheap in order to make high profits. Where is the balance in this standard?

The equable marketing system of antiquity aimed at bringing about fair division of labor and facilitating transportation of tribute. It was surely not for profit or commodity trade.

23

CICERO

Against Verres

Marcus Tullius Cicero* (106–43 B.C.E.) was one of the great orators and statesmen of the late Roman Republic. He was admired especially for the legal arguments he made for or against other Romans, usually public figures, brought before the courts. In this oration, Cicero spoke against a corrupt governor of Sicily, Caius Verres.† Cicero contrasted his own career as a Roman governor with that of Verres. What does Cicero's criticism of Verres, and his brief autobiography, tell you about Roman governance?

Thinking Historically

Like any primary source, this document is only a small piece of the past. In this case, it is a small part of one of many speeches Cicero wrote against Verres, and Cicero spoke about many other figures in many other cases. He also wrote volumes of letters, political philosophy, and diverse orations. Cicero was one of perhaps four million Romans when he prosecuted Verres in 70 B.C.E. Consequently, we must be very careful in generalizing from such a small fragment from the period. Nevertheless, a careful reading reveals certain facts about Roman society that are indisputable and certain facts that are highly likely. What are some of these?

If you compare this single source from Rome with the single source from China in selection 22, what conclusions can you draw about the different systems of government in Rome and China?

. . . At the height of the summer, governors of Sicily are accustomed to move around. This is because they feel that the best season for inspecting their province is the time when the grain is on the threshing-floor. For that is when the workers are all gathered together, so that the size

*SIH suh roh
†KY uhs VEHR uhs

Cicero, "Against Verres" (II, 5), from *On Government*, trans. Michael Grant (London: Penguin, 1993), 29–31, 32–34, 45–46, 82–85.

of the slave households can be reliably estimated, and the sort of work they are doing can be most easily seen. Yet at this time of year, when all other governors travel about, this novel type of commander, Verres, instead remained stationary, and had a camp set up for him at the city of Syracuse, and indeed in its most agreeable section. Precisely at the entrance of the harbour, where the gulf turns in from the sea-coast towards the city, he pitched a series of pavilions; they were constructed of fine linen, stretched on poles. Moving out of the governor's residence — the former palace of King Hiero[1] — he established himself on this new site so completely that, throughout all this time, it was impossible for anyone to catch a glimpse of him in the outside world.

Moreover, the only people allowed into this new dwelling of his were people whose job it was to share, or minister to, his sensualities. Here flocked all the women with whom he had had relations (and the number of them, at Syracuse, is past belief). Here assembled, also, the people whom Verres deemed worthy to be his friends — worthy, that is to say, to share the life of revelry in which he indulged. And Verres's son, too, by now a grown man, spent his time with men and women of the same type. His own character might incline him to be different from his father. But habit and upbringing made him his father's true son, all the same. . . .

Dressed in a purple Greek cloak and a tunic down to the ankles, Verres spent all this period having a good time with his women. However, while he was thus engaged, the absence of the chief magistrate from the Forum, the lack of any legal decisions and hearings, caused no one to feel in any way offended or displeased. Where Verres was staying, on the coast, there resounded a constant din of female voices and vocalists. In the Forum, on the other hand, laws and lawsuits had ceased to exist. But nobody minded. Men did not worry at all because, with Verres away, the law and the courts were suspended. On the contrary, his absence, they felt, was sparing them violence and brutality, and the savage, unprovoked plundering of their possessions. . . .

Next came his behavior when he had become a grown man. . . . I shall . . . only refer . . . to two recent matters, which will enable you to form your own idea about the rest of what was happening.

One was an entirely notorious fact, known to all the world: so well known that, during the consulships of Lucius Licinius Lucullus and Marcus Aurelius Cotta, every plainest rustic, from any country town, who came to Rome on legal business was aware of it. This fact that everyone learnt was that every single decision which Verres pronounced as city praetor had been made on the prompting of the prostitute Chelidon, and according to her wishes. A second matter that everyone knew about was this. Verres had, by this time, left the city, in his

[1]Hiero II, king of Syracuse (270–215 B.C.E.).

military commander's cloak. He had already offered his vows relating to his period of office and the welfare of the state. And yet time after time he got himself carried back to the city in a litter after darkness had fallen, in order to commit adultery with a woman who had a husband; though she was also available to everyone else. It was a proceeding entirely opposed to morality, to the auspices, to every principle of religion and human behaviour.

Heavens above, what different attitudes men have from one another, and what different intentions! Take my own case. If it is not true that I, when assuming the offices with which the Roman people has up to now honoured me, have felt the most solemn obligation to carry out my duties with the utmost conscientiousness, then, gentlemen, I will feel obliged, voluntarily, to sacrifice all the goodwill that you and our country have been kind enough to lavish upon my plans and hopes for the future! When I was elected quaestor,[2] I felt that the post had not only been conferred on me, but was a solemn trust committed into my hands. When I was carrying out the duties of my quaestorship in Sicily, I was convinced that all men's eyes were turned upon myself, and myself alone. It seemed to me that my own person, and my office, were set upon a stage, acting before an audience which was nothing less than the whole of the world. And so I denied myself all the amenities which are permitted to the incumbents of such offices, not only for the gratification of out-of-the-way tastes but even to satisfy the most orthodox and indispensable requirements. . . . Now I am an aedile elect.

In return for the labour and worry . . . I shall be the recipient of certain privileges. I shall have the right to speak early in the Senate. I shall be entitled to wear a purple-bordered toga, and sit in a curule chair.[3] I shall be permitted a portrait bust, as my memorial for later generations. And yet, over and above all these things, gentlemen—as I hope for the favour of all the gods in heaven—I must assure you of something else. Certainly, I am very happy that the Roman people has honoured me with this post. And yet my happiness is overtaken by a feeling of consuming anxiety. What I am anxious about is that men should not just think that I was given this office because it had to go to one or another of the candidates. What I want is that they should believe that the people came to a correct decision, and that the appointment went to the right man.

But, in contrast, Verres, consider yourself. I do not propose to talk about the circumstances of your election as praetor. But think of the moment when your election was announced, when the crier declared that you had been invested with this high office, by the votes of the entire Assembly, its senior and junior sections alike. I cannot see how, on

---

[2]A comparatively junior rung on the official ladder.
[3]An ivory folding seat, reserved for senior, "curule" officials.

that occasion, the very sound of the crier's voice could have failed to inspire you with a feeling that a share in the government of your country had been entrusted into your hands—so that for this one, forthcoming, year at least you would have to keep away from the houses of prostitutes! . . .

Let me now tell you, also, of Verres's novel scheme for extracting loot—which he was the first man ever to devise. The normal practice had been that all communities should make provision for their own fleet's costs, comprising food and pay and all other such expenditure. This was done by supplying their commander with the necessary sum. Let us bear in mind that he, for his part, was never likely to venture to incur the danger that he would be charged with misappropriation by people in Rome. For it was his obligation to submit accounts to his fellow-citizens. Thus his conduct of his duties at all times involved not only work but personal risk. This, I repeat, was the invariable practice, not only in Sicily but in every other of our provinces as well. Indeed, it even applied to the pay and expenses of our Italian allies, and of the Latins too, during the period when we used to employ them as auxiliary troops.

Verres, however, was the first man, ever since our imperial rule began, to have ordered that all these funds should be counted out by the provincial communities, to himself in person, and looked after by individuals who were his own nominees. Now, why you chose to introduce this innovation, changing a custom that was so longstanding and universal, must be perfectly clear to all. It must be clear enough, too, why, although it would have been so manifestly convenient to leave the handling of the money in other hands, you nevertheless preferred to do nothing of the kind; and why you were willing to take over, personally, a function which was not only tiresome and troublesome but made you the object of suspicions of the most disagreeable nature.

Other schemes for making money, too, were set on foot by Verres. In this connection you should note, gentlemen, how many opportunities of the kind the naval situation alone supplied, quite apart from anything else. For cities were only too ready to pay Verres to exempt them from the requirement of providing sailors. Enlisted men could secure discharge for a fee. Then the pay they would have been due to receive would be diverted by Verres to himself, while at the same time he would fail to hand over to all the rest the pay to which they were entitled. . . .

Concerning the torments inflicted on other Roman citizens I prefer just to offer a general, comprehensive description, rather than considering them one by one. While Verres was governor, the prison built at Syracuse by the cruel despot Dionysius I, and known as the Stone Quarries, was the place where Roman citizens had to live. If the thought or sight of any of them caused Verres displeasure, the man was immediately thrown into the Quarries. I can see, gentlemen, that this makes you all very angry.

. . . Verres, how you could have had the nerve to use that place of confinement for foreign malefactors and criminals and pirates and enemies of Rome to incarcerate Roman citizens, in substantial numbers. It is remarkable that the prospect of your future trial never occurred to you, nor the thought of a gathering such as this, at which such a mass of listeners are staring at you with censorious, hostile gaze. How strange that the greatness of the Roman people never entered your mind or presented itself to your imagination, not to speak, as I said, of this great concourse that you might have to face. That you would never again have to appear before their eyes, never re-enter the Forum of the Roman nation, never again be obliged to submit to the authority of our laws and our courts, was surely more than you could have hoped for. . . .

If it had been some monarch, or foreign people or nation, that had treated Roman citizens in this way, we should surely be taking official measures to punish those responsible, and dispatch our armies against them. For we could not possibly have endured such a disgraceful slur upon the honour of Rome without exacting vengeance and punishment. Remember all those important wars upon which our ancestors embarked, because Roman citizens were said to have been insulted, Roman ship-masters placed under arrest, Roman traders subjected to robbery. Yet I, on this occasion, am not complaining because these merchants were arrested, I am not declaring it unendurable that they were robbed. My accusation is that, after their ships and slaves and trading goods had been taken away from them, they were hurled into prison, and in that prison, although Roman citizens, they were killed.

My theme, then, is the brutal execution of that multitude of Roman citizens. And I am speaking about it in Rome itself, before this vast gathering of Romans. I am speaking to a jury composed of senators, members of the most eminent body in the state. I am speaking in the Forum of our Roman people. Yet, if my audience were Scythians instead, what I am saying would move even their barbarian hearts. For so magnificent is our empire, so greatly is the name of Rome respected among all the nations of the world, that it is not felt permissible for any man whatsoever to treat our citizens with such savagery. . . .

REFLECTIONS

We have compared Han China and ancient Rome on many topics. We began by noting that their empires straddled Eurasia about the same time, that they were a similar size with about the same number of people, that they were both based on agricultural technologies that supported emperors, large land-owning classes, and soldiers, and exploited subordinate populations. In selection 18, Adshead laid out these and other broad similarities and then explored a wide range of differences. Some of these differences seem to have been more important than others in making China different from Rome: using a language based on characters, perhaps, more than eating rice. Some differences seem quite profound in their effects. Both Adshead and Lloyd, in selection 21, contrasted Chinese and Greco-Roman thinking patterns and both related different modes of thinking to different types of social organizations.

The idea that different cultures think differently—not just think about different things, but actually think differently—is a periodic theory of anthropologists and social scientists. The French philosopher Lucien Levy-Bruhl wrote *How Natives Think* in 1910 to argue that "natives" had a "pre-logical mentality" of "mystical participation." Most historians and philosophers since have been wary of the implied prejudice in the idea that "natives" do not think logically and of the falsity of the assumption that their behavior is not practical. Levy-Bruhl was dismissed by many later social scientists as a representative of the European colonial attitude toward colonized peoples. Nevertheless, Levy-Bruhl had a profound influence in the development in the twentieth century of the sociology of knowledge, a field of philosophy and social science that explored the ways in which the social position of the knower shaped what was known. The intellectual debate flared recently with the publication of sociologist Marshall Sahlins's *How "Natives" Think: About Captain Cook, For Example* (1996) in which he argued that "natives" thought differently and that scholars who said otherwise were the ones who imposed a distinctly Western emphasis on logic and reason on others in the world who thought differently.

Han China, of course, was nothing like a "primitive" society. Yet the debate about logical/scientific versus symbolic/associational thinking that is raised by Adshead and Lloyd echoes the early debate that gave birth to the sociology of knowledge. In considering the possibility of deep human differences in thought or behavior, one always has to be careful of easy generalizations that fit current prejudices. In the 1950s and 1960s, after World War II, when China was struggling just to feed its population and the Japanese economy exported only cheap toys, social scientists argued that the social consciousness of Confucian cultures led them to become communist or collectivist, but prevented them from becoming capitalist or prosperous. Then, when Japan, Korea, and Taiwan became economic powerhouses in the 1980s, social scientists compared the advantages of the Confucian "Asian tigers" with the presumed cultural inhibitions of the slower economies of India and Southeast Asia. Inevitably, we construct our historical comparisons to understand how we have arrived at where we are. The problem of constructing a good comparison begins with the problem of knowing where we are.

Women in Classical Societies

India, China, and the Mediterranean,
500 B.C.E. – 500 C.E.

HISTORICAL CONTEXT

In Chapter 1 we saw how the earliest city societies or "civilizations," which emerged about five thousand years ago, often created patriarchies where fathers ruled families, kings ruled societies, priests administered for gods, and state officials, soldiers, and police preserved laws favoring men. The patriarchies that developed in the ancient world continued through the classical age down to the recent past, if not the present.

Nevertheless, not all patriarchies were alike. Some allowed women greater freedom or autonomy. Yet, they did have one thing in common—change. In the thousand years between 500 B.C.E. and 500 C.E. the roles of women did not remain constant in any society or civilization.

Historians call this period the "classical age" because it produced some of the enduring works of a number of the world's major civilizations, some of which we read in Chapters 3 and 4. In this chapter, we will read more of these works, partly to savor their authors' vision and insights and to understand the reasons for their wide acclaim. But we will also use these writings as windows on classical social life. We will ask specifically what they tell us about the comparative and changing roles of women in the classical age.

THINKING HISTORICALLY
Considering Historical Moment and Historical Process

We can think of history as moment or process. Most popular history attempts to capture a moment. Plays, movies, even our own imaginations usually try to capture moments: what it was like to live in ancient Rome, witness the assassination of Caesar or the preaching of Jesus. The appeal of a good primary source is that it can immerse us in its particular historical moment. In the previous two chapters we also used primary sources to compare two moments in different cultures—Rome with China, Greece with India, for instance—as if these moments could stand in for the whole history of a culture or civilization.

We also study history to understand how things change: How did the Roman Empire decline? How did Christianity spread? This is the study of history as process. Here we must also use primary sources (since that is, by definition, all we have of the past), but since each one represents only a particular moment we have to either examine it for evidence of change or gather many to see the changes that occurred from one moment to the next.

In this chapter we will be studying both historical moments and historical processes in the history of women in classical antiquity. We will read the efforts of historians to understand the process of change in women's history during this period. And we will examine primary sources—written and visual—that reflect moments of that past. We will also be comparing one document with another. But in addition to comparing a document from Rome, for instance, with one from China, we will also be considering how each document might reflect a particular stage or period in the longer process of the history of its civilization and of the history of women generally. We do this to understand and practice two different ways of thinking about the past.

SARAH SHAVER HUGHES
AND BRADY HUGHES

Women in the Classical Era

Sarah and Brady Hughes are modern historians. This selection is part
of their essay on the history of women in the ancient world. They
write here of the classical era in India, China, Greece, and Rome. All
of these were patriarchal societies, but how were they different? The
authors also mention later Greek Hellenistic society and pre-Roman
Etruscan society. How do these two societies round out your understanding of women in the classical era? What seem to be the conditions or causes that improved the status of women in some societies
and periods?

Thinking Historically

Notice that from the first sentence, the authors are interested in understanding the historical process, specifically how the role of women
changed over time. In what societies do they see change? Did the roles
of women improve or decline in these societies during this period?
How do the authors use primary sources to show change?

India

Women's rights deteriorated after the Vedic* period (1600–800 B.C.E.).
No one has been able to prove why this happened. Scholarly interest
has focused on women's exclusion from performing Hindu rituals,
which was in effect by 500 B.C.E. . . . Julia Leslie thinks that women's
exclusion resulted from intentional mistranslation of the Vedas by male
scholars, as the rituals became more complicated and as the requirement for property ownership was more rigorously enforced at a time
when women could not own property.

*VAY dihk

Sarah Shaver Hughes and Brady Hughes, "Women in Ancient Civilizations," in *Women's History in Global Perspective*, vol. II, ed. Bonnie G. Smith (Urbana: University of Illinois Press, published with the American Historical Association, 2005), 26–30 minus deletions and 36–40 minus deletions.

The falling age of marriage for Indian women is another illustration of their loss of rights. In 400 B.C.E. about sixteen years was a normal age for a bride at marriage; between 400 B.C.E. and 100 C.E. it fell to pre-puberty; and after 100 C.E. pre-puberty was favored. These child marriages also affected women's religious roles. Because girls married before they could finish their education, they were not qualified to perform ritual sacrifices. Furthermore, wives' legal rights eroded. As child wives, they were treated as minors. Then their minority status lengthened until they were lifetime minors as wards of their husbands. Finally, women were prohibited any independence and were always under men's control: their fathers, husbands, or sons. By 100 C.E. Hindu texts defined women with negative characteristics, stating, for example, that women would be promiscuous unless controlled by male relatives. While Indian women were losing their independence, Indian men continued to glorify their wives and mothers. A wife was the essence of the home, a man was not complete without a wife, and sons were expected to respect their mothers more than their fathers. As Romila Thapar sums up these contradictions, "The symbol of the woman in Indian culture has been a curious intermeshing of low legal status, ritual contempt, sophisticated sexual partnership, and deification."

One of the causes for this deterioration of women's rights and independence was the increasing rigidity of Hinduism under the influence of the Brahmans. By 600 B.C.E. sects were springing up that opposed Brahman power and ostentatiously omitted some of the Hindu essentials, such as priests, rituals and ceremonies, animal sacrifices, and even caste distinctions. Jainism and Buddhism are two of the sects that have survived. They were especially attractive to women. Jainism, the older religion, gained prominence with the efforts of its last prophet, Mahavira, who lived at the end of the sixth century B.C.E. Jains sought to live without passion and to act "correctly." One could achieve liberation only by living within a monastery or nunnery. Women who sought to join a nunnery found that the Jains had no membership restrictions. Many women entered and found new and exciting roles that were for the first time open to them. . . .

Mahavira's contemporary, Gautama Siddhartha* (the Buddha), began the religion that eventually spread throughout Asia. Among studies of Buddhist women, the early years have been a focus of interest. While Buddhism had no priests, it relied on celibate monks, who were initially homeless, except in the monsoon season, and had to beg for their necessities as they spread their ideas. The Buddha was reluctant to allow women to become nuns. He refused even the women in

*GAW tah moh   sih DAHR thah

his family who sought to become nuns until he was reminded repeatedly by his aunt and his disciple Ananda of his stated principle that anyone could attain enlightenment. The Buddha then reluctantly accepted women followers, and they, like monks, eventually lived in their own self-governing celibate monasteries. . . .

China

. . . For Chinese women the ideas of Confucius (551–479 B.C.E.) have been most influential. There is little mention of women in his *Analects*. His neo-Confucian interpreters corrected this omission, however. They made explicit men's desire for a woman's subordination to her family, her husband, and her sons. For example, Lieh Nu Chuan (also known as Liu Hsiang, 80–87 B.C.E.) wrote *The Biographies of Eminent Chinese Women*, in which he included 125 biographies of women from the peasant class to the emperor's wife, taken from prehistoric legends to the early years of the Han dynasty.

Although the purpose of these biographical sketches was to provide moral instruction in the passive ideals of Confucian womanhood, translator Albert Richard O'Hara's analysis of the women's actions reveals their influence on events that were important to them. The traditional Chinese interpretation of the genre is evident in one of the best-known biographies, that of the widowed mother of Mencius (Meng K'o, or Meng-tzu), whose stern supervision and self-sacrifice were shown to have shaped her son's character and philosophy. This tale drives home the point that a woman's highest ambitions should be fulfilled indirectly through the talents of her sons. Pan Chao,[1] a female scholar in the first century C.E., wrote *The Seven Feminine Virtues* as a Confucian manual for girls' behavior. Its prescriptions of humility, meekness, modesty, and hard work continued to be copied by generations of young women until the twentieth century. . . .

Occasionally, imperial women seized power to govern when acting as regent for an underage emperor. Usually regents exercised this power cautiously behind the scenes because there was much opposition to women's open governance. Two famous empresses ruled openly, however, and sought to transfer royal descent to their own natal families. The first, Empress Lu, violated every canon of Confucian femininity. The widow of Gaodi, the first Han emperor (ruled 202–195 B.C.E.), Empress Lu acted swiftly and brutally to eliminate competitors at court during the near-fifteen years of her rule as regent for her son, her grandson, and another adopted infant grandson. By retaining power

---

[1]Ban Zhao in selection 26. [Ed.]

until her death in 181 B.C.E., she expected that her own nephews would succeed her. Instead, a civil war over the succession ended the period of peaceful prosperity, low taxes, and lessened punishment for crimes that had made her reign popular with the Chinese people. . . .

Greece

Classical Greece has long been admired for its political theories, philosophy, science, and the arts. Until recently, Greek social history was largely ignored. Slavery, homosexuality, and subordination of women are topics once dismissed as insignificant but now recognized as important to understanding the culture. In the classical period there were actually many "Greeces," with distinct societies developing in the city-states of Athens, Sparta, and Thebes. Gender patterns varied considerably among these cities. Sparta's aristocratic women, for example, were often left alone to acquire wealth and some autonomy when their mercenary husbands soldiered elsewhere. To some Athenian men such as Aristotle, Spartan women were thought to be despicable, licentious, greedy, and the reason for Sparta's decline.

Aristotle and other Athenian men dominate the discourse from classical Greece. Their male descriptions tell how Athenian society secluded elite women, denigrated and exploited them, and made them the legal dependents of men. Because no women's writings survive, only indirect evidence suggests how Athenian wives escaped their lives of hard work in the isolated, dark rooms that their husbands imagined necessary to preserve their chastity. But as drawn on vases, groups of Athenian women read to one another, spun and wove, shared child care, or talked. Women are shown in public processions and getting water from wells. Bits of documentary records show respectable married women earning their livings as wet nurses, farm workers, and retail vendors. Most records reveal the lives of privileged women, yet many Athenian women were slaves. Exposure of unwanted female babies was one internal source of slaves, for the rescuer of such an infant became her owner. Athenian enslavement of females was exceptional in its celebration of prostitution in literary and artistic records. One explanation for the large number of slave sex workers may be the Athenians' desire to attract sailors and merchants to their port.

Research on women in the Hellenistic period concentrates on Greek women living in Egypt. These women were much more assertive and influential than their sisters in either contemporary Greece or later Rome. Women in the ruling Ptolemaic family often actually ruled Egypt, some as regents, others as queens. Cleopatra VII (69–30 B.C.E.), one of the best-known women in ancient history, guided her country from a tributary position in the Roman Empire into a partnership with

Marc Antony that might have led to Egypt's domination of the eastern Mediterranean. Non-elite women had unusual freedom. They owned property (including land), participated in commerce, produced textiles, were educated, and enjoyed careers as artists, poets, and farmers. But some women were slaves. . . .

Rome

As late as the sixth century B.C.E., Rome was dominated by its northern neighbors, the Etruscans. Although no body of Etruscan literature exists, scholars have sought evidence of women's lives from inscriptions and art found in their tombs. Upper-class Etruscan women were more autonomous and privileged than contemporary Greek women. Paintings of husbands and wives feasting together horrified Greek males, who only allowed prostitutes to attend their banquets. Etruscan women were not restricted to their homes as Greek women were and attended the games at gymnasiums. In Italy, all women left votive statues of women in sacred places, probably as a fertility offering, but only Etruscan statues included a nursing child, suggesting an affection for children that paralleled the affectionate touching between couples occasionally shown in their art. Finally, Etruscan women had personal names, in contrast to Greek women, who were known first as their fathers' daughters and later as their husbands' wives.

The Romans did not duplicate the autonomy of women in Etruscan society. Roman women legally were constrained within a highly patriarchal agricultural system organized around clans. A father could kill or sell his children into slavery without fear of legal action. Husbands could kill their wives if they were caught in adultery. Women did not speak in public meetings. They could not buy and sell property without their male relatives' approval. Legally treated as minors, women were first the responsibility of their fathers, then of their husbands, and finally of appointed guardians. Rome was a warrior society and a male republic. Men even dominated the state religion, with the exception of the six Vestal Virgins who served as priestesses. Roman society remained staunchly male until conquests brought wealth to Italy in the second century B.C.E. Changes that accompanied the booty of empire gave women a measure of economic and marital independence that is illustrated by the loosening of legal restrictions against women's property ownership.

The paterfamilias, the oldest male in the family, had complete *manus* (legal control) over his children. In marriage, manus passed from the paterfamilias to the new husband. Among other things, that meant the husband then controlled all of his wife's property. Before the first century B.C.E. some Roman marriages were made without transferring manus to the husband; the wife and her property would remain under her father's control, whose approval was theoretically required for the daughter to buy or sell property. Susan Treggiari explains how this enabled many women to gain control over their property:

> Given ancient expectation of life, it is probable that many women were fatherless for a relatively long period of their married lives. The pattern . . . for the middle ranks of Roman society is that girls married in their late teens and men in their mid- to late twenties. If expectation of life at birth is put between twenty and thirty, then 46 percent of fifteen-year-olds had no father left alive. The percentage grows to 59 percent of twenty-year-olds and 70 percent of twenty-five-year-olds. So there is about a 50 percent chance that a woman was already fatherless at the time of her first marriage.

Upon a father's death, manus was transferred to a guardian, and women began to choose as their guardians men who agreed with them. By the later years of the Roman Republic, therefore, many women bought and sold land as they pleased. Rome's expansion contributed to this change as it fueled a growing market in real and personal property.

In the third century B.C.E., Rome began two centuries of conquests that eventually placed most of the land surrounding the Mediterranean under Roman administration or in the hands of client states. Roman wives farmed while citizen-soldiers of the Republic were on campaigns, sometimes for more than a decade. Successful wars enriched a Roman elite who accumulated estates worked by male and female slaves as small farmers sold their lands and moved to the city with their wives and children. Elite Romans, both men and women, possessed large estates, luxurious urban houses, much rental property, and many slaves. By 50 B.C.E., Rome had a population of approximately one million. Slaves poured into Italy after successful campaigns, when the defeated enemy was enslaved. As the Romans conquered country after country, they brutalized the captured women, enslaving many. Ruling queens in subdued countries were inevitably replaced with either indigenous male elites or Roman officials. Queen Boudicca of Britain, for example, led a revolt that ended in her death in the first century C.E. Queen Zenobia of Palmyra's invasion of the empire in the third century C.E. was so well organized that Roman authors praised her. Cleopatra of Egypt committed suicide when her plan to make Egypt a regional partner of Rome failed.

Roman women did not publicly speak in the Forum (where men debated civic affairs), with the notable exception of Hortensia in 43 B.C.E. She was the spokesperson for a demonstration of wealthy women who protested taxation without representation for civil wars they did not support. Elite women usually indirectly influenced political decisions through networks of politicians' wives. During the civil wars of the first century B.C.E., wives of some tyrants even made temporary political decisions. On a wider scale, middle-class and elite women took advantage of the turmoil at the end of the Republic to acquire businesses, as analysis of Pompeii shows. Prostitution flowered in Rome with the inflow of slaves, both male and female. A small part of the elite lived in the self-indulgent luxury that became famous in literature. In a brief period of two generations at the end of the first century B.C.E., Roman elite women eschewed children and family responsibilities for a glamorous and self-absorbed life of parties and lovers. In this period men and women were openly adulterous. This "café society" flourished in the chaos of civil wars that nearly destroyed the prestige of the elite and killed or exiled many of them.

This era of chaos ended during the reign of the emperor Augustus (ruled 27 B.C.E.–14 C.E.), who sought to stabilize Roman society in part by reducing women's freedoms. Women were criticized for adultery, wearing too much makeup, having immodest dress and conduct, and especially for refusing to have children. Augustus procured laws that intended to remove control of marriage and reproduction from the family and allow the state to regulate marriage and reproduction. He attempted to penalize women between the ages of twenty and fifty and men over the age of twenty-five who did not marry and have children by denying them the right to inherit wealth. Furthermore, women were not to be released from male guardianship until they had three children. The Augustan laws made the state the regulator of private behavior and attempted to raise the birthrate of citizens while accepting some of the social changes that had modified the patriarchal society of the old Roman Republic. Augustus sought political support from conservative males by decreasing the autonomy of women who had less political influence than men.

Comparing Women's Status in Various Societies

As discussed earlier, the major literate civilizations of the ancient world were patriarchal. Later records from preliterate societies of the ancient period indicate that women in such societies could be more independent and have a higher status (for example, in many Southeast Asian and African societies). An appearance of universal subordination of women results from focusing only on early literate civilizations while ignoring the lives of women in nonliterate societies.

In the twentieth century, individual choice in personal relationships has replaced family selection of spouses in many societies, although arranged marriages persist in some cultures. In the ancient patriarchal world, however, the family chose spouses for their daughters and sons. Women lived with few civil rights in male-dominated societies. In inter-

preting ancient women's lives, scholars are faced with two contradictory images. The harsh portrayal is that women were sold by their fathers or brothers to husbands who abused them and that they were
considered to have the intellectual capacity of a child, perpetually dependent on a male. Alternatively, some documents reveal women who
were loved by their parents, husbands, and children. These women
could use the love and affection of their male relatives to gain personal
advantages that society would legally deny them. More likely, both explanations accurately reflect aspects of women's lives. Women negotiated a daily balance of gender power in personal relationships, often ignoring disadvantageous laws or ritual regulations, but those laws and
regulations could also fall with terrible force on any woman in the ancient patriarchal world.

25

R. K. NARAYAN

From The Ramayana

The Ramayana is a classic Indian epic that originated as an oral tradition between 1500 and 400 B.C.E., and was first recorded in the first
century C.E. by the poet Valmiki. The poem celebrates the virtues of
Prince Rama and his wife Sita, who eventually came to be worshiped
as deities in the Hindu pantheon. Exiled from his father's kingdom,
Rama goes to live in the forest, and Sita, a dutiful and devoted wife,
follows him. Sita is abducted by Ravana, an evil king who holds her
prisoner in his kingdom. Rama eventually defeats Ravana with the
help of the god Hanuman and brings his beloved Sita back to his own
kingdom, which he rightfully regains. But before Rama can fully accept Sita as his queen, she must prove that she has remained loyal to
him during her captivity.

There are innumerable versions and variations on this basic story,
which is divided into distinct episodes, two of which you will read
here. The first selection, the story of Ahalya and Gautama, serves as a
prologue to the main tale of Rama and Sita, and focuses on female
loyalty. We skip over the main body of the epic and pick up at the end

R. K. Narayan, *The Ramayana* (Harmondsworth: Penguin Books, 1977), 20–22, 161–64.

of the story in the second selection, in which Sita proves her fidelity to
Rama. The assurance of a wife's loyalty to her husband was (and still
is) an important requirement in patriarchal societies in which men preserve their family lines by ensuring the legitimacy of their sons.

How are the stories of Ahalya and Gautama and of Rama and Sita
similar? Why are the women punished? What seem to be the lessons
of these stories? What do these stories reveal about classical Indian
ideas of women, sexuality, and chastity?

Thinking Historically

In the previous selection, Sarah and Brady Hughes made a distinction
between Vedic and post-Vedic Indian history. In which period would
you place this story of Rama and Sita? Any document represents a
moment in history. Yet this story has been told in many versions over
the centuries. This version is by the modern Indian novelist R. K.
Narayan. Does it then reflect modern Indian values? Narayan writes
about his modern Indian audience in the introduction: "Everyone of
whatever age, outlook, education, or station in life knows the essential
part of the epic and adores the main figures in it—Rama and Sita."
Narayan based his version on an eleventh-century c.e. version. What
does the continued appeal of this story suggest about the history of
patriarchy in India?

While passing over slightly raised ground beside the walls of the fort,
Rama noticed a shapeless slab of stone, half buried vertically in the
ground; when he brushed past, the dust of his feet fell on it, and transformed it, that very instant, into a beautiful woman. As the woman did
obeisance and stood aside respectfully, Viswamithra introduced her to
Rama. "If you have heard of Sage Gautama, whose curse resulted in
great Indra's body being studded with a thousand eyes, all over. . . .
This lady was his wife, and her name is Ahalya." And he told Rama her
story.

Ahalya's Story

Brahma once created, out of the ingredients of absolute beauty, a
woman, and she was called Ahalya (which in the Sanskrit language
means non-imperfection). God Indra, being the highest god among the
gods, was attracted by her beauty and was convinced that he alone was
worthy of claiming her hand. Brahma, noticing the conceit and pre-
sumptuousness of Indra, ignored him, sought out Sage Gautama, and
left him in charge of the girl. She grew up in his custody, and when the

time came the sage took her back to Brahma and handed her over to him.

Brahma appreciated Gautama's purity of mind and heart (never once had any carnal thought crossed his mind), and said, "Marry her, she is fit to be your wife, or rather you alone deserve to be her husband." Accordingly, she was married, blessed by Brahma and other gods. Having spent her childhood with Gautama, Ahalya knew his needs and so proved a perfect wife, and they lived happily.

Indra, however, never got over his infatuation for Ahalya, and often came in different guises near to Gautama's *ashram*, waiting for every chance to gaze and feast on Ahalya's form and figure; he also watched the habits of the sage and noticed that the sage left his ashram at the dawn of each day and was away for a couple of hours at the river for his bath and prayers. Unable to bear the pangs of love any more, Indra decided to attain the woman of his heart by subterfuge. One day, hardly able to wait for the sage to leave at his usual hour, Indra assumed the voice of a rooster, and woke up the sage, who, thinking that the morning had come, left for the river. Now Indra assumed the sage's form, entered the hut, and made love to Ahalya. She surrendered herself, but at some stage realized that the man enjoying her was an imposter; but she could do nothing about it. Gautama came back at this moment, having intuitively felt that something was wrong, and surprised the couple in bed. Ahalya stood aside filled with shame and remorse; Indra assumed the form of a cat (the most facile animal form for sneaking in or out) and tried to slip away. The sage looked from the cat to the woman and was not to be deceived. He arrested the cat where he was with these words:

"Cat, I know you; your obsession with the female is your undoing. May your body be covered with a thousand female marks, so that in all the worlds, people may understand what really goes on in your mind all the time." Hardly had these words left his lips when every inch of Indra's body displayed the female organ. There could be no greater shame for the proud and self-preening Indra.

After Indra slunk away, back to his world, Gautama looked at his wife and said, "You have sinned with your body. May that body harden into a shapeless piece of granite, just where you are. . . ." Now in desperation Ahalya implored, "A grave mistake has been committed. It is in the nature of noble souls to forgive the errors of lesser beings. Please . . . I am already feeling a weight creeping up my feet. Do something . . . please help me. . . ."

Now the sage felt sorry for her and said, "Your redemption will come when the son of Dasaratha, Rama, passes this way at some future date. . . ."

"When? Where?" she essayed to question, desperately, but before the words could leave her lips she had become a piece of stone.

Indra's predicament became a joke in all the worlds at first, but later proved noticeably tragic. He stayed in darkness and seclusion and could never appear before men or women. This caused much concern to all the gods, as his multifarious duties in various worlds remained suspended, and they went in a body to Brahma and requested him to intercede with Gautama. By this time, the sage's resentment had vanished. And he said in response to Brahma's appeal, "May the thousand additions to Indra's features become eyes." Indra thereafter came to be known as the "thousand-eyed god."

Viswamithra concluded the story and addressed Rama. "O great one, you are born to restore righteousness and virtue to mankind and eliminate all evil. At our yagna, I saw the power of your arms, and now I see the greatness of the touch of your feet."

Rama said to Ahalya, "May you seek and join your revered husband, and live in his service again. Let not your heart be burdened with what is past and gone."

On their way to Mithila, they stopped to rest at Gautama's hermitage, and Viswamithra told the sage, "Your wife is restored to her normal form, by the touch of Rama's feet. Go and take her back, her heart is purified through the ordeal she has undergone." All this accomplished, they moved on, leaving behind the scented groves and forest, and approached the battlemented gates of Mithila City.

[The epic goes on to tell the story of Sita's abduction by the evil King Ravana. Rama defeats Ravana, and Sita is brought back home.]

Conclusion

After the death of Ravana, Rama sent Hanuman as his emissary to fetch Sita. Sita was overjoyed. She had been in a state of mourning all along, completely neglectful of her dress and appearance, and she immediately rose to go out and meet Rama as she was. But Hanuman explained that it was Rama's express wish that she should dress and decorate herself before coming to his presence.

A large crowd pressed around Rama. When Sita eagerly arrived, after her months of loneliness and suffering, she was received by her husband in full view of a vast public. She felt awkward but accepted this with resignation. But what she could not understand was why her lord seemed preoccupied and moody and cold. However, she prostrated herself at his feet, and then stood a little away from him, sensing some strange barrier between herself and him.

Rama remained brooding for a while and suddenly said, "My task is done. I have now freed you. I have fulfilled my mission. All this effort has been not to attain personal satisfaction for you or me. It was to vindicate the honour of the Ikshvahu race and to honour our ancestors' codes and values. After all this, I must tell you that it is not customary to admit back to the normal married fold a woman who has resided all alone in a stranger's house. There can be no question of our living together again. I leave you free to go where you please and to choose any place to live in. I do not restrict you in any manner."

On hearing this, Sita broke down. "My trials are not ended yet," she cried. "I thought with your victory all our troubles were at an end . . . ! So be it." She beckoned to Lakshmana and ordered, "Light a fire at once, on this very spot."

Lakshmana hesitated and looked at his brother, wondering whether he would countermand the order. But Rama seemed passive and acquiescent. Lakshmana, ever the most unquestioning deputy, gathered faggots and got ready a roaring pyre within a short time. The entire crowd watched the proceedings, stunned by the turn of events. The flames rose to the height of a tree; still Rama made no comment. He watched. Sita approached the fire, prostrated herself before it, and said, "O Agni, great god of fire, be my witness." She jumped into the fire.

From the heart of the flame rose the god of fire, bearing Sita, and presented her to Rama with words of blessing. Rama, now satisfied that he had established his wife's integrity in the presence of the world, welcomed Sita back to his arms.

Rama explained that he had to adopt this trial in order to demonstrate Sita's purity beyond a shadow of a doubt to the whole world. This seemed a rather strange inconsistency on the part of one who had brought back to life and restored to her husband a person like Ahalya, who had avowedly committed a moral lapse; and then there was Sugreeva's wife, who had been forced to live with Vali, and whom Rama commended as worthy of being taken back by Sugreeva after Vali's death. In Sita's case Ravana, in spite of repeated and desperate attempts, could not approach her. She had remained inviolable. And the fiery quality of her essential being burnt out the god of fire himself, as he had admitted after Sita's ordeal.

26

BAN ZHAO

Lessons for Women

Just as the epic poem *The Ramayana* created ideals for men, and women in India, the teachings of Confucius (561–479 B.C.E.) provided the Chinese and other Asian peoples with ideals of private and public conduct. Confucius's teachings emphasized the importance of filial piety, or the duty of children to serve and obey their parents, as well as to exercise restraint and treat others as one would like to be treated (see selection 19 for excerpts from Confucius's *Analects*). Ban Zhao* (45–116 C.E.) (Pan Chao in selection 24) was the leading female Confucian scholar of classical China. Born into a literary family and educated by her mother, she was married at the age of fourteen. After her husband's death she finished writing her brother's history of the Han dynasty and served as imperial historian to Emperor Han Hedi (r. 88–105 C.E.) and as an advisor to the Empress-Dowager Deng.

Ban Zhao is best remembered, however, for her *Lessons for Women*, which she wrote to fill a gap in Confucian literature. With their emphasis on the responsibilities of the son to the father and on the moral example of a good ruler, the writings of Confucius virtually ignored women. Ban Zhao sought to rectify that oversight by applying Confucian principles to the moral instruction of women. In what ways would Ban Zhao's *Lessons* support Chinese patriarchy? In what ways might they challenge the patriarchy or make it less oppressive for women? What similarities are there between the Confucian and Indian ideas of women's proper role?

Thinking Historically

This text came from a particular historical moment—in fact a moment that we can date with greater accuracy and assurance than any of the Confucian writings. Still, there are two reasons why we might be persuaded that it speaks for a longer period of Chinese history than its single moment of appearance. One reason is that, like *The Ramayana*, it is a classic text that has been retold for generations. We can imagine that its message was continually reinforced in the

*bahn ZHOW

Pan Chao: Foremost Woman Scholar of China, trans. Nancy Lee Swann (New York: Century Co., 1932), 82–90.

retelling. Second, there are clues in the text itself that these ideas are not entirely new. What are those clues?

This may seem to be a very patriarchal text. Yet it is written by a woman. How do you account for that? Some have said that Ban Zhao was actually modifying Confucian patriarchal values by stressing the bond between husband and wife rather than the traditional Confucian bond between father and son or parents and daughter-in-law. Can you see any evidence of such emphasis in the text of the document?

I, the unworthy writer, am unsophisticated, unenlightened, and by nature unintelligent, but I am fortunate both to have received not a little favor from my scholarly Father, and to have had a cultured mother and instructresses upon whom to rely for a literary education as well as for training in good manners. More than forty years have passed since at the age of fourteen I took up the dustpan and the broom in the Cao family.[1] During this time with trembling heart I feared constantly that I might disgrace my parents, and that I might multiply difficulties for both the women and the men of my husband's family. Day and night I was distressed in heart, but I labored without confessing weariness. Now and hereafter, however, I know how to escape from such fears.

Being careless, and by nature stupid, I taught and trained my children without system. Consequently I fear that my son Gu may bring disgrace upon the Imperial Dynasty by whose Holy Grace he has unprecedentedly received the extraordinary privilege of wearing the Gold and the Purple, a privilege for the attainment of which by my son, I a humble subject never even hoped. Nevertheless, now that he is a man and able to plan his own life, I need not again have concern for him. But I do grieve that you, my daughters, just now at the age for marriage, have not at this time had gradual training and advice; that you still have not learned the proper customs for married women. I fear that by failure in good manners in other families you will humiliate both your ancestors and your clan. I am now seriously ill, life is uncertain. As I have thought of you all in so untrained a state, I have been uneasy many a time for you. At hours of leisure I have composed . . . these instructions under the title, "Lessons for Women." In order that you may have something wherewith to benefit your persons, I wish every one of you, my daughters each to write out a copy for yourself.

From this time on every one of you strive to practice these lessons.

[1]Her husband's family. [Ed.]

Humility

On the third day after the birth of a girl the ancients observed three customs: first to place the baby below the bed; second to give her a potsherd[2] with which to play; and third to announce her birth to her ancestors by an offering. Now to lay the baby below the bed plainly indicated that she is lowly and weak, and should regard it as her primary duty to humble herself before others. To give her potsherds with which to play indubitably signified that she should practice labor and consider it her primary duty to be industrious. To announce her birth before her ancestors clearly meant that she ought to esteem as her primary duty the continuation of the observance of worship in the home.

These three ancient customs epitomize woman's ordinary way of life and the teachings of the traditional ceremonial rites and regulations. Let a woman modestly yield to others; let her respect others; let her put others first, herself last. Should she do something good, let her not mention it; should she do something bad let her not deny it. Let her bear disgrace; let her even endure when others speak or do evil to her. Always let her seem to tremble and to fear. When a woman follows such maxims as these then she may be said to humble herself before others.

Let a woman retire late to bed, but rise early to duties; let her not dread tasks by day or by night. Let her not refuse to perform domestic duties whether easy or difficult. That which must be done, let her finish completely, tidily, and systematically. When a woman follows such rules as these, then she may be said to be industrious.

Let a woman be correct in manner and upright in character in order to serve her husband. Let her live in purity and quietness of spirit, and attend to her own affairs. Let her love not gossip and silly laughter. Let her cleanse and purify and arrange in order the wine and the food for the offerings to the ancestors. When a woman observes such principles as these, then she may be said to continue ancestral worship.

No woman who observes these three fundamentals of life has ever had a bad reputation or has fallen into disgrace. If a woman fails to observe them, how can her name be honored; how can she but bring disgrace upon herself?

Husband and Wife

The Way of husband and wife is intimately connected with Yin and Yang and relates the individual to gods and ancestors. Truly it is the great principle of Heaven and Earth, and the great basis of human rela-

---

[2]A piece of broken pottery. [Ed.]

tionships. Therefore the "Rites"[3] honor union of man and woman; and in the "Book of Poetry"[4] the "First Ode" manifests the principle of marriage. For these reasons the relationship cannot but be an important one.

If a husband be unworthy, then he possesses nothing by which to control his wife. If a wife be unworthy, then she possesses nothing with which to serve her husband. If a husband does not control his wife, then the rules of conduct manifesting his authority are abandoned and broken. If a wife does not serve her husband, then the proper relationship between men and women and the natural order of things are neglected and destroyed. As a matter of fact the purpose of these two[5] is the same.

Now examine the gentlemen of the present age. They only know that wives must be controlled, and that the husband's rules of conduct manifesting his authority must be established. They therefore teach their boys to read books and study histories. But they do not in the least understand that husbands and masters must also be served, and that the proper relationship and the rites should be maintained. Yet only to teach men and not to teach women—is that not ignoring the essential relation between them? According to the "Rites," it is the rule to begin to teach children to read at the age of eight years, and by the age of fifteen years they ought then to be ready for cultural training. Only why should it not be that girls' education as well as boys' be according to this principle?

Respect and Caution

As Yin and Yang are not of the same nature, so man and woman have different characteristics. The distinctive quality of the Yang is rigidity; the function of the Yin is yielding. Man is honored for strength; a woman is beautiful on account of her gentleness. Hence there arose the common saying: "A man though born like a wolf may, it is feared, become a weak monstrosity; a woman though born like a mouse may, it is feared, become a tiger."

Now for self-culture nothing equals respect for others. To counteract firmness nothing equals compliance. Consequently it can be said that the Way of respect and acquiescence is woman's most important principle of conduct. So respect may be defined as nothing other than holding on to that which is permanent; and acquiescence nothing other

---

[3]*The Classic of Rites.* [Ed.]

[4]*The Classic of Odes.* [Ed.]

[5]The controlling of women by men, and the serving of men by women. [Ed.]

than being liberal and generous. Those who are steadfast in devotion know that they should stay in their proper places; those who are liberal and generous esteem others, and honor and serve them.

If husband and wife have the habit of staying together, never leaving one another, and following each other around within the limited space of their own rooms, then they will lust after and take liberties with one another. From such action improper language will arise between the two. This kind of discussion may lead to licentiousness. But of licentiousness will be born a heart of disrespect to the husband. Such a result comes from not knowing that one should stay in one's proper place.

Furthermore, affairs may be either crooked or straight; words may be either right or wrong. Straightforwardness cannot but lead to quarreling; crookedness cannot but lead to accusation. If there are really accusations and quarrels, then undoubtedly there will be angry affairs. Such a result comes from not esteeming others, and not honoring and serving them.

If wives suppress not contempt for husbands, then it follows that such wives rebuke and scold their husbands. If husbands stop not short of anger, then they are certain to beat their wives. The correct relationship between husband and wife is based upon harmony and intimacy, and conjugal love is grounded in proper union. Should actual blows be dealt, how could matrimonial relationship be preserved? Should sharp words be spoken, how could conjugal love exist? If love and proper relationship both be destroyed, then husband and wife are divided.

Womanly Qualifications

A woman ought to have four qualifications: (1) womanly virtue; (2) womanly words; (3) womanly bearing; and (4) womanly work. Now what is called womanly virtue need not be brilliant ability, exceptionally different from others. Womanly words need be neither clever in debate nor keen in conversation. Womanly appearance requires neither a pretty nor a perfect face and form. Womanly work need not be work done more skillfully than that of others.

To guard carefully her chastity; to control circumspectly her behavior; in every motion to exhibit modesty; and to model each act on the best usage, this is womanly virtue.

To choose her words with care; to avoid vulgar language; to speak at appropriate times; and not to weary others with much conversation, may be called the characteristics of womanly words.

To wash and scrub filth away; to keep clothes and ornaments fresh and clean; to wash the head and bathe the body regularly, and to keep the person free from disgraceful filth, may be called the characteristics of womanly bearing.

With whole-hearted devotion to sew and to weave; to love not gossip and silly laughter; in cleanliness and order to prepare the wine and food for serving guests, may be called the characteristics of womanly work.

These four qualifications characterize the greatest virtue of a woman. No woman can afford to be without them. In fact they are very easy to possess if a woman only treasures them in her heart. The ancients had a saying: "Is love afar off? If I desire love, then love is at hand!" So can it be said of these qualifications.

Implicit Obedience

Whenever the mother-in-law says, "Do not do that," and if what she says is right, unquestionably the daughter-in-law obeys. Whenever the mother-in-law says, "Do that," even if what she says is wrong, still the daughter-in-law submits unfailingly to the command. Let a woman not act contrary to the wishes and the opinions of parents-in-law about right and wrong; let her not dispute with them what is straight and what is crooked. Such docility may be called obedience which sacrifices personal opinion. Therefore the ancient book, "A Pattern for Women," says: "If a daughter-in-law who follows the wishes of her parents-in-law is like an echo and shadow, how could she not be praised?"

27

ARISTOPHANES

From Lysistrata

*Lysistrata** is often considered the best play of the comic Athenian playwright Aristophanes.[†] Written in the midst of the Peloponnesian War (431–404 B.C.E.), which concluded with the capitulation of Athens and the end of the Athenian golden age, Aristophanes imagines the women of Athens, Sparta, and other Greek city-states coming together

*lih sih STRAH tuh
[†]air ih STAH fuh neez

Aristophanes, *Lysistrata*, trans. Douglas Parker (New York: Signet, 2001), 55–58.

to force their husbands to make peace by means of a sex strike. The successful strategy of the women follows the plan of the Athenian Lysistrata to refuse sexual intercourse with their husbands or anyone else until the war is ended. Aristophanes suggests that their motive is partly personal—their men are gone and some of their sons are dead. But the play also allows Aristophanes to use women's voices to express misgivings about the war. In this selection, from midway in the play, Lysistrata berates the male politicians for the war and their ineptitude.

Nothing like this happened, of course. But even an overtly farcical and comical play reflects something of the world that produced it. What does the play tell you about the role of women in Athens or in other Greek city-states? How do the lives of Greek women compare to the lives of women in China or India?

Thinking Historically

Lysistrata appeared at a critical moment in the Athenian Peloponnesian War with Sparta, after the annihilation of the Athenian expeditionary forces in Sicily in 413 B.C.E. but before the overthrow of the Athenian constitution in 411. The play prefigures the domestic collapse that followed the external disaster. This was a moment of crisis for Greek politics. But was it also one for women? We do not know. It is interesting that Greek women were generally more independent in Sparta than Athens, and enjoyed greater autonomy in the Hellenistic period that followed the Peloponnesian War than in the Athenian golden age. A moment of crisis is likely to suggest such extreme, though admittedly impossible or improbable, solutions, but what evidence do you see in this selection that Athenian women may have had long-lasting sources of power that had not just appeared overnight?

COMMISSIONER   Might I ask where you women conceived this concern about War and Peace?

LYSISTRATA   *Loftily.* We shall explain.

COMMISSIONER   *Making a fist.* Hurry up, and you won't get hurt.

LYSISTRATA   Then *listen*. And do try to keep your hands to yourself.

COMMISSIONER   *Moving threateningly toward her.* I can't. Righteous anger forbids restraint, and decrees . . .

KLEONIKE   *Brandishing her chamber pot.* Multiple fractures?

COMMISSIONER   *Retreating.* Keep those croaks for yourself, you old crow! *To Lysistrata.* All right, lady, I'm ready. Speak.

KYSISTRATA   I shall proceed: When the War began, like the prudent, dutiful wives that we are, we tolerated you men, and endured your actions in silence. (Small wonder—you wouldn't let us say boo.) You were not precisely the answer to a matron's prayer—we knew you too well, and found out more.

Too many times, as we sat in the house, we'd hear that you'd done it again—manhandled another affair of state with your usual staggering incompetence. Then, masking our worry with a nervous laugh, we'd ask you, brightly, "How was the Assembly today, dear? Anything in the minutes about Peace?" And my husband would give his stock reply. "What's that to you? Shut up!" And I did.

KLEONIKE   *Proudly. I never shut up!*

COMMISSIONER   I trust you were shut up. Soundly.

LYSISTRATA   Regardless, *I* shut up. And then we'd learn that you'd passed another decree, fouler than the first, and we'd ask again: "Darling, how *did* you manage anything so idiotic?" And my husband, with his customary glare, would tell me to spin my thread, or else get a clout on the head. And of course he'd quote from Homer: Yᵉ *menne must husband yᵉ warre.*[1]

COMMISSIONER   Apt and irrefutably right.

LYSISTRATA   *Right,* you miserable misfit? To keep us from giving advice while you fumbled the City away in the Senate? Right, indeed!

But this time was really too much: Wherever we went, we'd hear you engaged in the same conversation:

"What Athens needs is a Man." "But there isn't a Man in the country." "You can say that again."

There was obviously no time to lose. We women met in immediate convention and passed a unanimous resolution: To work in concert for safety and Peace in Greece. We have valuable advice to impart, and if you can possibly deign to emulate our silence, and take your turn as audience, we'll rectify you—we'll straighten you out and set you right.

COMMISSIONER   *You'll* set *us* right? You go too far. I cannot permit such a statement to . . .

LYSISTRATA   Shush.

COMMISSIONER   I categorically decline to shush for some confounded woman, who wears—as a constant reminder of congenital inferiority, an injunction to public silence—a veil!

Death before such dishonor!

---

[1] From *The Iliad*—"Men must wage war."

LYSISTRATA   *Removing her veil.* If that's the only obstacle . . .
   I feel you need a new panache, so take the veil, my dear Commissioner, and drape it thus—and SHUSH!

As she winds the veil around the startled Commissioner's head, Kleonike and Myrrhine, with carding-comb and wool-basket, rush forward and assist in transforming him into a woman.

KLEONIKE   Accept, I pray, this humble comb.

MYRRHINE   Receive this basket of fleece as well.

LYSISTRATA   Hike up your skirts, and card your wool, and gnaw your beans—and stay at home! While we rewrite Homer:
   Yᵉ WOMEN *must WIVE* yᵉ *warre!*[2]

To the Chorus of Women, as the Commissioner struggles to remove his new outfit.
   Women, weaker vessels, arise!
   Put down your pitchers.
   It's our turn, now. Let's supply our friends with some moral support.

The Chorus of Women dances to the same tune as the Men, but with much more confidence.

CHORUS OF WOMEN   *Singly.*
   Oh, yes! I'll dance to bless their success.
   Fatigue won't weaken my will. Or my knees.
   I'm ready to join in any jeopardy.
      with girls as good as *these!*
   Tutte. A tally of their talents
   convinces me they're giants
   of excellence. To commence:
   there's Beauty, Duty, Prudence, Science,
   Self-Reliance, Compliance, Defiance,
   and Love of Athens in balanced alliance
      with Common Sense!

[2]Women must wage war!

28

LIVY

Women Demonstrate against the Oppian Law

In 215 B.C.E., after suffering a disastrous defeat by Hannibal of Carthage in the Second Punic War, Rome desperately needed to raise money to replenish its armies. Roman citizens met the emergency with various taxes and sacrifices, among them the Oppian law, which prohibited women from buying certain luxury goods and limited the amount of gold they could possess, passing the remainder on to the state.

Twenty years later, the crisis a dim memory, Roman women demonstrated to bring an end to the Oppian law. The moment of confrontation in 195 B.C.E. offers a window into gender relations in the Roman republic. Livy* (64 or 59 B.C.E.–17 C.E.), a Roman historian writing at the beginning of the first century C.E., provides us with the following account of the women's protest. What does the debate tell you about the relative power and position of women in this period? Do the women seem to be more or less powerful than the women of classical India, China, or Greece?

Thinking Historically

While this source and the much earlier *Lysistrata* both deal with women's protests, Livy was a historian, not a playwright. The women's protest against the Oppian law actually happened in 195 B.C.E. Cato† and Valerius actually gave these speeches. How did Cato think the lives of women had changed by 195 B.C.E.? How was Valerius's idea of women's history different from Cato's? Which of these interpretations of change comes closest to that of the modern historians in the first selection? Which interpretation do you think came closer to Livy's? Why do you think all of these authors are so interested in historical change? What were (or are) the political implications of emphasizing change or continuity?

*LIH vee
†KAY toh

Maureen B. Fant, trans., in Mary R. Lefkowitz and Maureen B. Fant, *Women's Lives in Greece and Rome*, 2nd ed. (Baltimore: The Johns Hopkins Press, 1982), 143–47.

Among the troubles of great wars, either scarcely over or yet to come, something intervened which, while it can be told briefly, stirred up enough excitement to become a great battle. Marcus Fundanius and Lucius Valerius, the tribunes of the people, brought a motion to repeal the Oppian law before the people. Gaius Oppius had carried this law as tribune at the height of the Punic War, during the consulship of Quintus Fabius and Tiberius Sempronius. The law said that no woman might own more than half an ounce of gold nor wear a multicoloured dress nor ride in a carriage in the city or in a town within a mile of it, unless there was a religious festival. The tribunes, Marcus and Publius Junius Brutus, were in favour of the Oppian law and said that they would not allow its repeal. Many noble men came forward hoping to persuade or dissuade them; a crowd of men, both supporters and opponents, filled the Capitoline Hill. The matrons, whom neither counsel nor shame nor their husbands' orders could keep at home, blockaded every street in the city and every entrance to the Forum. As the men came down to the Forum, the matrons besought them to let them, too, have back the luxuries they had enjoyed before, giving as their reason that the republic was thriving and that everyone's private wealth was increasing with every day. This crowd of women was growing daily, for now they were even gathering from the towns and villages. Before long they dared go up and solicit the consuls, praetors, and other magistrates; but one of the consuls could not be moved in the least, Marcus Porcius Cato, who spoke in favour of the law:

"If each man of us, fellow citizens, had established that the right and authority of the husband should be held over the mother of his own family, we should have less difficulty with women in general; now, at home our freedom is conquered by female fury, here in the Forum it is bruised and trampled upon, and, because we have not contained the individuals, we fear the lot. . . .

"Indeed, I blushed when, a short while ago, I walked through the midst of a band of women. Had not respect for the dignity and modesty of certain ones (not them all!) restrained me (so they would not be seen being scolded by a consul), I should have said, "What kind of behaviour is this? Running around in public, blocking streets, and speaking to other women's husbands! Could you not have asked your own husbands the same thing at home? Are you more charming in public with others' husbands than at home with your own? And yet, it is not fitting even at home (if modesty were to keep married women within the bounds of their rights) for you to concern yourselves with what laws are passed or repealed here." Our ancestors did not want women to conduct any—not even private—business without a guardian; they wanted them to be under the authority of parents, brothers, or husbands; we (the gods help us!) even now let them snatch at the government and meddle in the Forum and our assemblies. What are they doing now on the streets and crossroads, if they are not persuading the tribunes to vote for repeal? . . .

"If they are victorious now, what will they not attempt? . . . As soon as they begin to be your equals, they will have become your superiors. . . .

"What honest excuse is offered, pray, for this womanish rebellion? 'That we might shine with gold and purple,' says one of them, 'that we might ride through the city in coaches on holidays and working-days, as though triumphant over the conquered law and the votes which we captured by tearing them from you; that there should be no limit to our expenses and our luxury.' . . .

"The woman who can spend her own money will do so; the one who cannot will ask her husband. Pity that husband—the one who gives in and the one who stands firm! What he refuses, he will see given by another man. Now they publicly solicit other women's husbands, and, what is worse, they ask for a law and votes, and certain men give them what they want. You there, you, are easily moved about things which concern yourself, your estate, and your children; once the law no longer limits your wife's spending, you will never do it by yourself. Fellow citizens, do not imagine that the state which existed before the law was passed will return. A dishonest man is safer never accused than acquitted, and luxury, left alone, would have been more acceptable than it will be now, as when wild animals are first chafed by their chains and then released. I vote that the Oppian law should not, in the smallest measure, be repealed; whatever course you take, may all the gods make you happy with it."

After this, when the tribunes of the people, who had declared that they would oppose the motion to repeal, had added a few remarks along the same lines, Lucius Valerius spoke on behalf of the motion which he himself had brought:

"[Cato] used up more words castigating the women than he did opposing the motion, and he left in some uncertainty whether the women had done the deeds which he reproached on their own or at our instigation. I shall defend the motion, not ourselves, against whom the consul has hurled this charge, more for the words than for the reality of the accusation. He has called this assemblage 'secession' and sometimes 'womanish rebellion,' because the matrons have publicly asked you, in peacetime when the state is happy and prosperous, to repeal a law passed against them during the straits of war. . . .

"What, may I ask, are the women doing that is new, having gathered and come forth publicly in a case which concerns them directly? Have they never appeared in public before this? Allow me to unroll your own *Origines* before you. Listen to how often they have done so —always for the public good. From the very beginning—the reign of Romulus—when the Capitoline had been taken by the Sabines and there was fighting in the middle of the Forum, was not the battle halted by the women's intervention between the two lines? How about this? After the kings had been expelled, when the Volscian legions and their general, Marcius Coriolanus, had pitched camp at the fifth milestone, did not the matrons turn away the forces which would have buried the city? When Rome was in the hands of the Gauls, who ransomed it? Indeed the matrons agreed unanimously to turn their gold over to the public need. Not to go too far back in history, in the most recent war, when we needed funds, did not the widows' money assist the treasury? . . . You say these cases are different. I am not here to say they are the same; it is enough to prove that nothing new has been done. Indeed, as no one is amazed that they acted in situations affecting men and women alike, why should we wonder that they have taken action in a case which concerns themselves? What, after all, have they done? We have proud ears indeed, if, while masters do not scorn the appeals of slaves, we are angry when honourable women ask something of us . . .

"Who then does not know that this is a recent law, passed twenty years ago? Since our matrons lived for so long by the highest standards of behaviour without any law, what risk is there that, once it is repealed, they will yield to luxury? For if the law were an old one, or if it had been passed to restrain feminine licence, there might be reason to fear that repeal would incite them. The times themselves will show you why the law was passed. Hannibal was in Italy, victorious at Cannae. Already he held Tarentum, Arpi, and Capua. He seemed on the verge of moving against Rome. Our allies had gone over to him. We had no reserve troops, no allies at sea to protect the fleet, no funds in the treasury. Slaves were being bought and armed, on condition that the price be paid their owners when the war was over. The contractors had declared that they would provide, on that same day of payment (after the war), the grain and other supplies the needs of war demanded. We were giving our slaves as rowers at our own expense, in proportion to our property rating. We were giving all our gold and silver for public use, as the senators had done first. Widows and children were donating their funds to the treasury. We were ordered to keep at home no more than a certain amount of wrought and stamped gold and silver. . . . To whom is it not clear that poverty and misfortune were the authors of that law of yours, since all private wealth had to be turned over to public use, and that it was to remain in effect only as long as the reason for its writing did? . . .

"Shall it be our wives alone to whom the fruits of peace and tranquility of the state do not come? . . . Shall we forbid only women to wear purple? When you, a man, may use purple on your clothes, will you not allow the mother of your family to have a purple cloak, and will your horse be more beautifully saddled than your wife is garbed? . . .

"[Cato] has said that, if none of them had anything, there would be no rivalry among individual women. By Hercules! All are unhappy and indignant when they see the finery denied them permitted to the wives of the Latin allies, when they see them adorned with gold and purple, when those other women ride through the city and they follow on foot, as though the power belonged to the other women's cities, not to their own. This could wound the spirits of men; what do you think it could do to the spirits of women, whom even little things disturb? They cannot partake of magistracies, priesthoods, triumphs, badges of office, gifts, or spoils of war; elegance, finery and beautiful clothes are women's badges, in these they find joy and take pride, this our forebears called the women's world. When they are in mourning, what, other than purple and gold, do they take off? What do they put on again when they have completed the period of mourning? What do they add for public prayer and thanksgiving other than still greater ornament? Of course, if you repeal the Oppian law, you will not have the power to prohibit that which the law now forbids; daughters, wives, even some men's sisters will be less under your authority — never, while her men are well, is a woman's slavery cast off; and even they hate the freedom created by widowhood and orphanage. They prefer their adornment to be subject to your judgment, not the law's; and you ought to hold them in marital power and guardianship, not slavery; you should prefer to be called fathers and husbands to masters. The consul just now used odious terms when he said 'womanish rebellion' and 'secession.' For there is danger — he would have us believe — that they will seize the Sacred Hill as once the angry plebeians did, or the Aventine. It is for the weaker sex to submit to whatever you advise. The more power you possess, all the more moderately should you exercise your authority."

When these speeches for and against the law had been made, a considerably larger crowd of women poured forth in public the next day; as a single body they besieged the doors of the Brutuses, who were vetoing their colleagues' motion, and they did not stop until the tribunes took back their veto. After that there was no doubt but that all the tribes would repeal the law. Twenty years after it was passed, the law was repealed.

29

Fayum Portraits

Some of the most vivid and best-preserved images of women from antiquity come from the Fayum region of Egypt and date from the first century B.C.E. to the third century C.E. These are the beautifully painted and distinctive mummy portraits of inhabitants of Hellenistic and Roman Egypt, portraits usually painted while the subjects were alive and interred with them after death. The practice of painting tomb portraits in encaustic (that is, with hot pigmented wax) on wooden panels was a fairly common one in the region, and Egypt's extremely dry climate ensured the survival of many of these ancient works.

Figures 5.1 and 5.2 show portraits of women buried in Fayum, while Figure 5.3 depicts one "Ammonius from Antinoe," a young man from a town near Fayum. We do not know their ethnic background, although it is likely that they were either Roman settlers in Egypt or descendants of Egypt's Hellenistic rulers and colonists from Macedonia after Alexander the Great conquered Egypt. What clues *do* these visual sources offer about their subjects?

Sarah and Brady Hughes argue in their selection that Greek women living in Egypt during the Hellenistic period "were much more assertive than their sisters in either contemporary Greece or later Rome" (see page 159) and that even "non-elite women had unusual freedom. They owned property (including land), participated in commerce, produced textiles, were educated, and enjoyed careers as artists, poets and farmers." Do Figures 5.1 and 5.2 appear to support this argument? Why or why not?

Thinking Historically

Consider these images, individually and collectively. How would you describe the subjects' expressions? Content? Anxious? Serene? Fatalistic? Sad? What, if anything, can each tell us about the historical moment in which they were created? What are their limitations as evidence about their subjects? Can/Do these portraits tell us anything meaningful about those who sat for them?

The practice of painting the face of the deceased on a shroud, panel, or actual sarcophagus goes back to the time of the ancient pharaohs. Ammonius is holding an ankh, the ancient Egyptian hieroglyph that symbolized life force and eternal life, and one often carried as a good luck charm or amulet by the Hellenistic and Roman

Figure 5.1 Portrait of a Fayum Woman with Large Gold Necklace.

Source: The Detroit Institute of Arts, USA, Gift of Julius H. Haass/The Bridgeman Art Library International.

inhabitants of Egypt. How do you account for the popularity of ancient Egyptian religious traditions among Egypt's Greco-Roman populations? What might the ankh and the practice of tomb portraiture tell us about process in the history of women and religion in antiquity?

Figure 5.2 Portrait of Fayum Woman with White Earrings.

Source: Louvre, Paris, France, Lauros/Giraudon/The Bridgeman Art Library International.

Figure 5.3 Portrait of "Ammonius from Antinoe," with Ankh.
Source: Visual Arts Library (London)/Alamy.

REFLECTIONS

Thirty years ago the historian Joan Kelly ignited the study of women's history with an essay that asked: "Did Women Have a Renaissance?" Questioning whether the great eras in men's history were also great eras for women, she found that men's achievements often came at the expense of women. We have seen how the urban revolution fit this pattern. The rise of cities, the creation of territorial states, the invention of writing, and the development of complex societies, all beginning about five thousand years ago, accompanied the development of patriarchal institutions and ideas. Similarly, the rise of classical cultures, cities, and states about twenty-five hundred years ago seems to have cemented patriarchy.

Chinese classical culture may have been the most patriarchal. In China, the rise of the state undermined feudal nobilities where women's role depended more on family status than gender. In India, too, the state formation of the post-Vedic period may have undercut earlier matrilineal societies.

Roman and Greek women were affected differently by the rise of the state. The establishment of civil society in fifth-century Greece certainly undermined the power of familial clans and tribes, and with them the prestige and power of well-connected women. Most city-states confined women to the domestic sphere while male citizens controlled the public business of government. Nevertheless, the women of Sparta were less cloistered than the women of Athens, and the women of Rome enjoyed greater use of the public outdoors as early as 195 B.C.E.

Thus, if we compare China, India, and both Greece and Rome as a single "Mediterranean" society, the fortunes of women deteriorated during the classical period in China and India, but improved in the Mediterranean. The protest of Roman women against the Oppian law in 195 B.C.E. went far beyond the possibilities, if not the feared fantasies, of the classical Greeks. The upper-class Roman women Livy knew could own and inherit property and run businesses. All Roman women in the first century had access to the street, the marketplace, and other public spaces. They could not, however, participate in politics except informally as influential wives, mothers, and courtesans. Women would have to wait almost another two thousand years to vote and hold office.

In this chapter we see that capturing the moment and assessing change are not mutually exclusive. Nor are comparison and understanding change. We can compare how different societies change over the same period, and that knowledge can very usefully lead us to more sophisticated questions. What enabled Roman women, especially in the Empire, to achieve rights and liberties that were not available before or elsewhere? Was there a connection between the rights of women in the Empire and the loss of the rights that ordinary men had enjoyed in the earlier Republic? What Roman or Mediterranean social or cultural institutions lessened the patriarchal pressures that prevailed in other urban-based states? What was the impact of Christianity for Roman women? We will explore at least the last of these in the next chapter.

6

From Tribal
to Universal Religion

Hindu-Buddhist and Judeo-Christian Traditions, 1000 B.C.E.–100 C.E.

HISTORICAL CONTEXT

From 1000 B.C.E. to 100 C.E. two major religious traditions, one centered in the Middle East and the other in northern India, split into at least four major religious traditions, so large that today they are embraced by a majority of the inhabitants of the world. Each of the two original traditions, Hinduism and Judaism, were in 1000 B.C.E. highly restricted in membership. Neither sought converts but instead ministered to members of their own tribe and castes. This chapter explores how these two essentially inward-looking religions created universal religions, open to all. It is a story not only of the emergence of Christianity and Buddhism but also of the development of modern Judaic and Hindu religions.

Remarkably, both of these traditions moved from tribal to universal religions; even more remarkable are the common elements, given their different routes along that path. While Hinduism cultivated a psychological approach to spiritual enlightenment out of a priestly religion of obligation, Judaism developed an abiding faith in historical providence from a disastrous history.

As you read the selections in this chapter, notice over the course of the first millennium B.C.E. how both core religions created new faiths and the reform of the old. Notice also the fundamentally different ways these two great religious traditions changed. Finally, observe how the later offspring religions, Buddhism and Christianity, preached ideas that were already current, but not dominant, in the "parental" traditions.

THINKING HISTORICALLY
Detecting Change in Primary Sources

Understanding how religions change or evolve is especially difficult because of the tendency of religious adherents to emphasize the timelessness of their truths. Fortunately, religious commitment and belief do not require a denial of historical change. Indeed, many adherents have found strength in all manifestations of the sacred — the specific and historical as well as the universal and eternal.

Whether motives are primarily religious or secular, however, the historical study of religion offers a useful window on understanding large-scale changes in human behavior. Since religions tend to conserve, repeat, and enshrine, change is more gradual than in many other aspects of human thought and behavior: fashion, say, or technology. Thus, when religions develop radically new ideas or institutions, we can learn much about human resistance and innovation by studying the circumstances.

Because religions typically prefer conservation over innovation, changes are often grafted on to old formulations. Historians who want to understand when and how change occurred must sometimes discover and unmask new ideas and ways of doing things that have been assimilated into the tradition.

The easiest way to see change in primary sources is to compare a number of them composed in different historical periods. However, sometimes we are able to see examples of change in a single document. A written source may, for instance, originate in more than one oral account and the writer may combine them both even though one is later than the other and they represent different ideas. A manuscript might also pick up errors or updates as it is rewritten for the next generation. We will see examples of both of these changes and others in the documents in this chapter.

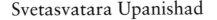

$$30$$

Svetasvatara Upanishad

In Chapter 3 selections from the Hindu Vedas* and Upanishads[†] help introduce some basic ideas in Hinduism: the belief that animals and human castes were created out of the primal sacrifice of the god Purusha in the Vedas, the complementary ideas of karma and reincarnation in the Upanishads, and, lastly, the identification of Brahman and *atman* (self and God) also in the Upanishads.

Take a look at the same selections again to understand the changing nature of Hinduism from the earliest Vedas to the latest Upanishads. For example, we see in selection 11 the interest of the Aryan invaders of India in defining and justifying caste differences and the supremacy of the Brahman priests as masters of sacrifice, prayers, rituals, and sacred hymns.

The authors of the Upanishads were less interested in sacrifice and priestly rituals and more absorbed by philosophical questions. Thus, selection 12 on karma and reincarnation spells out the idea of justice and a philosophy of nature that reflects the interests of a later settled society. Finally, selection 13 on the identity of Brahman and *atman* reflects an even more meditative Upanishad that virtually ignores the role of priests. This meditative tradition may have existed in early Hinduism, but there is far more evidence of its expression in the Upanishads (after 800 B.C.E.) than in the earlier Vedas.

The *Svetasvatara*[‡] Upanishad selection included here reflects an additional step along the path from the religion of priests, sacrifice, and caste obligation to individualized spirituality. Here the idea of the transmigration of souls from one body to another in an endless cycle of reincarnations — an idea that developed after the Vedas — is challenged by the idea that the individual who seeks Brahman might break out of the wheel of life. How would this idea of escaping reincarnation diminish the power of Brahman priests? How does it minimize the importance of caste and karma?

*VAY duhz
[†]oo PAH nee shahdz
[‡]sveh tah SVAH tah ruh

Svetasvatara Upanishad in *The Upanishads: The Breath of the Eternal*, trans. Swami Prabhavananda and Frederick Manchester (Hollywood: The Vedanta Society of Southern California, 1948; New York: Mentor Books, 1957), 118–21.

Thinking Historically

Recognizing changes in the Hindu tradition is more difficult than in the Judaic tradition. The literature of Judaism is full of historical references: names of historical figures and even dates. Hindu sacred literature, as you can tell from this brief introduction, shows virtually no interest in historical names and dates. Because time in India was conceived as cyclical, rather than linear, and the cycles of the Indian time scheme were immense, determining the exact time an event occurred was less important in Hindu thought than understanding its eternal meaning.

Consequently, our analysis of the changes in Hinduism is more logical than chronological. We can therefore speak of a long-term historical process even though we cannot date each step.

The oldest of the thirteen universally recognized Upanishads, all of which were composed between 800 and 400 B.C.E., are the Brihad Aranyaka and the Chandogya (from which selections 12 and 13 on *atman* and Brahman are taken). The *Svetasvatara* is one of the last of the thirteen, composed closer to 400 B.C.E. What is the idea of time suggested by this Upanishad?

This vast universe is a wheel. Upon it are all creatures that are subject to birth, death, and rebirth. Round and round it turns, and never stops. It is the wheel of Brahman. As long as the individual self thinks it is separate from Brahman, it revolves upon the wheel in bondage to the laws of birth, death, and rebirth. But when through the grace of Brahman it realizes its identity with him, it revolves upon the wheel no longer. It achieves immortality.

He who is realized by transcending the world of cause and effect, in deep contemplation, is expressly declared by the scriptures to be the Supreme Brahman. He is the substance, all else the shadow. He is the imperishable. The knowers of Brahman know him as the one reality behind all that seems. For this reason they are devoted to him. Absorbed in him, they attain freedom from the wheel of birth, death, and rebirth.

The Lord supports this universe, which is made up of the perishable and the imperishable, the manifest and the unmanifest. The individual soul, forgetful of the Lord, attaches itself to pleasure and thus is bound. When it comes to the Lord, it is freed from all its fetters.

Mind and matter, master and servant — both have existed from beginningless time. The Maya which unites them has also existed from beginningless time. When all three — mind, matter, and Maya — are known as one with Brahman, then is it realized that the Self is infinite and has no part in action. Then is it revealed that the Self is all.

Matter is perishable. The Lord, the destroyer of ignorance, is imperishable, immortal. He is the one God, the Lord of the perishable and of all souls. By meditating on him, by uniting oneself with him, by identifying oneself with him, one ceases to be ignorant.

Know God, and all fetters will be loosed. Ignorance will vanish. Birth, death, and rebirth will be no more. Meditate upon him and transcend physical consciousness. Thus will you reach union with the lord of the universe. Thus will you become identified with him who is One without a second. In him all your desires will find fulfillment.

The truth is that you are always united with the Lord. But you must *know* this. Nothing further is there to know. Meditate, and you will realize that mind, matter, and Maya (the power which unites mind and matter) are but three aspects of Brahman, the one reality.

Fire, though present in the firesticks, is not perceived until one stick is rubbed against another. The Self is like that fire: It is realized in the body by meditation on the sacred syllable OM.[1]

Let your body be the stick that is rubbed, the sacred syllable OM the stick that is rubbed against it. Thus shall you realize God, who is hidden within the body as fire is hidden within the wood.

Like oil in sesame seeds, butter in cream, water in the river bed, fire in tinder, the Self dwells within the soul. Realize him through truthfulness and meditation.

Like butter in cream is the Self in everything. Knowledge of the Self is gained through meditation. The Self is Brahman. By Brahman is all ignorance destroyed.

To realize God, first control the outgoing senses and harness the mind. Then meditate upon the light in the heart of the fire — meditate, that is, upon pure consciousness as distinct from the ordinary consciousness of the intellect. Thus the Self, the Inner Reality, may be seen behind physical appearance.

Control your mind so that the Ultimate Reality, the self-luminous Lord, may be revealed. Strive earnestly for eternal bliss.

With the help of the mind and the intellect, keep the senses from attaching themselves to objects of pleasure. They will then be purified by the light of the Inner Reality, and that light will be revealed.

The wise control their minds, and unite their hearts with the infinite, the omniscient, the all-pervading Lord. Only discriminating souls practice spiritual disciplines. Great is the glory of the self-luminous being, the Inner Reality.

Hear, all ye children of immortal bliss, also ye gods who dwell in the high heavens: Follow only in the footsteps of the illumined ones,

---

[1]Sacred symbol for God and the sound chanted in meditation. [Ed.]

and by continuous meditation merge both mind and intellect in the eternal Brahman. The glorious Lord will be revealed to you.

Control the vital force. Set fire to the Self within by the practice of meditation. Be drunk with the wine of divine love. Thus shall you reach perfection.

Be devoted to the eternal Brahman. Unite the light within you with the light of Brahman. Thus will the source of ignorance be destroyed, and you will rise above karma.

Sit upright, holding the chest, throat, and head erect. Turn the senses and the mind inward to the lotus of the heart. Meditate on Brahman with the help of the syllable OM. Cross the fearful currents of the ocean of worldliness by means of the raft of Brahman — the sacred syllable OM.

With earnest effort hold the senses in check. Controlling the breath, regulate the vital activities. As a charioteer holds back his restive horses, so does a persevering aspirant hold back his mind.

Retire to a solitary place, such as a mountain cave or a sacred spot. The place must be protected from the wind and rain, and it must have a smooth, clean floor, free from pebbles and dust. It must not be damp, and it must be free from disturbing noises. It must be pleasing to the eye and quieting to the mind. Seated there, practice meditation and other spiritual exercises.

As you practice meditation, you may see in vision forms resembling snow, crystals, smoke, fire, lightning, fireflies, the sun, the moon. These are signs that you are on your way to the revelation of Brahman.

As you become absorbed in meditation, you will realize that the Self is separate from the body and for this reason will not be affected by disease, old age, or death.

31

Buddhism: Gotama's Discovery

Gotama Siddhartha* (c. 563–483 B.C.E.), known to history as the Buddha, was the son of a Hindu Kshatriya prince in northern India. This selection tells a traditional story about his youth. Because his father was warned by "Brahman soothsayers" that young Gotama would leave his home to live among the seekers in the forest, his father kept the boy distracted in the palace, the sufferings of people outside hidden from him. This selection begins when the prince, or *raja*, finally agrees to let Gotama tour outside the palace.

What does Gotama discover? What seems to be the meaning of these discoveries for him? How is his subsequent thought or behavior similar to that of other Hindus in the era? How is the message of this story similar to the lessons of the Upanishads, especially the *Svetasvatara* Upanishad?

Thinking Historically

None of the stories we have of the Buddha was written during his lifetime. For some four hundred years, stories of the Buddha were passed by word of mouth before they were put into writing. Can you see any signs in this story that it was memorized and told orally? When the stories were finally written down, some were no doubt more faithful to the Buddha's actual words and experience than others. What elements in this story would most likely reflect the historical experience of Gotama? What parts of the story would most likely be added later by people who worshiped the Buddha?

Now the young lord Gotama, when many days had passed by, bade his charioteer make ready the state carriages, saying: "Get ready the carriages, good charioteer, and let us go through the park to inspect the pleasaunce." "Yes, my lord," replied the charioteer, and harnessed the state carriages and sent word to Gotama: "The carriages are ready, my lord; do now what you deem fit." Then Gotama mounted a state carriage and drove out in state into the park.

*GAH tah mah sih DAHR thah

"The Life of Gotama the Buddha," trans. E. H. Brewster, in Clarence H. Hamilton, *Buddhism* (1926; reprint, New York: Routledge, 1952).

Now the young lord saw, as he was driving to the park, an aged man as bent as a roof gable, decrepit, leaning on a staff, tottering as he walked, afflicted and long past his prime. And seeing him Gotama said: "That man, good charioteer, what has he done, that his hair is not like that of other men, nor his body?"

"He is what is called an aged man, my lord."

"But why is he called aged?"

"He is called aged, my lord, because he has not much longer to live."

"But then, good charioteer, am I too subject to old age, one who has not got past old age?"

"You, my lord, and we too, we all are of a kind to grow old; we have not got past old age."

"Why then, good charioteer, enough of the park for today. Drive me back hence to my rooms."

"Yea, my lord," answered the charioteer, and drove him back. And he, going to his rooms, sat brooding sorrowful and depressed, thinking, "Shame then verily be upon this thing called birth, since to one born old age shows itself like that!"

Thereupon the rāja sent for the charioteer and asked him: "Well, good charioteer, did the boy take pleasure in the park? Was he pleased with it?"

"No, my lord, he was not."

"What then did he see on his drive?"

(And the charioteer told the rāja all.)

Then the rāja thought thus: We must not have Gotama declining to rule. We must not have him going forth from the house into the homeless state. We must not let what the brāhman soothsayers spoke of come true.

So, that these things might not come to pass, he let the youth be still more surrounded by sensuous pleasures. And thus Gotama continued to live amidst the pleasures of sense.

Now after many days had passed by, the young lord again bade his charioteer make ready and drove forth as once before. . . .

And Gotama saw, as he was driving to the park, a sick man, suffering and very ill, fallen and weltering in his own water, by some being lifted up, by others being dressed. Seeing this, Gotama asked: "That man, good charioteer, what has he done that his eyes are not like others' eyes, nor his voice like the voice of other men?"

"He is what is called ill, my lord."

"But what is meant by ill?"

"It means, my lord, that he will hardly recover from his illness."

"But am I too, then, good charioteer, subject to fall ill; have I not got out of reach of illness?"

"You, my lord, and we too, we are all subject to fall ill; we have not got beyond the reach of illness."

"Why then, good charioteer, enough of the park for today. Drive me back hence to my rooms." "Yea, my lord," answered the charioteer, and drove him back. And he, going to his rooms, sat brooding sorrowful and depressed, thinking: Shame then verily be upon this thing called birth, since to one born decay shows itself like that, disease shows itself like that.

Thereupon the rāja sent for the charioteer and asked him: "Well, good charioteer, did the young lord take pleasure in the park and was he pleased with it?"

"No, my lord, he was not."

"What did he see then on his drive?"

(And the charioteer told the rāja all.)

Then the rāja thought thus: We must not have Gotama declining to rule; we must not have him going forth from the house to the homeless state; we must not let what the brāhman soothsayers spoke of come true.

So, that these things might not come to pass, he let the young man be still more abundantly surrounded by sensuous pleasures. And thus Gotama continued to live amidst the pleasures of sense.

Now once again, after many days . . . the young lord Gotama . . . drove forth.

And he saw, as he was driving to the park, a great concourse of people clad in garments of different colours constructing a funeral pyre. And seeing this he asked his charioteer: "Why now are all those people come together in garments of different colours, and making that pile?"

"It is because someone, my lord, has ended his days."

"Then drive the carriage close to him who has ended his days."

"Yea, my lord," answered the charioteer, and did so. And Gotama saw the corpse of him who had ended his days and asked: "What, good charioteer, is ending one's days?"

"It means, my lord, that neither mother, nor father, nor other kinsfolk will now see him, nor will he see them."

"But am I too then subject to death, have I not got beyond reach of death? Will neither the rāja, nor the ranee, nor any other of my kin see me more, or shall I again see them?"

"You, my lord, and we too, we are all subject to death; we have not passed beyond the reach of death. Neither the rāja, nor the ranee, nor any other of your kin will see you any more, nor will you see them."

"Why then, good charioteer, enough of the park for today. Drive me back hence to my rooms."

"Yea, my lord," replied the charioteer, and drove him back.

And he, going to his rooms, sat brooding sorrowful and depressed, thinking: Shame verily be upon this thing called birth, since to one born the decay of life, since disease, since death shows itself like that!

Thereupon the rāja questioned the charioteer as before and as before let Gotama be still more surrounded by sensuous enjoyment. And thus he continued to live amidst the pleasures of sense.

Now once again, after many days . . . the lord Gotama . . . drove forth.

And he saw, as he was driving to the park, a shaven-headed man, a recluse, wearing the yellow robe. And seeing him he asked the charioteer, "That man, good charioteer, what has he done that his head is unlike other men's heads and his clothes too are unlike those of others?"

"That is what they call a recluse, because, my lord, he is one who has gone forth."

"What is that, 'to have gone forth'?"

"To have gone forth, my lord, means being thorough in the religious life, thorough in the peaceful life, thorough in good action, thorough in meritorious conduct, thorough in harmlessness, thorough in kindness to all creatures."

"Excellent indeed, friend charioteer, is what they call a recluse, since so thorough is his conduct in all those respects, wherefore drive me up to that forthgone man."

"Yea, my lord," replied the charioteer and drove up to the recluse. Then Gotama addressed him, saying, "You master, what have you done that your head is not as other men's heads, nor your clothes as those of other men?"

"I, my lord, am one who has gone forth."

"What, master, does that mean?"

"It means, my lord, being thorough in the religious life, thorough in the peaceful life, thorough in good actions, thorough in meritorious conduct, thorough in harmlessness, thorough in kindness to all creatures."

"Excellently indeed, master, are you said to have gone forth since so thorough is your conduct in all those respects." Then the lord Gotama bade his charioteer, saying: "Come then, good charioteer, do you take the carriage and drive it back hence to my rooms. But I will even here cut off my hair, and don the yellow robe, and go forth from the house into the homeless state."

"Yea, my lord," replied the charioteer, and drove back. But the prince Gotama, there and then cutting off his hair and donning the yellow robe, went forth from the house into the homeless state.

Now at Kapilavatthu, the rāja's seat, a great number of persons, some eighty-four thousand souls, heard of what prince Gotama had done and thought: Surely this is no ordinary religious rule, this is no common going forth, in that prince Gotama himself has had his head shaved and has donned the yellow robe and has gone forth from the house into the homeless state. If prince Gotama has done this, why then should not we also? And they all had their heads shaved and donned the yellow robes; and in imitation of the Bodhisat [Buddha] they went forth from the house into the homeless state. So the Bodhisat went forth from the house into the homeless state. So the Bodhisat went up on his rounds through the villages, towns, and cities accompanied by that multitude.

Now there arose in the mind of Gotama the Bodhisat, when he was meditating in seclusion, this thought: That indeed is not suitable for me that I should live beset. 'Twere better were I to dwell alone, far from the crowd.

So after a time he dwelt alone, away from the crowd. Those eighty-four thousand recluses went one way, and the Bodhisat went another way.

Now there arose in the mind of Gotama the Bodhisat, when he had gone to his place and was meditating in seclusion, this thought: Verily, this world had fallen upon trouble — one is born, and grows old, and dies, and falls from one state, and springs up in another. And from the suffering, moreover, no one knows of any way to escape, even from decay and death. O, when shall a way of escape from this suffering be made known — from decay and from death?

32

The Buddha's First Sermon

This is said to be the Buddha's first sermon, delivered shortly after he achieved enlightenment. It contains the essence of Buddhist thought: the four noble truths, the eightfold path, and the middle way. The middle way is the course between the extremes of the pursuit of pleasure and the pursuit of pain. It is defined by an eightfold path, eight steps to a peaceful mind. The four noble truths might be summarized as the following:

1. Life is sorrow.
2. Sorrow is the result of selfish desire.
3. Selfish desire can be destroyed.
4. It can be destroyed by following the eightfold path.

The Buddhist Tradition in India, China and Japan, ed. William Theodore de Bary (New York: Random House, 1969), 16–17.

What do these ideas mean? What was considered the value of a "middle way"? In what ways did the eightfold path offer a spiritual discipline? What answers did the four noble truths provide?

Thinking Historically

Notice how the tone and style of this document are different from the preceding one. Which source reads more like the report of a witness or someone close to the events described? Which reads more like an idealization or myth? Why is it likely that a report would be written before an idealization or myth?

Thus I have heard. Once the Lord was at Vrānasī, at the deer park called Iwipatana. There he addressed the five monks:

There are two ends not to be served by a wanderer. What are these two? The pursuit of desires and of the pleasure which springs from desire, which is base, common, leading to rebirth, ignoble, and unprofitable; and the pursuit of pain and hardship, which is grievous, ignoble, and unprofitable. The Middle Way of the Tathāgata avoids both these ends. It is enlightened, it brings clear vision, it makes for wisdom, and leads to peace, insight, enlightenment, and Nirvāna. What is the Middle Way? . . . It is the Noble Eightfold Path — Right Views, Right Resolve, Right Speech, Right Conduct, Right Livelihood, Right Effort, Right Mindfulness, and Right Concentration. This is the Middle Way. . . .

And this is the Noble Truth of Sorrow. Birth is sorrow, age is sorrow, disease is sorrow, death is sorrow; contact with the unpleasant is sorrow, separation from the pleasant is sorrow, every wish unfulfilled is sorrow — in short all the five components of individuality are sorrow.

And this is the Noble Truth of the Arising of Sorrow. It arises from craving, which leads to rebirth, which brings delight and passion, and seeks pleasure now here, now there — the craving for sensual pleasure, the craving for continued life, the craving for power.

And this is the Noble Truth of the Stopping of Sorrow. It is the complete stopping of that craving, so that no passion remains, leaving it, being emancipated from it, being released from it, giving no place to it.

And this is the Noble Truth of the Way which Leads to the Stopping of Sorrow. It is the Noble Eightfold Path — Right Views, Right Resolve, Right Speech, Right Conduct, Right Livelihood, Right Effort, Right Mindfulness, and Right Concentration.

33

Buddhism and Caste

This story, part of the Buddhist canon that was written between one hundred and four hundred years after his death, tells of a confrontation between the Buddha and Brahmans, members of the Hindu priestly caste. This encounter would have been common. Why would it be important? How would you expect most Brahmans to react to the Buddha's opposition to caste? Would some Brahmans be persuaded by the Buddha's arguments? How and why would the appeal of Buddhism be more universal than Hinduism?

Thinking Historically

Notice the mention of Greece and the dialogue style of this selection. If, as some scholars have suggested, there may be Greek influence here, which Greek writer would they be referring to? How might this Greek influence help us find an approximate date for this writing?

Once when the Lord was staying at Sāvatthī there were five hundred brāhmans from various countries in the city . . . and they thought: "This ascetic Gautama preaches that all four classes are pure. Who can refute him?"

At that time there was a young brāhman named Assalāyana in the city . . . a youth of sixteen, thoroughly versed in the Vedas . . . and in all brāhmanic learning. "He can do it!" thought the brāhmans, and so they asked him to try; surrounded by a crowd of brāhmans, he went to the Lord, and, after greeting him, sat down and said:

"Brāhmans maintain that only they are the highest class, and the others are below them. They are white, the others black; only they are pure, and not the others. Only they are the true sons of Brahmā, born from his mouth, born of Brahmā, creations of Brahmā, heirs of Brahmā. Now what does the worthy Gautama say to that?"

"Do the brāhmans really maintain this, Assalāyana, when they're born of women just like anyone else, of brāhman women who have their periods and conceive, give birth and nurse their children, just like any other women?"

The Buddhist Tradition in India, China and Japan, ed. William Theodore de Bary (New York: Random House, 1969), 49–51.

"For all you say, this is what they think. . . ."

"Have you ever heard that in the lands of the Greeks and Kambojas and other peoples on the borders there are only two classes, masters and slaves, and a master can become a slave and vice versa?"

"Yes, I've heard so."

"And what strength or support does that fact give to the brāhmans' claim?"

"Nevertheless, that is what they think."

"Again if a man is a murderer, a thief, or an adulterer, or commits other grave sins, when his body breaks up on death does he pass on to purgatory if he's a kshatriya,[1] vaishya,[2] or shūdra,[3] but not if he's a brāhman?"

"No, Gautama. In such a case the same fate is in store for all men, whatever their class."

"And if he avoids grave sin, will he go to heaven if he's a brāhman, but not if he's a man of the lower classes?"

"No, Gautama. In such a case the same reward awaits all men, whatever their class."

"And is a brāhman capable of developing a mind of love without hate or ill-will, but not a man of the other classes?"

"No, Gautama. All four classes are capable of doing so."

"Can only a brāhman go down to a river and wash away dust and dirt, and not men of the other classes?"

"No, Gautama, all four classes can."

"Now suppose a king were to gather together a hundred men of different classes and to order the brāhmans and kshatriyas to take kindling wood of sāl, pine, lotus, or sandal, and light fires, while the low-class folk did the same with common wood. What do you think would happen? Would the fires of the high-born men blaze up brightly . . . and those of the humble fail?"

"No, Gautama. It would be alike with high and lowly. . . . Every fire would blaze with the same bright flame." . . .

"Suppose there are two young brāhman brothers, one a scholar and the other uneducated. Which of them would be served first at memorial feasts, festivals, and sacrifices, or when entertained as guests?"

"The scholar, of course; for what great benefit would accrue from entertaining the uneducated one?"

"But suppose the scholar is ill-behaved and wicked, while the uneducated one is well-behaved and virtuous?"

"Then the uneducated one would be served first, for what great benefit would accrue from entertaining an ill-behaved and wicked man?"

---

[1]kuh SHAH tree uh   Warrior. [Ed.]
[2]VAH eesh uh   Free peasant, artisan, or producer. [Ed.]
[3]SHOO druh   Serf. [Ed.]

"First, Assalāyana, you based your claim on birth, then you gave up birth for learning, and finally you have come round to my way of thinking, that all four classes are equally pure!"

At this Assalāyana sat silent . . . his shoulders hunched, his eyes cast down, thoughtful in mind, and with no answer at hand.

$$\boxed{34}$$

The Bible: History, Laws, and Psalms

Just as the caste-based Hinduism of ancient Aryan tribes gave rise to universal Buddhism after 500 B.C.E., so did the Judaism of the tribe of Abraham give birth to universalist Christianity. Judaism was already an ancient religion by the time of Jesus. It traced its roots back (perhaps two thousand years) to Abraham himself who, according to tradition, made a contract (or covenant) with God to worship him and him alone.

This commitment to one god, and one god only, was to mark the ancient Jews as unique. No other people in the ancient world were monotheistic. The people of Mesopotamia, Egypt, India, and the Mediterranean accepted various ancestral and natural gods. Only the Egyptians for a brief moment (around 1300 B.C.E.) preached the singularity of god, in this case the sun god Aton, but that was soon renounced. Since such a belief was unusual, the descendants of Abraham had difficulty accepting it. In their wanderings throughout the land of the Tigris and Euphrates rivers, from Abraham's native Ur to Egypt, the Jews came into contact with many different religious beliefs; some were even tempted by foreign gods. (See Map 6.1.) However, by around 1300 B.C.E., Abraham's descendants escaped Egyptian domination, crossed the Red Sea, and with the help of Moses renewed their covenant with God in the Ten Commandments. Even then, stories were told of Jews who worshiped the Golden Calf and other idols and of the displeasure of the God of Abraham. "I am a jealous God," he told his people. "Thou shall not take other gods before you."

Such is the story told in the books of the Hebrew Bible, written after the Jews settled in Jerusalem and the surrounding area sometime

---

Gen. 1:1–2:25, 17:1–14; Exod. 19:1–20:18; Lev. 1:1–9; Ps. 23:1–6; Amos 5:21–24. All biblical selections are from the King James Version.

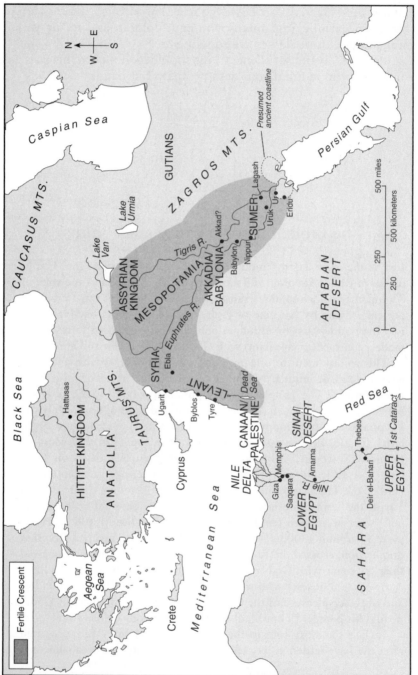

Map 6.1 The Ancient Near East, 4000–1000 B.C.E.

after 1000 B.C.E. They wrote of their history since the time of Abraham, and even of the ages before the patriarch, stretching back to the beginning of the world. By about 900 B.C.E., in the heyday of Jewish kingship, Kings Saul, David, and Solomon ruled large parts of what is today Israel, Palestine, and Jordan. The book we know as the Old Testament included their histories, the laws of the two Jewish kingdoms Judah and Israel, and various other writings (songs, psalms, and philosophy).

As you read these first selections from the Bible (Genesis, Exodus, Leviticus, and Psalms), note how they are similar to, and different from, the Vedas and Upanishads of Hinduism. How, for instance, is the story of the beginning of the world different from the sacrifice of Purusha? Why is an understanding of history more important to the Jews than it was to the Hindus? Compare the role of morality in the religion of Jews and Hindus. In what sense is the morality of Judaism universal and that of Hinduism caste based? How is the Judaic emphasis on morality also different from Buddhist ideas?

Thinking Historically

Since the books of the Hebrew Bible were composed over a long period of time, from about 900 B.C.E. to about 165 B.C.E., we might expect to see changes in emphasis, especially since this period was such a tumultuous one in Jewish history. The immediate descendants of Abraham were a nomadic pastoral people — shepherds, Psalm 23 reminds us, though this beautiful psalm attributed to King David was written in an urban, monarchal stage of Jewish history. Leviticus, too, echoes an earlier pastoral life where animal sacrifice, and the worship by shepherds generally, was still practiced.

When did morality replace sacrifice as the sign of respect to the God of Abraham? Was it around 1300 B.C.E., the traditional date for the reception by Moses of the Ten Commandments? Or is the existence of Leviticus, perhaps five hundred years later, a sign that sacrifice was still practiced? The sentiments of Amos (783–743 B.C.E.) suggest a later rejection not only of animal sacrifice but also of moral obedience that was not truly felt.

When did monotheism (the belief in one god) become unequivocal, unquestioned? Since this was a new idea, there must have been a time when it wasn't held. Some scholars see signs of an earlier polytheism (belief in many gods) in the book of Genesis itself. For instance, in Genesis 3:5 we find, "ye shall be as gods," and in Genesis 3:22, "And the Lord God said: Behold the man has become like one of us."

Certainly the beginning of Genesis is no-nonsense monotheism, majestically so: "In the beginning God created the heaven and the earth." But scholars have pointed out that this opening is followed by another story of origin beginning at Chapter 2, Verse 4, that not only tells the story over again, but does so without the intense declarative monotheism. They date this document at about 850 B.C.E. and the section from 1:1 to 2:3 at about 650 B.C.E. Compare the language in Genesis 1 to 2:3 with the section that begins at 2:4. Using the categories from the previous selection, reporting versus idealizing or myth-making, which selection from Genesis seems more idealized, which more like a report? Which version would probably be closer to the oral story-telling tradition? Which reflects the style of a sophisticated, urban, philosophical culture? Which is more monotheistic: God or Lord God?

If we can see increased emphasis on monotheism from 850 to 650 B.C.E., we might also see in these selections the transition from the religion of a tribe of shepherds to that of a political kingdom. What evidence do you see that a pastoral religion of animal sacrifice became a religion of law, or even internalized morality?

Finally, notice there is no heaven here — no afterlife. God promised Abraham land and prosperity. Even today, a belief in personal immortality is more accepted by Christians than Jews. Still, we will explore the development of that idea in Judaism in the second century B.C.E.

Genesis

Chapter 1

1 In the beginning God created the heaven and the earth. 2 And the earth was without form, and void; and darkness was upon the face of the deep. And the Spirit of God moved upon the face of the waters. 3 And God said, Let there be light: and there was light. 4 And God saw the light, and it was good: and God divided the light from the darkness. 5 And God called the light Day, and the darkness he called Night. And the evening and the morning were the first day.

6 And God said, Let there be a firmament in the midst of the waters, and let it divide the waters. 7 And God made the firmament, and divided the waters which were under the firmament from the waters which were above the firmament: and it was so. 8 And God called the firmament Heaven. And the evening and the morning were the second day.

9 And God said, Let the waters under the heaven be gathered together unto one place, and let the dry land appear: and it was so. 10 And God called the dry land Earth; and the gathering together of the water called he Seas: and God saw it was good. 11 And God said, Let the earth bring forth grass, the herb yielding seed, and the fruit tree

yielding fruit after his kind, whose seed is in itself, upon the earth: and it was so. 12 And the earth brought forth grass, and herb yielding seed after his kind, and the tree yielding fruit, whose seed was in itself, after his kind: and God saw it was good. 13 And the evening and the morning were the third day.

14 And God said, Let there be lights in the firmament of the heaven to divide the day from the night; and let them be for signs, and for seasons, and for days, and years: 15 And let them be for lights in the firmament of the heaven to give light upon the earth: and it was so. 16 And God made two great lights; the greater light to rule the day, and the lesser light to rule the night: he made the stars also. 17 And God set them in the firmament of the heaven to give light upon the earth, 18 And to rule over the day and over the night, and to divide the light from the darkness: and God saw that it was good. 19 And the evening and the morning were the fourth day.

20 And God said, Let the waters bring forth abundantly the moving creatures that hath life, and fowl that may fly above the earth in the open firmament of heaven. 21 And God created great whales, and every living creature that moveth, which the waters brought forth abundantly, after their kind, and every winged fowl after his kind: and God saw that it was good. 22 And God blessed them, saying, Be fruitful, and multiply, and fill the waters in the seas, and let fowl multiply in the earth. 23 And the evening and the morning were the fifth day.

24 And God said, Let the earth bring forth the living creature after his kind, cattle, and creeping thing, and beast of the earth after his kind: and it was so. 25 And God made the beast of the earth after his kind, and cattle after their kind, and every thing that creepeth upon the earth after his kind: and God saw that it was good.

26 And God said, Let us make man in our image, after our likeness: and let them have dominion over the fish of the sea, and over the fowl of the air, and over the cattle, and over all the earth, and over every creeping thing that creepeth upon the earth. 27 So God created man in his own image, in the image of God created he him: male and female created he them. 28 And God blessed them, and God said unto them, Be fruitful, and multiply, and replenish the earth, and subdue it: and have dominion over the fish of the sea, and over the fowl of the air, and over every living thing that moveth upon the earth.

29 And God said, Behold, I have given you every herb bearing seed, which is upon the face of all the earth, and every tree, in which is the fruit of a tree yielding seed; to you it shall be for meat. 30 And to every beast of the earth, and to every fowl of the air, and to every thing that creepeth upon the earth, wherein there is life, I have given every green herb for meat: and it was so. 31 And God saw every thing that he had made, and, behold, it was very good. And the evening and the morning were the sixth day.

Chapter 2

1 Thus the heavens and the earth were finished, and all the host of them. 2 And on the seventh day God ended his work which he had made; and he rested on the seventh day from all his work which he had made. 3 And God blessed the seventh day, and sanctified it: because that in it he had rested from all this work which God created and made.

4 These are the generations of the heavens and of the earth when they were created, in the day that the Lord God made the earth and the heavens. 5 And every plant of the field before it was in the earth, and every herb of the field before it grew: for the Lord God had not caused it to rain upon the earth, and there was not a man to till the ground. 6 But there went up a mist from the earth, and watered the whole face of the ground. 7 And the Lord God formed man of the dust of the ground, and breathed into his nostrils the breath of life; and man became a living soul.

8 And the Lord God planted a garden eastward in Eden; and there he put the man whom he had formed. 9 And out of the ground made the Lord God to grow every tree that is pleasant to the sight, and good for food; and the tree of life also in the midst of the garden, and the tree of knowledge of good and evil. 10 And a river went out of Eden to water the garden; and from thence it was parted, and became into four heads. 11 The name of the first is Pison: that is it which compasseth the whole land of Havilah, where there is gold; 12 And the gold of the land is good: there is bdellium and the onyx stone. 13 And the name of the second river is Gihon: the same is it that compasseth the whole land of Ethiopia. 14 And the name of the third river is Hiddekel: that is it which goeth toward the east of Assyria. And the fourth river is Euphrates. 15 And the Lord God took the man, and put him into the garden of Eden to dress it and to keep it. 16 And the Lord God commanded the man, saying, Of every tree of the garden thou mayest freely eat: 17 But of the tree of the knowledge of good and evil, thou shalt not eat of it: for in the day that thou eatest thereof thou shalt surely die.

18 And the Lord God said, It is not good that the man should be alone; I will make him a help meet for him. 19 And out of the ground the Lord God formed every beast of the field, and every fowl of the air; and brought them unto Adam to see what he would call them: and whatsoever Adam called every living creature, that was the name thereof. 20 And Adam gave names to all cattle, and to the fowl of the air, and to every beast of the field; but for Adam there was not found a help meet for him. 21 And the Lord God caused a deep sleep to fall upon Adam, and he slept; and he took one of his ribs, and closed up the flesh instead thereof. 22 And the rib, which the Lord God had taken from man, made he a woman, and brought her unto the man. 23 And Adam said, This is now bone of my bones, and flesh of my flesh: she

shall be called Woman, because she was taken out of man. 24 Therefore shall a man leave his father and his mother, and shall cleave unto his wife: and they shall be one flesh. 25 And they were both naked, the man and his wife, and were not ashamed.

Chapter 17

1 And when Abram was ninety years old and nine, the Lord appeared to Abram, and said unto him, I am the Almighty God; walk before me, and be thou perfect. 2 And I will make my covenant between me and thee, and will multiply thee exceedingly. 3 And Abram fell on his face: and God talked with him, saying, 4 As for me, behold, my covenant is with thee, and thou shalt be a father of many nations. 5 Neither shall thy name any more be called Abram, but thy name shall be Abraham; for a father of many nations I have made thee. 6 And I will make thee exceeding fruitful, and I will make nations of thee, and kings shall come out of thee. 7 And I will establish my covenant between me and thee and thy seed after thee in their generations, for an everlasting covenant, to be a God unto thee and to thy seed after thee. 8 And I will give unto thee, and to thy seed after thee, the land wherein thou art a stranger, all the land of Canaan, for an everlasting possession; and I will be their God. 9 And God said unto Abraham. Thou shalt keep my covenant therefore, thou, and thy seed after thee in their generations.

10 This is my covenant, which he shall keep, between me and you and thy seed after thee; Every man child among you shall be circumcised.

11 And ye shall circumcise the flesh of your foreskin; and it shall be a token of the covenant betwixt me and you. 12 And he that is eight days old shall be circumcised among you, every man child in your generations, he that is born in the house, or bought with money of any stranger, which is not of thy seed. 13 He that is born in thy house, and he that is bought with thy money, must needs be circumcised: and my covenant shall be in your flesh for an everlasting covenant. 14 And the uncircumcised man child whose flesh of his foreskin is not circumcised, that soul shall be cut off from his people; he hath broken my covenant.

Exodus

Chapter 19

1 In the third month, when the children of Israel were gone forth out of the land of Egypt, the same day came they into the wilderness of Sinai.

2 For they were departed from Rephidim, and were come to the desert of Sinai, and had pitched in the wilderness; and there Israel

camped before the mount. 3 And Moses went up unto God, and the Lord called unto him out of the mountain, saying, Thus shalt thou say to the house of Jacob, and tell the children of Israel; 4 Ye have seen what I did unto the Egyptians, and how I bare you on eagles' wings, and brought you unto myself. 5 Now therefore, if ye will obey my voice indeed, and keep my covenant, then ye shall be a peculiar treasure unto me above all people: for all the earth is mine: 6 And ye shall be unto me a kingdom of priests, and a holy nation. These are the words which thou shalt speak unto the children of Israel.

7 And Moses came and called for the elders of the people, and laid before their faces all these words which the Lord commanded him. 8 And all the people answered together, and said, All that the Lord hath spoken we will do. And Moses returned the words of the people unto the Lord. 9 And the Lord said unto Moses, Lo, I come unto thee in a thick cloud, that the people may hear when I speak with thee, and believe thee for ever. And Moses told the words of the people unto the Lord.

Chapter 20

1 And God spake all these words, saying,

2 I am the Lord thy God, which have brought thee out of the land of Egypt, out of the house of bondage. 3 Thou shalt have no other gods before me.

4 Thou shalt not make unto thee any graven image, or any likeness of any thing that is in heaven above, or that is in the earth beneath, or that is in the water under the earth: 5 Thou shalt not bow down thyself to them, nor serve them: for I the Lord thy God am a jealous God, visiting the iniquity of the fathers upon the children unto the third and fourth generation of them that hate me; 6 And showing mercy unto thousands of them that love me, and keep my commandments.

7 Thou shalt not take the name of the Lord thy God in vain: for the Lord will not hold him guiltless that taketh his name in vain.

8 Remember the sabbath day, to keep it holy. 9 Six days shalt thou labor, and do all thy work: 10 But the seventh day is the sabbath of the Lord thy God: in it thou shalt not do any work, thou, nor thy son, nor thy daughter, nor thy manservant, nor thy maidservant, nor thy cattle, nor thy stranger that is within thy gates: 11 For in six days the Lord made heaven and earth, the sea, and all that in them is, and rested the seventh day: wherefore the Lord blessed the sabbath day, and hallowed it.

12 Honor thy father and thy mother: that thy days may be long upon the land which the Lord thy God giveth thee.

13 Thou shalt not kill.

14 Thou shalt not commit adultery.

15 Thou shalt not steal.

16 Thou shalt not bear false witness against thy neighbor.

17 Thou shalt not covet thy neighbor's house; thou shalt not covet thy neighbor's wife, nor his manservant, nor his maidservant, nor his ox, nor his ass, nor any thing that is thy neighbor's.

18 And all the people saw the thunderings, and the lightnings, and the noise of the trumpet, and the mountain smoking: and when the people saw it, they removed, and stood afar off.

Leviticus

Chapter 1

1 And the Lord called unto Moses, and spake unto him out of the tabernacle of the congregation, saying, 2 Speak unto the children of Israel, and say unto them, If any man of you bring an offering unto the Lord, ye shall bring your offering of the cattle, even of the herd, and of the flock.

3 If his offering be a burnt sacrifice of the herd, let him offer a male without blemish: he shall offer it of his own voluntary will at the door of the tabernacle of the congregation before the Lord. 4 And he shall put his hand upon the head of the burnt offering; and it shall be accepted for him to make atonement for him. 5 And he shall kill the bullock before the Lord: and the priests, Aaron's sons, shall bring the blood, and sprinkle the blood round about upon the altar that is by the door of the tabernacle of the congregation. 6 And he shall flay the burnt offering, and cut it into his pieces. 7 And the sons of Aaron the priest shall put fire upon the altar, and lay the wood in order upon the fire: 8 And the priests, Aaron's sons, shall lay the parts, the head, and the fat, in order upon the wood that is on the fire which is upon the altar: 9 But his inwards and his legs shall he wash in water: and the priest shall burn all on the altar, to be a burnt sacrifice, an offering made by fire, of a sweet savor unto the Lord.

Psalm 23

1 The Lord is my shepherd; I shall not want.

2 He maketh me to lie down in green pastures: He leadeth me beside the still waters.

3 He restoreth my soul: He leadeth me in the paths of righteousness for his name's sake.

4 Yea, though I walk through the valley of the shadow of death, I will fear no evil: for thou art with me; Thy rod and thy staff they comfort me.

5 Thou preparest a table before me in the presence of mine enemies: Thou anointest my head with oil; my cup runneth over.

6 Surely goodness and mercy shall follow me all the days of my life:
And I will dwell in the house of the Lord for ever.

Amos

Chapter 5

21 I hate, I despise your feast days, and I will not delight in your
solemn assemblies.

22 Though you offer me burnt offerings and your meat offerings, I
will not accept them: neither will I regard the peace offerings of your
fat beasts.

23 Take thou away from me the noise of thy songs; for I will not
hear the melody of thy viols.

24 But let judgment run down as waters, and righteousness as a
mighty stream.

$$\boxed{35}$$

The Bible: Prophets and Apocalypse

The golden days of Jewish kings were not to last. Powerful empires
rose up to challenge and dominate the Jews: the Assyrians in 800
B.C.E., the Babylonians around 600 B.C.E., then the Medes, the Persians, the armies of Alexander the Great, his successor states — ruled
by his generals and their descendants — and then the Romans after 64
B.C.E. The Babylonians were among the worst of the invaders. They
conquered Jerusalem, destroyed the temple, and brought Jews as
hostages to Babylon. In 538 B.C.E. Cyrus, king of the Persians, allowed
Jews to return to Jerusalem and even rebuild the temple. But the Jews
never regained their kingdom or independence (except for brief periods), and the Greek Seleucid* rulers after Alexander proved to be in-
tolerant of non-Greek forms of worship.

*sel OO sihd

Dan. 12:1–13 King James.

Ironically, it was during this period of conquest and dispersal that Judaism began to develop the elements of a universal religion. The Babylonian destruction of the temple and population transfer made the religion of Yahweh less dependent on place. Virtually all religions of the ancient world were bound to a particular place, usually the sacred temple where the god was thought to reside. Judaism remained a religion of the descendants of Abraham and his son Israel, and the period after 600 B.C.E. was one of intense cultivation of that identity. But much of the Hebrew Bible was composed in exile, as a way of recalling a common history, reaffirming a common identity, predicting a common future. The prophets foresaw a brighter future or explained how the violation of the covenant had brought God's wrath on the people.

One of the great prophets of the exile and the postexile period was Daniel, described as one of the young men who was brought to Babylon by Nebuchadnezzar,* conqueror of Jerusalem in 586 B.C.E. The Book of Daniel begins by recounting that conquest. In Babylon Nebuchadnezzar asked Daniel to reveal the meaning of a dream. You will read his response below.

Daniel is the first to foretell of an apocalyptic end to history and the first to envision personal immortality. Previous prophets had predicted a new independent kingdom of Judah or they had predicted God's punishment of his people, but Daniel prophesied that God would come down to reign on earth forever, judging the living and the dead for all eternity. These ideas — an end to history, the Last Judgment, the Kingdom of God, eternal life or damnation — became more important later in Christianity than in Judaism, where these notions never entered the mainstream. But their appearance in Daniel shows the way in which Judaic ideas became more universal over the course of the first millennium B.C.E. Why would Daniel's ideas open the Judaic tradition to non-Jews or people not descended from Abraham? How would Daniel's prophecy affect his contemporaries? How would it affect you?

Thinking Historically

When did the idea of an afterlife enter Judaism? To answer this question we have to date the Book of Daniel, which is a bit more complex than it would seem. As mentioned, the book is presented as the prophecy of a Daniel who was taken from Jerusalem to Babylon around 586 B.C.E. If there was such a Daniel and he was a prophet, the version we have shows signs of continual updating. In the initial prophecy for Nebuchadnezzar and in similar instances reported throughout the Book of Daniel, the author predicts the string of empires that determined the fate of the Jews from the Babylonian to the

*neh boo kuhd NEH zur

Median to the Persian to the Greek under Alexander to the Seleucid (Alexander's successors). This is the meaning of the gold, silver, bronze, iron, clay sequence. In each case, the prophecy is vague (and sometimes inaccurate) when referring to the Babylonian period but very specific and exact about the period of iron and clay (the Seleucids). When Daniel speaks of the signs of the last days, his veiled references clearly refer to events during the reign of the Seleucid ruler Antiochus IV. He distinctly sees the desecration of the temple by Antiochus as the key event that will bring about God's eternal kingdom. Antiochus, who ruled from 175 to 163 B.C.E., pressured the Jews to accept Greek gods. In 168 B.C.E. he polluted the temple by slaughtering pigs on the altar and then erecting a statue of the Greek god Zeus — the event that Daniel predicts will bring on God's last judgment.

What would be the purpose of putting this prophecy in the writings of someone who had lived hundreds of years earlier? How does the age of Daniel's message give it added impact? When and why would the author of the Book of Daniel have predicted that the end of the world would occur 1290 days after an event in 168 B.C.E.? When and why would he have written "blessed are those who wait 1335 days"?

Daniel

Daniel Interprets the Dream of Nebuchadnezzar (Chapter 2)

Thou, O king, sawest, and behold a great image. This great image, whose brightness was excellent, stood before thee; and the form thereof was terrible.

32 This image's head was of fine gold, his breast and his arms of silver, his belly and his thighs of brass,

33 His legs of iron, his feet part of iron and part of clay.

34 Thou sawest till that a stone was cut out without hands, which smote the image upon his feet that were of iron and clay, and brake them to pieces.

35 Then was the iron, the clay, the brass, the silver, and the gold, broken to pieces together, and became like the chaff of the summer threshing floors; and the wind carried them away, that no place was found for them: and the stone that smote the image became a great mountain, and filled the whole earth.

36 This is the dream; and we will tell the interpretation thereof before the king.

37 Thou, O king, art a king of kings: for the God of heaven hath given thee a kingdom, power, and strength, and glory.

38 And wheresoever the children of men dwell, the beasts of the field and the fowls of the heaven hath he given into thine hand, and hath made thee ruler over them all. Thou art this head of gold.

39 And after thee shall arise another kingdom inferior to thee,[1] and another third kingdom of brass,[2] which shall bear rule over all the earth.

40 And the fourth kingdom[3] shall be strong as iron: forasmuch as iron breaketh in pieces and subdueth all things: and as iron that breaketh all these, shall it break in pieces and bruise.

41 And whereas thou sawest the feet and toes, part of potters' clay, and part of iron, the kingdom shall be divided;[4] but there shall be in it of the strength of the iron, forasmuch as thou sawest the iron mixed with miry clay.

42 And as the toes of the feet were part of iron, and part of clay, so the kingdom shall be partly strong, and partly broken.

43 And whereas thou sawest iron mixed with miry clay, they shall mingle themselves with the seed of men:[5] but they shall not cleave one to another, even as iron is not mixed with clay.

44 And in the days of these kings shall the God of heaven set up a kingdom, which shall never be destroyed: and the kingdom shall not be left to other people, but it shall break in pieces and consume all these kingdoms, and it shall stand for ever.

45 Forasmuch as thou sawest that the stone was cut out of the mountain without hands, and that it brake in pieces the iron, the brass, the clay, the silver, and the gold; the great God hath made known to the king what shall come to pass hereafter: and the dream is certain, and the interpretation thereof sure.

Daniel Sees the End of the Age of Iron and Clay (Chapter 11)

28 Then shall he[6] return into his land[7] with great riches and his heart shall be against the holy covenant;[8] and he shall do exploits, and return to his own land.

---

[1]Media, or Mede, Empire. Iranians who defeated Babylonians and ruled in the Middle East to 550 B.C.E. [Ed.]

[2]Persia, 550–330 B.C.E. [Ed.]

[3]Greek empire of Alexander the Great, 330–323 B.C.E. [Ed.]

[4]The Middle Eastern portion of Alexander's empire was divided after his death in 323 B.C.E. by his generals: Seleucus in Palestine and Syria and Ptolemy in Egypt. The kingdom of the Seleucids (iron) was stronger than the Ptolemy (clay). These two dynasties lasted until conquered by Rome and Persian Parthia. [Ed.]

[5]Probably refers to mixing of peoples and cultures in Alexander's and his successors' empire. [Ed.]

[6]Antiochus IV, the Seleucid emperor from 175 to 161 B.C.E., ruled Palestine, Syria, and Alexander's eastern empire, which included Jerusalem. [Ed.]

[7]Antiochus IV returned to Jerusalem after his first war with Egypt, 170 B.C.E. [Ed.]

[8]Antiochus stole Temple treasures and massacred many Jews, 169 B.C.E. [Ed.]

29 At the time appointed he shall return, and come toward the south;[9] but it shall not be as the former, or as the latter.

30 For the ships of Chittim[10] shall come against him: therefore he shall be grieved, and return, and have indignation against the holy covenant: so shall he do; he shall even return, and have intelligence with them that forsake[11] the holy covenant.

31 And arms shall stand on his part, and they shall pollute the sanctuary of strength, and shall take away the daily sacrifice, and they shall place the abomination that maketh desolate.[12]

32 And such as do wickedly against the covenant shall he corrupt by flatteries: but the people that do know their God shall be strong, and do exploits.

33 And they that understand among the people shall instruct many: yet they shall fall by the sword, and by flame, by captivity, and by spoil, many days.

34 Now when they shall fall, they shall be helped with a little help:[13] but many shall cleave to them with flatteries.[14]

35 And some of them of understanding shall fall, to try them, and to purge, and to make them white, even to the time of the end: because it is yet for a time appointed.

36 And the king shall do according to his will; and he shall exalt himself, and magnify himself above every god,[15] and shall speak marvelous things against the God of gods, and shall prosper till the indignation be accomplished: for that that is determined shall be done.

37 Neither shall he regard the God of his fathers, nor the desire of women, nor regard any god: for he shall magnify himself above all.

38 But in his estate shall he honour the God of forces: and a god whom his fathers knew not shall he honour with gold, and silver, and with precious stones, and pleasant things.

39 Thus shall he do in the most strong holds with a strange god, whom he shall acknowledge and increase with glory: and he shall cause them to rule over many, and shall divide the land for gain.

40 And at the time of the end shall the king of the south[16] push at him: and the king of the north shall come against him like a whirlwind,

---

[9]The second war of Antiochus IV with Egypt in 168 B.C.E. was not successful. [Ed.]

[10]Cyprus. Here it means ships of Romans, generally, who blocked him. [Ed.]

[11]Jews like Jason the high priest, who favored Greek customs. [Ed.]

[12]The army of Antiochus broke down the temple walls, desecrated the interior, and installed Greek statues. [Ed.]

[13]While many Jews chose martyrdom, some received the help of Judas Maccabeus, leader of the opposition to Antiochus. [Ed.]

[14]Some of the followers of Judas Maccabeus were insincere. [Ed.]

[15]Antiochus had himself declared "Epiphanes," or God Manifest. [Ed.]

[16]Ptolemy VI Philometor (Egypt) initiated the third Egyptian war, against Antiochus. [Ed.]

with chariots, and with horsemen, and with many ships; and he shall enter into the countries, and shall overflow and pass over.

41 He shall enter also into the glorious land, and many countries shall be overthrown: but these shall escape out of his hand, even Edom, and Moab, and the chief of the children of Ammon.

42 He shall stretch forth his hand also upon the countries: and the land of Egypt shall not escape.

43 But he shall have power over the treasures of gold and of silver, and over all the precious things of Egypt: and the Libyans and the Ethiopians shall be at his steps.

44 But tidings out of the east and out of the north[17] shall trouble him: therefore he shall go forth with great fury to destroy, and utterly to make away many.

45 And he shall plant the tabernacles of his palace between the seas in the glorious holy mountain;[18] yet he shall come to his end,[19] and none shall help him.

Then Shall Come the End of Days (Chapter 12)

1 And at that time shall Michael[20] stand up, the great prince which standeth for the children of thy people: and there shall be a time of trouble, such as never was since there was a nation even to that same time: and at that time thy people shall be delivered, every one that shall be found written in the book.

2 And many of them that sleep in the dust of the earth shall awake, some to everlasting life, and some to shame and everlasting contempt.

3 And they that be wise shall shine as the brightness of the firmament; and they that turn many to righteousness as the stars for ever and ever.

4 But thou, O Daniel, shut up the words, and seal the book, even to the time of the end: many shall run to and fro, and knowledge shall be increased.

5 Then I Daniel looked, and, behold, there stood other two, the one on this side of the bank of the river, and the other on that side of the bank of the river.

6 And one said to the man clothed in linen, which was upon the waters of the river, How long shall it be to the end of these wonders?

7 And I heard the man clothed in linen, which was upon the waters of the river, when he held up his right hand and his left hand unto

---

[17]Antiochus spent his last year in war with Armenia and Parthia (Persia). [Ed.]
[18]In Palestine. [Ed.]
[19]Antiochus IV died at Tabae in Persia in 163 B.C.E. [Ed.]
[20]Protective angel of Israel. [Ed.]

heaven, and sware by him that liveth for ever that it shall be for a time, times, and an half; and when he shall have accomplished to scatter the power of the holy people, all these things shall be finished.

8 And I heard, but I understood not: then said I, O my Lord, what shall be the end of these things?

9 And he said, Go thy way, Daniel: for the words are closed up and sealed till the time of the end.

10 Many shall be purified, and made white, and tried; but the wicked shall do wickedly: and none of the wicked shall understand; but the wise shall understand.

11 And from the time that the daily sacrifice shall be taken away, and the abomination that maketh desolate set up, there shall be a thousand two hundred and ninety days.

12 Blessed is he that waiteth, and cometh to the thousand three hundred and five and thirty days.

13 But go thou thy way till the end be: for thou shalt rest, and stand in thy lot at the end of the days.

36

Christianity: Jesus according to Matthew

The related ideas first enunciated in Daniel — the coming end of the world or the Kingdom of God, the Last Judgment, individual immortality or life after death — were to become central to the branch of Judaism that produced Christianity. Along with Judaic monotheism and the insistence of the prophets (like Amos) on internalized morality, the idea of personal responsibility and eternal salvation or damnation gave Christianity an appeal that would eventually reach far beyond the children of Abraham.

In this selection from the Gospel of Matthew, the evangelist recounts Jesus speaking of the apocalypse and there is a note of urgency here. Like Daniel, Jesus speaks of the signs that the end is at hand. Yet, in the same chapter, sometimes in the same paragraph, Matthew recounts Jesus telling his listeners that there is plenty of time before the end.

Matt. 24:1–41 King James.

What accounts for this apparent contradiction? If you were in the audience listening to Jesus, what idea would motivate you more — the fact that the end of the world is rapidly approaching or that it is generations away? If you were taking notes for the daily newspaper, which message would get the headline? If you were writing a history of Jesus for future generations, which message would you emphasize?

Thinking Historically

Matthew was writing about forty years after Jesus died. If he had been among those who heard Jesus speak, he took a long time to write it down. It is more likely that the author of this gospel is a second-generation evangelist, drawing on an earlier source, now lost. He may have had access to an earlier eyewitness account, or to a collection of sayings of Jesus.

We know that Matthew updated the words of Jesus for the benefit of those Christians living after 70 C.E. Notice, for example, Matthew's reference to Daniel in 24:15: Jesus tells his listeners that when they see the abomination of the temple of which Daniel spoke, they should flee into the mountains to prepare for the end. But we know today that Daniel was speaking of the desecration of the temple by Antiochus IV in 168 B.C.E. Matthew, unaware of the historical context of Daniel and writing after the Roman destruction of the temple in 70 C.E., believed that Roman destruction was the event Daniel was predicting. So Matthew updates the message of Jesus for future generations by including the temple desecration for the readers of his gospel ("whoso readeth, let him understand"). This is one of the ways we know that Matthew was written after 70 C.E. Jesus would not have referred to an event which was for his audience forty years into the future, and expect his audience to understand his reference. In addition to the Daniel reference, which parts of this selection would most likely have been updated by Matthew? Which quotations of Jesus were apt to need updating?

Matthew

Chapter 24

1 And Jesus went out, and departed from the temple: and his disciples came to him for to show him the buildings of the temple. 2 And Jesus said unto them, See ye not all these things? verily I say unto You, There shall not be left here one stone upon another, that shall not be thrown down. 3 And as he sat upon the Mount of Olives, the disciples came unto him privately, saying, Tell us, when shall these things be? and what shall be the sign of thy coming, and of the end of the world?

4 And Jesus answered and said unto them, Take heed that no man deceive you. 5 For many shall come in my name, saying, I am Christ; and shall deceive many. 6 And ye shall hear of wars and rumors of wars: see that ye be not troubled: for all these things must come to pass, but the end is not yet. 7 For nation shall rise against nation, and kingdom against kingdom: and there shall be famines, and pestilences, and earthquakes, in divers places. 8 All these are the beginning of sorrows. 9 Then shall they deliver you up to be afflicted, and shall kill you: and ye shall be hated of all nations for my name's sake. 10 And then shall many be offended, and shall betray one another, and shall hate one another. 11 And many false prophets shall rise, and shall deceive many. 12 And because iniquity shall abound, the love of many shall wax cold. 13 But he that shall endure unto the end, the same shall be saved. 14 And this gospel of the kingdom shall be preached in all the world for a witness unto all nations; and then shall the end come.

15 When ye therefore shall see the abomination of desolation, spoken of by Daniel the prophet, stand in the holy place (whoso readeth, let him understand), 16 Then let them which be in Judea flee into the mountains: 17 Let him which is on the housetop not come down to take any thing out of his house: 18 Neither let him which is in the field return back to take his clothes. 19 And woe unto them that are with child, and to them that give suck in those days! 20 But pray ye that your flight be not in the winter, neither on the sabbath day: 21 For then shall be great tribulation, such as was not since the beginning of the world to this time, no, nor ever shall be. 22 And except those days should be shortened, there should no flesh be saved: but for the elect's sake those days shall be shortened. 23 Then if any man shall say unto you, Lo, here is Christ, or there; believe it not. 24 For there shall arise false Christs, and false prophets, and shall show great signs and wonders; insomuch that, if it were possible, they shall deceive the very elect. 25 Behold, I have told you before. 26 Wherefore if they shall say unto you, Behold, he is in the desert; go not forth: behold he is in the secret chambers; believe it not. 27 For as the lightning cometh out of the east, and shineth even unto the west; so shall also the coming of the Son of man be. 28 For wheresoever the carcass is, there will the eagles be gathered together.

29 Immediately after the tribulation of those days shall the sun be darkened, and the moon shall not give her light, and the stars shall fall from heaven, and the powers of the heavens shall be shaken: 30 And then shall appear the sign of the Son of man in heaven: and then shall all the tribes of the earth mourn, and they shall see the Son of man coming in the clouds of heaven with power and great glory. 31 And he shall send his angels with a great sound of a trumpet, and they shall gather together his elect from the four winds, from one end of heaven to the other. 32 Now learn a parable of the fig tree; When his branch

is yet tender, and putteth forth leaves, ye know that summer is nigh: 33 So likewise ye, when ye shall see all these things, know that it is near, even at the doors. 34 Verily I say unto you, This generation shall not pass, till all these things be fulfilled. 35 Heaven and earth shall pass away, but my words shall not pass away.

36 But of that day and hour knoweth no man, no, not the angels of heaven, but my Father only. 37 But as the days of Noe [Noah] were, so shall also the coming of the Son of man be. 38 For as in the days that were before the flood they were eating and drinking, marrying and giving in marriage, until the day that Noe entered into the ark, 39 And knew not until the flood came, and took them all away; so shall also the coming of the Son of man be. 40 Then shall two be in the field; the one shall be taken, and the other left. 41 Two women shall be grinding at the mill; the one shall be taken, and the other left.

REFLECTIONS

The layers of revision are etched more sharply in Daniel and Matthew than in the Hindu and Buddhist documents because dates, chronology, and time sequences were far more important to the Judeo-Christian tradition. It was, and is, a tradition committed to the belief that God works in time; that there is a beginning, middle, and end to things; and that it is crucially important for humans to know where they are in the providential timeline. A modern skeptic might be bothered by the way the author or authors of Daniel turn history into prophecy. But for the Jews of the 160s B.C.E., the need to get the dates right and be ready for the end of days was far more important than checking who predicted what when.

Ironically, the precise prophecy of Daniel transcended its historical moorings when it was used by the author of Matthew in an effort to update the prophecy of Jesus, and it has been used regularly by every generation since with a different "king of the south" and new supporting cast. But if the Judeo-Christian tradition has left a legacy of apocalyptic warnings and millennial musings, it has also given us the interest and the tools that have shaped this chapter. The need to date, to find the actual words, to peel away the layers of rust that obfuscate an authentic past — that is a fine legacy indeed.

We have seen how Hinduism produced Buddhism and how Judaism generated Christianity, but neither Hinduism nor Judaism ended two thousand years ago. In fact, both "parental" religions underwent profound changes as well. Both became more universal, less dependent on particular places or people, and less limited to caste, region, or tribe.

We saw in the Upanishads how, around 500 B.C.E., Hinduism became almost monotheistic in its worship of Brahman. Similarly, about three hundred years later, Hindu devotional cults that centered on two of the other deities of the Hindu pantheon (Vishnu — especially in his incarnation as Krishna — and Shiva) developed. Reread the last eight stanzas of selection 14 from the *Bhagavad Gita* (written about 200 B.C.E.) to see how the worship of Vishnu/Krishna became enormously appealing to masses of Indian people.

At about the time of Jesus, Judaism also underwent a transformation that has continued until this day. A process that began with the destruction of the first temple and the captivity in Babylon in the sixth century B.C.E. — the development of a Judaism independent of a particular temple or place — was revived after the Romans destroyed the second temple in 70 C.E. The Roman conquest created a much greater diaspora (migration or dispersal) of Jews throughout the world than what the Babylonian conquest had spawned. Among new exiles throughout the world, Judaism became a religion of rabbis (teachers) rather than of temple priests. So great was this transformation of Judaism that one might argue, with Alan Segal in *Rebecca's Children,* that "the time of Jesus marks the birth of not one but two great religions in the West, Judaism and Christianity. . . . So great is the contrast between previous Jewish religious systems and rabbinism."[1]

And yet neither Judaism nor Hinduism became missionary religions; neither sought converts aggressively. Christianity and Buddhism did, however, and that is the subject of the next chapter.

---

[1]Alan F. Segal, *Rebecca's Children: Judaism and Christianity in the Roman World* (Cambridge: Harvard University Press, 1986), 1.

7

Encounters and Conversions: Monks, Merchants, and Monarchs

*Expansion of Salvation Religions,
400 B.C.E.–1400 C.E.*

HISTORICAL CONTEXT

From their beginnings, Buddhism and Christianity were less tribal and more universal than their parental religions, Hinduism and Judaism, because they offered universal salvation to their followers. The teachings of Jesus and the Buddha emphasized personal religious experience over the dictates of caste, ancestry, and formal law, making their ideas more likely to spread beyond their cultures of origin. Both religions, however, had relatively small followings at the deaths of their founders. How, then, did they win millions of converts within the next few hundred years? Similarly, how did Islam, founded in 622 C.E., spread from the Arabian peninsula to embrace the Berbers of North Africa, the Visigoths of Spain, Syrians, Persians, Turks, Central Asians, Indians, and even the western Chinese by 750 C.E.? What was happening throughout Eurasia that explained these successes? In this chapter we explore how both an array of powerful and charismatic individuals—religious figures, political leaders, and even merchants and traders—and specific economic, political, and social conditions helped to broaden the appeal of the salvation religions and find larger audiences for their gospels.

Religious thinkers loosened the new religions from their parental ties, often changing them as they spread them. St. Paul almost single-handedly separated Jesus from his Jewish roots, presenting him as the Son of God who was sacrificed for the sins of humankind, not just the

Jewish people. Similarly, Mahayana Buddhists taught that Buddha was more than a teacher and spiritual guide whom one could imitate; he was a savior, responsive to prayer and worship. Sufi shaykhs spread Islam in remote rural areas by incorporating local beliefs and practices into Islamic teachings.

Religious leaders weren't the only ones spreading faith; merchants and traders also played a crucial role. The spread of universal faiths and common cultures over great distances owed much to the roads and maritime transport of the Roman and Chinese empires, as well as the Persian, central Asian, and Indian states in between. But it was also a product of the Silk Road, or roads, that connected China with Rome after 100 B.C.E. (see Map 7.1, p. 223). The expansion of the great religious traditions was the work of merchants as well as monks; gods traveled in camel caravans, and holy images were carried on rolls of silk.

Contact alone, however, is not enough to explain why people converted to Christianity, Buddhism, and Islam. The appeals to salvation beyond this world testified to difficult times. Nomadic pastoral peoples undermined the stability of empires already weakened by public debt, class antagonisms, dwindling crop yields, and disease. Populations declined from 200–800 C.E. and did not reach earlier levels again until about 1000 C.E. in Europe and China. People sought spiritual reassurance as well as economic alliances that would protect them in uncertain times. When those in power adopted new religions, it often benefited others to follow their lead, securing a network of influence for new religious movements.

THINKING HISTORICALLY
Studying Religion in Historic Context

In the previous chapter we looked for evidence of change in primary religious documents. In this chapter we take the historical study of religion a step further by examining how religions developed in the larger historical context of political, economic, and social change. Religions evolve not only according to an inner theological dynamic but also in response to changes within the broader society. Our study of the expansion of Buddhism, Christianity, and Islam provides a particularly useful set of questions about the relationship of religion to other historical forces. When we ask how these great salvation religions spread, we must consider how religious ideas are different from other ideas. How are such ideas affected by political, social, and economic forces, and how are these forces affected by religious ideas?

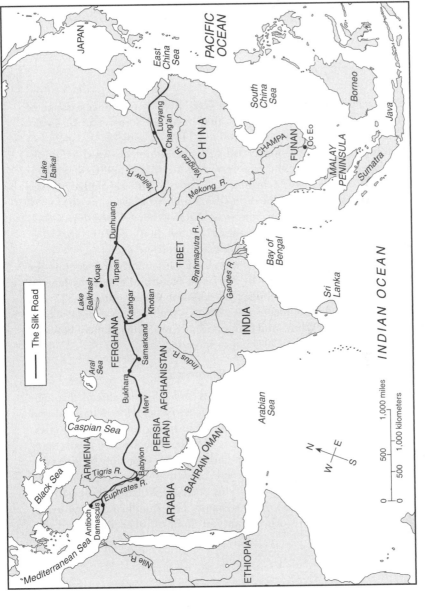

Map 7.1 The Silk Road.

37

JERRY H. BENTLEY

The Spread of World Religions

In this selection, modern historian Jerry Bentley examines a range of cultural and religious encounters that occurred across Eurasia in the period between 400 B.C.E. and 400 C.E. He first explores the spread of Buddhism from India northward to China and southward to Southeast Asia, highlighting the importance of merchants and trade in seeding new conversions. According to Bentley, what accounted for the initial resistance to Buddhism in China and the resounding success of Indian ideas and faiths in Southeast Asia? What relationships developed between religious and political leaders that aided the spread of Buddhism? Where do you see instances of cultural exchange?

Bentley then examines the spread of Christianity throughout the Roman Empire, from its rocky start as a faction of rebellious Jews to its eventual legalization under the emperor Constantine in 313 C.E. What specific developments does Bentley highlight to explain Christianity's success? What similarities and differences were there between the way Buddhism and Christianity spread?

Thinking Historically

In addition to describing *how* cultures and religions spread throughout Eurasia during this period, Bentley also asks *why*. What makes a people convert to a "foreign" religion? In trying to answer this question, he distinguishes three patterns of religious conversion: voluntary association, syncretism, or assimilation, and conversion by pressure. Obviously, these categories overlap, and it is often difficult to tell whether a conversion is voluntary or coerced. Which of these patterns best describes the spread of Christianity and Buddhism? How useful do you find these categories? Can you think of other patterns of religious conversion?

. . . Buddhism benefited enormously from the commercial traffic that crossed the silk roads. Once it arrived on the trade routes, Buddhism

Jerry H. Bentley, *Old World Encounters: Cross-Cultural Contacts and Exchanges in Pre-Modern Times* (Oxford: Oxford University Press, 1993), 47–53, 60–64.

found its way very quickly indeed to distant lands. Merchants proved to be an efficient vector of the Buddhist faith, as they established diaspora communities in the string of oasis towns—Merv, Bukhara, Samarkand, Kashgar, Khotan, Kuqa, Turpan, Dunhuang—that served as lifeline of the silk roads through central Asia. (See Map 7.1.) The oases depended heavily on trade for their economic survival, and they quickly accommodated the needs and interests of the merchants whom they hosted. They became centers of high literacy and culture; they organized markets and arranged for lodging, care of animals, and storage of merchandise; and they allowed their guests to build monasteries and bring large contingents of Buddhist monks and copyists into their communities. Before too long—perhaps as early as the first or even the second century B.C.E.—the oasis dwellers themselves converted to Buddhism.

Thus a process of conversion through voluntary association with well-organized foreigners underwrote the first major expansion of Buddhism outside India. Buddhist merchants linked the oases to a large and cosmopolitan world, and the oases became enormously wealthy by providing useful services for the merchants. It is not at all surprising that inhabitants of the small oasis communities would gradually incline toward the beliefs and values of the numerous Buddhist merchants who traveled the silk roads and enriched the oases.

Once established in oasis communities, Buddhism had the potential to spread both to nomadic peoples on the steppes of central Asia and even to China, a land of long-settled civilization with its own long-established cultural traditions. Buddhism realized this potential only partially, however, and only in gradual fashion. As a faith foreign to China and generally despised by Chinese during its early centuries there, Buddhism had a certain attraction for nomadic peoples who themselves had quite difficult relations with the Chinese. In other words, Buddhism exercised a kind of countercultural appeal to nomads who loathed the Chinese, but who also desired and even depended upon trade with China. Yet many nomadic peoples found it difficult to accept Buddhism; they did not have traditions of literacy to accommodate Buddhist moral and theological teachings, and their mobility made it impossible to maintain fixed monastic communities. As a result, many nomadic peoples held to their native shamanist cults, and others turned to Manichaeism[1] or Nestorian Christianity.[2] Meanwhile, some of those

---

[1]man ih KEE ih zuhm   Third-century Persian religion; belief that the body is trapped in darkness searching for the light. [Ed.]

[2]Fifth-century Syrian faith that spread to India, central Asia, and China; belief in the human nature of Jesus. [Ed.]

who adopted Buddhism did so at a very late date. Among the Mongols, for example, Buddhism did not become a popular faith until the sixteenth century. When nomadic peoples became involved in commerce, however, or when they established themselves as rulers of settled lands that they conquered, they frequently adopted Buddhism through a process of conversion through voluntary association. These patterns were quite prominent in central Asia and northern China during the era of the ancient silk roads.

The career of the monk and missionary Fotudeng especially helps to illuminate the voluntary conversion of nomadic peoples to Buddhism. Fotudeng probably came from Kuqa, an oasis town on the Silk Road in modern Xinjiang. He became a priest at an early age, traveled through central Asia, visited Kashmir, and set out to do missionary work in northern China during the early fourth century. He went to Dunhuang in order to improve his Chinese, then continued on to Luoyang about the year 310. There he caught the attention of Shi Le, the ruler of the nomadic Jie people (western allies of the Xiongnu), who controlled most of northern China during the fourth century. Fotudeng realized early on that he would not get very far with Shi Le by lecturing him on fine points of Buddhist philosophy, but he had a reputation for working miracles, which he used to the advantage of his mission. He dazzled Shi Le by producing bright blue lotus blossoms from his monk's begging bowl and by looking into his palm to see the reflection of distant events. Among his more utilitarian talents were rainmaking, healing, and prophecy. Fotudeng helped Shi Le plan military campaigns by foreseeing the outcome and devising clever strategies to ensure success. As a result of his miraculous talents, Fotudeng won widespread fame, and people from distant regions worshipped him. When he died about the year 345, he reportedly had ten thousand disciples and the erection of 893 temples to his credit.

Thus did a process of voluntary conversion help to establish Buddhism in northern China. The nomadic Jie settled in northern China and became deeply engaged in the political and economic affairs of a large and complex world. Fotudeng represented the culture of that larger world and brought talents useful for Jie rulers as they entered its life. He parlayed his personal relationship with Shi Le into official approval for his efforts to spread Buddhist values and even to found Buddhist institutions in northern China. Hence, his work not only illuminates the voluntary conversion of nomadic peoples but also helps to explain the early presence of the Buddhist faith in China.

The establishment of Buddhism in China was an even more difficult and gradual affair than its spread among nomadic peoples. Indeed, it required half a millennium for Buddhism to attract a large popular following in China. There as in Persia, the foreign faith could not immediately attract many followers away from indigenous cultural traditions, in this case principally Confucianism and Daoism. Even in its early years in China, Buddhism encountered determined resistance from Confucian and Daoist quarters. Representatives of the native Chinese traditions charged that Buddhism detracted from the authority of the state, that monasteries were unproductive and useless drags on the economy, that Buddhism itself was a barbarian faith inferior to Chinese traditions, and that the monastic life violated the natural order of society and disrupted family life. Not surprisingly, then, during its early centuries in China, Buddhism remained largely the faith of foreigners: merchants, ambassadors, refugees, hostages, and missionaries. . . .

As an alien cultural tradition that did not resonate in China, Buddhism could easily have experienced the same fate there that it did in Persia: It could have survived in the quarters inhabited by foreign merchants as an expatriate faith, perhaps even for centuries, without attracting much interest from the larger host community. The explanation for Buddhism's remarkable spread as a popular faith in east Asia begins with the voluntary conversion of elites, which enabled the foreign tradition to gain a foothold in Chinese society. In the north, where Buddhism first established its presence in China, voluntary conversion reflected the political interests of ruling elites. In most cases they were nomads, such as the Jie whom Fotudeng served so well, or the Toba rulers of the Northern Wei dynasty (386–534). After an initial period of tension and uncertain relations, it dawned on both Buddhists and rulers that an alliance could serve the interests of both parties. Buddhist monasteries provided ideological and economic support for established ruling houses: They recognized the legitimacy of the Jie and Toba rule; they facilitated long-distance trade, which figured prominently in the local economy; and they served as a conduit for the importation of exotic and luxury goods that symbolized the special status of the ruling elites. Meanwhile, the dynasties patronized the Buddhists in return, participated in their rituals, and protected the interests of their monasteries.

Like the oasis dwellers of central Asia, then, the ruling elites of northern China made common cause with representatives of a foreign cultural tradition who had extensive political and commercial links in the larger world. This sort of voluntary conversion was the only way by which Buddhism could find a place in Chinese society. Buddhists entered China in numbers too small to bring about a massive social transformation by way of pressure or assimilation. Only by winning the favor and protection of elites could the early Buddhists ensure their survival in China. . . .

Meanwhile, as Buddhism found tentative footing in China, both Buddhism and Hinduism attracted the attention of elites and won converts in southeast Asia. As in China, the carriers of Indian cultural traditions were mostly merchants. During the late centuries B.C.E., Indian traders began to sail the seas and visit the coastal towns of southeast Asia. Even during those remote centuries, there was considerable incentive for merchants to embark upon long and often dangerous voyages. According to an ancient Gujarati story, for example, men who went to Java never returned—but if by chance they did return, they brought with them wealth enough to provide for seven generations. By the early centuries C.E., southeast Asian mariners themselves traveled to India as well as to other southeast Asian sites. The resulting networks of trade and communication invigorated not only the economic but also the political and cultural life of southeast Asia.

Among the principal beneficiaries of early trade between India and southeast Asia were the political and cultural traditions of India. Merchants from the subcontinent established diaspora communities, into which they invited Hindu and Buddhist authorities. Local chiefs controlled commerce at the trading sites they ruled, and they quickly became introduced to the larger world of the Indian Ocean. The ruler of an important trading site was no longer a "frog under a coconut shell," as the Malay proverb has it, but, rather, a cultural and commercial broker of some moment. Trade and external alliances enabled local rulers to organize states on a larger scale than ever before in southeast Asia. The first of these well represented in historical sources—though by no means the only early state in southeast Asia—was Funan, founded along the Mekong River in the first century C.E. Through its main port, Oc Eo, Funan carried on trade with China, Malaya, Indonesia, India, Persia, and indirectly with Mediterranean lands. By the end of the second century, similar trading states had appeared in the Malay peninsula and Champa (southern Vietnam).

Indian influence ran so deep in these states that they and their successors for a millennium and more are commonly referred to as the "Indianized states of southeast Asia." Indian traditions manifested their influence in many different ways. In a land previously governed by charismatic individuals of great personal influence, for example, rulers adopted Indian notions of divine kingship. They associated themselves with the cults of Siva, Visnu, or the Buddha, and they claimed both foreign and divine authority to legitimize their rule. They built walled cities with temples at the center, and they introduced Indian music and ceremonies into court rituals. They brought in Hindu and Buddhist advisers, who reinforced the sense of divinely sanctioned rule. They took Sanskrit names and titles for themselves, and they used Sanskrit as the language of law and bureaucracy. Indian influence was so extensive, in fact, that an earlier generation of historians suggested that vast armadas of Indians had colonized southeast Asia—a view now regarded as complete fiction. More recent explanations of the Indianization process place more emphasis on southeast Asian elites who for their own purposes associated themselves as closely as possible with the

Hindu and Buddhist traditions. They certainly found no lack of willing and talented tutors; the quality of Sanskrit literature produced in southeast Asia argues for the presence there of many sophisticated and well-educated representatives of Indian cultural traditions. But high interest in foreign traditions on the part of southeast Asian elites drove the process of Indianization.

By no means did indigenous cultures fade away or disappear. During the early years after their arrival in southeast Asia, Indian traditions worked their influence mostly at the courts of ruling elites, and not much beyond. Over a longer term, however, Indian and native traditions combined to fashion syncretic cultural configurations and to bring about social conversion on a large scale. . . . In any case, though, the voluntary conversion of local elites to Hinduism and Buddhism decisively shaped the cultural development of southeast Asia.

. . .

Of all the religions that established themselves in the Roman empire, . . . none succeeded on such a large scale or over such a long term as Christianity. (See Map 7.2.) Its early experience thus calls for some discussion.

Christianity had many things in common with other religions that became widely popular in the Roman empire. It offered an explanation of the world and the cosmic order, one that endowed history with a sense of purpose and human life with meaning. It addressed the needs and interests of individuals by holding out the prospect of personal immortality, salvation, and perpetual enjoyment of a paradisiacal existence. It established high standards of ethics and morality, well suited to the needs of a complex, interdependent, and cosmopolitan world where peoples of different races and religions intermingled on a systematic basis. It was a religion of the cities, efficiently disseminated throughout the empire along established routes of trade and communication. It welcomed into its ranks the untutored and unsophisticated as well as the more privileged classes. It even shared with the other religions several of its ritual elements, such as baptism and the community meal. In many ways, then, early Christianity reflected the larger cultural world of the early Roman empire.

During its first three centuries, Christianity developed under a serious political handicap. The earliest Christians were associated with parties of rebellious Jews who resisted Roman administration in Palestine. Later Christians, even gentiles, refused to honor the Roman emperor and state in the fashion deemed appropriate by imperial authorities. As a result, Christians endured not only social contempt and scorn but also organized campaigns of persecution. Meanwhile, the Roman state generously patronized many of the empire's pagan cults: in exchange for public honor and recognition, the emperors and other

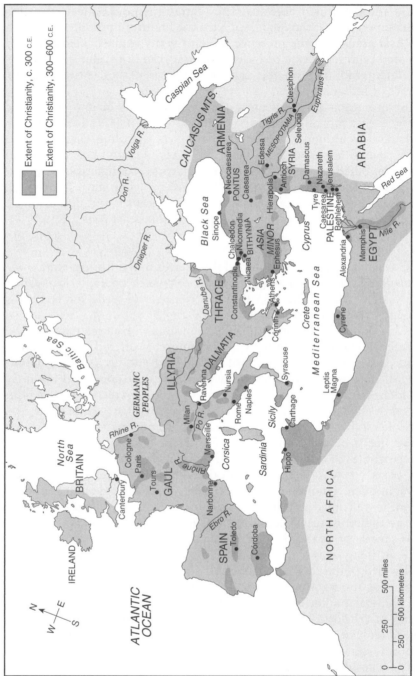

Map 7.2 The Spread of Christianity, 300–600 C.E.

important political figures provided financial sponsorship for rituals, festivals, and other pagan activities.

Nevertheless, Christianity benefited from the work of zealous missionaries who were able to persuade individuals and small groups that the Christians' god possessed awesome and unique powers. They communicated this message most effectively among the popular masses by acquiring a reputation for the working of miracles—healing illnesses, casting out demons, bestowing blessings on the faithful—that demonstrated the powers at their god's disposal. [Historian] Ramsay MacMullen has recently argued, in fact, that fear of pain and punishment, desire for blessings, and belief in miracles were the principal inducements that attracted pagans to Christianity in the period before the conversion of Constantine about the year 312 C.E.

A bit of information survives on one of the more effective of the early Christian missionaries, Gregory the Wonderworker, and it illustrates the importance of miracles for the building of the early Christian community. Gregory had studied with the great Origen,[3] and he wrote several formal theological treatises. For present purposes, though, his significance arises from his work in the Roman province of Pontus (north central Anatolia) during the 240s. Early accounts of his mission record one miracle after another. Gregory's prayers prevented a pagan deity from exercising his powers, but upon request Gregory summoned the deity to his pagan temple, thus demonstrating his superior authority; as a result, the caretaker of the temple converted to Christianity. On several occasions individuals interrupted Gregory's public teaching; each time, Gregory exorcized a demon from the offensive party, provoking widespread amazement and winning converts in the process. Gregory moved boulders, diverted a river in flood, and dried up an inconveniently located lake. By the end of his campaign, Gregory had brought almost every soul of the town of Neocaesarea into the ranks of the Christians, and surrounding communities soon joined the bandwagon. As in the case of Fotudeng in north China, Gregory's reputation as a miracle worker seized the attention of his audiences and helped him to promote his faith among pagans.

Did the conversions brought about by Christian miracle workers represent cases of conversion through voluntary association? To some extent, this interpretation seems plausible, in that converts voluntarily adopted Christianity as the cultural alternative that best reflected the realities of the larger world—for example by offering access to powers not available to others. A reputation for the ability to work miracles helped missionaries to dramatize the benefits and blessings that Christianity promised to individuals and suggested that Christianity possessed

[3]Biblical scholar and Christian theologian, c. 185–254. [Ed.]

an unusually effective capacity to explain and control the world. In other ways, however, the winning of early Christian converts differed from the more common pattern of conversion through voluntary association. Converts came from all ranks of society, not just those of merchants, rulers, and others who had extensive dealings with representatives from the larger world. Moreover, until the conversion of the emperor Constantine and the legalization of Christianity, there were some powerful disincentives to conversion, so that potential converts to the new faith had to weigh heavy political, social, and economic risks against the personal and spiritual benefits offered by Christianity.

On balance, then, it seems to me that the category of conversion through voluntary association helps at least in a limited way to explain the early spread of Christianity in the Mediterranean basin. From the viewpoint of Roman society as a whole, however, rather than that of individual citizens, early conversion to Christianity benefited especially from two additional developments that accompanied the process of conversion through voluntary association. In the first place, until the fourth century, Christianity spread largely through a process of syncretism. In the second place, following the conversion of Constantine, Christianity gained state sponsorship, and a process of conversion by political, social, and economic pressure consolidated the new faith as a securely institutionalized church. Both of these developments warrant some attention.

The decline of long-established pagan cults afforded an opportunity for Christianity to extend its influence by way of syncretism. Beginning in the third century, the pagan cults suffered progressively more difficult financial problems as the Roman economy went into serious decline. The Roman state could no longer afford to support the cults on the generous basis of centuries past. Wealthy individuals continued to provide a great deal of aid, but their sponsorship was more erratic and precarious than that of the state.

As the pagan cults failed to provide for the needs and interests of their followers, Christianity offered a meaningful alternative that was the more acceptable for its resemblance to the cults. In their rituals and their assumptions about the natural world, the early Christians very much reflected the larger culture of the late Roman empire. Like devotees of the pagan cults, they offered their sacraments as great mysteries, and there were pagan analogues to many of their rituals, such as the intonation of divine language, the use of special garments and paraphernalia, and even the observance of ceremonies like baptism and a community meal open only to initiates. Christians appropriated the power and authority associated with pagan heroes by emphasizing the virtues of a saint or martyr with similar attributes. Eventually, Christians even baptized pagan philosophy and festivals, which served as new links between pagan and Christian cultures: St. Augustine transformed Neoplatonism into a powerful Christian philosophy, and the birthdate of the unconquered pagan sun god became Christmas, the birthdate also of Jesus. Thus from a very early date, Christianity appealed to Mediterranean peoples partly because of its syncretic capacity: It came in familiar dress, and it dealt with many of the same concerns addressed by the pagan cults.

The conversion of Constantine amplified the effects of syncretism by inaugurating a process of officially sponsored conversion that ultimately resulted in the cultural transformation of the entire Roman empire. Constantine favored Christians from the moment that he consolidated his hold on the imperial throne. In the year 313 he issued his famous edict of toleration, which for the first time recognized Christianity as a legal religion in the Roman empire. At some indeterminate point, Constantine himself converted to Christianity. Constantine's personal example of course did not lead to immediate Christianization of the Roman empire, or even of the army that the emperor directly supervised. In several ways, though, it brought long-term changes that favored the Christians' efforts. It brought immediate material benefits, as Constantine and his successors underwrote the construction of churches and showered Christians with financial support. It also brought an intangible but nonetheless important social benefit: Christianity gained more public respect than it had ever previously enjoyed. As a result, ambitious and reputable individuals of increasing prominence joined Christian ranks—especially because Christians received preferential consideration for high imperial posts. Finally, the legalization of their religion allowed Christians to promote their faith more publicly and more aggressively than ever before. From its earliest days, the Christian community had produced combative and confrontational spokesmen. After Constantine's edict of toleration allowed Christians to promote their faith publicly, they relentlessly attacked the pagan cults, sometimes sparking episodes of personal violence, forcible conversion of individuals, and destruction of pagan temples and images.

State sponsorship provided Christianity with the material and political support required to bring about social conversion on a large scale. Christianity quickly became the official and only legally tolerated religion of the Roman empire: Already by the late fourth century, the emperors had begun to prohibit observance of pagan cults. By no means, however, did the various pagan religions forfeit their claims to cultural allegiance. Pagan spokesmen resisted efforts to destroy their cults, and thanks to syncretism, their values and rituals to some extent survived in Christian dress. Nevertheless, by the late fourth century, Christianity had won a cultural and institutional initiative over paganism that it would never relinquish. . . .

38

Pliny Consults the Emperor Trajan

The inhabitants of an average city of the ancient Mediterranean worshiped dozens of gods, though usually one was thought to be a special guardian of the populace and a protector of the state. Cities of the Roman Empire added deities and cults from conquered and distant territories, creating a bewildering array. General tolerance prevailed. No one cared which gods an individual worshiped. Only Rome, as the capital of the empire, might require worship of a state god, including, at times, the emperor himself. But aside from this matter of loyalty to the state, one's religious convictions were one's own affair.

Christians ran afoul of the law and practice not only by refusing the demonstration of loyalty to the state but also by aggressively denying the validity of all other gods — an attitude that many found distasteful.

Like the Jews, Christians were alternately persecuted and ignored. Roman oppression broke out when Nero blamed Christians for the great fire in Rome in 64 C.E. but then abated under the moderate rule of Trajan.

A brief correspondence between Pliny,* serving as governor of Bithynia (in modern Turkey), and the Emperor Trajan† from about the year 111 C.E. has survived, throwing light on official Roman policy toward Christians of that era. What does Pliny's letter to Trajan tell you about official Roman policy? What do you think of Trajan's answer?

Thinking Historically

Pliny is enforcing policy while at the same time he is personally repelled by the Christians. Try to distinguish these elements in Pliny's mind. What does he see as their legal guilt, and what does he find personally distasteful? How do you explain Pliny's confusion about whether he should punish former Christians? What does Pliny know about the Christians?

Pliny mentions that some of the accused Christians admitted that they had been Christians but were no longer. Were they telling the truth? What do you think?

*PLIH nee
†TRAY juhn

Pliny, Letters 10:96–97, in *Pliny Secundus: Letters and Panegyricus,* Loeb Classical Library, vol. II, trans. Betty Radice (Cambridge: Harvard University Press, 1959), 285, 287, 289, 291, 293.

Pliny to the Emperor Trajan

It is my custom to refer all my difficulties to you, Sir, for no one is better able to resolve my doubts and to inform my ignorance.

I have never been present at an examination of Christians. Consequently, I do not know the nature or the extent of the punishments usually meted out to them, nor the grounds for starting an investigation and how far it should be pressed. Nor am I at all sure whether any distinction should be made between them on the grounds of age, or if young people and adults should be treated alike; whether a pardon ought to be granted to anyone retracting his beliefs, or if he has once professed Christianity, he shall gain nothing by renouncing it; and whether it is the mere name of Christian which is punishable, even if innocent of crime, or rather the crimes associated with the name.

For the moment this is the line I have taken with all persons brought before me on the charge of being Christians. I have asked them in person if they are Christians, and if they admit it, I repeat the question a second and third time, with a warning of the punishment awaiting them. If they persist, I order them to be led away for execution; for, whatever the nature of their admission, I am convinced that their stubbornness and unshakeable obstinacy ought not to go unpunished. There have been others similarly fanatical who are Roman citizens. I have entered them on the list of persons to be sent to Rome for trial.

Now that I have begun to deal with this problem, as so often happens, the charges are becoming more widespread and increasing in variety. An anonymous pamphlet has been circulated which contains the names of a number of accused persons. Among these I considered that I should dismiss any who denied that they were or ever had been Christians when they had repeated after me a formula of invocation to the gods and had made offerings of wine and incense to your statue (which I had ordered to be brought into court for this purpose along with the images of the gods), and furthermore had reviled the name of Christ: none of which things, I understand, any genuine Christian can be induced to do.

Others, whose names were given to me by an informer, first admitted the charge and then denied it; they said that they had ceased to be Christians two or more years previously, and some of them even twenty years ago. They all did reverence to your statue and the images of the gods in the same way as the others, and reviled the name of Christ. They also declared that the sum total of their guilt or error amounted to no more than this: They had met regularly before dawn on a fixed day to chant verses alternately among themselves in honour of Christ as if to a god, and also to bind themselves by oath, not for any criminal purpose, but to abstain from theft, robbery and adultery, to commit no breach of trust and not to deny a deposit when called upon to restore it. After this ceremony it had been their custom to disperse and re-assemble later to take food of an ordinary, harmless kind; but they had in fact given up this practice since my edict, issued on your instructions, which banned all political societies. This made me decide it was all the more necessary to extract the truth by torture from two slave-women, whom they call deaconesses. I found nothing but a degenerate sort of cult carried to extravagant lengths.

I have therefore postponed any further examination and hastened to consult you. The question seems to me to be worthy of your consideration, especially in view of the number of persons endangered; for a great many individuals of every age and class, both men and women, are being brought to trial, and this is likely to continue. It is not only the towns, but villages and rural districts too which are infected through contact with this wretched cult. I think though that it is still possible for it to be checked and directed to better ends, for there is no doubt that people have begun to throng the temples which had been almost entirely deserted for a long time; the sacred rites which had been allowed to lapse are being performed again, and flesh of sacrificial victims is on sale everywhere, though up till recently scarcely anyone could be found to buy it. It is easy to infer from this that a great many people could be reformed if they were given an opportunity to repent.

Trajan to Pliny

You have followed the right course of procedure, my dear Pliny, in your examination of the cases of persons charged with being Christians, for it is impossible to lay down a general rule to a fixed formula. These people must not be hunted out; if they are brought before you and the charge against them is proved, they must be punished, but in the case of anyone who denies that he is a Christian, and makes it clear that he is not by offering prayers to our gods, he is to be pardoned as a result of his repentance however suspect his past conduct may be. But pamphlets circulated anonymously must play no part in any accusation. They create the worst sort of precedent and are quite out of keeping with the spirit of our age.

39

EUSEBIUS

From Life of Constantine

If Christians were persecuted by Roman officials and emperors, and despised by the thoughtful and powerful elite of Roman society, how then did Christianity ever succeed?

Part of the answer lies in the location of these Christians. They were more concentrated in urban than rural areas (the Latin word *pagan* meant "rural" before it meant "unchristian") and managed to gain significant advocates among the powerful elite.

No more powerful spokesman could be found than a Roman emperor, and so a short answer to the question of how Christianity succeeded must be "the Emperor Constantine" (288–337 C.E.). The emperor's historian Eusebius* (260–339 C.E.) recognized both the importance of the emperor and the role of the empire in the success of Christianity in winning the Roman Empire:

> At the same time one universal power, the Roman Empire arose and flourished, while the enduring and implacable hatred of nation against nation was now removed; and as the knowledge of one god and one way of religion and salvation, even the doctrine of Christ, was made known to all mankind; so at the same time the entire dominion of the Roman Empire being invested in a single sovereign, profound peace reigned throughout the world. And thus, by the express appointment of the same God, two roots of blessing, the Roman Empire and the doctrine of Christian piety, sprang up together for the benefit of men.[1]

In 312 C.E., Constantine, who ruled Gaul and Britain, was about to invade Italy and try to gain the throne of the western empire by defeating Maxentius, who ruled Rome. In his *Life of Constantine,* Eusebius, who knew the emperor, tells a story that must have circulated at the time to explain Constantine's support of Christianity.

---

*yoo SAY bee uhs
[1]Eusebius, *Oration in Praise of Constantine,* xv, 4. [Ed.]

P. Schaff and H. Wace, eds. *The Library of Nicene and Post-Nicene Fathers,* vol. I, *Church History, Life of Constantine, Oration in Praise of Constantine* (New York: The Christian Literature Company, 1890), 489–91.

Thinking Historically

What do you think of Eusebius's explanation for Constantine's acceptance of Christianity? What does Constantine's reasoning say about how people of his day chose their religious beliefs and loyalties? How would the conversion of the emperor encourage others to become Christians? What, if anything, might have slowed the advance of Christianity after 312 c.e.?

Being convinced, however, that he needed some more powerful aid than his military forces could afford him, on account of the wicked and magical enchantments which were so diligently practiced by the tyrant [Maxentius], he sought Divine assistance, deeming the possession of arms and a numerous soldiery of secondary importance, but believing the cooperating power of Deity invincible and not to be shaken. He considered, therefore, on what God he might rely for protection and assistance. While engaged in this enquiry, the thought occurred to him, that, of the many emperors who had preceded him, those who had rested their hopes in a multitude of gods, and served them with sacrifices and offerings, had in the first place been deceived by flattering predictions, and oracles which promised them all prosperity, and at last had met with an unhappy end, while not one of their gods had stood by to warn them of the impending wrath of heaven; while one alone who had pursued an entirely opposite course, who had condemned their error, and honored the Supreme God during his whole life, had found him to be the Saviour and Protector of his empire, and the Giver of every good thing. Reflecting on this, and well weighing the fact that they who had trusted in many gods had also fallen by manifold forms of death, without leaving behind them either family or offspring, stock, name, or memorial among men: while the God of his father had given to him, on the other hand, manifestations of his power and very many tokens: and considering farther that those who had already taken arms against the tyrant, and had marched to the battle-field under the protection of a multitude of gods, had met with a dishonorable end (for one of them had shamefully retreated from the contest without a blow, and the other, being slain in the midst of his own troops, became, as it were, the mere sport of death); reviewing, I say, all these considerations, he judged it to be folly indeed to join in the idle worship of those who were no gods, and after such convincing evidence, to err from the truth; and therefore felt it incumbent on him to honor his father's God alone.

Accordingly he called on Him with earnest prayer and supplications that he would reveal to him who He was, and stretch forth His right hand to help him in his present difficulties. And while he was thus praying with fervent entreaty, a most marvelous sign appeared to him from heaven, the account of which it might have been hard to believe had it been related by any other person. But since the victorious emperor himself long afterwards declared it to the writer of this history, when he was honored with his acquaintance and society, and confirmed his statement by an oath, who could hesitate to accredit the relation, especially since the testimony of after-time has established its truth? He said that about noon, when the day was already beginning to decline, he saw with his own eyes the trophy of a cross of light in the heavens, above the sun, and bearing the inscription, CONQUER BY THIS. At this sight he himself was struck with amazement, and his whole army also, which followed him on this expedition, and witnessed the miracle.

He said, moreover, that he doubted within himself what the import of this apparition could be. And while he continued to ponder and reason on its meaning, night suddenly came on; then in his sleep the Christ of God appeared to him with the same sign which he had seen in the heavens, and commanded him to make a likeness of that sign which he had seen in the heavens, and to use it as a safeguard in all engagements with his enemies.

At the dawn of day he arose, and communicated the marvel to his friends: and then, calling together the workers in gold and precious stones, he sat in the midst of them, and described to them the figure of the sign he had seen, bidding them represent it in gold and precious stones. And this representation I myself have had an opportunity of seeing. . . .

The emperor constantly made use of this sign of salvation as a safeguard against every adverse and hostile power, and commanded that others similar to it should be carried at the head of all his armies.

These things were done shortly afterwards. But at the time above specified, being struck with amazement at the extraordinary vision, and resolving to worship no other God save Him who had appeared to him, he sent for those who were acquainted with the mysteries of His doctrines, and enquired who that God was, and what was intended by the sign of the vision he had seen.

They affirmed that He was God, the only begotten Son of the one and only God: that the sign which had appeared was the symbol of immortality, and the trophy of that victory over death which He had gained in time past when sojourning on earth. They taught him also the causes of His advent, and explained to him the true account of His incarnation. Thus he was instructed in these matters, and was impressed with wonder at the divine manifestation which had been presented to his sight. Comparing, therefore, the heavenly vision with the interpretation given, he found his judgment confirmed; and, in the persuasion that the knowledge of these things had been imparted to him by Divine teaching, he determined thenceforth to devote himself to the reading of the inspired writings.

40

Buddhism in China:
From The Disposition of Error

When Buddhist monks traveled from India to China they came to a culture with different philosophical and religious traditions. In China, ancestor worship, which did not exist for Indians who believed in reincarnation, was a very important religious tradition. The leading Chinese philosopher was Confucius, who said very little about religion but stressed the need for respect: sons to fathers (filial piety), wives to husbands, children to parents, students to teachers, youngsters to elders, everyone to the emperor, the living to the deceased. More spiritual and meditative was the religion developed by the followers of a contemporary of Confucius, Lao Tze,* whose *Dao De Jing* (The Book of the Way) prescribed the peace that came from an acceptance of natural flows and rhythms. "Practice non-action" was the Daoist method.

The Disposition of Error is a Buddhist guide for converting the Chinese. While the author and date are uncertain, this kind of tract was common under the Southern Dynasties (420–589 C.E.). The author uses a frequently asked questions (FAQ) format that enables us to see what the Chinese—mainly Confucian—objections were to Buddhism, as well as what they considered good Buddhist answers.

What were the main Chinese objections to Buddhism? Why were Buddhist ideas of death such a stumbling block for Chinese Confucians? Were Confucian ideas about care of the body and hair only superficial concerns, or did they reflect basic differences between Confucianism and Buddhism?

---

*low TSAY

Hung-ming Chi, in Taishō daizōkyō, LII, 1–7, quoted in William Theodore de Bary, ed., *The Buddhist Tradition in India, China and Japan* (New York: Random House, 1969), 132–37.

Thinking Historically

Notice how the Buddhist Mou Tzu answers Chinese questions about Buddhism with both Confucian and Daoist ideas. Which answers do you think were most effective? Would Chinese converts to Buddhism become more Confucian or Daoist? Was conversion to Buddhism a greater challenge to traditional Chinese ideas or behavior?

Why Is Buddhism Not Mentioned in the Chinese Classics?

The questioner said: If the way of the Buddha is the greatest and most venerable of ways, why did Yao, Shun, the Duke of Chou, and Confucius not practice it? In the Five Classics one sees no mention of it. You, sir, are fond of the *Book of Odes* and the *Book of History*, and you take pleasure in rites and music. Why, then, do you love the way of the Buddha and rejoice in outlandish arts? Can they exceed the Classics and commentaries and beautify the accomplishments of the sages? Permit me the liberty, sir, of advising you to reject them.

Mou Tzu said: All written works need not necessarily be the words of Confucius, and all medicine does not necessarily consist of the formulae of [the famous physician] P'ien-ch'üeh. What accords with principle is to be followed, what heals the sick is good. The gentleman-scholar draws widely on all forms of good, and thereby benefits his character. Tzu-kung [a disciple of Confucius] said, "Did the Master have a permanent teacher?" Yao served Yin Shou, Shun served Wu-ch'eng, the Duke of Chou learned from Lü Wang, and Confucius learned from Lao Tzu. And none of these teachers is mentioned in the Five Classics. Although these four teachers were sages, to compare them to the Buddha would be like comparing a white deer to a unicorn, or a swallow to a phoenix. Yao, Shun, the Duke of Chou, and Confucius learned even from such teachers as these. How much less, then, may one reject the Buddha, whose distinguishing marks are extraordinary and whose superhuman powers know no bounds! How may one reject him and refuse to learn from him? The records and teachings of the Five Classics do not contain everything. Even if the Buddha is not mentioned in them, what occasion is there for suspicion?

Why Do Buddhist Monks Do Injury to Their Bodies?

The questioner said: The *Classic of Filial Piety* says, "Our torso, limbs, hair, and skin we receive from our fathers and mothers. We dare not do them injury." When Tseng Tzu was about to die, he bared his hands and feet.[1] But now the monks shave their heads. How this violates the sayings of the sages and is out of keeping with the way of the filially pious! . . .

Mou Tzu said: . . . Confucius has said, "He with whom one may follow a course is not necessarily he with whom one may weigh its merits." This is what is meant by doing what is best at the time. Furthermore, the *Classic of Filial Piety* says, "The kings of yore possessed the ultimate virtue and the essential Way." T'ai-po cut his hair short and tattooed his body, thus following of his own accord the customs of Wu and Yüeh and going against the spirit of the "torso, limbs, hair, and skin" passage.[2] And yet Confucius praised him, saying that his might well be called the ultimate virtue.

Why Do Monks Not Marry?

The questioner said: Now of felicities there is none greater than the continuation of one's line, of unfilial conduct there is none worse than childlessness. The monks forsake wife and children, reject property and wealth. Some do not marry all their lives. How opposed this conduct is to felicity and filial piety! . . .

Mou Tzu said: . . . Wives, children, and property are the luxuries of the world, but simple living and inaction are the wonders of the Way. Lao Tzu has said, "Of reputation and life, which is dearer? Of life and property, which is worth more?" . . . Hsü Yu and Ch'ao-fu dwelt in a tree. Po I and Shu Ch'i starved in Shou-yang, but Confucius praised their worth, saying, "They sought to act in accordance with humanity and they succeeded in acting so." One does not hear of their being ill-spoken of because they were childless and propertyless. The monk practices the Way and substitutes that for the pleasures of disporting himself in the world. He accumulates goodness and wisdom in exchange for the joys of wife and children.

Death and Rebirth

The questioner said: The Buddhists say that after a man dies he will be reborn. I do not believe in the truth of these words. . . .

Mou Tzu said: . . . The spirit never perishes. Only the body decays. The body is like the roots and leaves of the five grains, the spirit is like the seeds and kernels of the five grains. When the roots and leaves

---

[1]To show he had preserved them intact from all harm.

[2]Uncle of King Wen of the Chou who retired to the barbarian land of Wu and cut his hair and tattooed his body in barbarian fashion, thus yielding his claim to the throne to King Wen.

come forth they inevitably die. But do the seeds and kernels perish? Only the body of one who has achieved the Way perishes. . . .

Someone said: If one follows the Way one dies. If one does not follow the Way one dies. What difference is there?

Mou Tzu said: You are the sort of person who, having not a single day of goodness, yet seeks a lifetime of fame. If one has the Way, even if one dies one's soul goes to an abode of happiness. If one does not have the Way, when one is dead one's soul suffers misfortune.

Why Should a Chinese Allow Himself to Be Influenced by Indian Ways?

The questioner said: Confucius said, "The barbarians with a ruler are not so good as the Chinese without one." Mencius criticized Ch'en Hsiang for rejecting his own education to adopt the ways of [the foreign teacher] Hsü Hsing, saying, "I have heard of using what is Chinese to change what is barbarian, but I have never heard of using what is barbarian to change what is Chinese." You, sir, at the age of twenty learned the way of Yao, Shun, Confucius, and the Duke of Chou. But now you have rejected them, and instead have taken up the arts of the barbarians. Is this not a great error?

Mou Tzu said: . . . What Confucius said was meant to rectify the way of the world, and what Mencius said was meant to deplore one-sidedness. Of old, when Confucius was thinking of taking residence among the nine barbarian nations, he said, "If a gentleman-scholar dwells in their midst, what baseness can there be among them?" . . . The Commentary says, "The north polar star is in the center of heaven and to the north of man." From this one can see that the land of China is not necessarily situated under the center of heaven. According to the Buddhist scriptures, above, below, and all around, all beings containing blood belong to the Buddha-clan. Therefore I revere and study these scriptures. Why should I reject the Way of Yao, Shun, Confucius, and the Duke of Chou? Gold and jade do not harm each other, crystal and amber do not cheapen each other. You say that another is in error when it is you yourself who err.

Why Must a Monk Renounce Worldly Pleasures?

The questioner said: Of those who live in the world, there is none who does not love wealth and position and hate poverty and baseness, none who does not enjoy pleasure and idleness and shrink from labor and fatigue. . . . But now the monks wear red cloth, they eat one meal a day, they bottle up the six emotions, and thus they live out their lives. What value is there in such an existence?

Mou Tzu said: Wealth and rank are what man desires, but if he cannot obtain them in a moral way, he should not enjoy them. Poverty and meanness are what man hates, but if he can only avoid them by departing from the Way, he should not avoid them. Lao Tzu has said, "The five colors make men's eyes blind, the five sounds make men's ears deaf, the five flavors dull the palate, chasing about and hunting make men's minds mad, possessions difficult to acquire bring men's conduct to an impasse. The sage acts for his belly, not for his eyes." Can these words possibly be vain? Liu-hsia Hui would not exchange his way of life for the rank of the three highest princes of the realm. Tuan-kan Mu would not exchange his for the wealth of Prince Wen of Wei. . . . All of them followed their ideas, and cared for nothing more. Is there no value in such an existence?

Does Buddhism Have No Recipe for Immortality?

The questioner said: The Taoists say that Yao, Shun, the Duke of Chou, and Confucius and his seventy-two disciples did not die, but became immortals. The Buddhists say that men must all die, and that none can escape. What does this mean?

Mou Tzu said: Talk of immortality is superstitious and unfounded; it is not the word of the sages. Lao Tzu says, "Even Heaven and earth cannot be eternal. How much the less can man!" Confucius says, "The wise man leaves the world, but humanity and filial piety last forever." I have observed the six arts and examined the commentaries and records. According to them, Yao died, Shun had his [death place at] Mount Ts'ang-wu, Yü has his tomb on K'uai-chi, Po I and Shu Ch'i have their grave in Shou-yang. King Wen died before he could chastise Chou, King Wu died without waiting for King Ch'eng to grow up. We read of the Duke of Chou that he was reburied, and of Confucius that [shortly before his death] he dreamed of two pillars. [As for the disciples of Confucius], Po-yü died before his father, of Tzu Lu it is said that his flesh was chopped up and pickled.

41

From The Lotus Sutra

Buddhist monks won Chinese converts not by confronting the worldly practicality of Confucianism, but by emphasizing the mystical side of Buddhism, which was also found in Chinese Daoism. Still, it is unlikely that a heavily monastic religion like orthodox Buddhism would have swept across the family-centered Confucian cultures of East Asia. Though orthodox monastic Buddhism was successful in the Indian-influenced cultures of Southeast Asia, it was a more accommodative Buddhism, called Mahayana* or "the greater vehicle," that attracted many Chinese, Koreans, and Japanese.

Like Christianity, Mahayana Buddhism promised salvation from the ills of this world. The agents who brought this salvation to masses of people were called bodhisattvas,[†] enlightened ones who generously stopped at the brink of nirvana so that they could help others.

The Lotus Sutra—a sutra is a preaching, sermon, or other religious writing that Buddhists learn, practice, and repeat—is one of the classic texts of Mahayana Buddhism. While its origins are lost, it was translated into Chinese first in 255 C.E. and frequently thereafter, with greatest effect by Kumarajiva, a Central Asian monk and scholar, in 406 C.E. This selection is a translation of Kumarajiva's popular version. The first half of the selection (from Chapter 25 of the *Sutra*) introduces the bodhisattva named "Perceiver of the World's Sounds." The second half (from the last chapter, 28) tells of the bodhisattva named "Universal Worthy" and the importance of *The Lotus Sutra* itself. According to the *Sutra*, what does a bodhisattva do? How does one gain help from a bodhisattva? What do you think would be the appeal of Mahayana Buddhism?

Thinking Historically

The spread of both Christianity and Mahayana Buddhism suggests the attraction of salvation religions across Eurasia in this period. How were the appeals of Christianity and Mahayana Buddhism similar? How were they different? Did they appeal to the same or different sorts of people? How was the historical context of each expansion similar or different?

*mah hah YAH nuh
[†]boh dee SAHT vuh

The Lotus Sutra, trans. Burton Watson (New York: Columbia University Press, 1993), 298–300, 319–22.

25

The Universal Gateway of the Bodhisattva Perceiver of the World's Sounds

At that time the bodhisattva Inexhaustible Intent immediately rose from his seat, bared his right shoulder, pressed his palms together and, facing the Buddha, spoke these words: "World-Honored One, this Bodhisattva Perceiver of the World's Sounds—why is he called Perceiver of the World's Sounds?"

The Buddha said to Bodhisattva Inexhaustible Intent: "Good man, suppose there are immeasurable hundreds, thousands, ten thousands, millions of living beings who are undergoing various trials and suffering. If they hear of this bodhisattva Perceiver of the World's Sounds and single-mindedly call his name, then at once he will perceive the sound of their voices and they will all gain deliverance from their trials.

"If someone, holding fast to the name of Bodhisattva Perceiver of the World's Sounds, should enter a great fire, the fire could not burn him. This would come about because of this bodhisattva's authority and supernatural power. If one were washed away by a great flood and called upon his name, one would immediately find himself in a shallow place.

"Suppose there were a hundred, a thousand, ten thousand, a million living beings who, seeking for gold, silver, lapis lazuli, seashell, agate, coral, amber, pearls, and other treasures, set out on the great sea. And suppose a fierce wind should blow their ship off course and it drifted to the land of rakshasa demons.[1] If among those people there is even just one who calls the name of Bodhisattva Perceiver of the World's Sounds, then all those people will be delivered from their troubles with the rakshasas. This is why he is called Perceiver of the World's Sounds.

"If a person who faces imminent threat of attack should call the name of Bodhisattva Perceiver of the World's Sounds, then the swords and staves wielded by his attackers would instantly shatter into so many pieces and he would be delivered.

"Though enough yakshas[2] and rakshasas to fill all the thousand-millionfold world should try to come and torment a person, if they hear him calling the name of Bodhisattva Perceiver of the World's Sounds, then these evil demons will not even be able to look at him with their evil eyes, much less do him harm.

"Suppose there is a person who, whether guilty or not guilty, has had his body imprisoned in fetters and chains, cangue and lock. If he calls the name of Bodhisattva Perceiver of the World's Sounds, then all

---

[1]Evil spirits of Hindu mythology. [Ed.]
[2]Native spirits; maybe demons. [Ed.]

his bonds will be severed and broken and at once he will gain deliverance.

"Suppose, in a place filled with all the evil-hearted bandits of the thousand-millionfold world, there is a merchant leader who is guiding a band of merchants carrying valuable treasures over a steep and dangerous road, and that one man shouts out these words: 'Good men, do not be afraid! You must single-mindedly call on the name of Bodhisattva Perceiver of the World's Sounds. This bodhisattva can grant fearlessness to living beings. If you call his name, you will be delivered from these evil-hearted bandits!' When the band of merchants hear this, they all together raise their voices, saying, 'Hail to the Bodhisattva Perceiver of the World's Sounds!' And because they call his name, they are at once able to gain deliverance. Inexhaustible Intent, the authority and supernatural power of the bodhisattva and mahasattva Perceiver of the World's Sounds are as mighty as this!

"If there should be living beings beset by numerous lusts and cravings, let them think with constant reverence of Bodhisattva Perceiver of the World's Sounds and then they can shed their desires. If they have great wrath and ire, let them think with constant reverence of Bodhisattva Perceiver of the World's Sounds and then they can shed their ire. If they have great ignorance and stupidity, let them think with constant reverence of Bodhisattva Perceiver of the World's Sounds and they can rid themselves of stupidity.

"Inexhaustible Intent, the bodhisattva Perceiver of the World's Sounds possesses great authority and supernatural powers, as I have described, and can confer many benefits. For this reason, living beings should constantly keep the thought of him in mind.

"If a woman wishes to give birth to a male child, she should offer obeisance and alms to Bodhisattva Perceiver of the World's Sounds and then she will bear a son blessed with merit, virtue, and wisdom. And if she wishes to bear a daughter, she will bear one with all the marks of comeliness, one who in the past planted the roots of virtue and is loved and respected by many persons. . . . "

28
Encouragements of the Bodhisattva Universal Worthy

At that time Bodhisattva Universal Worthy, famed for his freely exercised transcendental powers, dignity and virtue, in company with great bodhisattvas in immeasurable, boundless, indescribable numbers, arrived from the east. . . .

When [Bodhisattva Universal Worthy] arrived in the midst of Mount Gridhrakuta in the saha world, he bowed his head to the ground in obeisance to Shakyamuni Buddha, circled around him to the right seven times, and said to the Buddha: "World-Honored One, when I was in the land of the Buddha King Above Jeweled Dignity and Virtue, from far away I heard the Lotus Sutra being preached in this saha world. In company with this multitude of immeasurable, boundless hundreds, thousands, ten thousands, millions of bodhisattvas I have come to listen to and accept it. I beg that the World-Honored One will preach it for us. And good men and good women in the time after the Thus Come One[3] has entered extinction—how will they be able to acquire this Lotus Sutra?"

The Buddha said to Bodhisattva Universal Worthy: "If good men and good women will fulfill four conditions in the time after the Thus Come One has entered extinction, then they will be able to acquire this Lotus Sutra. First, they must be protected and kept in mind by the Buddhas. Second, they must plant the roots of virtue. Third, they must enter the stage where they are sure of reaching enlightenment. Fourth, they must conceive a determination to save all living beings. If good men and good women fulfill these four conditions, then after the Thus Come One has entered extinction they will be certain to acquire this sutra."

At that time Bodhisattva Universal Worthy said to the Buddha: "World-Honored One, in the evil and corrupt age of the last five-hundred-year period, if there is someone who accepts and upholds this sutra, I will guard and protect him, free him from decline and harm, see that he attains peace and tranquility, and make certain that no one can spy out and take advantage of his shortcomings. . . .

"Whether that person is walking or standing, if he reads and recites this sutra, then at that time I will mount my six-tusked kingly white elephant and with my multitude of great bodhisattvas will proceed to where he is. I will manifest myself, offer alms, guard and protect him, and bring comfort to his mind. I will do this because I too want to offer alms to the Lotus Sutra. If when that person is seated he ponders this sutra, at that time too I will mount my kingly white elephant and manifest myself in his presence. If that person should forget a single phrase or verse of the Lotus Sutra, I will prompt him and join him in reading and reciting so that he will gain understanding. At that time the person who accepts, upholds, reads, and recites the Lotus Sutra will be able to see my body, will be filled with great joy, and will apply himself with greater diligence than ever. Because he has seen me, he will immediately acquire samadhis and dharanis.[4] These are called the repetition dharani, the hundred, thousand, ten thousand, million repetition dharani,

---

[3]A title for the Buddha. [Ed.]
[4]States of ecstasy and mantras, incantations, and prayers. [Ed.]

and the Dharma sound expedient dharani. He will acquire dharanis such as these.

"World-Honored One, in that later time, in the evil and corrupt age of the last five-hundred-year period, if monks, nuns, laymen believers or laywomen believers who seek out, accept, uphold, read, recite, and transcribe this Lotus Sutra should wish to practice it, they should do so diligently and with a single mind for a period of twenty-one days. When the twenty-one days have been fulfilled, I will mount my six-tusked white elephant and, with immeasurable numbers of bodhisattvas surrounding me and with this body that all living beings delight to see, I will manifest myself in the presence of the person and preach the Law for him, bringing him instruction, benefit, and joy. . . .

If there are those who accept, uphold, read, and recite this sutra, memorize it correctly, understand its principles, and practice it as the sutra prescribes, these persons should know that they are carrying out the practices of Universal Worthy himself. In the presence of immeasurable, boundless numbers of Buddhas they will have planted good roots deep in the ground, and the hands of the Thus Come Ones will pat them on the head.

"If they do no more than copy the sutra, when their lives come to an end they will be reborn in the Trayastrimsha heaven. At that time eighty-four thousand heavenly women, performing all kinds of music, will come to greet them. Such persons will put on crowns made of seven treasures and amidst the ladies-in-waiting will amuse and enjoy themselves. How much more so, then, if they accept, uphold, read, and recite the sutra, memorize it correctly, understand its principles, and practice it as the sutra prescribes. If there are persons who accept, uphold, read, and recite the sutra and understand its principles, when the lives of these persons come to an end, they will be received into the hands of a thousand Buddhas, who will free them from all fear and keep them from falling into the evil paths of existence. Immediately they will proceed to the Tushita heaven, to the place of Bodhisattva Maitreya. Bodhisattva Maitreya possesses the thirty-two features and is surrounded by a multitude of great bodhisattvas. He has hundreds, thousands, ten thousands, millions of heavenly women attendants, and these persons will be reborn in their midst. Such will be the benefits and advantages they enjoy."

42

From the Koran

In the centuries following the expansion of Christianity and Buddhism, a new monotheistic salvation religion, Islam, originated in Arabia and rapidly spread over much of the same area. (See Map 7.3.) The new faith centered on the Koran (or Qu'ran), which is said by Islamic believers, or Muslims, to be the word of God as spoken by the Angel Gabriel to the Prophet Muhammad about 610 C.E. Muhammad then recited these words so that others could memorize them or write them down. After Muhammad's death (632), these writings and memories were gathered together to form the Koran (literally "Recitation").

The chapters (or *surahs*) of the Koran, 114 in all, are organized by length, the longest first. This means that the earliest pieces, which are among the shortest, are found at the end of the book. We begin with an exception to this rule, *surah* 1, "The Opening," followed by numbers 99, 109, and 112. We also include excerpts from the later *surahs*, number 2, "The Cow,"[1] and number 4, "Women." What beliefs do these *surahs* convey? How are they similar to, or different from, other religious writings you have read? Why might Islam be called a salvation religion?

Thinking Historically

The early *surahs* (those with higher numbers) almost certainly reflect the concerns of early Islam. What are these concerns? The later *surahs* (such as 2 and 4) were probably written after Muhammad, threatened by the ruling tribes, had fled Mecca and taken control of the government of Medina. They may even have been written after Muhammad's death when his successors struggled with problems of governance. Judging from these later chapters, what kinds of issues most concerned leaders of the Muslim community?

---

[1]The title "The Cow" refers to verses 67–73 in *surah* 2 of the Koran (not included here), which tell of a dispute between Moses and the Israelites. After Moses tells the Israelites that God wants them to sacrifice a cow, they hesitate by asking a number of questions as to what kind of cow. Muslim meaning is that one should submit to God, not debate his commands.

Chapters 1, 91, 109, and 112: *Approaching the Qu'ran: The Early Revelations*, trans. Michael Sells (Ashland, OR: White Cloud Press, 1999), 42, 108, 128, 136. Chapters 2 and 4: *The New On-Line Translation of the Qur'an*, the Noor Foundation, http://www.islamusa .org/.

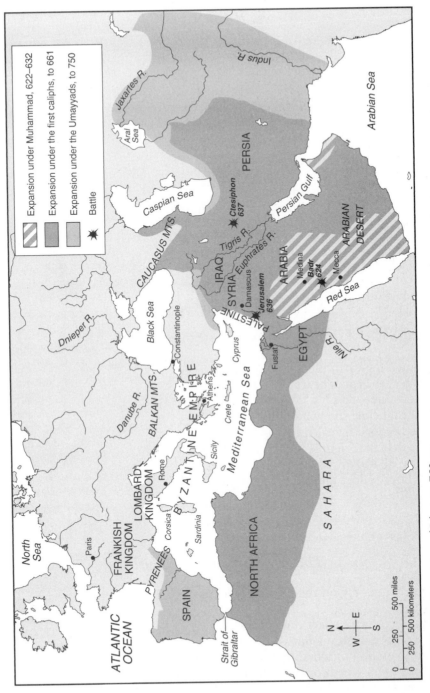

Map 7.3 The Expansion of Islam to 750 C.E.

Legend:
- Expansion under Muhammad, 622–632
- Expansion under the first caliphs, to 661
- Expansion under the Umayyads, to 750
- ✳ Battle

ATLANTIC OCEAN

North Sea

FRANKISH KINGDOM

Paris

PYRENEES

SPAIN

Strait of Gibraltar

NORTH AFRICA

SAHARA

Sardinia

Corsica

Rome

LOMBARD KINGDOM

BALKAN MTS.

Danube R.

Dnieper R.

Black Sea

Constantinople

BYZANTINE EMPIRE

Athens

Sicily

Crete

Cyprus

Mediterranean Sea

Fustat

EGYPT

Nile R.

Red Sea

PALESTINE

Jerusalem 636

Damascus

SYRIA

Mecca

Medina

Badr 624

ARABIA

ARABIAN DESERT

Caspian Sea

CAUCASUS MTS.

Tigris R.

Euphrates R.

Ctesiphon 637

IRAQ

PERSIA

Persian Gulf

Aral Sea

Jaxartes R.

Indus R.

Arabian Sea

N W E S

0   250   500 miles
0 250 500 kilometers

251

Surah 1
The Opening

In the name of God
    the Compassionate the Caring
Praise be to God
    lord sustainer of the worlds
the Compassionate the Caring
master of the day of reckoning
To you we turn to worship
    and to you we turn in time of need
Guide us along the road straight
the road of those to whom you are giving
    not those with anger upon them
    not those who have lost the way

Surah 99
The Quaking

In the Name of God the Compassionate the Caring

When the earth is shaken, quaking
When the earth bears forth her burdens
And someone says "What is with her?"
At that time she will tell her news
As her lord revealed her
At that time people will straggle forth
    to be shown what they have done
Whoever does a mote's weight good will see it
Whoever does a mote's weight wrong will see it

Surah 109
Those Who Reject the Faith

In the Name of God the Compassionate the Caring

Say: You who reject the faith
I do not worship what you worship
and you do not worship what I worship
I am not a worshipper of what you worship
You are not a worshipper of what I worship
A reckoning for you and a reckoning for me

Surah 112
Sincerity / Unity

In the Name of God the Compassionate the Caring

Version 1
> Say he is God, one
> God forever
> Not begetting, unbegotten,
>   and having as an equal none

Version 2
> Say he is God, one
> God the refuge
> Not begetting, unbegotten,
>   and having as an equal none

Version 3
> Say he is God, one
> God the rock
> Not begetting, unbegotten,
>   and having as an equal none

Surah 2
The Cow

Section 22

177. It is not the sole virtue that you turn your faces to the east or the west but true virtue is theirs, who believe in Allâh, the Last Day, the angels, the Book, and in the Prophets, and who give away their wealth (and substance) out of love for Him, to the near of kin, the orphans, the needy, the wayfarer and to those who ask (in charity) and in ransoming the slaves; and who observe the Prayer, who go on presenting the *Zakât* (the purifying alms) and those who always fulfill their pledges and agreements when they have made one, and those who are patiently persevering in adversity and distress and (steadfast) in times of war. It is these who have proved truthful (in their promises and in their faith) and it is these who are strictly guarded against evil.

178. O you who believe! equitable retaliation has been ordained for you in (the matter of) the slain. (Everyone shall pay for his own crime), the freeman (murderer) for the freeman (murdered), and the slave (murderer) for the slave (murdered), and the female (murderer) for the female (murdered), but who has been granted any remission by his

(aggrieved) brother (or family) then pursuing (of the matter) shall be done with equity and fairness, and the payment (of the blood money) to him (the heir) should be made in a handsome manner. This is an alleviation from your Lord and a mercy. But he who exceeds the limits after this (commandment), for him is a grievous punishment.

179. O people of pure and clear wisdom! your very life lies in (the law of) equitable retaliation, (you have been so commanded) so that you may enjoy security.

180. It has been prescribed for you at the time of death to any one of you, that if the (dying) person is leaving considerable wealth behind, to make a will to his parents and the near of kin to act with equity and fairness. This is an obligation incumbent on those who guard against evil.

181. He who alters it (the will) after he has heard it, (should know that) it is those that alter it who shall bear the burden of sin. Allâh indeed is All-Hearing, All-Knowing.

182. If anyone apprehends that the testator is partial or follows a sinful course there will be no blame on him provided he sets things right (and so brings about reconciliation) between them (the parties concerned under the will). Surely, Allâh is Great Protector, Ever Merciful.

Section 23

183. O you who believe! you are bound to observe fasting as those before you (followers of the Prophets) were bound, so that you may guard against evil.

184. (You are required to fast) for a prescribed number of days. But if anyone of you is sick or is on a journey he shall fast (to make up) the prescribed number in other days. And for those who are able to fast is an expiation (as thanksgiving) the feeding of a poor person (daily for the days of fasting). And he who volunteers (extra) good, (will find that) it is even better for him. And that you observe fasting is better for you, if you only know.

185. The (lunar) month of _Ramadzân_ is that in which the Qur'ân (started to be) revealed as a guidance for the whole of mankind with its clear evidences (providing comprehensive) guidance and the Discrimination (between right and wrong). Therefore he who shall witness the month, should fast (for full month) during it, but he who is sick or is on a journey shall fast (to make up) the prescribed number in other days. Allâh wishes facility for you and does not wish hardship for you. (This facility is given to you) that you may complete the number (of required fasts) and you may exalt the greatness of Allâh for His having guided you, and that you may render thanks (to Him). . . .

187. (Though during Fasting you must abstain from all the urges of nature including the sexual urge) it is made lawful for you on the nights

of the fasts to approach and lie with your wives (for sexual relationship). They are (a sort of) garment for you and you are (a sort of) garment for them. Allâh knows that you have been doing injustice to yourselves (by restricting conjugal relations with your wives even at night),
so He turned to you with mercy and provided you relief; now enjoy
their company (at night during *Ramadzân*) and seek what Allâh has ordained for you. Eat and drink till the white streak of the dawn becomes
distinct to you from the black streak (of the darkness), then complete
the fast till nightfall. And you shall not lie with them (your wives) while
you perform *I'tikâf* (while you are secluding in the mosque for prayer
and devotion to God). These are the limits (imposed) by Allâh so do
not approach these (limits). Thus does Allâh explain His commandments
for people that they may become secure against evil. . . .

Section 24

190. And fight in the cause of Allâh those who fight and persecute
you, but commit no aggression. Surely, Allâh does not love the aggressors.

191. And slay them (the aggressors against whom fighting is made
incumbent) when and where you get the better of them, in disciplinary
way, and turn them out whence they have turned you out. (Killing is
bad but) lawlessness is even worse than carnage. But do not fight them
in the precincts of *Masjid al-Harâm* (the Holy Mosque at Makkah) unless they fight you therein. Should they attack you (there) then slay
them. This indeed is the recompense of such disbelievers.

192. But if they desist (from aggression) then, behold, Allâh is indeed Great Protector, Ever Merciful.

193. And fight them until persecution is no more and religion is
(freely professed) for Allâh. But if they desist (from hostilities) then (remember) there is no punishment except against the unjust (who still
persist in persecution). . . .

195. And spend in the cause of Allâh and do not cast yourselves
into ruin with your own hands, and do good to others, and verily Allâh
loves the doers of good to others.

196. Accomplish the *Hajj** (the Greater Pilgrimage to Makkah)
and the *'Umrah* (the minor pilgrimage) for the sake of Allâh. But if you
are kept back, then (offer) whatever sacrifice is easily available, and do
not shave your heads (as is prescribed for the Pilgrims) till the offering
reaches its destination (in time, or place). And whosoever of you is sick
and has an ailment of his head (necessitating shaving before time) then
he should make an expiation either by fasting or alms-giving or by
making a sacrifice. When you are in peaceful conditions then he, who

*HAH juh

would avail himself of the *'Umrah* (a visit to the *Ka'bah* or a minor *Hajj*) together with the *Hajj* (the Greater Pilgrimage and thus performs *Tammattu'*) should make whatever offering is easily available; and whosoever finds none (for an offering) should fast for three days during (the days of) the pilgrimage and (for) seven (days) when he returns (home)—these are ten complete (days of fasting in all). This is for him whose family does not reside near the *Masjid al-Harâm* (the Holy Mosque at Makkah). Take Allâh as a shield, and know that Allâh is Severe in retribution (if you neglect your duties).

Section 25

197. The months of performing the *Hajj* are well Known; so whoever undertakes to perform the *Hajj* in them (should remember that) there is (to be) no obscenity, nor abusing, nor any wrangling during the (time of) *Hajj*. And whatever good you do Allâh knows it. And take provisions for yourselves. Surely, the good of taking provision is guarding (yourselves) against the evil (of committing sin and begging). Take Me alone as (your) shield, O people of pure and clear wisdom!

198. There is no blame on you that you seek munificence from your Lord (by trading during the time of *Hajj*). When you pour forth (in large numbers) from 'Arafât then glorify Allâh (with still more praises) near *Mash'aral-Harâm* (Holy Mosque in *Muzdalifah*), and remember Him (with gratitude) as He has guided you, though formerly you were certainly amongst the astray. . . .

Surah 4
Women

Section 1

1. O you people! take as a shield your Lord Who created you from a single being. The same stock from which He created the man He created his spouse, and through them both He caused to spread a large number of men and women. O people! regard Allâh with reverence in Whose name you appeal to one another, and (be regardful to) the ties of relationship (particularly from the female side). Verily, Allâh ever keeps watch over you.

2. And give the orphans their property and substitute not (your) worthless things for (their) good ones, nor consume their property mingling it along with your own property, for this indeed is a great sin.

3. And if (you wish to marry them and) you fear that you will not be able to do justice to the orphan girls then (marry them not, rather) marry of women (other than these) as may be agreeable to you, (you

may marry) two or three or four (provided you do justice to them), but if you fear that you will not be able to deal (with all of them) equitably then (confine yourselves only to) one, or (you may marry) that whom your right hands possess (your female captives of war). That is the best way to avoid doing injustice.

4. And give the women their dowers unasked, willingly and as agreed gift. But if they be pleased to remit you a portion thereof, of their own free will, then take it with grace and pleasure.

Section 2

11. Allâh prescribes (the following) law (of inheritance) for your children. For male is the equal of the portion of two females; but if they be all females (two or) more than two, for them is two thirds of what he (the deceased) has left; and if there be only one, for her is the half and for his parents, for each one of the two is a sixth of what he has left, if he (the deceased) has a child; but if he has no child and his parents only be his heirs, then for the mother is one third (and the rest two thirds is for the father); but if there be (in addition to his parents) his brothers (and sisters) then there is one sixth for the mother after (the payment of) any bequest he may have bequeathed or (still more important) of any debt (bequests made by the testator and his debts shall however be satisfied first). Your fathers and your children, you do not know which of them deserve better to benefit from you. (This) fixing (of portions) is from Allâh. Surely, Allâh is All-Knowing, All-Wise.

12. And for you is half of that which your wives leave behind, if they have no child; but if they have a child, then for you is one fourth of what they leave behind, after (the payment of) any bequest they may have bequeathed or (still more important) of any (of their) debt. And for them (your wives) is one fourth of what you leave behind if you have no child; but if you leave a child, then, for them is an eighth of what you leave after (the payment of) any bequest you have bequeathed or (still more important) of any debt. And if there be a man or a woman whose heritage is to be divided and he (or she—the deceased) has no child and he (or she) has (left behind) a brother or a sister then for each one of the twain is a sixth; but if they be more than one then they are (equal) sharers in one third after the payment of any bequest bequeathed or (still more important) of any debt (provided such bequest made by the testator and the debt) shall be without (any intent of) being harmful (to the interests of the heirs). This is an injunction from Allâh, and Allâh is All-Knowing, Most Forbearing.

13. These are the limits (of the law imposed) by Allâh, and who obeys Allâh and His Messenger He will admit them into Gardens served with running streams; therein they shall abide for ever; and that is a great achievement.

14. But whoso disobeys Allâh and His Messenger and transgresses the limits imposed by Him He will make him enter Fire where he shall abide long, and for him is a humiliating punishment.

15. As to those of your women who commit sexual perversity, call in four of you to witness against them, and if they bear witness then confine them to their houses, until death overtakes them or Allâh makes for them a way out.

16. And if two of your males commit the same (act of indecency), then punish them both, so if they repent and amend (keeping their conduct good) then turn aside from them, verily Allâh is Oft-Returning (with compassion), Ever Merciful.

43

Peace Terms with Jerusalem (636)

The expansion of Islam was far more rapid and more forceful than the expansion of Christianity and Buddhism. By 636, Arab armies had conquered many of the lands previously held by the Byzantine and Persian empires. Merchants and holy men would spread the faith even further afield at a later stage. But by 750 an Arab-dominated Muslim government controlled Eurasia from the strait of Gibraltar to the western borders of India and China. (See Map 7.3 on page 251.)

How much of this early expansion was military conquest and how much religious conversion? To help us answer this question, we look at an early peace treaty after the conquest of Jerusalem from the Byzantine (called "Roman") Empire.

As the Arabian force for Judeo-Christian monotheism, Muslims had a strong sentimental attachment to Jerusalem. In the first years of the faith, Muhammad and his followers prayed facing Jerusalem, Al Quds (the Holy City, as it is still called in Arabic). In 624, Mecca was substituted as the *qibla* or direction to face for prayer. At the time of Muhammad's death (632), his followers controlled most of Arabia. His successor (or *caliph*), Abu Bakr (r. 632–634), regained control of

"Peace Terms with Jerusalem (636)," in *Islam from the Prophet Muhammad to the Conquest of Constantinople*, ed. and trans. Bernard Lewis, vol. I, *Politics and War* (New York: Harper & Row, 1974), 235–36. Originally published in Al Tabari, *Tarik al-Rusulcwa'l muluk*, Vol. I (Leiden: Brill), 2405–6.

the tribes that tried to withdraw from the alliance after the prophet's death and turned to the conquest of Iraq and Syria. The second caliph, Omar (634–644), negotiated the surrender of the Byzantine forces that controlled Jerusalem after the defeat of Byzantine armies in 636. This document, written by the caliph and directed to the Christian community of Jerusalem, set the terms for continued Christian presence in the city. Many of these terms were continuations of past practice. The *jizya* was a tax or tribute that non-Muslims paid Muslim governments for protection. Jews had been expelled from Jerusalem under Roman administration, a policy continued under the Byzantine Christian administration, and reinstated in this document, though Omar later allowed Jews to reside in the city.

The Muslim sources tell us that the inhabitants of Jerusalem appealed to Omar to take control of Jerusalem. What evidence do you see in these terms that would make that story plausible? What would both sides, Muslim and Christian, seem to gain by these terms?

Thinking Historically

A forceful expansion does not preclude voluntary conversion. There are many stories of Christians, Zoroastrians, and others converting to Islam. What might be some of the reasons why one would convert to Islam before or after the Arab conquest? What might be a reason that Muslims would *not* want people of other religions to convert?

In the name of God the Merciful and the Compassionate.

This is the safe-conduct accorded by the servant of God 'Umar, the Commander of the Faithful, to the people of Aelia [Jerusalem].

He accords them safe-conduct for their persons, their property, their churches, their crosses, their sound and their sick, and the rest of their worship.

Their churches shall neither be used as dwellings nor destroyed. They shall not suffer any impairment, nor shall their dependencies, their crosses, nor any of their property.

No constraint shall be exercised against them in religion nor shall any harm be done to any among them.

No Jew shall live with them in Aelia.[1]

The people of Aelia must pay the *jizya* in the same way as the people of other cities.

---

[1]Aelia Capitolina was the name given to Jerusalem by Roman emperor Hadrian after he suppressed the second Jewish revolt in 132–135 (the first revolt was 66–70). He also expelled Jews from the city and banned them from living there. [Ed.]

They must expel the Romans[2] and the brigands from the city. Those who leave shall have safe-conduct for their persons and property until they reach safety. Those who stay shall have safe-conduct and must pay the *jizya* like the people of Aelia.

Those of the people of Aelia who wish to remove their persons and effects and depart with the Romans and abandon their churches and their crosses shall have safe-conduct for their persons, their churches, and their crosses, until they reach safety.

The country people who were already in the city before the killing of so-and-so may, as they wish, remain and pay the *jizya* the same way as the people of Aelia or leave with the Romans or return to their families. Nothing shall be taken from them until they have gathered their harvest.

This document is placed under the surety of God and the protection [*dhimma*] of the Prophet, the Caliphs and the believers, on condition that the inhabitants of Aelia pay the *jizya* that is due from them.

Witnessed by Khālid ibn al-Walīd, 'Amr ibn al-Āṣ, 'Abd al-Raḥmān ibn 'Awf, Muāwiya ibn Abī Sufyān, the last of whom wrote this document in the year 15 [636].

---

[2]Byzantine soldiers and officials.

44

From The Glorious Victories of 'Āmda Ṣeyon, King of Ethiopia

The sweeping expansion of Islam in the seventh and eighth centuries did not mean the end of Christian or Buddhist expansion. It did, however, signal a new emphasis on military conflicts, especially between Christian and Muslim states. The Crusaders' struggle over Jerusalem was one of the most well known of those battles (and we will examine it in Chapter 10). But there were many other conflicts on the borders between Christendom and the Muslim world, several

---

The Glorious Victories of 'Āmda Ṣeyon: King of Ethiopia, trans. G. W. B. Huntingford (London: Oxford University Press, 1965), 53–65.

occurring between the earliest Christian state, Ethiopia, and the surrounding Muslim states of Egypt and Sudan in the north and west and the growing Arab trading colonies on the coast of the eastern horn of Africa (modern Eritrea, Djibouti, and Somalia). In the fourteenth century, Ethiopia became engaged in a series of conflicts with the Muslim areas to its east. This was also the period in which Ethiopian history was first written down in the "Glory of the Kings," which began with Menelik I, by legend the son of the Queen of Sheba and the Biblical King Solomon, whom she met on a visit to Palestine about 1000 B.C.E. *The Glorious Victories of 'Āmda Ṣeyon* is one of these histories.

'Āmda Ṣeyon* was a fourteenth-century Ethiopian monarch who extended the kingdom to something like its present boundaries. This selection describes the battles he waged in 1329. How important is religion in these conflicts? How would you characterize the Christianity of 'Āmda Ṣeyon?

Thinking Historically

When we think of religions moving from one place to another, we sometimes make the mistake of assuming that a fixed set of ideas or practices moves without changing. In fact, when a religion moves, it changes. It constantly adapts to the new circumstances and new environment. In a later section of the history of 'Āmda Ṣeyon, the author refers to the monarch's two queens, the younger and the elder, as well as his courtesans. Clearly, the king's Christianity contained elements of traditional African polygamy or monarchical privilege, or both. Ethiopian Christianity was also unique in its insistence that its rulers were descended from Jewish kings as well as its early conversion to Christianity. What signs of this unique identity do you see in this selection? In what other ways does this Christianity seem different from others you know or have studied? What might account for those differences?

Let us write, with the help of our Lord Jesus Christ, of the power and the victory which God wrought by the hands of 'Āmda Ṣeyon king of Ethiopia, whose throne-name is Gabra Masqal, in the eighteenth year of his reign, and in the year 516 of the Era of Mercy. Let us write then this book trusting in the Father who helps, in the Son who consoles, and in the Holy Spirit who guides and seeks help from the Holy Trinity, "for," says the Apostle James, "if any one lacketh wisdom, let him

*AHM duh   SAY uhn

ask from God, who giveth generously to all, and he shall not be spurned." And so we also seek help from the Father, the Son, and the Holy Spirit, that they may guard us for ever. Amen.

Now the king of Ethiopia, whose name was 'Āmda Ṣeyon, heard that the king of the Rebels had revolted, and in (his) arrogance was unfaithful to him, making himself great, like the Devil who set himself above his creator and exalted himself like the Most High. The king of the Rebels, whose name was Sabradin, was full of arrogance towards his lord 'Āmda Ṣeyon, and said; "I will be king over all the land of Ethiopia; I will rule the Christians according to my law, and I will destroy their churches." And having said this, he arose and set out and came to the land of the Christians, and killed some of them; and those who survived, both men and women, he took prisoner and converted them to his religion. . . .

But the feet cannot become the head, nor the earth the sky, nor the servant the master. That perverse one, the son of a viper, of the seed of a serpent, the son of a stranger from the race of Satan, thought (covetously) of the throne of David and said, "I will rule in Ṣeyon," for pride entered into his heart, as (into) the Devil his father. He said, "I will make the Christian churches into mosques for the Moslems, and I will convert to my religion the king of the Christians together with his people, and I will nominate him governor of one (province), and if he refuses to be converted to my religion I will deliver him to the herdsmen who are called Warjeḥ that they make him a herder of camels. As for the queen Žān Mangeśā, the wife of the king, I will make her work at the mill. And I will make Mar'ādē his capital city my capital also. And I will plant there plants of *čāt*, because the Moslems love that plant, and (it is) a gift which he sent to the king."

And he gave permission to his soldiers to kill everyone, for the rebellious servant made himself equal to his lord, and vain were his thoughts and vain his words.

Now when the king (of Ethiopia) heard of the Rebel's insults to him, he was very angry, and moved by his wrath sent to him a messenger to tell him, in these words, "Of your truth, did you or did you not burn the churches of God and kill the Christians? And those who survived, did you make them turn to your religion, which is not as the religion of Christ, but (is) that of the Devil your father? Do you not know what I myself formerly accomplished when your brother Ḥaqadin took by force one of my young servants named Te'eyentay? (This is what I did:) . . .

[Āmda Ṣeyon then goes on to describe his glorious military victories over Sabradin's brother and other Moslem armies.]

But I defeated them through the strength of Jesus Christ, and also their master, the son of your brother, by name Darāder. Him I killed; and to you also I will do the same, for I will cast you from your throne, and with the help of God I will cause you to vanish from the earth. If you have killed ten Christians, then I will kill from among your side a thousand Moslems; and if you kill a thousand, then I will kill many thousands through the power of God."

When he heard this from the king's messenger, that accursed and evil man of Satan, the enemy of truth and adversary of the faith of Christ, a stranger to God, far from the glory of the Son, and divorced from the constitution of the Holy Spirit, sent word to the king (of Ethiopia) and said, "I will not come to your place; I will not stand before you (as a supplicant); and if you come against me I will not fear you, because I have more soldiers than you, who can fight with the sword, with the knife, with horses, with the bow, with the shield, with the spear, with the *dembus,* that is, the iron staff, with javelins, and with arrows. If you wish to come against me, come, the road is open. But if you do not come, I will make war on you." . . .

The messengers whom the king had sent to that Rebel returned to him the whole answer of the renegade, that rebel against righteousness. Hearing the insults of the evil man, the king called together (his) commanders . . . telling them to prepare for war. Then he ordered to be brought out from his treasury gold and silver and fine clothing which he had looted, and adorned each of his soldiers, from the (most) senior to the (most) junior; for in his time gold and silver were (as numerous) as stones, and precious raiment (as common) as the leaves of the trees (or) the grass of the field. So having adorned them, he sent them forth to war against the evil Sabradin on the 24th day of Yakātit, saying to them, "May God give you strength and victory, and may He help you." And obeying the king, a detachment from the corps called Takuelā marched out joyfully and in five days came to the headquarters of that Rebel. The greater part however did not arrive because of the badness of the country, and the roughness and even absence of roads. But the detachment which arrived found him ready for war, and they fought with him and forced him out of his residence; and he fled before them. And they defeated him through the power of God. And after this the rest of the king's army arrived, and destroyed the capital of the Rebel's kingdom, and killed a very great number of his soldiers. As for (the Rebel) himself, he fled from them, and they pursued him till sunset; but he escaped them, (going by) a different road. God threw him down from his glory; as it is said in the Book of God, "He humbleth the great, and exalteth the lowly."

Then the army of the king set forth and attacked the camp of the Rebel. They looted the (Rebel) king's treasure houses and (took) gold and silver and fine clothes and jewels without number. They killed men and women, old men and children; the corpses of the slain filled a large space. And those who survived were made prisoners, and there were left none but those who had escaped with that evil man. But the soldiers could not find a place to camp because of the foul smell of the corpses; and they went to another place and made their camp there. Then they sent word to the king saying, "(There is) good news for you, O king, for we have defeated your enemy who set himself up (to rule) over your kingdom. We your soldiers have killed those who remained, even the women and slaves, and have left only those who fled. Also we have looted his treasure-houses, (taking) gold and silver and fine raiment and precious stones and vessels of bronze, iron, tin, and glass without number. All this we have given to the (people) of Šagurā, of Zaber, and of the Medra Zēgā, according to their ability to carry it. As for him, he has escaped us through his trickery by another road."

The king, hearing that the Rebel had escaped, went into the tabernacle and approached the altar; seizing the horns of the altar he implored mercy of Jesus Christ saying, "Hear the petition of my heart and reject not the prayer of my lips, and shut not the gates of Thy mercy because of my sins, but send me Thy good angel to guide me on my road to pursue mine enemy who has set himself above Thy sheep and above Thy holy name." And having said this, he gave an offering to the church of coloured hangings for the altar, and went out. Then he sent other troops, those called Dāmot, Saqalt, Gondar, and Hadyā, cavalry and foot-soldiers, strong and skilled in war, powerful without comparison in warfare and battle; he sent their commander Ṣagā Krestos to Bēgamedr to make war in the land of the renegades who are like Jews, the crucifiers, of Samēn and Waggarā and Ṣalamt and Ṣagadē who were formerly Christian. Because like the Jews, the crucifiers, they denied Christ, he sent troops to destroy and devastate them and subject them to the rule of Christ. . . .

The king set out with the troops which were with him on the 6th day of Magābit, and going by the road of the right came to a country called Dawāro. The governor of this country, by name Ḥaydarā, in his words professed to love the king but in secret had evil designs, like Judas the traitor who sold his Lord. He spoke with two tongues, for he said to that rebel Sabradin, "If he (the king of Ethiopia) comes against you I will come with my soldiers (to you); and if he comes against me, come with your soldiers (to me); we will fight him together and destroy him utterly with his army." The king continued his march and came to Gālā on the 28th day of Miyāzyā; here he celebrated the feast of Easter, the resurrection of Christ, with joy and happiness. Here he left his camp and the queen Mangeśā, and set out to attack the district of Samāryā, where he killed many men, took their women and their livestock, and captured much booty. The next day he left his army secretly and set out on a journey of two days, riding a horse and accompanied by twenty-seven young horsemen unaccustomed to war and battles. He spent the night there with (these) few soldiers, eating no food, drinking no water, not ungirding his loins, and not sleeping. He did not even lie down that night, not from fear, but because of his experience as a soldier; though he trusted not in the number of his horses or his men, nor in the bow and spear, for (as) David said, "The king is not saved by the number of his soldiers, and the horse is a deceit for safety; not in my bow or spear do I trust to be saved." In the same manner Āmda Ṣeyon did not rely on numbers, and with only a few he was not afraid, but put his trust in God his Lord.

Now when he disappeared his soldiers went from place to place weeping and saying, "Woe unto us, for we know not what has become of our lord (nor) whether he is alive or not." At daylight the king arose and set out on the road, and while on the march met with the soldiers who were seeking him and weeping together. Then the king returned to his camp with much booty. After this, the troops which he had previously sent to make war on the Rebel (Sabradin) returned, and reported how they had fought and defeated (the enemy); and the king forthwith gave thanks to God.

When he learned that the king had been joined by (the rest of) his troops, that Rebel was filled with fear, and not knowing where to turn, for fear had taken possession of him, he sent to the queen saying, "I have done wrong to my lord the king, I have wrought injustice against him, and it is better that I fall into his hands than into the hands of a stranger. I will come myself and surrender to him, that he may do what he will to me." Thereupon the queen went to tell (the king) the whole of the message from that Rebel Sabradin, whose acts, like his name "broken judgement," consist of insults, mad rage, errors, contentions, and arrogance. When the king heard this message which the Rebel had sent to the queen, he was exceedingly angry, and said to the queen, "Do you send him a message and say: 'If you come, or if you do not come, it will not trouble me; but if you go to a distant country I will pursue you through the power of God. And if you go into a cave, or if you (just) run away, I will not leave you alone nor will I return to my capital till I have taken you.'"

Now when he received this message, (Sabradin) set out and came to the king, and stood before him. And the king asked him, saying, "Why have you behaved thus to me? The gifts which you (formerly) sent to me you have given to your servants; and the multitude of goods of silver and gold which I gave to the poor you have taken away. Those who traded with me you have bound in chains; and what is worse, you have aspired to the throne of my kingdom, in imitation of the Devil your father who wished to be the equal of his creator." When that Rebel heard these words of the king he was at a loss for an answer in the greatness of his fear, for he was afraid of the king's presence; and he answered, "Do with me according to your will." And immediately the soldiers who were on the left and right of the king stood forth in anger and said, "This man is not worthy of life, for he has burnt the churches of

God, he has slain Christians, and those whom he did not kill he has compelled to accept his religion. (Moreover) he desired to ascend the high mountain of the kingdom." And some said, "Let us slay him with the edge of the sword"; others said, "Let us stone him to death"; and others again, "Let us burn him with fire that he may disappear from the earth." And they said to the king, "Think not, O king, that he comes to you honestly and freely, for he trusts in his magic art." And so saying, they lifted from his bosom and arm a talisman and revealed the *sena kini* of his magic. Then said the king, "Can your talismans deliver you from my hands in which God has imprisoned you?" And he gave orders for his two hands to be bound with iron chains; he did not wish him to be killed, for he is merciful and forbearing. (Thus) was taken the Rebel in the net which he himself had woven, and in the snare which he himself had set, as said David, "He delved and dug a pit, and hath fallen into the pit which he made himself; his sins shall descend upon the crown of his head. God hath lowered him from his glory, for every one that maketh himself great shall be abased, and he that abaseth himself shall be honoured."

REFLECTIONS

Understanding religion in social and historical context may be particularly difficult for those of us raised in a culture that thinks of religion as belief rather than behavior. For many of us the relationship between individual religious ideas, faith, or belief, on the one hand, and religious social identity, membership, or behavior, on the other hand, is difficult to understand. Inevitably our own religious experiences and cultural background affect how we understand others and their religious beliefs. If we have strong beliefs, we expect intelligent, sensitive people to have similar beliefs. If they do not, we expect them to be easily persuaded when exposed to ideas that we find compelling. This may be a particularly American expectation. American culture, even in its secular forms, is a product of the Protestant reformation and Christian efforts to create a "city on a hill," as a beacon to the world.

Belief has always meant a lot to Christians. Ever since St. Paul organized a church based purely on faith—all you have to do is believe, he said—the particulars of belief have splintered Christianity into a thousand sects. But most religions did not evolve this way. Even other religions that have scriptural authorities—Judaism, Islam, Buddhism, Hinduism, to a certain extent—have devoted less attention to defining doctrine and rooting out heretics than they have to regulating daily life within the larger society. Among them only Islam displays a similar zeal to convert nonbelievers, but there is no set of doctrines, no credo, required of the Muslim besides the profession of faith in God and his Prophet. The schism of Islam between Sunnis and Shi'ites is deep, but it is historical and communal rather than intellectual or doctrinal. Jews, Buddhists, and Hindus do not evangelize and would be hard-pressed to answer if asked by potential recruits what to believe. For most people throughout the history of the world, religion was defined by birth; beliefs came later.

We started the chapter with religious conversion and ended it with religious warfare. A story that began with wandering monks and merchants, sharing ideas and building communities, concludes with armies wiping out women and children. It is hard to believe that soldiers thought they could convert souls by separating them from their bodies.

When did persuasion turn to enforcement? When did religion become the business of soldiers and kings? Perhaps it was when religion became a matter of state. Many early states were concerned with ensuring the proper observance of rituals, but usually only for their own subjects. Most ancient empires that governed foreign peoples allowed their subjects to administer their own religious affairs provided these affairs did not undermine political or social stability. Judaism, for example, did not present a threat to the Roman Empire as long as it remained a national religion in its own territory, and one willing to accept Roman law. When some Jews, called Christians, not only moved about the empire but sought to convert Roman citizens and caused them to neglect Roman gods, the state stepped in.

The combination of state and monotheistic religion could and did result in a potentially lethal intolerance. Indeed, the medieval history of Christian Crusade and Muslim Jihad bristles with battles of true believers. But when did that begin? The initial expansion of Islam has sometimes been seen as the first storm of mounted believers ready to convert or kill all in their path. Increasingly, however, this appears to be an age-old Christian myth. Recent histories argue that the initial seventh-century conquest was driven more by Arab tribal raiding traditions and antiforeign nationalism than it was by religious zeal. Arab armies gained more from the taxes and labor of subject populations than they would from religious equals. Conversions probably came later.

The historian Richard Bulliet shows how the Iranian conversions to Islam only took off a hundred years after the Arab conquest. Between 750 and 850, the percentage of Iranians who were Muslim rose from 10 percent to 90 percent. Clearly the Arab armies that conquered Iran in 648 did not shout "convert or die." Bulliet shows that conversion of Iranians to Islam followed a standard bell curve typical of the adoption of successful consumer products like high-definition televisions. That raises another question. In converting, did people merely choose to join the socially dominant group? Or were ideas and personal religious feelings more important factors?

8

Medieval Civilizations

European, Islamic, and Chinese
Societies, 600–1400 C.E.

HISTORICAL CONTEXT

In the centuries after 200 C.E., an influx of nomadic peoples from the grasslands of Eurasia into the Roman and Han Chinese empires brought an end to the classical civilizations. In their wake, three distinct civilizations developed: European Christian, Islamic (after 622 C.E.), and Chinese. Of the three, the Chinese was most like its preceding classical civilization; in some ways the Sui dynasty (589–618) revived the institutions of the Han. The greatest change occurred in Western Europe, especially the former urban areas of the Roman Empire, some of which virtually disappeared. The area from Byzantium to the Indus River was radically transformed by the rise of Islam, but a foreign observer might have been struck more by the continuity of urban growth and material progress than by the change of faith in Western Asia from the classical to Muslim period.

In any case, these three worlds of Eurasia in the Middle Ages were vastly different from each other. The goal of this chapter is to explore some of those differences.

THINKING HISTORICALLY
Distinguishing Social, Economic,
Political, and Cultural Aspects

Comparing civilizations is a daunting undertaking; there are so many variables one must keep in mind. Consequently, when historians compare civilizations, or any social system, they first break them down into parts. Most commonly, historians distinguish between the political,

268

economic, social, and cultural features of a system. The political refers to how a society or civilization is governed, the economic to how it supports itself, the social to how it organizes population groups, including families, and the cultural to how it explains and represents itself, including its religion.

In this chapter, you are asked to be systematic in distinguishing among these features for each of the three main civilizations. We will break them down to compare each part — for example, European and Chinese politics, Muslim and Chinese culture — but also to see how the parts of each civilization make a whole: for example, how Chinese politics and Chinese culture fit together.

45

Feudalism: An Oath of Homage and Fealty

This primary source is from France, selected to illustrate one of the important institutions of Europe in the Middle Ages: feudalism. This document details the mutual obligation between a feudal lord and his vassal. In this case, the feudal lord is a religious institution, the monastery of St. Mary of Grasse. Acting for the monastery and its lands is the abbot, Leo. The vassal who holds the properties of the monastery as a fief, and in return pledges homage and fealty, is Bernard Atton, viscount of Carcassonne.* The year is 1110.

What exactly does the viscount of Carcassonne promise to do? What is Leo the abbot's responsibility on behalf of the monastery? How new or old does this agreement appear to be? What else does this document tell you about the relationship of lords and vassals in European feudalism?

Thinking Historically

Using the distinctions suggested in the chapter introduction, how would you characterize this agreement? In short, is it an economic, political, social, or cultural agreement? Because it obviously has more

*cahr cas OHN

"Charter of Homage and Fealty of the Viscount of Carcassone, 1110," in D. C. Munro, *Translations and Reprints from the Original Sources of European History*, vol. IV, bk. 3 (Philadelphia: University of Pennsylvania Press, 1897), 18–20.

than one of these elements, how might you argue for each of the four characterizations?

What would be the closest equivalent to this sort of agreement today? Would you characterize the modern equivalent as economic, political, social, or cultural?

In the name of the Lord, I, Bernard Atton, Viscount of Carcassonne, in the presence of my sons, Roger and Trencavel, and of Peter Roger of Barbazan, and William Hugo, and Raymond Mantellini, and Peter de Vietry, nobles, and of many other honorable men, who had come to the monastery of St. Mary of Grasse, to the honor of the festival of the august St. Mary; since lord Leo, abbot of the said monastery, has asked me, in the presence of all those above mentioned, to acknowledge to him the fealty and homage for the castles, manors, and places which the patrons, my ancestors, held from him and his predecessors and from the said monastery as a fief, and which I ought to hold as they held, I have made to the lord abbot Leo acknowledgment and homage as I ought to do.

Therefore, let all present and to come know that I the said Bernard Atton, lord and viscount of Carcassonne, acknowledge verily to thee my lord Leo, by the grace of God, abbot of St. Mary of Grasse, and to thy successors that I hold and ought to hold as a fief, in Carcassonne, the following: . . . Moreover, I acknowledge that I hold from thee and from the said monastery as a fief the castle of Termes in Narbonne; and in Minerve the castle of Ventaion, and the manors of Cassanolles, and of Ferral and Aiohars; and in Le Rogès, the little village of Longville; for each and all of which I make homage and fealty with hands and with mouth to thee my said lord abbot Leo and to thy successors, and I swear upon these four gospels of God that I will always be a faithful vassal to thee and to thy successors and to St. Mary of Grasse in all things in which a vassal is required to be faithful to his lord, and I will defend thee, my lord, and all thy successors, and the said monastery and the monks present and to come and the castles and manors and all your men and their possessions against all malefactors and invaders, at my request and that of my successors at my own cost; and I will give to thee power over all the castles and manors above described, in peace and in war, whenever they shall be claimed by thee or by thy successors.

Moreover I acknowledge that, as a recognition of the above fiefs, I and my successors ought to come to the said monastery, at our own expense, as often as a new abbot shall have been made, and there do homage and return to him the power over all the fiefs described above. And when the abbot shall mount his horse I and my heirs, viscounts of

Carcassonne, and our successors ought to hold the stirrup for the honor of the dominion of St. Mary of Grasse; and to him and all who come with him, to as many as two hundred beasts, we should make the abbot's purveyance in the borough of St. Michael of Carcassonne, the first time he enters Carcassonne, with the best fish and meat and with eggs and cheese, honorably according to his will, and pay the expense of the shoeing of the horses, and for straw and fodder as the season shall require.

And if I or my sons or their successors do not observe to thee or to thy successors each and all the things declared above, and should come against these things, we wish that all the aforesaid fiefs should by that very fact be handed over to thee and to the said monastery of St. Mary of Grasse and to thy successors.

I, therefore, the aforesaid lord Leo, by the grace of God, abbot of St. Mary of Grasse, receive thy homage and fealty for all the fiefs of castles and manors and places which are described above; in the way and with the agreements and understandings written above; and likewise I concede to thee and thy heirs and their successors, the viscounts of Carcassonne, all the castles and manors and places aforesaid, as a fief, along with this present charter, divided through the alphabet. And I promise to thee and thy heirs and successors, viscounts of Carcassonne, under the religion of my order, that I will be a good and faithful lord concerning all those things described above.

Moreover, I, the aforesaid viscount, acknowledge that the little villages of [twelve are listed] with the farmhouse of Mathus and the chateaux of Villalauro and Claromont, with the little villages of St. Stephen of Surlac, and of Upper and Lower Agrifolio, ought to belong to the said monastery, and whoever holds anything there holds from the same monastery, as we have seen and have heard read in the privileges and charters of the monastery, and as was there written.

Made in the year of the Incarnation of the Lord 1110, in the reign of Louis. Seal of [the witnesses named in paragraph one, Bernard Atton and abbot Leo] who has accepted this acknowledgment of the homage of the said viscount.

And I, the monk John, have written this charter at the command of the said lord Bernard Atton, viscount of Carcassonne and of his sons, on the day and year given above, in the presence and witness of all those named above.

46

Manorialism: Duties of a Villein

Manorialism is another term used to describe medieval European civilization. It concerns the life around the manor houses that were the centers of life in the countryside. Manors were owned by feudal lords whose income derived, at least in good part, from the work of free peasants and dependent serfs (*villeins*).*

This document, from England in 1307, delineates the duties required of a villein, John of Cayworth, to the lord of the manor, Battle Abbey. What duties does the abbey require of John of Cayworth? What does he get in return? In what ways is this document similar to the previous one? In what ways is it different?

Thinking Historically

How is the social status of John of Cayworth different from that of Bernard Atton in the previous selection? What would you imagine about the differences in their economic welfare?

What would be the modern equivalent of this document? Would you call that modern equivalent economic, political, social, or cultural? Which word best characterizes this document?

They say that John of Cayworth holds one house and thirty acres of land, and he owes 2 *s.*[1] a year at Easter and Michaelmas, and he owes one cock and two hens at Christmas worth 4 *s.*

And he ought to harrow for two days at the sowing at Lent with one man and his own horse and harrow, the value of the work is 4 *d.*;[2] and he receives from the lord on each day three meals worth 3 *d.*; and the lord will thus lose 1 *d.*; and so this harrowing is worth nothing to the service of the lord.

And he ought to carry the manure of the lord for two days with one cart using his own two oxen, the work to value 8 *s.*, and he receives from the lord three meals of the above value each day; and so the work is worth 3 *d.* clear.

*vih LAYN
[1]Shilling, a British measure of money traditionally worth ½₀ of a pound. [Ed.]
[2]Pence, smallest measure of British currency traditionally worth ½₂ of a shilling. "d." comes from Roman *denarius*. [Ed.]

"Services Due from a Villein, 1307," in *Customals of Battle Abbey*, ed. S. R. Scargill-Bird (The Camden Society, 1887), 19–23.

And he should find one man for two days to mow the meadow of the lord, who can mow an estimated one acre and a half: the value of mowing one acre is 6 *d.*; and the total is 9 *d.*; and he receives for each day three meals of the above value, and thus the mowing is worth 4 *d.* clear.

And he ought to collect and carry that same hay which he has mowed, the value of the work is 3 *d.* And he has from the lord two meals to one man worth 1½ *d.*; thus the work is worth 1½ *d.* clear.

And he ought to carry the hay of the lord for one day with one cart and three animals of his own, the price of the work is 6 *d.*; and he has from the lord three meals worth 2½ *d.*; and thus the work has a value of 3½ *d.* clear.

And he ought to carry in the autumn beans or oats for two days with one cart and three of his own animals, the price of the work is 12 *d.*; and he has from the lord three meals of the above price for each day, and thus the work is worth 7 *d.* clear.

And he ought to carry wood from the woods of the lord to the manor house for two days in summer with one cart and three of his own animals, the price of the work is 9 *d.*; and he receives from the lord for each day three meals of the above price. And so the work is worth 4 *d.* clear.

And he ought to find one man for two days to cut heath, the price of the work is 4 [*d.*]; and he will have three meals for each day of the above price; and so the lord loses if he receives the work 1 *d.*; and thus that cutting is worth nothing to the work of the lord.

And he ought to carry the heath that he has cut, the price of the work is 5 *d.*; and he receives from the lord three meals of the price of 2½ *d.*; and thus the work is worth 2½ *d.* clear.

And he ought to carry to Battle [Abbey] two times in the summer half a load of grain each time, the price of the work is 4 *d.*; and he will receive in the manor each time one meal worth 2 *d.*; and thus the work is worth 2 *d.* clear.

The sum of the rents, with the price of the chickens is 2 *s.* 4 *d.*; the sum of the value of the work is 2 *s.* 3½ *d.*; owed from the said John per year. . . .

And it must be noted that all the aforesaid villeins may not marry their daughters nor have their sons tonsured, nor can they cut down timber growing on the lands they hold, without the personal approval of the bailiff or servant of the lord, and then for building and no other purpose.

And after the death of any one of the aforesaid villeins the lord will have as a heriot the best animal that he had; if, however, he had no living beast, the lord will have no heriot, as they say.

The sons or daughters of the aforesaid villeins will give to enter the tenement after the death of their ancestors as much as they gave in rent per year.

47

From the Magna Carta

The Magna Carta was a contract between King John of England and his nobles (or "liegemen") in which the king agreed to recognize certain rights and liberties of the nobility. In return the nobles accepted certain obligations to the king. What were some of these rights and obligations? Can you tell from these provisions what some of the nobles' complaints had been? Did the signing of this agreement in 1215 improve the position of the common people, women, or foreigners? What does the document tell you about English society in the early thirteenth century?

Thinking Historically

This is obviously a political document, as it details the mutual obligations of King John and his nobles, the barons. But in addition to political matters, it covers a number of issues that might be considered economic, social, and cultural. Which items would you characterize as falling into one of those categories?

What does the Magna Carta have in common with the other European documents on feudalism and manorialism? What does this commonality tell you about European society in the Middle Ages?

John, by the grace of God, King of England, Lord of Ireland, Duke of Normandy and Aquitaine, and Count of Anjou: To the Archbishops, Bishops, Abbots, Earls, Barons, Justiciaries, Foresters, Sheriffs, Reeves, Ministers, and all Bailiffs and others, his faithful subjects, Greeting. Know ye that in the presence of God, and for the health of Our soul, and the souls of Our ancestors and heirs, to the honor of God, and the exaltation of Holy Church, and amendment of Our Kingdom, by the advice of Our reverend Fathers, Stephen, Archbishop of Canterbury, Primate of all England, and Cardinal of the Holy Roman Church; Henry, Archbishop of Dublin; William of London, Peter of Winchester, Jocelin of Bath and Glastonbury, Hugh of Lincoln, Walter of Worcester, William of Coventry, and Benedict of Rochester, Bishops; Master Pandulph, the Pope's subdeacon and familiar; Brother Aymeric, Master

"Magna Carta," trans. E. P. Cheney, in *Translations and Reprints from the Original Sources of European History*, ed. D. C. Munro, vol. I, bk. 6 (Philadelphia: University of Pennsylvania Press, 1897), 6–15, passim.

of the Knights of the Temple in England; and the noble persons, William Marshal, Earl of Pembroke; William, Earl of Salisbury; William, Earl of Warren; William, Earl of Arundel; Alan de Galloway, Constable of Scotland; Warin Fitz-Gerald, Peter Fitz-Herbert, Hubert de Burgh, Seneschal of Poitou, Hugh de Neville, Matthew Fitz-Herbert, Thomas Basset, Alan Basset, Philip Daubeny, Robert de Roppelay, John Marshal, John Fitz-Hugh, and others, Our liegemen:

1. We have, in the first place, granted to God, and by this Our present Charter confirmed for Us and Our heirs forever — That the English Church shall be free and enjoy her rights in their integrity and her liberties untouched. And that We will this so to be observed appears from the fact that We of Our own free will, before the outbreak of the dissensions between Us and Our barons, granted, confirmed, and procured to be confirmed by Pope Innocent III the freedom of elections, which if considered most important and necessary to the English Church, which Charter We will both keep Ourself and will it to be kept with good faith by Our heirs forever. We have also granted to all the free men of Our kingdom, for Us and Our heirs forever, all the liberties underwritten, to have and to hold to them and their heirs of Us and Our heirs.

2. If any of Our earls, barons, or others who hold of Us in chief by knight's service shall die, and at the time of his death his heir shall be of full age and owe a relief[1] he shall have his inheritance by ancient relief; to wit, the heir or heirs of an earl of an entire earl's barony, £100; the heir or heirs of a baron of an entire barony, £100; the heir or heirs of a knight of an entire knight's fee, 100s. at the most; and he that owes less shall give less, according to the ancient custom of fees.

3. If, however, any such heir shall be under age and in ward, he shall, when he comes of age, have his inheritance without relief or fine.

4. The guardian of the land of any heir thus under age shall take therefrom only reasonable issues, customs, and services, without destruction or waste of men or property; and if We shall have committed the wardship of any such land to the sheriff or any other person answerable to Us for the issues thereof, and he commit destruction or waste, We will take an amends from him, and the land shall be committed to two lawful and discreet men of that fee, who shall be answerable for the issues to Us or to whomsoever We shall have assigned them. And if We shall give or sell the wardship of any such land to anyone, and he commit destruction or waste upon it, he shall lose the wardship, which shall be committed to two lawful and discreet men of that fee, who shall, in like manner, be answerable unto Us as has been aforesaid.

---

[1]A form of tax. [Ed.]

5. The guardian, so long as he shall have the custody of the land, shall keep up and maintain the houses, parks, fishponds, pools, mills, and other things pertaining thereto, out of the issues of the same, and shall restore the whole to the heir when he comes of age, stocked with ploughs and tillage, according as the season may require and the issues of the land can reasonably bear.

6. Heirs shall be married without loss of station, and the marriage shall be made known to the heir's nearest of kin before it be contracted.

7. A widow, after the death of her husband, shall immediately and without difficulty have her marriage portion and inheritance. She shall not give anything for her marriage portion, dower, or inheritance which she and her husband held on the day of his death, and she may remain in her husband's house for forty days after his death, within which time her dower shall be assigned to her.

8. No widow shall be compelled to marry so long as she has a mind to live without a husband, provided, however, that she give security that she will not marry without Our assent, if she holds of Us, or that of the lord of whom she holds, if she holds of another.

9. Neither We nor Our bailiffs shall seize any land or rent for any debt so long as the debtor's chattels are sufficient to discharge the same; nor shall the debtor's sureties be distrained so long as the debtor is able to pay the debt. If the debtor fails to pay, not having the means to pay, then the sureties shall answer the debt, and, if they desire, they shall hold the debtor's lands and rents until they have received satisfaction of the debt which they have paid for him, unless the debtor can show that he has discharged his obligation to them.

10. If anyone who has borrowed from the Jews any sum of money, great or small, dies before the debt has been paid, the heir shall pay no interest on the debt so long as he remains under age, of whomsoever he may hold. If the debt shall fall into Our hands, We will take only the principal sum named in the bond. . . .

13. The City of London shall have all her ancient liberties and free customs, both by land and water. Moreover, We will and grant that all other cities, boroughs, towns, and ports shall have their liberties and free customs.

14. For obtaining the common counsel of the kingdom concerning the assessment of aids (other than in the three cases aforesaid) or of scutage, We will cause to be summoned, severally by Our letters, the archbishops, bishops, abbots, earls, and great barons; We will also cause to be summoned, generally, by Our sheriffs and bailiffs, all those who hold lands directly of Us, to meet on a fixed day, but with at least forty days' notice, and at a fixed place. In all letters of such summons We will explain the cause thereof. The summons being thus made, the business shall proceed on the day appointed, according to the advice of

those who shall be present, even though not all the persons summoned have come. . . .

16. No man shall be compelled to perform more service for a knight's fee or other free tenement than is due therefrom.

17. Common Pleas shall not follow Our Court, but shall be held in some certain place. . . .

20. A free man shall be amerced[2] for a small fault only according to the measure thereof, and for a great crime according to its magnitude, saving his position; and in like manner a merchant saving his trade, and a villein saving his tillage, if they should fall under Our mercy. None of these amercements shall be imposed except by the oath of honest men of the neighborhood.

21. Earls and barons shall be amerced only by their peers, and only in proportion to the measure of the offense.

22. No amercement shall be imposed upon a clerk's[3] lay property, except after the manner of the other persons aforesaid, and without regard to the value of his ecclesiastical benefice.

23. No village or person shall be compelled to build bridges over rivers except those bound by ancient custom and law to do so. . . .

28. No constable or other of Our bailiffs shall take corn or other chattels of any man without immediate payment, unless the seller voluntarily consents to postponement of payment.

29. No constable shall compel any knight to give money in lieu of castle-guard when the knight is willing to perform it in person or (if reasonable cause prevents him from performing it himself) by some other fit man. Further, if We lead or send him into military service, he shall be quit of castle-guard for the time he shall remain in service by Our command.

30. No sheriff or other of Our bailiffs, or any other man, shall take the horses or carts of any free man for carriage without the owner's consent.

31. Neither We nor Our bailiffs will take another man's wood for Our castles or for any other purpose without the owner's consent. . . .

35. There shall be one measure of wine throughout Our kingdom, and one of ale, and one measure of corn, to wit, the London quarter, and one breadth of dyed cloth, russets, and haberjets[4] to wit, two cells within the selvages. As with measure so shall it also be with weights. . . .

38. In the future no bailiff shall upon his own unsupported accusation put any man to trial without producing credible witnesses to the truth of the accusation.

[2]Fined. [Ed.]
[3]Clergyman. [Ed.]
[4]Types of cloth. [Ed.]

39. No free man shall be taken, imprisoned, disseised,[5] outlawed, banished, or in any way destroyed, nor will We proceed against or prosecute him, except by the lawful judgment of his peers and by the law of the land.

40. To no one will We sell, to none will We deny or delay, right or justice.

41. All merchants shall have safe conduct to go and come out of and into England, and to stay in and travel through England by land and water for purposes of buying and selling, free of illegal tolls, in accordance with ancient and just customs, except, in time of war, such merchants as are of a country at war with Us. If any such be found in Our dominion at the outbreak of war, they shall be attached, without injury to their persons or goods, until it be known to Us or Our Chief Justiciary how Our merchants are being treated in the country at war with Us, and if Our merchants be safe there, then theirs shall be safe with Us.

42. In the future it shall be lawful (except for a short period in time of war, for the common benefit of the realm) for anyone to leave and return to Our kingdom safely and securely by land and water, saving his fealty to Us. Excepted are those who have been imprisoned or outlawed according to the law of the land, people of the country at war with Us, and merchants, who shall be dealt with as aforesaid. . . .

52. If anyone has been disseised or deprived by Us, without the legal judgment of his peers, of lands, castles, liberties, or rights, We will immediately restore the same, and if any dispute shall arise thereupon, the matter shall be decided by judgment of the twenty-five barons mentioned below in the clause for securing the peace. With regard to all those things, however, of which any man was disseised or deprived, without legal judgment of his peers, by King Henry Our Father or Our Brother King Richard, and which remain in Our warranty, We shall have respite during the term commonly allowed to the Crusaders, except as to those matters on which a plea had arisen, or an inquisition had been taken by Our command, prior to Our taking the Cross. Immediately after Our return from Our pilgrimage, or if by chance We should remain behind from it, We will at once do full justice.

---

[5]Dispossessed. [Ed.]

48

Islam: Sayings Ascribed to the Prophet

For Muslims the Koran was the word of God. Therefore no other writing was comparable. Nevertheless, when Muslims engaged in politics, considered laws, or studied social, economic, cultural, or other issues they could also refer to a body of writing called *hadiths,* or the sayings of the Prophet. These were writings attributed to Muhammad's contemporaries that described the decisions, acts, and the statements of the Prophet of Islam and the religion's first governor. What likely effect would the sayings included here have on the thinking of a devout Muslim? Under what circumstances would he or she be likely to be rebellious?

Thinking Historically

Most of these sayings deal with religion and government. What attitude toward politics do they express? If this selection was all you had to construct a Muslim idea of government, what would it be? How are these political ideas different from those in medieval Europe? What accounts for the differences?

I charge the Caliph[1] after me to fear God, and I commend the community of the Muslims to him, to respect the great among them and have pity on the small, to honor the learned among them, not to strike them and humiliate them, not to oppress them and drive them to unbelief, not to close his doors to them and allow the strong to devour the weak.

The Imams[2] are of Quraysh;[3] the godly among them rulers of the godly, and the wicked among them rulers of the wicked. If Quraysh gives a crop-nosed Ethiopian slave authority over you, hear him and obey him as long as he does not force any of you to choose between his Islam and his neck. And if he does force anyone to choose between his Islam and his neck, let him offer his neck.

[1]KAY lihf   Successor to the prophet; supreme authority. [Ed.]

[2]A leader, especially in prayer; clergyman. [Ed.]

[3]An aristocratic trading clan of Mecca; hostile to Muhammad, but after his death regained prominence. That religious leaders come from Quraysh was agreed after victory of the Meccan faction in 661. [Ed.]

Al-Muttaqi, *Kanz al'Ummal,* quoted in *Islam from the Prophet Muhammad to the Capture of Constantinople,* ed. and trans. Bernard Lewis, vol. I (New York: Harper, 1974), 150–51.

Hear and obey, even if a shaggy-headed black slave is appointed over you.

Whosoever shall try to divide my community, strike off his head.

If allegiance is sworn to two Caliphs, kill the other.

He who sees in his ruler something he disapproves should be patient, for if anyone separates himself from the community, even by a span, and dies, he dies the death of a pagan.

Obey your rulers, whatever happens. If their commands accord with the revelation I brought you, they will be rewarded for it, and you will be rewarded for obeying them; if their commands are not in accord with what I brought you, they are responsible and you are absolved. When you meet God, you will say, "Lord God! No evil." And He will say, "No evil!" And you will say, "Lord God! Thou didst send us Prophets, and we obeyed them by Thy leave; and Thou didst appoint over us Caliphs, and we obeyed them by Thy leave; and Thou didst place over us rulers, and we obeyed them for Thy sake." And He will say, "You speak truth. They are responsible, and you are absolved."

If you have rulers over you who ordain prayer and the alms tax and the Holy War for God, then God forbids you to revile them and allows you to pray behind them.

If anyone comes out against my community when they are united and seeks to divide them, kill him, whoever he may be.

He who dies without an Imam dies the death of a pagan, and he who throws off his obedience will have no defense on the Day of Judgment.

Do not revile the Sultan, for he is God's shadow on God's earth. Obedience is the duty of the Muslim man, whether he like it or not, as long as he is not ordered to commit a sin. If he is ordered to commit a sin, he does not have to obey.

The nearer a man is to government, the further he is from God; the more followers he has, the more devils; the greater his wealth, the more exacting his reckoning.

He who commends a Sultan in what God condemns has left the religion of God.

AL-TANUKHI

A Government Job

Al-Tanukhi* (d. 994) was a judge in Baghdad. In this selection, he relates the story of his great uncle Abu Qasim's† response when he asked him why he gave up a government job. What does Abu Qasim's story tell you about the job of government officials in Muslim Baghdad in the tenth century? How was government in Muslim Baghdad different from government in medieval Europe? How were ideas of government different?

Thinking Historically

This story concerns a political post, but in what ways is the story an economic one as well? Would you say the lesson of the story is political, economic, or religious?

How did you come to repent of being in Government service, Abu Qasim? I once asked, What was the cause?

This was the cause, said my great-uncle. Abu Ali Jubbai (the great Rationalist theologian) used to stay with me when he came to Ahwaz. I was Clerk to the Ahwaz municipality as well as deputy Finance Minister, so that all business used to pass through my hands. I really ran the whole place. Once a year, when the Land Tax collections began, Abu Ali Jubbai used to come to Ahwaz to arrange to have the taxes due from certain persons, who over the years had come to regard themselves as his dependents, added to the Land Tax on his own private estate at Jubba. Everybody treated him with the highest honor and respect whenever he came to town. As a rule he would only stay with me; and I used to settle his business with the Governor. The Governor, of course, was not always a friend of mine, nor was he always a man who realized Abu Ali's position, or else the amount at which his assessment was fixed would have been even lower than it was. But he would always remit at least half or a third of the tax due from him.

*ahl tah NOO kee
†ah BOO kah SEEM

Judge Muhassin Tanukhi, "Resurrections of Loquacity or Table-talk (10th century)," in Eric Schroeder, *Muhammad's People: A Tale by Anthology* (Portland, ME: Bond Wheelwright Company, 1955), 566–68.

Returning to Jubba, Abu Ali never kept for himself any of the money which in an ordinary case would have been taken in taxes from an estate like his. He used to deduct from the gross amount the sum he was to pay to Government, and then distribute the remainder among the members of his religious following, stipulating in return that each of them should entertain for a whole year one of the poor students who attended his lectures; the actual expense these students put them to was small, not a fifth of the amount due which Abu Ali's high standing had sufficed to get remitted. Then he would go to his own house, and there take out of the revenues of his estate a full tithe, which he used to give in alms among the poor people of his village, Pool, where he maintained his disciples. And he did all this every year.

On one occasion, he was staying with me at the usual season, I had done what he wanted in the matter of his Land Tax, and we were sitting talking in the evening.

Abu Ali, I said to him, are you afraid of the consequences to me in the Hereafter of the profession I am following?

How could I but be anxious, Abu Qasim? he replied. For be sure of this: if you should die employed as you now are, you will never breathe the fragrance of the Garden.

Why not? I asked. How am I guilty? I am only an accountant — I act merely as a copyist, an employee of the Treasury. It may be that somebody will come to me with a grievance, some man whose Land Tax has been unduly raised; and if I reduce it for him and set matters straight, he is only too glad to give me a present. At times perhaps I may appropriate something which really belongs to the Sovereign; but it only represents a share in the booty of the Muslims, to which I have a right.

Abu Qasim, he rejoined, GOD IS NOT DECEIVED. Tell me this: is it not you who appoints the land surveyors and sends them out to make their surveys, which are supposed to be accurate? And don't they go out into the country, and raise the acreage figures by ten or twenty per cent, with pen on paper, and then hand in these falsifications of theirs, and do you not make up your assessment registers on the basis of these same falsifications? And then hand over these registers to the Collector's officer, and tell him that unless he produces so much money at the Collector's Office within so many days his hands will be nailed to his feet?

Yes, I admitted.

And then the officer sets out with his escort of soldiers, horse and foot, his despatch riders and speed-up men, and flogs and cuffs and fetters? and all the time he is acting on your instructions. For if you bid him let a man off, or give him time, he does that; whereas if you give no such permission he is merciless until the man pays up.

Yes, said I.

And then the money is deposited at the Collector's Office, and the receipt forms are issued to him from your office, with your mark on them?

Yes, said I.

Then what part of the whole business, asked Abu Ali, is not of your undertaking? What part are you not answerable for? Beware of God, or you are lost. Give up your Government job. Provide for your future.

From such exhortations, from such grave warnings he would not desist until at last I burst into tears.

You are not more highly favored, he then said, nor more highly placed than Ja'far ibn Harb was: he held high office at court, his privileges and rank were almost those of a Vizier; and he was also an orthodox Believer, and a famous scholar, the author of more than one book which is still read. And yet Ja'far, when he was in office, and riding one day in a superb cavalcade, on the very crest of pomp and circumstance, suddenly heard a man reading the verse: *IS NOT THE HOUR YET COME WHEN ALL WHO TRULY BELIEVE MUST BE BROKEN AND CONTRITE OF HEART AT THE VERY MENTION OF GOD AND OF TRUTH REVEALED?* Ay, the hour is come! Ja'far exclaimed. Over and over again he said it, weeping. And he dismounted, and stripped off his dress, and waded into Tigris until the water came up to his neck. Nor did he come out again until he had given away everything he owned to atone for wrongs he had done, in reparations, pious foundations, and alms, doing everything that his system of Belief demanded, or that he thought his duty. Some passer-by, who saw him standing in the water and was told his story, gave him a shirt and a pair of breeches to cover his coming out; and he put them on. He gave himself to study and devotion from then until his death.

After a moment, Abu Ali said to me: Go, and do thou likewise, Abu Qasim. But if you cannot bring yourself to go the whole way, at least repent of being an official.

What Jubbai said made a great impression on me. I resolved that I would repent, that I would give up my job. For some time I conducted my affairs with this in view; and when I saw an opportunity of getting out of Government service, I repented, my mind made up that I would never take public office again.

50

Egyptian Invitation

This document is an invitation issued by the sultan of Egypt between 1280 and 1290. Egypt had been a part of the Muslim world since the Arab invasion under Omar in 639. Like other Arab dominions, Egypt was ruled by the Umayyad caliphate in Damascus before 747 and then nominally by the Abbasid caliphate in Baghdad after 750. (See Map 7.3.) But other powers created dynasties that effectively ruled Egypt after 868: first Turks, then Persians, then the North African Fatimids (910–1171), followed by the Kurdish Ayyubid dynasty founded in 1174 by Saladin that lasted until the Mongol invasion. The last Ayyubid ruler was murdered in 1250 and was replaced as sultan (political leader) by his Mamluk slave general. The use of purchased or captured non-Muslim slaves as soldiers gave Muslim rulers loyal forces that had no ties to other tribal leaders. Converted to Islam, well trained, and given considerable power and authority, these Mamluk troops and administrators owed everything to the Sultan. Between 1250 and 1517, two dynasties of Mamluks ruled Egypt. At first, Mamluk status was strictly nonhereditary, and their sons were prevented from sharing power. Eventually, however, Mamluk dynasties were grafted onto the tribal structure.

To whom is this invitation addressed? What did the Sultan hope to achieve by issuing it? What does the content of the document tell us about Mamluk Egyptian society? Every society needs soldiers and merchants. Using this document and those you have read from Europe, compare the Mamluk Egyptian method of supplying this need with the method of medieval Europe.

Thinking Historically

The purpose of this invitation is clearly economic. Yet this economic purpose has political, social, and cultural dimensions as well. What are these other dimensions? How is economics related to other aspects of medieval Islamic society?

A decree has been issued, may God exalt the Sultan's exalted command, and may his [the Sultan's] justice keep the subjects in assured protection. He requests the prayers of the people of both east and west

Islam from the Prophet Muhammad to the Conquest of Constantinople, ed. and trans. Bernard Lewis, vol. II, *Religion and Society* (New York: Harper & Row, 1974), 166–68.

for his thriving reign, and let all of them be sincere. He offers a genuine welcome to those who come to his realm, as to the garden of Eden, by whatever gate they may choose to enter, from Iraq, from Persia, from Asia Minor, from the Ḥijāz, from India, and from China. Whoever wishes to set forth — the distinguished merchants, the men of great affairs, and the small traders, from the countries enumerated and also those which have not been enumerated — and whoever wishes to enter our realms may sojourn or travel at will and to come to our country of broad lands and leafy shades, then let him, like those whom God has destined for this, make firm resolve on this worthy and beneficial act, and let him come to a country whose inhabitants have no need either of supplies or reserves of food, for it is an earthly paradise for those who dwell in it, and a consolation for those who are far from their own homes, a delight of which the eye does not weary, a place from which one is never driven by excessive cold, for one lives there in perpetual spring and permanent well-being. It is enough to say that one of its descriptions is that it is God's beauty spot on His earth. God's blessing accrues in the baggage of whoever does a good deed by lending or receives a good deed by borrowing. Another of its features is that anyone who comes there hoping for anything, gets what he wants, for it is a land of Islam, with armies whose swords are beyond reproach. For justice has made its lands prosper and has multiplied its inhabitants. The buildings have increased so that it is a land of great cities. The needy is at ease there, and does not fear the violence of the creditors, for demands there are not exacting and deferments easily obtained. The rest of the people and all the merchants have no fear there of any oppression, for justice protects.

Whoever becomes aware of this our decree, among the merchants who live in Yemen and India and China and Sind and elsewhere, let them prepare to travel and come to our country, where they will find the reality better than the word and will see a beneficence beyond the mere fulfillment of their promises and will sojourn in "a fair land under a forgiving Lord" [Qur'ān, xxxv, 15] and in comfort deserving of gratitude (for only the grateful is rewarded) and in security of person and property, and felicity which illuminates their circumstances and fulfills their hopes. They will receive from us all the justice that they expect. Our justice responds to those who call on it, has procedure which will be praised by their way of life, will leave their property to their descendants, and will protect and preserve them so that they will take shelter under its shadow and be protected. Whoever brings merchandise with him, such as spices and other articles imported by the Kārimī[1]

---

[1]An association of merchants in Egypt and Arabia, engaged in the eastern trade.

merchants, will suffer no unjust impost nor be subjected to any burden-some demand, for [our] justice will leave with them what is desirable and remove what is burdensome. If anyone brings [white] male slaves [mamlūk] or slave-girls, he will find their sale price beyond his expecta-tions and [will be accorded] the tolerance in fixing a profitable price which is customarily accorded to those who import such slaves from near and all the more from distant lands; for our desire is directed to-ward the increase of our troops, and those who import mamlūks have gained a title to our generosity. Let whoever can do so increase his im-port of mamlūks, and let him know that the purpose in demanding them is to increase the armies of Islam. For thanks to them, Islam today is in glory with flag unfurled and the Sultan al-Manṣūr [Qalawun]. The mamlūk who is thus imported is removed from darkness to light. Yes-terday he was blamed for unbelief; today he is praised for faith and fights for Islam against his own tribe and people.

This is our decree for all traveling merchants to whose knowledge it comes, "They seek the bounty of God, while others fight in the cause of God." [Qur'ān, lxxiii, 20] Let them read in it the orders which will ease their task; let them be guided by its star, nourished by its wisdom. Let them mount the neck of the hope which impels them to leave their homes and stretch out their hands in prayer for him who wishes people to come to his country, so that they may benefit from his generosity in all clarity and in all beneficence; and let them take advantage of the oc-casions for profit, for they are ripe for picking. These true promises are sent to them to confirm their high hopes and reaffirm to them that the noble rescript is valid, by the command of God, in accordance with what the pens have written, and [God is] the best Guarantor.

51

ICHISADA MIYAZAKI

The Chinese Civil Service Exam System

The Chinese civil service examination system originated fourteen hundred years ago, making it the first in the world. As a device for ensuring government by the brightest young men, regardless of class or social standing, it may also be viewed as one of the world's earliest democratic systems. It was not perfect. Like democratic systems in the West only two hundred years ago, it excluded women. The system also put enormous pressure on young boys of ambitious families.

This selection consists of two passages from a book by a noted modern Japanese historian of China. The first passage concerns the elaborate early preparations for the exams.

What did young boys have to learn? In what ways was their education different from your own? What effects did the examination system have on the goals and values of young people?

Thinking Historically

The Chinese examination system was primarily a political system, a way for the emperor to rule most effectively, employing the most talented administrators. In what sense did this system make China more "democratic" than the political systems of Western Europe or the Muslim world? In what sense was it less so? Did it become more or less democratic over the course of Chinese history? How did its purpose change from the Tang dynasty to the Sung dynasty?

Like any political system, the civil service system had a major impact on other aspects of life — social, economic, and cultural. How did it affect Chinese society, families, class differences, boys and girls? What were the economic effects of the system? How did it influence Chinese cultural values, ideas, and education?

Judging from this excerpt and your readings about Western Europe and the Islamic world, what was the single most important difference between Chinese and Western European civilizations? Between Chinese and Muslim civilization?

Ichisada Miyazaki, *China's Examination Hell*, trans. Conrad Schirokauer (New York: Weatherhill, 1976), 13–17, 111–16, passim.

Preparing for the Examinations

Competition for a chance to take the civil service examinations began, if we may be allowed to exaggerate only a little, even before birth. On the back of many a woman's copper mirror the five-character formula "Five Sons Pass the Examinations" expressed her heart's desire to bear five successful sons. Girls, since they could not take the examinations and become officials but merely ran up dowry expenses, were no asset to a family; a man who had no sons was considered to be childless. People said that thieves warned each other not to enter a household with five or more girls because there would be nothing to steal in it. The luckless parents of girls hoped to make up for such misfortune in the generation of their grandchildren by sending their daughters into marriage equipped with those auspicious mirrors.

Prenatal care began as soon as a woman was known to be pregnant. She had to be very careful then, because her conduct was thought to have an influence on the unborn child, and everything she did had to be right. She had to sit erect, with her seat and pillows arranged in exactly the proper way, to sleep without carelessly pillowing her head on an arm, to abstain from strange foods, and so on. She had to be careful to avoid unpleasant colors, and she spent her leisure listening to poetry and the classics being read aloud. These preparations were thought to lead to the birth of an unusually gifted boy.

If, indeed, a boy was born the whole family rejoiced, but if a girl arrived everyone was dejected. On the third day after her birth it was the custom to place a girl on the floor beneath her bed, and to make her grasp a tile and a pebble so that even then she would begin to form a lifelong habit of submission and an acquaintance with hardship. In contrast, in early times when a boy was born arrows were shot from an exorcising bow in the four directions of the compass and straight up and down. In later times, when literary accomplishments had become more important than the martial arts, this practice was replaced by the custom of scattering coins for servants and others to pick up as gifts. Frequently the words "First-place Graduate" were cast on those coins, to signify the highest dreams of the family and indeed of the entire clan.

It was thought best for a boy to start upon his studies as early as possible. From the very beginning he was instructed almost entirely in the classics, since mathematics could be left to merchants, while science and technology were relegated to the working class. A potential grand official must study the Four Books, the Five Classics, and other Confucian works, and, further, he must know how to compose poems and write essays. For the most part, questions in civil service examinations did not go beyond these areas of competence.

When he was just a little more than three years old, a boy's education began at home, under the supervision of his mother or some other suitable person. Even at this early stage the child's home environment exerted a great effect upon his development. In cultivated families, where books were stacked high against the walls, the baby sitter taught the boy his first characters while playing. As far as possible these were characters written with only a few strokes.

First a character was written in outline with red ink on a single sheet of paper. Then the boy was made to fill it in with black ink. Finally he himself had to write each character. At this stage there was no special need for him to know the meanings of the characters.

After he had learned in this way to hold the brush and to write a number of characters, he usually started on the *Primer of One Thousand Characters*. This is a poem that begins:

> Heaven is dark, earth is yellow,
> The universe vast and boundless . . .

It consists of a total of two hundred and fifty lines, and since no character is repeated, it provided the student with a foundation of a thousand basic ideograms.

Upon completing the *Primer*, a very bright boy, who could memorize one thing after another without difficulty, would go on to a history text called *Meng Ch'iu* (*The Beginner's Search*) and then proceed to the Four Books and the Five Classics normally studied in school. If rumors of such a prodigy reached the capital, a special "tough examination" was held, but often such a precocious boy merely served as a plaything for adults and did not accomplish much in later life. Youth examinations were popular during the Sung dynasty, but declined and finally were eliminated when people realized how much harm they did to the boys.

Formal education began at about seven years of age (or eight, counting in Chinese style). Boys from families that could afford the expense were sent to a temple, village, communal, or private school staffed by former officials who had lost their positions, or by old scholars who had repeatedly failed the examinations as the years slipped by. Sons of rich men and powerful officials often were taught at home by a family tutor in an elegant small room located in a detached building, which stood in a courtyard planted with trees and shrubs, in order to create an atmosphere conducive to study.

A class usually consisted of eight or nine students. Instruction centered on the Four Books, beginning with the *Analects*, and the process of learning was almost entirely a matter of sheer memorization. With their books open before them, the students would parrot the teacher, phrase by phrase, as he read out the text. Inattentive students, or those who amused themselves by playing with toys hidden in their sleeves, would be scolded by the teacher or hit on the palms and thighs with his fan-shaped "warning ruler." The high regard for discipline was reflected in the saying, "If education is not strict, it shows that the teacher is lazy."

Students who had learned how to read a passage would return to their seats and review what they had just been taught. After reciting it a hundred times, fifty times while looking at the book and fifty with the book face down, even the least gifted would have memorized it. At first the boys were given twenty to thirty characters a day, but as they became more experienced they memorized one, two, or several hundred each day. In order not to force a student beyond his capacity, a boy who could memorize four hundred characters would be assigned no more than two hundred. Otherwise he might become so distressed as to end by detesting his studies.

Along with the literary curriculum, the boys were taught proper conduct, such as when to use honorific terms, how to bow to superiors and to equals, and so forth — although from a modern point of view their training in deportment may seem somewhat defective, as is suggested by the incident concerning a high-ranking Chinese diplomat in the late Ch'ing dynasty who startled Westerners by blowing his nose with his fingers at a public ceremony.

It was usual for a boy to enter school at the age of eight and to complete the general classical education at fifteen. The heart of the curriculum was the classics. If we count the number of characters in the classics that the boys were required to learn by heart, we get the following figures:

Analects	11,705
Mencius	34,685
Book of Changes	24,107
Book of Documents	25,700
Book of Poetry	39,234
Book of Rites	99,010
Tso Chuan	196,845

The total number of characters a student had to learn, then, was 431,286.

The *Great Learning* and the *Doctrine of the Mean*, which together with the *Analects* and the *Mencius* constitute the Four Books, are not counted separately, since they are included in the *Book of Rites*. And, of course, those were not 431,286 *different* characters: Most of the ideographs would have been used many times in the several texts. Even so, the task of having to memorize textual material amounting to more than 400,000 characters is enough to make one reel. They required exactly six years of memorizing, at the rate of two hundred characters a day.

After the students had memorized a book, they read commentaries, which often were several times the length of the original text, and practiced answering questions involving passages selected as examination topics. On top of all this, other classical, historical, and literary works had to be scanned, and some literary works had to be examined carefully, since the students were required to write poems and essays modeled upon them. Anyone not very vigorous mentally might well become sick of it all halfway through the course.

Moreover, the boys were at an age when the urge to play is strongest, and they suffered bitterly when they were confined all day in a classroom as though under detention. Parents and teachers, therefore, supported a lad, urging him on to "become a great man!" From ancient times, many poems were composed on the theme, "If you study while young, you will get ahead." The Sung emperor Chen-tsung wrote such a one:

> To enrich your family, no need to buy good land:
> Books hold a thousand measures of grain.
> For an easy life, no need to build a mansion:
> In books are found houses of gold.
> Going out, be not vexed at absence of followers:
> In books, carriages and horses form a crowd.
> Marrying, be not vexed by lack of a good go-between:
> In books there are girls and faces of jade.
> A boy who wants to become a somebody
> Devotes himself to the classics, faces the window, and reads.

In later times this poem was criticized because it tempted students with the promise of beautiful women and riches, but that was the very reason it was effective.

Nonetheless, in all times and places students find shortcuts to learning. Despite repeated official and private injunctions to study the Four Books and Five Classics honestly, rapid-study methods were devised with the sole purpose of preparing candidates for the examinations. Because not very many places in the classics were suitable as subjects for examination questions, similar passages and problems were often repeated. Aware of this, publishers compiled collections of examination answers, and a candidate who, relying on these compilations, guessed successfully during the course of his own examinations could obtain a good rating without having worked very hard. But if he guessed wrong he faced unmitigated disaster because, unprepared, he would have submitted so bad a paper that the officials could only shake their heads and fail him. Reports from perturbed officials caused the government to issue frequent prohibitions of the publication of such collections of model answers, but since it was a profitable business with a steady demand, ways of issuing them surreptitiously were arranged, and time and again the prohibitions rapidly became mere empty formalities.

An Evaluation of the Examination System

Did the examination system serve a useful purpose? . . .

The purpose of instituting the examinations, some fourteen hundred years ago under the Sui rulers, was to strike a blow against government by the hereditary aristocracy, which had prevailed until then, and to establish in its place an imperial autocracy. The period of disunion lasting from the third to the sixth century was the golden age of the Chinese aristocracy: during that time it controlled political offices in central and local governments. . . .

The important point in China, as in Japan, was that the power of the aristocracy seriously constrained the emperor's power to appoint officials. He could not employ men simply on the basis of their ability, since any imperial initiative to depart from the traditional personnel policy evoked a sharp counterattack from the aristocratic officials. This was the situation when the Sui emperor, exploiting the fact that he had reestablished order and that his authority was at its height, ended the power of the aristocracy to become officials merely by virtue of family status. He achieved this revolution when he enacted the examination system (and provided that only its graduates were to be considered qualified to hold government office), kept at hand a reserve of such officials, and made it a rule to use only them to fill vacancies in central and local government as they occurred. This was the origin of the examination system.

The Sui dynasty was soon replaced by the T'ang, which for the most part continued the policies of its predecessor. Actually, as the T'ang was in the process of winning control over China, a new group of aristocrats appeared who hoped to transmit their privileges to their descendants. To deal with this problem the emperor used the examination system and favored its *chin-shih*[1] trying to place them in important posts so that he could run the government as he wished. The consequence was strife between the aristocrats and the *chin-shih*, with the contest gradually turning in favor of the latter. Since those who gained office simply through their parentage were not highly regarded, either by the imperial government or by society at large, career-minded aristocrats, too, seem to have found it necessary to enter officialdom through the examination system. Their acceptance of this hard fact meant a real defeat for the aristocracy.

The T'ang can be regarded as a period of transition from the aristocratic government inherited from the time of the Six Dynasties to the purely bureaucratic government of future regimes. The examination

[1]Highest degree winners. [Ed.]

system made a large contribution to what was certainly a great advance for China's society, and in this respect its immense significance in Chinese history cannot be denied. Furthermore, that change was begun fourteen hundred years ago, at about the time when in Europe the feudal system had scarcely been formed. In comparison, the examination system was immeasurably progressive, containing as it did a superb idea the equal of which could not be found anywhere else in the world at that time.

This is not to say that the T'ang examination system was without defects. First, the number of those who passed through it was extremely small. In part this was an inevitable result of the limited diffusion of China's literary culture at a time when printing had not yet become practical and hand-copied books were still both rare and expensive, thus restricting the number of men able to pursue scholarly studies. Furthermore, because the historical and economic roots of the new bureaucratic system were still shallow, matters did not always go smoothly and sometimes there were harsh factional conflicts among officials. The development of those conflicts indicates that they were caused by the examination system itself and constituted a second serious defect.

As has been indicated, a master-disciple relationship between the examiner and the men he passed was established, much like that between a political leader and his henchmen, while the men who passed the examination in the same year considered one another as classmates and helped one another forever after. When such combinations became too strong, factions were born.

These two defects of the examination system were eliminated during the Sung regime. For one thing, the number of men who were granted degrees suddenly rose, indicating a similar rise in the number of candidates. This was made possible by the increase in productive power and the consequent accumulation of wealth, which was the underlying reason that Chinese society changed so greatly from the T'ang period to the Sung. A new class appeared in China, comparable to the bourgeoisie in early modern Europe. In China this newly risen class concentrated hard on scholarship, and with the custom of this group, publishers prospered mightily. The classic books of Buddhism and Confucianism were printed; the collected writings of contemporaries and their discourses and essays on current topics were published; and the government issued an official gazette, so that in a sense China entered upon an age of mass communications. As a result learning was so widespread that candidates for the examinations came from virtually every part of the land, and the government could freely pick the best among them to form a reserve of officials.

In the Sung dynasty the system of conducting the examinations every three years was established. Since about three hundred men were selected each time, the government obtained an average of one hundred men a year who were qualified for the highest government positions. Thus the most important positions in government were occupied by *chin-shih*, and no longer were there conflicts between men who differed in their preparatory backgrounds, such as those between *chin-shih* and non–*chin-shih* that had arisen in the T'ang period.

Another improvement made during the Sung period was the establishment of the palace examination as the apex of the normal examination sequence. Under the T'ang emperors the conduct of the examinations was completely entrusted to officials, but this does not mean that emperors neglected them, because they were held by imperial order. It even happened that Empress Wu (r. 684–705) herself conducted the examinations in an attempt to win popularity. . . .

The position of the emperor in the political system changed greatly from T'ang times to Sung. No longer did the emperor consult on matters of high state policy with two or three great ministers deep in the interior of the palace, far removed from actual administrators. Now he was an autocrat, directly supervising all important departments of government and giving instructions about every aspect of government. Even minor matters of personnel needed imperial sanction. Now the emperor resembled the pivot of a fan, without which the various ribs of government would fall apart and be scattered. The creation of the palace examination as the final examination, given directly under the emperor's personal supervision, went hand in hand with this change in his function in the nation's political machinery and was a necessary step in the strengthening of imperial autocracy.

Thus, the examination system changed, along with Chinese society as a whole. Created to meet an essential need, it changed in response to that society's demand. It was most effective in those early stages when, first in the T'ang period, it was used by the emperor to suppress the power of the aristocracy, and then later, in the Sung period, when the cooperation of young officials with the *chin-shih* was essential for the establishment of imperial autocracy. Therefore, in the early Sung years *chin-shih* enjoyed very rapid promotion; this was especially true of the first-place *chin-shih*, not a few of whom rose to the position of chief councilor in fewer than ten years.

52

LIU TSUNG-YUAN

Camel Kuo the Gardener

Liu Tsung-yuan* (773–819) was one of the great writers of the T'ang dynasty (618–907). He was especially loved for his scenes of nature, a topic he uses here for an allegory about government. What is the message of the allegory?

Thinking Historically

Are the ideas of government expressed here more like those of Confucius or Lao Tzu? How do you think Liu Tsung-yuan felt about the civil service system? Can we assume that Chinese government was practiced as the author desired, or that it was not?

How does this view of government differ from that of Western European or Muslim societies? In what sense is it more typically Chinese?

Whatever name Camel Kuo may have had to begin with is not known. But he was a hunchback and walked in his bumpy way with his face to the ground, very like a camel, and so that was what the country folk called him. When Camel Kuo heard them he said, "Excellent. Just the right name for me." — And he forthwith discarded his real name and himself adopted "Camel" also.

He lived at Feng-lo, to the west of Ch'ang-an. Camel was a grower of trees by profession; and all the great and wealthy residents of Ch'ang-an who planted trees for their enjoyment or lived off the sale of their fruit would compete for the favour of his services. It was a matter of observation that when Camel Kuo had planted a tree, even though it was uprooted from elsewhere, there was never a one but lived, and grew strong and glossy, and fruited early and abundantly. Other growers, however they spied on him and tried to imitate his methods, never could achieve his success.

*lee OU   tsung WAHN

Liu Tsung-yuan, "Camel Kuo the Gardener," in *Anthology of Chinese Literature*, ed. and trans. Cyril Birch (New York: Grove Press, 1965), 258–59.

Once, when questioned on the point, Camel replied: "I cannot make a tree live for ever or flourish. What I *can* do is comply with the nature of the tree so that it takes the way of its kind. When a tree is planted its roots should have room to breathe, its base should be firmed, the soil it is in should be old, and the fence around it should be close. When you have it this way, then you must neither disturb it nor worry about it, but go away and not come back. If you care for it like this when you plant it, and neglect it like this *after* you have planted it, then its nature will be fulfilled and it will take the way of its kind. And so all *I* do is avoid harming its growth — I have no power to make it grow; I avoid hindering the fruiting — I have no power to bring it forward or make it more abundant.

"With other growers it is not the same. They coil up the roots and they use fresh soil. They firm the base either too much or not enough. Or if they manage to avoid these faults, then they dote too fondly and worry too anxiously. They inspect the tree every morning and cosset it every night; they cannot walk away from it without turning back for another look. The worst of them will even scrape off the bark to see if it is still living, or shake the roots to test whether they are holding fast. And with all this the tree gets further every day from what a tree should be. This is not mothering but smothering, not affection but affliction. This is why they cannot rival my results: what other skill can I claim?"

"Would it be possible to apply this philosophy of yours to the art of government?" asked the questioner.

"My only art is the growing of trees," said Camel Kuo in answer. "Government is not my business. But living here in the country I have seen officials who go to a lot of trouble issuing orders as though they were deeply concerned for the people; yet all they achieve is an increase of misfortune. Morning and evening runners come yelling, 'Orders from the government: plough at once! Sow right away! Harvest inspection! Spin your silk! Weave your cloth! Raise your children! Feed your livestock!' Drums roll for assembly, blocks are struck to summon us. And we the common people miss our meals to receive the officials and still cannot find the time: how then can we expect to prosper our livelihood and find peace in our lives? This is why we are sick and weary; and in this state of affairs I suppose there may be some resemblance to my profession?"

"Wonderful!" was the delighted cry of the man who had questioned him. "The art I sought was of cultivating trees; the art I found was of cultivating men. Let this be passed on as a lesson to all in office!"

53

FAN ZHONGYAN

Rules for the
Fan Lineage's Charitable Estate

From the time of the Sung dynasty (960–1279), many wealthy Chinese families formed charitable trusts for their descendants. One of the first men to set up such a trust was Fan Zhongyan (989–1052), an important political official.

This selection presents the rules that Fan set down for the way in which his descendants would share the income from his estate. What activities did the lineage support? What other activities would have been left to individual families? Why would lineages be more common among wealthy than poor families?

Thinking Historically

Lineage was both a social and economic organization. What impact would these lineages have on Chinese social life? Would they strengthen or weaken Chinese families? How might they affect Chinese economic life?

How did lineages make Chinese society different from that of Western Europe? Were there similar social institutions in Islamic society? Is there a modern equivalent?

1. One pint of rice per day may be granted for each person whom a branch has certified to be one of its members. (These quantities refer to polished rice. If hulled rice is used, the amount should be increased proportionately.)

2. Children of both sexes over five years of age are counted in the total.

3. Female servants may receive rice if they have borne children by men in the lineage and the children are over fifteen or they themselves are over fifty.

4. One bolt of silk for winter clothing may be granted for each individual, except children between five and ten years of age who may receive half a bolt.

Fan Zhongyan, *Fan Wengzheng gong ji*, in *Chinese Civilization: A Sourcebook*, 2nd ed., ed. and trans. Patricia Buckley Ebrey (New York: The Free Press, 1993), 155–56.

5. Each branch may receive a rice ration for a single slave, but not any silk.

6. Every birth, marriage, death, or other change in the number of lineage members must immediately be recorded.

7. Each branch should make a list of those entitled to grain rations. At the end of the month the manager should examine these requests. He must not make any prior arrangements or exceed the stipulated monthly rations. The manager should also keep his own register in which he records the quantity due each branch based on the number of its members. If the manager spends money wastefully or makes advance payments to anyone, the branches have the authority to require him to pay an indemnity.

8. For the expenses of marrying a daughter, thirty strings of cash may be granted, unless the marriage is a second one, in which case twenty strings may be granted.

9. For the expenses of taking a first wife, twenty strings may be granted (but nothing for a second wife).

10. Lineage members who become officials may receive the regular rice and silk grants and the special grants for weddings and funerals if they are living at home awaiting a post, awaiting selection, or mourning their parents. They may also receive the grants if they leave their families at home while they serve in Sichuan, Gwangdong, or Fujien, or for any other good reason.

11. For the expenses of mourning and funerals in the various branches, if the deceased is a senior member, when mourning begins, a grant of ten strings of cash may be made, and a further fifteen at the time of the burial. For more junior members, the figures are five and ten strings respectively. In the case of low-ranking members or youths under nineteen, seven strings for both expenses; for those under fifteen, three strings; for those under ten, two strings. No grant should be made for children who die before seven, or slaves or servants.

12. If any relatives through marriage living in the district face dire need or unexpected difficulties, the branches should jointly determine the facts and discuss ways to provide assistance from the income of the charitable estate.

13. A stock of rice should be stored by the charitable estate from year to year. The monthly rations and the grants of silk for winter clothing should start with the tenth month of 1050. Thereafter, during each year with a good harvest, two years' worth of grain rations should be hulled and stored. If a year of dearth occurs, no grants should be made except for the rice rations. Any surplus over and above the two years' reserve should be used first for funeral and mourning expenses, then marriage expenses. If there is still a remainder, winter clothes may be issued. However, if the surplus is not very large, the priorities should be discussed, and the amount available divided up and granted in equi-

table proportions. If grants cannot be made to all entitled to them, they should be made first to those who have suffered bereavement, next to those with weddings. In cases where more than one death has occurred at the same time, senior members take precedence over junior ones. Where the relative seniority of those concerned is the same, the grant should be made on the basis of which death or burial took place first. If, after paying out the rations and the allowances for marriages and burials, a surplus still remains, it must not be sold off, but hulled and put into storage for use as rations for three or more years. If there is a danger that the stored grain might go bad, it may be sold off and replaced with fresh rice after the autumn harvest. All members of the branches of the lineage will carefully comply with the above rules.

Tenth month, 1050. Academician of the Zizheng Hall, Vice-president of the Board of Rites, and Prefect of Hangzhou, Fan. Sealed.

REFLECTIONS

Whatever particular period or region historians work on — in the case of this chapter, medieval Europe, Islam, and China — they also tend to specialize in particular kinds of documents and related aspects of life. They are social historians, or economic historians, or cultural historians. As a matter of fact, most of them would characterize their work even more precisely than that. A particular social historian might prefer to be called a historian of gender or a historian of the family. A political historian might be a diplomatic historian. A cultural historian might be a historian of religion, or even of medieval Christianity, or of Christian anti-Semitism. As in the sciences, historians are able to dig deeper and learn more by specializing. And, as in any field, the more you specialize, the more you discover you do not know, the more questions you have, and the more you can learn.

All of this begins, however, with some basic categories, like those we have used in this chapter. That is why you were asked to think in terms of political, economic, social, and cultural history.

To pull together and compare some of the characterizations you made from the selections in this chapter, make a chart: Write the names of the three civilizations — European, Islamic, and Chinese — across the top of the page, and the categories social, economic, political, and cultural down the left margin, allowing a quarter page for each. Try to fill in as many of the blocks as you can. You might use more than one characterization for each. For instance, in the box for social aspects of European civilization you would, no doubt, write "feudalism." You might also write "nobles," "monasteries," "fealty and homage," "vassals defend," and "sons inherit status." Or your style of observing and characterizing might lead you to such notes as "churches can be land-lords," "lots of witnesses," and "they were very formal." All of these descriptions are correct: Just make sure your comments are about society, social behavior, social relationships, social organization, or various social elements — class, family, men and women, population, and age. Repeat this exercise with the other three categories. These are by no means exclusive, but try not to use the same words in describing, say, a social and an economic aspect.

After you have filled in as many of the blanks as you can, you can make comparisons in a number of interesting ways. (You have already done some of this, but here you can be more systematic.) First, compare how one category, say society, is different in Europe and Islam, or Europe and China, or China and Islam. You might, for example, say that European society was less centralized than Chinese or Islamic society or that the extended family was more important in China.

After doing the same for economics, politics, and culture, notice how the four categories of any civilization fit together. How does the type of society in medieval Europe, for instance, "fit" medieval Europe's economy? This interaction is what constitutes a civilization. See if you used a word repetitively in characterizing each of the four aspects of a particular civilization. Then try to categorize the civilization as a whole.

Now you are ready to compare each of these civilizations to another one. These characterizations may be general, or they may be qualified and later modified, but at the very least you now have a general starting point for more in-depth analysis of these three great civilizations in future chapters.

Love and Marriage

Medieval Europe, India, and Japan, 400–1200 C.E.

HISTORICAL CONTEXT

Love and marriage, love and marriage,
Go together like a horse and carriage.
This I tell ya, brother,
You can't have one without the other.[1]

Despite the lyrics of the song, love and marriage had little to do with each other throughout most of human history. Parents arranged marriages with their own economic needs foremost. Few people had the time to cultivate the idea of romantic love. One group who did, the ancient Greeks, wrote of love as a sickness; its symptoms were sweaty palms, palpitating heart, blushing complexion, and stammering speech. Marriage cured the disease, ending all symptoms, returning the couple to the steady sanity of daily life. But the idea of love as affliction, accident, or attack (symbolized by the random shot of Cupid's arrow) was evidently too enticing to disappear with the end of the classical world. Cultivated in the religious poetry of the Islamic world, ideas of fevered emotional dedication revived in Europe in the Middle Ages.

A thousand years ago, romantic love was experienced by very few people—often members of a leisure class who seemed to have time on their hands. And the set of ideas, feelings, and actions they exhibited might strike modern readers as rather bizarre. We have to look closely to see the roots of one of our favorite modern emotions.

[1]Written by Sammy Cahn and Jimmy Van Heusen.

THINKING HISTORICALLY
Analyzing Cultural Differences

In the previous chapter, we distinguished among the economic, social, political, and cultural aspects of a society. In this chapter we will examine cultural aspects alone. Actually, culture is never alone, any more than are economics, politics, or social behavior. Culture is nothing less than all our thoughts and feelings and the way we express them by the way we walk, talk, dream, and read history books. Even love, a single ingredient of a culture, is related to aspects of behavior, economics, and even politics. Yet we will isolate this one cultural piece—love—to see how its meaning is different in different cultures. We will analyze these differences to understand better the different cultures and also to understand something about the history of love.

$$\boxed{54}$$

KEVIN REILLY

Love in Medieval Europe, India, and Japan

We hesitantly introduce this piece as a secondary source. It might be better called a tertiary source because it is based so much on the work of others and is part of a chapter in a college textbook. Nevertheless, it sets the stage for our discussion about love. The selection begins with the classic argument that romantic love was a product of medieval Europe, originating in the troubadour tradition of southern France around the twelfth century. The story of Ulrich von Liechtenstein, although probably not typical, details all the facets of the new idea of love, as well as the courts of chivalry that developed its code of behavior. What, according to this interpretation, are the elements of romantic love? How is it similar to, or different from, other kinds of love? How does it relate to sex and marriage? How is the medieval Indian tradition of *bhakti* different from European romantic love? How were medieval Hindu ideas of sex different from Christian ideas of sex? How was the Japanese idea of love during the Heian* period (794–1185) different from European romantic love? How was it similar?

*hay AHN

Kevin Reilly, *The West and the World*, 3rd ed. (Princeton, N.J.: Markus Wiener, 1997), 279–80, 282–83, 287–92.

Thinking Historically

Every culture encompasses a wide variety of ideas and behavior at any one time, making it difficult to argue that a certain idea or behavior defines the culture as a whole. Nevertheless, if there were no commonalities there could be no culture. One way to understand what makes one culture different from another is to discount the extreme behavior at the fringes and focus on what most people think or do. But another way is to compare the extremes of one culture with the extremes of another, on the assumption that the extremists of any culture will magnify the culture's main trait. You might think of Ulrich von Liechtenstein as an extreme example of medieval European ideas of romantic love. A question to ask after you read about other societies is: Could there have been an Ulrich elsewhere? Could medieval India or Japan have produced an Ulrich? If not, why not?

Notice also that this selection highlights particular social classes as well as particular cultures. How do cultures and classes interact to form the ideal of romantic love in Europe and something both similar and different in Japan?

In the Service of Woman

In the twelfth century the courtly love tradition of the troubadours traveled north into France and Germany, and it became a guide to behavior for many young knights.

We are lucky to have the autobiography of one of these romantic knights, a minor noble who was born in Austria about 1200. His name was Ulrich von Liechtenstein, and he called his autobiography, appropriately enough, *In the Service of Woman*.[1]

At an early age Ulrich learned that the greatest honor and happiness for a knight lay in the service of a beautiful and noble woman. He seems to have realized, at least subconsciously, that true love had to be full of obstacles and frustrations in order to be spiritually ennobling. So at the age of twelve Ulrich chose as the love of his life a princess. She was a perfect choice: Far above him socially, she was also older than Ulrich and already married. Ulrich managed to become a page in her court so that he could see her and touch the same things that she touched. Sometimes he was even able to steal away to his room with the very water that she had just washed her hands in, and he would secretly drink it.

By the age of seventeen Ulrich had become a knight and took to the countryside to joust the tournaments wearing the lady's colors. Finally

---

[1]Paraphrased from Martin Hunt, *The National History of Love* (New York: Alfred A. Knopf, 1959), 132–39. Quotations from Hunt.

after a number of victories, Ulrich gained the courage to ask his niece to call on the lady and tell her that he wanted to be a distant, respectful admirer. The princess would have none of it. She told Ulrich's niece that she was repulsed by Ulrich's mere presence, that he was low class and ugly—especially with that harelip of his. On hearing her reply Ulrich was overjoyed that she had noticed him. He went to have his harelip removed, recuperated for six weeks, and wrote a song to the princess. When the lady heard of this she finally consented to let Ulrich attend a riding party she was having, suggesting even that he might exchange a word with her if the opportunity arose. Ulrich had his chance. He was next to her horse as she was about to dismount, but he was so tongue-tied that he couldn't say a word. The princess thought him such a boor that she pulled out a lock of his hair as she got off her horse.

Ulrich returned to the field for the next three years. Finally the lady allowed him to joust in her name, but she wouldn't part with as much as a ribbon for him to carry. He sent her passionate letters and songs that he had composed. She answered with insults and derision. In one letter the princess derided Ulrich for implying that he had lost a finger while fighting for her when he had actually only wounded it slightly. Ulrich responded by having a friend hack off the finger and send it to the lady in a green velvet case. The princess was evidently so impressed with the power that she had over Ulrich that she sent back a message that she would look at it every day—a message that Ulrich received as he had the others—"on his knees, with bowed head and folded hands."

More determined than ever to win his lady's love, Ulrich devised a plan for a spectacular series of jousts, in which he challenged all comers on a five-week trip. He broke eight lances a day in the service of his princess. After such a showing, the princess sent word that Ulrich might at last visit her, but that he was to come disguised as a leper and sit with the other lepers who would be there begging. The princess passed him, said nothing, and let him sleep that night out in the rain. The following day she sent a message to Ulrich that he could climb a rope to her bedroom window. There she told him that she would grant no favors until he waded across the lake; then she dropped the rope so that he fell into the stinking moat.

Finally, after all of this, the princess said that she would grant Ulrich her love if he went on a Crusade in her name. When she learned that he was making preparations to go, she called it off and offered her love. After almost fifteen years Ulrich had proved himself to the princess.

What was the love that she offered? Ulrich doesn't say, but it probably consisted of kisses, an embrace, and possibly even a certain amount of fondling. Possibly more, but probably not. That was not the point. Ulrich had not spent fifteen years for sex. In fact, Ulrich had not spent fifteen years to win. The quest is what kept him going. His real reward was in the suffering and yearning. Within two years Ulrich was after another perfect lady.

Oh yes. We forgot one thing. Ulrich mentions that in the middle of his spectacular five-week joust, he stopped off for three days to visit the wife and kids. He was married? He was married. He speaks of his wife with a certain amount of affection. She was evidently quite good at managing the estate and bringing up the children. But what were these mundane talents next to the raptures of serving the ideal woman? Love was certainly not a part of the "details of crops, and cattle, fleas and fireplaces, serfs and swamp drainage." In fact, Ulrich might expect that his wife would be proud of him if she knew what he was up to. The love of the princess should make Ulrich so much more noble and esteemed in his wife's eyes.

Courtly Love

The behavior of Ulrich von Liechtenstein reflected in exaggerated form a new idea of love in the West. Historians have called it "courtly love" because it developed in the courts of Europe, where noble ladies and knights of "quality" came together. For the first time since the Greeks a man could idealize a woman, but only if he minimized her sexuality. The evidence is overwhelming that these spiritual affairs would ideally never be consummated.

It is difficult for us to understand how these mature lords and ladies could torture themselves with passionate oaths, feats of endurance, fainting spells when they heard their lover's name or voice, in short the whole repertoire of romance, and then refrain from actually consummating that love. Why did they insist on an ideal of "pure love" that allowed even naked embraces but drew the line at intercourse, which they called "false love"? No doubt the Christian antipathy for sex was part of the problem. Earlier Christian monks had practiced a similar type of *agape*, Christianity had always taught that there was a world of difference between love and lust. The tendency of these Christian men to think of their ladies as replicas of the Virgin Mother also made sex inappropriate, if not outright incestuous.

But these lords and ladies were also making a statement about their "class" or good breeding. They were saying (as did Sigmund Freud almost a thousand years later) that civilized people repress their animal lust. They were distinguishing themselves from the crude peasants and soldiers around them who knew only fornication and whoring and raping. They were cultivating their emotions and their sensitivity, and priding themselves on their self-control. They were privileged (as members of the upper class) to know that human beings were capable of loyalty and love and enjoying beauty without behaving like animals. They were telling each other that they were refined, that they had "class." . . .

Further, despite the new romanticized view of the woman (maybe because of it), wives were just as excluded as they had always been. Noble, uplifting love, genuine romantic love, could not be felt for someone who swept the floor any more than it could be felt *by* someone whose life was preoccupied with such trivia. The lords and one of their special ladies, Marie, the countess of Champagne, issued the following declaration in 1174:

> We declare and we hold as firmly established that love cannot exert its power between two people who are married to each other. For lovers give each other everything freely, under no compulsion of necessity, but married people are in duty bound to give in to each other's desires and deny themselves to each other in nothing.[2]

The Court of Love

The proclamation was one of many that were made by the "courts of love" that these lords and ladies established in order to settle lovers' quarrels—and to decide for themselves the specifics of the new morality. . . .

No one did more to formulate these rules than Andreas Capellanus. Andreas not only summarized the numerous cases that came before the court, but he used these decisions to write a manual of polite, courtly love. He called his influential book *A Treatise on Love and Its Remedy*, a title that indicated his debt to Sappho and the Greek romantic idea of love as a sickness. Andreas, however, did not think that he was advocating a "romantic" idea of love. The word was not even used in his day. He considered himself to be a modern twelfth-century Ovid—merely updating the Roman's *Art of Love*. He called himself Andreas the Lover and, like Ovid, considered himself an expert on all aspects of love.

But Andreas only used the same word as Ovid. The similarity ended there. The "aspects" of love that Andreas taught concerned the loyalty of the lovers, courteous behavior, the spiritual benefits of "pure love," the importance of gentleness, the subservience of the man to his lover, and the duties of courtship. There is none of Ovid's preoccupation with the techniques of seduction. Andreas is not talking about sex. In fact, he clearly advises against consummating the relationship.

Ovid made fun of infatuation and silly emotional behavior, but urged his readers to imitate such sickness in order to get the woman in bed. Andreas valued the passionate emotional attachment that Ovid mocked. Sincerity and honesty were too important to Andreas to dream

---

[2] Andreas, *Tractatus de Amore,* 1:6, 7th Dialogue. Quoted in Hunt, 143–44.

of trickery, deceit, or pretense. Love, for Andreas, was too noble an emotion, too worthy a pursuit, to be put on like a mask. In short, the Roman had been after sexual gratification; the Christian wanted to refine lives and cleanse souls. They both called it love, but Andreas never seemed to realize that they were not talking the same language.

A Medieval Indian Alternative: Mystical Eroticism

Sometimes the best way to understand our own traditions is to study those of a different culture. It is difficult, for instance, for us to see Christian sexual morality as unusual because it has shaped our culture to such a great extent.

There have been alternatives, however. One of the most remarkable was the Indian ecstatic religion of the Middle Ages. Here the erotic played a central role, not as temptation to be shunned but as a source of salvation. Most medieval temple sculpture was erotic. The temples at Khajuraho and Orissa are full of sexual imagery: sensuous nudes and embracing couples. The temple architecture itself suggests fertility and reproduction. The temple sculptures, like the popular story *Gita Govinda* of the twelfth century, tell of the loves of the god Krishna. He is shown scandalizing young women, dancing deliriously, and bathing with scores of admirers. Krishna's erotic appeal is a testament to his charisma. He is "divine in proportion to his superiority as a great lover."

> Worshippers were encouraged to commit excesses during festivals as the surest way to achieve . . . ecstasy, the purging climax of the orgiastic feast, the surmounting of duality.[3]

Among the most popular forms of medieval Hindu worship were the *bhakti* cults, which originated in devotion to Krishna in the *Bhagavad Gita*. *Bhakti* cults underline the difference between Indian and European devotion. While the Christian church discouraged spiritual love that might easily lead to "carnal love," the Indian *bhakti* sects encouraged rituals of ecstasy and sensual love precisely because they obliterated moral distinctions. The ecstatic union with the divine Krishna, Vishnu, or Shiva enabled the worshiper to transcend the limitations of self and confining definitions of good and evil.

Thus, Indian ecstatic religion sought sexual expression as a path to spiritual fulfillment. It is interesting that the word *bhakti* meant sex as well as worship, while we use the word "devotion" to mean worship and love. Hindu eroticism had nothing to do with the private expression of romantic love. In fact, it was the opposite. While romantic love depended

[3]Richard Lannoy, *The Speaking Tree: A Study of Indian Culture and Society* (Oxford: Oxford University Press, 1971), 64.

on the development of the individual personality and the cultivation of individual feelings, *bhakti* depended on the loss of self in the sexual act.

Bhakti cults differed from the European courtly love tradition in one other important respect. They were not expressions of upper-class control. They were popular expressions of religious feeling. In essence they were directed against the dominating *brahman* and *kshatriya* castes because they challenged the importance of caste distinctions altogether. The ecstatic communion with the deity that they preached was open to all, regardless of caste. They appealed even to women and untouchables, as well as to farmers and artisans.

As Christianity did in Europe, popular Hinduism of the Middle Ages replaced a classical formal tradition with a spiritual passion. Ovid's *Art of Love* and the *Kama Sutra* were mechanical, passionless exercises for tired ruling classes. Both India and Europe turned to more emotionally intense religious experiences in the Middle Ages. Perhaps the classical ideals seemed sterile after the spread of salvation religions like Christianity, Buddhism, and revived Hinduism. The similarity between Christian and Hindu emotionalism may be a product of uncertain times, barbarian threats, and diseases that stalked the Eurasian continent. But the differences between Christian courtly love and *bhakti* cults were also profound. In India, sexual passion was an avenue to spiritual salvation. In Christian Europe sexual passion was at best a dead end, and at worst a road to hell.

Polygamy, Sexuality, and Style: A Japanese Alternative

At the same time that feudal Europe was developing a code of chivalry that romanticized love and almost desexualized marriage, the aristocracy of feudal Japan was evolving a code of polygamous sexuality without chivalry and almost without passion. We know about the sexual lives of Japanese aristocrats between 950 and 1050—the apex of the Heian period—through a series of remarkable novels and diaries, almost all of which were written by women. These first classics of Japanese literature, like *The Tale of Genji* and *The Pillow Book*, were written by women because Japanese men were still writing the "more important" but less-informative laws and theological studies in Chinese (just as Europeans still wrote in a Latin that was very different from the everyday spoken language).

When well-born Japanese in the Heian court spoke of "the world" they were referring to a love affair, and the novels that aristocratic women like Murasaki Shikibu or Sei Shonagon had time to compose in the spoken language were full of stories of "the world."

In *The World of the Shining Prince* Ivan Morris distinguishes three types of sexual relationships between men and women of the Heian aristocracy. (Homosexuality among the court ladies was "probably quite common," he writes, "as in any society where women were obliged to live in continuous and close proximity," but male homosexuality among "warriors, priests, and actors" probably became prevalent in later centuries.) The first type of heterosexual relationship was between the male aristocrat and his "principal wife." She was often several years older than her boy-husband and frequently served more as a guardian than as a bride. She was always chosen for her social standing, usually to cement a political alliance between ruling families. Although the match must frequently have been loveless, her status was inviolate; it was strictly forbidden, for instance, for a prince to exalt a secondary wife to principal wife. Upon marriage the principal wife would normally continue to live with her family, visited by her husband at night, until he became the head of his own household on the death or retirement of his father. Then the principal wife would be installed with all of her servants and aides as the head of the north wing of her husband's residence. An aristocratic woman (but never a peasant woman) might also become a secondary wife or official concubine. If she were officially recognized as such (much to the pleasure of her family), she might be moved into another wing of the official residence (leading to inevitable conflicts with the principal wife and other past and future secondary wives), or she might be set up in her own house. The arrangements were virtually limitless. The third and most frequent type of sexual relationship between men and women was the simple (or complex) affair—with a lady at court, another man's wife or concubine, but usually with a woman of a far lower class than the man. Ivan Morris writes of this kind of relationship:

> Few cultured societies in history can have been as tolerant about sexual relations as was the world of *The Tale of Genji*. Whether or not a gentleman was married, it redounded to his prestige to have as many affairs as possible; and the palaces and great mansions were full of ladies who were only too ready to accommodate him if approached in the proper style. From reading the *Pillow Book* we can tell how extremely commonplace these casual affairs had become in court circles, the man usually visiting the girl at night behind her screen of state and leaving her at the crack of dawn.[4]

That emphasis on "the proper style" is what distinguishes the sexuality of medieval Japan from that of ancient Rome, and reminds us of the medieval European's display of form—the aristocracy's mark of "class." Perhaps because the sexuality of the Heian aristocracy was potentially more explosive than the repressed rituals of European chivalry, style was that much more important. Polygamous sexuality could be practiced

[4]Ivan Morris, *The World of the Shining Prince: Court Life in Ancient Japan* (Baltimore: Penguin Books, 1969), 237.

without tearing the society apart (and destroying aristocratic dominance in the process) only if every attention were given to style. Listen, for instance, to what the lady of *The Pillow Book* expected from a good lover:

> A good lover will behave as elegantly at dawn as at any other time. He drags himself out of bed with a look of dismay on his face. The lady urges him on: "Come, my friend, it's getting light. You don't want anyone to find you here." He gives a deep sigh, as if to say that the night has not been nearly long enough and that it is agony to leave. Once up, he does not instantly pull on his trousers. Instead he comes close to the lady and whispers whatever was left unsaid during the night. Even when he is dressed, he still lingers, vaguely pretending to be fastening his sash.
>
> Presently he raises the lattice, and the two lovers stand together by the side door while he tells her how he dreads the coming day, which will keep them apart; then he slips away. The lady watches him go, and this moment of parting will remain among her most charming memories.
>
> Indeed, one's attachment to a man depends largely on the elegance of his leave-taking. When he jumps out of bed, scurries about the room, tightly fastens his trouser-sash, rolls up the sleeves of his Court cloak, over-robe, or hunting costume, stuffs his belongings into the breast of his robe and then briskly secures the outer sash—one really begins to hate him.[5]

The stylistic elegance of the lover's departure was one of the principal themes of Heian literature. Perhaps no situation better expressed the mood of the Japanese word *aware* (a word that was used over a thousand times in *The Tale of Genji*), which meant the poignant or the stylishly, even artistically, sorrowful—a style of elegant resignation. The word also suggests the mood of "the lady in waiting" and even the underlying anguish and jealousy of a precariously polygamous existence for the women consorts and writers of the Japanese feudal age. The ladies of the court were trained in calligraphy, poetry, and music; they were dressed in elaborate, colorful silks, painted with white faces and black teeth, and rewarded by sexual attention that always had to be justified by its cultured style. . . .

Aristocracies have behaved in similar ways throughout the world, and throughout history. They demonstrate their "class" or "good breeding" with elaborate rituals that differentiate their world from the ordinary. But the example of aristocratic Heian Japan a thousand years ago points to some of the differences between Japanese and Christian culture. The Japanese developed rituals of courtship and seduction for the leisured few that were sexually satisfying and posed no threat to

---

[5]*The Pillow Book of Sei Shonagon,* trans. Ivan Morris (Baltimore: Penguin Books, 1971), 49–50.

marriage. They were rituals that showed artistic refinement rather than sexual "purity" or chastity. They could be sexual because Japanese culture did not disparage sexuality. Rather it disparaged lack of "taste." The affair did not threaten marriage because the culture did not insist on monogamy. The new sexual interest could be carried on outside or inside the polygamous estate of the Japanese aristocrat. Perhaps the main difference, then, is that the Japanese aristocrat invented stylized sex rather than romantic love.

55

ULRICH VON LIECHTENSTEIN

The Service of Ladies

This selection is drawn from Ulrich von Liechtenstein's own account of his adventures. After over ten years of service, as a page and then a distant admirer, in 1226, Ulrich undertook a spectacular series of jousts to impress and win his lady, the princess. In the course of a five-week itinerary in northern Italy and southern German-speaking areas in which he took on all comers, he claims to have broken three hundred and seven lances. In the first part of this selection he details his preparation for the traveling tournament. In the second part of the selection, he tells of a brief interruption in his jousting for a stop at home. What does this selection tell you about Ulrich's ideas of love and marriage?

Thinking Historically

Sometimes the best entry point for analyzing cultural differences is to begin with the surprising or incomprehensible. If we can refrain from merely dismissing what seems beyond the pale, this can be an opportunity to understand how cultures can be truly different from our own.

Even a moderately careful reading of the two selections from Ulrich's autobiography should evoke some surprise. In the first selection, Ulrich sketches a visual image of himself on horseback that is far from our expectations. Imagine what he must have looked like. Imagine how others must have seen him. Recognizing that this was not some Halloween prank, that others proceeded to joust with him rather than laugh him out of town, we are forced to rethink what his outfit and

Ulrich von Liechtenstein, *The Service of Ladies*, trans. J. W. Thomas (Suffolk, England and Rochester, N.Y.: The Boydell Press, 2004; published by arrangement with University of North Carolina Press, Chapel Hill, 1969), 46–49, 85–86.

presentation meant to him and those in his society. The recognition that the meaning of an act (like donning women's clothing) could be vastly different in Europe of the thirteenth century from what it is today offers the entry to comparative analysis.

We may also note that there are many things in Ulrich's description of love that are not at all surprising. This may be because they have become second nature to our own society. Certainly some of the elements of romantic love, which were fresh in Ulrich's day, have become clichés in modern film and television. What do you make of the elements of this story that are familiar? What do you make of those that surprise you?

"My service must be God's command.
Now let me tell you what I've planned.
I'll take on woman's dress and name
and thus disguised will strive for fame.
Sweet God protect me and sustain!
I'll travel with a knightly train
up to Bohemia from the sea.
A host of knights shall fight with me.

"This very winter I shall steal
out of the land and shall conceal
my goal from everyone but you.
I'll travel as a pilgrim who
to honor God is bound for Rome
(no one will question this at home).
I'll stop in Venice and shall stay
in hiding till the first of May.

"I'll carefully remain unseen
but deck myself out like a queen;
it should be easy to acquire
some lovely feminine attire
which I'll put on—now hear this last—
and when St. George's day is past,
the morning afterwards, I'll ride
(I pray that God is on my side)

"from the sea to Mestre, near
by Venice. He who breaks a spear
with me to serve, by tourneying,
his lady fair will get a ring

of gold and it will be quite nice.
I'll give it to him with this advice,
that he present it to his love,
the one he's in the service of.

"Messenger, I'll make the trip
so there will never be a slip
and no one possibly can guess
whose form is hid beneath the dress.
For I'll be clad from head to toe
in woman's garb where'er I go,
fully concealed from people's eyes.
They'll see me only in disguise.

"If you would please me, messenger,
then travel once again to her.
Just tell her what I have in mind
and ask if she will be so kind
as to permit that I should fight
throughout this journey as her knight.
It's something she will not repent
and I'll be glad of her assent."

He rode at once to tell her this
and swore upon his hope of bliss
my loyalty would never falter,
that I was true and would not alter.
He told my plan in full detail
and said, "My lady, should you fail
to let him serve and show your trust
in him, it wouldn't seem quite just."

"Messenger," she spoke, "just let
him have this message, don't forget.
This trip, if I have understood
you right, will surely do him good
and he will win a rich reward
in praise from many a lady and lord.
Whether it helps with me or not,
from others he will gain a lot."

The messenger was pleased and sure.
He found me by the river Mur
at Liechtenstein where I was then.
'T was nice to have him there again.

I spoke, "O courtly youth, now tell
me if the lady's feeling well.
For, if my darling's doing fine,
then shall rejoice this heart of mine."

He spoke, "She's fair and happy too;
she bade me bring this word to you
about your journey. If you should
go through with it 't will do you good
and, whether it helps with her or not,
from others you will gain a lot.
She certainly supports your aim
and says that you'll be rich in fame."

I listened to the news he had,
and heart and body both were glad.
It was a joy for me to know
my undertaking pleased her so.
I didn't linger but began
at once to carry out my plan
and was quite happy, I admit,
that he also approved of it.

I soon was ready, I assure
you, to begin my knightly tour.
I started out as pilgrim dressed
and left the land. I thought it best
to take a staff and pouch at least,
for looks (I got them from a priest);
one would have thought me bound for Rome.
I prayed God bring me safely home.

I got to Venice without delay
and found a house in which to stay,
right on the edge of town, a place
where none would ever see my face
who might have recognized me there.
I was as cautious everywhere
and all the winter long I hid.
But let me tell you what I did:

I had some woman's clothing made
to wear throughout the masquerade.
They cut and sewed for me twelve skirts
and thirty fancy lady's shirts.

I bought two braids for my disguise,
the prettiest they could devise,
and wound them with some pearls I got
which didn't cost an awful lot.

I bade the tailors then prepare
three velvet cloaks for me to wear,
all white. The saddles too on which
the master labored, stitch by stitch,
were silver white. As for a king
was made the saddle covering,
long and broad and gleaming white.
The bridles all were rich and bright.

The tailors sewed for every squire
(there were a dozen) white attire.
A hundred spears were made for me
and all as white as they could be.
But I need not continue so,
for all I wore was white as snow
and everything the squires had on
was just as white as any swan.

My shield was white, the helmet too.
I had them make ere they were through
a velvet cover for each steed
as armor. These were white, indeed,
as was the battle cape which I
should wear for jousting by and by,
the cloth of which was very fine.
I was quite pleased to call it mine.

At last I had my horses sent
to me (none knew just where they went)
and got some servants, as I'd planned,
each native to a foreign land.
They carefully did not let slip
a thing about my coming trip
and I took heed that those who came
to serve me never learned my name.

. . .

They rode toward me with armor on;
I had not waited long to don
a rich and splendid battle dress.

Von Ringenberg with full success
broke off a spear on me. The one
I jousted with when this was done
I knocked down backwards off his horse,
which made him feel ashamed, of course.

The spears I broke then numbered four.
On the field had come no more
with armor on and lance in hand
and so I stopped. At my command
the servants gave six rings away.
I sought the inn where I should stay
and found a pretty hostel there;
I got some other things to wear.

I changed my clothing under guard,
and then the hostel door was barred.
I took with me a servant who
would not say anything, I knew.
We stole away without a sound
and rode with joy to where I found
my dearest wife whom I adore;
I could not ever love her more.

She greeted me just as a good
and loving woman always should
receive a husband she holds dear.
That I had come to see her here
had made her really very pleased.
My visit stilled her grief and eased
her loneliness. We shared our bliss,
my sweet and I, with many a kiss.

She was so glad to see her knight,
and I had comfort and delight
till finally the third day came;
to give me joy was her sole aim.
When dawn appeared it was the third.
I dressed, an early mass was heard,
I prayed God keep me from transgressing,
and then received a friendly blessing.

Right after that I took my leave,
lovingly, you may believe,
and rode with joyful heart to where

I'd left my servants unaware.
I entered Gloggnitz hastily
and found them waiting there for me,
prepared to journey on again.
At once we left the city then.

We rode to Neunkirchen gaily decked
and were received as I'd expect
of those whose manners are refined.
Each knight was courteous and kind
who waited there with spear and shield.
When I came riding on the field
I found them all prepared, adorned
with trappings no one would have scorned.

Nine waited there, not more nor less,
to joust with me, in battle dress.
I saw them and it wasn't long
till I'd donned armor, bright and strong.
The first to come I'd heard much of;
his great desire was ladies' love.
It was Sir Ortold von Graz, a name
already widely known to fame.

All that he wore was of the best.
The good man cut me in the chest
so strong and skilful was his joust;
through shield and armor went the thrust.
When I beheld the wound indeed
and saw that it began to bleed
I hid it quickly with my coat
before the other knights took note.

I broke nine lances there in haste
and found my inn. I dared not waste
much time before I got in bed.
I sent nine rings of golden red
to each of them who with his spear
had earned from me a present here.
My injuries were deftly bound
by a doctor whom my servants found.

56

ANDREAS CAPELLANUS

From The Art of Courtly Love

Andreas Capellanus (Andreas the Chaplain) compiled this guide to courtly love between 1184 and 1186. He probably intended his book to update Ovid's *Art of Love*, as discussed in selection 54, but his approach reflects many of the new ideas of love circulating among the upper classes of Europe in the twelfth century. Andreas says that love is suffering, but also that it is wonderful. What does he mean? Compare his ideas about sex and marriage to those of Ulrich von Liechtenstein. The bishop of Paris condemned Andreas's ideas in 1277, but do they seem religious or Christian in any way? Notice the author's attention to passion and proper behavior. How does he combine or balance the two?

Thinking Historically

How unusual are these ideas about love? Do you think that most people in most societies would agree with these ideas or are they unique? How might these ideas be considered European?

Introduction to the Treatise on Love

We must first consider what love is, whence it gets its name, what the effect of love is, between what persons love may exist, how it may be acquired, retained, increased, decreased, and ended, what are the signs that one's love is returned, and what one of the lovers ought to do if the other is unfaithful.

What Love Is

Love is a certain inborn suffering derived from the sight of and excessive meditation upon the beauty of the opposite sex, which causes each one to wish above all things the embraces of the other and by common desire to carry out all of love's precepts in the other's embrace.

That love is suffering is easy to see, for before the love becomes equally balanced on both sides there is no torment greater, since the

---

Andreas Capellanus, *The Art of Courtly Love*, trans. John J. Parry (New York: Columbia University Press, 1990), 28–32, 159–86.

lover is always in fear that his love may not gain its desire and that he is wasting his efforts. He fears, too, that rumors of it may get abroad, and he fears everything that might harm it in any way, for before things are perfected a slight disturbance often spoils them. If he is a poor man, he also fears that the woman may scorn his poverty; if he is ugly, he fears that she may despise his lack of beauty or may give her love to a more handsome man; if he is rich, he fears that his parsimony in the past may stand in his way. To tell the truth, no one can number the fears of one single lover. This kind of love, then, is a suffering which is felt by only one of the persons and may be called "single love." But even after both are in love the fears that arise are just as great, for each of the lovers fears that what he has acquired with so much effort may be lost through the effort of someone else, which is certainly much worse for a man than if, having no hope, he sees that his efforts are accomplishing nothing, for it is worse to lose the things you are seeking than to be deprived of a gain you merely hope for. The lover fears, too, that he may offend his loved one in some way; indeed he fears so many things that it would be difficult to tell them.

That this suffering is inborn I shall show you clearly, because if you will look at the truth and distinguish carefully you will see that it does not arise out of any action; only from the reflection of the mind upon what it sees does this suffering come. For when a man sees some woman fit for love and shaped according to his taste, he begins at once to lust after her in his heart; then the more he thinks about her the more he burns with love, until he comes to a fuller meditation. Presently he begins to think about the fashioning of the woman and to differentiate her limbs, to think about what she does, and to pry into the secrets of her body, and he desires to put each part of it to the fullest use. Then after he has come to this complete meditation, love cannot hold the reins, but he proceeds at once to action; straightway he strives to get a helper to find an intermediary. He begins to plan how he may find favor with her, and he begins to seek a place and a time opportune for talking; he looks upon a brief hour as a very long year, because he cannot do anything fast enough to suit his eager mind. It is well known that many things happen to him in this manner. This inborn suffering comes, therefore, from seeing and meditating. Not every kind of meditation can be the cause of love, an excessive one is required; for a restrained thought does not, as a rule, return to the mind, and so love cannot arise from it.

Between What Persons Love May Exist

Now, in love you should note first of all that love cannot exist except between persons of opposite sexes. Between two men or two women love can find no place, for we see that two persons of the same sex are not at all fitted for giving each other the exchanges of love or for practicing the acts natural to it. Whatever nature forbids, love is ashamed to accept.

What the Effect of Love Is

Now it is the effect of love that a true lover cannot be degraded with any avarice. Love causes a rough and uncouth man to be distinguished for his handsomeness; it can endow a man even of the humblest birth with nobility of character; it blesses the proud with humility; and the man in love becomes accustomed to performing many services gracefully for everyone. O what a wonderful thing is love, which makes a man shine with so many virtues and teaches everyone, no matter who he is, so many good traits of character! There is another thing about love that we should not praise in few words: it adorns a man, so to speak, with the virtue of chastity, because he who shines with the light of one love can hardly think of embracing another woman, even a beautiful one. For when he thinks deeply of his beloved the sight of any other woman seems to his mind rough and rude.

If One of the Lovers Is Unfaithful to the Other

If one of the lovers should be unfaithful to the other, and the offender is the man, and he has an eye to a new love affair, he renders himself wholly unworthy of his former love, and she ought to deprive him completely of her embraces.

But what if he should be unfaithful to his beloved—not with the idea of finding a new love, but because he has been driven to it by an irresistible passion for another woman? What, for instance, if chance should present to him an unknown woman in a convenient place or what if at a time when Venus is urging him on to that which I am talking about he should meet with a little strumpet or somebody's servant girl? Should he, just because he played with her in the grass, lose the love of his beloved? We can say without fear of contradiction that just for this a lover is not considered unworthy of the love of his beloved unless he indulges in so many excesses with a number of women that we may conclude that he is overpassionate. But if whenever he becomes acquainted with a woman he pesters her to gain his end, or if he attains his object as a result of his efforts, then rightly he does deserve to be deprived of his former love, because there is strong presumption that he has acted in this way with an eye toward a new one, especially where he has strayed with a woman of the nobility or otherwise of an honorable estate.

I know that once when I sought advice I got the answer that a true lover can never desire a new love unless he knows that for some definite and sufficient reason the old love is dead; we know from our own experience that this rule is very true. We have fallen in love with a woman of the most admirable character, although we have never had, or hope to have, any fruit of this love. For we are compelled to pine away for love of a woman of such lofty station that we dare not say one word about it, nor dare we throw ourself upon her mercy, and so at length we are forced to find our body shipwrecked. But although rashly and without foresight we have fallen into such great waves in this tempest, still we cannot think about a new love or look for any other way to free ourself.

But since you are making a special study of the subject of love, you may well ask whether a man can have a pure love for one woman and a mixed or common love with another. We will show you, by an unanswerable argument, that no one can feel affection for two women in this fashion. For although pure love and mixed love may seem to be very different things, if you will look at the matter properly you will see that pure love, so far as its substance goes, is the same as mixed love and comes from the same feeling of the heart. The substance of the love is the same in each case, and only the manner and form of loving are different, as this illustration will make clear to you. Sometimes we see a man with a desire to drink his wine unmixed, and at another time his appetite prompts him to drink only water or wine and water mixed; although his appetite manifests itself differently, the substance of it is the same and unchanged. So likewise when two people have long been united by pure love and afterwards desire to practice mixed love, the substance of the love remains the same in them, although the manner and form and the way of practicing it are different. . . .

The Rules of Love

Let us come now to the rules of love, and I shall try to present to you very briefly those rules which the King of Love[1] is said to have proclaimed with his own mouth and to have given in writing to all lovers. . . .

I. Marriage is no real excuse for not loving.
II. He who is not jealous cannot love.
III. No one can be bound by a double love.
IV. It is well known that love is always increasing or decreasing.
V. That which a lover takes against the will of his beloved has no relish.
VI. Boys do not love until they arrive at the age of maturity.
VII. When one lover dies, a widowhood of two years is required of the survivor.
VIII. No one should be deprived of love without the very best of reasons.

[1]King Arthur of Britain. [Ed.]

IX.   No one can love unless he is impelled by the persuasion of love.

X.   Love is always a stranger in the home of avarice.

XI.   It is not proper to love any woman whom one should be ashamed to seek to marry.

XII.   A true lover does not desire to embrace in love anyone except his beloved.

XIII.   When made public love rarely endures.

XIV.   The easy attainment of love makes it of little value; difficulty of attainment makes it prized.

XV.   Every lover regularly turns pale in the presence of his beloved.

XVI.   When a lover suddenly catches sight of his beloved his heart palpitates.

XVII.   A new love puts to flight an old one.

XVIII.   Good character alone makes any man worthy of love.

XIX.   If love diminishes, it quickly fails and rarely revives.

XX.   A man in love is always apprehensive.

XXI.   Real jealousy always increases the feeling of love.

XXII.   Jealousy, and therefore love, are increased when one suspects his beloved.

XXIII.   He whom the thought of love vexes, eats and sleeps very little.

XXIV.   Every act of a lover ends in the thought of his beloved.

XXV.   A true lover considers nothing good except what he thinks will please his beloved.

XXVI.   Love can deny nothing to love.

XXVII.   A lover can never have enough of the solaces of his beloved.

XXVIII.   A slight presumption causes a lover to suspect his beloved.

XXIX.   A man who is vexed by too much passion usually does not love.

XXX.   A true lover is constantly and without intermission possessed by the thought of his beloved.

XXXI.   Nothing forbids one woman being loved by two men or one man by two women.

KALIDASA

From Shakuntala

Kalidasa (c. 400 C.E.) was one of the greatest Indian dramatists. His play *Shakuntala*, a classic of the Hindu literary tradition, tells the story of a love between a king and a hermit girl. The two fall passionately in love with each other although they have barely exchanged words. Despite their different stations in life, they are equally overcome by *kama*, one of the four great forces in the Hindu culture—the force of love and physical attraction. In this selection from Act 3 (of seven acts), Shakuntala is urged by her friends, Priyamvadā and Anasuya, who say they "don't know what it is to be in love," to write a letter to the king, who overhears their conversation. In what ways is this similar to European ideas of romantic love? In what ways is it different?

Thinking Historically

The description of feelings in this selection might seem overly florid, but the emotions are not unfamiliar to a modern reader. Can you think of a play or film that is similar to this? What is the similarity? Is there any unfamiliar aspect? If you were to present this story to a modern American audience, how might you change it? Why?

PRIYAMVADĀ: Compose a love letter and I'll hide it in a flower. I'll deliver it to his hand on the pretext of bringing a gift from our offering to the deity.

ANASŪYĀ: This subtle plan pleases me. What does Shakuntalā say?

SHAKUNTALĀ: I'll try my friend's plan.

PRIYAMVADĀ: Then compose a poem to declare your love!

SHAKUNTALĀ: I'm thinking, but my heart trembles with fear that he'll reject me.

KING [IN HIDING]: (*delighted*):
The man whom you fear will reject you
waits longing to love you, timid girl—
a suitor may be lucky or cursed,
but his goodness of fortune always wins.

Kalidasa, *Shakuntala*, Act III, trans. Barbara Stoler Miller, in *Theater of Memory: The Plays of Kalidasa*, ed. Barbara Stoler Miller (New York: Columbia University Press, 1984), 114–18.

BOTH FRIENDS: Why do you devalue your own virtues? Who would keep autumn moonlight from cooling the body by covering it with a bit of cloth?

SHAKUNTALĀ (*smiling*): I'm following your advice. (*She sits thinking*)

KING: As I stare at her, my eyes forget to blink.
She arches an eyebrow
struggling to compose the verse—
the down rises on her cheek,
showing the passion she feels.

SHAKUNTALĀ: I have thought of a song, but there's nothing I can write it on.

PRIYAMVADĀ: Engrave the letters with your nails on this lotus leaf! It's as delicate as a parrot's breast.

SHAKUNTALĀ (*miming what Priyamvadā described*): Listen and tell me if this makes sense!

BOTH FRIENDS: We're both paying attention.

SHAKUNTALĀ (*sings*):
I don't know your heart,
but day and night Love
violently burns my limbs
with desire for you, cruel man.

KING (*Having been listening to them, entering suddenly*):
Love torments you, slender girl,
but he utterly consumes me—
daylight makes the moon fade
when it folds the white lotus.

BOTH FRIENDS (*Looking, rising with delight*): Welcome to the swift success of love's desire!
(*Shakuntalā tries to rise.*)

KING: Don't strain yourself!
Limbs on a couch of crushed flowers
and fragrant tips of lotus stalks
are too frail from suffering
to perform ceremonial acts . . .

ANASŪYĀ: We've heard that kings have many loves. Will our beloved friend become a sorrow to her relatives after you've spent your time with her?

KING: Noble lady, enough of this! I may have many wives, but my royal line rests on two foundations: the sea-bound earth and this friend of yours!

BOTH FRIENDS: We are assured.

PRIYAMVADĀ (*casting a glance*): Anasūyā this fawn is looking for its mother. Let's take it to her!
(*They both begin to leave.*)

SHAKUNTALĀ: Come back! Don't leave me unprotected!

BOTH FRIENDS: The protector of the earth is at your side.

SHAKUNTALĀ: Why have they gone?

KING: Don't be alarmed! A servant worships at your side.
   Shall I set moist winds in motion
   with lotus-leaf fans to cool your pain,
   or put your pale red lotus feet on my lap
   and stroke them, voluptuous girl?

SHAKUNTALĀ: I cannot sin against those I respect! (*standing as if she wants to leave*)

KING: Beautiful Shakuntalā, the day is still hot.
   Why leave this couch of flowers
   and its shield of lotus leaves
   to venture into the heat
   with your frail wan limbs?
   (*Saying this, he forces her to turn around.*)

SHAKUNTALĀ: Puru king, control yourself! Though I'm burning with love I'm not free to give myself to you.

KING: Don't fear your elders! The father of your family knows the law. When he finds out, he will not fault you. Many kings' daughters first marry in secret and their fathers bless them.

SHAKUNTALĀ: Release me! I must ask my friends' advice!

KING: Yes, I shall release you.

SHAKUNTALĀ: When?

KING:
   Only let my thirsting mouth
   gently drink from your lips,
   the way a bee sips nectar
   from a fragile virgin blossom.

58

MIRABAI
Bhakti Poems

Mirabai (b. c. 1550) was one of the great poets of the medieval Indian Bhakti or Hindu devotional tradition. Bhakti philosophers and poets expressed a Hinduism suffused with love for the deity. Typically, Mirabai's religious experience of personal love represented a form of protest against the religious formalism of caste and the authority of Brahmin sacrifice. According to legend, Mirabai refused to consummate her marriage to a king because she had fallen in love with the god Khrishna, who was often pictured as the deep blue "dark Lord" and the lifter of mountains. How is Mirabai's imagery similar to that of medieval European courtly love? How is it different?

Thinking Historically

India was not the only society that produced women who expressed an almost sexual passion toward a god. The great Muslim mystic Rabia al-Adawiyya (b. c. 717) and the Sufis used similar language, and St. Teresa of Avila (1515–1582) is perhaps the best known among Christian devotees who wrote with an almost erotic passion. The Hindu celebration of *kama* and the development of Bhakti Hinduism were particularly Indian. Still, can you think of cases in your own culture where love of a deity faded into, or felt like, love for another person? How about Ulrich's "worship" of the princess? How unique is this Indian cultural form after all?

Colored by Devotion to Krishna

The motif of being dyed with the color of devotion to the Dark Lord is common in bhakti poetry, as is dancing before him. The poison cup refers to an incident when the Rānā tried to poison her, but the only effect was to make her glow with the beauty of Krishna. The "mountain lifter" is a reference to one of Krishna's miracles.

[From Mīrābāī, in Parashurām Caturvedī, *Mīrābāī kī Padāvalī*, no. 37, trans. by J.S.H. and M.J.]

Poems of Mirabai, trans. John S. Hawley and Mark Juergensmeyer, in *Sources of Indian Tradition*, vol. I, *From the Beginning to 1800*, 2nd ed., ed. Ainslee Embree (New York: Columbia University Press, 1988), 365–69.

326

I'm colored with the color of dusk, O Rānā
   colored with the color of my Lord.
Drumming out the rhythm on the drums, I danced,
   dancing in the presence of the saints,
      colored with the color of my Lord.
They thought me mad for the Wily One,
   raw for my dear dark love,
      colored with the color of my Lord.
The Rānā sent me a poison cup:
   I didn't look, I drank it up,
      colored with the color of my Lord.
The clever Mountain Lifter is the Lord of Mīrā.
   Life after life he's true—
      colored with the color of my Lord.

Marriage with Krishna

This poem echoes Mīrā's consciousness of having been married to
Krishna in previous births. She is filled with longing for him and is begging him to unite with her now in this life.

[From Mīrābāī, *Mīrābāī Kī Padāvalī*, no. 51, trans. by J.S.H. and M. J.]

I have talked to you, talked,
   Dark Lifter of Mountains,
About this old love,
   from birth after birth.
Don't go, don't,
   Lifter of Mountains,
Let me offer a sacrifice—myself—
   beloved,
      to your beautiful face.
Come, here in the courtyard,
   Dark Lord,
The women are singing auspicious wedding songs;
My eyes have fashioned
   an altar of pearl tears,
And here is my sacrifice:
   the body and mind
of Mīrā,
   the servant who clings to your feet,
      through life after life,
         a virginal harvest for you to reap.

Life without Krishna

Mīrā's love for Krishna leads to the enmity of her family, but at the same time gives her a refuge to which she can escape.

[From Mīrābāī, *Mīrābāī kī Padāvalī*, no. 42, trans. by J. S. H. and M. J.]

Life without Hari is no life, friend,
And though my mother-in-law fights,
   my sister-in-law teases,
   the *rānā* is angered,
A guard is stationed on the stoop outside,
   and a lock is mounted on the door,
How can I abandon the love I have loved
   in life after life?
Mīrā's Lord is the clever Mountain-Lifter:
   Why would I want anyone else?

The Sound of Krishna's Flute

Muralī is the bamboo flute that is one of Krishna's chief symbols. It is the medium through which Krishna entrances the women of Braj, calling them to love. Sometimes the flute is pictured as a woman herself, with more immediate access to Krishna than has anyone else. So the sound of the flute fills Mīrā with the intense pain of longing for love, a longing that is one of the constant themes of love poetry in the Indian tradition.

[From Mīrābāī, no. 166, trans. by J.S.H. and M. J.]

Muralī sounds on the banks of the Jumna,
Muralī snatches away my mind;
My senses cut away from their moorings—
Dark waters, dark garments, Dark Lord.
I listen close to the sounds of Muralī
And my body withers away—
Lost thoughts, lost even the power to think.
   Mīrā's Lord, clever Mountain-Lifter,
   Come quick, snatch away my pain.

59

MURASAKI SHIKIBU

From The Tale of Genji

The Tale of Genji is, by some measures, the world's first novel. It was written by Murasaki Shikibu, a woman at the Japanese court, probably in the first decade after the year 1000. During the Heian period (794–1185) of Japanese history, women in the Japanese aristocracy differentiated their culture from the Chinese one that had dominated it since the seventh century.

While Japanese men were still using a dated form of Chinese for official documents, women like Lady Murasaki were fashioning the Japanese language into an effective and contemporary medium of communication. As ladies of the court, they also had the experience and leisure for writing intriguing, richly evocative stories.

The Tale of Genji is about Prince Genji—an attractive, talented, and sensitive son of the emperor—and his love interests. This chapter, occurring near the end of the novel, tells of one of Prince Genji's many flirtations. It also reveals much about the culture of the Japanese court. Notice the cultivation of music, dance, and poetry among the court nobility. What, if anything, does this display of sensitivity have to do with ideas of love and marriage? What signs do you see here of the persistence of Chinese culture in Heian Japan?

Also, notice the absence of monogamy in the court. The emperor is married but has taken in turn three consorts: Kokiden, Kiritsubo, and now Fujitsubo. What is the relationship between marriage and sex in this society? What does that tell you about the mores of the time?

Thinking Historically

Would you call this a story of romantic love? In what ways is the love Lady Murasaki describes similar to or different from the love Andreas Capellanus describes in selection 56? What aspects of Heian Japanese culture are different from the culture of medieval Europe? Is the dominant-upper class idea of love in Japan during this period different from that of Europe?

Murasaki Shikibu, *The Tale of Genji*, trans. Arthur Waley (1929; reprint, Garden City, N.Y.: Anchor Books, 1955), 201–10.

About the twentieth day of the second month the Emperor gave a Chinese banquet under the great cherry-tree of the Southern Court. Both Fujitsubo and the Heir Apparent were to be there. Kokiden, although she knew that the mere presence of the Empress was sufficient to spoil her pleasure, could not bring herself to forgo so delightful an entertainment. After some promise of rain the day turned out magnificent; and in full sunshine, with the birds singing in every tree, the guests (royal princes, noblemen, and professional poets alike) were handed the rhyme words which the Emperor had drawn by lot, and set to work to compose their poems. It was with a clear and ringing voice that Genji read out the word "Spring" which he had received as the rhyme-sound of his poem. Next came To no Chujo who, feeling that all eyes were upon him and determined to impress himself favourably on his audience, moved with the greatest possible elegance and grace; and when on receiving his rhyme he announced his name, rank, and titles, he took great pains to speak pleasantly as well as audibly. Many of the other gentlemen were rather nervous and looked quite pale as they came forward, yet they acquitted themselves well enough. But the professional poets, particularly owing to the high standard of accomplishment which the Emperor's and Heir Apparent's lively interest in Chinese poetry had at that time diffused through the Court, were very ill at ease; as they crossed the long space of the garden on their way to receive their rhymes they felt utterly helpless. A simple Chinese verse is surely not much to ask of a professional poet; but they all wore an expression of the deepest gloom. One expects elderly scholars to be somewhat odd in their movements and behaviour, and it was amusing to see the lively concern with which the Emperor watched their various but always uncouth and erratic methods of approaching the Throne. Needless to say a great deal of music had been arranged for. Towards dusk the delightful dance known as the Warbling of Spring Nightingales was performed, and when it was over the Heir Apparent, remembering the Festival of Red Leaves, placed a wreath on Genji's head and pressed him so urgently that it was impossible for him to refuse. Rising to his feet he danced very quietly a fragment of the sleeve-turning passage in the Wave Dance. In a few moments he was seated again, but even into this brief extract from a long dance he managed to import an unrivalled charm and grace. Even his father-in-law who was not in the best of humour with him was deeply moved and found himself wiping away a tear.

"And why have we not seen To no Chujo?" said the Heir Apparent. Whereupon Chujo danced the Park of Willow Flowers, giving a far more complete performance than Genji, for no doubt he knew that he would be called upon and had taken trouble to prepare his dance. It was a great success and the Emperor presented him with a cloak, which everyone said was a most unusual honour. After this the other young noblemen who were present danced in no particular order, but it was now so dark that it was impossible to discriminate between their performances.

Then the poems were opened and read aloud. The reading of Genji's verses was continually interrupted by loud murmurs of applause. Even the professional poets were deeply impressed, and it may well be imagined with what pride the Emperor, to whom at times Genji was a source of consolation and delight, watched him upon such an occasion as this. Fujitsubo, when she allowed herself to glance in his direction, marvelled that even Kokiden could find it in her heart to hate him. "It is because he is fond of me; there can be no other reason," she decided at last, and the verse, "Were I but a common mortal who now am gazing at the beauty of this flower, from its sweet petals not long should I withhold the dew of love," framed itself on her lips, though she dared not utter it aloud.

It was now very late and the banquet was over. The guests had scattered. The Empress and the Heir Apparent had both returned to the Palace—all was still. The moon had risen very bright and clear, and Genji, heated with wine, could not bear to quit so lovely a scene. The people at the Palace were probably all plunged in a heavy sleep. On such a night it was not impossible that some careless person might have left some door unfastened, some shutter unbarred. Cautiously and stealthily he crept towards Fujitsubo's apartments and inspected them. Every bolt was fast. He sighed; here there was evidently nothing to be done. He was passing the loggia of Kokiden's palace when he noted that the shutters of the third arch were not drawn. After the banquet Kokiden herself had gone straight to the Emperor's rooms. There did not seem to be anyone about. A door leading from the loggia into the house was standing open, but he could hear no sound within. "It is under just such circumstances as this that one is apt to drift into compromising situations," thought Genji. Nevertheless he climbed quietly on to the balustrade and peeped. Everyone must be asleep. But no; a very agreeable young voice with an intonation which was certainly not that of any waiting-woman or common person was softly humming the last two lines of the *Oborozuki-yo*.[1] Was not the voice coming towards him? It seemed so, and stretching out his hand he suddenly found that he was grasping a lady's sleeve. "Oh, how you frightened me!" she cried. "Who is it?" "Do not be alarmed," he whispered. "That both of us were not content to miss the beauty of this departing night is proof more clear than the half-clouded moon that we were meant to meet," and as he recited the words he took her gently by the hand and led her into the house, closing the door behind them. Her surprised and puzzled air fascinated him. "There is someone there," she whispered

---

[1] A famous poem by Oye no Chisato (ninth century): "What so lovely as a night when the moon though dimly clouded is never wholly lost to sight!"

tremulously, pointing to the inner room. "Child," he answered, "I am allowed to go wherever I please and if you send for your friends they will only tell you that I have every right to be here. But if you will stay quietly here. . . ." It was Genji. She knew his voice and the discovery somewhat reassured her. She thought his conduct rather strange, but she was determined that he should not think her prudish or stiff. And so because he on his side was still somewhat excited after the doings of the evening, while she was far too young and pliant to offer any serious resistance, he soon got his own way with her.

Suddenly they saw to their discomfiture that dawn was creeping into the sky. She looked, thought Genji, as though many disquieting reflections were crowding into her mind. "Tell me your name," he said. "How can I write you unless you do? Surely this is not going to be our only meeting?" She answered with a poem in which she said that names are of this world only and he would not care to know hers if he were resolved that their love should last till worlds to come. It was a mere quip and Genji, amused at her quickness, answered, "You are quite right. It was a mistake on my part to ask." And he recited the poem: "While still I seek to find on which blade dwells the dew, a great wind shakes the grasses of the level land." "If you did not repent of this meeting," he continued, "you would surely tell me who you are. I do not believe that you want. . . ." But here he was interrupted by the noise of people stirring in the next room. There was a great bustle and it was clear that they would soon be starting out to fetch Princess Kokiden back from the palace. There was just time to exchange fans in token of their new friendship before Genji was forced to fly precipitately from the room. In his own apartments he found many of his gentlemen waiting for him. Some were awake, and these nudged one another when he entered the room as though to say, "Will he never cease these disreputable excursions?" But discretion forbad them to show that they had seen him and they all pretended to be fast asleep. Genji too lay down, but he could not rest. He tried to recall the features of the lady with whom he had just spent so agreeable a time. Certainly she must be one of Kokiden's sisters. Perhaps the fifth or sixth daughter, both of whom were still unmarried. . . . But at present he could think of no way to make sure. She had not behaved at all as though she did not want to see him again. Why then had she refused to give him any chance of communicating with her? In fact he worried about the matter so much and turned it over in his mind with such endless persistency that it soon became evident he had fallen deeply in love with her. Nevertheless no sooner did the recollection of Fujitsubo's serious and reticent demeanour come back to his mind than he realized how incomparably more she meant to him than this light-hearted lady.

That day the after-banquet kept him occupied till late at night. At the Emperor's command he performed on the thirteen-stringed zithern and had an even greater success than with his dancing on the day before. At dawn Fujitsubo retired to the Emperor's rooms. Disappointed in his hope that the lady of last night would somewhere or somehow make her appearance on the scene, he sent for Yoshikiyo and Koremitsu with whom all his secrets were shared and bade them keep watch upon the lady's family. When he returned next day from duty at the Palace they reported that they had just witnessed the departure of several coaches which had been drawn up under shelter in the Courtyard of the Watch. "Among a group of persons who seemed to be the domestic attendants of those for whom the coaches were waiting two gentlemen came threading their way in a great hurry. These we recognized as Shii no Shosho and Uchuben, so there is little doubt that the carriages belonged to Princess Kokiden. For the rest we noted that the ladies were by no means ill-looking and that the whole party drove away in three carriages." Genji's heart beat fast. But he was no nearer than before to finding out which of the sisters it had been. Supposing her father, the Minister of the Right, should hear anything of this, what a to-do there would be! It would indeed mean his absolute ruin. It was a pity that while he was about it he did not stay with her till it was a little lighter. But there it was! He did not know her face, but yet he was determined to recognize her. How? . . . He still had her fan. It was a folding fan with ribs of hinoki-wood and tassels tied in a splice-knot. One side was covered with silverleaf on which was painted a dim moon, giving the impression of a moon reflected in water. It was a device which he had seen many times before, but it had agreeable associations for him, and continuing the metaphor of the "grass on the moor" which she had used in her poem, he wrote on the fan—"Has mortal man ever puzzled his head with such a question before as to ask where the moon goes to when she leaves the sky at dawn?" And he put the fan safely away. . . .

Fugitive as their meeting had been, it had sufficed to plunge the lady whose identity Prince Genji was now seeking to establish into the depths of despair; for in the fourth month she was to become the Heir Apparent's wife. Turmoil filled her brain. Why had not Genji visited her again? He must surely know whose daughter she was. But how should he know which daughter? Besides, her sister Kokiden's house was not a place where, save under very strange circumstances, he was likely to feel at all at his ease. And so she waited in great impatience and distress; but of Genji there was no news.

About the twentieth day of the third month her father, the Minister of the Right, held an archery meeting in which most of the young noblemen and princes were present. It was followed by a wistaria feast. The cherry blossom was for the most part over, but two trees, which the Minister seemed somehow to have persuaded to flower later than all the rest, were still an enchanting sight. He had had his house rebuilt only a short time ago when celebrating the initiation of his grand-daughters, the children of Kokiden. It was now a magnificent building and not a thing in it but was of the very latest fashion. He had invited Genji when he had met him at the Palace only a few days before and was extremely annoyed when he did not appear. . . . It was very late indeed when at last he [Genji] made his appearance at the party. He was dressed in a cloak of thin Chinese fabric, white outside but lined with yellow. His robe was of a deep wine-red colour with a very long train. The dignity and grace with which he carried this fancifully regal attire in a company where all were dressed in plain official robes were indeed remarkable, and in the end his presence perhaps contributed more to the success of the party than did the fragrance of the Minister's boasted flowers. His entry was followed by some very agreeable music. It was already fairly late when Genji, on the plea that the wine had given him a headache, left his seat and went for a walk. He knew that his two stepsisters, the daughters of Kokiden, were in the inner apartments of the palace. He went to the eastern portico and rested there. It was on this side of the house that the wistaria grew. The wooden blinds were raised and a number of ladies were leaning out of the window to enjoy the blossoms. They had hung bright-coloured robes and shawls over the windowsill just as is done at the time of the New Year dancing and other gala days and were behaving with a freedom of allure which contrasted very oddly with the sober decorum of Fujitsubo's household. "I am feeling rather overpowered by all the noise and bustle of the flower-party," Genji explained. "I am very sorry to disturb my sisters, but I can think of nowhere else to seek refuge . . ." and advancing towards the main door of the women's apartments, he pushed back the curtain with his shoulder. . . . A scent of costly perfumes pervaded the room; silken skirts rustled in the darkness. There could be little doubt that these were Kokiden's sisters and their friends. Deeply absorbed, as indeed was the whole of his family, in the fashionable gaieties of the moment, they had flouted decorum and posted themselves at the window that they might see what little they could of the banquet which was proceeding outside. Little thinking that his plan could succeed, yet led on by delightful recollections of his previous encounter, he advanced towards them chanting in a careless undertone the song:

> At Ishikawa, Ishikawa
> A man from Koma [Korea] took my belt away . . .

But for "belt" he substituted "fan" and by this means he sought to discover which of the ladies was his friend. "Why, you have got it wrong! I never heard of *that* Korean," one of them cried. Certainly it was not she. But there was another who though she remained silent seemed to him to be sighing softly to herself. He stole towards the curtain-of-state behind which she was sitting and taking her hand in his at a venture he whispered the poem: "If on this day of shooting my arrow went astray, 'twas that in dim morning twilight only the mark had glimmered in my view." And she, unable any longer to hide that she knew him, answered with the verse: "Had it been with the arrows of the heart that you had shot, though from the moon's slim bow no brightness came, would you have missed your mark?" Yes, it was her voice. He was delighted, and yet . . .

REFLECTIONS

Cultural comparisons, formerly a staple of historical studies, have come under harsh criticism in recent years, and for good reason. The ambitious general histories and philosophical anthropologies written at the beginning of the twentieth century were full of gross generalizations about the "essence" of various cultures and the advantages of one civilization over another. These grand overviews, predating serious empirical studies of African, Asian, and Latin American societies, invariably argued that such "pre-modern," or "traditional," societies lacked some critical cultural attribute honed in Europe that enabled Europeans to conquer the world after 1500. It goes without saying that these sweeping interpretations were written by Europeans and their North American descendants.

The comparative history of love got caught up in the whirlwind with historians and anthropologists, seeking to explain European expansion, industrialization, and modernization, arguing that conjugal love—the nonromantic familial variety—created family units in Europe and America that were different from those in other parts of the world. They saw the Western family as the stimulus of modern society. Still others found the Western practices of dating, mate choosing, and individual decision making unique.

Toward the end of the twentieth century, in a postcolonial age that had grown skeptical of Western claims of objectivity, cultural comparisons were seen for what they often were—thinly veiled exercises in self-aggrandizement and implicit rationales for Western domination. For example, Western scientific racism, in which the reigning Western anthropologists and scientists divided the world by cranial sizes, nose width, or culture-bound intelligence tests (always putting themselves on top), came crashing down, after its rationale was exposed as the foundation for the horrific genocides of World War II.

There is a growing debate about the strategy of explaining Western growth and dominance by looking for Western traits that non-Western cultures lacked. But whether or not such a strategy is wise, we would be foolish to stop trying to compare cultures. Cultures are rich reposi-tories of human thought and behavior; they differ over time and across the globe; and the process of comparison is essential to learning and creating knowledge. In any case, historical comparisons should not be about establishing which culture is better or worse. Culture, almost by definition, is good for the particular society in which it arises. That people in different parts of the world have found different ways of deal-ing with the same human problems should not surprise us. To call some better than others is meaningless.

What we can learn from cultural comparison is something about the malleability of human nature and the range of options available to us. We also learn much about ourselves when we peer at another face in the mirror. The differences leap out at us over time as well as space. In some ways, Ulrich's mirror is as foreign as Genji's. In other ways it is not. Both reflect elements of our own culture, call it European, West-ern, global, or something else. In response to an age of prejudice and cultural stereotyping, many well-intentioned people choose to deny or celebrate cultural differences. A far wiser course is to understand what these differences reveal about our world and us.

The First Crusade

Muslims, Christians, and Jews during the First Crusade, 1095–1099 C.E.

HISTORICAL CONTEXT

In the eleventh century the Seljuk Turks, recently converted to Islam, emerged from the grasslands of central Asia to conquer much of the land held by the weakened Caliphate at Baghdad, the Egyptian Fatimid Caliphate, and the Byzantine Empire. By 1095 the Seljuks controlled the important cities of Baghdad and Jerusalem and threatened to take Constantinople.

Alexius, the Byzantine emperor, appealed to the Roman pope for help and found a receptive audience. Pope Urban II was continuing recent papal efforts to strengthen the Roman church's power over the scattered nobles and princes of European feudal society. He sought to reform the church of abuses such as the sale of church offices, and to bring peace to the fractious countryside, riddled with private armies of knights that fought each other or preyed on Christian peasants. Urban II's efforts to revitalize Christendom found a mission in the Seljuk occupation of Jerusalem, and in 1095 the First Crusade began with his urgent call for Christians to rout the new Muslim occupiers of the Holy Land. (See Map 10.1.)

The Crusades were an important chapter in the religious and military history — or more broadly, the cultural and political history — of both European and Islamic civilizations. They brought large numbers of European Christians and Muslims into contact with each other in a struggle and dialogue that would last for centuries.

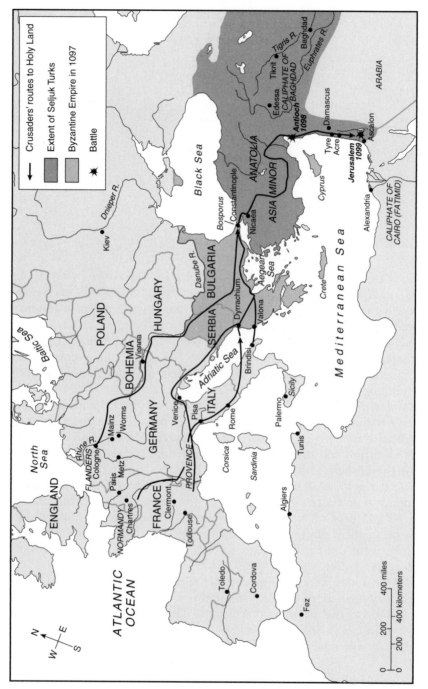

Map 10.1 The First Crusade, 1096–1099.

THINKING HISTORICALLY
Analyzing and Writing Narrative

When most people think of history, they think of narrative—the story itself. Narrative settles on specific details—one at a time—neither indiscriminately nor as examples of general laws, but usually chronologically, as they happen, woven in a chain of cause and effect. The "truth" of narrative is different from that of social science, which aspires to generality. The social scientist writes, "Holy wars among states are a dime a dozen." The narrative historian immerses us in the specific details of the battle: "The Duke's trumpets sounded, the shimmering line swayed forward, the long lances came down to point at the foe, their pennons shadowing the ground before them." A good narrative has the appeal of a good story: It places the reader on the scene, enables us to feel the drama of the moment, to experience what happened as it happened.

In this chapter you will read a number of brief narratives about the Crusades. You will analyze each narrative for what it tells you and to reflect on the way the story conveys that information, and then you will be encouraged to write your own narrative.

Keep in mind that narrative, or storytelling, is only one way of providing information. Storytelling is often considered a low-level skill, less sophisticated than analysis or synthesis. In college classes instructors will often say: "Don't just tell me the story" when they want you to analyze or make comparisons. Most professional historians write analytical books devoted to answering a particular historical question or challenging an interpretation. Generally historians only write narratives for a popular audience, not for each other. But the power of narrative is so strong some have even suggested that we might be hardwired for story telling—that we ought to be aware of how this form of knowing and presenting affects our understanding of historical events.

60

FULCHER OF CHARTRES

Pope Urban at Clermont

The Chronicle of Fulcher of Chartres is one of the few firsthand accounts of the First Crusade. Born in 1059, Fulcher was present at the Council of Clermont, where Pope Urban II issued his call for the First Crusade in 1095. In response to Urban's plea, Fulcher joined the army of Robert of Normandy, Stephen of Blois, and Robert of Flanders. He then joined Baldwin of Boulogne in Edessa (see Map 10.1, p. 338), the first Crusader state, and later visited Jerusalem after its capture by the Crusaders. In 1100 when Baldwin became King of Jerusalem, Fulcher returned to the Holy City to become his chaplain. There he wrote his history from 1101 until about 1128. The reliability of Fulcher's Chronicles, therefore, depends on his important contacts as well as his own observations.

Why, according to Fulcher, did Pope Urban II call the Council of Clermont? What did he hope to accomplish? How important among the pope's concerns was the capture of Jerusalem? How important was strengthening the Church?

Thinking Historically

What indications do you see in Urban's speech that the call to capture Jerusalem was only part of his agenda, perhaps even an afterthought? Fulcher's account of the speech and his section on "events after the council" mainly address the issue of Jerusalem. That emphasis is appropriate in a history of the crusade. A historical narrative must follow a particular thread. If Fulcher was writing a history of church reforms rather than of the First Crusade, what kind of "events after the council" might he have included?

A narrative, or story, is different from an explanation. What do you think were the causes of the First Crusade, based on what you have read so far? How is your answer an explanation rather than a narrative? How would you make your answer more of a narrative?

The First Crusade: The Chronicle of Fulcher of Chartres and Other Source Materials, 2nd ed., ed. Edward Peters (Philadelphia: University of Pennsylvania Press, 1998), 49–55.

I. The Council of Clermont

1. In the year 1095 from the Lord's Incarnation, with Henry reigning in Germany as so-called emperor,[1] and with Philip as king in France, manifold evils were growing in all parts of Europe because of wavering faith. In Rome ruled Pope Urban II, a man distinguished in life and character, who always strove wisely and actively to raise the status of the Holy Church above all things.

2. He saw that the faith of Christianity was being destroyed to excess by everybody, by the clergy as well as by the laity. He saw that peace was altogether discarded by the princes of the world, who were engaged in incessant warlike contention and quarreling among themselves. He saw the wealth of the land being pillaged continuously. He saw many of the vanquished, wrongfully taken prisoner and very cruelly thrown into foulest dungeons, either ransomed for a high price or, tortured by the triple torments of hunger, thirst, and cold, blotted out by a death hidden from the world. He saw holy places violated; monasteries and villas burned. He saw that no one was spared of any human suffering, and that things divine and human alike were held in derision.

3. He heard, too, that the interior regions of Romania, where the Turks ruled over the Christians, had been perniciously subjected in a savage attack.[2] Moved by long-suffering compassion and by love of God's will, he descended the mountains to Gaul, and in Auvergne he called for a council to congregate from all sides at a suitable time at a city called Clermont. Three hundred and ten bishops and abbots, who had been advised beforehand by messengers, were present.

4. Then, on the day set aside for it, he called them together to himself and, in an eloquent address, carefully made the cause of the meeting known to them. In the plaintive voice of an aggrieved Church, he expressed great lamentation, and held a long discourse with them about the raging tempests of the world, which have been mentioned, because faith was undermined.

5. One after another, he beseechingly exhorted them all, with renewed faith, to spur themselves in great earnestness to overcome the Devil's devices and to try to restore the Holy Church, most unmercifully weakened by the wicked, to its former honorable status.

---

[1]Henry IV (1056–1106). Fulcher uses the term "so-called emperor," since Henry was not recognized as rightful emperor by adherents of Gregory VII and Urban II.

[2]This refers to the Seljuk conquest of Anatolia, probably to Manzikert, 1071.

II. *The Decree of Pope Urban in the Council*

1. "Most beloved brethren," he said, "by God's permission placed over the whole world with the papal crown, I, Urban, as the messenger of divine admonition, have been compelled by an unavoidable occasion to come here to you servants of God. I desired those whom I judged to be stewards of God's ministries to be true stewards and faithful, with all hypocrisy rejected.[3]

2. "But with temperance in reason and justice being remote, I, with divine aid, shall strive carefully to root out any crookedness or distortion which might obstruct God's law. For the Lord appointed you temporarily as stewards over His family to serve it nourishment seasoned with a modest savor. Moreover, blessed will you be if at last the Overseer find you faithful.[4]

3. "You are also called shepherds; see that you are not occupied after the manner of mercenaries. Be true shepherds, always holding your crooks in your hands; and sleeping not, guard on every side the flock entrusted to you.

4. "For if through your carelessness or negligence, some wolf seizes a sheep, you doubtless will lose the reward prepared for you by our Lord.[5] Nay, first most cruelly beaten by the whips of the lictors, you afterwards will be angrily cast into the keeping of a deadly place.

5. "Likewise, according to the evangelical sermon, you are the 'salt of the earth.'[6] But if you fail, it will be disputed wherewith it was salted. O how much saltiness, indeed, is necessary for you to salt the people in correcting them with the salt of wisdom, people who are ignorant and panting with desire after the wantonness of the world; so that, unsalted, they might not be rotten with sins and stink whenever the Lord might wish to exhort them.

6. "For if because of the sloth of your management, He should find in them worms, that is, sin, straightway, He will order that they, despised, be cast into the dungheap. And because you could not make restoration for such a great loss, He will banish you, utterly condemned in judgment, from the familiarity of His love.

7. "It behooves saltiness of this kind to be wise, provident, temperate, learned, peace-making, truth-seeking, pious, just, equitable, pure. For how will the unlearned be able to make men learned, the intemper-

---

[3]Reference to I Corinthians 4:1, 2.
[4]Reference to Matthew 24:45, 46.
[5]Reference to John 10:12–16.
[6]Matthew 5:13.

ate make temperate, the impure make them pure? If one despises peace, how will he appease? Or if one has dirty hands, how will he be able to wipe the filth off another one defiled? For it is read, 'If the blind lead the blind, both shall fall into a ditch.'[7]

8. "Set yourselves right before you do others, so that you can blamelessly correct your subjects. If you wish to be friends of God, gladly practice those things which you feel will please Him.

9. "Especially establish ecclesiastical affairs firm in their own right, so that no simoniac heresy will take root among you. Take care lest the vendors and moneychangers, flayed by the scourges of the Lord, be miserably driven out into the narrow streets of destruction.[8]

10. "Uphold the Church in its own ranks altogether free from all secular power. See that the tithes of all those who cultivate the earth are given faithfully to God; let them not be sold or held back.

11. "Let him who has seized a bishop be considered an outlaw. Let him who has seized or robbed monks, clerics, nuns and their servants, pilgrims, or merchants, be excommunicated. Let the robbers and burners of homes and their accomplices, banished from the Church, be smitten with excommunication.

12. "It must be considered very carefully, as Gregory says, by what penalty he must be punished who seizes other men's property, if he who does not bestow his own liberally is condemned to Hell. For so it happened to the rich man in the well-known Gospel, who on that account was not punished because he had taken away the property of others, but because he had misused that which he had received.

13. "And so by these iniquities, most beloved, you have seen the world disturbed too long; so long, as it was told to us by those reporting, that perhaps because of the weakness of your justice in some parts of your provinces, no one dares to walk in the streets with safety, lest he be kidnapped by robbers by day or thieves by night, either by force or trickery, at home or outside.

14. "Wherefore the Truce,[9] as it is commonly called, now for a long time established by the Holy Fathers, must be renewed. In admonition, I entreat you to adhere to it most firmly in your own bishopric. But if anyone affected by avarice or pride breaks it of his own free will, let him be excommunicated by God's authority and by the sanction of the decrees of this Holy Council."

[7]Matthew 15:14.

[8]Reference to John 2:15.

[9]Truce of God—Cessation of all feuds from Wednesday evening to Monday morning in every week and during church festivals, ordered by the Church in 1041. This was proclaimed anew at the Council of Clermont.

III. *The Pope's Exhortation Concerning the Expedition to Jerusalem*

1. These and many other things having been suitably disposed of, all those present, both clergy and people, at the words of Lord Urban, the Pope, voluntarily gave thanks to God and confirmed by a faithful promise that his decrees would be well kept. But straightway he added that another thing not less than the tribulation already spoken of, but even greater and more oppressive, was injuring Christianity in another part of the world, saying:

2. "Now that you, O sons of God, have consecrated yourselves to God to maintain peace among yourselves more vigorously and to uphold the laws of the Church faithfully, there is work to do, for you must turn the strength of your sincerity, now that you are aroused by divine correction, to another affair that concerns you and God. Hastening to the way, you must help your brothers living in the Orient, who need your aid for which they have already cried out many times.

3. "For, as most of you have been told, the Turks, a race of Persians,[10] who have penetrated within the boundaries of Romania[11] even to the Mediterranean to that point which they call the Arm of Saint George, in occupying more and more of the lands of the Christians, have overcome them, already victims of seven battles, and have killed and captured them, have overthrown churches, and have laid waste God's kingdom. If you permit this supinely for very long, God's faithful ones will be still further subjected.

4. "Concerning this affair, I, with suppliant prayer—not I, but the Lord—exhort you, heralds of Christ, to persuade all of whatever class, both knights and footmen, both rich and poor, in numerous edicts, to strive to help expel that wicked race from our Christian lands before it is too late.

5. "I speak to those present, I send word to those not here; moreover, Christ commands it. Remission of sins will be granted for those going thither, if they end a shackled life either on land or in crossing the sea, or in struggling against the heathen. I, being vested with that gift from God, grant this to those who go.

6. "O what a shame, if a people, so despised, degenerate, and enslaved by demons would thus overcome a people endowed with the trust of almighty God, and shining in the name of Christ! O how many evils will be imputed to you by the Lord Himself, if you do not help those who, like you, profess Christianity!

---

[10]Really Seljuk Turks who conquered lands from east to west by way of Persia.

[11]Fulcher uses the term *Romania* to refer to the Anatolian as well as to the European provinces of the Byzantine Empire, but here, of course, he means the Anatolian. The Seljuks called the state which they founded here *Rum*.

7. "Let those," he said, "who are accustomed to wage private wars wastefully even against Believers, go forth against the Infidels in a battle worthy to be undertaken now and to be finished in victory. Now, let those, who until recently existed as plunderers, be soldiers of Christ; now, let those, who formerly contended against brothers and relations, rightly fight barbarians; now, let those, who recently were hired for a few pieces of silver, win their eternal reward. Let those, who wearied themselves to the detriment of body and soul, labor for a twofold honor. Nay, more, the sorrowful here will be glad there, the poor here will be rich there, and the enemies of the Lord here will be His friends there.

8. "Let no delay postpone the journey of those about to go, but when they have collected the money owed to them and the expenses for the journey, and when winter has ended and spring has come, let them enter the crossroads courageously with the Lord going on before."

IV. The Bishop of Puy and the Events after the Council

1. After these words were spoken, the hearers were fervently inspired. Thinking nothing more worthy than such an undertaking, many in the audience solemnly promised to go, and to urge diligently those who were absent. There was among them one Bishop of Puy, Ademar by name, who afterwards, acting as vicar-apostolic, ruled the whole army of God wisely and thoughtfully, and spurred them to complete their undertaking vigorously.

2. So, the things that we have told you were well established and confirmed by everybody in the Council. With the blessing of absolution given, they departed; and after returning to their homes, they disclosed to those not knowing, what had taken place. As it was decreed far and wide throughout the provinces, they established the peace, which they call the Truce, to be upheld mutually by oath.

3. Many, one after another, of any and every occupation, after confession of their sins and with purified spirits, consecrated themselves to go where they were bidden.

4. Oh, how worthy and delightful to all of us who saw those beautiful crosses, either silken or woven of gold, or of any material, which the pilgrims sewed on the shoulders of their woolen cloaks or cassocks by the command of the Pope, after taking the vow to go. To be sure, God's soldiers, who were making themselves ready to battle for His honor, ought to have been marked and fortified with a sign of victory. And so by embroidering the symbol [of the cross] on their clothing in recognition of their faith, in the end they won the True Cross itself. They imprinted the ideal so that they might attain the reality of the ideal.

5. It is plain that good meditation leads to doing good work and that good work wins salvation of the soul. But, if it is good to mean well, it is better, after reflection, to carry out the good intention. So, it is best to win salvation through action worthy of the soul to be saved. Let each and everyone, therefore, reflect upon the good, that he makes better in fulfillment, so that, deserving it, he might finally receive the best, which does not diminish in eternity.

6. In such a manner Urban, a wise man and reverenced,
Meditated a labor, whereby the world florescenced.

For he renewed peace and restored the laws of the Church to their former standards; also he tried with vigorous instigation to expel the heathen from the lands of the Christians. And since he strove to exalt all things of God in every way, almost everyone gladly surrendered in obedience to his paternal care. . . .

61

Chronicle of Solomon bar Simson

Solomon bar Simson (who is known only from this chronicle) provides the most complete of the Hebrew chronicles of the First Crusade. He takes up the story after Pope Urban II's appeal. Franks and Germans have organized their armies of knights, suppliers, aides, and followers, and have set off for Jerusalem by way of Constantinople. Why did these Crusaders stop at Mainz* and other German cities to murder Jews?

Thinking Historically

This narrative, like the previous selection, includes quotations from speeches. How can you tell that some of these quotations do not contain the exact words that were spoken?

Solomon bar Simson's narrative contains another element that, while absent from modern histories, is found in other narratives of the Crusades and is especially pronounced here. This is not just a narra-

---

*myntz

"Chronicle of Solomon bar Simson," in *The Jews and the Crusaders: The Hebrew Chronicles of the First and Second Crusades*, ed. and trans. Shlomo Eidelberg (Madison: University of Wisconsin Press, 1977), 21–26.

tive of human action and intention, but it interprets divine action and intention as well. Why is this narrative strategy necessary for this author? If you were writing a narrative of the Crusades today, would you want to tell both of these stories, or only the human one? Why?

I will now recount the event of this persecution in other martyred communities as well—the extent to which they clung to the Lord, God of their fathers, bearing witness to His Oneness to their last breath.

In the year four thousand eight hundred and fifty-six, the year one thousand twenty-eight of our exile, in the eleventh year of the cycle Ranu, the year in which we anticipated salvation and solace, in accordance with the prophecy of Jeremiah: "Sing with gladness for Jacob, and shout at the head of the nations," etc.—this year turned instead to sorrow and groaning, weeping and outcry. Inflicted upon the Jewish People were the many evils related in all the admonitions; those enumerated in Scripture as well as those unwritten were visited upon us.

At this time arrogant people, a people of strange speech, a nation bitter and impetuous, Frenchmen and Germans, set out for the Holy City, which had been desecrated by barbaric nations, there to seek their house of idolatry and banish the Ishmaelites and other denizens of the land and conquer the land for themselves. They decorated themselves prominently with their signs, placing a profane symbol—a horizontal line over a vertical one—on the vestments of every man and woman whose heart yearned to go on the stray path to the grave of their Messiah. Their ranks swelled until the number of men, women, and children exceeded a locust horde covering the earth; of them it was said: "The locusts have no king [yet go they forth all of them by bands]." Now it came to pass that as they passed through the towns where Jews dwelled, they said to one another: "Look now, we are going a long way to seek out the profane shrine and to avenge ourselves on the Ishmaelites, when here, in our very midst, are the Jews—they whose forefathers murdered and crucified him for no reason. Let us first avenge ourselves on them and exterminate them from among the nations so that the name of Israel will no longer be remembered, or let them adopt our faith and acknowledge the offspring of promiscuity."

When the Jewish communities became aware of their intentions, they resorted to the custom of our ancestors, repentance, prayer, and charity. The hands of the Holy Nation turned faint at this time, their hearts melted, and their strength flagged. They hid in their innermost rooms to escape the swirling sword. They subjected themselves to great endurance, abstaining from food and drink for three consecutive days and nights, and then fasting many days from sunrise to sunset, until their skin was shriveled and dry as wood upon their bones. And they cried out loudly and bitterly to God.

But their Father did not answer them; He obstructed their prayers, concealing Himself in a cloud through which their prayers could not pass, and He abhorred their tent, and He removed them out of His sight—all of this having been decreed by Him to take place "in the day when I visit"; and this was the generation that had been chosen by Him to be His portion, for they had the strength and the fortitude to stand in His Sanctuary, and fulfill His word, and sanctify His Great Name in His world. It is of such as these that King David said: "Bless the Lord, ye angels of His, ye almighty in strength, that fulfil His word," etc.

That year, Passover fell on Thursday, and the New Moon of the following month, Iyar, fell on Friday and the Sabbath. On the eighth day of Iyar, on the Sabbath, the foe attacked the community of Speyer and murdered eleven holy souls who sanctified their Creator on the holy Sabbath and refused to defile themselves by adopting the faith of their foe. There was a distinguished, pious woman there who slaughtered herself in sanctification of God's Name. She was the first among all the communities of those who were slaughtered. The remainder were saved by the local bishop without defilement [i.e., baptism], as described above.

On the twenty-third of Iyar they attacked the community of Worms.[1] The community was then divided into two groups; some remained in their homes and others fled to the local bishop seeking refuge. Those who remained in their homes were set upon by the steppe-wolves who pillaged men, women, and infants, children, and old people. They pulled down the stairways and destroyed the houses, looting and plundering; and they took the Torah Scroll, trampled it in the mud, and tore and burned it. The enemy devoured the children of Israel with open maw.

Seven days later, on the New Moon of Sivan—the very day on which the Children of Israel arrived at Mount Sinai to receive the Torah—those Jews who were still in the court of the bishop were subjected to great anguish. The enemy dealt them the same cruelty as the first group and put them to the sword. The Jews, inspired by the valor of their brethren, similarly chose to be slain in order to sanctify the Name before the eyes of all, and exposed their throats for their heads to be severed for the glory of the Creator. There were also those who took their own lives, thus fulfilling the verse: "The mother was dashed in pieces with her children." Fathers fell upon their sons, being slaughtered upon one another, and they slew one another—each man his kin, his wife and children; bridegrooms slew their betrothed, and merciful

---

[1]Town in the Holy Roman Empire (now Germany). [Ed.]

women their only children. They all accepted the divine decree whole-heartedly and, as they yielded up their souls to the Creator, cried out: "Hear, O Israel, the Lord is our God, the Lord is One." The enemy stripped them naked, dragged them along, and then cast them off, sparing only a small number whom they forcibly baptized in their profane waters. The number of those slain during the two days was approximately eight hundred—and they were all buried naked. It is of these that the Prophet Jeremiah lamented: "They that were brought up in scarlet embrace dunghills." I have already cited their names above. May God remember them for good.

When the saints, the pious ones of the Most High, the holy community of Mainz, whose merit served as shield and protection for all the communities and whose fame had spread throughout the many provinces, heard that some of the community of Speyer had been slain and that the community of Worms had been attacked a second time, and that the sword would soon reach them, their hands became faint and their hearts melted and became as water. They cried out to the Lord with all their hearts, saying: "O Lord, God of Israel, will You completely annihilate the remnant of Israel? Where are all your wonders which our forefathers related to us, saying: 'Did You not bring us up from Egypt and from Babylonia and rescue us on numerous occasions?' How, then, have You now forsaken and abandoned us, O Lord, giving us over into the hands of evil Edom so that they may destroy us? Do not remove Yourself from us, for adversity is almost upon us and there is no one to aid us."

The leaders of the Jews gathered together and discussed various ways of saving themselves. They said: "Let us elect elders so that we may know how to act, for we are consumed by this great evil." The elders decided to ransom the community by generously giving of their money and bribing the various princes and deputies and bishops and governors. Then, the community leaders who were respected by the local bishop approached him and his officers and servants to negotiate this matter. They asked: "What shall we do about the news we have received regarding the slaughter of our brethren in Speyer and Worms?" They [the Gentiles] replied: "Heed our advice and bring all your money into our treasury. You, your wives, and your children, and all your belongings shall come into the courtyard of the bishop until the hordes have passed by. Thus will you be saved from the errant ones."

Actually, they gave this advice so as to herd us together and hold us like fish that are caught in an evil net, and then to turn us over to the enemy, while taking our money. This is what actually happened in the end, and "the outcome is proof of the intentions." The bishop assembled his ministers and courtiers—mighty ministers, the noblest in the land—for the purpose of helping us; for at first it had been his desire to save us with all his might, since we had given him and his ministers and servants a large bribe in return for their promise to help us. Ultimately, however, all the bribes and entreaties were of no avail to protect us on the day of wrath and misfortune.

It was at this time that Duke Godfrey [of Bouillon], may his bones be ground to dust, arose in the hardness of his spirit, driven by a spirit of wantonness to go with those journeying to the profane shrine, vowing to go on this journey only after avenging the blood of the crucified one by shedding Jewish blood and completely eradicating any trace of those bearing the name "Jew," thus assuaging his own burning wrath. To be sure, there arose someone to repair the breach—a God-fearing man who had been bound to the most holy of altars—called Rabbi Kalonymos, the *Parnass*[2] of the community of Mainz. He dispatched a messenger to King Henry in the kingdom of Pula, where the king had been dwelling during the past nine years, and related all that had happened.

The king was enraged and dispatched letters to all the ministers, bishops, and governors of all the provinces of his realm, as well as to Duke Godfrey, containing words of greeting and commanding them to do no bodily harm to the Jews and to provide them with help and refuge. The evil duke then swore that he had never intended to do them harm. The Jews of Cologne nevertheless bribed him with five hundred *zekukim* of silver, as did the Jews of Mainz. The duke assured them of his support and promised them peace.

However, God, the maker of peace, turned aside and averted His eyes from His people, and consigned them to the sword. No prophet, seer, or man of wise heart was able to comprehend how the sin of the people infinite in number was deemed so great as to cause the destruction of so many lives in the various Jewish communities. The martyrs endured the extreme penalty normally inflicted only upon one guilty of murder. Yet, it must be stated with certainty that God is a righteous judge, and we are to blame.

Then the evil waters prevailed. The enemy unjustly accused them of evil acts they did not do, declaring: "You are the children of those who killed our object of veneration, hanging him on a tree, and he himself had said: 'There will yet come a day when my children will come and avenge my blood.' We are his children and it is therefore obligatory for us to avenge him since you are the ones who rebel and disbelieve in him. Your God has never been at peace with you. Although He intended to deal kindly with you, you have conducted yourselves improperly before Him. God has forgotten you and is no longer desirous of you since you are a stubborn nation. Instead, He has departed from you and has taken us for His portion, casting His radiance upon us."

---

[2] Reference to the Greek mountain Parnassus, perhaps meaning "mainstay" of the community. [Ed.]

When we heard these words, our hearts trembled and moved out of their places. We were dumb with silence, abiding in darkness, like those long dead, waiting for the Lord to look forth and behold from heaven.

And Satan—the Pope of evil Rome—also came and proclaimed to all the nations believing in that stock of adultery—these are the stock of Seir[3]—that they should assemble and ascend to Jerusalem so as to conquer the city, and journey to the tomb of the superstition whom they call their god. Satan came and mingled with the nations, and they gathered as one man to fulfill the command, coming in great numbers like the grains of sand upon the seashore, the noise of them clamorous as a whirlwind and a storm. When the drops of the bucket had assembled, they took evil counsel against the people of the Lord and said: "Why should we concern ourselves with going to war against the Ishmaelites dwelling about Jerusalem, when in our midst is a people who disrespect our god—indeed, their ancestors are those who crucified him. Why should we let them live and tolerate their dwelling among us? Let us commence by using our swords against them and then proceed upon our stray path."

The heart of the people of our God grew faint and their spirit flagged, for many sore injuries had been inflicted upon them and they had been smitten repeatedly. They now came supplicating to God and fasting, and their hearts melted within them. But the Lord did as He declared, for we had sinned before Him, and He forsook the sanctuary of Shiloh—the Temple-in-Miniature—which He had placed among His people who dwelt in the midst of alien nations. His wrath was kindled and He drew the sword against them, until they remained but as the flagstaff upon the mountaintop and as the ensign on the hill, and He gave over His nation into captivity and trampled them underfoot. See, O Lord, and consider to whom Thou hast done thus: to Israel, a nation despised and pillaged, Your chosen portion! Why have You uplifted the shield of its enemies, and why have they gained in strength? Let all hear, for I cry out in anguish; the ears of all that hear me shall be seared: How has the staff of might been broken, the rod of glory—the sainted community comparable to fine gold, the community of Mainz! It was caused by the Lord to test those that fear Him, to have them endure the yoke of His pure fear. . . .

---

[3] An enemy of ancient Israel.

62

ANNA COMNENA

From The Alexiad

Anna Comnena was the daughter of Emperor Alexius (r. 1081–1118) of Byzantium. Threatened on three sides—by the Seljuk Turks to the east, the Norman Kingdom of southern Italy to the west, and rebellions to the north—Alexius appealed for aid to Pope Urban II of Rome in 1095. He expected a mercenary army, but because the pope saw a chance to send a massive force against Muslim occupiers of Jerusalem as well as against those threatening Constantinople, Alexius instead received an uncontrollable ragtag force of Christians and Crusaders that included his Norman enemies, led by Bohemond.

Princess Anna, the emperor's daughter, recalled the story of the First Crusade's appearance in Byzantium some forty years later in her history titled *The Alexiad* after her father. According to Anna, how did Alexius respond to the approach of the Crusader army? Did Alexius fear the Franks more than he feared the Turks?

Thinking Historically

This is a third perspective on the history of the First Crusade—the view of a Christian ally of Rome, more directly threatened than the Roman church by the Muslim armies. Yet, Byzantium and Rome were also at odds. Since 1054, they had accepted a parting of ways, theologically and institutionally. And with the advancing Frankish armies, Anna and Alexius were not sure whether they were facing friend or foe. How does Anna's critical perspective change our idea of the Crusaders? How might her idea of the Franks change our narrative of the early stage of the crusade?

Notice how this narrative combines a sequence of events with generalizations (often about the "race" or nature of the Franks) to explain specific events. Does a narrative history have to include generalizations as well as a sequence of specific events? Can the events alone provide sufficient explanation?

Anna Comnena, *The Alexiad of the Princess Anna Comnena*, trans. Elizabeth A. S. Dawes (London: Routledge & Kegan Paul Ltd., 1967), 247–52. Reprinted in William H. McNeill and Schuyler O. Houser, *Medieval Europe* (Oxford: Oxford University Press, 1971), 135–40.

Before he had enjoyed even a short rest, he heard a report of the approach of innumerable Frankish armies. Now he dreaded their arrival for he knew their irresistible manner of attack, their unstable and mobile character and all the peculiar natural and concomitant characteristics which the Frank retains throughout; and he also knew that they were always agape for money, and seemed to disregard their truces readily for any reason that cropped up. For he had always heard this reported of them, and found it very true. However, he did not lose heart, but prepared himself in every way so that, when the occasion called, he would be ready for battle. And indeed the actual facts were far greater and more terrible than rumour made them. For the whole of the West and all the barbarian tribes which dwell between the further side of the Adriatic and the pillars of Heracles, had all migrated in a body and were marching into Asia through the intervening Europe, and were making the journey with all their household. The reason of this upheaval was more or less the following. A certain Frank, Peter by name, nicknamed Cucupeter, had gone to worship at the Holy Sepulchre and after suffering many things at the hands of the Turks and Saracens who were ravaging Asia, he got back to his own country with difficulty. But he was angry at having failed in his object, and wanted to undertake the same journey again. However, he saw that he ought not to make the journey to the Holy Sepulchre alone again, lest worse things befall him, so he worked out a cunning plan. This was to preach in all the Latin countries that "the voice of God bids me announce to all the Counts in France" that they should all leave their homes and set out to worship at the Holy Sepulchre, and to endeavour wholeheartedly with hand and mind to deliver Jerusalem from the hand of Hagarenes.[1] And he really succeeded. For after inspiring the souls of all with this quasi-divine command he contrived to assemble the Franks from all sides, one after the other, with arms, horses and all the other paraphernalia of war. And they were all so zealous and eager that every highroad was full of them. And those Frankish soldiers were accompanied by an unarmed host more numerous than the sand or the stars, carrying palms and crosses on their shoulders, women and children, too, came away from their countries and the sight of them was like many rivers streaming from all sides, and they were advancing towards us through Dacia generally with all their hosts. Now the coming of these many peoples was preceded by a locust which did not touch the wheat, but made a terrible attack on the vines. This was really a presage as the diviners of the time interpreted it, and meant that this enormous Frankish army would, when it came, refrain from interference in Christian affairs, but fall very heavily upon the barbarian

---

[1] Saracens, who were considered "children of Hagar" (cf. Gen. 16). [Ed.]

Ishmaelites who were slaves to drunkenness, wine, and Dionysus.[2] For this race is under the sway of Dionysus and Eros,[3] rushes headlong into all kind of sexual intercourse, and is not circumcised either in the flesh or in their passions. It is nothing but a slave, nay triply enslaved, to the ills wrought by Aphrodite. For this reason they worship and adore Astarte and Ashtaroth[4] too and value above all the image of the moon, and the golden figure of Hobar[5] in their country. Now in these symbols Christianity was taken to be the corn because of its wineless and very nutritive qualities; in this manner the diviners interpreted the vines and the wheat. However let the matter of the prophecy rest.

The incidents of the barbarians' approach followed in the order I have described, and persons of intelligence could feel that they were witnessing a strange occurrence. The arrival of these multitudes did not take place at the same time nor by the same road (for how indeed could such masses starting from different places have crossed the straits of Lombardy all together?). Some first, some next, others after them and thus successively all accomplished the transit, and then marched through the Continent. Each army was preceded, as we said, by an unspeakable number of locusts; and all who saw this more than once recognized them as forerunners of the Frankish armies. When the first of them began crossing the straits of Lombardy sporadically the Emperor summoned certain leaders of the Roman forces, and sent them to the parts of Dyrrachium and Valona[6] with instructions to offer a courteous welcome to the Franks who had crossed, and to collect abundant supplies from all the countries along their route; then to follow and watch them covertly all the time, and if they saw them making any foraging-excursions, they were to come out from under cover and check them by light skirmishing. These captains were accompanied by some men who knew the Latin tongue, so that they might settle any disputes that arose between them.

Let me, however, give an account of this subject more clearly and in due order. According to universal rumour Godfrey,[7] who sold his country, was the first to start on the appointed road; this man was very rich and very proud of his bravery, courage and conspicuous lineage; for every Frank is anxious to outdo the others. And such an upheaval

---

[2]Anna's account of the beliefs of the Muslims was highly biased. Muhammad forbade his followers to drink intoxicating liquors.

[3]Dionysus was the Greek god associated with wine and revelry; Eros was the patron of lovers, and son of Aphrodite, goddess of love.

[4]Names of the Semitic goddess of fertility.

[5]I.e., Hathor, the Egyptian goddess of love, usually depicted with the head of a cow. (N.B. Idol worship was strictly forbidden by Islamic law.)

[6]Ports on the Adriatic, directly opposite the heel of Italy in modern Albania.

[7]Godfrey of Bouillon, the duke of Lower Lorraine (c. 1060–1100). To raise money for the Crusade, he sold two of his estates, and pledged his castle at Bouillon to the bishop of Liège.

of both men and women took place then as had never occurred within human memory, the simpler-minded were urged on by the real desire of worshipping at our Lord's Sepulchre, and visiting the sacred places; but the more astute, especially men like Bohemund and those of like mind, had another secret reason, namely, the hope that while on their travels they might by some means be able to seize the capital [Constantinople] itself, looking upon this as a kind of corollary. And Bohemund disturbed the minds of many nobler men by thus cherishing his old grudge against the Emperor. Meanwhile Peter, after he had delivered his message, crossed the straits of Lombardy before anybody else with eighty thousand men on foot, and one hundred thousand on horseback, and reached the capital by way of Hungary.[8] For the Frankish race, as one may conjecture, is always very hotheaded and eager, but when once it has espoused a cause, it is uncontrollable.

The Emperor, knowing what Peter had suffered before from the Turks, advised him to wait for the arrival of the other Counts, but Peter would not listen for he trusted the multitude of his followers, so he crossed and pitched his camp near a small town called Helenopolis.[9] After him followed the Normans numbering ten thousand, who separated themselves from the rest of the army and devastated the country round Nicaea, and behaved most cruelly to all. For they dismembered some of the children and fixed others on wooden spits and roasted them at the fire, and on persons advanced in age they inflicted every kind of torture. But when the inhabitants of Nicaea became aware of these doings, they threw open their gates and marched out upon them, and after a violent conflict had taken place they had to dash back inside their citadel as the Normans fought so bravely. And thus the latter recovered all the booty and returned to Helenopolis. Then a dispute arose between them and the others who had not gone out with them, as is usual in such cases, for the minds of those who stayed behind were aflame with envy, and thus caused a skirmish after which the headstrong Normans drew apart again, marched to Xerigordus[10] and took it by assault. When the Sultan[11] heard what had happened, he dispatched Elchanes[12] against them with a substantial force. He came, and recaptured Xerigordus and sacrificed some of the Normans to the sword, and took others captive, at the same time laid plans to catch those who had remained behind with Cucupeter. He placed ambushes in suitable spots so that any coming from the camp in the direction of Nicaea would fall into them unexpectedly and be killed. Besides this, as he knew the Franks' love of money, he sent for two active-minded men

---

[8]Peter's contingent probably numbered about twenty thousand including noncombatants.
[9]I.e., Peter moved his forces across the Bosphorus and into Asia Minor.
[10]A castle held by the Turks.
[11]Qilij Arslan I, ruled 1092–1106.
[12]An important Turkish military commander.

and ordered them to go to Cucupeter's camp and proclaim there that the Normans had gained possession of Nicaea, and were now dividing everything in it. When this report was circulated among Peter's followers, it upset them terribly. Directly [When] they heard the words "partition" and "money" they started in a disorderly crowd along the road to Nicaea, all but unmindful of their military experience and the discipline which is essential for those starting out to battle. For, as I remarked above, the Latin race is always very fond of money, but more especially when it is bent on raiding a country; it then loses its reason and gets beyond control. As they journeyed neither in ranks nor in squadrons, they fell foul of the Turkish ambuscades near the river Dracon and perished miserably. And such a large number of Franks and Normans were the victims of the Ishmaelite sword, that when they piled up the corpses of the slaughtered men which were lying on either side they formed, I say, not a very large hill or mound or a peak, but a high mountain as it were, of very considerable depth and breadth—so great was the pyramid of bones. And later men of the same tribe as the slaughtered barbarians built a wall and used the bones of the dead to fill the interstices as if they were pebbles, and thus made the city their tomb in a way. This fortified city is still standing today with its walls built of a mixture of stones and bones. When they had all in this way fallen prey to the sword, Peter alone with a few others escaped and reentered Helenopolis,[13] and the Turks who wanted to capture him, set fresh ambushes for him. But when the Emperor received reliable information of all this, and the terrible massacre, he was very worried lest Peter should have been captured. He therefore summoned Constantine Catacalon Euphorbenus (who has already been mentioned many times in this history), and gave him a large force which was embarked on ships of war and sent him across the straits to Peter's succour. Directly the Turks saw him land they fled. Constantine, without the slightest delay, picked up Peter and his followers, who were but few, and brought them safe and sound to the Emperor. On the Emperor's reminding him of his original thoughtlessness and saying that it was due to his not having obeyed his, the Emperor's, advice that he had incurred such disasters, Peter, being a haughty Latin, would not admit that he himself was the cause of the trouble, but said it was the others who did not listen to him, but followed their own will, and he denounced them as robbers and plunderers who, for that reason, were not allowed by the Saviour to worship at His Holy Sepulchre. Others of the Latins, such as Bohemund and men of like mind, who had long cherished a desire for the Roman Empire, and wished to win it for themselves, found a pretext in Peter's preaching, as I have said, deceived the more single-

[13]According to other accounts of the battle, Peter was in Constantinople at the time.

minded, caused this great upheaval and were selling their own estates under the pretence that they were marching against the Turks to redeem the Holy Sepulchre.

FULCHER OF CHARTRES
The Siege of Antioch

We return here to Fulcher's Chronicles (Book I, Chapters 16 and 17). Antioch, in northern Syria, was the largest and most formidable Muslim-controlled city on the Crusaders' route to Jerusalem. After laying siege to the city for more than two years, the Crusader forces had suffered losses that seriously reduced their strength and morale. After their initial success, what events seem to have caused these reversals? What were the strengths and weaknesses of the Crusader armies?

Thinking Historically

Like the narrative of Solomon bar Simson, this narrative operates on two levels: the human and the divine. Notice how Fulcher attempts to interpret both of these narrative lines, separately and in their interaction. How much of Fulcher's narrative recounts God's work? How much recounts the work of the Crusaders? How does he combine these two threads? Of course, modern historians are normally limited to the human thread. Try to write a narrative that shows how the human Crusaders conquered Antioch.

XVI. The Wretched Poverty of the Christians and the Flight of the Count of Blois

1. In the year of the Lord 1098, after the region all around Antioch had been wholly devastated by the multitude of our people, the strong as well as the weak were more and more harassed by famine.

The First Crusade: The Chronicle of Fulcher of Chartres and Other Source Materials, 2nd ed., ed. Edward Peters (Philadelphia: University of Pennsylvania Press, 1998), 73–75.

2. At that time, the famished ate the shoots of beanseeds growing in the fields and many kinds of herbs unseasoned with salt; also thistles, which, being not well cooked because of the deficiency of firewood, pricked the tongues of those eating them; also horses, asses, and camels, and dogs and rats. The poorer ones ate even the skins of the beasts and seeds of grain found in manure.

3. They endured winter's cold, summer's heat, and heavy rains for God. Their tents became old and torn and rotten from the continuation of rains. Because of this, many of them were covered by only the sky.

4. So like gold thrice proved and purified sevenfold by fire, long predestined by God, I believe, and weighed by such a great calamity, they were cleansed of their sins. For even if the assassin's sword had not failed, many, long agonizing, would have voluntarily completed a martyr's course. Perhaps they borrowed the grace of such a great example from Saint Job, who, purifying his soul by the torments of his body, ever held God fast in mind. Those who fight with the heathen, labor because of God.

5. Granting that God—who creates everything, regulates everything created, sustains everything regulated, and rules by virtue—can destroy or renew whatsoever He wishes, I feel that He assented to the destruction of the heathen after the scourging of the Christians. He permitted it, and the people deserved it, because so many times they cheaply destroyed all things of God. He permitted the Christians to be killed by the Turks, so that the Christians would have the assurance of salvation; the Turks, the perdition of their souls. It pleased God that certain Turks, already predestined for salvation, were baptized by priests. "For those whom He predestined, He also called and glorified."

6. So what then? There were some of our men, as you heard before, who left the siege because it brought so much anguish; others, because of poverty; others, because of cowardice; others, because of fear of death; first the poor and then the rich.

7. Stephen, Count of Blois, withdrew from the siege and returned home to France by sea. Therefore all of us grieved, since he was a very noble man and valiant in arms. On the day following his departure, the city of Antioch was surrendered to the Franks. If he had persevered, he would have rejoiced much in the victory with the rest. This act disgraced him. For a good beginning is not beneficial to anyone unless it be well consummated. I shall cut short many things in the Lord's affairs lest I wander from the truth, because lying about them must be especially guarded against.

8. The siege lasted continuously from this same month of October, as it was mentioned, through the following winter and spring until June. The Turks and Franks alternately staged many attacks and counter-attacks; they overcame and were overcome. Our men, however, triumphed more often than theirs. Once it happened that many of the fleeing Turks fell into the Fernus River, and being submerged in it,

they drowned. On the near side of the river, and on the far side, both forces often waged war alternately.

9. Our leaders constructed castles before the city, from which they often rushed forth vigorously to keep the Turks from coming out [of the city]. By this means, the Franks took the pastures from their animals. Nor did they get any help from Armenians outside the city, although these Armenians often did injury to our men.

XVII. The Surrender of the City of Antioch

1. When it pleased God that the labor of His people should be consummated, perhaps pleased by the prayers of those who daily poured out supplications and entreaties to Him, out of His compassion He granted that through a fraud of the Turks the city be returned to the Christians in a secret surrender. Hear, therefore, of a fraud, and yet not a fraud.

2. Our Lord appeared to a certain Turk, chosen beforehand by His grace, and said to him: "Arise, thou who sleepest! I command thee to return the city to the Christians." The astonished man concealed that vision in silence.

3. However, a second time, the Lord appeared to him: "Return the city to the Christians," He said, "for I am Christ who command this of thee." Meditating what to do, he went away to his ruler, the prince of Antioch, and made that vision known to him. To him the ruler responded: "You do not wish to obey the phantom, do you, stupid?" Returning, he was afterwards silent.

4. The Lord again appeared to him, saying: "Why hast thou not fulfilled what I ordered thee? Thou must not hesitate, for I, who command this, am Lord of all." No longer doubting, he discreetly negotiated with our men, so that by his zealous plotting they might receive the city.

5. He finished speaking, and gave his son as hostage to Lord Bohemond, to whom he first directed that discourse, and whom he first persuaded. On a certain night, he sent twenty of our men over the wall by means of ladders made of ropes. Without delay, the gate was opened. The Franks, already prepared, entered the city. Forty of our soldiers, who had previously entered by ropes, killed sixty Turks found there, guards of the tower. In a loud voice, altogether the Franks shouted: "God wills it! God wills it!" For this was our signal cry, when we were about to press forward on any enterprise.

6. After hearing this, all the Turks were extremely terrified. Then, when the redness of dawn had paled, the Franks began to go forward to attack the city. When the Turks had first seen Bohemond's red banner on high, furling and unfurling, and the great tumult aroused on all sides, and the Franks running far and wide through the streets with their naked swords and wildly killing people, and had heard their horns sounding on the top of the wall, they began to flee here and there,

bewildered. From this scene, many who were able fled into the citadel situated on a cliff.

7. Our rabble wildly seized everything that they found in the streets and houses. But the proved soldiers kept to warfare, in following and killing the Turks.

64

IBN AL-QALANISI

From The Damascus Chronicle

Here we switch to a Muslim view of the events of 1098 and 1099: especially the battles of Antioch, Jerusalem, and Ascalon (modern Ashkelon, Israel). Ibn al-Qalanisi* (d. 1160) was a scholar in Damascus, Syria. How does his account of the battle for Antioch differ from the previous selection by Fulcher of Chartres? How do you resolve these differences?

Thinking Historically

We noticed how the medieval Christian historian provided two historical threads—the human and divine. How does this Muslim account integrate the threads of human action and divine will?

Modern historians restrict their accounts to human action but they seek to include the view of both sides in a conflict. How do you integrate both sides into your narrative? Also, what signs do you see here of a possible second conflict, this one between Muslims?

A.H. 491

(9th December, 1097, to 27th November, 1098)

At the end of First Jumādā (beginning of June, 1098) the report arrived that certain of the men of Antioch among the armourers in the train of the amīr Yāghī Siyān had entered into a conspiracy against Antioch and

---

*IH buhn   ahl kahl ah NEE see

H. A. R. Gibb, *The Damascus Chronicle of the Crusades*, extracted and translated from the *Chronicle of Ibn al-Qalanisi* (Mineola, N.Y.: Dover Publications, 2002), 44–49.

had come to an agreement with the Franks to deliver the city up to them, because of some ill-usage and confiscations which they had formerly suffered at his hands. They found an opportunity of seizing one of the city bastions adjoining the Jabal, which they sold to the Franks, and thence admitted them into the city during the night. At daybreak they raised the battle cry, whereupon Yāghī Siyān took to flight and went out with a large body, but not one person amongst them escaped to safety. When he reached the neighbourhood of Armanāz, an estate near Ma 'arrat Masrīn, he fell from his horse to the ground. One of his companions raised him up and remounted him, but he could not maintain his balance on the back of the horse, and after falling repeatedly he died. As for Antioch, the number of men, women, and children, killed, taken prisoner, and enslaved from its population is beyond computation. About three thousand men fled to the citadel and fortified themselves in it, and some few escaped for whom God had decreed escape.

In Sha'bān (July) news was received that al-Afdal, the commander-in-chief (amīr al-juyūsh), had come up from Egypt to Syria at the head of a strong 'askar.[1] He encamped before Jerusalem, where at that time were the two amīrs Sukmān and Il-Ghāzī, sons of Ortuq, together with a number of their kinsmen and followers and a large body of Turks, and sent letters to them, demanding that they should surrender Jerusalem to him without warfare or shedding of blood. When they refused his demand, he opened an attack on the town, and having set up mangonels[2] against it, which effected a breach in the wall, he captured it and received the surrender of the Sanctuary of David[3] from Sukmān. On his entry into it, he shewed kindness and generosity to the two amīrs, and set both them and their supporters free. They arrived in Damascus during the first ten days of Shawwāl (September), and al-Afdal returned with his 'askar to Egypt.

In this year also the Franks set out with all their forces to Ma'arrat al-Nu'mān,[4] and having encamped over against it on 29th Dhu'l-Hijja (27th November), they opened an attack on the town and brought up a tower and scaling-ladders against it.

Now after the Franks had captured the city of Antioch through the devices of the armourer, who was an Armenian named Fīrūz,[5] on the eve

---

[1]Small military force of slaves and freed men, under Muslim amirs. [Ed.]

[2]A catapult that could hurl large stones as far as four hundred feet to break down a wall. [Ed.]

[3]The Citadel of Jerusalem.

[4]Ma'arrat al-Numān or Ma'arat al-Numān: Syrian city south of Antioch. Conquest of Antioch did not provide enough food so crusaders marched on to this next city on route to Jerusalem. There they massacred the population of 10,000–20,000 and by some accounts cannibalized some of them. [Ed.]

[5]In the text Nairūz.

of Friday, 1st Rajab (night of Thursday 3rd June), and a series of reports were received confirming this news, the armies of Syria assembled in uncountable force and proceeded to the province of Antioch, in order to inflict a crushing blow upon the armies of the Franks. They besieged the Franks until their supplies of food were exhausted and they were reduced to eating carrion; but thereafter the Franks, though they were in the extremity of weakness, advanced in battle order against the armies of Islām, which were at the height of strength and numbers, and they broke the ranks of the Muslims and scattered their multitudes. The lords of the pedigree steeds[6] were put to flight, and the sword was unsheathed upon the footsoldiers who had volunteered for the cause of God, who had girt themselves for the Holy War, and were vehement in their desire to strike a blow for the Faith and for the protection of the Muslims. This befel on Tuesday, the [twenty] sixth of Rajab, in this year (29th June, 1098).

A.H. 492

(28th November, 1098, to 16th November, 1099)

In Muharram of this year (December, 1098), the Franks made an assault on the wall of Ma'arrat al-Nu'mān from the east and north. They pushed up the tower until it rested against the wall, and as it was higher, they deprived the Muslims of the shelter of the wall. The fighting raged round this point until sunset on 14th Muharram (11th December), when the Franks scaled the wall, and the townsfolk were driven off it and took to flight. Prior to this, messengers had repeatedly come to them from the Franks with proposals for a settlement by negotiation and the surrender of the city, promising in return security for their lives and property, and the establishment of a [Frankish] governor amongst them, but dissension among the citizens and the fore-ordained decree of God prevented acceptance of these terms. So they captured the city after the hour of the sunset prayer, and a great number from both sides were killed in it. The townsfolk fled to the houses of al-Ma'arra, to defend themselves in them, and the Franks, after promising them safety, dealt treacherously with them. They erected crosses over the town, exacted indemnities from the townsfolk, and did not carry out any of the terms upon which they had agreed, but plundered everything that they found, and demanded of the people sums which they could not pay. On Thursday 17th Safar (13th January, 1099) they set out for Kafr Tāb.

Thereafter they proceeded towards Jerusalem, at the end of Rajab (middle of June) of this year, and the people fled in panic from their

[6]Literally "of the short-haired and swift-paced."

abodes before them. They descended first upon al-Ramla, and captured it after the ripening of the crops. Thence they marched to Jerusalem, the inhabitants of which they engaged and blockaded, and having set up the tower against the city they brought it forward to the wall. At length news reached them that al-Afdal was on his way from Egypt with a mighty army to engage in the Holy War against them, and to destroy them, and to succour and protect the city against them. They therefore attacked the city with increased vigour, and prolonged the battle that day until the daylight faded, then withdrew from it, after promising the inhabitants to renew the attack upon them on the morrow. The townsfolk descended from the wall at sunset, whereupon the Franks renewed their assault upon it, climbed up the tower, and gained a footing on the city wall. The defenders were driven down, and the Franks stormed the town and gained possession of it. A number of the townsfolk fled to the sanctuary [of David], and a great host were killed. The Jews assembled in the synagogue, and the Franks burned it over their heads. The sanctuary was surrendered to them on guarantee of safety on the 22nd of Sha'bān (14th July) of this year, and they destroyed the shrines and the tomb of Abraham. Al-Afdal arrived with the Egyptian armies, but found himself forestalled, and having been reinforced by the troops from the Sāhil,[7] encamped outside Ascalon on 14th Ramadān (4th August), to await the arrival of the fleet by sea and of the Arab levies. The army of the Franks advanced against him and attacked him in great force. The Egyptian army was thrown back towards Ascalon, al-Afdal himself taking refuge in the city. The swords of the Franks were given mastery over the Muslims, and death was meted out to the footmen, volunteers, and townsfolk, about ten thousand souls, and the camp was plundered. Al-Afdal set out for Egypt with his officers, and the Franks besieged Ascalon, until at length the townsmen agreed to pay them twenty thousand dinars as protection money, and to deliver this sum to them forthwith. They therefore set about collecting this amount from the inhabitants of the town, but it befel that a quarrel broke out between the [Frankish] leaders, and they retired without having received any of the money. It is said that the number of the people of Ascalon who were killed in this campaign—that is to say of the witnesses, men of substance, merchants, and youths, exclusive of the regular levies—amounted to two thousand seven hundred souls.

---

[7]The Sāhil was the general name given to the coastal plain and the maritime towns, from Ascalon to Bairūt.

65

RAYMOND OF ST. GILES,
COUNT OF TOULOUSE

The Capture of Jerusalem by the Crusaders

The author of this letter or proclamation was the secular military leader chosen by Pope Urban II to lead the crusade. By the time of the capture of Jerusalem in 1099, he was certainly—with the Norman Bohemond and a couple other nobles—among the top military leaders. How does he account for their capture of Jerusalem? How would you explain it? Raymond tells how immediately after conquering Jerusalem, the Crusaders went to meet an Egyptian army (mistakenly identified as Babylonian) at Ascalon. How does Raymond explain their success? How did Ibn al-Qalanisi explain it? How might you explain it?

Thinking Historically

A letter can read much like a historical narrative, as does this one by Raymond of St. Giles. The author clearly wants to tell his readers what has happened. But this letter addressed to the pope, his bishops, and "the whole Christian people" is as much a testament to God's work as it is a history. Why does this make it difficult to construct the human narrative? Which events could you confidently include in your history of the crusade?

To lord Paschal, pope of the Roman church, to all the bishops, and to the whole Christian people, from the archbishop of Pisa, duke Godfrey, now, by the grace of God, defender of the church of the Holy Sepulchre, Raymond, count of St. Giles, and the whole army of God, which is in the land of Israel, greeting.

Multiply your supplications and prayers in the sight of God with joy and thanksgiving, since God has manifested His mercy in fulfilling by our hands what He had promised in ancient times. For after the capture of Nicaea, the whole army, made up of more than three hundred thousand soldiers, departed thence. And, although this army was so

---

Raymond of St. Giles, Count of Toulouse, "The Capture of Jerusalem by the Crusaders," in D. C. Munro, ed., *Translations and Reprints from the Original Sources of European History*, 4th ed., vol. I, bk. 4 (New York: AMC Press, Inc., 1971), 8–12.

great that it could have in a single day covered all Romania and drunk up all the rivers and eaten up all the growing things, yet the Lord conducted them amid so great abundance that a ram was sold for a penny and an ox for twelve pennies or less. Moreover, although the princes and kings of the Saracens rose up against us, yet, by God's will, they were easily conquered and overcome. Because, indeed, some were puffed up by these successes, God opposed to us Antioch, impregnable to human strength. And there He detained us for nine months and so humbled us in the siege that there were scarcely a hundred good horses in our whole army. God opened to us the abundance of His blessing and mercy and led us into the city, and delivered the Turks and all of their possessions into our power.

Inasmuch as we thought that these had been acquired by our own strength and did not worthily magnify God who had done this, we were beset by so great a multitude of Turks that no one dared to venture forth at any point from the city. Moreover, hunger so weakened us that some could scarcely refrain from eating human flesh. It would be tedious to narrate all the miseries which we suffered in that city. But God looked down upon His people whom He had so long chastised and mercifully consoled them. Therefore, He at first revealed to us, as a recompense for our tribulation and as a pledge of victory, His lance which had lain hidden since the days of the apostles. Next, He so fortified the hearts of the men, that they who from sickness or hunger had been unable to walk, now were endued with strength to seize their weapons and manfully to fight against the enemy.

After we had triumphed over the enemy, as our army was wasting away at Antioch from sickness and weariness and was especially hindered by the dissensions among the leaders, we proceeded into Syria, stormed Barra and Marra, cities of the Saracens, and captured the fortresses in that country. And while we were delaying there, there was so great a famine in the army that the Christian people now ate the putrid bodies of the Saracens.[1] Finally, by the divine admonition, we entered into the interior of Hispania,[2] and the most bountiful, merciful and victorious hand of the omnipotent Father was with us. For the cities and fortresses of the country through which we were proceeding sent ambassadors to us with many gifts and offered to aid us and to surrender their walled places. But because our army was not large and it was the unanimous wish to hasten to Jerusalem, we accepted their pledges and made them tributaries. One of the cities forsooth, which

---

[1]Radulph of Caen, another Crusader chronicler, wrote, "In Ma'arra our troops boiled pagan adults alive in cooking-pots; they impaled children on spits and devoured them grilled." [Ed.]

[2]Probably a metaphor for an extremely fertile Muslim land, as Muslim Spain was known to be. [Ed.]

was on the sea-coast, had more men than there were in our whole army. And when those at Antioch and Laodicea and Archas heard how the hand of the Lord was with us, many from the army who had remained in those cities followed us to Tyre. Therefore, with the Lord's companionship and aid, we proceeded thus as far as Jerusalem.

And after the army had suffered greatly in the siege, especially on account of the lack of water, a council was held and the bishops and princes ordered that all with bare feet should march around the walls of the city, in order that He who entered it humbly in our behalf might be moved by our humility to open it to us and to exercise judgment upon His enemies. God was appeased by this humility and on the eighth day after the humiliation He delivered the city and His enemies to us. It was the day indeed on which the primitive church was driven thence, and on which the festival of the dispersion of the apostles is celebrated. And if you desire to know what was done with the enemy who were found there, know that in Solomon's Porch and in his temple our men rode in the blood of the Saracens up to the knees of their horses.

Then, when we were considering who ought to hold the city, and some moved by love for their country and kinsmen wished to return home, it was announced to us that the king of Babylon had come to Ascalon with an innumerable multitude of soldiers. His purpose was, as he said, to lead the Franks, who were in Jerusalem, into captivity, and to take Antioch by storm. But God had determined otherwise in regard to us.

Therefore, when we learned that the army of the Babylonians was at Ascalon, we went down to meet them, leaving our baggage and the sick in Jerusalem with a garrison. When our army was in sight of the enemy, upon our knees we invoked the aid of the Lord, that He who in our other adversities had strengthened the Christian faith, might in the present battle break the strength of the Saracens and of the devil and extend the kingdom of the church of Christ from sea to sea, over the whole world. There was no delay; God was present when we cried for His aid, and furnished us with so great boldness, that one who saw us rush upon the enemy would have taken us for a herd of deer hastening to quench their thirst in running water. It was wonderful, indeed, since there were in our army not more than 5,000 horsemen and 15,000 foot-soldiers, and there were probably in the enemy's army 100,000 horsemen and 400,000 foot-soldiers. Then God appeared wonderful to His servants. For before we engaged in fighting, by our very onset alone, He turned this multitude in flight and scattered all their weapons, so that if they wished afterwards to attack us, they did not have the weapons in which they trusted. There can be no question how great the spoils were, since the treasures of the king of Babylon were captured. More than 100,000 Moors perished there by the sword. Moreover, their panic was so great that about 2,000 were suffocated at the gate of the city. Those who perished in the sea were innumerable. Many were entangled in the thickets. The whole world was certainly fighting for us, and if many of ours had not been detained in plundering the camp, few of the great multitude of the enemy would have been able to escape from the battle.

And although it may be tedious, the following must not be omitted: On the day preceding the battle the army captured many thousands of camels, oxen, and sheep. By the command of the princes these were divided among the people. When we advanced to battle, wonderful to relate, the camels formed in many squadrons and the sheep and oxen did the same. Moreover, these animals accompanied us, halting when we halted, advancing when we advanced, and charging when we charged. The clouds protected us from the heat of the sun and cooled us.

Accordingly, after celebrating the victory, the army returned to Jerusalem. Duke Godfrey remained there; the count of St. Giles, Robert, count of Normandy, and Robert, count of Flanders, returned to Laodicea. There they found the fleet belonging to the Pisans and to Bohemond. After the archbishop of Pisa had established peace between Bohemond and our leaders, Raymond prepared to return to Jerusalem for the sake of God and his brethren.

Therefore, we call upon you of the Catholic Church of Christ and of the whole Latin church to exult in the so admirable bravery and devotion of your brethren, in the so glorious and very desirable retribution of the omnipotent God, and in the so devoutly hoped-for remission of all our sins through the grace of God. And we pray that He may make you—namely, all bishops, clerks, and monks who are leading devout lives, and all the laity—to sit down at the right hand of God, who liveth and reigneth God for ever and ever. And we ask and beseech you in the name of our Lord Jesus, who has ever been with us and aided us and freed us from all our tribulations, to be mindful of your brethren who return to you, by doing them kindnesses and by paying their debts, in order that God may recompense you and absolve you from all your sins and grant you a share in all the blessings which either we or they have deserved in the sight of the Lord. Amen.

66

IBN AL-ATHIR
The Conquest of Jerusalem

Ibn al-Athir* (1160–1233) was an influential Arab historian who wrote a history of the first three crusades, having witnessed the third himself. The following selection, taken from his work *The Perfect History*, is one of the most authoritative, roughly contemporaneous histories of the First Crusade from the Muslim perspective. What reason does al-Athir give for the Egyptian capture of Jerusalem from the Turks? Why were the Franks successful in wresting Jerusalem and other lands from Muslim control? What is the significance of the poem at the end of the selection?

Thinking Historically

There are always more than two sides to a story, but it is certainly useful to have battle descriptions from two sides of a conflict. In constructing your own narrative of the battle of Jerusalem, you might first look for points of agreement. On what points does Ibn al-Athir agree with other accounts you have read? How else would you decide which elements from each account to include in your narrative?

Taj ad-Daula Tutūsh was the Lord of Jerusalem but had given it as a feoff to the amīr Suqmān ibn Artūq the Turcoman. When the Franks defeated the Turks at Antioch the massacre demoralized them, and the Egyptians, who saw that the Turkish armies were being weakened by desertion, besieged Jerusalem under the command of al-Afdal ibn Badr al-Jamali. Inside the city were Artūq's sons, Suqmān and Ilghazi, their cousin Sunij and their nephew Yaquti. The Egyptians brought more than forty siege engines to attack Jerusalem and broke down the walls at several points. The inhabitants put up a defense, and the siege and fighting went on for more than six weeks. In the end the Egyptians forced the city to capitulate, in Sha'bān 489/August 1096. Suqmān, Ilghazi, and their friends were well treated by al-Afdal, who gave them

*IH buhn   ahl AH tuhr

Francesco Gabrieli, ed., *Arab Historians of the Crusades: Selected and Translated from the Arabic Sources*, ed. and trans. E. J. Costello. Islamic World Series (Berkeley: University of California Press, 1969), 10–12.

large gifts of money and let them go free. They made for Damascus and then crossed the Euphrates. Suqmān settled in Edessa and Ilghazi went on into Iraq. The Egyptian governor of Jerusalem was a certain Iftikhār ad-Daula, who was still there at the time of which we are speaking.

After their vain attempt to take Acre by siege, the Franks moved on to Jerusalem and besieged it for more than six weeks. They built two towers, one of which, near Sion, the Muslims burnt down, killing everyone inside it. It had scarcely ceased to burn before a messenger arrived to ask for help and to bring the news that the other side of the city had fallen. In fact Jerusalem was taken from the north on the morning of Friday 22 Sha'bān 492/July 15, 1099. The population was put to the sword by the Franks, who pillaged the area for a week. A band of Muslims barricaded themselves into the Oratory of David and fought on for several days. They were granted their lives in return for surrendering. The Franks honoured their word, and the group left by night for Ascalon. In the Masjid al-Aqsa the Franks slaughtered more than 70,000 people, among them a large number of Imams and Muslim scholars, devout and ascetic men who had left their homelands to live lives of pious seclusion in the Holy Place. The Franks stripped the Dome of the Rock of more than forty silver candelabra, each of them weighing 3,600 drams, and a great silver lamp weighing forty-four Syrian pounds, as well as a hundred and fifty smaller silver candelabra and more than twenty gold ones, and a great deal more booty. Refugees from Syria reached Baghdād in Ramadan, among them the qadi Abu Sa'd al-Hárawi. They told the Caliph's ministers a story that wrung their hearts and brought tears to their eyes. On Friday they went to the Cathedral Mosque and begged for help, weeping so that their hearers wept with them as they described the sufferings of the Muslims in that Holy City: the men killed, the women and children taken prisoner, the homes pillaged. Because of the terrible hardships they had suffered, they were allowed to break the fast. . . .

It was the discord between the Muslim princes, as we shall describe, that enabled the Franks to overrun the country. Abu l-Muzaffar al-Abiwardi composed several poems on this subject, in one of which he says:

> We have mingled blood with flowing tears, and there is no room left in us for pity[?]
> To shed tears is a man's worst weapon when the swords stir up the embers of war.
> Sons of Islām, behind you are battles in which heads rolled at your feet.
> Dare you slumber in the blessed shade of safety, where life is as soft as an orchard flower?

How can the eye sleep between the lids at a time of disasters that would waken any sleeper?

While your Syrian brothers can only sleep on the backs of their chargers, or in vultures' bellies!

Must the foreigners feed on our ignominy, while you trail behind you the train of a pleasant life, like men whose world is at peace?

When blood has been spilt, when sweet girls must for shame hide their lovely faces in their hands!

When the white swords' points are red with blood, and the iron of the brown lances is stained with gore!

At the sound of sword hammering on lance young children's hair turns white.

This is war, and the man who shuns the whirlpool to save his life shall grind his teeth in penitence.

This is war, and the infidel's sword is naked in his hand, ready to be sheathed again in men's necks and skulls.

This is war, and he who lies in the tomb at Medina seems to raise his voice and cry: "O sons of Hashim!

I see my people slow to raise the lance against the enemy: I see the Faith resting on feeble pillars.

For fear of death the Muslims are evading the fire of battle, refusing to believe that death will surely strike them."

Must the Arab champions then suffer with resignation, while the gallant Persians shut their eyes to their dishonour?

67

Letter from a Jewish Pilgrim in Egypt

The following letter was written in 1100 by an anonymous Jewish pilgrim from Alexandria, unable to make his pilgrimage to Jerusalem because of the ongoing war. How does the letter's author regard the Egyptian Sultan? How does he view the struggle between the Sultan and the Franks? What does this suggest about the lives of Jews under Muslim rule during this time period?

"Contemporary Letters on the Capture of Jerusalem by the Crusaders," trans. S. D. Goitein, *Journal of Jewish Studies*, vol. 3, no. 4 (London: Jewish Chronicle Publications, 1952), 162–77.

Thinking Historically

What does this letter add to your understanding of the Crusaders' capture of Jerusalem? How would you write a narrative of the First Crusade that took advantage of Christian, Muslim, and Jewish sources?

In Your name, You Merciful.

If I attempted to describe my longing for you, my Lord, my brother *and cousin,*—may God prolong your days and make permanent your honour, success, happiness, health, and welfare; and . . . subdue your enemies—all the paper in the world would not suffice. My longing will but increase and double, just as the days will grow and double. May *the Creator of the World* presently make us meet together in joy when I return under His guidance to my homeland *and to the inheritance of my Fathers* in complete happiness, *so that we rejoice and be happy through His great mercy and His vast bounty; and thus may be His will!*

You may remember, my Lord, that many years ago I left our country to seek God's mercy and help in my poverty, to behold Jerusalem and return thereupon. However, when I was in Alexandria God brought about circumstances which caused a slight delay. Afterwards, however, "the sea grew stormy," and many armed bands made their appearance in Palestine; *"and he who went forth and he who came had no peace,"* so that hardly one survivor out of a whole group came back to us from Palestine and told us that scarcely anyone could save himself from those armed bands, since they were so numerous and were gathered round . . . every town. There was further the journey through the desert, among [the bedouins] and whoever escaped from the one, fell into the hands of the other. Moreover, mutinies [spread throughout the country and reached] even Alexandria, so that we ourselves were besieged several times and the city was ruined; . . . the end however *was good,* for the Sultan—may God bestow glory upon his victories—conquered the city and caused justice to abound in it in a manner unprecedented in the history of any king in the world; not even a dirham was looted from anyone. Thus I had come to hope that because of his justice and strength God would give the land into his hands, and I should thereupon go to Jerusalem in safety and tranquility. For this reason I proceeded from Alexandria to Cairo, in order to start [my journey] from there.

When, however, God had given Jerusalem, the blessed, into his hands this state of affairs continued for too short a time to allow for making a journey there. The Franks arrived and killed everybody in the city, whether of *Ishmael or of Israel*; and the few who survived the slaughter were made prisoners. Some of these have been ransomed since, while others are still in captivity in all parts of the world.

Now, all of us had anticipated that our Sultan—may God bestow glory upon his victories—would set out against them [the Franks] with his troops and chase them away. But time after time our hope failed. Yet, to this very present moment we do hope that God will give his [the Sultan's] enemies into his hands. For it is inevitable that the armies will join in battle this year; and, if God grants us victory through him [the Sultan] and he conquers Jerusalem—and so it may be, with God's will—I for one shall not be amongst those who will linger, but shall go there to behold the city; and shall afterwards return straight to you—if God wills it. My salvation is in God, for this [is unlike] the other previous occasions [of making a pilgrimage to Jerusalem]. God, indeed, will exonerate me, since at my age I cannot afford to delay and wait any longer; I want to return home under any circumstances, if I still remain alive—whether I shall have seen Jerusalem or have given up the hope of doing it—both of which are possible.

You know, of course, my Lord, what has happened to us in the course of the last five years: the plague, the illnesses, and ailments have continued unabated for four successive years. As a result of this the wealthy became impoverished and a great number of people died *of the plague*, so that entire families perished in it. I, too, was affected with a grave illness, from which I recovered only about a year ago; then I was taken ill the following year so that (on the margin) for four years I have remained.... He who has said: *The evil diseases of Egypt* ... he who hiccups does not live ... ailments and will die ... otherwise ... will remain alive.

REFLECTIONS

The First Crusade (1095–1099) only marks the beginning of a protracted conflict between Christians and Muslims that continued until, perhaps, the eighteenth century. In the Holy Land there were crusades intermittently over the next forty years culminating in what was called the Second Crusade from 1147–1149. Meanwhile, the conquest of Muslims in Spain, which had been equated with the crusade by Pope Urban II, continued, as did frequent crusades into Eastern Europe.

The establishment of Latin kingdoms in Palestine could not be maintained without continual reinforcements, and they were vulnerable to Muslim attack. In 1187 Saladin reconquered most of Palestine, including Jerusalem, for the Muslims, a trauma for the Christians that led to the Third Crusade (1189–1192) and German Crusade

(1197–1198) by which Christians retook settlements on the coast. Popular enthusiasm continued in the Children's Crusade (1212) and the Crusade of the Shepherds (1251). The armies of the Fourth Crusade (1202–1204) were diverted to Constantinople, which they sacked in 1204. A Fifth Crusade (1217–1229) recovered Jerusalem, which was retaken by the Muslims in 1244, leading to crusades initiated by King Louis IX of France. Other crusading armies invaded Egypt, Tunisia, Muslim Spain, northwest Africa, southern France, Poland, Latvia, Germany, Russia, the Mongol Empire, Finland, Bosnia, and Italy, against papal enemies and Eastern Orthodox Christians as well as Muslims. Recent histories of the Crusades have ended their narratives in 1521, 1560, 1588, and 1798, according to Jonathan Riley-Smith who ends the recent *Oxford History of the Crusades* with images of the crusades in twentieth-century wars. Does the imagery of the Crusades still animate our wars?

While Americans, like President George W. Bush, learned the effects of using the term *crusade* in the context of American aspirations in the Middle East, the interference of Western forces in the region is a constant reminder to Muslims of a long history of Western intervention that began with the First Crusade. In Syria, Lebanon, Jordan, Palestine, and Israel one can still see crusader castles looming over the landscape and meet the descendants and coreligionists of the founders of Crusader states. From the perspective of many Muslims, unquestioned U.S. support of Israel, especially in Jerusalem, is a direct continuation of the Crusades. On more than one occasion, leaders of Middle Eastern countries have pictured themselves as a modern-day Saladin, the twelfth-century Kurdish Muslim warrior from Tikrit, Iraq, who retook Jerusalem in 1187, eighty-eight years after the events described by Raymond of St. Giles and Ibn al-Athir.

Writing a narrative of the First Crusade is difficult enough given the many sides to the conflict. Anna Comnena and the orthodox Christians of Byzantium had a very different perspective than the Franks or Roman Christian Crusaders of Western Europe. Nor were Muslims a single force of opposition. The Seljuk Turks had different interests than the Caliph of Baghdad, and, contrary to the opinion of Raymond St. Giles, the Fatimid Egyptian forces at Ascalon were neither Biblical Babylonians nor Abbasids from Baghdad. Then too there were Jews, and those in Germany may have had different interests from those in Egypt, despite an agreement about Christian crusading. Still, there are more sources than we have been able to explore here, and more interpretations than we have been able to include.

After trying your hand at writing a narrative of the First Crusade, you might think of how narratives are constructed. Each story leaves out some information to include other information, lest it read like a phone book. How do you decide whose "numbers" to include? To stimulate your thoughts about narrative choices, you might choose a subject a little closer to home where you have greater knowledge of the primary sources. Try a narrative of your own life up to now. If you dare, ask someone close to you to point out what you missed or over-emphasized.

11

Raiders of Steppe and Sea: Vikings and Mongols

Eurasia and the Atlantic, 750–1350 C.E.

HISTORICAL CONTEXT

Ever since the first urban settlements emerged five thousand years ago, they have been at risk of attack. The domestication of the horse and the development of sailing ships about four thousand years ago increased that risk. Much of ancient history is the story of the conflict between settled peoples and raiders on horseback or sailors on fleet ships. Eventually — between the third and fifth centuries C.E. — the great empires of Rome and Han dynasty China succumbed to raiding nomadic tribes from central Asia. As nomadic peoples settled themselves, new waves of raiders appeared.

In the previous chapter, we explored the impact of the Seljuk Turks who conquered cities in the Middle East that had been taken hundreds of years earlier by Arab armies on horseback. At about the same time as the Turks emerged from central Asia to threaten settlements south of the great Eurasian steppe grasslands, a new force from the north, Viking raiders on sailing ships, burst across the northern seas to attack the coastal enclaves and river cities of Europe and what came to be known in their wake as Russia. As generations oscillated between raiding and trading, new waves of Norsemen explored the edges of known waters to plant new settlements as far west as Iceland, Greenland, and North America. (See Map 11.1.) Who were these people? What did they hope to accomplish? How were they different from the land-raiders who preceded them?

At about the time that the Vikings were becoming farmers and grandfathers, around the year 1200, the Eurasian steppe exploded with its last and largest force of nomadic tribesmen on horseback: the

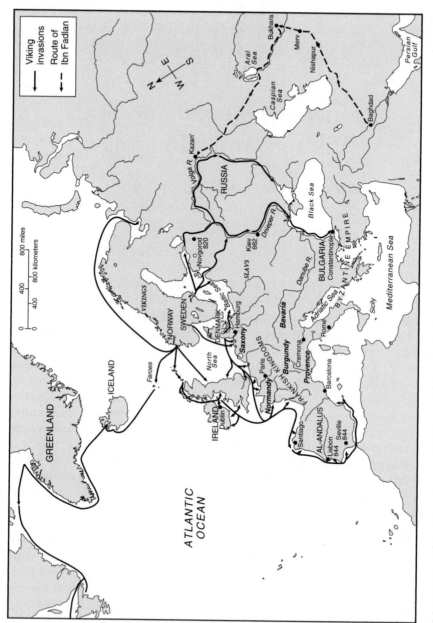

Map 11.1 Viking Invasions and Voyages of the Ninth and Tenth Centuries.

Mongols. Between the election of Chingis [or Genghis] Khan* (c. 1162–1227) as the Khan of Khans in 1206 and the Black Death of 1350 (or the end of the Mongol Yuan dynasty in China in 1368), the Mongols swept across Eurasia and created the largest empire the world had ever seen. (See Map 11.2.) Who were the Mongols? What made them so successful? How were they similar to, and different from, the Norsemen?

What was the impact of these raiding peoples on settled societies? How did they change each other? How did they change themselves? How did they create some of the conditions necessary for the modern world to come into being?

THINKING HISTORICALLY
Distinguishing Historical Understanding from Moral Judgments

The ancient Greeks called non-Greeks "barbarians" (because their languages contained "bar-bar"-like sounds that seemed foreign, untutored, and, thus, uncivilized). Since then the terms *barbarian* and *civilized* have been weighted with the same combination of descriptive and moral meaning. In the nineteenth century it was even fashionable among historians and anthropologists to distinguish between nomadic peoples and settled, urban peoples with the terms *barbarian* and *civilized*. As our first reading (and perhaps modern common sense) makes clear, rural or nomadic people are not necessarily less "moral" than city people; technological development is hardly the same thing as moral development (or the opposite).

What connection, if any, is there between history and morality? Stories of the past are frequently used to celebrate or condemn past individuals or groups. Sometimes we find past behavior shocking or reprehensible. Is it logical or proper to make moral judgments about the past? Can historians find answers to moral questions by studying the past?

Perhaps the place to begin is by recognizing that just as the "is" is different from the "ought," so too the "was" is different from the "should have been." Historians must begin by finding out what was. Our own moral values may lead us to ask certain questions about the past, but the historian's job is only to find out what happened. We will see in the following selections how difficult it has been for past observers to keep their own moral judgments from coloring their

*chihn GIHZ   kahn

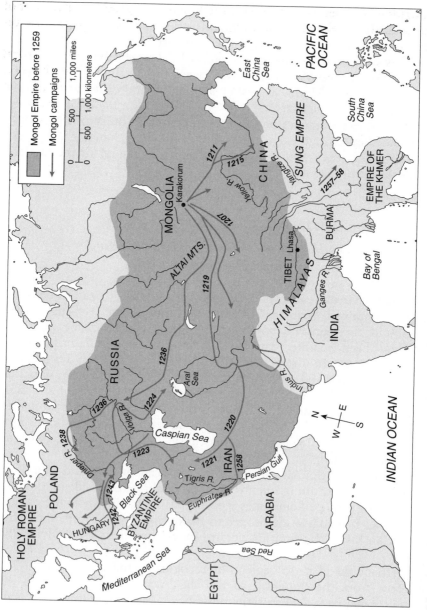

Map 11.2 Mongol Invasions of the Thirteenth Century.

descriptions of peoples and events they found disagreeable. This part of our study may help us realize how our own moral feelings affect our responses.

Then, assuming we have established the facts fairly, can our moral sentiments legitimately come into play? As "consumers" of history, readers, and thinking people, we cannot avoid making judgments about the past. Under what conditions are such judgments fair, helpful, or appropriate? We will explore this much larger and more complex question in this chapter.

68

GREGORY GUZMAN

Were the Barbarians a Negative or Positive Factor in Ancient and Medieval History?

Gregory Guzman is a modern world historian. In this essay he asks some questions about the peoples who have been called "barbarians." How were the lives of pastoral nomads different from those of settled people? How did the horse shape life on the steppe? How effective were these herders as rulers of settled societies? What were the achievements of the pastoral nomads?

Thinking Historically

Why, according to Guzman, have most histories of the barbarians made them look bad? How have city people or historians let their own prejudices block an appreciation of the achievements of pastoralists?

According to the general surveys of ancient and medieval history found in most textbooks, barbarian peoples and/or primitive savages repeatedly invaded the early Eurasian civilized centers in Europe, the Middle East, India, and China. All accounts of the early history of these four

---

Gregory Guzman, "Were the Barbarians a Negative or Positive Factor in Ancient and Medieval History?" *The Historian* L (August 1988): 558–72.

civilizations contain recurrent references to attacks by such familiar and famous barbarians as the Hittites, Hyksos, Kassites, Aryans, Scythians, Sarmatians, Hsiung-nu, Huns, Germans, Turks, and Mongols, and they also record the absorption and assimilation of these Inner Asian barbarian hordes into the respective cultures and lifestyles of the more advanced coastal civilizations. The early sources generally equate the barbarians with chaos and destruction. The barbarians are presented as evil and despicable intruders, associated only with burning, pillaging, and slaughtering, while the civilized peoples are portrayed as the good and righteous forces of stability, order, and progress.

But it must be remembered that most of these early sources are not objective; they are blatantly one-sided, biased accounts written by members of the civilized societies. Thus, throughout recorded history, barbarians have consistently received bad press — bad PR to use the modern terminology. By definition, barbarians were illiterate, and thus they could not write their own version of events. All written records covering barbarian-civilized interaction came from the civilized peoples at war with the barbarians — often the sedentary peoples recently defeated and overwhelmed by those same barbarians. Irritated and angered coastal historians tended to record and emphasize only the negative aspects of their recent interaction with the barbarians. These authors tended to condemn and denigrate the way their barbarian opponents looked and to associate them with the devil and evil, rather than to report with objectivity what actually happened. For example, the Roman historian Ammianus Marcellinus, whose description is distorted by hatred and fear, described the barbarians as "two-footed beasts, seemingly chained to their horses from which they take their meat and drink, never touching a plough and having no houses." While living in Jerusalem, St. Jerome also left a vivid description of the Huns who ". . . filled the whole earth with slaughter and panic alike as they flittered hither and thither on their swift horses. . . . They were at hand everywhere before they were expected; by their speed they outstripped rumor, and they took pity neither upon religion nor rank nor age nor wailing childhood. Those who had just begun to live were compelled to die. . . ."

Such reports obviously made the barbarians look bad, while their nomadic habits and practices, which differed from those of the sedentary coastal peoples, were clearly portrayed as inferior and less advanced: the incarnation of evil itself. These horror-filled and biased descriptions were not the accounts of weak and defenseless peoples. Rather, they were written by the citizens of the most advanced and powerful states and empires in Europe, the Middle East, India, and China. The individual barbarian tribes were, nevertheless, able to attack and invade these strong and well-organized civilized states with relative impunity — pillaging and killing almost at will.

Several important questions, not addressed by the ancient and medieval historians, need to be answered here. Who were these barbarians?

Why and how did they manage to repeatedly defeat and overwhelm so easily the wealthiest and most advanced civilizations of the day? And why were they so vehemently condemned and hated in recorded history, if these barbarian Davids were able to consistently defeat such mighty Goliath civilized centers? Since the rich and populous civilized states enjoyed tremendous advantages in the confrontations, why have the barbarians so often been denied the popular role of the underdog?

In the process of answering those questions, this study would like to suggest that maybe the barbarians were not really the "bad guys." While they may not deserve to be called the "good guys," they made a much more positive contribution to human civilization than presented in the grossly distorted written sources. The barbarians deserve much more credit than they have been given, for they created a complex pastoral lifestyle as an alternative to sedentary agriculture, and in that achievement they were not subhuman savages only out to loot, pillage, and destroy. As this study will show, the barbarians played a much more positive and constructive role in the development and diffusion of early human history than that with which they are usually credited.

Before proceeding further, it is necessary to identify these much-maligned barbarians and describe how their way of life and their basic practices differed from those of the sedentary coastal peoples in order to better evaluate the barbarian role and its impact on the history of humanity.

In terms of identity, the barbarians were the steppe nomads of Inner Asia or Central Eurasia. This area represents one of the toughest and most inhospitable places in the world in which to survive. The climate of the interior of the large Eurasian landmass is not moderated by the distant seas, resulting in extremes of climate, of hot and cold, wet and dry. It is an area of ice, forest, desert, and mountains — with bitter winds, dust, and poor soil. Unlike the coastal regions with their dependable moisture and warmth, the soil of Inner Asia was too cold, poor, and dry for agriculture; thus the sedentary urban lifestyle of the coastal civilized centers was not an option in the Eurasian heartland. The people living there had to be tough to endure such a hostile environment, where they constantly fought both nature and other people for survival.

Due to necessity, the people of Inner Asia were nomads, wandering in search of food and pasture, and they became herdsmen, shepherds, and warriors. These steppe nomads, the barbarians of recorded history, were frequently nothing more than migrants looking for new homes; these people needed little encouragement to seek safety, security, and better living conditions in the warm, rich, and fertile coastal civilization centers. Thus the steppe barbarians were not always savage marauders coming only to loot and pillage. Many of the so-called barbarian invaders constituted a surplus population which harsh Inner Asia could not support, or they represented whole tribes being pushed out of their ancestral homeland by stronger tribes behind them. At any rate, these repeated waves of nomadic peoples leaving the steppes soon encountered the coastal civilizations.

These Inner Asian barbarians were more or less harmless outsiders until the horse dramatically changed their lifestyle on the vast steppes. They adopted the pastoral system as the best way of providing for basic needs. The natural pasture provided by the steppe grassland proved ideal for grazing large herds and flocks of animals. Soon their whole life revolved around their animals; they became shepherds, herders, and keepers of beasts. . . .

The dominant feature of this emerging barbarian pastoralism was its mounted nature; it was essentially a horse culture by 1000 B.C. At first small horses were kept only for food and milk, but bigger horses eventually led to riding. Once an accomplished fact, mounted practices dramatically changed the lifestyle of the barbarian steppe peoples. Horseback riding made the tending of scattered herds faster and less tiring, and it enlarged the size of herds while increasing the range of pastoral movement. It also made possible, when necessary, the total migration of entire tribes and clans. Mastery of the horse reduced the vast expanses of steppe pasturage to more manageable proportions. Steppe nomads moved twice a year between traditional winter and summer pastures; the spring and fall were spent moving between the necessary grazing grounds. All peoples and possessions moved with regularity; the nomads became used to living in the saddle, so to speak.

The horse thus became the center of pastoral life on the steppes. The barbarian nomads could literally live off their animals which provided meat, milk, and hides for clothing, coverings, boots, etc. Tools and weapons were made from the bones and sinews, and dried dung was used as fuel. The barbarians ate, sold, negotiated, slept, and took care of body functions in the saddle as indicated in the following quotations: "From their horses, by day and night every one of that nation buys and sells, eats and drinks, and bowed over the narrow neck of the animal relaxes in a sleep so deep as to be accompanied by many dreams." "All the time they let themselves be carried by their horses. In that way they fight wars, participate in banquets, attend public and private business. On their back, they move, stand still, carry on trade, and converse." These mounted practices led to the emergence of the centaur motif in Middle Eastern art, as the civilized people tended to view the horse and rider as one inseparable unit.

Military action also became an integral part of nomadic steppe life. Warfare was simply cavalry action by the pastoral herdsmen who served as soldiers for the duration of the conflict. Steppe military service differed little from the normal, on-the-move pastoral life. Large-scale steppe alliances were hard to organize and even harder to hold together among the independent nomads. Such temporary alliances, called hordes, rose swiftly to great strength and power, but they usually declined and disintegrated just as quickly.

At any rate, these barbarian nomads were tough and hardy warriors. The horse gave them speed and mobility over both the light and heavily armed infantry of the civilized centers, but for this speed and mobility the barbarians gave up any type of defensive armor. They learned to guide their horses with their knees, since both arms needed to be free for the bow and arrow, their primary offensive weapon. By 1000 B.C. the compound bow was in common use by barbarians. This shorter bow could be handled with ease from horseback, and arrows could be shot up to three hundred yards with accuracy. As steppe hunters, all barbarians made excellent archers.

Early civilized armies had no cavalry. The famous Macedonian phalanx and the formidable Roman legions contained only light and heavily armed infantry. At first these brave foot soldiers had no tactical maneuvers to face and contain a barbarian cavalry charge. Even more devastating was the storm of arrows raining down upon them long before they could engage in the traditional hand-to-hand combat. The formidable steppe cavalry thus subjected civilized defenses to continuous pressure. Every nomad with a horse and bow was a potential frontline soldier who was tough, resourceful, and ferocious, whereas only a small percentage of the civilized population was equipped and trained for war. The nomadic lifestyle and the speed of the horse eliminated the need for expensive and heavy metal armor and its accompanying technological skills. Cavalry tactics gave an initial military advantage to the barbarians and the mounted horsemen won most of the early battles. The best defense against barbarian cavalry was an insurmountable obstacle, a wall. Ten- to twenty-foot-high walls of dirt, wood, or stone were built around cities and along some frontiers, i.e., the Great Wall of China. The old statement that Rome fell because China built a wall may not be such a simple overstatement after all.

Since they had the military advantage of cavalry tactics, the steppe nomads attacked and conquered various coastal civilizations with regularity. In a typical conquest, the victorious barbarians were the new military/political rulers. These new rulers possessed strengths obvious to all. The barbarians had vigorous and dynamic leadership; good, able, and charismatic leadership had been needed to organize the independent nomads into an effective horde in the first place. The new rulers had the complete loyalty of their followers; their group identity based on common blood and ancestors resulted in an intense personal and individual allegiance and commitment.

The first century after the initial conquest was usually an era of dynamic leadership, good government, and economic prosperity, as nomadic strengths mixed with the local advances and practices of that civilization. The new ruling family was often a fusion of the best of both sides as the barbarian victors married into the previous ruling dynasty. This brought forth an age of powerful and successful rulers, and produced an era of energetic leadership, good government, low taxes, agricultural revival, and peace. . . .

After this early period of revitalized and dynamic rule, slow decline usually set in. Royal vigor and ability sank as the rulers became soft, both mentally and physically. Without physical exercise and self-discipline, the rulers became overindulgent, instantly acquiring everything they wanted — excessive amounts of food or drink, harems, puppets, and yes-men as advisers. At the same time court rivalries and internal divisiveness began to emerge once the strong unity required for the conquest was no longer needed. A rivalry that often arose was between the ruler and various groups of his followers — his military, his bureaucracy, his harem (especially the queen mothers), his conquered subjects, and his old nomadic supporters. His steppe horsemen began to give first loyalty to their new family land rather than to their individual leader who was now weak, impaired, and soft. Such internal rivalries weakened the central government and led to chaos and civil wars. Thus, a civilized center was ripe for the next series of invasions and conquest by the next group of unified, tough, and well-led barbarians who would, in turn, be assimilated and absorbed in this process of ongoing revitalization of stagnant civilizations.

Despite the usual negative view and definition of barbarians provided by the sedentary civilized peoples, the steppe nomads had developed a complex pastoral and nomadic society. They were tough and hardy horsemen whose cavalry tactics gave them the military advantage for several centuries. The barbarians used this advantage, and their periodic attacks on civilization centers caused destruction, sometimes severe destruction. But the barbarian role in mankind's history was not always negative. The barbarians can and should be viewed as representing a dynamic and vital element in human history for they periodically revived many stagnating coastal civilizations. Many of these sedentary centers flourished, growing rich and powerful. In the process they also became conservative, settled into a fixed routine. Preferring the status quo, they tended to use old answers and ways to face new problems and issues, and as a consequence they lost the vitality and flexibility required for healthy and progressive growth.

The barbarians were active and dynamic. In their conquests of civilized centers, they frequently destroyed and eliminated the old and outdated and preserved and passed on only the good and useful elements. Sometimes, the mounted invaders also introduced new ideas and practices. Some of these new barbarian innovations (horseback riding, archery, trousers, and boots, etc.) fused with the good and useful practices of the sedentary peoples. Old and new practices and processes merged, and provided viable alternatives to the old, outdated civilized ways which had failed or outlived their usefulness. This fusion brought forth dynamic creativity and development. The ongoing encounters with barbarian strangers inevitably fostered innovation and progress in the civilized centers — due to their need to adjust in order to survive. . . .

It can be argued that barbarians also played a positive role in the spread and diffusion of civilization itself. The four major Eurasian civilization centers were separated from each other by deserts, mountains, and the vast expanses of the steppe heartland of Inner Asia. In its early stages each civilization was somewhat isolated from the others. Overland trade and contact was possible only through the barbarian steppe highway which stretched over five thousand miles across Eurasia, from Hungary to Manchuria. There was little early sea contact between the four sedentary centers, as naval travel was longer and more dangerous than the overland routes.

Thus the steppe barbarians were the chief agency through which the ideas and practices of one civilization were spread to another before 1500 A.D. According to [historian] William H. McNeill, there was much conceptual diffusion carried along the steppe highway by the barbarians. Writing originated in the ancient Middle East. The concept, not the form, of writing then spread eastward from the Middle East, as the Indian and Chinese forms and characters were significantly different than Middle Eastern cuneiform. The making and use of bronze and chariots also spread from the Middle East to Europe, India, and China. Chariots were introduced to China, on the eastern end of the steppe highway, a few centuries after their appearance in the Middle East. Needless to say, this type of early cultural diffusion is difficult to document with any degree of certainty, but enough evidence exists to make it highly probable, even if not scientifically provable.

The late medieval period provides even more examples of cultural diffusion via the movement of barbarians along the Inner Asian steppe highway. The great Eurasian *Pax Mongolica* opened the way for much cultural cross-fertilization in the late-thirteenth and early-fourteenth centuries. Chinese inventions like gunpowder and printing made their way to the Middle East and Europe in this period. Records show that Chinese artillerymen accompanied the Mongol armies into the Middle East. Papal envoys like John of Plano Carpini and William of Rubruck traveled to the Mongol capital of Karakorum in the 1240s and 1250s. In the 1280s, Marco Polo brought with him from Kublai Khan's court in China a Mongol princess to be the bride of the Mongol Khan of Persia. . . .

This cultural interaction and exchange between Eurasian coastal civilizations ended with the collapse of the Mongol Khanates in Persia and China in the mid-fourteenth century. The barbarian Mongols, therefore, provided the last period of great cultural cross-fertilization before the modern age.

Historical evidence that exists enables one to argue that the barbarian nomads played an active and positive role in the history of mankind. The barbarian invaders revitalized stagnant and decaying civilizations and were responsible for a certain amount of cultural diffusion between emerging ancient and medieval civilizations. The traditional portrayal of barbarians as mere marauders and destroyers is misleading and incorrect. Unfortunately this is the usual role they are given when historians center their study of the past narrowly on the civilized centers and the biased written sources produced by those peoples. All too often historians tend to adopt and reflect the biases and values of their subjects under study, and thus continue to denigrate and condemn all barbarians without objectively evaluating their real contributions to human development. The study of the steppe nomads, the barbarians, is just as valid a topic for historical analysis as the traditional study of coastal sedentary civilizations. Only by knowing and understanding the pastoral barbarian can historians accurately evaluate the constant interaction between the two lifestyles and come to understand the full picture of humanity's early growth and development in the ancient and medieval periods of Eurasian history.

$$\boxed{69}$$

IBN FADLAN

The Viking Rus

In 921 C.E. the Muslim caliph of Baghdad sent Ibn Fadlan* on a mission to the King of the Bulgars.[1] The Muslim king of the Bulgars may have been looking for an alliance with the caliph of Baghdad against the Khazars, sandwiched between them, just west of the Caspian Sea. North and west of the Bulgars was the area that became Ukraine and Russia. The Volga River, which had its source in the Ural Mountains,

---

*IH buhn   fahd LAHN

[1]These Bulgars, with a Muslim king, had recently been forced north of the Caspian Sea (while other Bulgars moved west to what is today Bulgaria where they were converted to Christianity by Byzantium).

Albert Stanburrough Cook, "Ibn Fadlan's Account of Scandinavian Merchants on the Volga in 922," in *Journal of English and Germanic Philology*, vol. 22, no. 1 (1923): 56–63.

flowed north through this land into the Baltic Sea. In the eighth and ninth centuries this area was inhabited by various tribes, many of which spoke early Slavic languages. At some point these tribes were united under the command of a people called the Rus. The origins of the Rus are disputed, but most experts believe that they were either Vikings or the descendants of Vikings and Slavs.

Ibn Fadlan provides our earliest description of these Rus (or Northmen, as he calls them here), whom he encountered on the Volga near the modern city of Kazan' during his trip to the Bulgar king. (See Map 11.1 on page 376 for his route.) They or their ancestors had sailed downriver from the Baltic Sea on raiding and trading expeditions. What does Ibn Fadlan tell us about these Scandinavian raiders who gave their name to Russia?

Thinking Historically

Notice Ibn Fadlan's moral judgments about the Viking Rus. Notice your own moral judgments. How are Ibn Fadlan's judgments different from your own? What do you think accounts for those differences?

I saw how the Northmen had arrived with their wares, and pitched their camp beside the Volga. Never did I see people so gigantic; they are tall as palm trees, and florid and ruddy of complexion. They wear neither camisoles nor *chaftans*, but the men among them wear a garment of rough cloth, which is thrown over one side, so that one hand remains free. Every one carries an axe, a dagger, and a sword, and without these weapons they are never seen. Their swords are broad, with wavy lines, and of Frankish make. From the tip of the finger-nails to the neck, each man of them is tattooed with pictures of trees, living beings, and other things. The women carry, fastened to their breast, a little case of iron, copper, silver, or gold, according to the wealth and resources, of their husbands. Fastened to the case they wear a ring, and upon that a dagger, all attached to their breast. About their necks they wear gold and silver chains. If the husband possesses ten thousand dirhems, he has one chain made for his wife; if twenty thousand, two; and for every ten thousand, one is added. Hence it often happens that a Scandinavian woman has a large number of chains about her neck. Their most highly prized ornaments consist of small green shells, of one of the varieties which are found in [the bottoms of] ships. They make great efforts to obtain these, paying as much as a dirhem for such a shell, and stringing them as a necklace for their wives.

They are the filthiest race that God ever created. They do not wipe themselves after going to stool, nor wash themselves after a nocturnal pollution, any more than if they were wild asses.

They come from their own country, anchor their ships in the Volga, which is a great river, and build large wooden houses on its banks. In every such house there live ten or twenty, more or fewer. Each man has a couch, where he sits with the beautiful girls he has for sale. Here he is as likely as not to enjoy one of them while a friend looks on. At times several of them will be thus engaged at the same moment, each in full view of the others. Now and again a merchant will resort to a house to purchase a girl, and find her master thus embracing her, and not giving over until he has fully had his will.

Every morning a girl comes and brings a tub of water, and places it before her master. In this he proceeds to wash his face and hands, and then his hair, combing it out over the vessel. Thereupon he blows his nose, and spits into the tub, and, leaving no dirt behind, conveys it all into this water. When he has finished, the girl carries the tub to the man next [to] him, who does the same. Thus she continues carrying the tub from one to another till each of those who are in the house has blown his nose and spit into the tub, and washed his face and hair.

As soon as their ships have reached the anchorage, every one goes ashore, having at hand bread, meat, onions, milk, and strong drink, and betakes himself to a high, upright piece of wood, bearing the likeness of a human face; this is surrounded by smaller statues, and behind these there are still other tall pieces of wood driven into the ground. He advances to the large wooden figure, prostrates himself before it, and thus addresses it: "O my Lord, I am come from a far country, bringing with me so and so many girls, and so and so many pelts of sable" [or, marten]; and when he has thus enumerated all his merchandise, he continues, "I have brought thee this present," laying before the wooden statue what he has brought, and saying: "I desire thee to bestow upon me a purchaser who has gold and silver coins, who will buy from me to my heart's content, and who will refuse none of my demands." Having so said, he departs. If his trade then goes ill, he returns and brings a second, or even a third present. If he still continues to have difficulty in obtaining what he desires, he brings a present to one of the small statues, and implores its intercession, saying: "These are the wives and daughters of our lord." Continuing thus, he goes to each statue in turn, invokes it, beseeches its intercession, and bows humbly before it. If it then chances that his trade goes swimmingly, and he disposes of all his merchandise, he reports: "My lord has fulfilled my desire; now it is my duty to repay him." Upon this, he takes a number of cattle and sheep, slaughters them, gives a portion of the meat to the poor, and carries the rest before the large statue and the smaller ones that surround it, hanging the heads of the sheep and cattle on the large piece of wood which is planted in the earth. When night falls, dogs come and devour it all. Then he who has so placed it exclaims: "I am well pleasing to my lord; he has consumed my present."

If one of their number falls sick, they set up a tent at a distance, in which they place him, leaving bread and water at hand. Thereafter they never approach nor speak to him, nor visit him the whole time, especially if he is a poor person or a slave. If he recovers and rises from his sick bed, he returns to his own. If he dies, they cremate him; but if he is a slave they leave him as he is till at length he becomes the food of dogs and birds of prey.

If they catch a thief or a robber, they lead him to a thick and lofty tree, fasten a strong rope round him, string him up, and let him hang until he drops to pieces by the action of wind and rain.

I was told that the least of what they do for their chiefs when they die, is to consume them with fire. When I was finally informed of the death of one of their magnates, I sought to witness what befell. First they laid him in his grave — over which a roof was erected — for the space of ten days, until they had completed the cutting and sewing of his clothes. In the case of a poor man, however, they merely build for him a boat, in which they place him, and consume it with fire. At the death of a rich man, they bring together his goods, and divide them into three parts. The first of these is for his family; the second is expended for the garments they make; and with the third they purchase strong drink, against the day when the girl resigns herself to death, and is burned with her master. To the use of wine they abandon themselves in mad fashion, drinking it day and night; and not seldom does one die with the cup in his hand.

When one of their chiefs dies, his family asks his girls and pages: "Which one of you will die with him?" Then one of them answers, "I." From the time that he [or she] utters this word, he is no longer free: should he wish to draw back, he is not permitted. For the most part, however, it is the girls that offer themselves. So, when the man of whom I spoke had died, they asked his girls, "Who will die with him?" One of them answered, "I." She was then committed to two girls, who were to keep watch over her, accompany her wherever she went, and even, on occasion, wash her feet. The people now began to occupy themselves with the dead man — to cut out the clothes for him, and to prepare whatever else was needful. During the whole of this period, the girl gave herself over to drinking and singing, and was cheerful and gay.

When the day was now come that the dead man and the girl were to be committed to the flames, I went to the river in which his ship lay, but found that it had already been drawn ashore. Four corner-blocks of birch and other woods had been placed in position for it, while around were stationed large wooden figures in the semblance of human beings. Thereupon the ship was brought up, and placed on the timbers above mentioned. In the mean time the people began to walk to and fro, uttering words which I did not understand. The dead man, meanwhile, lay at a distance in his grave, from which they had not yet removed him. Next they brought a couch, placed it in the ship, and covered it with Greek cloth of gold, wadded and quilted, with pillows of the same material. There came an old crone, whom they call the angel of death, and spread the articles mentioned on the couch. It was she who attended to the sewing of the garments, and to all the equipment; it was she, also, who was to slay the girl. I saw her; she was dark, . . . thick-set, with a lowering countenance.

When they came to the grave, they removed the earth from the wooden roof, set the latter aside, and drew out the dead man in the loose wrapper in which he had died. Then I saw that he had turned quite black, by reason of the coldness of that country. Near him in the grave they had placed strong drink, fruits, and a lute; and these they now took out. Except for his color, the dead man had not changed. They now clothed him in drawers, leggings, boots, and a *kurtak* and *chaftan* of cloth of gold, with golden buttons, placing on his head a cap made of cloth of gold, trimmed with sable! Then they carried him into a tent placed in the ship, seated him on the wadded and quilted covering, supported him with the pillows, and, bringing strong drink, fruits, and basil, placed them all beside him. Then they brought a dog, which they cut in two, and threw into the ship; laid all his weapons beside him; and led up two horses which they chased until they were dripping with sweat, whereupon they cut them in pieces with their swords, and threw the flesh into the ship. Two oxen were then brought forward, cut in pieces, and flung into the ship. Finally they brought a cock and a hen, killed them, and threw them in also.

The girl who had devoted herself to death meanwhile walked to and fro, entering one after another of the tents which they had there. The occupant of each tent lay with her, saying, "Tell your master, 'I [the man] did this only for love of you.'"

When it was now Friday afternoon, they led the girl to an object which they had constructed, and which looked like the framework of a door. She then placed her feet on the extended hands of the men, was raised up above the framework, and uttered something in her language, whereupon they let her down. Then again they raised her, and she did as at first. Once more they let her down, and then lifted her a third time, while she did as at the previous times. They then handed her a hen, whose head she cut off and threw away; but the hen itself they cast into the ship. I inquired of the interpreter what it was that she had done. He replied: "The first time she said, 'Lo, I see here my father and mother'; the second time, 'Lo, now I see all my deceased relatives sitting'; the third time, 'Lo, there is my master, who is sitting in Paradise. Paradise is so beautiful, so green. With him are his men and boys. He calls me, so bring me to him.'" Then they led her away to the ship.

Here she took off her two bracelets, and gave them to the old woman who was called the angel of death, and who was to murder her. She also drew off her two anklets, and passed them to the two serving-maids, who were the daughters of the so-called angel of death. Then they lifted her into the ship, but did not yet admit her to the tent. Now men came up with shields and staves, and handed her a cup of strong drink. This she took, sang over it, and emptied it. "With this," so the interpreter told me, "she is taking leave of those who are dear to her." Then another cup was handed her, which she also took, and began a lengthy song. The crone admonished her to drain the cup without lingering, and to enter the tent where her master lay. By this time, as it seemed to me, the girl had become dazed [or, possibly, crazed]; she made as though she would enter the tent, and had brought her head forward between the tent and the ship, when the hag seized her by the head, and dragged her in. At this moment the men began to beat upon their shields with the staves, in order to drown the noise of her outcries, which might have terrified the other girls, and deterred then from seeking death with their masters in the future. Then six men followed into the tent, and each and every one had carnal companionship with her. Then they laid her down by her master's side, while two of the men seized her by the feet and two by the hands. The old woman known as the angel of death now knotted a rope around her neck, and handed the ends to two of the men to pull. Then with a broad-bladed dagger she smote her between the ribs, and drew the blade forth while the two men strangled her with the rope till she died.

The next of kin to the dead man now drew near, and, taking a piece of wood, lighted it, and walked backwards toward the ship holding the stick in one hand, with the other placed upon his buttocks (he being naked), until the wood which had been piled under the ship was ignited. Then the others came up with staves and firewood, each one carrying a stick already lighted at the upper end, and threw it all on the pyre. The pile was soon aflame, then the ship, finally the tent, the man, and the girl, and everything else in the ship. A terrible storm began to blow up, and thus intensified the flames, and gave wings to the blaze.

At my side stood one of the Northmen, and I heard him talking with the interpreter, who stood near him. I asked the interpreter what the Northman had said, and received this answer: "'You Arabs,' he said, must be a stupid set! You take him who is to you the most revered and beloved of men, and cast him into the ground, to be devoured by creeping things and worms. We, on the other hand, burn him in a twinkling, so that he instantly, without a moment's delay, enters into Paradise.' At this he burst out into uncontrollable laughter, and then continued: 'It is the love of the Master [God] that causes the wind to blow and snatch him away in an instant.'" And, in very truth, before an hour had passed, ship, wood, and girl had with the man, turned to ashes.

Thereupon they heaped over the place where the ship had stood something like a rounded hill, and erecting on the centre of it a large birchen post, wrote on it the name of the deceased, along with that of the king of the Northmen. Having done this, they left the spot.

$$\boxed{70}$$

BARRY CUNLIFFE

The Western Vikings

The Vikings who sailed down the rivers of Russia to raid, trade, and settle came mainly from eastern Scandinavia — what is today Sweden and Finland. Their cousins in western Scandinavia sailed to the south and west. In this selection from a wide-ranging history of the European Atlantic world, the author, a modern archaeologist, discusses the expansion of Western Vikings — mainly Danes and Norwegians — into the Atlantic. How would you compare the expansion of the Western Vikings with that of the Eastern Vikings into what became Russia?

Thinking Historically

The modern historian lets us hear enough from the medieval victims of the Vikings for us to feel their fear, and his list of destroyed cities and massacred peoples registers the horror they must have unleashed in their era. But Cunliffe also gives us information that enables us to put the Viking attacks in some perspective. What is that information? What perspective on the Vikings does the reading give you?

The Coming of the Northmen

About 790 Beaduheard, the king's reeve at Dorchester in southern Britain, got news that three foreign ships had landed at Portland and, assuming them to be traders, he went to welcome them. He was wrong.

Barry Cunliffe, *Facing the Ocean: The Atlantic and Its Peoples* (Oxford: Oxford University Press, 2001), 482–83, 488–95, 499, 514–16.

They were raiders from Scandinavia and he died for his mistake. The Dorset landing was a foretaste. A few years later, in 793, the raiding began in earnest with the attack on the monastery of St Cuthbert on Lindisfarne: "Never before has such terror appeared in Britain as we have now suffered from a pagan race, nor was it thought that such an in-road from the sea could be made. Behold, the church of St Cuthbert spattered with the blood of the priests of God, despoiled of all its ornaments; a place more venerable than all in Britain is given as prey to pagan people." So wrote the English cleric Alcuin at the court of Charlemagne. Many more raids followed around the coasts of Britain and Ireland. The Franks were soon to suffer, so too the Bretons. By the 840s Viking war bands were exploring further south along the Atlantic coasts. A vast fleet of 150 ships sailed up the Garonne and plundered almost to Toulouse. Then it moved onwards to attack Galicia and Lisbon before sailing into the Guadalquivir. Here, from their base on the Isla Menor, the Vikings pillaged Seville but were severely mauled by the Moors. Those captured were hanged from the city's palm trees, and two hundred Viking heads were sent by the Emir to his allies in Tangier as an effective witness to his military prowess. Undeterred, the Viking force continued through the Straits of Gibraltar harassing the coasts as they sailed to the mouth of the Rhône where, on an island in the Camargue, a base was established for raiding upriver into the heart of France and across the sea to the coasts of Italy. In 861 they returned to their base on the Loire. The expedition had been "at once profitable and honourable."

The Mediterranean venture, while a notable feat, was of little lasting consequence. But meanwhile, in the north, raids and settlement had reached significant proportions. Some indication of what was going on is given by the pained lamentation of Ermentarius, a monk at Noirmoutier, writing in the 860s:

> The number of ships increases, the endless flood of Vikings never ceases to grow bigger. Everywhere Christ's people are the victims of massacre, burning, and plunder. The Vikings overrun all that lies before them, and no one can withstand them. They seize Bordeaux, Périgueux, Limoges, Angoulême, Toulouse; Angers, Tours, and Orleans are made deserts. Ships past counting voyage up the Seine . . . Rouen is laid waste, looted, and burnt; Paris, Beauvais, Meaux are taken, Melun's stronghold is razed to the ground, Chartres occupied, Evreux and Bayeux looted, and every town invested. . . .

Why the Raids of the Northmen Began

The raids of the Danes and Norwegians began in the last decade of the eighth century, and over the next seventy years rose to a devastating crescendo. No single factor was responsible for unleashing the fury, but there can be little doubt that the overseas ventures became possible only after the longship had reached its peak of excellence by the middle of the eighth century. The Scandinavian landscape demanded good shipping. The long Atlantic coastline of Norway, with its deeply indented fjords, was accessible with ease only by sea, while the sounds and islands of Denmark had, for millennia, been bound together by boat. The Baltic, too, was a cradle for navigation — a great inland sea providing ease of access between the extensive littorals and their productive hinterlands, and to the river routes penetrating far south across the North European Plain. Throughout Scandinavia settlements favoured the sea coasts and the inland lakes and waterways. They faced the open water and kept their backs to the forest. Thus communities depended upon ships for their livelihood, their rulers able to maintain their power only by command of the sea. In such a world it is easy to see how the ship became a symbol of authority, honed to perfection to reflect the status of the elite. A ship, either real or symbolic, might also accompany its owner in his burial. . . . By the early years of the ninth century, all the features characteristic of the classic Viking ship had been brought together, creating fast and highly efficient seagoing vessels suitable for carrying men across the ocean in search of land and plunder.

. . . In the course of the eighth century, trade between continental Europe and England developed apace, with well-established links leading northwards to the Baltic. In this way the volume of mercantile traffic in the southern North Sea increased dramatically, while the rulers of Denmark became increasingly aware of the wealth to be had to the south. Through the various traders who visited the Scandinavian ports they would also have learnt the political geography of western Europe — most notably the whereabouts of its rich, isolated monasteries and the distracting factional disputes endemic among its ruling households. To the Scandinavian elite there was much prestige to be had in leading a successful raid: the spoils would enrich the begetters and would bind followers closer to their leader. In the competitive emulation which accompanied the early raiding expeditions the number, intensity, and duration of the raids inevitably escalated.

Another, quite different, factor at work was the desire for new land to settle. With a growing population the narrow coastal zone of Norway was too restricted a territory to provide the social space needed for enterprising sons to establish themselves. The only solution was to find new territories overseas in Britain and Ireland, and further afield on the more remote islands of the north Atlantic. For the most part what was sought was new farmland, like the home territories, where families could set up new farms with plenty of space around for expansion by successive generations. It was this that the north Atlantic could supply in plenty. What England had to offer was rather different but no less acceptable — well-run estates which new Scandinavian lords could leave largely undisturbed, simply taking the profits.

Another incentive to moving overseas was the possibility of setting up merchant colonies emulating those that were so successful in the Baltic and along the eastern coasts of the North Sea. York, already a developing English market, was taken over by the Northmen in 866 and rapidly expanded to become the principal entrepôt in northern Britain, while an entirely new port-of-trade was established at Dublin and soon became a centre for Irish Sea commerce. In all of these ventures the ship was vital.

It would be wrong to give the impression that overseas activities were narrowly focused: trading could soon turn into raiding, while raiding could dissipate itself into settlement. One was never exclusive of the other. This is evocatively summed up in an account of the lifestyle of Svein Asleifarson recorded in the twelfth-century *Orkneyinga Saga*, no doubt referring wistfully to a long-gone era when Vikings behaved like Vikings:

> In the spring he had more than enough to occupy him, with a great deal of seed to sow which he saw to carefully himself. Then when the job was done, he would go off plundering in the Hebrides and in Ireland on what he called his "spring-trip," then back home just after midsummer where he stayed till the cornfields had been reaped and the grain was safely in. After that he would go off raiding again, and never came back till the first month of winter was ended. This he used to call his "autumn trip."

The Vikings in the West: A Brief Progress

. . . *Viking* is the word frequently used by the English sources to describe raiders and settlers from Scandinavia, while the Carolingian sources prefer *Northmen*. Both words include, without differentiation, Danes and Norwegians. Until the mid-ninth century it is possible to make a broad distinction between Norwegians, who settled northern and western Scotland and the Northern and Western Isles and were active in the Irish Sea, and Danes, who raided the North Sea and Channel coasts, but thereafter the distinction becomes blurred.

The progress of the settlement of north-western Britain by the Norwegians is unrecorded, but contact began as early as the seventh century and it is quite likely that the colonization was largely completed during the course of the eighth century. The newly settled areas provided the springboard for attacks on Ireland and the Irish Sea coasts, becoming increasingly widespread and frequent in the period 795–840.

The rich and unprotected monasteries were the target. Iona was attacked three times, in 795, 802, and 806, in the first flush of activity. Thereafter raids thrust further and further south — 821 Wexford, 822 Cork, and 824 the isolated monastery of Skelling Michael in the Atlantic off the Kerry coast. Having picked off the vulnerable coastal communities the attacks then began to penetrate inland, but usually no more than 30 kilometres or so from the safety of navigable water. These early attacks were opportunistic hit-and-run affairs, meeting no significant organized opposition.

Meanwhile in the North Sea the Danes adopted similar tactics. In 820 a massive Danish fleet of two hundred vessels threatened Saxony, and in three successive years, beginning in 834, the great trading port of Dorestad was devastated. Frisia became the immediate focus of contention. In 838 the Danish king Harik demanded of the Frankish king Louis that "The Frisians be given over to him" — a request that was roundly refused. The vulnerability of the coast was vividly brought home when, in 835, the monastery of St-Philibert on the island of Noirmoutier south of the Loire estuary was attacked. England suffered only sporadic raids at first, but these intensified in the 830s. . . .

The events of 840–865 saw the Scandinavians working the full length of the Atlantic zone from the Rhine to Gibraltar and beyond, but they were at their most active and most persistent along the major rivers — the Seine, the Thames, the Loire, and the Garonne — feeding off the cities that owed their wealth and well-being to their command of the river routes. The rivers that brought them their commercial advantage through access to the sea now brought men who sought to take it for themselves.

The 860s saw a change of pace from raid to settlement, accompanied by intensified and co-ordinated opposition by those whose land the Northmen were intent on taking. The Franks were the first to come to terms with the new reality by building fortified bridges across the rivers Seine and Loire, by fortifying towns and monasteries, and by paying tribute to groups of Vikings in return for protection or military services. These tactics protected the heart of the kingdom while leaving the lower reaches of the two rivers to the roving bands of invaders who had now taken up residence in the areas. The strategy kept Frankia free from further incursions until a new wave of attacks began on Paris in 885. . . .

Towards the end of the tenth century, with the rise of a strong dynasty in Denmark under Harald Bluetooth and his son, Sven Forkbeard, a new phase of Viking raiding was initiated, and once more it was the Atlantic coastal regions as far south as Iberia that took the brunt of the attack. England was particularly vulnerable. In 991 Sven Forkbeard led his first raid against the English, his activities culminating in the conquest of the kingdom in 1013. Three years later, after his death, his son Knut was formally recognized as king of England. Dynastic squabbles and claims and counter-claims to the English throne rumbled on throughout the eleventh century, but the failure of the threatened Danish conquest of England to materialize in 1085 was the effective end of the Viking episode. Occasional Norwegian expeditions to the Northern and Western Isles were the last ripples, three centuries after the Viking wave first struck.

The Northmen and the Atlantic Communities

That the impact of the Scandinavians on the Atlantic communities was profound and lasting there can be no doubt, but sufficient will have been said to show that it varied significantly from region to region.

In lightly inhabited or empty lands like the Northern and Western Isles, the Faroes, Iceland, and Greenland, Scandinavian culture was directly transplanted in its entirety and flourished much in the style of the Norwegian homeland, but elsewhere the Scandinavian component fused with indigenous culture. In regions where the local systems were well established and comparatively stable, as in eastern England and the maritime region of France (soon to become Normandy), the new order emerged imperceptibly from the old with little disruption to the social or economic balance, but in other areas, like Ireland, where warfare between rival factions of the elite was endemic, the Scandinavian presence was a catalyst for widespread change. Here the ferocity of the Irish warlords matched their own. For this reason the small enclaves established at harbours around the coast remained small, developing as isolated trading colonies in an otherwise hostile landscape. Apart from certain areas of the north-east, large-scale land-taking and settlement was not possible. Much the same pattern can be seen in south-west Wales.

The Scandinavian settlements of the Irish Sea zone chose good docking facilities, initially to serve as protected anchorages for the vessels of the early raiders, but these quickly developed as trading centres, making the Irish Sea the major focus of exchange in the Scandinavian maritime system. From here ships might go south to Andalucía, north to Iceland and beyond, or around Britain eastwards to the Baltic. In this way the Irish Sea became the hub of a complex network of communications built upon the long-distance exchange systems which had already been established in the preceding centuries.

In Brittany a rather different pattern of interaction emerged. Here the long-term hostility between the Bretons and the Franks provided a situation in which raiding and mercenary activity could profitably be maintained, while the internecine warfare that broke out in both kingdoms in the painful periods when succession was being contested offered the raiders further opportunities for easy intervention.

Throughout this time the Loire formed the focus of Scandinavian activity and Nantes was often in their control, but there is, as yet, little evidence that a major trading enclave developed here. It may simply have been that the political turmoil in the region allowed warfare in its various modes to provide the necessary economic underpinning to sustain Viking society. From the Breton point of view the Scandinavian presence, disruptive though it was, was an important factor in helping to maintain their independence from the Franks.

South of the Loire, Viking military activity was sporadic and superficial, at least in so far as the historical record allows us to judge, but given their interest in trade it is difficult to believe that there were not regular visits by merchants to the Gironde and Garonne and along the Atlantic seaboard of Iberia. In this they would simply have been following the routes plied by their predecessors.

Some measure of the integration of the multifaceted maritime system that emerged is provided by a wreck excavated at Skuldelev in the Danish fjord of Roskilde. It was one of six that had been sunk to block the fjord from seaward attack some time in the late eleventh or early twelfth century. The vessel was a typical Viking longship suitable for carrying fifty to sixty warriors. Dendrochronology has shown that the ship had been built about 1060 at, or in the vicinity of, Dublin. What service it saw as a raiding vessel in the seas around Britain and France we will never know, but its final resting place 2,200 kilometres from the yard in which it had been built is a vivid reminder of the capacity of the sea in bringing the communities of Atlantic Europe ever closer together.

71

Eirik's Saga

Scandinavian seafarers spread out in all directions in the tenth century. While Swedes and Finns sailed down the rivers of Russia to the Black and Caspian seas, Danes conquered and colonized from England down the coast of France into the Mediterranean as far as Italy, North Africa, and Arabia. The Vikings of Norway sailed mainly

"Eirik's Saga," in *The Vinland Sagas: The Norse Discovery of America*, trans. and introduction by Magnus Magnusson and Hermann Palsson (Harmondsworth, Middlesex, England: Penguin Books, 1965), 75–78.

westward, colonizing Iceland, Greenland, and North America (certainly Newfoundland but likely further south). The Norsemen discovered Iceland in about 860 and began settlement some fourteen years later. By 930, Iceland contained the families and retainers of many lords who fled Western Norway to escape the conquering Harald Fairhair.

Eirik the Red (950–1003) came to Iceland with his family in 960 after his father had to flee Norway because of "some killings." In turn, Eirik was exiled from Iceland in 982 after he committed murder in the heat of two quarrels. Exile meant searching for a settlement even further west, leading Eirik to Greenland. While not the first to see or land in Greenland, Eirik established the first colony there.

This excerpt from "Eirik's Saga," written about 1260, insofar as it captures the oral tradition, gives us an idea of Viking thought in the tenth century. Does this account change your idea of Viking society? How? How does it contribute to your understanding of the Viking expansion?

Thinking Historically

How does this internal view of Viking society inevitably change our moral perspective from that of an outsider? How might the religious differences between Ibn Fadlan and this author lead to different moral perspectives?

There was a warrior king called Olaf the White, who was the son of King Ingjald. Olaf went on a Viking expedition to the British Isles, where he conquered Dublin and the adjoining territory and made himself king over them. He married Aud the Deep-Minded, the daughter of Ketil Flat-Nose; they had a son called Thorstein the Red.

Olaf was killed in battle in Ireland, and Aud and Thorstein the Red then went to the Hebrides. There Thorstein married Thurid, the daughter of Eyvind the Easterner; they had many children.

Thorstein the Red became a warrior king, and joined forces with Earl Sigurd the Powerful, together they conquered Caithness, Sutherland, Ross, and Moray, and more than half of Argyll. Thorstein ruled over these territories as king until he was betrayed by the Scots and killed in battle.

Aud the Deep-Minded was in Caithness when she learned of Thorstein's death; she had a ship built secretly in a forest, and when it was ready she sailed away to Orkney. There she gave away in marriage Groa, daughter of Thorstein the Red.

After that, Aud set out for Iceland; she had twenty freeborn men aboard her ship. She reached Iceland and spent the first winter with her brother Bjorn at Bjarnarhaven. Then she took possession of the entire Dales district between Dogurdar River and Skraumuhlaups River, and made her home at Hvamm. She used to say prayers at Kross Hills; she had crosses erected there, for she had been baptized and was a devout Christian.

Many well-born men, who had been taken captive in the British Isles by Vikings and were now slaves, came to Iceland with her. One of them was called Vifil; he was of noble descent. He had been taken prisoner in the British Isles and was a slave until Aud gave him his freedom.

When Aud gave land to members of her crew, Vifil asked her why she did not give him some land like the others. Aud replied that it was of no importance, and said that he would be considered a man of quality wherever he was. She gave him Vifilsdale, and he settled there. He married, and had two sons called Thorbjorn and Thorgeir; they were both promising men, and grew up with their father.

Eirik Explores Greenland

There was a man called Thorvald, who was the father of Eirik the Red. He and Eirik left their home in Jaederen because of some killings and went to Iceland. They took possession of land in Hornstrands, and made their home at Drangar. Thorvald died there, and Eirik the Red then married Thjodhild, and moved south to Haukadale; he cleared land there and made his home at Eirikstead, near Vatnshorn.

Eirik's slaves started a landslide that destroyed the farm of a man called Valthjof, at Valthjofstead; so Eyjolf Saur, one of Valthjof's kinsmen, killed the slaves at Skeidsbrekkur, above Vatnshorn. For this, Eirik killed Eyjolf Saur; he also killed Hrafn the Dueller, at Leikskalar. Geirstein and Odd of Jorvi, who were Eyjolf's kinsmen, took action over his killing, and Eirik was banished from Haukadale.

Eirik then took possession of Brok Island and Oxen Island, and spent the first winter at Tradir, in South Island. He lent his bench-boards to Thorgest of Breidabolstead. After that, Eirik moved to Oxen Island, and made his home at Eirikstead. He then asked for his bench-boards back, but they were not returned; so Eirik went to Breidabolstead and seized them. Thorgest pursued him, and they fought a battle near the farmstead at Drangar. Two of Thorgest's sons and several other men were killed there.

After this, both Eirik and Thorgest maintained a force of fighting-men at home. Eirik was supported by Styr Thorgrimsson, Eyjolf of Svin Island, Thorbjorn Vifilsson, and the sons of Thorbrand of Alptafjord;

Thorgest was supported by Thorgeir of Hitardale, Aslak of Langadale and his son Illugi, and the sons of Thord Gellir.

Eirik and his men were sentenced to outlawry at the Thorsness Assembly. He made his ship ready in Eiriksbay, and Eyjolf of Svin Island hid him in Dimunarbay while Thorgest and his men were scouring the islands for him.

Thorbjorn Vifilsson and Styr and Eyjolf accompanied Eirik out beyond the islands, and they parted in great friendship; Eirik said he would return their help as far as it lay within his power, if ever they had need of it. He told them he was going to search for the land that Gunnbjorn, the son of Ulf Crow, had sighted when he was driven westwards off course and discovered the Gunnbjarnar Skerries; he added that he would come back to visit his friends if he found this country.

Eirik put out to sea past Snæfells Glacier, and made land near the glacier that is known as Blaserk. From there he sailed south to find out if the country were habitable there. He spent the first winter on Eiriks Island, which lies near the middle of the Eastern Settlement. In the spring he went to Eiriksfjord, where he decided to make his home. That summer he explored the wilderness to the west and gave names to many landmarks there. He spent the second winter on Eiriks Holms, off Hvarfs Peak. The third summer he sailed all the way north to Snæfell and into Hrafnsfjord, where he reckoned he was farther inland than the head of Eiriksfjord. Then he turned back and spent the third winter on Eiriks Island, off the mouth of Eiriksfjord.

He sailed back to Iceland the following summer and put in at Breidafjord. He stayed the winter with Ingolf of Holmlatur. In the spring he fought a battle with Thorgest of Breidabolstead and was defeated. After that a reconciliation was arranged between them.

That summer Eirik set off to colonize the country he had discovered; he named it *Greenland*, for he said that people would be much more tempted to go there if it had an attractive name.

72

The Poetic Edda, Selections from the Havamol

The Poetic Edda constitutes a collection of poems, songs, stories, and proverbs from the rich body of Nordic mythology. In addition to the Edda, there are the Sagas — the historic stories like selection 71 and the epic tales of gods, giants, heroes, and the end of the world. Much of the Sagas have enriched the imaginations of generations from the operas of Richard Wagner to *The Lord of the Rings*. The Edda are shorter and less well known, but more immediately accessible than the grand stories. The Havamol is the part of *The Poetic Edda* that contains an abundance of practical guidance and moral lessons. These poems were part of an oral tradition in northern Europe for centuries before they were written down about the eleventh century. This version was translated from an Icelandic poetic Edda of the thirteenth century. What do these brief poems tell you about the culture and life of the people who told and wrote them?

Thinking Historically

Of all Norse, Viking, or Icelandic literature, the poems of the Havamol most directly express moral values. What do they tell you about the moral values of their authors? The Havamol has sometimes been compared to other books of wisdom literature, including the book of Proverbs in the Hebrew Bible. No single book can represent the ideas of an entire people throughout time and space. However, to the extent that these selections can stand for the ideas of the Vikings, how would you characterize their ideas of morality? What if any of these values do you see reflected in the behavior of the people described by Ibn Fadlan? How were the Vikings different from the barbarians who toppled the Roman and Han empires in the third to sixth centuries?

The Poetic Edda, trans. from the Icelandic with an introduction and notes by Henry Adams Bellows (Princeton, N.J.: Princeton University Press, 1936). Scanned at sacred-texts.com, April–July 2001, available online at http://www.sacred-texts.com/neu/poe/poe04.htm.

1. Within the gates | ere a man shall go,
(Full warily let him watch,)
Full long let him look about him;
For little he knows | where a foe may lurk,
And sit in the seats within.

3. Fire he needs | who with frozen knees
Has come from the cold without;
Food and clothes | must the farer have,
The man from the mountains come.

4. Water and towels | and welcoming speech
Should he find who comes, to the feast;
If renown he would get, | and again be greeted,
Wisely and well must he act.

5. Wits must he have | who wanders wide,
But all is easy at home;
At the witless man | the wise shall wink
When among such men he sits.

34. Crooked and far | is the road to a foe,
Though his house on the highway be;
But wide and straight | is the way to a friend,
Though far away he fare.

35. Forth shall one go, | nor stay as a guest
In a single spot forever;
Love becomes loathing | if long one sits
By the hearth in another's home.

36. Better a house, | though a hut it be,
A man is master at home;
A pair of goats | and a patched-up roof
Are better far than begging.

38. Away from his arms | in the open field
A man should fare not a foot;
For never he knows | when the need for a spear
Shall arise on the distant road.

39. If wealth a man | has won for himself,
Let him never suffer in need;
Oft he saves for a foe | what he plans for a friend,
For much goes worse than we wish.

78. Cattle die, | and kinsmen die,
And so one dies one's self;
One thing now | that never dies,
The fame of a dead man's deeds.

81. Give praise to the day at evening, | to a woman on her pyre,
To a weapon which is tried, | to a maid at wed lock,
To ice when it is crossed, | to ale that is drunk.

82. When the gale blows hew wood, | in fair winds seek the water;
Sport with maidens at dusk, | for day's eyes are many;
From the ship seek swiftness, | from the shield protection,
Cuts from the sword, | from the maiden kisses.

90. The love of women | fickle of will
Is like starting o'er ice | with a steed unshod,
A two-year-old restive | and little tamed,
Or steering a rudderless | ship in a storm,
Or, lame, hunting reindeer | on slippery rocks.

91. Clear now will I speak, | for I know them both,
Men false to women are found;
When fairest we speak, | then falsest we think,
Against wisdom we work with deceit.

92. Soft words shall he speak | and wealth shall he offer
Who longs for a maiden's love,
And the beauty praise | of the maiden bright;
He wins whose wooing is best.

139. I ween that I hung | on the windy tree,
Hung there for nights full nine;
With the spear I was wounded, | and offered I was
To Othin, myself to myself,
On the tree that none | may ever know
What root beneath it runs.

73

From The Secret History
of the Mongols

This Mongol account records the early years of Mongol expansion under Chingis Khan, the founder of the empire. Born Temujin in 1155 or 1167, the young son of a minor tribal chieftain attracted the support of Mongol princes in the years between 1187 and 1206 through a series of decisive military victories over other tribes and competing Mongol claimants to the title of Great Khan.

The Mongols were illiterate before the time of Chingis Khan, who adopted the script of the Uighurs, one of the more literate peoples of the steppe. Thus the *Secret History* was written in Mongolian with Uighur letters. The only surviving version is a fourteenth-century Chinese translation. The author is unknown, but the book provides detailed accounts of the early years of Temujin and ends with the reign of his son and successor, Ogodai, in 1228 — only a year after his father's death.

Because so much about the Mongols was written by their literate enemies, *The Secret History* is an invaluable resource: It is clearly an "insider's" account of the early years of Mongol expansion. While it includes mythic elements — it begins with the augury of the birth of a blue wolf to introduce Chingis Khan — *The Secret History* is, without doubt, an authentic representation of a Mongol point of view.

In this selection, you will read three passages. The first describes a meeting in about 1187 of several tribal leaders who agree that the twenty-year-old Temujin should become Great Khan (Chingis Khan). What do these tribal leaders expect to gain from this alliance under Temujin? What do they offer in return?

The second passage deals with an early Mongol victory in 1202 over the neighboring Tatars, a tribe that Europeans often confused with the Mongols. How merciful or harsh does Chingis Khan seem?

The third passage recounts the story of an important Mongol victory over the Naiman in 1204. What does this section tell you about the sources of Mongol military strength?

How does this "insider's" view of the Mongols provide unique information or a perspective that would be unattainable from non-Mongols?

Adapted by K. Reilly from R. P. Lister, *Genghis Khan* (New York: Barnes & Noble, 1993), 99–100, 136–39, 166–76, 191–93. While this volume is a retelling of the almost indecipherable *The Secret History of the Mongols* in Lister's own words, the selections that follow simplify without contextualizing or explaining the original work. More scholarly editions, trans. and ed. Francis Woodman Cleaves (Cambridge, Mass.: Harvard University Press, 1982) and Paul Kahn (San Francisco: North Point Press, 1984) are less accessible.

Thinking Historically

What moral values does this selection reveal? Do the Mongols think of themselves as "moral" people? Is the author-historian interested in describing what happened objectively, or in presenting an unblemished, sanitized view?

In what ways does this written Mongol history make you more sympathetic to the Mongols? Notice that the "Mongols Conquer the Naiman" passage begins with an account of the Naiman. How fair does the Mongol author seem to be toward the Naiman? Would this be a good source for understanding the Naiman? Do you think the Mongol authors described the Naiman more accurately than Chinese or Europeans described the Mongols?

The Choosing of the Khan

. . . A general council of all the chieftains was called, and the three most notable men among them, Prince Altan, Khuchar, and Sacha Beki, came forward. They addressed Temujin formally, in the following manner:

> We will make you Khan; you shall ride at our head, against our foes.
> We will throw ourselves like lightning on your enemies;
> We will bring you their finest women and girls, their rich tents like palaces.
> From all the peoples and nations we will bring you the fair girls and the high-stepping horses;
> When you hunt wild beasts, we will drive them towards you; we will encircle them, pressing hard at their heels.
>
> If on the day of battle we disobey you,
> Take our flocks from us, our women and children, and cast our worthless heads on the steppe.
> If in times of peace we disobey you,
> Part us from our men and our servants, our wives and our sons;
> Abandon us and cast us out, masterless, on the forsaken earth. . . .

Mongol Conquest of Tatars

. . . Temujin came up against the Tatars at Dalan Namurgas, on the Khalkha, east of Buir Nor, and defeated them in battle. They fell back; the Mongol armies pursued them, slaying and capturing them in large numbers.

The princes, Altan, Khuchar, and Daritai, were less assiduous in the pursuit. Finding a great number of animals roaming the steppes in the absence of their Tatar owners, they followed the usual custom of rounding them up, and collecting anything that took their fancy in the abandoned Tatar camps.

Temujin, having issued a clear order [against looting], could not tolerate their disobedience. He detached portions of his army, placed them under the command of Jebe and Khubilai, and sent them off after the disobedient princes, with orders to take away from them everything they had captured. The outcome was what might have been expected. Prince Altan and Khuchar, retiring in haste with as much of their booty as they could take with them, departed from their allegiance to him. They re-established themselves as independent chieftains, entering into such arrangements with Ong Khan, Jamukha, and other rulers as seemed desirable.

Daritai, however, seeing a little more clearly than the others, submitted to having his booty taken away from him.

Owing to his determined pursuit of the Tatars, Temujin found that he had a very considerable number of Tatar prisoners. They were kept under guard in the Mongol camp, and for the most part they were not greatly perturbed by their situation. Some of the chieftains might expect to be executed, but the lesser men had a reasonable hope of surviving. Some might have to serve as warriors under the Mongols, or even be enslaved, but a slave of talents could always hope to become a warrior again.

Temujin held a council to decide what to do with them. It was a great matter, and nobody was present at this council but his own family. The Khan's intention [was] to wipe out his enemies on a large scale. . . .

Belgutai had . . . made friends among the Tatar prisoners. One of these was Yeke Charan, the principal Tatar leader. . . . When Yeke Charan asked him what decision the family council had come to, Belgutai did not hesitate to tell him.

"We agreed to measure you against the linchpin,"[1] he said.

Yeke Charan told his fellow prisoners of the Khan's decision. Having nothing to lose, they rose up against their guards and fought their way out of the camp, taking with them what weapons they could seize. They gathered themselves together on a hilltop in a tight formation of fierce warriors. Men who are going to be killed whatever happens, and know it, fight well. The destruction of the Tatars, which was in due course accomplished, cost many Mongol lives.

Temujin was remarkably lenient towards Belgutai.

"Because Belgutai revealed the decision of the family council," he said, "Our army suffered great losses. From now on, Belgutai will take

---

[1]This was not an unknown procedure, though it had never been applied on quite such a vast scale. Prisoners were led past the wheel of a wagon. Those who were taller than the linchpin were beheaded; the children, who were smaller, survived to be taken into the Mongol armies when they grew up.

no part in the council. While it is being held, he will remain outside, keeping order in the camp, and he will sit in judgment during that time over the quarrelsome, the thieves, and the liars. When the council is finished and the wine is all drunk, then Belgutai can come in."

He ordered at the same time that Daritai should be banned from the family councils, for disobeying his *yasakh*.[2] . . .

Mongols Conquer the Naiman

When the news was brought to [the Naiman] Tayang Khan that someone claiming to be Ong Khan had been slain at the Neikun watercourse, his mother, Gurbesu, said: "Ong Khan was the great Khan of former days. Bring his head here! If it is really he, we will sacrifice to him."

She sent a message to Khorisu, commanding him to cut the head off and bring it in. When it was brought to her, she recognised it as that of Ong Khan. She placed it on a white cloth, and her daughter-in-law carried out the appropriate rites. . . . A wine-feast was held and stringed instruments were played. Gurbesu, taking up a drinking-bowl, made an offering to the head of Ong Khan.

When the sacrifice was made to it, the head grinned.

"He laughs!" Tayang Khan cried. Overcome by religious awe, he flung the head on the floor and trampled on it until it was mangled beyond recognition.

The great general Kokse'u Sabrakh was present at these ceremonies, and observed them without enthusiasm. It was he who had been the only Naiman general to offer resistance to Temujin and Ong Khan on their expedition against Tayang Khan's brother Buyiruk.

"First of all," he remarked, "you cut off the head of a dead ruler, and then you trample it into the dust. What kind of behaviour is this? Listen to the baying of those dogs: It has an evil sound. The Khan your father, Inancha Bilgei, once said: 'My wife is young, and I, her husband, am old. Only the power of prayer has enabled me to beget my son, this same Tayang. But will my son, born a weakling, be able to guard and hold fast my common and evil-minded people?'

"Now the baying of the dogs seems to announce that some disaster is at hand. The rule of our queen, Gurbesu, is firm; but you, my Khan, Torlukh Tayang, are weak. It is truly said of you that you have no thought for anything but the two activities of hawking and driving game, and no capacity for anything but these."

Tayang Khan was accustomed to the disrespect of his powerful general, but he was stung into making a rash decision.

[2]Order, law.

"There are a few Mongols in the east. From the earliest days this old and great Ong Khan feared them, with their quivers; now they have made war on him and driven him to death. No doubt they would like to be rulers themselves. There are indeed in Heaven two shining lights, the sun and the moon, and both can exist there; but how can there be two rulers here on earth? Let us go and gather those Mongols in."

His mother Gurbesu said: "Why should we start making trouble with them? The Mongols have a bad smell; they wear black clothes. They are far away, out there; let them stay there. Though it is true," she added, "that we could have the daughters of their chieftains brought here; when we had washed their hands and feet, they could milk our cows and sheep for us."

Tayang Khan said: "What is there so terrible about them? Let us go to these Mongols and take away their quivers."

"What big words you are speaking," Kokse'u Sabrakh said. "Is Tayang Khan the right man for it? Let us keep the peace."

Despite these warnings, Tayang Khan decided to attack the Mongols. It was a justifiable decision; his armies were stronger, but time was on Temujin's side. Tayang sought allies, sending a messenger to Alakhu Shidigichuri of the Onggut, in the south, the guardians of the ramparts between Qashin and the Khingan. "I am told that there are a few Mongols in the east," he said. "Be my right hand! I will ride against them from here, and we will take their quivers away from them."

[Alakhu Shidigichuri's] reply was brief: "I cannot be your right hand." He in his turn sent a message to Temujin. "Tayang Khan of the Naiman wants to come and take away your quivers. He sent to me and asked me to be his right hand. I refused. I make you aware of this, so that when he comes your quivers will not be taken away."[3]

When he received Alakhu's message Temujin, having wintered near Guralgu, was holding one of his . . . roundups of game on the camel-steppes of Tulkinche'ut, in the east. The beasts had been encircled by the clansmen and warriors; the chieftains were gathered together, about to begin the great hunt.

"What shall we do now?" some of them said to each other. "Our horses are lean at this season."

. . . The snow had only lately left the steppe; the horses had found nothing to graze on during these recent months. Their ribs stuck out and they lacked strength.

The Khan's youngest brother, Temuga, spoke up. . . .

---

[3]Temujin, grateful for this warning, sent him five hundred horses and a thousand sheep. His friendship with Alakhu was valuable to him at a later time.

"How can that serve as an excuse," he said, "that the horses are lean? My horses are quite fat enough. How can we stay sitting here, when we receive a message like that?"

Prince Belgutai spoke. . . .

"If a man allows his quivers to be taken away during his lifetime, what kind of an existence does he have? For a man who is born a man, it is a good enough end to be slain by another man, and lie on the steppe with his quiver and bow beside him. The Naiman make fine speeches, with their many men and their great kingdom. But suppose, having heard their fine speeches, we ride against them, would it be so difficult to take their quivers away from them? We must mount and ride; it is the only thing to do."

Temujin was wholly disposed to agree with these sentiments. He broke off the hunt, set the army in motion, and camped near Ornu'u on the Khalkha. Here he paused for a time while he carried out a swift re-organisation of the army. A count was held of the people; they were divided up into thousands, hundreds, and tens, and commanders of these units were appointed. Also at this time he chose his personal body-guards, the seventy day-guards and eighty night-guards. . . .

Having reorganised the army, he marched away from the mountainside of Ornu'u on the Khalkha, and took the way of war against the Naiman.

The spring of the Year of the Rat [1204] was by now well advanced. During this westward march came the Day of the Red Disc, the sixteenth day of the first moon of summer. On this day, the moon being at the full, the Khan caused the great yak's-tail banner to be consecrated, letting it be sprinkled with fermented mare's milk, with the proper observances.

They continued the march up the Kerulen, with Jebe and Khubilai in the van. When they came on to the Saari steppes, they met with the first scouts of the Naiman. There were a few skirmishes between the Naiman and Mongol scouts; in one of these, a Mongol scout was captured, a man riding a grey horse with a worn saddle. The Naiman studied this horse with critical eyes, and thought little of it. "The Mongols' horses are inordinately lean," they said to each other.

The Mongol army rode out on to the Saari steppes, and began to deploy themselves for the forthcoming battle. . . . Dodai Cherbi, one of the newly appointed captains, put a proposal before the Khan.

"We are short in numbers compared to the enemy; besides this, we are exhausted after the long march, our horses in particular. It would be a good idea to settle in this camp, so that our horses can graze on the steppe, until they have had as much to eat as they need. Meanwhile, we can deceive the enemy by making puppets and lighting innumerable fires. For every man, we will make at least one puppet, and we will burn fires in five places. It is said that the Naiman people are very numerous, but it is rumoured also that their king is a weakling, who has never left his tents. If we keep them in a state of uncertainty about our numbers, with our puppets and our fires, our geldings can stuff themselves till they are fat."

The suggestion pleased Temujin, who had the order passed on to the soldiers to light fires immediately. Puppets were constructed and placed all over the steppe, some sitting or lying by the fires, some of them even mounted on horses.

At night, the watchers of the Naiman saw, from the flanks of the mountain, fires twinkling all over the steppe. They said to each other: "Did they not say that the Mongols were very few? Yet they have more fires than there are stars in Heaven."

Having previously sent to Tayang Khan news of the lean grey horse with the shabby saddle, they now sent him the message: "The warriors of the Mongols are camped out all over the Saari steppes. They seem to grow more numerous every day; their fires outnumber the stars."

When this news was brought to him from the scouts, Tayang Khan was at the watercourse of Khachir. He sent a message to his son Guchuluk.

"I am told that the geldings of the Mongols are lean, but the Mongols are, it seems, numerous. Once we start fighting them, it will be difficult to draw back. They are such hard warriors that when several men at once come up against one of them, he does not move an eyelid; even if he is wounded, so that the black blood flows out, he does not flinch. I do not know whether it is a good thing to come up against such men.

"I suggest that we should assemble our people and lead them back to the west, across the Altai; and all the time, during this retreat, we will fight off the Mongols as dogs do, by running in on them from either side as they advance. Our geldings are too fat; in this march we shall make them lean and fit. But the Mongols' lean geldings will be brought to such a state of exhaustion they will vomit in the Mongols' faces."

On receiving this message, Guchuluk Khan, who was more warlike than his father, said: "That woman Tayang has lost all his courage, to speak such words. Where does this great multitude of Mongols come from? Most of the Mongols are with Jamukha, who is here with us. Tayang speaks like this because fear has overcome him. He has never been farther from his tent than his pregnant wife goes to urinate. He has never dared to go so far as the inner pastures where the knee-high calves are kept." So he expressed himself on the subject of his father, in the most injurious and wounding terms.

When he heard these words, Tayang Khan said: "I hope the pride of this powerful Guchuluk will not weaken on the day when the clash of arms is heard and the slaughter begins. Because once we are committed to battle against the foe, it will be hard to disengage again."

Khorisu Beki, a general who commanded under Tayang Khan, said: "Your father, Inancha Bilgei, never showed the back of a man or the haunch of a horse to opponents who were just as worthy as these. How can you lose your courage so early in the day? We would have done better to summon your mother Gurbesu to command over us. It is a pity that Kokse'u Sabrakh has grown too old to lead us. Our army's discipline has become lax. For the Mongols, their hour has come. It is finished! Tayang, you have failed us." He belted on his quiver and galloped off.

Tayang Khan grew angry. "All men must die," he said. "Their bodies must suffer. It is the same for all men. Let us fight, then."

So, having created doubt and dismay, and lost the support of some of his best leaders, he decided to give battle. He broke away from the watercourse of Khachir, marched down the Tamir, crossed the Orkhon and skirted the eastern flanks of the mountain Nakhu. When they came to Chakirma'ut, Temujin's scouts caught sight of them and brought back the message: "The Naiman are coming!"

The Battle of Chakirma'ut

When the news was brought to Temujin he said: "Sometimes too many men are just as big a handicap as too few."

Then he issued his general battle orders. "We will march in the order 'thick grass,' take up positions in the 'lake' battle order, and fight in the manner called 'gimlet.'"[4] He gave Kasar the command of the main army, and appointed Prince Otchigin to the command of the reserve horses, a special formation of great importance in Mongol warfare.

The Naiman, having advanced as far as Chakirma'ut, drew themselves up in a defensive position on the foothills of Nakhu, with the mountain behind them. . . . The Mongols forced their scouts back on to the forward lines, and then their forward lines back on to the main army, and drove tightly knit formations of horsemen again and again into the Naiman ranks. The Naiman, pressed back on themselves, could do nothing but retreat gradually up the mountain. Many of their men . . . hardly had the chance to fight at all, but were cut down in an immobile mass of men as soon as the Mongols reached them.

Tayang Khan, with his advisers, also retreated up the mountain as the day advanced. From the successive spurs to which they climbed, each one higher than the last, they could see the whole of this dreadful disaster as it took place below them.

Jamukha was with Tayang Khan. . . .

"Who are those people over there," Tayang Khan asked him, "who throw my warriors back as if they were sheep frightened by a wolf, who come huddling back to the sheepfold?"

---

[4]These were the names of various tactical disciplines in which he had drilled his army.

Jamukha said: "My *anda*[5] Temujin has four hounds whom he brought up on human flesh, and kept in chains. They have brows of copper, snouts like chisels, tongues like bradawls, hearts of iron, and tails that cut like swords. They can live on dew, and ride like the wind. On the day of battle they eat the flesh of men. You see how, being set loose, they come forward slavering for joy. Those two are Jebe and Khubilai; those two are Jelmei and Subetai. That is who those four hounds are."

He pointed out to him also the Uru'ut and the Mangqut, who, as Tayang Khan remarked, seemed to bound like foals set loose in the morning, when, after their dams have suckled them, they frisk around her on the steppe. "They hunt down men who carry lances and swords," he said. "Having struck them down, they slay them, and rob them of all they possess. How joyful and boisterous they look, as they ride forward!"

"Who is it coming up there in the rear," Tayang Khan asked him, "who swoops down on our troops like a ravening falcon?"

"That is my *anda* Temujin. His entire body is made of sounding copper; there is no gap through which even a bodkin could penetrate. There he is, you see him? He advances like an eagle about to seize his prey. You said formerly that if you once set eyes on the Mongols you would not leave so much of them as the skin of a lamb's foot. What do you think of them now?"

By this time the chieftains were standing on a high spur. Below them, the great army of the Naiman, Jamukha's men with them, were retreating in confusion, fighting desperately as the Mongols hemmed them in.

"Who is that other chieftain," Tayang asked Jamukha, "who draws ever nearer us, in a dense crowd of men?"

"Mother Hoelun brought up one of her own sons on human flesh. He is nine feet tall; he eats a three-year-old cow every day. If he swallows an armed man whole, it makes no difference to his appetite. When he is roused to anger, and lets fly with one of his *angqu'a* [forked] arrows, it will go through ten or twenty men. His normal range is a thousand yards; when he draws his bow to its fullest extent, he shoots over eighteen hundred yards. He is mortal, but he is not like other mortals; he is more than a match for the serpents of Guralgu. He is called Kasar."

They were climbing high up the mountain now, to regroup below its summit. Tayang Khan saw a new figure among the Mongols.

"Who is that coming up from the rear?" he asked Jamukha.

"That is the youngest son of Mother Hoelun. He is called Otchigin [Odeigin] the Phlegmatic. He is one of those people who go to bed

---

[5]Sworn brother, blood brother, declared ally.

early and get up late. But when he is behind the army, with the reserves, he does not linger; he never comes too late to the battle lines."

"We will climb to the peak of the mountain," Tayang Khan said.

Jamukha, seeing that the battle was lost, slipped away to the rear and descended the mountain, with a small body of men. One of these he sent to Temujin with a message. "Say this to my *anda*. Tayang Khan, terrified by what I have told him, has completely lost his senses. He has retreated up the mountain as far as he can. He could be killed by one harsh word. Let my *anda* take note of this: They have climbed to the top of the mountain, and are in no state to defend themselves any more. I myself have left the Naiman."

Since the evening was drawing on, Temujin commanded his troops in the forefront of the attack to draw back. Bodies of men were sent forward on the wings, east and west, to encircle the summit of Mount Nakhu. There they stood to arms during the night. During the night, the Naiman army tried to break out of the encircling ring. Bodies of horsemen plunged down the mountainside in desperate charges; many fell and were trampled to death, the others were slain. In the first light they were seen lying about the mountain in droves, like fallen trees. Few were left defending the peak; they put up little resistance to the force sent up against them.

$$\boxed{74}$$

JOHN OF PLANO CARPINI
History of the Mongols

Chingis Khan united the tribes of the steppe and conquered northern China, capturing Peking by 1215. He then turned his armies against the West, conquering the tribes of Turkestan and the Khorezmian Empire, the great Muslim power of central Asia, by 1222 and sending an army around the Caspian Sea into Russia. In 1226, he turned again to the East, subduing and destroying the kingdom of Tibet before he

John of Plano Carpini, "History of the Mongols," in *Mission to Asia: Narratives and Letters of the Franciscan Missionaries in Mongolia and China in the Thirteenth and Fourteenth Centuries*, trans. a nun of Stanbrook Abbey, ed. Christopher Dawson (1955; reprint, New York: Harper & Row, 1966), 60–69.

died in 1227. One historian, Christopher Dawson, summarizes the career of Chingis Khan this way:

> In spite of the primitive means at his disposal, it is possible that [Chingis Khan] succeeded in destroying a larger portion of the human race than any modern expert in total warfare. Within a dozen years from the opening of his campaign against China, the Mongol armies had reached the Pacific, the Indus, and the Black Sea, and had destroyed many of the great cities in India. For Europe especially, the shock was overwhelming.

European fears intensified in 1237 as the principal Mongol armies under Batu Khan systematically destroyed one Russian city after another. In April 1241, one Mongol army destroyed a combined force of Polish and German armies, while another defeated the Hungarian army and threatened Austria. In 1245, desperate to learn as much as possible about Mongol intentions, Pope Innocent IV sent a mission to the Mongols. For this important task, he sent two Franciscan monks — one of whom was John of Plano Carpini — with two letters addressed to the Emperor of the Tartars (a compounded error that changed the Tatars, the Mongols' enemy, into the denizens of Tartarus, or Hell).

In May, the barefoot sixty-five-year-old Friar John reached Batu's camp on the Volga River, from which he was relayed to Mongolia by five fresh horses a day in order to reach the capital at Karakorum in time for the installation of the third Great Khan, Guyuk (r. 1246–1248) in July and August.

In this selection from his *History of the Mongols*, John writes of his arrival in Mongolia for the installation of Guyuk (here written as Cuyuc). In what ways does John's account change or expand your understanding of the Mongols? Was John a good observer? How does he compensate for his ignorance (as an outside observer) of Mongol society and culture? In what ways does he remain a victim of his outsider status?

Thinking Historically

How would you characterize John's moral stance towards the Mongols? Consider your own moral judgment, if any, of the Mongols. How is it related to your historical understanding?

... On our arrival Cuyuc had us given a tent and provisions, such as it is the custom for the Tartars to give, but they treated us better than other envoys. Nevertheless we were not invited to visit him for he had not yet been elected, nor did he yet concern himself with the government. The translation of the Lord Pope's letter, however, and the things I had said had been sent to him by Bati. After we had stayed there for five or six days he sent us to his mother where the solemn court was assembling. By the time we got there a large pavilion had already been put up made of white velvet, and in my opinion it was so big that more than two thousand men could have got into it. Around it had been erected a wooden palisade, on which various designs were painted. On the second or third day we went with the Tartars who had been appointed to look after us and there all the chiefs were assembled and each one was riding with his followers among the hills and over the plains round about.

On the first day they were all clothed in white velvet, on the second in red — that day Cuyuc came to the tent — on the third day they were all in blue velvet, and on the fourth in the finest brocade. In the palisade round the pavilion were two large gates, through one of which the Emperor alone had the right to enter and there were no guards placed at it although it was open, for no one dare enter or leave by it; through the other gate all those who were granted admittance entered and there were guards there with swords and bows and arrows. . . . The chiefs went about everywhere armed and accompanied by a number of their men, but none, unless their group of ten was complete, could go as far as the horses; indeed those who attempted to do so were severely beaten. There were many of them who had, as far as I could judge, about twenty marks' worth of gold on their bits, breastplates, saddles, and cruppers. The chiefs held their conference inside the tent and, so I believe, conducted the election. All the other people however were a long way away outside the aforementioned palisade. There they remained until almost midday and then they began to drink mare's milk and they drank until the evening, so much that it was amazing to see. We were invited inside and they gave us mead as we would not take mare's milk. They did this to show us great honour, but they kept on plying us with drinks to such an extent that we could not possibly stand it, not being used to it, so we gave them to understand that it was disagreeable to us and they left off pressing us.

Outside were Duke Jerozlaus of Susdal in Russia and several chiefs of the Kitayans and Solangi, also two sons of the King of Georgia, the ambassador of the Caliph of Baghdad, who was a Sultan, and more than ten other Sultans of the Saracens, so I believe and so we were told by the stewards. There were more than four thousand envoys there, counting those who were carrying tribute, those who were bringing gifts, the Sultans and other chiefs who were coming to submit to them, those summoned by the Tartars and the governors of territories. All these were put together outside the palisade and they were given drinks at the same time, but when we were outside with them we and Duke Jerozlaus were always given the best places. I think, if I remember rightly, that we had been there a good four weeks when, as I believe, the election took place; the result however was not made public at that time; the chief ground for my supposition was that whenever Cuyuc left the tent they sang before him and as long as he remained outside they dipped to him beautiful rods on the top of which was scarlet wool, which they did not do for any of the other chiefs. They call this court the Sira Orda.

Leaving there we rode all together for three or four leagues to another place, where on a pleasant plain near a river among the mountains another tent had been set up, which is called by them the Golden Orda, it was here that Cuyuc was to be enthroned on the feast of the Assumption of Our Lady. . . .

At that place we were summoned into the presence of the Emperor, and Chingay the protonotary wrote down our names and the names of those who had sent us, also the names of the chief of the Solangi and of others, and then calling out in a loud voice he recited them before the Emperor and all the chiefs. When this was finished each one of us genuflected four times on the left knee and they warned us not to touch the lower part of the threshold. After we had been most thoroughly searched for knives and they had found nothing at all, we entered by a door on the east side, for no one dare enter from the west with the sole exception of the Emperor or, if it is a chief's tent, the chief; those of lower rank do not pay much attention to such things. This was the first time since Cuyuc had been made Emperor that we had entered his tent in his presence. He also received all the envoys in that place, but very few entered his tent.

So many gifts were bestowed by the envoys there that it was marvellous to behold — gifts of silk, samite, velvet, brocade, girdles of silk threaded with gold, choice furs, and other presents. The Emperor was also given a sunshade or little awning such as is carried over his head, and it was all decorated with precious stones. . . .

Leaving there we went to another place where a wonderful tent had been set up all of red velvet, and this had been given by the Kitayans; there also we were taken inside. Whenever we went in we were given mead and wine to drink, and cooked meat was offered us if we wished to have it. A lofty platform of boards had been erected, on which the Emperor's throne was placed. The throne, which was of ivory, was wonderfully carved and there was also gold on it, and precious stones, if I remember rightly, and pearls. Steps led up to it and it was rounded behind. Benches were also placed round the throne, and here the ladies sat in their seats on the left; nobody, however, sat on the right, but the chiefs were on benches in the middle and the rest of the people sat beyond them. Every day a great crowd of ladies came.

Finally, after some time, John was to be brought again before the Emperor. When he heard from them that we had come to him he ordered us to go back to his mother, the reason being that he wished on the following day to raise his banner against the whole of the Western world — we were told this definitely by men who knew . . . — and he wanted us to be kept in ignorance of this. On our return we stayed for a few days, then we went back to him again and remained with him for a good month, enduring such hunger and thirst that we could scarcely keep alive, for the food provided for four was barely sufficient for one, moreover, we were unable to find anything to buy, for the market was a very long way off. If the Lord had not sent us a certain Russian, by name Cosmas, a goldsmith and a great favourite of the Emperor, who supported us to some extent, we would, I believe, have died, unless the Lord had helped us in some other way. . . .

After this the Emperor sent for us, and through Chingay his protonotary told us to write down what we had to say and our business, and give it to him. We did this and wrote out for him all that we said earlier to Bati. . . . A few days passed by; then he had us summoned again and told us through Kadac, the procurator of the whole empire, in the presence of Bala and Chingay his protonotaries and many other scribes, to say all we had to say: We did this willingly and gladly. Our interpreter on this as on the previous occasion was Temer, a knight of Jerozlaus': and there were also present a cleric who was with him and another cleric who was with the Emperor. On this occasion we were asked if there were any people with the Lord Pope who understood the writing of the Russians or Saracens or even of the Tartars. We gave answer that we used neither the Ruthenian nor Saracen writing; there were however Saracens in the country but they were a long way from the Lord Pope; but we said that it seemed to us that the most expedient course would be for them to write in Tartar and translate it for us, and we would write it down carefully in our own script and we would take both the letter and the translation to the Lord Pope. Thereupon they left us to go to the Emperor.

On St. Martin's day we were again summoned, and Kadac, Chingay, and Bala, the aforementioned secretaries, came to us and translated the letter for us word by word. When we had written it in Latin, they had it translated so that they might hear a phrase at a time, for they wanted to know if we had made a mistake in any word. When both letters were written, they made us read it once and a second time in case we had left out anything. . . .

It is the custom for the Emperor of the Tartars never to speak to a foreigner, however important he may be, except through an intermediary, and he listens and gives his answer, also through the intermediary. Whenever his subjects have any business to bring before Kadac, or while they are listening to the Emperor's reply, they stay on their knees until the end of the conversation, however important they may be. It is not possible nor indeed is it the custom for anyone to say anything about any matter after the Emperor has declared his decision. This Emperor not only has a procurator and protonotaries and secretaries, but all officials for dealing with both public and private matters, except that he has no advocates, for everything is settled according to the decision of the Emperor without the turmoil of legal trials. The other princes of the Tartars do the same in those matters concerning them.

The present Emperor may be forty or forty-five years old or more; he is of medium height, very intelligent, and extremely shrewd, and most serious and grave in his manner. He is never seen to laugh for a slight cause nor to indulge in any frivolity, so we were told by the Christians who are constantly with him. The Christians of his household also told us that they firmly believed he was about to become a Christian, and they have clear evidence of this, for he maintains Christian clerics and provides them with supplies of Christian things; in addition he always has a chapel before his chief tent and they sing openly and in public and beat the board for services after the Greek fashion like other Christians, however big a crowd of Tartars or other men be there. The other chiefs do not behave like this.

. . . on the feast of St. Brice [November 13th], they gave us a permit to depart and a letter sealed with the Emperor's seal, and sent us to the Emperor's mother. She gave each of us a fox-skin cloak, which had the fur outside and was lined inside, and a length of velvet; our Tartars stole a good yard from each of the pieces of velvet and from the piece given to our servant they stole more than half. This did not escape our notice, but we preferred not to make a fuss about it.

We then set out on the return journey. . . .

REFLECTIONS

The great Chinese artist Cheng Ssu-hsaio (1241–1318) continued to paint his delicate Chinese orchids in the years after the Mongol defeat of the Sung dynasty, under the alien rule of Khubilai Khan (r. 1260–1294), the fifth Great Khan and the founder of the Mongol Yuan dynasty of China. But when Cheng was asked why he always painted the orchids without earth around their roots, he replied that the earth had been stolen by the barbarians.

Just as it would be a mistake to see a fifth-generation Mongol ruler like Khubilai as a barbarian, it would also be a mistake to assume that Cheng's hardened resistance remained the norm. In fact, a younger generation of artists found opportunity and even freedom in Khubilai's China. Khubilai appointed some of the most famous Chinese painters of his era to positions of government — Ministries of War, Public

Works, Justice, Personnel, Imperial Sacrifices — actively recruiting the bright young men, artists and intellectuals, for his government. While some painters catered to the Mongol elite's inclination for paintings of horses, others relished the wider range of subjects allowed by a regime free of highly cultivated prejudices.

If conquest invariably brings charges of barbarism, it also eventually turns to issues of government and administration. Administrators need officials. Though Khubilai abolished the Chinese civil service examination system because it would have forced him to rely on Chinese officials, the Chinese language, and an educational system based on the Chinese classics, he actively sought ways of governing that were neither too Chinese nor too Mongolian. Typically, he promulgated a Chinese alphabet that was based on Tibetan, hoping that its phonetic symbols would make communication easier and less classical. Many of his achievements were unintended. While his officials continued to use Chinese characters and the Uighur script, the Yüan dynasty witnessed a flowering of literary culture, including theater and novels. For some, no doubt, the wind from the steppe blew away the dust and cobwebs that had accumulated for too long.

Our judgment of the Mongols depends to a great extent on the period of Mongol history we consider. But while it is easy to condemn Chingis Khan and the initial conquests and praise the later enlightened governance, two considerations come to mind. First, in the great sweep of history, many "barbarians" became benign, even indulgent, administrators. Second, the Mongols were not unique in making that transition.

Before the Mongols, the Vikings had already made the transition from raiding to trading and from conquering to colonizing. In fact, as Cunliffe points out, the Vikings had always been farmer-sailors who were as hungry for land as for plunder. Unlike the Mongols who were born on horses, continually picking up and remaking camp in new pastureland, the Vikings became nomadic in emergencies when a search for new settlements was necessary.

The memory of Viking assaults also faded faster than that of the Mongols. The Viking Rus had the Mongols to thank. The Rus of Viking cities like Novgorod became the national heroes of anti-Mongol Russian legend. The Viking Rus became the Russians. In Europe, too, the descendants of Vikings helped establish new national identities. The last great Viking king, Harald the Hard Ruler, "Thunderbolt of the North," won back his father's crown as King of Norway after preparing himself in Russian trading cities and Byzantine courts. He married a Russian princess and fought for the Byzantines in Asia Minor, Jerusalem, and the Caucasus Mountains. In 1066, this King of Norway lost his control of England when he was killed by an English earl. A few days later the new English king was killed by William Duke of

Normandy, a Viking son who had previously conquered much of France. Norman rule was to last over a hundred years, from 1066 to 1215, and create a new English identity.

In the North Atlantic and North America the Vikings traded with indigenous peoples whom they called "wretches" and later generations were to call Eskimos, Inuit, and Indians. But the land did not allow much contact and they learned very little from each other.

At the end of the day, history is neither moral nor immoral. History is what happened, for better or worse, and moralistic history is generally bad history. The Vikings and Mongols of our period were no more morally frozen in time than were the Christian and Muslim crusaders of the same era who visited such violence upon each other.

Just as the role of nomads and settlers changes over time, so does the degree to which a people are particularly aggressive or peaceful. It is hard to imagine a more fearful people than the Mongols of the thirteenth century or the Vikings of the tenth century. Yet modern Scandinavia, Iceland, and Mongolia are among the most peaceful places on the planet.

We can study societies or periods marked by unusually high levels of violence in order to understand the causes and avoid the repetition. History never offers simple lessons, but without its rich sources for explanation and reflection, we sail adrift bereft of markers or direction. Indeed, as history teaches us the consequences of our acts, we might say that without history there can hardly be morality.

The Black Death

Afro-Eurasia, 1346–1350 C.E.

HISTORICAL CONTEXT

The Mongol peace that made the Persian Ilkhanid dynasty (1256–1353) and the Chinese Yuan dynasty (1279–1368) sister empires nurtured a level of economic exchange and artistic communication greater than in the most cosmopolitan days of the early Roman/Han Silk Road. But the new caravan routes that spanned Central Asia could carry microbes as well as people. The plague that had long been endemic in country rats spread by fleas to city rats and other animals, including humans. As early as 1346, travelers reported millions killed in China, Central Asia, and the Middle East. In Europe and Egypt, approximately a third of the population perished. In some cities, the death toll was greater than half. This pandemic plague of 1348–1350 is sometimes called the Black Death, after the discolored wounds it caused.

THINKING HISTORICALLY
Considering Cause and Effect

The study of history, like the practice of medicine, is a process of understanding the causes of certain effects. In medicine the effects are diseases; in history they are more varied events. Nevertheless, understanding the causes of things is central to both disciplines. For medical specialists the goal of understanding causes is implicitly a part of the process of finding a cure. Historians rarely envision "cures" for social ills, but many believe that an understanding of cause and effect can improve society's chances of progress.

Still, the most hopeful medical researcher or historian would agree that the process of relating cause and effect, of finding causes and explaining effects, is fraught with difficulties. We will explore some of those difficulties in this chapter.

MARK WHEELIS

Biological Warfare at the 1346 Siege of Caffa

We are used to thinking of biological warfare as a recently developed threat. This article, published in a journal for public health professionals, suggests a longer history. According to the author, how and where did the Black Death originate? What was the significance of the Mongol siege of Caffa in 1346? The author draws on the contemporary account of the Black Death by Gabriele de Mussis. On what points does he agree and disagree with de Mussis?

Thinking Historically

The author of this selection, a professor of microbiology at the University of California, was trained as a bacterial physiologist and geneticist, but for more than the last ten years his research has concentrated on the history and control of biological weapons. Notice how he explains the causes of such events as the spread of plague and the infection at Caffa. Would you call his way of finding causes the method of a medical researcher or a historian, or does he employ the methods of both? If you see a distinction, try to note the places where he is thinking more like a medical scientist and those where he is thinking more like a historian.

The Black Death, which swept through Europe, the Near East, and North Africa in the mid-fourteenth-century, was probably the greatest public health disaster in recorded history and one of the most dramatic examples ever of emerging or reemerging disease. Europe lost an

Mark Wheelis, "Biological Warfare at the 1346 Siege of Caffa," *Emerging Infectious Diseases,* 8, no. 9 (September, 2002): 971–75. The journal is published by the U.S. Centers for Disease Control and Prevention (C.D.C.), Atlanta, and is also available online at http://www.cdc.gov/ncidod/EID/vol8no9/01-0536.htm.

estimated one quarter to one third of its population, and the mortality in North Africa and the Near East was comparable. China, India, and the rest of the Far East are commonly believed to have also been severely affected, but little evidence supports that belief.

A principal source on the origin of the Black Death is a memoir by the Italian Gabriele de' Mussis. This memoir has been published several times in its original Latin and has recently been translated into English (although brief passages have been previously published in translation). This narrative contains some startling assertions: that the Mongol army hurled plague-infected cadavers into the besieged Crimean city of Caffa, thereby transmitting the disease to the inhabitants; and that fleeing survivors of the siege spread plague from Caffa to the Mediterranean Basin. If this account is correct, Caffa should be recognized as the site of the most spectacular incident of biological warfare ever, with the Black Death as its disastrous consequence. After analyzing these claims, I have concluded that it is plausible that the biological attack took place as described and was responsible for infecting the inhabitants of Caffa; however, the event was unimportant in the spread of the plague pandemic.

Origin of the Fourteenth-Century Pandemic

The disease that caused this catastrophic pandemic has, since Hecker, generally been considered to have been a plague, a zoonotic disease caused by the gram-negative bacterium *Yersinia pestis,* the principal reservoir for which is wild rodents. The ultimate origin of the Black Death is uncertain — China, Mongolia, India, central Asia, and southern Russia have all been suggested. Known fourteenth-century sources are of little help; they refer repeatedly to an eastern origin, but none of the reports is firsthand. Historians generally agree that the outbreak moved west out of the steppes north of the Black and Caspian Seas, and its spread through Europe and the Middle East is fairly well documented (see Map 12.1). However, despite more than a century of speculation about an ultimate origin further east, the requisite scholarship using Chinese and central Asian sources has yet to be done. In any event, the Crimea clearly played a pivotal role as the proximal source from which the Mediterranean Basin was infected.

Historical Background to the Siege of Caffa

Caffa (now Feodosija, Ukraine) was established by Genoa in 1266 by agreement with the Kahn of the Golden Horde. It was the main port for the great Genoese merchant ships, which connected there to a coastal shipping industry to Tana (now Azov, Russia) on the Don

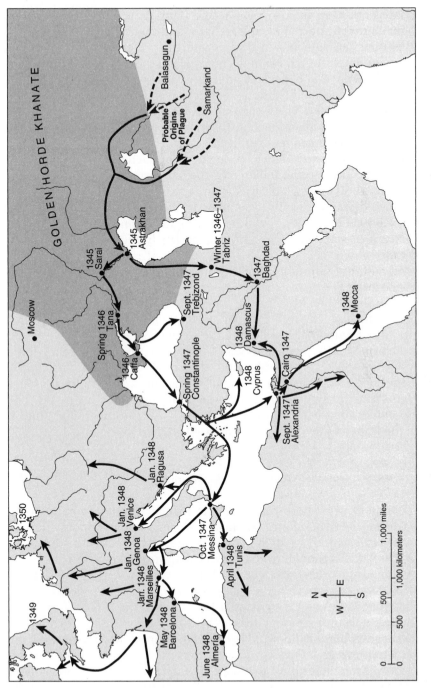

Map 12.1 Tentative Chronology of the Initial Spread of Plague in the Mid-Fourteenth Century.

River. Trade along the Don connected Tana to Central Russia, and overland caravan routes linked it to Sarai and thence to the Far East.

Relations between Italian traders and their Mongol hosts were uneasy, and in 1307 Toqtai, Kahn of the Golden Horde, arrested the Italian residents of Sarai, and besieged Caffa. The cause was apparently Toqtai's displeasure at the Italian trade in Turkic slaves (sold for soldiers to the Mameluke Sultanate). The Genoese resisted for a year, but in 1308 set fire to their city and abandoned it. Relations between the Italians and the Golden Horde remained tense until Toqtai's death in 1312.

Toqtai's successor, Özbeg, welcomed the Genoese back, and also ceded land at Tana to the Italians for the expansion of their trading enterprise. By the 1340s, Caffa was again a thriving city, heavily fortified within two concentric walls. The inner wall enclosed 6,000 houses, the outer 11,000. The city's population was highly cosmopolitan, including Genoese, Venetian, Greeks, Armenians, Jews, Mongols, and Turkic peoples.

In 1343 the Mongols under Janibeg (who succeeded Özbeg in 1340) besieged Caffa and the Italian enclave at Tana following a brawl between Italians and Muslims in Tana. The Italian merchants in Tana fled to Caffa (which, by virtue of its location directly on the coast, maintained maritime access despite the siege). The siege of Caffa lasted until February 1344, when it was lifted after an Italian relief force killed 15,000 Mongol troops and destroyed their siege machines. Janibeg renewed the siege in 1345 but was again forced to lift it after a year, this time by an epidemic of plague that devastated his forces. The Italians blockaded Mongol ports, forcing Janibeg to negotiate, and in 1347 the Italians were allowed to reestablish their colony in Tana.

Gabriele de' Mussis

Gabriele de' Mussis, born circa 1280, practiced as a notary in the town of Piacenza, over the mountains just north of Genoa. Tononi summarizes the little we know of him. His practice was active in the years 1300–1349. He is thought to have died in approximately 1356.

Although Henschel thought de' Mussis was present at the siege of Caffa, Tononi asserts that the Piacenza archives contain deeds signed by de' Mussis spanning the period 1344 through the first half of 1346. While this does not rule out travel to Caffa in late 1346, textual evidence suggests that he did not. He does not claim to have witnessed any of the Asian events he describes and often uses a passive voice for descriptions. After describing the siege of Caffa, de' Mussis goes on to say, "Now it is time that we passed from east to west to discuss all the things which we ourselves have seen. . . ."

The Narrative of Gabriele de' Mussis

The de' Mussis account is presumed to have been written in 1348 or early 1349 because of its immediacy and the narrow time period described. The original is lost, but a copy is included in a compilation of historical and geographic accounts by various authors, dating from approximately 1367. The account begins with an introductory comment by the scribe who copied the documents: "In the name of God, Amen. Here begins an account of the disease or mortality which occurred in 1348, put together by Gabrielem de Mussis of Piacenza."

The narrative begins with an apocalyptic speech by God, lamenting the depravity into which humanity has fallen and describing the retribution intended. It goes on:

". . . In 1346, in the countries of the East, countless numbers of Tartars and Saracens were struck down by a mysterious illness which brought sudden death. Within these countries broad regions, far-spreading provinces, magnificent kingdoms, cities, towns and settlements, ground down by illness and devoured by dreadful death, were soon stripped of their inhabitants. An eastern settlement under the rule of the Tartars called Tana, which lay to the north of Constantinople and was much frequented by Italian merchants, was totally abandoned after an incident there which led to its being besieged and attacked by hordes of Tartars who gathered in a short space of time. The Christian merchants, who had been driven out by force, were so terrified of the power of the Tartars that, to save themselves and their belongings, they fled in an armed ship to Caffa, a settlement in the same part of the world which had been founded long ago by the Genoese.

"Oh God! See how the heathen Tartar races, pouring together from all sides, suddenly invested the city of Caffa and besieged the trapped Christians there for almost three years. There, hemmed in by an immense army, they could hardly draw breath, although food could be shipped in, which offered them some hope. But behold, the whole army was affected by a disease which overran the Tartars and killed thousands upon thousands every day. It was as though arrows were raining down from heaven to strike and crush the Tartars' arrogance. All medical advice and attention was useless; the Tartars died as soon as the signs of disease appeared on their bodies: swellings in the armpit or groin caused by coagulating humours, followed by a putrid fever.

"The dying Tartars, stunned and stupefied by the immensity of the disaster brought about by the disease, and realizing that they had no hope of escape, lost interest in the siege. But they ordered corpses to be placed in catapults[1] and lobbed into the city in the hope that the intolerable stench would kill everyone inside.[2] What seemed like mountains of dead were thrown into the city, and the Christians could not hide or flee or escape from them, although they dumped as many of the bodies as they could in the sea. And soon the rotting corpses tainted the air and poisoned the water supply, and the stench was so overwhelming that hardly one in several thousand was in a position to flee the remains of the Tartar army. Moreover one infected man could carry the poison to others, and infect people and places with the disease by look alone. No one knew, or could discover, a means of defense.

"Thus almost everyone who had been in the East, or in the regions to the south and north, fell victim to sudden death after contracting this pestilential disease, as if struck by a lethal arrow which raised a tumor on their bodies. The scale of the mortality and the form which it took persuaded those who lived, weeping and lamenting, through the bitter events of 1346 to 1348 — the Chinese, Indians, Persians, Medes, Kurds, Armenians, Cilicians, Georgians, Mesopotamians, Nubians, Ethiopians, Turks, Egyptians, Arabs, Saracens, and Greeks (for almost all the East has been affected) — that the last judgement had come.

". . . As it happened, among those who escaped from Caffa by boat were a few sailors who had been infected with the poisonous disease. Some boats were bound for Genoa, others went to Venice and to other Christian areas. When the sailors reached these places and mixed with the people there, it was as if they had brought evil spirits with them: every city, every settlement, every place was poisoned by the contagious pestilence, and their inhabitants, both men and women, died suddenly. And when one person had contracted the illness, he poisoned his whole family even as he fell and died, so that those preparing to bury his body were seized by death in the same way. Thus death entered through the windows, and as cities and towns were depopulated their inhabitants mourned their dead neighbours."

The account closes with an extended description of the plague in Piacenza, and a reprise of the apocalyptic vision with which it begins.

---

[1]Technically trebuchets, not catapults. Catapults hurl objects by the release of tension on twisted cordage; they are not capable of hurling loads over a few dozen kilograms. Trebuchets are counter-weight-driven hurling machines, very effective for throwing ammunition weighing a hundred kilos or more.

[2]Medieval society lacked a coherent theory of disease causation. Three notions coexisted in a somewhat contradictory mixture: 1) disease was a divine punishment for individual or collective transgression: 2) disease was the result of "miasma," or the stench of decay: and 3) disease was the result of person-to-person contagion.

Commentary

In this narrative, de' Mussis makes two important claims about the siege of Caffa and the Black Death: that plague was transmitted to Europeans by the hurling of diseased cadavers into the besieged city of Caffa and that Italians fleeing from Caffa brought it to the Mediterranean ports.

Biological Warfare at Caffa

De' Mussis's account is probably secondhand and is uncorroborated; however, he seems, in general, to be a reliable source, and as a Piacenzian he would have had access to eyewitnesses of the siege. Several considerations incline me to trust his account: this was probably not the only, nor the first, instance of apparent attempts to transmit disease by hurling biological material into besieged cities; it was within the technical capabilities of besieging armies of the time; and it is consistent with medieval notions of disease causality.

Tentatively accepting that the attack took place as described, we can consider two principal hypotheses for the entry of plague into the city: it might, as de' Mussis asserts, have been transmitted by the hurling of plague cadavers; or it might have entered by rodent-to-rodent transmission from the Mongol encampments into the city.

Diseased cadavers hurled into the city could easily have transmitted plague, as defenders handled the cadavers during disposal. Contact with infected material is a known mechanism of transmission; for instance, among 284 cases of plague in the United States in 1970–1995 for which a mechanism of transmission could be reasonably inferred, 20 percent were thought to be by direct contact. Such transmission would have been especially likely at Caffa, where cadavers would have been badly mangled by being hurled, and many of the defenders probably had cut or abraded hands from coping with the bombardment. Very large numbers of cadavers were possibly involved, greatly increasing the opportunity for disease transmission. Since disposal of the bodies of victims in a major outbreak of lethal disease is always a problem, the Mongol forces may have used their hurling machines as a solution to their mortuary problem, in which case many thousands of cadavers could have been involved. de' Mussis's description of "mountains of dead" might have been quite literally true.

Thus it seems plausible that the events recounted by de' Mussis could have been an effective means of transmission of plague into the city. The alternative, rodent-to-rodent transmission from the Mongol encampments into the city, is less likely. Besieging forces must have camped at least a kilometer away from the city walls. This distance is necessary to have a healthy margin of safety from arrows and artillery and to provide space for logistical support and other military activities between the encampments and the front lines. Front-line location must have been approximately 250–300 m from the walls; trebuchets are known from modern reconstruction to be capable of hurling 100 kg more than 200 m, and historical sources claim 300 m as the working range of large machines. Thus, the bulk of rodent nests associated with the besieging armies would have been located a kilometer or more away from the cities, and none would have likely been closer than 250 m. Rats are quite sedentary and rarely venture more than a few tens of meters from their nest. It is thus unlikely that there was any contact between the rat populations within and outside the walls.

Given the many uncertainties, any conclusion must remain tentative. However, the considerations above suggest that the hurling of plague cadavers might well have occurred as de' Mussis claimed, and if so, that this biological attack was probably responsible for the transmission of the disease from the besiegers to the besieged. Thus, this early act of biological warfare, if such it were, appears to have been spectacularly successful in producing casualties, although of no strategic importance (the city remained in Italian hands, and the Mongols abandoned the siege).

Crimea as the Source of European and Near Eastern Plague

There has never been any doubt that plague entered the Mediterranean from the Crimea, following established maritime trade routes. Rat infestations in the holds of cargo ships would have been highly susceptible to the rapid spread of plague, and even if most rats died during the voyage, they would have left abundant hungry fleas that would infect humans unpacking the holds. Shore rats foraging on board recently arrived ships would also become infected, transmitting plague to city rat populations.

Plague appears to have been spread in a stepwise fashion, on many ships rather than on a few [see Map 12.1], taking over a year to reach Europe from the Crimea. This conclusion seems fairly firm, as the dates for the arrival of plague in Constantinople and more westerly cities are reasonably certain. Thus de' Mussis was probably mistaken in attributing the Black Death to fleeing survivors of Caffa, who should not have needed more than a few months to return to Italy.

Furthermore, a number of other Crimean ports were under Mongol control, making it unlikely that Caffa was the only source of infected ships heading west. And the overland caravan routes to the Middle East from Serai and Astrakhan insured that plague was also spreading south (Map 12.1), whence it would have entered Europe in any case. The siege of Caffa and its gruesome finale thus are unlikely to have been seriously implicated in the transmission of plague from the Black Sea to Europe.

Conclusion

Gabriele de' Mussis's account of the origin and spread of plague appears to be consistent with most known facts, although mistaken in its claim that plague arrived in Italy directly from the Crimea. His account of biological attack is plausible, consistent with the technology of the time, and it provides the best explanation of disease transmission into besieged Caffa. This thus appears to be one of the first biological attacks recorded and among the most successful of all time.

However, it is unlikely that the attack had a decisive role in the spread of plague to Europe. Much maritime commerce probably continued throughout this period from other Crimean ports. Overland caravan routes to the Middle East were also unaffected. Thus, refugees from Caffa would most likely have constituted only one of several streams of infected ships and caravans leaving the region. The siege of Caffa, for all of its dramatic appeal, probably had no more than anecdotal importance in the spread of plague, a macabre incident in terrifying times.

Despite its historical unimportance, the siege of Caffa is a powerful reminder of the horrific consequences when disease is successfully used as a weapon. The Japanese use of plague as a weapon in World War II and the huge Soviet stockpiles of *Y. pestis* prepared for use in an all-out war further remind us that plague remains a very real problem for modern arms control, six and a half centuries later.

$$\boxed{76}$$

GABRIELE DE' MUSSIS

Origins of the Black Death

Gabriele de' Mussis (d. 1356) was a lawyer who lived in the northern Italian city of Piacenza. The previous reading introduced you to de' Mussis and the importance of his history of the Black Death. Since Wheelis quoted abundantly from the story of the siege of Caffa, we pick up the story in de' Mussis's words of the spread of the plague to Europe where, as he wrote, he had direct evidence. How would you

The Black Death, trans. and ed. Rosemary Horrox (Manchester, England: Manchester University Press, 1994), 18–26.

rate de' Mussis as an eyewitness observer? According to his evidence, how did the Black Death spread in Italy? How deadly was it?

Thinking Historically

As in the previous selection, there are two causal chains in this account, but in this case they are not medical and historical. Rather, reminiscent of the readings on the First Crusade, they are divine and human chains of causation. What according to the author were the divine or religious causes of the Black Death? What were the human, physical, or scientific causes? What remedies does each type of cause call for?

Now it is time that we passed from east to west, to discuss all the things which we ourselves have seen, or known, or consider likely on the basis of the evidence, and, by so doing, to show forth the terrifying judgements of God. Listen everybody, and it will set tears pouring from your eyes. For the Almighty has said: "I shall wipe man, whom I created, off the face of the earth. Because he is flesh and blood, let him be turned to dust and ashes. My spirit shall not remain among man."

— "What are you thinking of, merciful God, thus to destroy your creation and the human race; to order and command its sudden annihilation in this way? What has become of your mercy; the faith of our fathers; the blessed virgin, who holds sinners in her lap; the precious blood of the martyrs; the worthy army of confessors and virgins; the whole host of paradise, who pray ceaselessly for sinners; the most precious death of Christ on the cross and our wonderful redemption? Kind God, I beg that your anger may cease, that you do not destroy sinners in this way, and, because you desire mercy rather than sacrifice, that you turn away all evil from the penitent, and do not allow the just to be condemned with the unjust."

— "I hear you, sinner, dropping words into my ears. I bid you weep. The time for mercy has passed. I, God, am called to vengeance. It is my pleasure to take revenge on sin and wickedness. I shall give my signs to the dying, let them take steps to provide for the health of their souls."

As it happened, among those who escaped from Caffa by boat were a few sailors who had been infected with the poisonous disease. Some boats were bound for Genoa, others went to Venice and to other Christian areas. . . .

— "We Genoese and Venetians bear the responsibility for revealing the judgements of God. Alas, once our ships had brought us to port we went to our homes. And because we had been delayed by tragic events, and because among us there were scarcely ten survivors from a thousand sailors, relations, kinsmen and neighbours flocked to us from all sides. But, to our anguish, we were carrying the darts of death. While they hugged and kissed us we were spreading poison from our lips even as we spoke."

When they returned to their own folk, these people speedily poisoned the whole family, and within three days the afflicted family would succumb to the dart of death. Mass funerals had to be held and there was not enough room to bury the growing numbers of dead. Priests and doctors, upon whom most of the care of the sick devolved, had their hands full in visiting the sick and, alas, by the time they left they too had been infected and followed the dead immediately to the grave. Oh fathers! Oh mothers! Oh children and wives! For a long time prosperity preserved you from harm, but one grave now covers you and the unfortunate alike. You who enjoyed the world and upon whom pleasure and prosperity smiled, who mingled joys with follies, the same tomb receives you and you are handed over as food for worms. Oh hard death, impious death, bitter death, cruel death, who divides parents, divorces spouses, parts children, separates brothers and sisters. We bewail our wretched plight. The past has devoured us, the present is gnawing our entrails, the future threatens yet greater dangers. What we laboured to amass with feverish activity, we have lost in one hour.

Where are the fine clothes of gilded youth? Where is nobility and the courage of fighters, where the mature wisdom of elders and the regal throng of great ladies, where the piles of treasure and precious stones? Alas! All have been destroyed; thrust aside by death. To whom shall we turn, who can help us? To flee is impossible, to hide futile. Cities, fortresses, fields, woods, highways and rivers are ringed by thieves — which is to say by evil spirits, the executioners of the supreme Judge, preparing endless punishments for us all.

We can unfold a terrifying event which happened when an army was camped near Genoa. Four of the soldiers left the force in search of plunder and made their way to Rivarolo on the coast, where the disease had killed all the inhabitants. Finding the houses shut up, and no one about, they broke into one of the houses and stole a fleece which they found on a bed. They then rejoined the army and on the following night the four of them bedded down under the fleece. When morning comes it finds them dead. As a result everyone panicked, and thereafter nobody would use the goods and clothes of the dead, or even handle them, but rejected them outright.

Scarcely one in seven of the Genoese survived. In Venice, where an inquiry was held into the mortality, it was found that more than 70 percent of the people had died, and that within a short period 20 out of 24 excellent physicians had died. The rest of Italy, Sicily, and Apulia and the neighbouring regions maintain that they have been virtually emptied of inhabitants. The people of Florence, Pisa, and Lucca, finding themselves bereft of their fellow residents, emphasise their losses. The Roman Curia at Avignon, the provinces on both sides of the Rhône, Spain,

France, and the Empire cry up their griefs and disasters — all of which makes it extraordinarily difficult for me to give an accurate picture.

By contrast, what befell the Saracens can be established from trust-worthy accounts. In the city of Babylon alone (the heart of the Sultan's power), 480,000 of his subjects are said to have been carried off by dis-ease in less than three months in 1348 — and this is known from the Sul-tan's register which records the names of the dead, because he receives a gold bezant for each person buried. I am silent about Damascus and his other cities, where the number of dead was infinite. In the other countries of the East, which are so vast that it takes three years to ride across them and which have a population of 10,000 for every one inhabitant of the west, it is credibly reported that countless people have died.

Everyone has a responsibility to keep some record of the disease and the deaths, and because I am myself from Piacenza I have been urged to write more about what happened there in 1348. . . .

I don't know where to begin. Cries and laments arise on all sides. Day after day one sees the Cross and the Host[1] being carried about the city, and countless dead being buried. The ensuing mortality was so great that people could scarcely snatch breath. The living made prepa-rations for their burial, and because there was not enough room for in-dividual graves, pits had to be dug in colonnades and piazzas, where nobody had ever been buried before. It often happened that man and wife, father and son, mother and daughter, and soon the whole house-hold and many neighbours, were buried together in one place. The same thing happened in Castell' Arquato and Viguzzolo and in the other towns, villages, cities, and settlements, and last of all in the Val Tidone, where they had hitherto escaped the plague.

Very many people died. One Oberto de Sasso, who had come from the infected neighbourhood around the church of the Franciscans, wished to make his will and accordingly summoned a notary and his neighbours as witnesses, all of whom, more than sixty of them, died soon after. At this time the Dominican friar Syfredo de Bardis, a man of prudence and great learning who had visited the Holy Sepulchre, also died, along with 23 brothers of the same house. There also died within a short time the Franciscan friar Bertolino Coxadocha of Piacenza, renowned for his learning and many virtues, along with 24 brothers of the same house, nine of them on one day; seven of the Augustinians; the Carmelite friar Francesco Todischi with six of his brethren; four of the order of Mary; more than sixty prelates and parish priests from the city and district of Piacenza; many nobles; countless young people; numberless women, particularly those who were pregnant. It is too dis-tressing to recite any more, or to lay bare the wounds inflicted by so great a disaster.

---

[1]The consecrated Eucharistic wafer. The reference is to priests taking the last sacrament to the dying.

Let all creation tremble with fear before the judgement of God. Let human frailty submit to its creator. May a greater grief be kindled in all hearts, and tears well up in all eyes as future ages hear what happened in this disaster. When one person lay sick in a house no one would come near. Even dear friends would hide themselves away, weeping. The physician would not visit. The priest, panic-stricken, administered the sacraments with fear and trembling.

Listen to the tearful voices of the sick: "Have pity, have pity, my friends. At least say something, now that the hand of God has touched me."

"Oh father, why have you abandoned me? Do you forget that I am your child?"

"Mother, where have you gone? Why are you now so cruel to me when only yesterday you were so kind? You fed me at your breast and carried me within your womb for nine months."

"My children, whom I brought up with toil and sweat, why have you run away?"

Man and wife reached out to each other, "Alas, once we slept happily together but now are separated and wretched."

And when the sick were in the throes of death, they still called out piteously to their family and neighbours, "Come here. I'm thirsty, bring me a drink of water. I'm still alive. Don't be frightened. Perhaps I won't die. Please hold me tight, hug my wasted body. You ought to be holding me in your arms."

At this, as everyone else kept their distance, somebody might take pity and leave a candle burning by the bed head as he fled. And when the victim had breathed his last, it was often the mother who shrouded her son and placed him in the coffin, or the husband who did the same for his wife, for everybody else refused to touch the dead body. . . .

I am overwhelmed, I can't go on. Everywhere one turns there is death and bitterness to be described. The hand of the Almighty strikes repeatedly, to greater and greater effect. The terrible judgement gains in power as time goes by.

— What shall we do? Kind Jesus, receive the souls of the dead, avert your gaze from our sins and blot out all our iniquities.

We know that whatever we suffer is the just reward of our sins. Now, therefore, when the Lord is enraged, embrace acts of penance, so that you do not stray from the right path and perish. Let the proud be humbled. Let misers, who withheld alms from the poor, blush for shame. Let the envious become zealous in almsgiving. Let lechers put aside their filthy habits and distinguish themselves in honest living. Let the raging and wrathful restrain themselves from violence. Let gluttons temper their appetites by fasting. Let the slaves of sloth arise and dress themselves in good works. Let adolescents and youths abandon their present delight in following fashion. Let there be good faith and equity among judges, and respect for the law among merchants. Let pettifogging lawyers study and grow wise before they put pen to paper. Let members of religious orders abandon hypocrisy. Let the dignity of prelates be put to better use. Let all of you hurry to set your feet on the way of salvation. And let the overweening vanity of great ladies, which so easily turns into voluptuousness, be bridled. It was against their arrogance that Isaiah inveighed: "Because the daughters of Sion are haughty, and have walked with stretched out necks and wanton glances of their eyes, and made a noise as they walked with their feet, and moved in a set pace. . . . Thy fairest men also shall fall by the sword: and thy valiant ones in battle. And her gates shall lament and mourn: and she shall sit desolate on the ground" [Isaiah 3.16–26]. This was directed against the pride of ladies and young people.

For the rest, so that the conditions, causes, and symptoms of this pestilential disease should be made plain to all, I have decided to set them out in writing. Those of both sexes who were in health, and in no fear of death, were struck by four savage blows to the flesh. First, out of the blue, a kind of chilly stiffness troubled their bodies. They felt a tingling sensation, as if they were being pricked by the points of arrows. The next stage was a fearsome attack which took the form of an extremely hard, solid boil. In some people this developed under the armpit and in others in the groin between the scrotum and the body. As it grew more solid, its burning heat caused the patients to fall into an acute and putrid fever, with severe headaches. As it intensified its extreme bitterness could have various effects. In some cases it gave rise to an intolerable stench. In others it brought vomiting of blood, or swellings near the place from which the corrupt humour arose: on the back, across the chest, near the thigh. Some people lay as if in a drunken stupor and could not be roused. Behold the swellings, the warning signs sent by the Lord.[2] All these people were in danger of dying. Some died on the very day the illness took possession of them, others on the next day, others — the majority — between the third and fifth day. There was no known remedy for the vomiting of blood. Those who fell into a coma, or suffered a swelling or the stink of corruption very rarely escaped. But from the fever it was sometimes possible to make a recovery. . . .

Truly, then was a time of bitterness and grief, which served to turn men to the Lord. I shall recount what happened. A warning was given by a certain holy person, who received it in a vision, that in cities, towns and other settlements, everyone, male and female alike, should gather in their parish church on three consecutive days and, each with a lighted candle in their hand, hear with great devotion the mass of the

---

[2]A pun: *bulla* is a swelling, but it is also the word for the papal seal, and hence for a papal document (or bull). De' Mussis is playing on the idea of the swelling characteristic of the plague being God's seal, notifying the victim of his imminent fate.

Blessed Anastasia, which is normally performed at dawn on Christmas day, and they should humbly beg for mercy, so that they might be delivered from the disease through the merits of the holy mass. Other people sought deliverance through the mediation of a blessed martyr; and others humbly turned to other saints, so that they might escape the abomination of disease. For among the aforesaid martyrs, some, as stories relate, are said to have died from repeated blows, and it was therefore the general opinion that they would be able to protect people against the arrows of death. Finally, in 1350, the most holy Pope Clement ordained a general indulgence, to be valid for a year, which remitted penance and guilt to all who were truly penitent and confessed. And as a result a numberless multitude of people made the pilgrimage to Rome, to visit with great reverence and devotion the basilicas of the blessed apostles Peter and Paul and St John.

Oh, most dearly beloved, let us therefore not be like vipers, growing ever more wicked, but let us rather hold up our hands to heaven to beg for mercy on us all, for who but God shall have mercy on us? With this, I make an end. May the heavenly physician heal our wounds — our spiritual rather than our bodily wounds. To whom be the blessing and the praise and the glory for ever and ever, Amen.

GIOVANNI BOCCACCIO

The Plague in Florence: *From* the Decameron

Giovanni Boccaccio* (1313–1375) was a poet in Florence, Italy, when the plague struck in 1348. His *Decameron*† is a collection of a hundred tales based on his experiences during the plague years. This selection is drawn from the Introduction. What does Boccaccio add to your understanding of the Black Death?

*boh KAH chee oh
†deh KAM uh rahn

Giovanni Boccaccio, *Decameron,* trans. G. H. McWilliam (Harmondsworth, England: Penguin, 1972), 50–58.

Thinking Historically

Compare Boccaccio's treatment of divine and human causes of the plague. Boccaccio not only muses on the causes of the plague; he also sees the plague as the cause of new forms of behavior. What were the behavioral effects of the plague according to Boccaccio?

I say, then, that the sum of thirteen hundred and forty-eight years had elapsed since the fruitful Incarnation of the Son of God, when the noble city of Florence, which for its great beauty excels all others in Italy, was visited by the deadly pestilence. Some say that it descended upon the human race through the influence of the heavenly bodies, others that it was a punishment signifying God's righteous anger at our iniquitous way of life. But whatever its cause, it had originated some years earlier in the East, where it had claimed countless lives before it unhappily spread westward, growing in strength as it swept relentlessly on from one place to the next.

In the face of its onrush, all the wisdom and ingenuity of man were unavailing. Large quantities of refuse were cleared out of the city by officials specially appointed for the purpose, all sick persons were forbidden entry, and numerous instructions were issued for safeguarding the people's health, but all to no avail. Nor were the countless petitions humbly directed to God by the pious, whether by means of formal processions or in any other guise, any less ineffectual. For in the early spring of the year we have mentioned, the plague began, in a terrifying and extraordinary manner, to make its disastrous effects apparent. It did not take the form it had assumed in the East, where if anyone bled from the nose it was an obvious portent of certain death. On the contrary, its earliest symptom, in men and women alike, was the appearance of certain swellings in the groin or the armpit, some of which were egg-shaped whilst others were roughly the size of the common apple. Sometimes the swellings were large, sometimes not so large, and they were referred to by the populace as *gavòccioli*. From the two areas already mentioned, this deadly *gavòcciolo* would begin to spread, and within a short time it would appear at random all over the body. Later on, the symptoms of the disease changed, and many people began to find dark blotches and bruises on their arms, thighs, and other parts of the body, sometimes large and few in number, at other times tiny and closely spaced. These, to anyone unfortunate enough to contract them, were just as infallible a sign that he would die as the *gavòcciolo* had been earlier, and as indeed it still was.

Against these maladies, it seemed that all the advice of physicians and all the power of medicine were profitless and unavailing. Perhaps the nature of the illness was such that it allowed no remedy; or perhaps those people who were treating the illness (whose numbers had increased enormously because the ranks of the qualified were invaded by people, both men and women, who had never received any training in medicine), being ignorant of its causes, were not prescribing the appropriate cure. At all events, few of those who caught it ever recovered, and in most cases death occurred within three days from the appearance of the symptoms we have described, some people dying more rapidly than others, the majority without any fever or other complications.

But what made this pestilence even more severe was that whenever those suffering from it mixed with people who were still unaffected, it would rush upon these with the speed of a fire racing through dry or oily substances that happened to be placed within its reach. Nor was this the full extent of its evil, for not only did it infect healthy persons who conversed or had any dealings with the sick, making them ill or visiting an equally horrible death upon them, but it also seemed to transfer the sickness to anyone touching the clothes or other objects which had been handled or used by its victims. . . .

Some people were of the opinion that a sober and abstemious mode of living considerably reduced the risk of infection. They therefore formed themselves into groups and lived in isolation from everyone else. Having withdrawn to a comfortable abode where there were no sick persons, they locked themselves in and settled down to a peaceable existence, consuming modest quantities of delicate foods and precious wines and avoiding all excesses. They refrained from speaking to outsiders, refused to receive news of the dead or sick, and entertained themselves with music and whatever other amusements they were able to devise.

Others took the opposite view, and maintained that an infallible way of warding off this appalling evil was to drink heavily, enjoy life to the full, go round singing and merrymaking, gratify all of one's cravings whenever the opportunity offered, and shrug the whole thing off as one enormous joke. Moreover, they practised what they preached to the best of their ability, for they would visit one tavern after another, drinking all day and night to immoderate excess; or alternatively (and this was their more frequent custom), they would do their drinking in various private houses, but only in the ones where the conversation was restricted to subjects that were pleasant or entertaining. Such places were easy to find, for people behaved as though their days were numbered, and treated their belongings and their own persons with equal abandon. Hence most houses had become common property, and any passing stranger could make himself at home as naturally as though he were the rightful owner. But for all their riotous manner of living, these people always took good care to avoid any contact with the sick.

In the face of so much affliction and misery, all respect for the laws of God and man had virtually broken down and been extinguished in our city. For like everybody else, those ministers and executors of the laws who were not either dead or ill were left with so few subordinates that they were unable to discharge any of their duties. Hence everyone was free to behave as he pleased.

There were many other people who steered a middle course between the two already mentioned, neither restricting their diet to the same degree as the first group, nor indulging so freely as the second in drinking and other forms of wantonness, but simply doing no more than satisfy their appetite. Instead of incarcerating themselves, these people moved about freely, holding in their hands a posy of flowers, or fragrant herbs, or one of a wide range of spices, which they applied at frequent intervals to their nostrils, thinking it an excellent idea to fortify the brain with smells of that particular sort; for the stench of dead bodies, sickness, and medicines seemed to fill and pollute the whole of the atmosphere.

Some people, pursuing what was possibly the safer alternative, callously maintained that there was no better or more efficacious remedy against a plague than to run away from it. Swayed by this argument, and sparing no thought for anyone but themselves, large numbers of men and women abandoned their city, their homes, their relatives, their estates, and their belongings, and headed for the countryside, either in Florentine territory or, better still, abroad. It was as though they imagined that the wrath of God would not unleash this plague against men for their iniquities irrespective of where they happened to be, but would only be aroused against those who found themselves within the city walls; or possibly they assumed that the whole of the population would be exterminated and that the city's last hour had come.

Of the people who held these various opinions, not all of them died. Nor, however, did they all survive. On the contrary, many of each different persuasion fell ill here, there, and everywhere, and having themselves, when they were fit and well, set an example to those who were as yet unaffected, they languished away with virtually no one to nurse them. It was not merely a question of one citizen avoiding another, and of people almost invariably neglecting their neighbours and rarely or never visiting their relatives, addressing them only from a distance; this scourge had implanted so great a terror in the hearts of men and women that brothers abandoned brothers, uncles their nephews, sisters their brothers, and in many cases wives deserted their husbands. But even worse, and almost incredible, was the fact that fathers and mothers refused to nurse and assist their own children, as though they did not belong to them.

Hence the countless numbers of people who fell ill, both male and female, were entirely dependent upon either the charity of friends (who were few and far between) or the greed of servants, who remained in short supply despite the attraction of high wages out of all proportion to the services they performed. Furthermore, these latter were men and women of coarse intellect and the majority were unused to such duties, and they did little more than hand things to the invalid when asked to do so and watch over him when he was dying. And in performing this kind of service, they frequently lost their lives as well as their earnings.

As a result of this wholesale desertion of the sick by neighbours, relatives, and friends, and in view of the scarcity of servants, there grew up a practice almost never previously heard of, whereby when a woman fell ill, no matter how gracious or beautiful or gently bred she might be, she raised no objection to being attended by a male servant, whether he was young or not. Nor did she have any scruples about showing him every part of her body as freely as she would have displayed it to a woman, provided that the nature of her infirmity required her to do so; and this explains why those women who recovered were possibly less chaste in the period that followed.

Moreover a great many people died who would perhaps have survived had they received some assistance. And hence, what with the lack of appropriate means for tending the sick, and the virulence of the plague, the number of deaths reported in the city whether by day or night was so enormous that it astonished all who heard tell of it, to say nothing of the people who actually witnessed the carnage. . . .

As for the common people and a large proportion of the bourgeoisie, they presented a much more pathetic spectacle, for the majority of them were constrained, either by their poverty or the hope of survival, to remain in their houses. Being confined to their own parts of the city, they fell ill daily in their thousands, and since they had no one to assist them or attend to their needs, they inevitably perished almost without exception. Many dropped dead in the open streets, both by day and by night, whilst a great many others, though dying in their own houses, drew their neighbours' attention to the fact more by the smell of their rotting corpses than by any other means. And what with these, and the others who were dying all over the city, bodies were here, there, and everywhere. . . .

[T]here were no tears or candles or mourners to honour the dead; in fact, no more respect was accorded to dead people than would nowadays be shown towards dead goats. For it was quite apparent that the one thing which, in normal times, no wise man had ever learned to accept with patient resignation (even though it struck so seldom and unobtrusively), had now been brought home to the feeble-minded as well, but the scale of the calamity caused them to regard it with indifference.

Such was the multitude of corpses (of which further consignments were arriving every day and almost by the hour at each of the churches), that there was not sufficient consecrated ground for them to be buried in, especially if each was to have its own plot in accordance with long-established custom. So when all the graves were full, huge trenches were excavated in the churchyards, into which new arrivals were placed in their hundreds, stowed tier upon tier like ships' cargo, each layer of corpses being covered over with a thin layer of soil till the trench was filled to the top.

But rather than describe in elaborate detail the calamities we experienced in the city at that time, I must mention that, whilst an ill wind was blowing through Florence itself, the surrounding region was no less badly affected. In the fortified towns, conditions were similar to those in the city itself on a minor scale; but in the scattered hamlets and the countryside proper, the poor unfortunate peasants and their families had no physicians or servants whatever to assist them, and collapsed by the wayside, in their fields, and in their cottages at all hours of the day and night, dying more like animals than human beings. Like the townspeople, they too grew apathetic in their ways, disregarded their affairs, and neglected their possessions. Moreover, they all behaved as though each day was to be their last, and far from making provision for the future by tilling their lands, tending their flocks, and adding to their previous labours, they tried in every way they could think of to squander the assets already in their possession. Thus it came about that oxen, asses, sheep, goats, pigs, chickens, and even dogs (for all their deep fidelity to man) were driven away and allowed to roam freely through the fields, where the crops lay abandoned and had not even been reaped, let alone gathered in. And after a whole day's feasting, many of these animals, as though possessing the power of reason, would return glutted in the evening to their own quarters without any shepherd to guide them.

But let us leave the countryside and return to the city. What more remains to be said, except that the cruelty of heaven (and possibly, in some measure, also that of man) was so immense and so devastating that between March and July of the year in question, what with the fury of the pestilence and the fact that so many of the sick were inadequately cared for or abandoned in their hour of need because the healthy were too terrified to approach them, it is reliably thought that over a hundred thousand human lives were extinguished within the walls of the city of Florence? Yet before this lethal catastrophe fell upon the city, it is doubtful whether anyone would have guessed it contained so many inhabitants.

Images of the Black Death

Contemporary accounts testify to the plague's terrifying physical, social, and psychological impact. Images from the period document the ravages of the epidemic as well, sometimes in gruesome detail. The engraving in Figure 12.1, for example, shows a plague victim covered in the dark blotches characteristic of the disease. The town in the back-

Figure 12.1 Plague Victim with Maiden, 1348.
Source: The Bridgeman Art Library International.

ground appears to be going up in flames while lightning flares in the sky above. What else do you think is going on in this image? Who is the woman depicted and what is she doing? If this is a group fleeing with their belongings from the burning town, do you think the plague victim is part of their entourage? What might be the significance of the flag they carry?

Figures 12.2 and 12.3 show two well-documented phenomena of the plague years: The first depicts a group of flagellants, members of a movement who wandered from town to town beating themselves with whips studded with iron nails in an effort to do penance for the sins they believed had brought on the plague. Written accounts confirm many elements in this picture: Flagellants usually carried crosses or banners with crosses on them, wore long pleated skirts, and went around bare-chested, the better to make their scourging as painful as possible. Figure 12.3 illustrates a similar impulse toward punishment as a means of coping with the plague, but this time the violence is

Figure 12.2 Flagellants, from a Fifteenth-Century Chronicle from Constance, Switzerland.
Source: © Bettmann/CORBIS.

Figure 12.3 The Burning of Jews in an Early Printed Woodcut.
Source: © Christel Gerstenberg/CORBIS.

directed outward, against Jews, so often the scapegoats in troubled times. Baseless accusations that Jews poisoned wells to spread the plague resulted in many such attacks against them during the period.

The final image, Figure 12.4, is one of a transi tomb from 1390. Transi tombs, which emerged during and after the plague era, were a major departure from standard funerary monuments that typically offered an idealized depiction of the deceased. Instead these tombs showed decaying or skeletal corpses covered with worms and other emblems of bodily corruption. Scholars differ over their meaning. How might you explain them?

Thinking Historically

What can these images tell us about fourteenth-century people's beliefs about the possible causes — medical or religious — of the plague? Think about the social and religious changes wrought by the plague recounted in the de' Mussis and Boccaccio readings. What evidence, if any, do you see in these images of these changes?

Figure 12.4   François de la Sarra, Tomb at La Sarraz, Switzerland, c. 1390.
Source: Reproduced courtesy of Harry N. Abrams, Inc.

79

AHMAD AL-MAQRIZI

The Plague in Cairo

Ahmad al-Maqrizi* (1364–1442) became a historian after pursuing a career as an administrator in post-plague Cairo. While he wrote his history of the plague period more than fifty years after the event, he probably had access to contemporary sources that are now lost to us. Compare al-Maqrizi's account of the plague in Cairo with the prior accounts of the plague in Italy. How was the experience of the Black Death in Cairo similar to, and different from, the experience in Florence?

Thinking Historically

Like Boccaccio, al-Maqrizi devotes more attention to the effects than to the causes of the Black Death. What effects were similar in Florence and Cairo? Al-Maqrizi discusses certain effects that were not mentioned in the Italian accounts. Which, if any, of these effects do you think also probably occurred in Italy?

In January 1349, there appeared new symptoms that consisted of spitting up of blood. The disease caused one to experience an internal fever, followed by an uncontrollable desire to vomit; then one spat up blood and died. The inhabitants of a house were stricken one after the other, and in one night or two, the dwelling became deserted. Each individual lived with this fixed idea that he was going to die in this way. He prepared for himself a good death by distributing alms; he arranged for scenes of reconciliation and his acts of devotion multiplied. . . .

By January 21, Cairo had become an abandoned desert, and one did not see anyone walking along the streets. A man could go from the Port Zuwayla to Bāb al-Nasr[1] without encountering a living soul. The dead were very numerous, and all the world could think of nothing else. Debris piled up in the streets. People went around with worried faces. Everywhere one heard lamentations, and one could not pass by any house without being overwhelmed by the howling. Cadavers

---

*ahk MAHD   ahl mah KREE zee
[1]This was apparently the busiest boulevard in medieval Cairo.

John Aberth, *The Black Death: The Great Mortality of 1348–1350, A Brief History with Documents* (Boston: Bedford/St. Martin's, 2005), 84–87.

formed a heap on the public highway, funeral processions were so many that they could not file past without bumping into each other, and the dead were transported in some confusion. . . .

One began to have to search for readers of the Koran for funeral ceremonies, and a number of individuals quit their usual occupations in order to recite prayers at the head of funeral processions. In the same way, some people devoted themselves to smearing crypts with plaster; others presented themselves as volunteers to wash the dead or carry them. These latter folk earned substantial salaries. For example, a reader of the Koran took ten *dirhams*.[2] Also, hardly had he reached the oratory when he slipped away very quickly in order to go officiate at a new [funeral]. Porters demanded 6 *dirhams* at the time they were engaged, and then it was necessary to match it [at the grave]. The gravedigger demanded fifty *dirhams* per grave. Most of the rest of these people died without having taken any profit from their gains. . . . Also families kept their dead on the bare ground, due to the impossibility of having them interred. The inhabitants of a house died by the tens and, since there wasn't a litter ready to hand, one had to carry them away in stages. Moreover, some people appropriated for themselves without scruple the immovable and movable goods and cash of their former owners after their demise. But very few lived long enough to profit thereby, and those who remained alive would have been able to do without. . . .

Family festivities and weddings had no more place [in life]. No one issued an invitation to a feast during the whole time of the epidemic, and one did not hear any concert. The *vizier*[3] lifted a third of what he was owed from the woman responsible [for collecting] the tax on singers. The call to prayer was canceled in various places, and in the exact same way, those places [where prayer] was most frequent subsisted on a *muezzin*[4] alone. . . .

The men of the [military] troop and the cultivators took a world of trouble to finish their sowing [of fields]. The plague emerged at the end of the season when the fields were becoming green. How many times did one see a laborer, at Gaza, at Ramleh, and along other points of the Syrian littoral,[5] guide his plow being pulled by oxen suddenly fall down dead, still holding in his hands his plow, while the oxen stood at their place without a conductor.

It was the same in Egypt: When the harvest time came, there remained only a very small number of *fellahs*.[6] The soldiers and their

[2]A silver coin used in the Muslim world.
[3]The chief minister of the caliph, or leader of the Muslim community.
[4]An official of the mosque who called the faithful to prayer from the minaret.
[5]The coastal plain of southern Palestine, where the most fertile land was located.
[6]Arabic word for ploughman or tiller, which also denoted the peasantry of Egypt and is the origin of the modern term, *fellahin*.

valets left for the harvest and attempted to hire workers, promising them half of the crop, but they could not find anyone to help them reap it. They loaded the grain on their horses, did the mowing themselves, but, being powerless to carry out the greatest portion of the work, they abandoned this enterprise.

The endowments[7] passed rapidly from hand to hand as a consequence of the multiplicity of deaths in the army. Such a concession passed from one to the other until the seventh or eighth holder, to fall finally [into the hands] of artisans, such as tailors, shoemakers, or public criers, and these mounted the horse, donned the [military] headdress, and dressed in military tunics.

Actually, no one collected the whole revenue of his endowment, and a number of holders harvested absolutely nothing. During the flooding of the Nile[8] and the time of the sprouting of vegetation, one could procure a laborer only with difficulty: On half the lands only did the harvest reach maturity. Moreover, there was no one to buy the green clover [as feed] and no one sent their horses to graze over the field. This was the ruin of royal properties in the suburbs of Cairo, like Matarieh, Hums, Siryaqus, and Bahtit. In the canton [administrative district] of Nay and Tanan, 1,500 *feddans*[9] of clover were abandoned where it stood: No one came to buy it, either to pasture their beasts on the place or to gather it into barns and use it as fodder.

The province of Upper Egypt was deserted, in spite of the vast abundance of cultivable terrain. It used to be that, after the land surface was cultivated in the territory of Asyūt,[10] 6,000 individuals were subject to payment of the property tax; now, in the year of the epidemic [1348–49], one could not count on more than 106 contributors. Nevertheless, during this period, the price of wheat did not rise past fifteen *dirhams* per *ardeb*.[11]

Most of the trades disappeared, for a number of artisans devoted themselves to handling the dead, while the others, no less numerous, occupied themselves in selling off to bidders [the dead's] movable goods and clothing, so well that the price of linen and similar objects fell by a fifth of their real value, at the very least, and still further until one found customers. . . .

Thus the trades disappeared: One could no longer find either a water carrier, or a laundress, or a domestic. The monthly salary of a

---

[7]Mamluk commanders and elite soldiers, like their Ayyubid predecessors, were paid out of the revenues of land grants, known as *iqtas* (similar to fiefs in Europe). With the dearth of labor caused by the Black Death, it became far more difficult to extract income from these estates.

[8]This usually took place between September and November of every year.

[9]A *feddan* is equivalent to 1.038 acres.

[10]Located along the Nile in Upper Egypt, about midway between Cairo and Aswan.

[11]An *ardeb* is equivalent to 5.62 bushels.

groom rose from thirty *dirhams* to eighty. A proclamation made in
Cairo invited the artisans to take up their old trades, and some of the
recalcitrants reformed themselves. Because of the shortage of men and
camels, a goatskin of water reached the price of eight *dirhams,* and in
order to grind an *ardeb* of wheat, one paid fifteen *dirhams.*

80

WILLIAM H. McNEILL

Consequences of the Black Death in Europe

In this selection, William H. McNeill, a leading world historian (see
selection 10), explores the psychological, cultural, and economic consequences of the Black Death in Europe. What, according to McNeill,
were these consequences? Which do you think were most important?

Thinking Historically

McNeill uses the term *consequences* rather than *effects*. Do the words
mean the same thing, or are his "consequences" too general to be attached to specific causes? In fact, he lists some of the major changes
that occurred in European culture and economy in the centuries after
the Black Death. Which of these consequences was likely caused by
the Black Death? In the last sentence of this selection, McNeill makes
a distinction between effects that depend on a single cause "alone"
and on causes that "contributed" to a broader effect. What does he
mean by this distinction?

Before pursuing this theme, however, it seems worth venturing a few remarks about the psychological, economic, and cultural consequences of
Europe's encounter with the plague in the fourteenth and succeeding centuries; and then we must survey as best we can the disease consequences
for Asia and Africa of the Mongol opening of the steppelands to regular
transit.

William H. McNeill, *Plagues and Peoples* (Garden City, N.Y.: Anchor Books, 1976), 161–65.

At the psychological and cultural level European reactions were obvious and varied. In face of intense and immediate crisis, when an outbreak of plague implanted fear of imminent death in an entire community, ordinary routines and customary restraints regularly broke down. In time, rituals arose to discharge anxiety in socially acceptable ways; but in the fourteenth century itself, local panic often provoked bizarre behavior. The first important effort at ritualizing responses to the plague took extreme and ugly forms. In Germany and some adjacent parts of Europe companies of Flagellants aimed at propitiating God's wrath by beating each other bloody and attacking Jews, who were commonly accused of spreading the pestilence. The Flagellants disdained all established authorities of church and state and, if accounts are to be believed, their rituals were well-nigh suicidal for the participants.

Attacks on German-Jewish communities inspired by Flagellants and others probably accelerated an eastward shift of centers of Jewish population in Europe. Poland escaped the first round of plague almost entirely, and though popular rioting against Jews occurred there too, royal authorities welcomed German Jews for the urban skills they brought into the country. The subsequent development of east European Jewry was therefore significantly affected (and the rise in the Vistula and Nieman valleys of a market-oriented agriculture, largely under Jewish management, was probably accelerated) by the fourteenth-century pattern of popular reaction to plague.

These and other violent episodes attest the initial impact of the plague on European consciousness. In time, the fear and horror of the first onset relaxed. Writers as diverse as Boccaccio, Chaucer, and William Langland all treated the plague as a routine crisis of human life — an act of God, like the weather. Perhaps the plague had other, more lasting, consequences for literature: scholars have suggested, for instance, that the rise of vernacular tongues as a medium for serious writing and the decay of Latin as a *lingua franca* among the educated men of western Europe was hastened by the die-off of clerics and teachers who knew enough Latin to keep that ancient tongue alive. Painting also responded to the plague-darkened vision of the human condition provoked by repeated exposure to sudden, inexplicable death. Tuscan painters, for instance, reacted against Giotto's serenity, preferring sterner, hieratic portrayals of religious scenes and figures. The "Dance of Death" became a common theme for art; and several other macabre motifs entered the European repertory. The buoyancy and self-confidence, so characteristic of the thirteenth century, when Europe's great cathedrals were abuilding, gave way to a more troubled age. Acute social tensions between economic classes and intimate acquaintance with sudden death assumed far greater importance for almost everyone than had been true previously.

The economic impact of the Black Death was enormous, though local differences were greater than an earlier generation of scholars assumed. In highly developed regions like northern Italy and Flanders, harsh collisions between social classes manifested themselves as the boom times of the thirteenth century faded into the past. The plague, by disrupting wage and price patterns sharply, exacerbated these conflicts, at least in the short run. Some ninety years ago Thorold Rogers argued that the Black Death had improved the lot of the lower classes and advanced freedom by destroying serfdom. His idea was that labor shortage caused by plague deaths allowed wage earners to bargain among rival would-be employers and thus improve their real wages. This view is no longer widely believed. Local circumstances differed widely. Employers died as well as laborers; and manpower shortages proved evanescent in those towns where a vigorous market economy did effect a short-term rise in real wages.

In time, of course, the initial perturbations created by the plague tended to diminish. All the same, two general displacements of European culture and society can be discerned in the latter fourteenth and fifteenth centuries that seem plausibly related to the terrifying, constantly renewed experience of plague.

When the plague was raging, a person might be in full health one day and die miserably within twenty-four hours. This utterly discredited any merely human effort to explain the mysteries of the world. The confidence in rational theology, which characterized the age of Aquinas (d. 1274), could not survive such experiences. A world view allowing ample scope to arbitrary, inexplicable catastrophe alone was compatible with the grim reality of plague. Hedonism and revival of one or another form of fatalistic pagan philosophy were possible reactions, though confined always to a few. Far more popular and respectable was an upsurge of mysticism, aimed at achieving encounter with God in inexplicable, unpredictable, intense, and purely personal ways. Hesychasm[1] among the Orthodox, and more variegated movements among Latin Christians — e.g., the practices of the so-called Rhineland mystics, of the Brethren of the Common Life, and of heretical groups like the Lollards of England — all gave expression to the need for a more personal, antinomian access to God than had been offered by Thomist theology and the previously recognized forms of piety. Recurrence of plague refreshed this psychological need until the mid-seventeenth century; hence it is no accident that all branches of organized Christianity — Orthodox, Catholic, and Protestant — made more room for personal mysticism and other forms of communion with God, even though ecclesiastical

---

[1]Mystical religious practice by Orthodox monks which involved certain repetitive movements and recitation of prayer. [Ed.]

authorities always remained uncomfortable when confronting too much private zeal.

Secondly, the inadequacy of established ecclesiastical rituals and administrative measures to cope with the unexampled emergency of plague had pervasively unsettling effects. In the fourteenth century, many priests and monks died; often their successors were less well trained and faced more quizzical if not openly antagonistic flocks. God's justice seemed far to seek in the way plague spared some, killed others; and the regular administration of God's grace through the sacraments (even when consecrated priests remained available) was an entirely inadequate psychological counterpoise to the statistical vagaries of lethal infection and sudden death. Anticlericalism was of course not new in Christian Europe; after 1346, however, it became more open and widespread, and provided one of the elements contributing to Luther's later success.

Because sacred rituals remained vigorously conservative, it took centuries for the Roman Church to adjust to the recurrent crises created by outbreaks of plague. Hence it was mainly in the period of the Counter-Reformation that psychologically adequate ceremonies and symbols for coping with recurrent lethal epidemics defined themselves. Invocation of St. Sebastian, who in early Christian centuries had already attracted to himself many of the attributes once assigned to Apollo, became central in Catholic rituals of prophylaxis against the plague. The suffering saint, whose death by arrows was symbolic of deaths dealt by the unseen arrows of pestilential infection, began to figure largely in religious art as well. A second important figure was St. Roch. He had a different character, being an exemplar and patron of the acts of public charity and nursing that softened the impact of plague in those cities of Mediterranean Europe that were most exposed to the infection.

Protestant Europe never developed much in the way of special rituals for meeting epidemic emergencies. The Bible had little to say about how to cope with massive outbreaks of infectious disease, and since plague seldom affected the North (though when it came it was sometimes exceptionally severe), Protestants lacked sufficient stimulus to such a development.

In contrast to the rigidities that beset the church, city governments, especially in Italy, responded rather quickly to the challenges presented by devastating disease. Magistrates learned how to cope at the practical level, organizing burials, safeguarding food deliveries, setting up quarantines, hiring doctors, and establishing other regulations for public and private behavior in time of plague. The ability of city authorities to react in these more or less effective ways was symptomatic of their general vigor — a vigor that made the centuries between 1350 and 1550 a sort of golden age for European city-states, especially Germany and Italy, where competition with any superior secular government was minimal.

Italian and German city governments and businessmen not only managed their own local affairs with general success, but also pioneered the development of a far more closely integrated inter-regional market economy that ran throughout all of Europe. Ere long these same cities also defined a more secularized style of life and thought that by 1500 attracted the liveliest attention throughout the continent. The shift from medieval to renaissance cultural values, needless to say, did not depend on the plague alone; yet the plague, and the generally successful way city authorities managed to react to its ravages, surely contributed something to the general transformation of European sensibility.

When we turn attention from Europe and ask what the new plague pattern may have meant elsewhere in the Old World, a troublesome void presents itself. Scholarly discussion of the Black Death in Europe, its course and consequences, is more than a century old; nothing remotely comparable exists for other regions of the earth. Yet it is impossible to believe that the plague did not affect China, India, and the Middle East; and it is even more implausible to think that human life on the steppe was not also brought under new and unexampled stress by the establishment of a persistent reservoir of bubonic infection among the rodents of the Eurasian grasslands all the way from Manchuria to the Ukraine.

To be sure, there is ample evidence that plague became and remained, as in Europe, a dreaded recurrent affliction throughout the Islamic world. Egypt and Syria shared the plague experience of other parts of the Mediterranean coastlands with which they remained always in close contact. About a third of Egypt's population seems to have died in the first attack, 1347–1349, and the plague returned to the Nile Valley at frequent intervals thereafter, appearing there most recently in the 1940s.

REFLECTIONS

History is always written backwards. We study the rearview mirror to see where we are going. What can the Black Death tell us about the possibility of pandemic disease in the future? Historians who are sometimes embarrassed by their present-mindedness can take refuge in the conventions of the discipline: Histories begin in the past and work chronologically toward the present; narratives seem to only tell the story, just as it happened. But both chronological and narrative presentations imply a chain of cause and effect where analysis might reveal chance or no relationship at all.

We can all easily fall prey to the logical fallacy called in Latin "*post hoc, ergo propter hoc*" (meaning literally "after this, therefore because of this"). Just because "B" came after "A" doesn't mean that "B" was caused by "A." Still it is only natural to cast around for this sort of simple, uncomplicated causation when your world is falling apart. Consider how de' Mussis, Boccaccio, or the Flagellants and Europeans shown in Figures 12.2 and 12.3 and discussed in the McNeill reading explained what was happening to them. Nevertheless, in our lives, as in our understanding of history, we can only see the past from the standpoint of the immediate present, and all roads seem to lead inexorably to Now. Though most of us like to think we can shape our future, we gain some comfort from believing that we couldn't have changed our past.

At least for the purposes of historical accuracy, how do we break this mindset? We have already suggested (in our introduction to the reading by McNeill) the importance of recognizing multiple causation. Rarely if ever is any event the result of a single cause. Even a single premeditated act of an individual can be usefully understood in terms of a myriad of factors. Anything as complex as a social movement, economic trend, political revolution, or cultural style results from a profound web of causes. When we ask about the causes of the Protestant Reformation or the Communist Revolution in China, we are clearly dealing with multiple factors, all of which were imporant to some degree in these developments.

Finally, it is important to keep in mind that historical causation always underplays the role of chance or accident. We know our personal lives are full of chance events. Do these unpredictable events become more predictable in larger social groups or over longer time periods? Sometimes we realize later that an event we thought was chance actually had causes. Might this be true more generally? Are chance events merely those we have not yet been able to explain?

We end, perhaps, with more questions than answers. This is because the study of history involves nothing less than the study of everything that has happened to all of the very complex creatures we call human beings. We can formulate certain scientific methods for studying the past. We can even use these methods to improve our understanding of the past. But we never have a single or final explanation of any of it.

On Cities

European, Chinese, Islamic,
and Mexican Cities, 1000–1550 C.E.

HISTORICAL CONTEXT

During the last five thousand years, cities have grown and multiplied, the world becoming increasingly urbanized. There have been interruptions in this process, however: the period of the Mongol invasions in the first half of the thirteenth century and the era of the Black Death, the plague that wiped out urban populations in the middle of the fourteenth century, for instance. But, by and large, the general course of world history has promoted the rise and expansion of cities and of urban over rural populations.

In this chapter, we ask what this increasing urbanization meant for those who lived in the cities and for those who did not. We compare cities in various parts of the world between 1000 and 1550. We will study primary and secondary sources, and you will be asked to note the ways in which these cities are similar and different.

THINKING HISTORICALLY
Evaluating a Comparative Thesis

Many of the chapters, even individual readings, in this volume have been comparative. Making comparisons is a critical skill in any disciplined thinking process. In the study of world history, comparisons are particularly important and potentially fruitful, since until recently the historical profession tended to study different nations' histories somewhat in isolation from each other or without reference to a broader comparative context.

Comparisons are not useful in and of themselves. They are merely a first step toward a thesis that attempts to explain the differences or similarities noticed. To say that something is bigger or smaller, hotter or colder, than something else, that one country is more densely populated or more religious than another, may or may not be obvious or interesting, but the observation is not meaningful in and of itself. The comparative observation becomes meaningful when it is explained by some general rule that covers both cases. Human behavior is too complex to attain what some call "covering laws" in science, but the effort to reach an explanation that covered both cases might be called a comparative thesis.

In history, there are many comparative theses. An example of one might run something like this: Canada has a more universal health care system than the United States because it has a longer tradition of mutual aid and trust in government. Now, one might agree or disagree with either the comparison or the explanation. If one disagrees with the comparison there is no need to go further. But if one agrees with the comparison, then one has to evaluate the comparative thesis.

In this chapter you will be asked to consider a comparative thesis about cities that is offered in the first reading. The other readings in the chapter will enable you to consider what evidence they offer for or against the initial comparison and its explanatory thesis.

$$\boxed{81}$$

FERNAND BRAUDEL

Towns and Cities

Fernand Braudel* (1902–1985) **was one of the great historians of the twentieth century, and the following selection, which provides a broad overview of medieval towns and cities throughout the world, is from one of his interpretative works of world history. According to Braudel, what were some of the distinctive characteristics of Western, or European, towns? Why did Western towns acquire these character-**

*broh DELL

Fernand Braudel, *The Structures of Everyday Life: The Limits of the Possible* (London: Collins, 1983), 509–15, 518–25.

istics? How does Braudel describe Chinese and Islamic cities? Why and how did these towns develop differently?

Thinking Historically

Braudel begins with a comparative judgment—that European towns "were marked by an unparalleled freedom." How does he explain this supposed difference between European towns and those of other societies? He offers a kind of covering law in the form of a "Western model" that relates urban freedom to a number of other features. He says these towns were autonomous, self-governing, bodies of largely middle-class citizens who thought of themselves as a community. They were not governed by a king, emperor, or territorial state, but, rather, governed themselves through a number of organizations. In addition to governing councils and militaries, these organizations included guilds, church groups, and various other voluntary societies in which citizens exercised real power over their lives. On an even broader level, Braudel attributes these differences to the long history of European feudalism and weak states, and to the rise of capitalism and a middle class.

As you read Braudel, try to weigh his evidence for both the comparison and the larger model. Does it appear from the reading that inhabitants of European towns had greater freedom than the people of other towns? If you agree with his comparison, try to evaluate his model. Do the elements of the model fit together? Was there a complex of features in Western society that did not occur elsewhere? What is his evidence for that comparative thesis? What else would you want to learn to challenge or confirm his thesis?

The Originality of Western Towns

. . . What were Europe's differences and original features? Its towns were marked by an unparalleled freedom. They had developed as autonomous worlds and according to their own propensities. They had outwitted the territorial state, which was established slowly and then only grew with their interested co-operation—and was moreover only an enlarged and often insipid copy of their development. They ruled their countrysides autocratically, regarding them exactly as later powers regarded their colonies, and treating them as such. They pursued an economic policy of their own via their satellites and the nervous system of urban relay points; they were capable of breaking down obstacles and creating or recreating protective privileges. Imagine what would happen if modern states were suppressed so that the Chambers of Commerce of the large towns were free to act as they pleased!

Even without resort to doubtful comparisons these long-standing realities leap to the eye. And they lead us to a key problem which can be formulated in two or three different ways: What stopped the other cities of the world from enjoying the same relative freedom? Or to take another aspect of the same problem, why was change a striking feature of the destiny of Western towns (even their physical existence was transformed) while the other cities have no history by comparison and seem to have been shut in long periods of immobility? Why were some cities like steam-engines while the others were like clocks, to parody Lévi-Strauss? Comparative history compels us to look for the reason for these differences and to attempt to establish a dynamic "model" of the turbulent urban evolution of the West, whereas a model representing city life in the rest of the world would run in a straight and scarcely broken line across time.

Free Worlds

Urban freedom in Europe is a classic and fairly well documented subject; let us start with it.

In a simplified form we can say:

1. The West well and truly lost its urban framework with the end of the Roman Empire. Moreover the towns in the Empire had been gradually declining since before the arrival of the barbarians. The very relative animation of the Merovingian period was followed, slightly earlier in some places, slightly later in others, by a complete halt.

2. The urban renaissance from the eleventh century was precipitated by and superimposed on a rise in rural vigour, a growth of fields, vineyards, and orchards. Towns grew in harmony with villages and clearly outlined urban law often emerged from the communal privileges of village groups. The town was often simply the country revived and remodeled. The names of a number of streets in Frankfurt (which remained very rural until the sixteenth century) recall the woods, clumps of trees, and marshland amid which the town grew up.

This rural rearrangement naturally brought to the nascent city the representatives of political and social authority: nobles, lay princes, and ecclesiastics.

3. None of this would have been possible without a general return to health and a growing monetary economy. Money, a traveler from perhaps distant lands (from Islam, according to Maurice Lombard), was the active and decisive force. Two centuries before Saint Thomas Aquinas, Alain de Lille said: "Money, not Caesar, is everything now." And money meant towns.

Thousands of towns were founded at this time, but few of them went on to brilliant futures. Only certain regions, therefore, were urbanized in depth, thus distinguishing themselves from the rest and playing a vitalizing role: such was the region between the Loire and the Rhine, for instance, or northern and central Italy, and certain key points on Mediterranean coasts. Merchants, craft guilds, industries, long-distance trade, and banks were quick to appear there, as well as a certain kind of bourgeoisie and even some sort of capitalism. The destinies of these very special cities were linked not only to the progress of the surrounding countryside but to international trade. Indeed, they often broke free of rural society and former political ties. The break might be achieved violently or amicably, but it was always a sign of strength, plentiful money, and real power.

Soon there were no states around these privileged towns. This was the case in Italy and Germany, with the political collapses of the thirteenth century. The hare beat the tortoise for once. Elsewhere—in France, England, Castile, even in Aragon—the earlier rebirth of the territorial state restricted the development of the towns, which in addition were not situated in particularly lively economic areas. They grew less rapidly than elsewhere.

But the main, the unpredictable thing was that certain towns made themselves into autonomous worlds, city-states, buttressed with privileges (acquired or extorted) like so many juridical ramparts. Perhaps in the past historians have insisted too much on the legal factors involved, for if such considerations were indeed sometimes more important than, or of equal importance to, geographical, sociological, and economic factors, the latter did count to a large extent. What is privilege without material substance?

In fact the miracle in the West was not so much that everything sprang up again from the eleventh century, after having been almost annihilated with the disaster of the fifth. History is full of examples of secular revivals, of urban expansion, of births and rebirths: Greece from the fifth to the second century B.C.E.; Rome perhaps; Islam from the ninth century; China under the Sungs. But these revivals always featured two runners, the state and the city. The state usually won and the city then remained subject and under a heavy yoke. The miracle of the first great urban centuries in Europe was that the city won hands down, at least in Italy, Flanders, and Germany. It was able to try the experiment of leading a completely separate life for quite a long time. This was a colossal event. Its genesis cannot be pinpointed with certainty, but its enormous consequences are visible.

Towns as Outposts of Modernity

It was on the basis of this liberty that the great Western cities, and other towns they influenced and to which they served as examples, built up a distinctive civilization and spread techniques which were new, or had been revived or rediscovered after centuries—it matters little which. The important thing is that these cities had the rare privilege of following through an unusual political, social, and economic experience.

In the financial sphere, the towns organized taxation, finances, public credit, customs, and excise. They invented public loans: the first issues of the Monte Vecchio in Venice could be said to go back to 1167, the first formulation of the Casa di San Giorgio to 1407. One after another, they reinvented gold money, following Genoa which may have minted the *genovino* as early as the late twelfth century. They organized industry and the guilds; they invented long-distance trade, bills of exchange, the first forms of trading companies and accountancy. They also quickly became the scene of class struggles. For if the towns were "communities" as has been said, they were also "societies" in the modern sense of the word, with their tensions and civil struggles: nobles against bourgeois; poor against rich ("thin people" *popolo magro* against "fat people" *popolo grosso*). The struggles in Florence were already more deeply akin to those of the industrial early nineteenth century than to the faction-fights of ancient Rome, as the drama of the Ciompi (1378) demonstrates.

This society divided from within also faced enemies from without— the worlds of the noble, prince, or peasant, of everybody who was not a citizen. The cities were the West's first focus for patriotism—and the patriotism they inspired was long to be more coherent and much more conscious than the territorial kind, which emerged only slowly in the first states. . . .

A new state of mind was established, broadly that of an early, still faltering, Western capitalism—a collection of rules, possibilities, calculations, the art both of getting rich and of living. It also included gambling and risk: the key words of commercial language, *fortuna, ventura, ragione, prudenza, sicurta*, define the risks to be guarded against. No question now of living from day to day as noblemen did, always putting up their revenues to try to meet the level of their expenditure, which invariably came first—and letting the future take care of itself. The merchant was economical with his money, calculated his expenditure according to his returns, his investments according to their yield. The hour-glass had turned back the right way. He would also be economical with his time: A merchant could already say that *chi tempo ha e tempo aspetta tempo perde*, which means much the same thing as "time is money."

Capitalism and towns were basically the same thing in the West. Lewis Mumford humorously claimed that capitalism was the cuckoo's egg laid in the confined nests of the medieval towns. By this he meant to convey that the bird was destined to grow inordinately and burst its tight framework (which was true), and then link up with the state, the conqueror of towns but heir to their institutions and way of thinking and completely incapable of dispensing with them. The important thing was that even when it had declined as a city the town continued to rule the roost all the time it was passing into the actual or apparent service of the prince. The wealth of the state would still be the wealth of the town: Portugal converged on Lisbon, the Netherlands on Amsterdam, and English primacy was London's primacy (the capital modelled England in its own image after the peaceful revolution of 1688). The latent defect in the Spanish imperial economy was that it was based on Seville—a controlled town rotten with dishonest officials and long dominated by foreign capitalists—and not on a powerful free town capable of producing and carrying through a really individual economic policy. Likewise, if Louis XIV did not succeed in founding a "royal bank," despite various projects (1703, 1706, 1709), it was because faced with the power of the monarch, Paris did not offer the protection of a town free to do what it wanted and accountable to no one.

Urban Patterns

Let us imagine we are looking at a comprehensive history of the towns of Europe covering the complete series of their forms from the Greek city-state to an eighteenth-century town—everything Europe was able to build at home and overseas, from Muscovy in the East to America in the West. . . .

Simplifying, one could say that the West has had three basic types of town in the course of its evolution: open towns, that is to say not differentiated from their hinterland, even blending into it (A); towns closed in on themselves in every sense, their walls marking the boundaries of an individual way of life more than a territory (B); finally towns held in subjection, by which is meant the whole range of known controls by prince or state (C).

Roughly, A preceded B, and B preceded C. But there is no suggestion of strict succession about this order. It is rather a question of directions and dimensions shaping the complicated careers of the Western towns. They did not all develop at the same time or in the same way. Later we will see if this "grid" is valid for classifying all the towns of the world.

Type A: the ancient Greek or Roman city was open to the surrounding countryside and on terms of equality with it. Athens accepted inside its walls as rightful citizens the Eupatrid horse-breeders as well as the vine-growing peasants so dear to Aristophanes. As soon as the smoke rose above the Pnyx, the peasant responded to the signal and attended the Assembly of the People, where he sat among his equals. At the beginning of the Peloponnesian war, the entire population of the Attic countryside evacuated itself to Athens where it took refuge while the Spartans ravaged the fields, olive groves, and houses. When the Spartans fell back at the approach of winter, the country people returned to their homes. The Greek city was in fact the sum of the town and its surrounding countryside. . . . Likewise, if one explores the ruins of Roman cities, one is in open country immediately outside the gates: There are no suburbs, which is as good as saying no industry or active and organized trades in their duly allotted place.

Type B: the closed city: the medieval town was the classic example of a closed city, a self-sufficient unit, an exclusive, Lilliputian empire. Entering its gates was like crossing one of the serious frontiers of the world today. You were free to thumb your nose at your neighbour from the other side of the barrier. He could not touch you. The peasant who uprooted himself from his land and arrived in the town was immediately another man. He was free—or rather he had abandoned a known and hated servitude for another, not always guessing the extent of it beforehand. But this mattered little. If the town had adopted him, he could snap his fingers when his lord called for him. And though obsolete elsewhere, such calls were still frequently to be heard in Silesia in the eighteenth century and in Muscovy up to the nineteenth.

Though the towns opened their gates easily it was not enough to walk through them to be immediately and really part of them. Full citizens were a jealous minority, a small town inside the town itself. A citadel of the rich was built up in Venice in 1297 thanks to the *serrata*, the closing of the Great Council to new members. The *nobili* of Venice became a closed class for centuries. Very rarely did anyone force its gates. The category of ordinary *cittadini*—at a lower level—was probably more hospitable. But the Signoria very soon created two types of citizen, one *de intus*, the other *de intus et extra*, the latter full, the former partial. Fifteen years' residence were still required to be allowed to apply for the first, twenty-five years for the second. A decree by the Senate in 1386 even forbade new citizens (including those who were full citizens) from trading directly in Venice with German merchants at the Fondego dei Todeschi or outside it. The ordinary townspeople were no less mistrustful or hostile to newcomers. According to Marin Sanudo, in June 1520, the street people attacked the peasants who had arrived from the mainland as recruits for the galleys or the army, crying "*Poltroni ande arar!*" "Back to the plough, shirkers!"

Of course Venice was an extreme example. Moreover, it owed the preservation of its own constitution until 1797 to an aristocratic and extremely reactionary regime, as well as to the conquest at the beginning of the fifteenth century of the Terra Firma, which extended its authority as far as the Alps and Brescia. It was the last *polis* in the West. But citizenship was also parsimoniously granted in Marseilles in the sixteenth century; it was necessary to have "ten years of domicile, to possess property, to have married a local girl." Otherwise the man remained amongst the masses of non-citizens of the town. This limited conception of citizenship was the general rule everywhere.

The main source of contention can be glimpsed throughout this vast process: to whom did industry and craft, their privileges and profits, belong? In fact they belonged to the town, to its authorities and to its merchant entrepreneurs. They decided if it were necessary to deprive, or to try to deprive, the rural area of the city of the right to spin, weave, and dye, or if on the contrary it would be advantageous to grant it these rights. Everything was possible in these interchanges, as the history of each individual town shows.

As far as work inside the walls was concerned (we can hardly call it industry without qualification), everything was arranged for the benefit of the craft guilds. They enjoyed exclusive contiguous monopolies, fiercely defended along the imprecise frontiers that so easily led to absurd conflicts. The urban authorities did not always have the situation under control. Sooner or later, with the help of money, they were to allow obvious, acknowledged, honorary superiorities, consecrated by money or power, to become apparent. The "Six Corps" (drapers, grocers, haberdashers, furriers, hosiers, goldsmiths) were the commercial aristocracy of Paris from 1625. In Florence it was the *arte dela lana* and the *Arte di Calimala* (engaged in dyeing fabric imported from the north, unbleached). But town museums in Germany supply the best evidence of these old situations. In Ulm, for example, each guild owned a picture hinged in triptych form. The side panels represented characteristic scenes of the craft. The centre, like a treasured family album, showed innumerable small portraits recalling the successive generations of masters of the guild over the centuries.

An even more telling example was the City of London and its annexes (running along its walls) in the eighteenth century, still the domain of fussy, obsolete, and powerful guilds. If Westminster and the suburbs were growing continually, noted a well-informed economist (1754), it was for obvious reasons: "These suburbs are free and present a clear field for every industrious citizen, while in its bosom London nourishes ninety-two of all sorts of those exclusive companies [guilds], whose numerous members can be seen adorning the Lord Mayor's Show every year with immoderate pomp." . . .

Type C: subjugated towns, of early modern times. Everywhere in Europe, as soon as the state was firmly established it disciplined the towns with instinctive relentlessness, whether or not it used violence. The Habsburgs did so just as much as the Popes, the German princes as much as the Medicis or the kings of France. Except in the Netherlands and England, obedience was imposed.

Take Florence as an example: The Medicis had slowly subjugated it, almost elegantly in Lorenzo's time. But after 1532 and the return of the Medicis to power the process accelerated. Florence in the seventeenth

century was no more than the Grand Duke's court. He had seized everything—money, the right to govern, and to distribute honours. From the
Pitti Palace, on the left bank of the Arno, a gallery—a secret passage in
fact—allowed the prince to cross the river and reach the Uffizi. This elegant gallery, still in existence today on the Ponte Vecchio, was the
thread from which the spider at the extremity of his web supervised the
imprisoned town. . . .

Different Types of Development

But we know, of course, that urban development does not happen of its
own accord: It is not an endogenous phenomenon produced under a
bell-jar. It is always the expression of a society which controls it from
within, but also from without, and in this respect, our classification is, I
repeat, too simple. That said, how does it work when applied outside
the narrow confines of Western Europe?

1. *Towns in colonial America.* We should say "in Latin America," because the English towns remained a separate case. They had to live by
their own resources and emerge from their wilderness to find a place in
the vast world; the real parallel for them is the medieval city. The
towns in Iberian America had a much simpler and more limited career.
Built like Roman camps inside four earth walls, they were garrisons lost
in the midst of vast hostile expanses, linked together by communications which were slow because they stretched across enormous empty
spaces. Curiously, at a period when the privileged medieval town had
spread over practically the whole of Europe, the ancient rule prevailed
in all Hispano-Portuguese America, apart from the large towns of
the viceroys: Mexico City, Lima, Santiago de Chile, San Salvador
(Bahia)—that is to say the official, already parasitical organisms.

There were scarcely any purely commercial towns in this part of
America, or if there were they were of minor importance. For example,
Recife—the merchants' town—stood next to aristocratic Olinda, town
of great plantation owners, *senhores de engenbos*,[1] and slave owners. It
was rather like Piraeus or Phalera in relation to Pericles' Athens.
Buenos Aires after its second foundation (the successful one in 1580)
was still a small market village—like Megara or Aegina. It had the misfortune to have nothing but Indian *bravos* round about, and its inhabitants complained of being forced to earn "their bread by the sweat of
their brow" in this America where the whites were *rentiers*.[2] But caravans of mules or large wooden carts arrived there from the Andes, from

[1] Men of talent. [Ed.]
[2] Property owners. [Ed.]

Lima, which was a way of acquiring Potosi silver. Sugar, and soon gold, came by sailing ship from Brazil. And contact with Portugal and Africa was maintained through the smuggling carried on by sailing ships bringing black slaves. But Buenos Aires remained an exception amidst the "barbarism" of nascent Argentina.

The American town was generally tiny, without these gifts from abroad. It governed itself. No one was really concerned with its fate. Its masters were the landowners who had their houses in the town, with rings for tethering their horses fixed on the front walls overlooking the street. These were the "men of property," os *homes bons* of the municipalities of Brazil, or the *hacendados* of the Spanish *cabildos*.[3] These towns were so many miniature versions of Sparta or of Thebes in the time of Epaminondas. It could safely be said that the history of the Western towns in America began again from zero. Naturally there was no separation between the towns and the hinterland and there was no industry to be shared out. Wherever industry appeared—in Mexico city, for example—it was carried on by slaves or semi-slaves. The medieval European town would not have been conceivable if its artisans had been serfs.

2. *How should Russian towns be classified?* One can tell at a glance that the towns that survived or grew up again in Muscovy after the terrible catastrophes of the Mongol invasion no longer lived according to the Western pattern. Although there were great cities among them, like Moscow or Novgorod, they were kept in hand sometimes brutally. In the sixteenth century a proverb still asked: "Who can set his face against God and the mighty Novgorod?" But the proverb was wrong. The town was harshly brought to heel in 1427 and again in 1477 (it had to deliver 300 cartloads of gold). Executions, deportations, confiscations followed in quick succession. Above all, these towns were caught up in the slow circulation of traffic over an immense, already Asiatic, still wild expanse. In 1650, as in the past, transport on the rivers or overland by sledge or by convoys of carts moved with an enormous loss of time. It was often dangerous even to go near villages, and a halt had to be called every evening in open country—as on the Balkan roads—deploying the carriages in a circle, with everyone on the alert to defend himself.

For all these reasons the Muscovy towns did not impose themselves on the vast surrounding countryside; quite the reverse. They were unable to dictate their wishes to a peasant world which was biologically extraordinarily strong, although poverty-stricken, restless, and perpetually on the move. The important fact was that "harvests per hectare in

[3]Town councils. [Ed.]

the European countries of the East remained constant on average, from the sixteenth to the nineteenth century"—at a low level. There was no healthy rural surplus and therefore no really prosperous town. Nor did the Russian towns have serving them those secondary towns that were a characteristic of the West and its lively trade.

Consequently, there were innumerable peasant serfs practically without land, insolvent in the eyes of their lords and even the state. It was of no importance whether they went to towns or to work in the houses of rich peasants. In the town they became beggars, porters, craftsmen, poor tradesmen, or very rarely merchants who got rich quickly. They might also stay put and become craftsmen in their own villages, or seek the necessary supplement to their earnings by becoming carriers or travelling pedlars. This irresistible tide of mendicancy could not be stemmed, and indeed it often served the interests of the landlord who gave it his blessing: All such artisans and traders remained his serfs whatever they did and however great their social success; they still owed him their dues.

These examples and others indicate a fate resembling what may after all have happened at the beginning of Western urbanization. Though a clearer case, it is comparable to the caesura[4] between the eleventh and thirteenth centuries, that interlude when almost everything was born of the villages and peasant vitality. We might call it an intermediate position between A and C, without the B type (the independent city) ever having arisen. The prince appeared too quickly, like the ogre in a fairy tale.

3. *Imperial towns in the East and Far East.* The same problems and ambiguities—only deeper—arise when we leave Europe and move east.

Towns similar to those in medieval Europe—masters of their fate for a brief moment—only arose in Islam when the empires collapsed. They marked some outstanding moments in Islamic civilization. But they only lasted for a time and the main beneficiaries were certain marginal towns like Cordoba, or the cities which were urban republics by the fifteenth century, like Ceuta before the Portuguese occupation in 1415, or Oran before the Spanish occupation in 1509. The usual pattern was the huge city under the rule of a prince or a Caliph: a Baghdad or a Cairo.

Towns in distant Asia were of the same type: imperial or royal cities, enormous, parasitical, soft, and luxurious—Delhi and Vijnayanagar, Peking and to some extent Nanking, though this was rather different. The great prestige enjoyed by the prince comes as no surprise to us.

---

[4]Pause. [Ed.]

And if one ruler was swallowed up by the city or more likely by his palace, another immediately took his place and the subjection continued. Neither will it surprise us to learn that these towns were incapable of taking over the artisanal trades from the countryside: They were both open towns and subject towns simultaneously. Besides, in India as in China, social structures already existing hampered the free movement of the towns. If the town did not win its independence, it was not only because of the bastinadoes[5] ordered by the mandarins or the cruelty of the prince to merchants and ordinary citizens. It was because society was prematurely fixed, crystallized in a certain mould.

In India, the caste system automatically divided and broke up every urban community. In China, the cult of the *gentes*[6] on the one hand was confronted on the other by a mixture comparable to that which created the Western town: Like the latter it acted as a melting-pot, breaking old bonds and placing individuals on the same level. The arrival of immigrants created an "American" environment, where those already settled set the tone and the way of life. In addition, there was no independent authority representing the Chinese town as a unit, in its dealings with the State or with the very powerful countryside. The rural areas were the real heart of living, active, and thinking China.

The town, residence of officials and nobles, was not the property of either guilds or merchants. There was no gradual "rise of the bourgeoisie" here. No sooner did a bourgeoisie appear than it was tempted by class betrayal, fascinated by the luxurious life of the mandarins. The towns might have lived their own lives, filled in the contours of their own destiny, if individual initiative and capitalism had had a clear field. But the tutelary State hardly lent itself to this. It did occasionally nod, intentionally or not: At the end of the sixteenth century a bourgeoisie seems to have emerged with a taste for business enterprise, and we can guess what part it played in the large iron-works near Peking, in the private porcelain workshops that developed in King-te-chen, and even more in the rise of the silk trade in Su-Chu, the capital of Kiang-tsu. But this was no more than a flash in the pan. With the Manchu conquest, the Chinese crisis was resolved in the seventeenth century in a direction completely opposed to urban freedoms.

Only the West swung completely over in favour of its towns. The towns caused the West to advance. It was, let us repeat, an enormous event, but the deep-seated reasons behind it are still inadequately explained. What would the Chinese towns have become if the junks had discovered the Cape of Good Hope at the beginning of the fifteenth century, and had made full use of such a chance of world conquest?

[5]Beatings (often on soles of the feet). [Ed.]
[6]People. [Ed.]

82

Charter of Henry I
for London, 1130–1133

In the last century types of cities have been distinguished by historians and sociologists who have recognized that European cities in the late Middle Ages were relatively independent of rulers and other cities due to charters of freedom. Town and city charters were frequently drawn up between European lords, princes, and kings, on the one hand, and the inhabitants, owners, or burghers, on the other. These charters, which were granted to the town for a fee, brought needed income to the lord or ruler while ensuring the ruler access to an active class of artisans, merchants, specialists, and luxury providers.

In this charter, for London, England, what does the king give to the townspeople? What powers does the king retain? What seems to have been the main concerns of the townspeople and king that are settled here?

Thinking Historically

Does this charter reflect King Henry's strength or his weakness? Would this sort of arrangement be more likely to develop in a feudal society like Europe than it would in a Mongol or Chinese empire? Why or why not? Does the charter support Braudel's comparative thesis?

Henry, by the grace of God, king of the English, to the archbishop of Canterbury, and to the bishops and abbots, and earls and barons and justices and sheriffs, and to all his liegemen, both French and English, of the whole of England, greeting. Know that I have granted to my citizens of London that they shall hold middlesex at "farm" for three hundred pounds "by tale" for themselves and their heirs from me and my heirs, so that the citizens shall appoint as sheriff from themselves whomsoever they may choose, and shall appoint from among themselves as justice whomsoever they choose to look after the pleas of my crown and the pleadings which arise in connexion with them. No other shall be justice over the same men of London. And the citizens shall not plead outside the walls of the city in respect of any plea; and they shall

Charter of Henry I for London (1130–1133), from *English Historical Documents*, vol. II, ed. David C. Douglas and George W. Greenaway (London: Eyre and Spottiswoode, Ltd., 1955), 945–46.

be quit of scot and of Danegeld[1] and the murder-fine. Nor shall any of them be compelled to offer trial by battle. And if any one of the citizens shall be impleaded in respect of the pleas of the crown, let him prove himself to be a man of London by an oath which shall be judged in the city. Let no one be billeted within the walls of the city, either of my household, or by the force of anyone else. And let all the men of London and their property be quit and free from toll and passage and lestage[2] and from all other customs throughout all England and at the seaports. And let the churches and barons and citizens hold and have well and in peace their sokes,[3] with all their customs, so that those who dwell in these sokes shall pay no customs except to him who possesses the soke, or to the steward whom he has placed there. And a man of London shall not be fined at mercy except according to his "were," that is to say, up to one hundred shillings: This applies to an offence which can be punished by a fine. And there shall no longer be "miskenning"[4] in the hustings court,[5] nor in the folk-moot,[6] nor in other pleas within the city. And the hustings court shall sit once a week, to wit, on Monday. I will cause my citizens to have their lands and pledges and debts within the city and outside it. And in respect of the lands about which they make claim to me, I will do them right according to the law of the city. And if anyone has taken toll or custom from the citizens of London, then the citizens of London may take from the borough or village where toll or custom has been levied as much as the man of London gave for toll, and more also may be taken for a penalty. And let all debtors to the citizens of London discharge their debts, or prove in London that they do not owe them; and if they refuse either to pay, or to come and make such proof, then the citizens to whom the debts are due may take pledges within the city either from the borough or from the village or from the county in which the debtor lives. And the citizens shall have their hunting chases, as well and fully as had their predecessors, to wit, in Chiltern and Middlesex and Surrey.

---

[1]A medieval land tax, originally levied to buy off raiding Danes (literally, "Dane's money"). First levied in England in 868, but generally discontinued in the twelfth century. [Ed.]

[2]Sometimes "lastage": a toll payable by traders attending fairs and markets. [Ed.]

[3]A right of local jurisdiction. [Ed.]

[4]A verbal error in making a formal oath. [Ed.]

[5]King's court or court of king's representatives. [Ed.]

[6]A general assembly of the people. [Ed.]

83

GREGORIO DATI

Corporations and Community in Florence

This is an account of the Italian city of Florence and its inhabitants from 1380 to 1405. While family identity was primary, residents of Florence were also members of many corporate organizations that served to channel their loyalty to the larger urban community. Among these were guilds and parish churches, as well as political, welfare, and religious organizations. On public holidays like the feast day of St. John the Baptist, the patron saint of Florence, these various groups would come together in a display of communal solidarity that was often more fraternal than the deliberations in the political arena. What seems to motivate people to participate in public acts and parades in Florence?

Thinking Historically

Would a chartered city be more or less likely than a city run by a king to hold these sorts of festivities? In what ways would you expect the politics of Florence to be similar to and different from those of London? What aspects of this account support Braudel's thesis?

When springtime comes and the whole world rejoices, every Florentine begins to think about organizing a magnificent celebration on the feast day of St. John the Baptist [June 24]. . . . For two months in advance, everyone is planning marriage feasts or other celebrations in honor of the day. There are preparations for the horse races, the costumes of the retinues, the flags, and the trumpets; there are the pennants and the wax candles and other things which the subject territories offer to the Commune. Messengers are sent to obtain provisions for the banquets, and horses come from everywhere to run in the races. The whole city is engaged in preparing for the feast, and the spirits of the young people and the women [are animated] by these preparations. . . . Everyone is filled with gaiety; there are dances and concerts and songfests and tournaments and other joyous activities. Up to the eve of the holiday, no one thinks about anything else.

Gregorio Dati, "*Istoria di Firenze dall'anno MCCCLXXX all'anno MCCCCV*" (History of Florence from 1380 to 1405) (Florence, 1735), in *The Society of Renaissance Florence*, ed. and trans. Gene Brucker (New York: Harper & Row, 1971), 75–78.

Early on the morning of the day before the holiday, each guild has a display outside of its shops of its fine wares, its ornaments, and jewels. There are cloths of gold and silk sufficient to adorn ten kingdoms. . . . Then at the third hour, there is a solemn procession of clerics, priests, monks, and friars, and there are so many [religious] orders, and so many relics of saints, that the procession seems endless. [It is a manifestation] of great devotion, on account of the marvelous richness of the adornments . . . and clothing of gold and silk with embroidered figures. There are many confraternities of men who assemble at the place where their meetings are held, dressed as angels, and with musical instruments of every kind and marvelous singing. They stage the most beautiful representations of the saints, and of those relics in whose honor they perform. They leave from S. Maria del Fiore [the cathedral] and march through the city and then return.

Then, after midday, when the heat has abated before sunset, all of the citizens assemble under [the banner of] their district, of which there are sixteen. Each goes in the procession in turn, the first, then the second, and so on with one district following the other, and in each group the citizens march two by two, with the oldest and most distinguished at the head, and proceeding down to the young men in rich garments. They march to the church of St. John [the Baptistery] to offer, one by one, a wax candle weighing one pound. . . . The walls along the streets through which they pass are all decorated, and there are . . . benches on which are seated young ladies and girls dressed in silk and adorned with jewels, pearls, and precious stones. This procession continues until sunset, and after each citizen has made his offering, he returns home with his wife to prepare for the next morning.

Whoever goes to the Piazza della Signoria on the morning of St. John's Day witnesses a magnificent, marvelous, and triumphant sight, which the mind can scarcely grasp. Around the great piazza are a hundred towers which appear to be made of gold. Some were brought on carts and others by porters. . . . [These towers] are made of wood, paper, and wax [and decorated] with gold, colored paints, and with figures. . . . Next to the rostrum of the palace [of the Signoria] are standards . . . which belong to the most important towns which are subject to the Commune: Pisa, Arezzo, Pistoia, Volterra, Cortona, Lucignano. . . .

First to present their offering, in the morning, are the captains of the Parte Guelfa, together with all of the knights, lords, ambassadors, and foreign knights. They are accompanied by a large number of the most honorable citizens, and before them, riding on a charger covered with a cloth . . . is one of their pages carrying a banner with the insignia of the Parte Guelfa. Then there follow the above-mentioned standards, each one carried by men on horseback . . . and they all go to make their offerings at the Baptistery. And these standards are given a tribute by the districts which have been acquired by the Commune of Florence. . . . The wax candles, which have the appearance of golden towers, are the tribute of the regions which in most ancient times were subject to the Florentines. In order of dignity, they are brought, one by one, to be offered to St. John, and on the following day, they are hung inside the church and there they remain for the entire year until the next feast day. . . . Then come . . . an infinite number of large wax candles, some weighing one hundred pounds and others fifty, some more and some less . . . carried by the residents of the villages [in the *contado*[1]] which offer them. . . .

Then the lord priors and their colleges come to make their offerings, accompanied by their rectors, that is, the podestà, the captain [of the *popolo*[2]], and the executor. . . . And after the lord [priors] come those who are participating in the horse race, and they are followed by the Flemings and the residents of Brabant who are weavers of woolen cloth in Florence. Then there are offerings by twelve prisoners who, as an act of mercy, have been released from prison . . . in honor of St. John, and these are poor people. . . . After all of these offerings have been made, men and women return home to dine. . . .

[1]Countryside. [Ed.]
[2]People. [Ed.]

MARCO POLO

From The Travels of Marco Polo

In *The Travels of Marco Polo,* the Venetian merchant recounted his travels across the Silk Road to Mongolia and China. According to his account he stayed in China from 1275 to 1292 before returning to Venice. In 1275, the Chinese Southern Song capital of Hangchou had just been conquered by Kubilai Khan, the grandson of Ghengis Khan. The Mongols were able to conquer China, but they could not radically change it. The structure and organization of towns and cities remained very much the way it had been under the Song. In addition to Hangchou, which Marco Polo calls Kinsay, he had been to the Mon-

Marco Polo, *The Travels of Marco Polo,* the Complete Yule-Currier ed., vol. 2 (New York: Dover, 1993), 185–206.

gol capital at Karakorum and to the Chinese cities of Peking and Changan. Why does he consider the city of Hangchou "the finest and the noblest in the world"? How does his description support that characterization? What do you see in this account of Hangchou that supports or challenges Braudel's comparison and thesis?

Thinking Historically

In what ways does the Hangchou that emerges from this document resemble London or Florence? In what ways was Hangchou significantly different? Does Marco Polo's description show signs that Chinese cities were autonomous or that they were not?

When you have left the city of Changan and have travelled for three days through a splendid country, passing a number of towns and villages, you arrive at the most noble city of Kinsay,[1] a name which is as much as to say in our tongue "The City of Heaven," as I told you before.

And since we have got thither I will enter into particulars about its magnificence; and these are well worth the telling, for the city is beyond dispute the finest and the noblest in the world. In this we shall speak according to the written statement which the Queen of this Realm sent to Bayan the conqueror of the country for transmission to the Great Kaan, in order that he might be aware of the surpassing grandeur of the city and might be moved to save it from destruction or injury. I will tell you all the truth as it was set down in that document. For truth it was, as the said Messer Marco Polo at a later date was able to witness with his own eyes. And now we shall rehearse those particulars.

First and foremost, then, the document stated the city of Kinsay to be so great that it hath an hundred miles of compass. And there are in it twelve thousand bridges of stone,[2] for the most part so lofty that a great fleet could pass beneath them. And let no man marvel that there are so many bridges, for you see the whole city stands as it were in the water and surrounded by water, so that a great many bridges are required to give free passage about it. [And though the bridges be so high, the approaches are so well contrived that carts and horses do cross them.]

The document aforesaid also went on to state that there were in this city twelve guilds of the different crafts, and that each guild had twelve thousand houses in the occupation of its workmen. Each of these houses contains at least twelve men, whilst some contain twenty and some forty,—not that these are all masters, but inclusive of the

---

[1]Kinsay simply means "capital." The current name is Hangchou. [Ed.]
[2]Generally assumed to be an exaggeration; one thousand would have been a lot. [Ed.]

journeymen who work under the masters. And yet all these craftsmen had full occupation, for many other cities of the kingdom are supplied from this city with what they require.

The document aforesaid also stated that the number and wealth of the merchants, and the amount of goods that passed through their hands, was so enormous that no man could form a just estimate thereof. And I should have told you with regard to those masters of the different crafts who are at the head of such houses as I have mentioned, that neither they nor their wives ever touch a piece of work with their own hands, but live as nicely and delicately as if they were kings and queens. The wives indeed are most dainty and angelical creatures! Moreover it was an ordinance laid down by the King that every man should follow his father's business and no other, no matter if he possessed 100,000 bezants.[3]

Inside the city there is a Lake which has a compass of some thirty miles:[4] and all round it are erected beautiful palaces and mansions, of the richest and most exquisite structure that you can imagine, belonging to the nobles of the city. There are also on its shores many abbeys and churches of the Idolaters. In the middle of the Lake are two Islands, on each of which stands a rich, beautiful, and spacious edifice, furnished in such style as to seem fit for the palace of an Emperor. And when any one of the citizens desired to hold a marriage feast, or to give any other entertainment, it used to be done at one of these palaces. And everything would be found there ready to order, such as silver plate, trenchers, and dishes [napkins and tablecloths], and whatever else was needful. The King made this provision for the gratification of his people, and the place was open to every one who desired to give an entertainment. . . .

The people are Idolaters; and since they were conquered by the Great Kaan they use paper money. [Both men and women are fair and comely, and for the most part clothe themselves in silk, so vast is the supply of that material, both from the whole district of Kinsay, and from the imports by traders from other provinces.] And you must know they eat every kind of flesh, even that of dogs and other unclean beasts, which nothing would induce a Christian to eat.

Since the Great Kaan occupied the city he has ordained that each of the twelve thousand bridges should be provided with a guard of ten men, in case of any disturbance, or of any being so rash as to plot treason or insurrection against him. [Each guard is provided with a hollow

[3]A gold coin struck at Byzantium (or Constantinople) and used throughout Europe from the ninth century. [Ed.]

[4]The circumference of the lake was more probably 30 li. A li was about a third of a mile, but it was sometimes used to mean a hundredth of a day's march. The entire circumference of the city could not have been more than 100 li. [Ed.]

instrument of wood and with a metal basin, and with a timekeeper to enable them to know the hour of the day or night. . . .

Part of the watch patrols the quarter, to see if any light or fire is burning after the lawful hours; if they find any they mark the door, and in the morning the owner is summoned before the magistrates, and unless he can plead a good excuse he is punished. Also if they find any one going about the streets at unlawful hours they arrest him, and in the morning they bring him before the magistrates. Likewise if in the daytime they find any poor cripple unable to work for his livelihood, they take him to one of the hospitals, of which there are many, founded by the ancient kings, and endowed with great revenues. Or if he be capable of work they oblige him to take up some trade. . . .

The Kaan watches this city with especial diligence because it forms the head of all Manzi;[5] and because he has an immense revenue from the duties levied on the transactions of trade therein, the amount of which is such that no one would credit it on mere hearsay.

All the streets of the city are paved with stone or brick, as indeed are all the highways throughout Manzi, so that you ride and travel in every direction without inconvenience. . . .

You must know also that the city of Kinsay has some three thousand baths, the water of which is supplied by springs. They are hot baths, and the people take great delight in them, frequenting them several times a month, for they are very cleanly in their persons. They are the finest and largest baths in the world; large enough for one hundred persons to bathe together.

And the Ocean Sea comes within twenty-five miles of the city at a place called Ganfu, where there is a town and an excellent haven, with a vast amount of shipping which is engaged in the traffic to and from India and other foreign parts, exporting and importing many kinds of wares, by which the city benefits. And a great river flows from the city of Kinsay to that sea-haven, by which vessels can come up to the city itself. This river extends also to other places further inland.

Know also that the Great Kaan hath distributed the territory of Manzi into nine parts, which he hath constituted into nine kingdoms. To each of these kingdoms a king is appointed who is subordinate to the Great Kaan, and every year renders the accounts of his kingdom to the fiscal office at the capital. This city of Kinsay is the seat of one of these kings, who rules over one hundred forty great and wealthy cities. For in the whole of this vast country of Manzi there are more than twelve hundred great and wealthy cities, without counting the towns and villages, which are in great numbers. And you may receive it for certain that in each of those twelve hundred cities the Great Kaan has a

[5]China. [Ed.]

garrison, and that the smallest of such garrisons musters one thousand men; whilst there are some of ten thousand, twenty thousand, and thirty thousand; so that the total number of troops is something scarcely calculable. . . . And all of them belong to the army of the Great Kaan.

I repeat that everything appertaining to this city is on so vast a scale, and the Great Kaan's yearly revenues therefrom are so immense, that it is not easy even to put it in writing, and it seems past belief to one who merely hears it told. But I *will* write it down for you. . . .

I must tell you that in this city there are 160 *tomans*[6] of fires, or in other words 160 *tomans* of houses. Now I should tell you that the *toman* is 10,000, so that you can reckon the total as altogether 1,600,000 houses, among which are a great number of rich palaces. There is one church only, belonging to the Nestorian Christians.

There is another thing I must tell you. It is the custom for every burgess of this city, and in fact for every description of person in it, to write over his door his own name, the name of his wife, and those of his children, his slaves, and all the inmates of his house, and also the number of animals that he keeps. And if any one dies in the house then the name of that person is erased, and if any child is born its name is added. So in this way the sovereign is able to know exactly the population of the city. And this is the practice also throughout all Manzi and Cathay.

And I must tell you that every hosteler who keeps an hostel for travellers is bound to register their names and surnames, as well as the day and month of their arrival and departure. And thus the sovereign hath the means of knowing, whenever it pleases him, who come and go throughout his dominions. And certes this is a wise order and a provident [one].

The position of the city is such that it has on one side a lake of fresh and exquisitely clear water (already spoken of), and on the other a very large river. The waters of the latter fill a number of canals of all sizes which run through the different quarters of the city, carry away all impurities, and then enter the Lake; whence they issue again and flow to the Ocean, thus producing a most excellent atmosphere. By means of these channels, as well as by the streets, you can go all about the city. Both streets and canals are so wide and spacious that carts on the one and boats on the other can readily pass to and fro, conveying necessary supplies to the inhabitants.

At the opposite side the city is shut in by a channel, perhaps forty miles in length, very wide, and full of water derived from the river aforesaid, which was made by the ancient kings of the country in order to relieve the river when flooding its banks. This serves also as a de-

---

[6]A *toman* is a Mongol measurement of ten thousand. [Ed.]

fence to the city, and the earth dug from it has been thrown inward, forming a kind of mound enclosing the city.

In this part are the ten principal markets, though besides these there are a vast number of others in the different parts of the town. The former are all squares of half a mile to the side, and along their front passes the main street, which is forty paces in width, and runs straight from end to end of the city, crossing many bridges of easy and commodious approach. At every four miles of its length comes one of those great squares of two miles (as we have mentioned) in compass. So also parallel to this great street, but at the back of the marketplaces, there runs a very large canal, on the bank of which toward the squares are built great houses of stone, in which the merchants from India and other foreign parts store their wares, to be handy for the markets. In each of the squares is held a market three days in the week, frequented by forty thousand or fifty thousand persons, who bring thither for sale every possible necessary of life, so that there is always an ample supply of every kind of meat and game, as of roebuck, red-deer, fallow-deer, hares, rabbits, partridges, pheasants, francolins, quails, fowls, capons, and of ducks and geese an infinite quantity; for so many are bred on the Lake that for a Venice groat of silver you can have a couple of geese and two couple of ducks. Then there are the shambles where the larger animals are slaughtered, such as calves, beeves, kids, and lambs, the flesh of which is eaten by the rich and the great dignitaries.

Those markets make a daily display of every kind of vegetables and fruits; and among the latter there are in particular certain pears of enormous size, weighing as much as ten pounds apiece, and the pulp of which is white and fragrant like a confection; besides peaches in their season both yellow and white, of every delicate flavour. . . .

All the ten marketplaces are encompassed by lofty houses, and below these are shops where all sorts of crafts are carried on, and all sorts of wares are on sale, including spices and jewels and pearls. Some of these shops are entirely devoted to the sale of wine made from rice and spices, which is constantly made fresh, and is sold very cheap.

Certain of the streets are occupied by the women of the town, who are in such a number that I dare not say what it is. They are found not only in the vicinity of the marketplaces, where usually a quarter is assigned to them, but all over the city. They exhibit themselves splendidly attired and abundantly perfumed, in finely garnished houses, with trains of waiting-women. These women are extremely accomplished in all the arts of allurement, and readily adapt their conversation to all sorts of persons, insomuch that strangers who have once tasted their attractions seem to get bewitched, and are so taken with their blandishments and their fascinating ways that they never can get these out of their heads. Hence it comes to pass that when they return home they

say they have been to Kinsay or the City of Heaven, and their only desire is to get back thither as soon as possible.

Other streets are occupied by the Physicians, and by the As-
trologers, who are also teachers of reading and writing; and an infinity
of other professions have their places round about those squares. In
each of the squares there are two great palaces facing one another, in
which are established the officers appointed by the King to decide differences arising between merchants, or other inhabitants of the quarter.
It is the daily duty of these officers to see that the guards are at their
posts on the neighbouring bridges, and to punish them at their discretion if they are absent. . . .

The natives of the city are men of peaceful character, both from education and from the example of their kings, whose disposition was the
same. They know nothing of handling arms, and keep none in their
houses. You hear of no feuds or noisy quarrels or dissensions of any
kind among them. Both in their commercial dealings and in their manu-
factures they are thoroughly honest and truthful, and there is such a degree of good will and neighbourly attachment among both men and
women that you would take the people who live in the same street to be
all one family.

And this familiar intimacy is free from all jealousy or suspicion
of the conduct of their women. These they treat with the greatest respect, and a man who should presume to make loose proposals to a
married woman would be regarded as an infamous rascal. They also
treat the foreigners who visit them for the sake of trade with great cor-
diality, and entertain them in the most winning manner, affording them
every help and advice on their business. But on the other hand they
hate to see soldiers, and not least those of the Great Kaan's garrisons,
regarding them as the cause of their having lost their native kings and
lords.

85

S. D. GOITEIN

Cairo: An Islamic City
in Light of the Geniza

The author of this selection provides an especially detailed picture of medieval Cairo due to an unusual discovery of documents. "The Geniza" refers to a treasure trove of documents maintained by a Jewish synagogue in Cairo from the tenth to thirteenth centuries. It contains correspondence, legal documents, receipts, inventories, prescriptions, and notes—written in Hebrew characters in the Arabic language—and offers a rare opportunity to review virtually everything a community wrote over a long period of time. It is an extremely valuable resource that can answer most questions about medieval society in Cairo.

In this selection, S. D. Goitein studies the documents for the insight they provide into city life in Cairo. What do the Geniza documents tell us about city life in Cairo? What would it have been like to live in medieval Cairo?

Thinking Historically

In what ways would life in medieval Cairo have been similar to or different from life in a city of medieval Europe or medieval China? What is the significance of the lack of public buildings and guilds in Cairo? In what ways was the Muslim identity larger or more cosmopolitan than European urban identities? How does this support or challenge Braudel's thesis?

... It is astounding how rarely government buildings are mentioned in the Geniza documents. There were the local police stations and prisons, as well as the offices where one received the licenses occasionally needed, but even these are seldom referred to. The Mint and the Exchange are frequently referred to, but at least the latter was only semi-public in character, since the persons working there were not on the government payroll. Taxes were normally collected by tax farmers. Thus there was little direct contact between the government and the

---

S. D. Goitein, "Cairo: An Islamic City in Light of the Geniza," in *Middle Eastern Cities*, ed. Ira M. Lapidus (Berkeley and Los Angeles: University of California Press, 1969), 90–95.

populace and consequently not much need for public buildings. The imperial palace and its barracks formed a city by itself, occasionally mentioned in Ayyūbid times, but almost never in the Fāṭimid period.

Government, although not conspicuous by many public buildings, was present in the city in many other ways. A city was governed by a military commander called *amīr*, who was assisted by the *wālī* or superintendent of the police. Smaller towns had only a *wālī* and no *amīr*. Very powerful, sometimes more powerful than the *amīr*, was the *qāḍī*, or judge, who had administrative duties in addition to his substantial judicial functions. The chief *qāḍī* often held other functions such as the control of the taxes or of a port, as we read with regard to Alexandria or Tyre. The city was divided into small administrative units called *rabʿ* (which is not the classical *rubʿ*, meaning quarter, but instead designates an area, or rather a compound). Each *rabʿ* had a superintendent called *ṣāḥib rabʿ* (pronounced rub), very often referred to in the Geniza papers. In addition to regular and mounted police there were plain clothesmen, or secret service men, called *aṣḥāb al-khabar*, "informants" who formed a government agency independent even of the *qāḍī*, a state of affairs for which there seem to exist parallels in more modern times.

An ancient source tells us that the vizier[1] al-Ma'mūn, mentioned above, instructed the two superintendents of the police of Fusṭāṭ[2] and Cairo, respectively, to draw up exact lists of the inhabitants showing their occupations and other circumstances and to permit no one to move from one house to another without notification of the police. This is described as an extraordinary measure aimed at locating any would-be assassins who might have been sent to the Egyptian capital by the Bāṭiniyya, an Ismāʿīlī group using murder as a political weapon. Such lists, probably with fewer details, no doubt were in regular use for the needs of taxation. In a letter from Sicily, either from its capital Palermo or from Mazara on its southwestern tip, the writer, an immigrant from Tunisia around 1063, informs his business friend in Egypt that he is going to buy a house and that he has already registered for the purpose in the *qānūn* (Greek *canon*) which must have designated an official list of inhabitants. With regard to non-Muslims, a differentiation was made between permanent residents and newcomers. Whether the same practice existed with respect to Muslims is not evident from the Geniza papers.

What were the dues that a town dweller had to pay to the government in his capacity as the inhabitant of a city, and what were the benefits that he derived from such payments? By right of conquest, the

---

[1]Prime minister. [Ed.]
[2]Old Cairo. [Ed.]

ground on which Fusṭāṭ stood belonged to the Muslims, that is, to the government (the same was the case in many other Islamic cities), and a ground rent, called *ḥikr*, had to be paid for each building. A great many deeds of sale, gift, and rent refer to this imposition. . . .

Besides the ground rent, every month a *ḥarāsa*, or "due for protection," had to be paid to the government. The protection was partly in the hands of a police force, partly in those of the superintendents of the compounds, and partly was entrusted to nightwatchmen, usually referred to as *ṭawwāfūn*, literally, "those that make the round," but known also by other designations. As we learn expressly from a Geniza source, the nightwatchmen, like the regular police, were appointed by the government (and not by a municipality or local body which did not exist). The amounts of the *ḥarāsa* in the communal accounts cannot be related to the value of the properties for which they were paid, but it is evident that they were moderate.

In a responsum[3] written around 1165, Rabbi Maimon, the father of Moses Maimonides,[4] states that the markets of Fusṭāṭ used to remain open during the nights, in contrast of course to what the writer was accustomed from having lived in other Islamic cities. In Fusṭāṭ, too, this had not been always the case. In a description of the festival of Epiphany from the year 941 in which all parts of the population took part, it is mentioned as exceptional that the streets were not closed during that particular night.

Sanitation must have been another great concern of the government, for the items "removal of rubbish" (called "throwing out of dust") and "cleaning of pipes" appear with great regularity in the monthly accounts preserved in the Geniza. One gets the impression that these hygienic measures were not left to the discretion of each individual proprietor of a house. The clay tubes bringing water (for washing purposes) to a house and those connecting it with a cesspool constantly needed clearing, and there are also many references to their construction. The amounts paid for both operations were considerable. The Geniza has preserved an autograph note by Maimonides permitting a beadle[5] to spend a certain sum on "throwing out of dust" (presumably from a synagogue). This may serve as an illustration for the fact that landlords may have found the payment of these dues not always easy.

In this context we may also draw attention to the new insights gained through the study of the documents from the Geniza about the

---

[3] A legal document. [Ed.]
[4] (1135–1204), a Jewish rabbi, physician, and philosopher in Spain and Egypt. [Ed.]
[5] A minor official. [Ed.]

social life of Cairo. Massignon[6] had asserted, and he was followed by many, that the life-unit in the Islamic city was the professional corporation, the guilds of the merchants, artisans, and scholars which had professional, as well as social and religious functions. No one would deny that this was true to a large extent for the sixteenth through the nineteenth centuries. However, there is not a shred of evidence that this was true for the ninth through the thirteenth centuries. . . .

The term "guild" designates a medieval union of craftsmen or traders which supervised the work of its members in order to uphold standards, and made arrangements for the education of apprentices and their initiation into the union. The guild protected its members against competition, and in Christian countries was closely connected with religion.

Scrutinizing the records of the Cairo Geniza or the Muslim handbooks of market supervision contemporary with them, one looks in vain for an Arabic equivalent of the term "guild." There was no such word because there was no such institution. The supervision of the quality of the artisans' work was in the hands of the state police, which availed itself of the services of trustworthy and expert assistants.

Regarding apprenticeship and admission to a profession, no formalities and no rigid rules are to be discovered in our sources. Parents were expected to have their sons learn a craft and to pay for their instruction, and the Geniza has preserved several contracts to this effect.

The protection of the local industries from the competition of newcomers and outsiders is richly documented by the Geniza records, but nowhere do we hear about a professional corporation fulfilling this task. It was the Jewish local community, the central Jewish authorities, the state police, or influential notables, Muslim and Jewish, who were active in these matters.

As to the religious aspect of professional corporation, the associations of artisans and traders in imperial Rome, or at least a part of them, bore a religious character and were often connected with the local cult of the town from which the founders of an association had originated. Similarly, the Christian guilds of the late Middle Ages had their patron saints and special rites. The fourteenth century was the heyday of Muslim corporations, especially in Anatolia (the present day Turkey), which adopted the doctrines and ceremonies of Muslim mystic brotherhoods. One looks in vain for similar combinations of artisanship and religious cult in the period and the countries under discussion. On the other hand, we find partnerships of Muslims and Jews both in workshops and in mercantile undertakings, for free partnerships were the normal form of industrial cooperation, and were common as well in commercial ventures. The classical Islamic city was a

---

[6]Louis Massignon (1883–1962), a French scholar of Islam. [Ed.]

free enterprise society, the very opposite of a community organized in rigid guilds and tight professional corporations.

Further, we have stated before that no formal citizenship existed. The question is, however, how far did people feel a personal attachment to their native towns. "Homesickness," says Professor Gibb in his translation of the famous traveler Ibn Baṭṭūṭa, "was hardly to be expected in a society so cosmopolitan as that of medieval Islam." Indeed the extent of travel and migration reflected in the Geniza is astounding. No less remarkable, however, is the frequency of expressions of longing for one's native city and the wish to return to it, as well as the fervor with which compatriots stuck together when they were abroad. On the other hand, I cannot find much of neighborhood factionalism or professional *esprit de corps*, both of which were so prominent in the later Middle Ages. Under an ever more oppressive military feudalism and government-regimented economy, life became miserable and insecure, and people looked for protection and assistance in their immediate neighborhood. In an earlier period, in a free-enterprise, competitive society, there was no place for such factionalism. A man felt himself to be the son of a city which provided him with the security, the economic possibilities, and the spiritual amenities which he needed.

86

BERNAL DÍAZ
Cities of Mexico

Bernal Díaz (1492–1580) accompanied Hernando Cortés* and the band of Spanish conquistadors who were the first Europeans to see the cities of the central Mexican plateau, dominated by the Aztec capital of Tenochtitlan,† or Mexico, in 1519. Later in life, he recalled what he saw in this account of *The Conquest of New Spain*. What impressed Díaz about the cities of Mexico? How, according to Díaz, were they different from the cities of Europe?

*kohr TEHZ
†teh NOHCH teet LAHN

Bernal Díaz, *The Conquest of New Spain*, trans. J. M. Cohen (London: Penguin Books, 1963), 214–20, 230–35.

Thinking Historically

The cities of Mexico provide the best example of how much cities could differ. Unlike the cities of Eurasia, or even Islamic Africa, the development of Mexican cities was entirely separate from and uninfluenced by the other cultures we have studied. Therefore, this description of Mexico, and the other cities of the Mexican plateau, like Iztapalapa and Coyoacan, is enormously useful to us.

In what respects were these cities different from others you have read about? What other cities do they most resemble? How does this selection support or challenge Braudel's comparison and thesis?

Next morning, we came to a broad causeway[1] and continued our march towards Iztapalapa. And when we saw all those cities and villages built in the water, and other great towns on dry land, and that straight and level causeway leading to Mexico, we were astounded. These great towns and *cues*[2] and buildings rising from the water, all made of stone, seemed like an enchanted vision from the tale of Amadis. Indeed, some of our soldiers asked whether it was not all a dream. It is not surprising therefore that I should write in this vein. It was all so wonderful that I do not know how to describe this first glimpse of things never heard of, seen, or dreamed of before.

When we arrived near Iztapalapa we beheld the splendour of the other *Caciques*[3] who came out to meet us, the lord of that city whose name was Cuitlahuac, and the lord of Culuacan, both of them close relations of Montezuma. And when we entered the city of Iztapalapa, the sight of the palaces in which they lodged us! They were very spacious and well built, of magnificent stone, cedar wood, and the wood of other sweet-smelling trees, with great rooms and courts, which were a wonderful sight, and all covered with awnings of woven cotton.

When we had taken a good look at all this, we went to the orchard and garden, which was a marvellous place both to see and walk in. I was never tired of noticing the diversity of trees and the various scents given off by each, and the paths choked with roses and other flowers, and the many local fruit-trees and rose-bushes, and the pond of fresh water. Another remarkable thing was that large canoes could come into the garden from the lake, through a channel they had cut, and their crews did not have to disembark. Everything was shining with lime and decorated with different kinds of stonework and paintings which were a marvel to gaze

---

[1]The causeway of Cuitlahuac, which separated the lakes of Chalco and Xochimilco.
[2]Spanish for temple; probably refers to pyramids. [Ed.]
[3]Taino for rulers. [Ed.]

on. Then there were birds of many breeds and varieties which came to
the pond. I say again that I stood looking at it, and thought that no land
like it would ever be discovered in the whole world, because at that time
Peru was neither known nor thought of. But today all that I then saw is
overthrown and destroyed; nothing is left standing.

The Entrance into Mexico

Early next day we left Iztapalapa with a large escort of these great
Caciques, and followed the causeway, which is eight yards wide and
goes so straight to the city of Mexico that I do not think it curves at all.
Wide though it was, it was so crowded with people that there was
hardly room for them all. Some were going to Mexico and others coming away, besides those who had come out to see us, and we could
hardly get through the crowds that were there. For the towers and the
cues were full, and they came in canoes from all parts of the lake. No
wonder, since they had never seen horses or men like us before!

With such wonderful sights to gaze on we did not know what to
say, or if this was real that we saw before our eyes. On the land side
there were great cities, and on the lake many more. The lake was
crowded with canoes. At intervals along the causeway there were many
bridges, and before us was the great city of Mexico [Tenochtitlan]. As
for us, we were scarcely four hundred strong, and we well remembered
the words and warnings of the people of Huexotzinco and Tlascala and
Tlamanalco, and the many other warnings we had received to beware
of entering the city of Mexico, since they would kill us as soon as they
had us inside. Let the interested reader consider whether there is not
much to ponder in this narrative of mine. What men in all the world
have shown such daring? But let us go on.

We marched along our causeway to a point where another small
causeway branches off to another city called Coyoacan, and there, beside some towerlike buildings, which were their shrines, we were met
by many more *Caciques* and dignitaries in very rich cloaks. The different chieftains wore different brilliant liveries, and the causeways were
full of them. Montezuma had sent these great *Caciques* in advance to
receive us, and as soon as they came before Cortes they told him in
their language that we were welcome, and as a sign of peace they
touched the ground with their hands and kissed it. . . .

Who could now count the multitude of men, women, and boys in
the streets, on the roof-tops and in canoes on the waterways, who had
come out to see us? It was a wonderful sight and, as I write, it all comes
before my eyes as if it had happened only yesterday.

They led us to our quarters, which were in some large houses capable of accommodating us all and had formerly belonged to the great

Montezuma's father, who was called Axayacatl. Here Montezuma now kept the great shrines of his gods, and a secret chamber containing gold bars and jewels. This was the treasure he had inherited from his father, which he never touched. Perhaps their reason for lodging us here was that, since they called us *Teules*[4] and considered us as such, they wished to have us near their idols. In any case they took us to this place, where there were many great halls, and a dais hung with the cloth of their country for our Captain, and matting beds with canopies over them for each of us.

On our arrival we entered the large court, where the great Montezuma was awaiting our Captain. Taking him by the hand, the prince led him to his apartment in the hall where he was to lodge, which was very richly furnished in their manner. Montezuma had ready for him a very rich necklace, made of golden crabs, a marvellous piece of work, which he hung round Cortes' neck. His captains were greatly astonished at this sign of honour.

After this ceremony, for which Cortes thanked him through our interpreters, Montezuma said: "Malinche,[5] you and your brothers are in your own house. Rest awhile." He then returned to his palace, which was not far off.

We divided our lodgings by companies, and placed our artillery in a convenient spot. Then the order we were to keep was clearly explained to us, and we were warned to be very much on the alert, both the horsemen and the rest of us soldiers. We then ate a sumptuous dinner which they had prepared for us in their native style.

So, with luck on our side, we boldly entered the city of Tenochtitlan or Mexico on 8 November in the year of our Lord 1519. . . .

I must now speak of the skilled workmen whom Montezuma employed in all the crafts they practised, beginning with the jewellers and workers in silver and gold and various kinds of hollowed objects, which excited the admiration of our great silversmiths at home. Many of the best of them lived in a town called Atzcapotzalco, three miles from Mexico. There were other skilled craftsmen who worked with precious stones and *chalchihuites*, and specialists in feather-work, and very fine painters and carvers. We can form some judgement of what they did then from what we can see of their work today. There are three Indians now living in the city of Mexico, named Marcos de

---

[4]Gods. [Ed.]

[5]mah LEEN cheh Also known as Malintzin and Doña Marina. According to Díaz, she was a daughter of a cacique who was given away as a slave after her mother remarried. She had learned Nahuatl as a youth and Yucatec Mayan as a slave. Thus, with the help of a Spanish sailor who had learned Mayan, Cortés could initially translate between Nahuatl and Spanish. Malinche also learned Spanish and became Cortés's translator and mistress, eventually giving birth to Cortés's son, Martin. [Ed.]

Aquino, Juan de la Cruz, and El Crespillo, who are such magnificent painters and carvers that, had they lived in the age of the Apelles of old,[6] or of Michael Angelo,[7] or Berruguete[8] in our own day, they would be counted in the same rank.

Let us go on to the women, the weavers and sempstresses, who made such a huge quantity of fine robes with very elaborate feather designs. These things were generally brought from some towns in the province of Cotaxtla, which is on the north coast, quite near San Juan de Ulua. In Montezuma's own palaces very fine cloths were woven by those chieftains' daughters whom he kept as mistresses; and the daughters of other dignitaries, who lived in a kind of retirement like nuns in some houses close to the great *cue* of Huichilobos,[9] wore robes entirely of featherwork. Out of devotion for that god and a female deity who was said to preside over marriage, their fathers would place them in religious retirement until they found husbands. They would then take them out to be married.

Now to speak of the great number of performers whom Montezuma kept to entertain him. There were dancers and stilt-walkers, and some who seemed to fly as they leapt through the air, and men rather like clowns to make him laugh. There was a whole quarter full of these people who had no other occupation. He had as many workmen as he needed, too, stonecutters, masons, and carpenters, to keep his houses in repair. . . .

When we had already been in Mexico for four days, . . . Cortés said it would be a good thing to visit the large square of Tlatelolco and see the great *cue* of Huichilobos. So he sent Aguilar, Doña Marina,[10] and his own young page Orteguilla, who by now knew something of the language, to ask for Montezuma's approval of this plan. On receiving his request, the prince replied that we were welcome to go, but for fear that we might offer some offence to his idols he would himself accompany us with many of his chieftains. Leaving the palace in his fine litter, when he had gone about half way, he dismounted beside some shrines, since he considered it an insult to his gods to visit their dwelling in a litter. Some of the great chieftains then supported him by the arms, and his principal vassals walked before him, carrying two staves, like sceptres raised on high as a sign that the great Montezuma was approaching. When riding in his litter he had carried a rod, partly of gold and partly of wood, held up like a wand of justice. The prince now climbed

---

[6]Famous Ancient Greek painter. [Ed.]

[7]Michelangelo (1476–1564), Renaissance master painter and sculptor. [Ed.]

[8]Berruguete is either Pedro (1450–1504) or his son, Alonso (1488–1561), both famous Spanish painters. [Ed.]

[9]Huitzilopochtli. Aztec god of sun and war; required human sacrifice. [Ed.]

[10]Same as Malinche (footnote 5). [Ed.]

the steps of the great *cue*, escorted by many *papas*,[11] and began to burn incense and perform other ceremonies for Huichilobos. . . .

On reaching the market-place, escorted by the many *Caciques* whom Montezuma had assigned to us, we were astounded at the great number of people and the quantities of merchandise, and at the orderliness and good arrangements that prevailed, for we had never seen such a thing before. The chieftains who accompanied us pointed everything out. Every kind of merchandise was kept separate and had its fixed place marked for it.

Let us begin with the dealers in gold, silver, and precious stones, feathers, cloaks, and embroidered goods, and male and female slaves who are also sold there. They bring as many slaves to be sold in that market as the Portuguese bring Negroes from Guinea. Some are brought there attached to long poles by means of collars round their necks to prevent them from escaping, but others are left loose. Next there were those who sold coarser cloth, and cotton goods and fabrics made of twisted thread, and there were chocolate merchants with their chocolate. In this way you could see every kind of merchandise to be found anywhere in New Spain, laid out in the same way as goods are laid out in my own district of Medina del Campo, a centre for fairs, where each line of stalls has its own particular sort. So it was in this great market. There were those who sold sisal cloth and ropes and the sandals they wear on their feet, which are made from the same plant. All these were kept in one part of the market, in the place assigned to them, and in another part were skins of tigers and lions, otters, jackals, and deer, badgers, mountain cats, and other wild animals, some tanned and some untanned, and other classes of merchandise.

There were sellers of kidney-beans and sage and other vegetables and herbs in another place, and in yet another they were selling fowls, and birds with great dewlaps,[12] also rabbits, hares, deer, young ducks, little dogs, and other such creatures. Then there were the fruiterers; and the women who sold cooked food, flour and honey cake, and tripe, had their part of the market. Then came pottery of all kinds, from big water-jars to little jugs, displayed in its own place, also honey, honey-paste, and other sweets like nougat. Elsewhere they sold timber too, boards, cradles, beams, blocks, and benches, all in a quarter of their own.

Then there were the sellers of pitch-pine for torches, and other things of that kind, and I must also mention, with all apologies, that they sold many canoe-loads of human excrement, which they kept in the creeks near the market. This was for the manufacture of salt and

---

[11] Aztec priests. [Ed.]
[12] Turkeys.

the curing of skins, which they say cannot be done without it. I know that many gentlemen will laugh at this, but I assure them it is true. I may add that on all the roads they have shelters made of reeds or straw or grass so that they can retire when they wish to do so, and purge their bowels unseen by passers-by, and also in order that their excrement shall not be lost. . . .

We went on to the great *cue*, and as we approached its wide courts, before leaving the market-place itself, we saw many more merchants who, so I was told, brought gold to sell in grains, just as they extract it from the mines. This gold is placed in the thin quills of the large geese of that country, which are so white as to be transparent. They used to reckon their accounts with one another by the length and thickness of these little quills, how much so many cloaks or so many gourds of chocolate or so many slaves were worth, or anything else they were bartering.

Now let us leave the market, having given it a final glance, and come to the courts and enclosures in which their great *cue* stood. Before reaching it you passed through a series of large courts, bigger I think than the Plaza at Salamanca. These courts were surrounded by a double masonry wall and paved, like the whole place, with very large smooth white flagstones. Where these stones were absent everything was whitened and polished, indeed the whole place was so clean that there was not a straw or a grain of dust to be found there.

When we arrived near the great temple and before we had climbed a single step, the great Montezuma sent six *papas* and two chieftains down from the top, where he was making his sacrifices, to escort our Captain; and as he climbed the steps, of which there were one hundred and fourteen, they tried to take him by the arms to help him up in the same way as they helped Montezuma, thinking he might be tired, but he would not let them near him.

The top of the *cue* formed an open square on which stood something like a platform, and it was here that the great stones stood on which they placed the poor Indians for sacrifice. Here also was a massive image like a dragon, and other hideous figures, and a great deal of blood that had been spilled that day. Emerging in the company of two *papas* from the shrine which houses his accursed images, Montezuma made a deep bow to us all and said: "My lord Malinche, you must be tired after climbing this great *cue* of ours." And Cortes replied that none of us was ever exhausted by anything. Then Montezuma took him by the hand, and told him to look at his great city and all the other cities standing in the water, and the many others on the land round the lake; and he said that if Cortes had not had a good view of the great market-place he could see it better from where he now was. So we stood there looking, because that huge accursed *cue* stood so high that it dominated everything. We saw the three causeways that led into

Mexico: the causeway of Iztapalapa by which we had entered four days before. . . . We saw the fresh water which came from Chapultepec to supply the city, and the bridges that were constructed at intervals on the causeways so that the water could flow in and out from one part of the lake to another. We saw a great number of canoes, some coming with provisions and others returning with cargo and merchandise; and we saw too that one could not pass from one house to another of that great city and the other cities that were built on the water except over wooden drawbridges or by canoe. We saw *cues* and shrines in these cities that looked like gleaming white towers and castles: a marvellous sight. All the houses had flat roofs, and on the causeways were other small towers and shrines built like fortresses.

Having examined and considered all that we had seen, we turned back to the great market and the swarm of people buying and selling. The mere murmur of their voices talking was loud enough to be heard more than three miles away. Some of our soldiers who had been in many parts of the world, in Constantinople, in Rome, and all over Italy, said that they had never seen a market so well laid out, so large, so orderly, and so full of people.

REFLECTIONS

Our selections certainly offer support for Braudel's thesis on the European city. London was hardly unique among European cities. The chartering of cities as independent corporations with their own laws, courts, and independent citizenry was a phenomenon repeated throughout Europe, especially in the West and the Mediterranean from the eleventh to the fifteenth century. The Florentine festival demonstrates how citizens came together in so many groups to celebrate their collective identity as citizens. Europe was a world without emperors, in which kings and lords were forced to bargain freedoms for favors.

Marco Polo unwittingly points to the power of the emperor, Song or Mongol, in imperial China. The capital city especially is designed and maintained according to his specifications. City life may be vibrant. There may even be enormous markets and wealthy merchants, but it is the emperor's city, not the merchants'. Rich merchants might train their sons to govern, but only as officials of the emperor.

Neither Chinese nor Muslim urban dwellers find their primary identities as citizens or even as residents of a particular city. They may be Cairenes, but they are Muslims first. Muslims had no need for self-governing cities when they could travel and work anywhere in the vast world of Islam.

Braudel struggled with American cities. North American towns, he thought, were re-creations of European towns. In Latin America, he classified Mexico City as similar to the imperial capitals of other parts of the world. Like Hangchou, Mexico City could be astonishingly rich, but it was not an autonomous entity under Aztecs or Spaniards. The readings were selected not to stack the deck, but to show what Braudel meant. Consequently, some qualifications of Braudel's thesis might be in order.

First, we should not assume that autonomous or communal cities were limited to Europe. Rather, they were a product of a feudal, or politically weak and decentralized, society, where urban populations could bargain for special privileges. We could find similar examples of urban autonomy among, for example, Japanese port cities during the Japanese feudal era of the fourteenth to sixteenth centuries. One of these, Sakai, was called the Venice of Japan. Not until after 1600 and the re-centralization of Japan under the Tokugawa administration were these independent cities brought to heel. In many ways, Tokugawa developments paralleled those of Europe, where centralized states also subordinated the independence of commercial cities after 1700.

Second, the absence of a movement for urban autonomy in Islamic and Chinese cities—important as it was in the time and places discussed in this chapter—was not universal. Chinese cities before the Mongol Yüan dynasty, especially in the earlier Sung dynasty, had developed an extremely prosperous commercial class. And while it is true that they did not gain (or seek) urban independence, they were content to exercise sufficient influence on the local representatives of the emperor. No appointed official could think lightly of ignoring the advice of Chinese merchants, the uniquely Chinese class of civil-service exam graduates, and the many Chinese guilds (one of the more important forces for self-government in Europe).

Third, while medieval Muslim cities encouraged little urban autonomy or identity, a prosperous class of merchants—always at the core of Islam—were nourished by more enlightened sultans and emirs. The Turkish historian Halil Inalcik writes that it was "the deliberate policy" of the Ottoman government, as it founded its successive capitals at Bursa in 1326, Edirne in 1402, and Istanbul in 1453, to create commercial and industrial centers, and that it consequently used every means—from tax exemptions to force—to attract and settle merchants and artisans in the new capitals. With the same end in view, Mehmed II encouraged the Jews of Europe to migrate to his new capital at Istanbul as they were being expelled from Spain and Portugal.

Braudel's thesis emphasizes the differences among cities, but as he well knew, one could emphasize the similarities as well. All cities distinguished themselves from the countryside which they controlled and exploited. All cities built and concentrated the wealth, achievements, and opportunities of the culture within their walls. All cities were greater engines of change than were villages, farm, and pasture. And some have argued that all cities promote patriarchy and class stratification.

Today about half the world's people live in cities. In 1800 only 3 percent of the world's population lived in cities. It is expected that by 2030, 60 percent of the world's population will be urban. Does that mean the lives of so many people will change in a similar way? Does it mean increasing patriarchy? Increasing exploitation of the countryside? Increasing inequality? Do significant choices need to be made about the types of cities we inhabit? Can we find ways to make our cities of the future our own?

14

Ecology, Technology, and Science

Europe, Asia, Oceania, and Africa,
500–1550 C.E.

HISTORICAL CONTEXT

Everyone knows that the world has changed drastically since the Middle Ages. And most people would agree that the most important and far-reaching changes have occurred in the fields of ecology, technology, and science. Global population has grown tenfold. The world has become a single ecological unit where microbes, migrants, and money travel everywhere at jet speed. In most parts of the world, average life expectancy has doubled; cities have mushroomed, supplanting farm and pasture. Machines have replaced the labor of humans and animals. Powers that were only imagined in the Middle Ages — elixirs to cure disease, energy to harness rivers, machines that could fly — are now commonplace. Other aspects of life — among them religion, political behavior, music, and art — have also evolved, but even these were affected significantly by advances in modern science and technology.

Have the changes been for good or ill? The signs of environmental stress are visible everywhere. The hole in the earth's protective ozone layer over Antarctica continues to expand. The North Pole floats in the summer. Ten-thousand-year-old glaciers are disappearing. The oceans are rising two to four inches every ten years. Our atmosphere contains more carbon gasses than it has for at least 650,000 years. The stored energy of millions of years burns to service the richest members of a couple of generations. Ancient aquifers are drained to water the lawns of desert cities.

Precisely what change or changes occurred? When did the cycle of change begin and what caused it? We will examine these questions here. You will read three substantial answers. Lynn White Jr. defines the transformation to modernity in largely technological and ecological terms, but emphasizes the role of cultural causes. Lynda Shaffer discusses technological and scientific changes as spreading through contact and trade. Jared Diamond writes of cultural failures to meet new natural and technological crises.

These explanations of long-term change differ most markedly in how they explain the roots of the transformation. White, a historian of medieval European technology, focuses on the role of medieval European religion: Christianity. Shaffer, a world historian, underscores the role of India and South Asia. Diamond, a professor of geography with numerous specializations in fields like physiology, evolutionary biology, and biogeography, finds a failure of will in many societies.

THINKING HISTORICALLY
Evaluating Grand Theories

Big questions deserve big answers — or at least grand theories. Here we consider three grand theories about the origins of our technological transformation and ecological difficulties, the links between environmental decline and the growth of technology and science, and the role of Western (European and American) economic growth in undermining the environment. Grand theories are especially speculative. They give us much to question and challenge. But their scope and freshness can often suggest new insights. Grand theories almost inevitably have elements that seem partly wrong and partly right. You will be encouraged to weigh some of the many elements in these theories. Then you can evaluate the theories, decide where you agree and disagree, and, perhaps, begin to develop your own grand theory as well.

87

LYNN WHITE JR.

The Historical Roots of
Our Ecological Crisis

This classic essay first appeared in the magazine *Science* in 1967 and
has since been reprinted and commented on many times. What do you
think of White's linkage of ecological crisis and Christianity? Which
of White's arguments and evidence do you find most persuasive?
Which do you find least convincing? Imagine a continuum that includes all of the world's people, from the most ecologically minded
"tree-huggers" on the left to the most damaging polluters and destroyers of the environment on the right. Where on that continuum would
you place the historical majority of Christians? Buddhists? Why?

Thinking Historically

A grand theory like this — that Christianity is responsible for our environmental problems — argues far more than can be proven in such a
brief essay. White concentrates on making certain kinds of connections
and marshaling certain kinds of evidence. In addition to weighing the
arguments he makes, consider the gaps in his argument. What sorts of
evidence would you seek to make White's theory more convincing?

A conversation with Aldous Huxley[1] not infrequently put one at the
receiving end of an unforgettable monologue. About a year before his
lamented death he was discoursing on a favorite topic: man's unnatural
treatment of nature and its sad results. To illustrate his point he told
how, during the previous summer, he had returned to a little valley in
England where he had spent many happy months as a child. Once it
had been composed of delightful grassy glades; now it was becoming
overgrown with unsightly brush because the rabbits that formerly kept
such growth under control had largely succumbed to a disease, myxo-
matosis, that was deliberately introduced by the local farmers to reduce

---

[1]Aldous Huxley (1894–1963), British author of novels, short stories, travel books, biog-
raphy, and essays. Best known for *Brave New World* (1932). [Ed.]

Lynn White Jr., "The Historical Roots of Our Ecological Crisis," *Science* 155 (March 1967):
1203–7.

the rabbits' destruction of crops. Being something of a Philistine,[2] I could be silent no longer, even in the interests of great rhetoric. I interrupted to point out that the rabbit itself had been brought as a domestic animal to England in 1176, presumably to improve the protein diet of the peasantry.

All forms of life modify their contexts. The most spectacular and benign instance is doubtless the coral polyp. By serving its own ends, it has created a vast undersea world favorable to thousands of other kinds of animals and plants. Ever since man became a numerous species he has affected his environment notably. The hypothesis that his fire-drive[3] method of hunting created the world's great grasslands and helped to exterminate the monster mammals of the Pleistocene from much of the globe is plausible, if not proved. For six millennia at least, the banks of the lower Nile have been a human artifact rather than the swampy African jungle which nature, apart from man, would have made it. The Aswan Dam, flooding five thousand square miles, is only the latest stage in a long process. In many regions terracing or irrigation, overgrazing, and the cutting of forests by Romans to build ships to fight Carthaginians or by Crusaders to solve the logistics problems of their expeditions have profoundly changed some ecologies. Observation that the French landscape falls into two basic types, the open fields of the north and the *bocage*[4] of the south and west, inspired Marc Bloch to undertake his classic study of medieval agricultural methods. Quite unintentionally, changes in human ways often affect nonhuman nature. It has been noted, for example, that the advent of the automobile eliminated huge flocks of sparrows that once fed on the horse manure littering every street.

The history of ecologic change is still so rudimentary that we know little about what really happened, or what the results were. The extinction of the European aurochs[5] as late as 1627 would seem to have been a simple case of overenthusiastic hunting. On more intricate matters it often is impossible to find solid information. For a thousand years or more the Frisians and Hollanders have been pushing back the North Sea, and the process is culminating in our own time in the reclamation

---

[2]An anti-intellectual (though obviously White is not; he was only impatient with Huxley's pedantry). [Ed.]

[3]Paleolithic hunters used fires to drive animals to their deaths. [Ed.]

[4]Full of groves or woodlands. Marc Bloch reasoned that the open fields north of the Loire River in France must have been plowed by teams of oxen and heavy plows because of the hard soil. In the south farmers could use scratch plows on the softer soil and therefore did not clear large fields, preserving more woodlands. [Ed.]

[5]A now extinct European wild ox believed to be the ancestor of European domestic cattle. [Ed.]

of the Zuider Zee.[6] What, if any, species of animals, birds, fish, shore life, or plants have died out in the process? In their epic combat with Neptune have the Netherlanders overlooked ecological values in such a way that the quality of human life in the Netherlands has suffered? I cannot discover that the questions have ever been asked, much less answered.

People, then, have often been a dynamic element in their own environment, but in the present state of historical scholarship we usually do not know exactly when, where, or with what effects man-induced changes came. As we enter the last third of the twentieth century, however, concern for the problem of ecologic backlash is mounting feverishly. Natural science, conceived as the effort to understand the nature of things, had flourished in several eras and among several peoples. Similarly there had been an age-old accumulation of technological skills, sometimes growing rapidly, sometimes slowly. But it was not until about four generations ago that Western Europe and North America arranged a marriage between science and technology, a union of the theoretical and the empirical approaches to our natural environment. The emergence in widespread practice of the Baconian creed that scientific knowledge means technological power over nature can scarcely be dated before about 1850, save in the chemical industries, where it is anticipated in the eighteenth century. Its acceptance as a normal pattern of action may mark the greatest event in human history since the invention of agriculture, and perhaps in nonhuman terrestrial history as well.

Almost at once the new situation forced the crystallization of the novel concept of ecology; indeed, the word *ecology* first appeared in the English language in 1873. Today, less than a century later, the impact of our race upon the environment has so increased in force that it has changed in essence. When the first cannons were fired, in the early fourteenth century, they affected ecology by sending workers scrambling to the forests and mountains for more potash, sulfur, iron ore, and charcoal, with some resulting erosion and deforestation. Hydrogen bombs are of a different order: A war fought with them might alter the genetics of all life on this planet. By 1285 London had a smog problem arising from the burning of soft coal, but our present combustion of fossil fuels threatens to change the chemistry of the globe's atmosphere as a whole, with consequences which we are only beginning to guess. With the population explosion, the carcinoma of planless urbanism, the now geological deposits of sewage and garbage, surely no creature other than man has ever managed to foul its nest in such short order.

---

[6]Once a Dutch lake, it was joined to the North Sea by a flood in the thirteenth century but has since been reclaimed by the building of a dam. [Ed.]

There are many calls to action, but specific proposals, however worthy as individual items, seem too partial, palliative, negative: Ban the bomb, tear down the billboards, give the Hindus contraceptives and tell them to eat their sacred cows. The simplest solution to any suspect change is, of course, to stop it, or, better yet, to revert to a romanticized past: Make those ugly gasoline stations look like Anne Hathaway's cottage or (in the Far West) like ghost-town saloons. The "wilderness area" mentality invariably advocates deep-freezing an ecology, whether San Gimignano or the High Sierra, as it was before the first Kleenex was dropped. But neither atavism nor prettification will cope with the ecologic crisis of our time.

What shall we do? No one yet knows. Unless we think about fundamentals, our specific measures may produce new backlashes more serious than those they are designed to remedy.

As a beginning we should try to clarify our thinking by looking, in some historical depth, at the presuppositions that underlie modern technology and science. Science was traditionally aristocratic, speculative, intellectual in intent; technology was lower-class, empirical, action-oriented. The quite sudden fusion of these two, toward the middle of the nineteenth century, is surely related to the slightly prior and contemporary democratic revolutions which, by reducing social barriers, tended to assert a functional unity of brain and hand. Our ecologic crisis is the product of an emerging, entirely novel, democratic culture. The issue is whether a democratized world can survive its own implications. Presumably we cannot unless we rethink our axioms.

The Western Traditions of Technology and Science

One thing is so certain that it seems stupid to verbalize it: Both modern technology and modern science are distinctively *Occidental*. Our technology has absorbed elements from all over the world, notably from China; yet everywhere today, whether in Japan or in Nigeria, successful technology is Western. Our science is the heir to all the sciences of the past, especially perhaps to the work of the great Islamic scientists of the Middle Ages, who so often outdid the ancient Greeks in skill and perspicacity: al-Rāzī in medicine, for example; or ibn-al-Haytham in optics; or Omar Khayyám in mathematics. Indeed, not a few works of such geniuses seem to have vanished in the original Arabic and to survive only in medieval Latin translations that helped to lay the foundations for later Western developments. Today, around the globe, all significant science is Western in style and method, whatever the pigmentation or language of the scientists.

A second pair of facts is less well recognized because they result from quite recent historical scholarship. The leadership of the West, both in technology and in science, is far older than the so-called Scientific Revolution of the seventeenth century or the so-called Industrial Revolution of the eighteenth century. These terms are in fact outmoded and obscure the true nature of what they try to describe — significant stages in two long and separate developments. By A.D. 1000 at the latest — and perhaps, feebly, as much as two hundred years earlier — the West began to apply water power to industrial processes other than milling grain. This was followed in the late twelfth century by the harnessing of wind power. From simple beginnings, but with remarkable consistency of style, the West rapidly expanded its skills in the development of power machinery, labor-saving devices, and automation. Those who doubt should contemplate that most monumental achievement in the history of automation: the weight-driven mechanical clock, which appeared in two forms in the early fourteenth century. Not in craftsmanship but in basic technological capacity, the Latin West of the later Middle Ages far outstripped its elaborate, sophisticated, and esthetically magnificent sister cultures, Byzantium and Islam. In 1444 a great Greek ecclesiastic, Bessarion, who had gone to Italy, wrote a letter to a prince in Greece. He is amazed by the superiority of Western ships, arms, textiles, glass. But above all he is astonished by the spectacle of waterwheels sawing timbers and pumping the bellows of blast furnaces. Clearly, he had seen nothing of the sort in the Near East.

By the end of the fifteenth century the technological superiority of Europe was such that its small, mutually hostile nations could spill out over all the rest of the world, conquering, looting, and colonizing. The symbol of this technological superiority is the fact that Portugal, one of the weakest states of the Occident, was able to become, and to remain for a century, mistress of the East Indies. And we must remember that the technology of Vasco da Gama and Albuquerque was built by pure empiricism, drawing remarkably little support or inspiration from science.

In the present-day vernacular understanding, modern science is supposed to have begun in 1543, when both Copernicus and Vesalius published their great works. It is no derogation of their accomplishments, however, to point out that such structures as the *Fabrica*[7] and the *De revolutionibus*[8] do not appear overnight. The distinctive Western tradition of science, in fact, began in the late eleventh century with a massive movement of translation of Arabic and Greek scientific works into Latin. A

[7]*De Humani Corporis Fabrica* (1543), an illustrated work on human anatomy based on dissections, was produced by Andreas Vesalius (1514–1564), a Flemish anatomist, at the University of Padua in Italy. [Ed.]

[8]*De revolutionibus orbium coelestium* (1543; On the Revolutions of Heavenly Bodies) was published by Nicolas Copernicus (1473–1543); it showed the sun as the center of a system around which the Earth revolved. [Ed.]

few notable books — Theophrastus, for example — escaped the West's avid new appetite for science, but within less than two hundred years effectively the entire corpus of Greek and Muslim science was available in Latin, and was being eagerly read and criticized in the new European universities. Out of criticism arose new observation, speculation, and increasing distrust of ancient authorities. By the late thirteenth century Europe had seized global scientific leadership from the faltering hands of Islam. It would be as absurd to deny the profound originality of Newton, Galileo, or Copernicus as to deny that of the fourteenth-century scholastic scientists like Buridan or Oresme on whose work they built. Before the eleventh century, science scarcely existed in the Latin West, even in Roman times. From the eleventh century onward, the scientific sector of Occidental culture has increased in a steady crescendo.

Since both our technological and our scientific movements got their start, acquired their character, and achieved world dominance in the Middle Ages, it would seem that we cannot understand their nature or their present impact upon ecology without examining fundamental medieval assumptions and developments.

Medieval View of Man and Nature

Until recently, agriculture has been the chief occupation even in "advanced" societies; hence, any change in methods of tillage has much importance. Early plows, drawn by two oxen, did not normally turn the sod but merely scratched it. Thus, cross-plowing was needed and fields tended to be squarish. In the fairly light soils and semiarid climates of the Near East and Mediterranean, this worked well. But such a plow was inappropriate to the wet climate and often sticky soils of northern Europe. By the latter part of the seventh century after Christ, however, following obscure beginnings, certain northern peasants were using an entirely new kind of plow, equipped with a vertical knife to cut the line of the furrow, a horizontal share to slice under the sod, and a moldboard to turn it over. The friction of this plow with the soil was so great that it normally required not two but eight oxen. It attacked the land with such violence that cross-plowing was not needed, and fields tended to be shaped in long strips.

In the days of the scratch-plow, fields were distributed generally in units capable of supporting a single family. Subsistence farming was the presupposition. But no peasant owned eight oxen: to use the new and more efficient plow, peasants pooled their oxen to form large plow-teams, originally receiving (it would appear) plowed strips in proportion to their contribution. Thus, distribution of land was based no longer on the needs of a family but, rather, on the capacity of a power machine to till the earth. Man's relation to the soil was profoundly changed. Formerly man had been part of nature; now he was the exploiter of nature. Nowhere else in the world did farmers develop any analogous agricultural implement. Is it coincidence that modern technology, with its ruthlessness toward nature, has so largely been produced by descendants of these peasants of northern Europe?

This same exploitive attitude appears slightly before A.D. 830 in Western illustrated calendars. In older calendars the months were shown as passive personifications. The new Frankish calendars, which set the style for the Middle Ages, are very different: They show men coercing the world around them — plowing, harvesting, chopping trees, butchering pigs. Man and nature are two things, and man is master.

These novelties seem to be in harmony with larger intellectual patterns. What people do about their ecology depends on what they think about themselves in relation to things around them. Human ecology is deeply conditioned by beliefs about our nature and destiny — that is, by religion. To Western eyes this is very evident in, say, India or Ceylon. It is equally true of ourselves and of our medieval ancestors.

The victory of Christianity over paganism was the greatest psychic revolution in the history of our culture. It has become fashionable today to say that, for better or worse, we live in "the post-Christian age." Certainly the forms of our thinking and language have largely ceased to be Christian, but to my eye the substance often remains amazingly akin to that of the past. Our daily habits of action, for example, are dominated by an implicit faith in perpetual progress which was unknown either to Greco-Roman antiquity or to the Orient. It is rooted in, and is indefensible apart from, Judeo-Christian teleology.[9] The fact that Communists share it merely helps to show what can be demonstrated on many other grounds: that Marxism, like Islam, is a Judeo-Christian heresy. We continue today to live, as we have lived for about seventeen hundred years, very largely in a context of Christian axioms.

What did Christianity tell people about their relations with the environment?

While many of the world's mythologies provide stories of creation, Greco-Roman mythology was singularly incoherent in this respect. Like Aristotle, the intellectuals of the ancient West denied that the visible world had had a beginning. Indeed, the idea of a beginning was impossible in the framework of their cyclical notion of time. In sharp contrast, Christianity inherited from Judaism not only a concept of time as nonrepetitive and linear but also a striking story of creation. By gradual stages a loving and all-powerful God had created light and darkness, the heavenly bodies, the earth and all its plants, animals, birds, and fishes. Finally, God had created Adam and, as an afterthought,

---

[9]The Biblical idea that God's purpose is revealed in his creation, that human history can be seen as the result of God's intentions. [Ed.]

Eve to keep man from being lonely. Man named all the animals, thus establishing his dominance over them. God planned all of this explicitly for man's benefit and rule: No item in the physical creation had any purpose save to serve man's purposes. And, although man's body is made of clay, he is not simply part of nature: He is made in God's image.

Especially in its Western form, Christianity is the most anthropocentric religion the world has seen. As early as the second century both Tertullian and Saint Irenaeus of Lyons were insisting that when God shaped Adam he was foreshadowing the image of the incarnate Christ, the Second Adam. Man shares, in great measure, God's transcendence of nature. Christianity, in absolute contrast to ancient paganism and Asia's religions (except, perhaps, Zoroastrianism), not only established a dualism of man and nature but also insisted that it is God's will that man exploit nature for his proper ends.

At the level of the common people this worked out in an interesting way. In Antiquity every tree, every spring, every stream, every hill had its own *genius loci*, its guardian spirit. These spirits were accessible to men, but were very unlike men; centaurs, fauns, and mermaids show their ambivalence. Before one cut a tree, mined a mountain, or dammed a brook, it was important to placate the spirit in charge of that particular situation, and to keep it placated. By destroying pagan animism, Christianity made it possible to exploit nature in a mood of indifference to the feelings of natural objects.

It is often said that for animism the Church substituted the cult of saints. True; but the cult of saints is functionally quite different from animism. The saint is not *in* natural objects; he may have special shrines, but his citizenship is in heaven. Moreover, a saint is entirely a man; he can be approached in human terms. In addition to saints, Christianity of course also had angels and demons inherited from Judaism and perhaps, at one remove, from Zoroastrianism. But these were all as mobile as the saints themselves. The spirits *in* natural objects, which formerly had protected nature from man, evaporated. Man's effective monopoly on spirit in this world was confirmed, and the old inhibitions to the exploitation of nature crumbled.

When one speaks in such sweeping terms, a note of caution is in order. Christianity is a complex faith, and its consequences differ in differing contexts. What I have said may well apply to the medieval West, where in fact technology made spectacular advances. But the Greek East, a highly civilized realm of equal Christian devotion, seems to have produced no marked technological innovation after the late seventh century, when Greek fire was invented. The key to the contrast may perhaps be found in a difference in the tonality of piety and thought which students of comparative theology find between the Greek and the Latin Churches. The Greeks believed that sin was intellectual blindness, and that salvation was found in illumination, orthodoxy — that is, clear thinking. The Latins, on the other hand, felt that sin was moral evil, and that salvation was to be found in right conduct. Eastern theology has been intellectualist. Western theology has been voluntarist. The Greek saint contemplates; the Western saint acts. The implications of Christianity for the conquest of nature would emerge more easily in the Western atmosphere.

The Christian dogma of creation, which is found in the first clause of all the Creeds, has another meaning for our comprehension of today's ecologic crisis. By revelation, God had given man the Bible, the Book of Scripture. But since God had made nature, nature also must reveal the divine mentality. The religious study of nature for the better understanding of God was known as natural theology. In the early Church, and always in the Greek East, nature was conceived primarily as a symbolic system through which God speaks to men: The ant is a sermon to sluggards; rising flames are the symbol of the soul's aspiration. This view of nature was essentially artistic rather than scientific. While Byzantium preserved and copied great numbers of ancient Greek scientific texts, science as we conceive it could scarcely flourish in such an ambience.

However, in the Latin West by the early thirteenth century natural theology was following a very different bent. It was ceasing to be the decoding of the physical symbols of God's communication with man and was becoming the effort to understand God's mind by discovering how his creation operates. The rainbow was no longer simply a symbol of hope first sent to Noah after the Deluge: Robert Grosseteste, Friar Roger Bacon, and Theodoric of Freiberg produced startlingly sophisticated work on the optics of the rainbow, but they did it as a venture in religious understanding. From the thirteenth century onward, up to and including Leibnitz and Newton, every major scientist, in effect, explained his motivations in religious terms. Indeed, if Galileo had not been so expert an amateur theologian he would have got into far less trouble: The professionals resented his intrusion. And Newton seems to have regarded himself more as a theologian than as a scientist. It was not until the late eighteenth century that the hypothesis of God became unnecessary to many scientists.

It is often hard for the historian to judge, when men explain why they are doing what they want to do, whether they are offering real reasons or merely culturally acceptable reasons. The consistency with which scientists during the long formative centuries of Western science said that the task and the reward of the scientist was "to think God's thoughts after him" leads one to believe that this was their real motivation. If so, then modern Western science was cast in a matrix of Christian theology. The dynamism of religious devotion, shaped by the Judeo-Christian dogma of creation, gave it impetus.

An Alternative Christian View

We would seem to be headed toward conclusions unpalatable to many Christians. Since both *science* and *technology* are blessed words in our contemporary vocabulary, some may be happy at the notions, first, that, viewed historically, modern science is an extrapolation of natural theology and, second, that modern technology is at least partly to be explained as an Occidental, voluntarist realization of the Christian dogma of man's transcendence of, and rightful mastery over, nature. But, as we now recognize, somewhat over a century ago science and technology — hitherto quite separate activities — joined to give mankind powers which, to judge by many of the ecologic effects, are out of control. If so, Christianity bears a huge burden of guilt.

I personally doubt that disastrous ecologic backlash can be avoided simply by applying to our problems more science and more technology. Our science and technology have grown out of Christian attitudes toward man's relation to nature which are almost universally held not only by Christians and neo-Christians but also by those who fondly regard themselves as post-Christians. Despite Copernicus, all the cosmos rotates around our little globe. Despite Darwin, we are *not*, in our hearts, part of the natural process. We are superior to nature, contemptuous of it, willing to use it for our slightest whim. The newly elected Governor of California,[10] like myself a churchman but less troubled than I, spoke for the Christian tradition when he said (as is alleged), "when you've seen one redwood tree, you've seen them all." To a Christian a tree can be no more than a physical fact. The whole concept of the sacred grove is alien to Christianity and to the ethos of the West. For nearly two millennia Christian missionaries have been chopping down sacred groves, which are idolatrous because they assume spirit in nature.

What we do about ecology depends on our ideas of the man-nature relationship. More science and more technology are not going to get us out of the present ecologic crisis until we find a new religion, or rethink our old one. The beatniks, who are the basic revolutionaries of our time, show a sound instinct in their affinity for Zen Buddhism, which conceives of the man-nature relationship as very nearly the mirror image of the Christian view. Zen, however, is as deeply conditioned by Asian history as Christianity is by the experience of the West, and I am dubious of its viability among us.

Possibly we should ponder the greatest radical in Christian history since Christ: Saint Francis of Assisi. The prime miracle of Saint Francis is the fact that he did not end at the stake, as many of his left-wing fol-

---

[10]Ronald Reagan, governor from 1967 to 1975.

lowers did. He was so clearly heretical that a General of the Franciscan Order, Saint Bonaventura, a great and perceptive Christian, tried to suppress the early accounts of Franciscanism. The key to an understanding of Francis is his belief in the virtue of humility — not merely for the individual but for man as a species. Francis tried to depose man from his monarchy over creation and set up a democracy of all God's creatures. With him the ant is no longer simply a homily for the lazy, flames a sign of the thrust of the soul toward union with God; now they are Brother Ant and Sister Fire, praising the Creator in their own ways as Brother Man does in his.

Later commentators have said that Francis preached to the birds as a rebuke to men who would not listen. The records do not read so: He urged the little birds to praise God, and in spiritual ecstasy they flapped their wings and chirped rejoicing. Legends of saints, especially the Irish saints, had long told of their dealings with animals but always, I believe, to show their human dominance over creatures. With Francis it is different. The land around Gubbio in the Apennines was being ravaged by a fierce wolf. Saint Francis, says the legend, talked to the wolf and persuaded him of the error of his ways. The wolf repented, died in the odor of sanctity, and was buried in consecrated ground.

What Sir Steven Ruciman calls "the Franciscan doctrine of the animal soul" was quickly stamped out. Quite possibly it was in part inspired, consciously or unconsciously, by the belief in reincarnation held by the Cathar heretics who at that time teemed in Italy and southern France, and who presumably had got it originally from India. It is significant that at just the same moment, about 1200, traces of metempsychosis are found also in Western Judaism, in the Provençal *Cabbala*. But Francis held neither to transmigration of souls nor to pantheism. His view of nature and of man rested on a unique sort of pan-psychism of all things animate and inanimate, designed for the glorification of their transcendent Creator, who, in the ultimate gesture of cosmic humility, assumed flesh, lay helpless in a manger, and hung dying on a scaffold.

I am not suggesting that many contemporary Americans who are concerned about our ecologic crisis will be either able or willing to counsel with wolves or exhort birds. However, the present increasing disruption of the global environment is the product of a dynamic technology and science which were originating in the Western medieval world against which Saint Francis was rebelling in so original a way. Their growth cannot be understood historically apart from distinctive attitudes toward nature which are deeply grounded in Christian dogma. The fact that most people do not think of these attitudes as Christian is irrelevant. No new set of basic values has been accepted in our society to displace those of Christianity. Hence we shall continue to have a worsening ecologic crisis until we reject the Christian axiom that nature has no reason for existence save to serve man.

The greatest spiritual revolutionary in Western history, Saint Francis, proposed what he thought was an alternative Christian view of nature and man's relation to it: He tried to substitute the idea of the equality of all creatures, including man, for the idea of man's limitless rule of creation. He failed. Both our present science and our present technology are so tinctured with orthodox Christian arrogance toward nature that no solution for our ecologic crisis can be expected from them alone. Since the roots of our trouble are so largely religious, the remedy must also be essentially religious, whether we call it that or not. We must rethink and refeel our nature and destiny. The profoundly religious, but heretical, sense of the primitive Franciscans for the spiritual autonomy of all parts of nature may point a direction. I propose Francis as a patron saint for ecologists.

┌─────┐
│ 88 │
└─────┘

Life of Boniface:
Converting the Hessians

This story about the Christian missionary Boniface was told in the *Life of Boniface*, written between 754 and 768, by Willibald, one of his students. The Hessians, previously converted to Christianity, had reverted to paganism, and Boniface traveled from England to Germany to reconvert them. Hessians were widely regarded by the early Christian missionaries to Germany as a difficult people to convert. Boniface's success became a guide for future missions. What does this account tell us about the nature of Hessian paganism? What does Boniface do to reconvert them to Christianity? What, if anything, does the story tell us about Christianity?

Thinking Historically

How does this primary source relate to Lynn White Jr.'s article? Does it support his argument? Can a single piece like this ever prove an argument like White's, or can it only illustrate it?

The Anglo-Saxon Missionaries in Germany, trans. C. H. Talbot (London: Sheed and Ward, 1954), 45–46.

Now many of the Hessians who at that time had acknowledged the Catholic faith were confirmed by the grace of the Holy Spirit and received the laying-on of hands. But others, not yet strong in the spirit, refused to accept the pure teachings of the Church in their entirety. Moreover, some continued secretly, others openly, to offer sacrifices to trees and springs, to inspect the entrails of victims; some practised divination, legerdemain,[1] and incantations; some turned their attention to auguries, auspices, and other sacrificial rites; whilst others, of a more reasonable character, forsook all the profane practices of heathenism and committed none of these crimes. With the counsel and advice of the latter persons, Boniface in their presence attempted to cut down, at a place called Gaesmere, . . . a certain oak of extraordinary size called by the pagans of olden times the Oak of Jupiter. Taking his courage in his hands (for a great crowd of pagans stood by watching and bitterly cursing in their hearts the enemy of the gods), he cut the first notch. But when he had made a superficial cut, suddenly the oak's vast bulk, shaken by a mighty blast of wind from above, crashed to the ground shivering its topmost branches into fragments in its fall. As if by the express will of God (for the brethren present had done nothing to cause it) the oak burst asunder into four parts, each part having a trunk of equal length. At the sight of this extraordinary spectacle the heathens who had been cursing ceased to revile and began, on the contrary, to believe and bless the Lord. Thereupon the holy bishop took counsel with the brethren, built an oratory from the timber of the oak and dedicated it to St. Peter the Apostle. He then set out on a journey to Thuringia, having accomplished by the help of God all the things we have already mentioned. Arrived there, he addressed the elders and the chiefs of the people, calling on them to put aside their blind ignorance and to return to the Christian religion which they had formerly embraced. . . .

[1]Sleight of hand.

89

Image from a Cistercian Manuscript, Twelfth Century

This image of a monk chopping down a tree while his lay servant prunes the branches is from a manuscript of the Cistercian order of monks, from the twelfth century. The Cistercians, more than other orders, spoke out in favor of conserving forest resources, but they also celebrated manual labor. Does this image indicate that the monks were in favor of forest clearance?

Thinking Historically

Does this image lend support to White's argument? Why or why not? If there were many such images, would visual evidence like this convince you of White's argument? Would it be more convincing if almost all European images of trees showed someone chopping them down and virtually no Chinese tree images showed that? In other words, how much visual evidence would convince you of White's interpretation?

Image from a Cistercian manuscript, 12th c., monk chopping tree (Dijon, Bibliothèque municipale, MS 173), duplicated in *Cambridge Illustrated History of the Middle Ages*, Robert Fossier, ed. (Cambridge: Cambridge University Press, 1997), 72.

Figure 14.1 Twelfth-Century Manuscript.
Source: Courtesy of Tresorier Principal Municipal, Dijon.

90

Image from a French Calendar, Fifteenth Century

This French calendar scene for March is from the early fifteenth century. What sorts of activities does it show? How does it relate specifically to White's argument about the changing images of European calendars? (See p. 501.) The top half of the calendar shows a zodiac. In what ways are these images of nature different from those in the bottom half?

Thinking Historically

What technologies are shown here? Were any of these technologies particularly recent or European? Does this image merely illustrate White's argument, or does it support it to some extent? What other visual evidence would you want to see in order to be persuaded by White's argument?

From *Les trés riches heures du duc de Berry*, Giraudon, Musée de Condé.

Figure 14.2 French Calendar Scene.

Source: Bridgeman-Giraudon/Art Resource, N.Y.

91

Image of a Chinese *Feng-Shui* Master

Although the Chinese celebrated the natural landscape in their paintings, they also created drawings that showcased their advanced technologies. The Chinese made and used the compass (as well as paper, printing, and gunpowder) long before Europeans. Instead of using it to subdue the natural world, however, they used it to find harmony with nature, specifically through the practice of *feng-shui.** *Feng-shui*, which literally means wind over water, is the Chinese art of determining the best position and placement of structures such as houses within the natural environment. In the following image we see a type of compass used in the work of a Chinese *feng-shui* master. Before building, the *feng-shui* master would use instruments like this to ascertain the flow of energy (*chi*) on the site, resulting in new buildings that would be in harmony with, rather than obstruct, this flow. How might a compass detect energy? How was the Chinese use of a compass-like device different from the modern scientific use of the compass?

Thinking Historically

An image has many elements to read. What information is revealed about Chinese society in this image, in addition to the scientific devices? What significance do you attach to the artist's depiction of humans and the natural setting? In what ways does this image support Lynn White Jr.'s argument? In what ways does it challenge his interpretation? On balance, do you find it more supportive or critical of White's position?

*fung SHWEE

Joseph Needham, *Science and Civilization in China*, vol. 2 (Cambridge: Cambridge University Press, 1956), 362.

Figure 14.3 Chinese *Feng-Shui* Master.

92

LYNDA NORENE SHAFFER

Southernization

The author of this selection began her career as a historian of China, but she is currently a world historian, having published books on Native American, Southeast Asian, and Chinese history. Shaffer coins the term *Southernization* to suggest that *Westernization* was preceded by an earlier "southern" process of technological expansion that eventually made it possible. Which of her examples of Southernization do you find most important in changing the world? Which least significant? Did India and Indian Ocean societies of the early Middle Ages play a role like that of the West today?

Thinking Historically

Shaffer did not write this essay to criticize Lynn White Jr., nor does her essay address precisely the same issues. Our exercise here is not the relatively simple task of weighing two debaters on a single issue. Rather, Shaffer's essay challenges some of the assumptions and arguments made by White and many other historians when they discuss the history of technology. What are some of the assumptions and arguments of White that Shaffer challenges? How might you use Shaffer to challenge White's grand theory? Which essay provides a more satisfying explanation of the origins of modern science and technology?

The term *Southernization* is a new one. It is used here to refer to a multifaceted process that began in Southern Asia and spread from there to various other places around the globe. The process included so many interrelated strands of development that it is impossible to do more here than sketch out the general outlines of a few of them. Among the most important that will be omitted from this discussion are the metallurgical, the medical, and the literary. Those included are the development of mathematics; the production and marketing of subtropical or tropical spices; the pioneering of new trade routes; the cultivation, processing, and marketing of southern crops such as sugar and cotton; and the development of various related technologies.

The term *Southernization* is meant to be analogous to *Westernization*. Westernization refers to certain developments that first occurred

Lynda Norene Shaffer, "Southernization," *Journal of World History* 5 (Spring 1994): 1–21.

in western Europe. Those developments changed Europe and eventually spread to other places and changed them as well. In the same way, southernization changed Southern Asia and later spread to other areas, which then underwent a process of change.

Southernization was well under way in Southern Asia by the fifth century C.E., during the reign of India's Gupta kings (320–535 C.E.). It was by that time already spreading to China. In the eighth century various elements characteristic of Southernization began spreading through the lands of the Muslim caliphates. Both in China and in the lands of the caliphate, the process led to dramatic changes, and by the year 1200 it was beginning to have an impact on the Christian Mediterranean. One could argue that within the Northern Hemisphere, by this time the process of Southernization had created an Eastern Hemisphere characterized by a rich south and a north that was poor in comparison. And one might even go so far as to suggest that in Europe and its colonies, the process of Southernization laid the foundation for Westernization.

The Indian Beginning

Southernization was the result of developments that took place in many parts of southern Asia, both on the Indian subcontinent and in Southeast Asia. By the time of the Gupta kings, several of its constituent parts already had a long history in India. Perhaps the oldest strand in the process was the cultivation of cotton and the production of cotton textiles for export. Cotton was first domesticated in the Indus River valley some time between 2300 and 1760 B.C.E., and by the second millennium B.C.E., the Indians had begun to develop sophisticated dyeing techniques. During these early millennia Indus River valley merchants are known to have lived in Mesopotamia, where they sold cotton textiles.

In the first century C.E. Egypt became an important overseas market for Indian cottons. By the next century there was a strong demand for these textiles both in the Mediterranean and in East Africa, and by the fifth century they were being traded in Southeast Asia. The Indian textile trade continued to grow throughout the next millennium. Even after the arrival of European ships in Asian ports at the turn of the sixteenth century, it continued unscathed. According to one textile expert, "India virtually clothed the world" by the mid-eighteenth century. The subcontinent's position was not undermined until Britain's Industrial Revolution, when steam engines began to power the production of cotton textiles.

Another strand in the process of Southernization, the search for new sources of bullion, can be traced back in India to the end of the

Mauryan Empire (321–185 B.C.E.). During Mauryan rule Siberia had been India's main source of gold, but nomadic disturbances in Central Asia disrupted the traffic between Siberia and India at about the time that the Mauryans fell. Indian sailors then began to travel to the Malay peninsula and the islands of Indonesia in search of an alternative source, which they most likely "discovered" with the help of local peoples who knew the sites. (This is generally the case with bullion discoveries, including those made by Arabs and Europeans.) What the Indians (and others later on) did do was introduce this gold to international trade routes.

The Indians' search for gold may also have led them to the shores of Africa. Although its interpretation is controversial, some archaeological evidence suggests the existence of Indian influence on parts of East Africa as early as 300 C.E. There is also one report that gold was being sought in East Africa by Ethiopian merchants, who were among India's most important trading partners.

The sixth-century Byzantine geographer Cosmas Indicopleustes described Ethiopian merchants who went to some location inland from the East African coast to obtain gold. "Every other year they would sail far to the south, then march inland, and in return for various made-up articles they would come back laden with ingots of gold." The fact that the expeditions left every other year suggests that it took two years to get to their destination and return. If so, their destination, even at this early date, may have been Zimbabwe. The wind patterns are such that sailors who ride the monsoon south as far as Kilwa can catch the return monsoon to the Red Sea area within the same year. But if they go beyond Kilwa to the Zambezi River, from which they might go inland to Zimbabwe, they cannot return until the following year.

Indian voyages on the Indian Ocean were part of a more general development, more or less contemporary with the Mauryan Empire, in which sailors of various nationalities began to knit together the shores of the "Southern Ocean," a Chinese term referring to all the waters from the South China Sea to the eastern coast of Africa. During this period there is no doubt that the most intrepid sailors were the Malays, peoples who lived in what is now Malaysia, Indonesia, the southeastern coast of Vietnam, and the Philippines.

Sometime before 300 B.C.E. Malay sailors began to ride the monsoons, the seasonal winds that blow off the continent of Asia in the colder months and onto its shores in the warmer months. Chinese records indicate that by the third century B.C.E. "Kunlun" sailors, the Chinese term for the Malay seamen, were sailing north to the southern coasts of China. They may also have been sailing west to India, through the straits now called Malacca and Sunda. If so they may have been the first to establish contact between India and Southeast Asia.

Malay sailors had reached the eastern coast of Africa at least by the first century B.C.E., if not earlier. Their presence in East African waters is testified to by the peoples of Madagascar, who still speak a Malayo-Polynesian language. Some evidence also suggests that Malay sailors had settled in the Red Sea area. Indeed, it appears that they were the first to develop a long-distance trade in a southern spice. In the last centuries B.C.E., if not earlier, Malay sailors were delivering cinnamon from South China Sea ports to East Africa and the Red Sea.

By about 400 C.E. Malay sailors could be found two-thirds of the way around the world, from Easter Island to East Africa. They rode the monsoons without a compass, out of sight of land, and often at latitudes below the equator where the northern pole star cannot be seen. They navigated by the wind and the stars, by cloud formations, the color of the water, and swell and wave patterns on the ocean's surface. They could discern the presence of an island some thirty miles from its shores by noting the behavior of birds, the animal and plant life in the water, and the swell and wave patterns. Given their manner of sailing, their most likely route to Africa and the Red Sea would have been by way of the island clusters, the Maldives, the Chagos, the Seychelles, and the Comoros.

Malay ships used balance lug sails, which were square in shape and mounted so that they could pivot. This made it possible for sailors to tack against the wind, that is, to sail into the wind by going diagonally against it, first one way and then the other. Due to the way the sails were mounted, they appeared somewhat triangular in shape, and thus the Malays' balance lug sail may well be the prototype of the triangular lateen, which can also be used to tack against the wind. The latter was invented by both the Polynesians to the Malays' east and by the Arabs to their west, both of whom had ample opportunity to see the Malays' ships in action.

It appears that the pepper trade developed after the cinnamon trade. In the first century C.E. southern India began supplying the Mediterranean with large quantities of pepper. Thereafter, Indian merchants could be found living on the island of Socotra, near the mouth of the Red Sea, and Greek-speaking sailors, including the anonymous author of the *Periplus of the Erythraean Sea*, could be found sailing in the Red Sea and riding the monsoons from there to India.

Indian traders and shippers and Malay sailors were also responsible for opening up an all-sea route to China. The traders' desire for silk drew them out into dangerous waters in search of a more direct way to its source. By the second century C.E. Indian merchants could make the trip by sea, but the route was slow, and it took at least two years to make a round trip. Merchants leaving from India's eastern coast rounded the shores of the Bay of Bengal. When they came to the Isthmus

of Kra, the narrowest part of the Malay peninsula, the ships were un-
loaded, and the goods were portaged across to the Gulf of Thailand.
The cargo was then reloaded on ships that rounded the gulf until they
reached Funan, a kingdom on what is now the Kampuchea-Vietnam
border. There they had to wait for the winds to shift, before embarking
upon a ship that rode the monsoon to China.

Some time before 400 C.E. travelers began to use a new all-sea route
to China, a route that went around the Malay peninsula and thus
avoided the Isthmus of Kra portage. The ships left from Sri Lanka and
sailed before the monsoon, far from any coasts, through either the Strait
of Malacca or the Strait of Sunda into the Java Sea. After waiting in the
Java Sea port for the winds to shift, they rode the monsoon to southern
China. The most likely developers of this route were Malay sailors, since
the new stopover ports were located within their territories.

Not until the latter part of the fourth century, at about the same
time as the new all-sea route began to direct commercial traffic through
the Java Sea, did the fine spices — cloves, nutmeg, and mace — begin to
assume importance on international markets. These rare and expensive
spices came from the Moluccas, several island groups about a thousand
miles east of Java. Cloves were produced on about five minuscule islands off the western coast of Halmahera; nutmeg and mace came from
only a few of the Banda Islands, some ten islands with a total area of
seventeen square miles, located in the middle of the Banda Sea. Until
1621 these Moluccan islands were the only places in the world able to
produce cloves, nutmeg, and mace in commercial quantities. The
Moluccan producers themselves brought their spices to the international
markets of the Java Sea ports and created the market for them.

It was also during the time of the Gupta kings, around 350 C.E.,
that the Indians discovered how to crystallize sugar. There is considerable disagreement about where sugar was first domesticated. Some
believe that the plant was native to New Guinea and domesticated
there, and others argue that it was domesticated by Southeast Asian
peoples living in what is now southern China. In any case, sugar cultivation spread to the Indian subcontinent. Sugar, however, did not become an important item of trade until the Indians discovered how to
turn sugarcane juice into granulated crystals that could be easily stored
and transported. This was a momentous development, and it may have
been encouraged by Indian sailing, for sugar and clarified butter (ghee)
were among the dietary mainstays of Indian sailors.

The Indians also laid the foundation for modern mathematics during the time of the Guptas. Western numerals, which the Europeans
called Arabic since they acquired them from the Arabs, actually come
from India. (The Arabs call them Hindi numbers.) The most significant
feature of the Indian system was the invention of the zero as a number
concept. The oldest extant treatise that uses the zero in the modern way

is a mathematical appendix attached to Aryabhata's text on astronomy, which is dated 499 C.E.

The Indian zero made the place-value system of writing numbers superior to all others. Without it, the use of this system, base ten or otherwise, was fraught with difficulties and did not seem any better than alternative systems. With the zero the Indians were able to perform calculations rapidly and accurately, to perform much more complicated calculations, and to discern mathematical relationships more aptly. These numerals and the mathematics that the Indians developed with them are now universal — just one indication of the global significance of Southernization.

As a result of these developments India acquired a reputation as a place of marvels, a reputation that was maintained for many centuries after the Gupta dynasty fell. As late as the ninth century Amr ibn Bahr al Jahiz (c. 776–868), one of the most influential writers of Arabic, had the following to say about India:

> As regards the Indians, they are among the leaders in astronomy, mathematics — in particular, they have Indian numerals — and medicine; they alone possess the secrets of the latter, and use them to practice some remarkable forms of treatment. They have the art of carving statues and painted figures. They possess the game of chess, which is the noblest of games and requires more judgment and intelligence than any other. They make Kedah swords, and excel in their use. They have splendid music. . . . They possess a script capable of expressing the sounds of all languages, as well as many numerals. They have a great deal of poetry, many long treatises, and a deep understanding of philosophy and letters; the book *Kalila wa-Dimna* originated with them. They are intelligent and courageous. . . . Their sound judgment and sensible habits led them to invent pins, cork, toothpicks, the drape of clothes, and the dyeing of hair. They are handsome, attractive, and forbearing; their women are proverbial; and their country produces the matchless Indian aloes which are supplied to kings. They were the originators of the science of *fikr*, by which a poison can be counteracted after it has been used, and of astronomical reckoning, subsequently adopted by the rest of the world. When Adam descended from Paradise, it was to their land that he made his way.

The Southernization of China

These Southern Asian developments began to have a significant impact on China after 350 C.E. The Han dynasty had fallen in 221 C.E., and for more than 350 years thereafter China was ruled by an ever-changing collection of regional kingdoms. During these centuries Buddhism became increasingly important in China, Buddhist monasteries spread throughout the disunited realm, and cultural exchange between India and China grew accordingly. By 581, when the Sui dynasty reunited the empire, processes associated with Southernization had already had a major impact on China. The influence of Southernization continued during the T'ang (618–906) and Sung (960–1279) dynasties. One might even go so far as to suggest that the process of Southernization underlay the revolutionary social, political, economic, and technological developments of the T'ang and Sung.

The Chinese reformed their mathematics, incorporating the advantages of the Indian system, even though they did not adopt the Indian numerals at that time. They then went on to develop an advanced mathematics, which was flourishing by the time of the Sung dynasty. Cotton and indigo became well established, giving rise to the blueblack peasant garb that is still omnipresent in China. Also in the Sung period the Chinese first developed cotton canvas, which they used to make a more efficient sail for ocean-going ships.

Although sugar had long been grown in some parts of southern China it did not become an important crop in this region until the process of Southernization was well under way. The process also introduced new varieties of rice. The most important of these was what the Chinese called Champa rice, since it came to China from Champa, a Malay kingdom located on what is now the southeastern coast of Vietnam. Champa rice was a drought-resistant, early ripening variety that made it possible to extend cultivation up well-watered hillsides, thereby doubling the area of rice cultivation in China. . . .

In southern China the further development of rice production brought significant changes in the landscape. Before the introduction of Champa rice, rice cultivation had been confined to lowlands, deltas, basins, and river valleys. Once Champa rice was introduced and rice cultivation spread up the hillsides, the Chinese began systematic terracing and made use of sophisticated techniques of water control on mountain slopes. Between the mid-eighth and the early twelfth century the population of southern China tripled, and the total Chinese population doubled. According to Sung dynasty household registration figures for 1102 and 1110 — figures that Sung dynasty specialists have shown to be reliable — there were 100 million people in China by the first decade of the twelfth century.

Before the process of Southernization, northern China had always been predominant, intellectually, socially, and politically. The imperial center of gravity was clearly in the north, and the southern part of China was perceived as a frontier area. But Southernization changed this situation dramatically. By 600, southern China was well on its way to becoming the most prosperous and most commercial part of the empire. The most telling evidence for this is the construction of the Grand Canal, which was completed around 610, during the Sui dynasty. Even though the rulers of the Sui had managed to put the pieces of the empire back together in 581 and rule the whole of China again from a single northern capital, they were dependent on the new southern crops. Thus it is no coincidence that this dynasty felt the need to build a canal that could deliver southern rice to northern cities.

The T'ang dynasty, when Buddhist influence in China was especially strong, saw two exceedingly important technological innovations — the invention of printing and gunpowder. These developments may also be linked to Southernization. Printing seems to have developed within the walls of Buddhist monasteries between 700 and 750, and subtropical Sichuan was one of the earliest centers of the art. The invention of gunpowder in China by Taoist alchemists in the ninth century may also be related to the linkages between India and China created by Buddhism. In 644 an Indian monk identified soils in China that contained saltpeter and demonstrated the purple flame that results from its ignition. As early as 919 C.E. gunpowder was used as an igniter in a flamethrower, and the tenth century also saw the use of flaming arrows, rockets, and bombs thrown by catapults. The earliest evidence of a cannon or bombard (1127) has been found in Sichuan, quite near the Tibetan border, across the Himalayas from India.

By the time of the Sung the Chinese also had perfected the "south-pointing needle," otherwise known as the compass. Various prototypes of the compass had existed in China from the third century B.C.E., but the new version developed during the Sung was particularly well suited for navigation. Soon Chinese mariners were using the south-pointing needle on the oceans, publishing "needle charts" for the benefit of sea captains, and following "needle routes" on the Southern Ocean.

Once the Chinese had the compass they, like Columbus, set out to find a direct route to the spice markets of Java and ultimately to the Spice Islands in the Moluccas. Unlike Columbus, they found them. They did not bump into an obstacle, now known as the Western Hemisphere, on their way, since it was not located between China and the Spice Islands. If it had been so situated, the Chinese would have found it some 500 years before Columbus.

Cities on China's southern coasts became centers of overseas commerce. Silk remained an important export, and by the T'ang dynasty it had been joined by a true porcelain, which was developed in China sometime before 400 C.E. China and its East Asian neighbors had a monopoly on the manufacture of true porcelain until the early eighteenth century. Many attempts were made to imitate it, and some of the resulting imitations were economically and stylistically important. China's southern ports were also exporting to Southeast Asia large quantities of ordinary consumer goods, including iron hardware, such as needles, scissors, and cooking pots. Although iron manufacturing was concentrated in the north, the large quantity of goods produced was a direct result of the size of the market in southern China and overseas. Until the

British Industrial Revolution of the eighteenth century, no other place ever equaled the iron production of Sung China.

The Muslim Caliphates

In the seventh century C.E., Arab cavalries, recently converted to the new religion of Islam, conquered eastern and southern Mediterranean shores that had been Byzantine (and Christian), as well as the Sassanian empire (Zoroastrian) in what is now Iraq and Iran. In the eighth century they went on to conquer Spain and Turko-Iranian areas of Central Asia, as well as northwestern India. Once established on the Indian frontier, they became acquainted with many of the elements of Southernization.

The Arabs were responsible for the spread of many important crops, developed or improved in India, to the Middle East, North Africa, and Islamic Spain. Among the most important were sugar, cotton, and citrus fruits. Although sugarcane and cotton cultivation may have spread to Iraq and Ethiopia before the Arab conquests, only after the establishment of the caliphates did these southern crops have a major impact throughout the Middle East and North Africa.

The Arabs were the first to import large numbers of enslaved Africans in order to produce sugar. Fields in the vicinity of Basra, at the northern end of the Persian Gulf, were the most important sugar-producing areas within the caliphates, but before this land could be used, it had to be desalinated. To accomplish this task, the Arabs imported East African (Zanj) slaves. This African community remained in the area, where they worked as agricultural laborers. The famous writer al Jahiz, whose essay on India was quoted earlier, was a descendant of Zanj slaves. In 869, one year after his death, the Zanj slaves in Iraq rebelled. It took the caliphate fifteen years of hard fighting to defeat them, and thereafter Muslim owners rarely used slaves for purposes that would require their concentration in large numbers.

The Arabs were responsible for moving sugarcane cultivation and sugar manufacturing westward from southern Iraq into other relatively arid lands. Growers had to adapt the plant to new conditions, and they had to develop more efficient irrigation technologies. By 1000 or so sugarcane had become an important crop in the Yemen; in Arabian oases; in irrigated areas of Syria, Lebanon, Palestine, Egypt, and the Mahgrib; in Spain; and on Mediterranean islands controlled by Muslims. By the tenth century cotton also had become a major crop in the lands of the caliphate, from Iran and Central Asia to Spain and the Mediterranean islands. Cotton industries sprang up wherever the plant was cultivated, producing for both local and distant markets. . . .

Under Arab auspices, Indian mathematics followed the same routes as the crops. Al-Kharazmi (c. 780–847) introduced Indian mathematics to the Arabic-reading world in his *Treatise on Calculation with the Hindu Numerals*, written around 825. Mathematicians within the caliphates then could draw upon the Indian tradition, as well as the Greek and Persian. On this foundation Muslim scientists of many nationalities, including al-Battani (d. 929), who came from the northern reaches of the Mesopotamian plain, and the Persian Omar Khayyám (d. 1123), made remarkable advances in both algebra and trigonometry.

The Arab conquests also led to an increase in long-distance commerce and the "discovery" of new sources of bullion. Soon after the Abbasid caliphate established its capital at Baghdad, the caliph al-Mansur (r. 745–75) reportedly remarked, "This is the Tigris; there is no obstacle between us and China; everything on the sea can come to us." By this time Arab ships were plying the maritime routes from the Persian Gulf to China, and they soon outnumbered all others using these routes. By the ninth century they had acquired the compass (in China, most likely), and they may well have been the first to use it for marine navigation, since the Chinese do not seem to have used it for this purpose until after the tenth century.

. . . Thus it was that the Arabs "pioneered" or improved an existing long-distance route across the Sahara, an ocean of sand rather than water. Routes across this desert had always existed, and trade and other contacts between West Africa and the Mediterranean date back at least to the Phoenician period. Still, the numbers of people and animals crossing this great ocean of sand were limited until the eighth century when Arabs, desiring to go directly to the source of the gold, prompted an expansion of trade across the Sahara. Also during the eighth century Abdul al-Rahman, an Arab ruler of Morocco, sponsored the construction of wells on the trans-Saharan route from Sijilmasa to Wadidara to facilitate this traffic. This Arab "discovery" of West African gold eventually doubled the amount of gold in international circulation. East Africa, too, became a source of gold for the Arabs. By the tenth century Kilwa had become an important source of Zimbabwean gold.

Developments after 1200: The Mongolian Conquest and the Southernization of the European Mediterranean

By 1200 the process of Southernization had created a prosperous south from China to the Muslim Mediterranean. Although mathematics, the pioneering of new ocean routes, and "discoveries" of bullion are not inextricably connected to locations within forty degrees of the equator, several crucial elements in the process of Southernization were closely linked to latitude. Cotton generally does not grow above the fortieth parallel. Sugar, cinnamon, and pepper are tropical or subtropical crops, and the fine spices will grow only on particular tropical islands. Thus for many centuries the more southern parts of Asia and the Muslim Mediterranean enjoyed the profits that these developments brought, while locations that were too far north to grow these southern crops were unable to participate in such lucrative agricultural enterprises.

The process of Southernization reached its zenith after 1200, in large part because of the tumultuous events of the thirteenth century. During that century in both hemispheres there were major transformations in the distribution of power, wealth, and prestige. In the Western Hemisphere several great powers went down. Cahokia (near East St. Louis, Illinois), which for three centuries had been the largest and most influential of the Mississippian mound-building centers, declined after 1200, and in Mexico Toltec power collapsed. In the Mediterranean the prestige of the Byzantine empire was destroyed when Venetians seized its capital in 1204. From 1212 to 1270 the Christians conquered southern Spain, except for Granada. In West Africa, Ghana fell to Sosso, and so did Mali, one of Ghana's allies. But by about 1230 Mali, in the process of seeking its own revenge, had created an empire even larger than Ghana's. At the same time Zimbabwe was also becoming a major power in southern Africa.

The grandest conquerors of the thirteenth century were the Central Asians. Turkish invaders established the Delhi sultanate in India. Mongolian cavalries devastated Baghdad, the seat of the Abbasid caliphate since the eighth century, and they captured Kiev, further weakening Byzantium. By the end of the century they had captured China, Korea, and parts of mainland Southeast Asia as well.

Because the Mongols were pagans at the time of their conquests, the western Europeans cheered them on as they laid waste to one after another Muslim center of power in the Middle East. The Mongols were stopped only when they encountered the Mamluks of Egypt at Damascus. In East Asia and Southeast Asia only the Japanese and the Javanese were able to defeat them. The victors in Java went on to found Majapahit, whose power and prestige then spread through maritime Southeast Asia.

Both hemispheres were reorganized profoundly during this turmoil. Many places that had flourished were toppled, and power gravitated to new locales. In the Eastern Hemisphere the Central Asian conquerors had done great damage to traditional southern centers just about everywhere, except in Africa, southern China, southern India, and maritime Southeast Asia. At the same time the Mongols' control of overland routes between Europe and Asia in the thirteenth and early fourteenth centuries fostered unprecedented contacts between Europeans and peoples from those areas that had long been southernized. Marco Polo's long sojourn in Yüan Dynasty China is just one example of such interaction.

Under the Mongols overland trade routes in Asia shifted north and converged on the Black Sea. After the Genoese helped the Byzantines to retake Constantinople from the Venetians in 1261, the Genoese were granted special privileges of trade in the Black Sea. Italy then became directly linked to the Mongolian routes. Genoese traders were among the first and were certainly the most numerous to open up trade with the Mongolian states in southern Russia and Iran. In the words of one Western historian, in their Black Sea colonies they "admitted to citizenship" people of many nationalities, including those of "strange background and questionable belief," and they "wound up christening children of the best ancestry with such uncanny names as Saladin, Hethum, or Hulugu."

Such contacts contributed to the Southernization of the Christian Mediterranean during this period of Mongolian hegemony. Although European conquerors sometimes had taken over sugar and cotton lands in the Middle East during the Crusades, not until some time after 1200 did the European-held Mediterranean islands become important exporters. Also after 1200 Indian mathematics began to have a significant impact in Europe. Before that time a few western European scholars had become acquainted with Indian numerals in Spain, where the works of al-Kharazmi, al-Battani, and other mathematicians had been translated into Latin. Nevertheless, Indian numerals and mathematics did not become important in western Europe until the thirteenth century after the book *Liber abaci* (1202), written by Leonardo Fibonacci of Pisa (c. 1170–1250), introduced them to the commercial centers of Italy. Leonardo had grown up in North Africa (in what is now Bejala, Algeria), where his father, consul over the Pisan merchants in that port, had sent him to study calculation with an Arab master.

In the seventeenth century, when Francis Bacon observed the "force and virtue and consequences of discoveries," he singled out three technologies in particular that "have changed the whole face and state of things throughout the world." These were all Chinese inventions — the compass, printing, and gunpowder. All three were first acquired by Europeans during this time of hemispheric reorganization.

It was most likely the Arabs who introduced the compass to Mediterranean waters, either at the end of the twelfth or in the thirteenth century. Block printing, gunpowder, and cannon appeared first in Italy in the fourteenth century, apparently after making a single great leap from Mongolian-held regions of East Asia to Italy. How this great leap was accomplished is not known, but the most likely scenario is one suggested by Lynn White Jr., in an article concerning how various other Southern (rather than Eastern) Asian technologies reached western

Europe at about this time. He thought it most likely that they were introduced by "Tatar" slaves, Lama Buddhists from the frontiers of China whom the Genoese purchased in Black Sea marts and delivered to Italy. By 1450 when this trade reached its peak, there were thousands of these Asian slaves in every major Italian city.

Yet another consequence of the increased traffic and communication on the more northern trade routes traversing the Eurasian steppe was the transmission of the bubonic plague from China to the Black Sea. The plague had broken out first in China in 1331, and apparently rats and lice infected with the disease rode westward in the saddlebags of Mongolian post messengers, horsemen who were capable of traveling one hundred miles per day. By 1346 it had reached a Black Sea port, whence it made its way to the Middle East and Europe.

During the latter part of the fourteenth century the unity of the Mongolian empire began to disintegrate, and new regional powers began to emerge in its wake. Throughout much of Asia the chief beneficiaries of imperial disintegration were Turkic or Turko-Mongolian powers of the Muslim faith. The importance of Islam in Africa was also growing at this time, and the peoples of Southeast Asia, from the Malay peninsula to the southern Philippines, were converting to the faith.

Indeed, the world's most obvious dynamic in the centuries before Columbus was the expansion of the Islamic faith. Under Turkish auspices Islam was even spreading into eastern Europe, a development marked by the Ottoman conquest of Constantinople in 1453. This traumatic event lent a special urgency to Iberian expansion. The Iberians came to see themselves as the chosen defenders of Christendom. Ever since the twelfth century, while Christian Byzantium had been losing Anatolia and parts of southeastern Europe to Islam, they had been retaking the Iberian peninsula for Christendom.

One way to weaken the Ottomans and Islam was to go around the North African Muslims and find a new oceanic route to the source of West African gold. Before the Portuguese efforts, sailing routes had never developed off the western shore of Africa, since the winds there blow in the same direction all year long, from north to south. (Earlier European sailors could have gone to West Africa, but they would not have been able to return home.)

The Portuguese success would have been impossible without the Chinese compass, Arabic tables indicating the declination of the noonday sun at various latitudes, and the lateen sail, which was also an Arab innovation. The Portuguese caravels were of mixed, or multiple, ancestry, with a traditional Atlantic hull and a rigging that combined the traditional Atlantic square sail with the lateen sail of Southern Ocean provenance. With the lateen sail the Portuguese could tack against the wind for the trip homeward.

The new route to West Africa led to Portugal's rounding of Africa and direct participation in Southern Ocean trade. While making the voyages to West Africa, European sailors learned the wind patterns and ocean currents west of Africa, knowledge that made the Columbian voyages possible. The Portuguese moved the sugarcane plant from Sicily to Madeira, in the Atlantic, and they found new sources of gold, first in West Africa and then in East Africa. Given that there was little demand in Southern Ocean ports for European trade goods, they would not have been able to sustain their Asian trade without this African gold.

The Rise of Europe's North

The rise of the north, or more precisely, the rise of Europe's northwest, began with the appropriation of those elements of Southernization that were not confined by geography. In the wake of their southern European neighbors, they became partially southernized, but they could not engage in all aspects of the process due to their distance from the equator. Full Southernization and the wealth that we now associate with northwestern Europe came about only after their outright seizure of tropical and subtropical territories and their rounding of Africa and participation in Southern Ocean trade. . . .

Even though the significance of indigenous developments in the rise of northwestern Europe should not be minimized, it should be emphasized that many of the most important causes of the rise of the West are not to be found within the bounds of Europe. Rather, they are the result of the transformation of western Europe's relationships with other regions of the Eastern Hemisphere. Europe began its rise only after the thirteenth-century reorganization of the Eastern Hemisphere facilitated its Southernization, and Europe's northwest did not rise until it too was reaping the profits of Southernization. Thus the rise of the North Atlantic powers should not be oversimplified so that it appears to be an isolated and solely European phenomenon, with roots that spread no farther afield than Greece. Rather, it should be portrayed as one part of a hemisphere-wide process, in which a northwestern Europe ran to catch up with a more developed south — a race not completed until the eighteenth century.

JARED DIAMOND

Easter Island's End

In comparison with the grand theories of White and Shaffer, an essay on a small island in the Pacific might seem to be an exercise in the recent vogue of small-bore "micro-history." It is not. Jared Diamond, author of *Guns, Germs, and Steel,* uses small examples to big effect. In this selection and in his larger book-length treatment, *Collapse: How Societies Choose to Fail or Succeed,* Diamond teases a global lesson from the history of tiny Easter Island. What is that lesson? What does Diamond's essay suggest about the causes of environmental decline? Are we in danger of duplicating the fate of Easter Island? How can we avoid the fate of Easter Island?

Thinking Historically

How does Diamond's essay challenge the thesis of Lynn White Jr.? Do you see in this essay an alternative grand theory for understanding our environmental problems? If so, what is that theory? Do you agree or disagree with it? Why or why not?

In just a few centuries, the people of Easter Island wiped out their forest, drove their plants and animals to extinction, and saw their complex society spiral into chaos and cannibalism. Are we about to follow their lead?

Among the most riveting mysteries of human history are those posed by vanished civilizations. Everyone who has seen the abandoned buildings of the Khmer, the Maya, or the Anasazi is immediately moved to ask the same question: Why did the societies that erected those structures disappear?

Their vanishing touches us as the disappearance of other animals, even the dinosaurs, never can. No matter how exotic those lost civilizations seem, their framers were humans like us. Who is to say we won't succumb to the same fate? Perhaps someday New York's skyscrapers will stand derelict and overgrown with vegetation, like the temples at Angkor Wat and Tikal.

Among all such vanished civilizations, that of the former Polynesian society on Easter Island remains unsurpassed in mystery and isola-

Jared Diamond, "Easter Island's End," *Discover* 16, no. 8 (August 1995).

tion. The mystery stems especially from the island's gigantic stone statues and its impoverished landscape, but it is enhanced by our associations with the specific people involved: Polynesians represent for us the ultimate in exotic romance, the background for many a child's, and an adult's, vision of paradise. My own interest in Easter was kindled over 30 years ago when I read Thor Heyerdahl's fabulous accounts of his Kon-Tiki voyage.

But my interest has been revived recently by a much more exciting account, one not of heroic voyages but of painstaking research and analysis. My friend David Steadman, a paleontologist, has been working with a number of other researchers who are carrying out the first systematic excavations on Easter intended to identify the animals and plants that once lived there. Their work is contributing to a new interpretation of the island's history that makes it a tale not only of wonder but of warning as well.

Easter Island, with an area of only 64 square miles, is the world's most isolated scrap of habitable land. It lies in the Pacific Ocean more than 2,000 miles west of the nearest continent (South America), 1,400 miles from even the nearest habitable island (Pitcairn). Its subtropical location and latitude — at 27 degrees south, it is approximately as far below the equator as Houston is north of it — help give it a rather mild climate, while its volcanic origins make its soil fertile. In theory, this combination of blessings should have made Easter a miniature paradise, remote from problems that beset the rest of the world.

The island derives its name from its "discovery" by the Dutch explorer Jacob Roggeveen, on Easter (April 5) in 1722. Roggeveen's first impression was not of a paradise but of a wasteland: "We originally, from a further distance, have considered the said Easter Island as sandy; the reason for that is this, that we counted as sand the withered grass, hay, or other scorched and burnt vegetation, because its wasted appearance could give no other impression than of a singular poverty and barrenness."

The island Roggeveen saw was a grassland without a single tree or bush over ten feet high. Modern botanists have identified only 47 species of higher plants native to Easter, most of them grasses, sedges, and ferns. The list includes just two species of small trees and two of woody shrubs. With such flora, the islanders Roggeveen encountered had no source of real firewood to warm themselves during Easter's cool, wet, windy winters. Their native animals included nothing larger than insects, not even a single species of native bat, land bird, land snail, or lizard. For domestic animals, they had only chickens. European visitors throughout the eighteenth and early nineteenth centuries estimated Easter's human population at about 2,000, a modest number considering the island's fertility. As Captain James Cook recognized during his brief visit in 1774, the islanders were Polynesians (a Tahitian man accompanying Cook was able to converse with them). Yet despite the Polynesians' well-deserved fame as a great seafaring people, the Easter Islanders who came out to Roggeveen's and Cook's ships did so by swimming or paddling canoes that Roggeveen described as "bad and frail." Their craft, he wrote, were "put together with manifold small planks and light inner timbers, which they cleverly stitched together with very fine twisted threads. . . . But as they lack the knowledge and particularly the materials for caulking and making tight the great number of seams of the canoes, these are accordingly very leaky, for which reason they are compelled to spend half the time in bailing." The canoes, only ten feet long, held at most two people, and only three or four canoes were observed on the entire island.

With such flimsy craft, Polynesians could never have colonized Easter from even the nearest island, nor could they have traveled far offshore to fish. The islanders Roggeveen met were totally isolated, unaware that other people existed. Investigators in all the years since his visit have discovered no trace of the islanders' having any outside contacts: not a single Easter Island rock or product has turned up elsewhere, nor has anything been found on the island that could have been brought by anyone other than the original settlers or the Europeans. Yet the people living on Easter claimed memories of visiting the uninhabited Sala y Gomez reef 260 miles away, far beyond the range of the leaky canoes seen by Roggeveen. How did the islanders' ancestors reach that reef from Easter, or reach Easter from anywhere else?

Easter Island's most famous feature is its huge stone statues, more than 200 of which once stood on massive stone platforms lining the coast. [See Figure 14.4.] At least 700 more, in all stages of completion, were abandoned in quarries or on ancient roads between the quarries and the coast, as if the carvers and moving crews had thrown down their tools and walked off the job. Most of the erected statues were carved in a single quarry and then somehow transported as far as six miles — despite heights as great as 33 feet and weights up to 82 tons. The abandoned statues, meanwhile, were as much as 65 feet tall and weighed up to 270 tons. The stone platforms were equally gigantic: up to 500 feet long and 10 feet high, with facing slabs weighing up to 10 tons.

Roggeveen himself quickly recognized the problem the statues posed: "The stone images at first caused us to be struck with astonishment," he wrote, "because we could not comprehend how it was possible that these people, who are devoid of heavy thick timber for making any machines, as well as strong ropes, nevertheless had been able to erect such images." Roggeveen might have added that the islanders had no wheels, no draft animals, and no source of power except their own muscles. How did they transport the giant statues for miles, even before erecting them? To deepen the mystery, the statues were still standing in

Figure 14.4   Easter Island Statues.
Source: © Westend61/Alamy.

1770, but by 1864 all of them had been pulled down, by the islanders themselves. Why then did they carve them in the first place? And why did they stop?

The statues imply a society very different from the one Roggeveen saw in 1722. Their sheer number and size suggest a population much larger than 2,000 people. What became of everyone? Furthermore, that society must have been highly organized. Easter's resources were scattered across the island: the best stone for the statues was quarried at Rano Raraku near Easter's northeast end; red stone, used for large crowns adorning some of the statues, was quarried at Puna Pau, inland in the southwest; stone carving tools came mostly from Aroi in the northwest. Meanwhile, the best farmland lay in the south and east, and the best fishing grounds on the north and west coasts. Extracting and redistributing all those goods required complex political organization. What happened to that organization, and how could it ever have arisen in such a barren landscape?

Easter Island's mysteries have spawned volumes of speculation for more than two and a half centuries. Many Europeans were incredulous that Polynesians — commonly characterized as "mere savages" — could have created the statues or the beautifully constructed stone platforms. In the 1950s, Heyerdahl argued that Polynesia must have been settled by advanced societies of American Indians, who in turn must have received civilization across the Atlantic from more advanced societies of the Old World. Heyerdahl's raft voyages aimed to prove the feasibility of such prehistoric transoceanic contacts. In the 1960s the Swiss writer Erich von Däniken, an ardent believer in Earth visits by extraterrestrial astronauts, went further, claiming that Easter's statues were the work of intelligent beings who owned ultramodern tools, became stranded on Easter, and were finally rescued.

Heyerdahl and von Däeniken both brushed aside overwhelming evidence that the Easter Islanders were typical Polynesians derived from Asia rather than from the Americas and that their culture (including their statues) grew out of Polynesian culture. Their language was Polynesian, as Cook had already concluded. Specifically, they spoke an eastern Polynesian dialect related to Hawaiian and Marquesan, a dialect isolated since about A.D. 400, as estimated from slight differences in vocabulary. Their fishhooks and stone adzes resembled early Marquesan models. Last year DNA extracted from 12 Easter Island skeletons was also shown to be Polynesian. The islanders grew bananas, taro, sweet potatoes, sugarcane, and paper mulberry — typical Polynesian crops, mostly of Southeast Asian origin. Their sole domestic animal, the chicken, was also typically Polynesian and ultimately Asian, as were the rats that arrived as stowaways in the canoes of the first settlers.

What happened to those settlers? The fanciful theories of the past must give way to evidence gathered by hardworking practitioners in three fields: archeology, pollen analysis, and paleontology. Modern archeological excavations on Easter have continued since Heyerdahl's 1955 expedition. The earliest radiocarbon dates associated with human activities are around A.D. 400 to 700, in reasonable agreement with the approximate settlement date of 400 estimated by linguists. The period of statue construction peaked around 1200 to 1500, with few if any statues erected thereafter. Densities of archeological sites suggest a large population; an estimate of 7,000 people is widely quoted by archeologists, but other estimates range up to 20,000, which does not seem implausible for an island of Easter's area and fertility.

Archeologists have also enlisted surviving islanders in experiments aimed at figuring out how the statues might have been carved and erected. Twenty people, using only stone chisels, could have carved even the largest completed statue within a year. Given enough timber and fiber for making ropes, teams of at most a few hundred people could have loaded the statues onto wooden sleds, dragged them over lubricated wooden tracks or rollers, and used logs as levers to maneuver them into a standing position. Rope could have been made from the fiber of a small native tree, related to the linden, called the hauhau. However, that tree is now extremely scarce on Easter, and hauling one statue would have required hundreds of yards of rope. Did Easter's now barren landscape once support the necessary trees? That question can be answered by the technique of pollen analysis, which involves boring out a column of sediment from a swamp or pond, with the most recent deposits at the top and relatively more ancient deposits at the bottom. The absolute age of each layer can be dated by radiocarbon methods. Then begins the hard work: examining tens of thousands of pollen grains under a microscope, counting them, and identifying the plant species that produced each one by comparing the grains with modern pollen from known plant species. For Easter Island, the bleary-eyed scientists who performed that task were John Flenley, now at Massey University in New Zealand, and Sarah King of the University of Hull in England.

Flenley and King's heroic efforts were rewarded by the striking new picture that emerged of Easter's prehistoric landscape. For at least 30,000 years before human arrival and during the early years of Polynesian settlement, Easter was not a wasteland at all. Instead, a subtropical forest of trees and woody bushes towered over a ground layer of shrubs, herbs, ferns, and grasses. In the forest grew tree daisies, the rope-yielding hauhau tree, and the toromiro tree, which furnishes a dense, mesquite-like firewood. The most common tree in the forest was a species of palm now absent on Easter but formerly so abundant that the bottom strata of the sediment column were packed with its pollen. The Easter Island palm was closely related to the still-surviving Chilean wine palm, which grows up to 82 feet tall and 6 feet in diameter. The tall, unbranched trunks of the Easter Island palm would have been ideal for transporting and erecting statues and constructing large canoes. The palm would also have been a valuable food source, since its Chilean relative yields edible nuts as well as sap from which Chileans make sugar, syrup, honey, and wine.

What did the first settlers of Easter Island eat when they were not glutting themselves on the local equivalent of maple syrup? Recent excavations by David Steadman, of the New York State Museum at Albany, have yielded a picture of Easter's original animal world as surprising as Flenley and King's picture of its plant world. Steadman's expectations for Easter were conditioned by his experiences elsewhere in Polynesia, where fish are overwhelmingly the main food at archeological sites, typically accounting for more than 90 percent of the bones in ancient Polynesian garbage heaps. Easter, though, is too cool for the coral reefs beloved by fish, and its cliff-girded coastline permits shallow-water fishing in only a few places. Less than a quarter of the bones in its early garbage heaps (from the period 900 to 1300) belonged to fish; instead, nearly one-third of all bones came from porpoises.

Nowhere else in Polynesia do porpoises account for even 1 percent of discarded food bones. But most other Polynesian islands offered animal food in the form of birds and mammals, such as New Zealand's now extinct giant moas and Hawaii's now extinct flightless geese. Most other islanders also had domestic pigs and dogs. On Easter, porpoises would have been the largest animal available — other than humans. The porpoise species identified at Easter, the common dolphin, weighs up to 165 pounds. It generally lives out at sea, so it could not have been hunted by line fishing or spearfishing from shore. Instead, it must have been harpooned far offshore, in big seaworthy canoes built from the extinct palm tree.

In addition to porpoise meat, Steadman found, the early Polynesian settlers were feasting on seabirds. For those birds, Easter's remoteness and lack of predators made it an ideal haven as a breeding site, at least until humans arrived. Among the prodigious numbers of seabirds that bred on Easter were albatross, boobies, frigate birds, fulmars, petrels, prions, shearwaters, storm petrels, terns, and tropic birds. With at least 25 nesting species, Easter was the richest seabird breeding site in Polynesia and probably in the whole Pacific. Land birds as well went into early Easter Island cooking pots.

Steadman identified bones of at least six species, including barn owls, herons, parrots, and rail. Bird stew would have been seasoned with meat from large numbers of rats, which the Polynesian colonists inadvertently brought with them; Easter Island is the sole known Polynesian island where rat bones outnumber fish bones at archeological sites. (In case you're squeamish and consider rats inedible, I still recall recipes for creamed laboratory rat that my British biologist friends used to supplement their diet during their years of wartime food rationing.)

Porpoises, seabirds, land birds, and rats did not complete the list of meat sources formerly available on Easter. A few bones hint at the possibility of breeding seal colonies as well. All these delicacies were cooked in ovens fired by wood from the island's forests.

Such evidence lets us imagine the island onto which Easter's first Polynesian colonists stepped ashore some 1,600 years ago, after a long canoe voyage from eastern Polynesia. They found themselves in a pristine paradise. What then happened to it? The pollen grains and the bones yield a grim answer.

Pollen records show that destruction of Easter's forests was well under way by the year 800, just a few centuries after the start of human settlement. Then charcoal from wood fires came to fill the sediment cores, while pollen of palms and other trees and woody shrubs decreased or disappeared, and pollen of the grasses that replaced the forest became more abundant. Not long after 1400 the palm finally became extinct, not only as a result of being chopped down but also because the now ubiquitous rats prevented its regeneration: of the dozens of preserved palm nuts discovered in caves on Easter, all had been chewed by rats and could no longer germinate. While the hauhau tree did not become extinct in Polynesian times, its numbers declined drastically until there weren't enough left to make ropes from. By the time Heyerdahl visited Easter, only a single, nearly dead toromiro tree remained on the island, and even that lone survivor has now disappeared. (Fortunately, the toromiro still grows in botanical gardens elsewhere.)

The fifteenth century marked the end not only for Easter's palm but for the forest itself. Its doom had been approaching as people cleared land to plant gardens; as they felled trees to build canoes, to transport and erect statues, and to burn; as rats devoured seeds; and probably as the native birds died out that had pollinated the trees' flowers and dispersed their fruit. The overall picture is among the most extreme examples of forest destruction anywhere in the world: the whole forest gone, and most of its tree species extinct.

The destruction of the island's animals was as extreme as that of the forest: without exception, every species of native land bird became extinct. Even shellfish were overexploited, until people had to settle for small sea snails instead of larger cowries. Porpoise bones disappeared abruptly from garbage heaps around 1500; no one could harpoon porpoises anymore, since the trees used for constructing the big seagoing canoes no longer existed. The colonies of more than half of the seabird species breeding on Easter or on its offshore islets were wiped out.

In place of these meat supplies, the Easter Islanders intensified their production of chickens, which had been only an occasional food item. They also turned to the largest remaining meat source available: humans, whose bones became common in late Easter Island garbage heaps. Oral traditions of the islanders are rife with cannibalism; the most inflammatory taunt that could be snarled at an enemy was "The flesh of your mother sticks between my teeth." With no wood available to cook these new goodies, the islanders resorted to sugarcane scraps, grass, and sedges to fuel their fires.

All these strands of evidence can be wound into a coherent narrative of a society's decline and fall. The first Polynesian colonists found themselves on an island with fertile soil, abundant food, bountiful building materials, ample lebensraum, and all the prerequisites for comfortable living. They prospered and multiplied.

After a few centuries, they began erecting stone statues on platforms, like the ones their Polynesian forebears had carved. With passing years, the statues and platforms became larger and larger, and the statues began sporting ten-ton red crowns — probably in an escalating spiral of one-upmanship, as rival clans tried to surpass each other with shows of wealth and power. (In the same way, successive Egyptian pharaohs built ever-larger pyramids. Today Hollywood movie moguls near my home in Los Angeles are displaying their wealth and power by building ever more ostentatious mansions. Tycoon Marvin Davis topped previous moguls with plans for a 50,000-square-foot house, so now Aaron Spelling has topped Davis with a 56,000-square-foot house.

All that those buildings lack to make the message explicit are ten-ton red crowns.) On Easter, as in modern America, society was held together by a complex political system to redistribute locally available resources and to integrate the economies of different areas.

Eventually Easter's growing population was cutting the forest more rapidly than the forest was regenerating. The people used the land for gardens and the wood for fuel, canoes, and houses — and, of course, for lugging statues. As forest disappeared, the islanders ran out of timber and rope to transport and erect their statues. Life became more uncomfortable — springs and streams dried up, and wood was no longer available for fires.

People also found it harder to fill their stomachs, as land birds, large sea snails, and many seabirds disappeared. Because timber for building seagoing canoes vanished, fish catches declined and porpoises disappeared from the table. Crop yields also declined, since deforestation allowed the soil to be eroded by rain and wind, dried by the sun, and its nutrients to be leeched from it. Intensified chicken production and cannibalism replaced only part of all those lost foods. Preserved statuettes with sunken cheeks and visible ribs suggest that people were starving.

With the disappearance of food surpluses, Easter Island could no longer feed the chiefs, bureaucrats, and priests who had kept a complex society running. Surviving islanders described to early European visitors how local chaos replaced centralized government and a warrior class took over from the hereditary chiefs. The stone points of spears and daggers, made by the warriors during their heyday in the 1600s and 1700s, still litter the ground of Easter today. By around 1700, the population began to crash toward between one-quarter and one-tenth of its former number. People took to living in caves for protection against their enemies. Around 1770 rival clans started to topple each other's statues, breaking the heads off. By 1864 the last statue had been thrown down and desecrated.

As we try to imagine the decline of Easter's civilization, we ask ourselves, "Why didn't they look around, realize what they were doing, and stop before it was too late? What were they thinking when they cut down the last palm tree?"

I suspect, though, that the disaster happened not with a bang but with a whimper. After all, there are those hundreds of abandoned statues to consider. The forest the islanders depended on for rollers and rope didn't simply disappear one day — it vanished slowly, over decades. Perhaps war interrupted the moving teams; perhaps by the time the carvers had finished their work, the last rope snapped. In the meantime, any islander who tried to warn about the dangers of progressive deforestation would have been overridden by vested interests of carvers, bureaucrats, and chiefs, whose jobs depended on continued deforestation. Our Pacific Northwest loggers are only the latest in a long line of loggers to cry, "Jobs over trees!" The changes in forest cover from year to year would have been hard to detect: yes, this year we cleared those woods over there, but trees are starting to grow back again on this abandoned garden site here. Only older people, recollecting their childhoods decades earlier, could have recognized a difference. Their children could no more have comprehended their parents' tales than my eight-year-old sons today can comprehend my wife's and my tales of what Los Angeles was like 30 years ago.

Gradually trees became fewer, smaller, and less important. By the time the last fruit-bearing adult palm tree was cut, palms had long since ceased to be of economic significance. That left only smaller and smaller palm saplings to clear each year, along with other bushes and treelets. No one would have noticed the felling of the last small palm.

By now the meaning of Easter Island for us should be chillingly obvious. Easter Island is Earth writ small. Today, again, a rising population confronts shrinking resources. We too have no emigration valve, because all human societies are linked by international transport, and we can no more escape into space than the Easter Islanders could flee into the ocean. If we continue to follow our present course, we shall have exhausted the world's major fisheries, tropical rain forests, fossil fuels, and much of our soil by the time my sons reach my current age.

Every day newspapers report details of famished countries — Afghanistan, Liberia, Rwanda, Sierra Leone, Somalia, the former Yugoslavia, Zaire — where soldiers have appropriated the wealth or where central government is yielding to local gangs of thugs. With the risk of nuclear war receding, the threat of our ending with a bang no longer has a chance of galvanizing us to halt our course. Our risk now is of winding down, slowly, in a whimper. Corrective action is blocked by vested interests, by well-intentioned political and business leaders, and by their electorates, all of whom are perfectly correct in not noticing big changes from year to year. Instead, each year there are just somewhat more people, and somewhat fewer resources, on Earth. It would be easy to close our eyes or to give up in despair. If mere thousands of Easter Islanders with only stone tools and their own muscle power sufficed to destroy their society, how can billions of people with metal tools and machine power fail to do worse? But there is one crucial difference. The Easter Islanders had no books and no histories of other doomed societies. Unlike the Easter Islanders, we have histories of the past — information that can save us. My main hope for my sons' generation is that we may now choose to learn from the fates of societies like Easter's.

REFLECTIONS

Grand theories are difficult to evaluate, as are these. In part the diffi-culty is that they cover so much. How many images or primary sources could ever establish that a particular set of Christian ideas affected the way Christians actually behaved? And yet we know, or believe, that ideas matter. How many South Asian crops, tools, skills, and ideas con-stitute a global technological, let alone a scientific, revolution? And yet we know past historians have overemphasized the impact of European independence and Westernization. How many histories of societal col-lapse do we need to understand the threats to our own? And yet, we know that the more knowledge of how others have struggled and failed or succeeded we possess, the better our own chances for survival.

At least two issues lie beneath the surface of the debate in this chapter. One is the issue of culture, specifically the importance of cul-tural or religious ideas in shaping human behavior. White argues that religious ideas have a profound impact on how societies behave. Shaf-fer's study of material things rather than ideas, and even of ideas as things, offers a different view. By her account economic growth and technological development proceed with little regard to religions, ide-ologies, or belief systems. For Diamond too, not only are Christian or monotheistic ideas irrelevant, but historical processes leave precious little room for thoughtful intervention.

Historians are always working between ideas and things. Histori-ans of ideas may have a tendency to see ideas shaping history, and his-torians of things (economic historians, for instance) may see ideas as mere rationalizations. But good historians are not predictable. Lynn White Jr. is perhaps best known for his book *Medieval Technology and Social Change* in which he argued, among other things, that the intro-duction of the stirrup into medieval Europe was the cause of the society and culture we call feudalism. While this idea is much debated today, one would have a hard time finding an example of a stronger argument of how a thing created a culture. Nor does Diamond, a professor of ge-ography and physiology, ignore the role of ideas. In addition to the case of Easter Island, he surveys the example of Viking collapse in Green-land in his recent book, *Collapse: How Societies Choose to Fail or Suc-ceed* (a title that suggests the power of will and ideas). The Vikings, he suggests, failed in Greenland because they were unable to change their culture in ways necessary to adapt to the new environment. For Diamond, ideas and political will offer the only hope against the blind destructiveness of entrenched interests and seemingly unstoppable his-torical processes.

Another issue below the surface of this debate is the relationship between ecology and economic development. We tend to think that one comes at the expense of the other. White criticizes Western (Christian) environmental behavior with the same lens that has allowed others to celebrate Western (Christian) economic development. This is a reason, by the way, why many contemporary world historians find both views too centered on the West or Europe. Lynda Shaffer's article on "Southernization" is in good part an effort to counter Europe-centered history with a more global version. But if Europe was not the source of modern technology, it was also not a source of our modern ecological predicament. Diamond is also critical of approaches that start and end in Europe. (His area of specialty is New Guinea.) Since he eliminated religious or cultural motives, his story of Easter Island can be read as an indictment of economic growth as the cause of ecological collapse. But the villain in Diamond's essay is not any kind of economic growth; it is the competitive economic exploitation of different tribes without any common plan or restraint. His message for our own predicament is to correct the anarchy of competing greedy corporations and interest groups with a common agenda and control.

Are not genuine economic growth and ecological balance mutually supportive? It is difficult to imagine long-term, healthy economic growth continuing while wrecking the environment. Similarly with environmental movements: White has us imagine that the true environmentalists are Buddhist mendicants and Hindu tree-huggers. But Buddhist monks might be content to cultivate their own gardens and ignore the rest of the world. After all, modern ecological political movements are largely products of rich societies with threatened environments. Might the most precarious ecologies display — by necessity — the greatest ecological concern? If that is the case, is the renewed popularity of environmental movements in our own age at least a sign of hope?

Acknowledgments

John Aberth. "Ahmad al-Maqrizi, the Plague in Cairo." From *The Black Death: The Great Mortality of 1348–1350* by John Aberth. Copyright © 2005 by Bedford/St. Martin's. Reproduced by permission of Bedford/St. Martin's.

S. A. M. Adshead. "China and Rome Compared." Excerpts from *China in World History.* Copyright © 2000. Reprinted by permission of Palgrave Macmillan.

Natalie Angier. "Furs for Evening, But Cloth Was the Stone Age Standby." From *The New York Times*, December 14, 1999. Copyright © 1999 by The New York Times. Reprinted with permission.

Anonymous. Excerpt from "Chandogya Upanishad." In *The Upanishads: Breath of the Eternal*, translated by Juan Mascaro. Copyright © by Juan Mascaro. Reprinted with permission of Penguin Books, Ltd.

Anonymous. Excerpt from *The Bhagavad-Gita: Caste and Self* translated by Barbara Stoler Miller. Copyright © 1986 by Barbara Stoler Miller. Used by permission of Bantam Books, a division of Random House, Inc.

Anonymous. Excerpt from *The Epic of Gilgamesh*, translated by N. K. Sanders. Copyright © 1972 by N. K. Sanders. Reprinted with the permission of Penguin Books, Ltd.

Anonymous. "The Rig-Veda: Sacrifice as Creation." Excerpt from *Sources of Indian Tradition*, Second Edition, by Ainslie T. Embree. Copyright © 1988 by Columbia University Press. Reprinted with the permission of the publisher.

Anonymous. "Svetasvatara Upanished." From *The Upanishads: Breath of the Eternal*, translated by Swami Prabhavananda and Frederick Manchester. Copyright © 1948, 1957 by The Vedanta Society of Southern California. Reprinted with permission.

Anonymous. "The Upanishads: Karma and Reincarnation." Excerpt from *The Hindu Tradition: Readings in Oriental Thought*, edited by Ainslie T. Embree. Copyright © 1966 by Random House, Inc. Used by permission of Random House, Inc.

Aristophanes. Excerpt from *Lysistrata*, edited by William Arrowsmith, translated by Douglass Parker. Copyright © 1964 by William Arrowsmith. Used by permission of Dutton Signet, a division of Penguin Group (USA) Inc.

Aristotle. "The Athenian Constitution." From *Aristotle, Politics and the Athenian Constitution*, translated by John Warrington. Copyright © 1959 by John Warrington. Reprinted with the permission of David Campbell Publishers, Ltd.

Ban Zhao. "Lessons for Women." From *Pan Chao: Foremost Woman Scholar of China, First Century A.D.: Background, Ancestry, Life and Writings of the Most Celebrated Chinese Woman of Letters*, translated by Nancy Lee Swann. Copyright © The East Asian Library and the Gest Collection, Princeton University. Reprinted by permission of Princeton University.

William Theodore De Bary. Excerpts from "The Buddha's First Sermon," "Buddhism and Caste," and "Buddhism in China" (Hung-ming chi, in Taisho daizokyo, LII, 1-7). From *The Buddhist Tradition in India, China and Japan* by William Theodore De Bary. Copyright © 1969 by William Theodore De Bary. Used by permission of Random House, Inc.

Jerry H. Bentley. "The Spread of World Religions." From *Old World Encounters: Cross-Cultural Contacts and Exchanges in Pre-Modern Times.* Copyright 1992 by Oxford University Press, Inc. Used by permission of Oxford University Press, Inc.

Giovanni Boccaccio. Excerpt from *The Decameron* by Boccaccio, translated by G. H. McWilliam (Penguin Classics 1972, Second Edition, 1995). Copyright © G. H. McWilliam 1972, 1995. Reprinted by permission of Penguin Books Ltd.

Elise Boulding. "Women and the Agricultural Revolution." From *The Underside of History: A View of Women through Time* (Boulder, Colo.: Westview Press, 1976). Copyright © 1976 by Elise Boulding. Reprinted by permission of the author.

Fernand Braudel. "Towns and Cities." Excerpt from *The Structures of Everyday Life: The Limits of the Possible* by Fernand Braudel (London: Collins, 1983). Copyright © 1983. Reprinted by permission Armand Colin Foreign Rights.

Andreas Capellanus. Excerpt from *The Art of Courtly Love,* translated by John J. Parry. Copyright © 1990 by Columbia University Press. Reprinted with the permission of the publisher.

"Chronicle of Solomon bar Simon." From *The Jews and the Crusaders: The Hebrew Chronicles of the First and Second Crusades* by Schlomo Eidelberg, editor and translator (The University of Wisconsin Press, 1977). © 1977. Reprinted with the permission of Schlomo Eidelberg.

Cicero. "Against Verres." From *On Government*, translated by Michael Grant. Copyright © Michael Grant Publications, Ltd. 1993. Reprinted with permission of Penguin Books Ltd.

Anna Comnena. Excerpt from *The Alexiad of Princess Anna Comnena*, translated by Elizabeth A. S. Dawes. Reprinted with the permission of Barnes and Noble Books, Totowa, New Jersey, 07512.

Barry Cunliffe. "The Western Vikings." Excerpts from *Facing the Ocean: The Atlantic and Its Peoples*. Copyright © 2001 Oxford University Press. Reprinted with permission.

Jared Diamond. "Easter Island's End." From *Discover,* volume 16, No. 8, August 1995. Copyright © 1995. Reprinted by permission of the author.

Bernal Díaz. Excerpt from *The Conquest of New Spain*, translated by J. M. Cohen. Copyright 1963 by J. M. Cohen. Reprinted with the permission of Penguin Books, Ltd.

Patricia Buckley Ebrey. "The Debate on Salt and Iron." Excerpt translated by Patricia Buckley Ebrey, in *Chinese Civilization: A Sourcebook*, Second Edition. Copyright © 1993 by Patricia Buckley Ebrey. Reprinted with the permission of The Free Press, a Division of Simon & Schuster Adult Publishing Group. All rights reserved.

Fan Zhongyan. "Rules for the Fan Lineage's Charitable Estate." From *Chinese Civilization: A Sourcebook*, Second Edition by Patricia Buckley Ebrey. Copyright © 1993 by Patricia Buckley Ebrey. Reprinted with the permission of The Free Press, A Division of Simon & Schuster Adult Publishing Group. All rights reserved.

Fulcher of Chartres. "Pope Urban at Clermont." "The Siege of Antioch." From *The First Crusade: The Chronicle of Fulcher of Chartres and Other Source Materials*, Second Edition, by Edward Peters, editor. Copyright © 1998. Reprinted by permission of the University of Pennsylvania Press.

H. A. R. Gibb. Excerpt from "The Damascus Chronicle of the Crusades." Extracted and Translated from the *Chronicle of Ibn al-Qalanisi*. Translated by H.A.R. Gibb. Published by Dover Publications, 2002.

S. D. Goitein. "Letter from a Jewish Pilgrim in Egypt." Excerpt from "Contemporary Letters on the Capture of Jerusalem by the Crusaders." Translated by S. D.

Goitein, *Journal of Jewish Studies*, volume 3, #4. Copyright © 1952 by S. G. Goitein. Reprinted by permission of the *Journal of Jewish Studies*. "Cairo: An Islamic City in Light of the Geniza." Translated and edited by Ira M. Lapidus. From *Middle Eastern Cities*. Copyright © 1969 by the Regents of the University of California Press. Reprinted by permission of the publisher.

Gregory Guzman. "Were the Barbarians a Negative or Positive Factor in Ancient and Medieval History?" From *The Historian*, August 1988. Reprinted with the permission of the author.

Gabriel de' Mussis. "Origins of the Black Death." From *The Black Death* by Rosemary Horrox. Copyright © 1994 Manchester University Press, Manchester, UK. Reprinted by permission.

Sarah Shaver Hughes and Brady Hughes. Excerpt from "Women in Ancient Civilizations." As published in *Women's History in Global Perspective*, vol. 2, pp. 26–30 and 36–40. Copyright © 1998 by Sarah Shaver Hughes and Brady Hughes. Reprinted with permission of the American Historical Association and the authors.

G. W. B. Huntingford. Excerpt from *The Glorious Victories of 'Āmda Seyon: King of Ethiopia*. Translated by G. W. B. Huntingford. Copyright © 1965. Published by Oxford University Press. Reprinted by permission.

Ibn al-Athir. "The Conquest of Jerusalem." Excerpt from *Arab Historians of the Crusades: Selected and Translated from the Arabic Sources*, edited and translated by E. J. Costello. Islamic World Series, 1969. Copyright © 1969 Routledge & Kegan Paul, Ltd. Reprinted by permission of Copyright Clearance Center, via the format Textbook.

John of Plano Carpini. Excerpt from *History of the Mongols*; Guyuk Khan, "Letter to Pope Innocent IV," excerpts from "Narrative of Brother Benedict the Pole," and excerpt from *The Journey of William of Rubrick* from *Mission to Asia: Narratives and Letters of the Franciscan Missionaries to Mongolia and China in the Thirteenth and Fourteenth Centuries*, translated by a nun of Stanbrook Abbey, edited by Christopher Dawson. Copyright © 1955. Reprinted with permission of The Continuum International Publishing Group.

Kalidasa. Excerpt from *Shakuntala*. Translated by Barbara Stoler Miller. From *Theatre of Memory: The Plays of Kalidasa*, edited by Barbara Stoler Miller. Copyright © 1984 Columbia University Press. Reprinted with permission.

Gerda Lerner. "The Urban Revolution: Origins of Patriarchy." From *The Creation of Patriarchy*. Copyright © 1986, 1987 by Gerda Lerner. Used by permission of Oxford University Press, Inc.

Bernard Lewis. "Peace Terms with Jerusalem," from "Al Tabari, Tarik al-Rusulcwa'I muluk" (Leiden: Brill), published in *Islam from the Prophet Muhammad to the Conquest of Constantinople*, edited and translated by Bernard Lewis. Vol. I: Politics and War. Excerpt from Vol II: Religion and Society. Published by Harper & Row, 1974.

Miriam Lichtheim. "Advice to the Young Egyptian: Be a Scribe." From *Ancient Egyptian Literature: A Book of Readings, Volume 2; The New Kingdom* by Miriam Lichtheim. Copyright © 1976 by the University of California Press Books. Reproduced with permission of University of California Press Books in the format Textbook via Copyright Clearance Center.

Liu Tsung-yuan. "Camel Kuo the Gardner" from *An Anthology of Chinese Literature: From Early Times to the Fourteenth Century*, edited by Cyril Birch.

Selected World History Titles in the *Bedford Series in History and Culture*

SPARTACUS AND THE SLAVE WARS
A Brief History with Documents
Translated, Edited, and with an Introduction by Brent D. Shaw, *University of Pennsylvania*

THE BLACK DEATH: THE GREAT MORTALITY OF 1348–1350
A Brief History with Documents
John Aberth, *Castleton State College*

CHRISTOPHER COLUMBUS AND THE ENTERPRISE OF THE INDIES
A Brief History with Documents
Geoffrey Symcox, *University of California, Los Angeles*, and Blair Sullivan, *University of California, Los Angeles*

VICTORS AND VANQUISHED
Spanish and Nahua Views of the Conquest of Mexico
Edited with an Introduction by Stuart B. Schwartz, *Yale University*

THE INTERESTING NARRATIVE OF THE LIFE OF OLAUDAH EQUIANO, **Written by Himself, With Related Documents, Second Edition**
Edited with an Introduction by Robert J. Allison, *Suffolk University*

SLAVE REVOLUTION IN THE CARIBBEAN, 1789–1804
A Brief History with Documents
Laurent Dubois, *Michigan State University*, and John D. Garrigus, *Jacksonville University*

SLAVERY, FREEDOM, AND THE LAW IN THE ATLANTIC WORLD
A Brief History with Documents
Sue Peabody, *Washington State University Vancouver*, and Keila Grinberg, *Universidade Federal do Estado do Rio de Janeiro / Universidade Candido Mendes*

MAO ZEDONG AND CHINA'S REVOLUTIONS
A Brief History with Documents
Timothy Cheek, *University of British Columbia*

For a complete list of titles in the Bedford Series in History and Culture, please visit bedfordstmartins.com/history.

TradeUp

Package any title from our sister companies at Holtzbrinck Publishers — at a discount of 50% off the regular price. To see a complete list of trade titles available for packaging, go to bedfordstmartins.com/tradeup.

 PICADOR